La bell' America

From *La Rivoluzione*
to the Great Depression:
An Italian Immigrant
Family Remembered

T0162029

Anthony M. Graziano

A LeapSci Book
Leapfrog Science and History
Leapfrog Press
Teaticket, Massachusetts

A LeapSci Book
Leapfrog Science and History

Published in 2009 in the United States by
Leapfrog Press LLC
PO Box 2110
Teaticket, MA 02536
www.leapfrogpress.com

Distributed in the United States and Canada by
Consortium Book Sales and Distribution
St. Paul, Minnesota 55114
www.cbsd.com

First Edition

Library of Congress Cataloging-in-Publication Data

Graziano, Anthony M., 1932-
  La bell'America : from la rivoluzione to the Great
Depression : an Italian immigrant family remembered /
Anthony M. Graziano. -- 1st ed.
      p. cm.
  "A LeapSci Book."
  Includes bibliographical references and index.
  ISBN 978-1-935248-01-9
  1. Italian Americans--New York (State)--History. 2.
Italian Americans--New York (State)--Social
conditions. 3. Italian Americans--New York
(State)--Biography. 4. United States--Emigration and immigration--History. 5.
Calabria (Italy)--Emigration and immigration. 6. Calabria (Italy)--Biography. 7.
Graziano, Anthony M., 1932---Family. 8. Graziano, Anthony M., 1932---Child-
hood and youth. I. Title.
  F130.I8G73 2009
  974.7'00451--dc22

    2009036972

Printed in the United States of America

To the memories of
Michele, Teresa,
and
Ferdinando,
and to the futures of
Tegenya, Benjamin, and Aaron Lucas

Table of Contents

Preface

From the 1880s through the 1920s, European immigrants flowed from their homes in poverty, oppression, and distress, bringing little more than hope and determination. It was a massive migration of 70 million people tossed by 19th-century Europe's monumental disruptions—overpopulation, disease, revolutions, and wars. They were pushed from Europe and pulled to the Americas. Half of them came to the United States, where few warm welcomes greeted them. Poor, ignorant of America's language and customs, uneducated, dressed in antiquated, often shabby clothing, they were easy targets for ridicule, exploitation, and blatant American xenophobia.

They landed at the bottom of the social heap, with few resources. However, millions succeeded in ways that were impossible to achieve in their original countries. In this book, I will remember a group of Southern Italians who came to the United States in the 1920s and settled into the small town of Nyack, just north of New York City. They drew from their personal strengths and from the opportunities offered by their new country. They brought a magnificent capacity for sustained, hard work, even at the meanest of labors, and a guiding idea that each person is responsible for his or her success or failure. They found in the United States a country of contrasts. Despite its brutal prejudice and barriers, America offered unimagined opportunities to work and earn a portion of the country's rich resources, including freedom and respect, neither of which had been available in the oppressive feudal society of their old country.

Their new country was generous—but it was also unforgiving, dangerous, and viciously rejecting of foreigners. "Here are wealth, freedom, and respect," it whispered to the immigrants. "They are all around you. Earn them, if you can, but be careful, because if you let us, we will destroy you in a minute!" The immigrants heard that voice and took their chances. They came to fear America for its cruelty, to love it for its generosity, and to wrestle with it for its opportunities. They adapted, survived, and succeeded.

But not all succeeded. Many were ground up by America's unforgiving nature and by paths ill chosen. In those who overcame the odds, personal strength combined well with a society that made room for them and offered its resources. They recognized and appreciated that, despite its hard surfaces and sharp edges, *la bell'America* offered a collective generosity not found anywhere else in the world. "*Dove c'è pane, c'è patria* (where there is bread, there is my country)," they said, and gave their allegiance to their adopted home. It is interesting how readily so many Italian immigrants developed a powerful sense of patriotism for the United States and rejected their commitment to the Italian nation while keeping strong ties with their Italian culture.

Those who immigrated in the 1920s, like my parents, found themselves at the bottom of the deep and destructive depression that wiped out so much for millions of Americans. But the immigrants whom I knew survived that decade of desperation, while so many other Americans, with many more resources, did not. How did they do it? I hope, in telling their stories, to shed some light on this.

Our small group of relatives and friends in the 1930s bore the family names Asaro, Barone, Biancinni, Cervodoro, Conace, Dattilo, D'Auria, Dellolio, Delpizzo, Fatale, Fiola, Gallo, Graziano, Lanzana, Maiorano, Paone, Pugliese, Raso, Renella, Serratore, Scheno, Sutera, and many others that I did not know of until much later. At times, I thought they were simply materialistic, migrating in order to share in America's wealth. But I came to understand that the United States allowed something far more important, the exercise of a deeply spiritual life, though not in the sense of religious faith. Most of the men I knew were not religious, although the women were. Men were spiritual in the sense of defining and maintaining life's most important task: nurturing those whom one loves. One gave thanks to those who earned them, our parents, in recognition that their hard labors in the factories, farms, road gangs, and sweatshops had brought it all about. A raised glass, "*a salute*" in chorus, the brief touch and light tinkling of glasses—musical notes floating over the table. What more is needed? The father sat proudly in his honored seat at the head of the table. Were his arms long enough, he would have encircled everyone there, and that is what it was all about—*la famiglia*, the circle of love that transcended everything else, crafted by those immigrants and celebrated each day. In today's more sophisticated, perhaps cynical world, theirs seems a naive philosophy:

"Protect, enjoy, and be loyal to your family above all, because nothing, not even God, is more important than your family.

"Work hard and succeed, because this great country, *la bell'America*, like no other in the world, will give you the chance to do that.

"Tend to your own business and take care of your family and yourself, because no one else—no God, church, union, or government—is going to do it for you."

My discussions of Italian history are not objective treatments of historical facts, and they might not fare well under the scrutiny of historians. I consulted historical sources for contexts that support the memories, attitudes, and opinions that were passed on to me by my parents and their

Figure 1.
The relative land areas of the Continental United States
and Italy (including Sicily and Sardinia).

Italian compatriots. My version of historical events has been informed by
their experiences, by the modifying process of time passing in my life, and,
undoubtedly, by some self-serving and unexamined needs of my own. My
versions of history, such as the long Italian Revolution or events surrounding World War I, are as those people understood them, or, rather, as I recall
and reconstruct what they passed on to me. There is also a good bit of edi-
torializing throughout this work; I do not claim dispassionate objectivity.

Italian immigrants viewed *l'America* as an overpowering colossus of a
country. Everything seemed big: the buildings, the streets, the noise, the
frenzy, and even the American people, jabbering in their foreign tongue.
New arrivals stepping onto the New York pavement must have felt the difference in size between themselves and everything else. For some, that sense
of a vast, overbearing country would never be shed. We might appreciate
the more abstract, perhaps fanciful, representation shown in Figure 1.

I have tried to present some phrases in the *Calabrese* dialect as it was spoken in my parents' time as best as I can remember them. My neighbor, Joseph Vircillo of Buffalo, helped me to recapture the Calabrese idiom. Professor Julia Cozzarelli of Ithaca College and my cousin Michael Bartolotti helped to correct Italian phrases. I thank them all for their generous assistance. However, responsibility for the final renditions—errors, inconsistencies, and all—is mine.

Relatives and friends have shared their memories and other mementos of our families in Italy and in Nyack. I thank Anthony Colistra, Maria Colistra Rosado, Elaine Conace, Theresa Lanzana Serratore, and Joseph Dattilo. A special note of gratitude goes to my cousins Elisabetta, Benedetta, and Michael Bartolotti; Anna Dattilo Ottaiano, Michael Dattilo, Theresa Dattilo Fiola, and Fred J. Graziano; to my niece Anne Graziano Keane, and to my lifelong virtual cousins, Theresa Conace, Mary Serratore Lynch, and Laura Serratore Ciliberto. They shared family photographs, newspaper clippings, old books, and stories of earlier times, wrote letters to me, filled out family questionnaires, tolerated my tape recorder, and patiently carried on late-night telephone conversations over the miles between us. Thank you.

I have not discussed my younger cousins, nieces, and nephews, not because I have forgotten them, but because they did not enter the story until much later. Perhaps someday one of them will pick up the tale and tell us more.

As I recounted the 1930s depression, I saw a disquieting familiarity, a resurrection of events that led to the Great Depression. They are with us again: a heavy national debt incurred by war, looting of the nation's resources by well-positioned businessmen, and a failure to share the country's wealth among the general population. We again have huge tax breaks for the wealthy but increased fees, taxes, and prices for everyone else. New laws give advantages to well-placed investors, big business is ever-more entwined with big government and the burgeoning war machine. Our schools, hospitals, bridges, and roads deteriorate as our wealth flies overseas. Americans' consumer debt is skyrocketing, home mortgage foreclosures are rapidly escalating, and we see a general failure to save. There is, too, a disturbing similarity of the vicious anti-immigration surge following World War I and our current obsession with Mexican "illegal immigration." These are cause for concern. We would be wise to pay attention.

I have written about many people and events, but this work is primarily the story of Michele Graziano, Teresa Dattilo Graziano, and their son, my brother, Ferdinando.

A.M.G.
Time Hill Farm
Chautauqua County, New York

I

Revolution and Promise

Chapter 1

The Turquoise Room (Nyack, 1935)

1. 1935

Dark turquoise paint covers the walls and woodwork, making the room gloomy despite the sunshine outside. Whatever is out there is yet unknown, featureless, like luminous fog. The world is here, in this room. A little boy, three years old, wears short pants and a shirt with four buttons at the waist to which the shorts are attached. His face is round, smooth, his expression troubled. Ruffled hair pokes down his forehead like little fingers. His short legs are sturdily rounded, and his feet press up on their toes, urgently leveraging him higher. Linoleum stretches away in all directions like a yellow desert.

He is leaning, glued to his mother's leg. She sits, silent, in an old wooden chair that has a rounded back with five spindles. One is broken, taped together, and can be moved back and forth inside its bandage. The old chair is scratched and rough and is missing a rung. One leg is too short, so the chair wobbles like an old man trying to keep his balance. It once had legs of equal length and glossy white paint with stenciled yellow and orange flowers, but now it is faded and chipped. It looks like it has been kicked around a lot; a poor, sad chair, like the room.

I remember dull yellow linoleum with worn spots that blossomed from the underside like flat red mushrooms. Black squares were outlined on it, and if you looked closely, you could see faded flowers in each. Carefully, I placed a foot on a square, but not my full weight, because you might sink in, down to that red stuff (and who could tell what that was and what it might do to you if it grabbed your foot).

The black squares marched away from me like a desert of bottomless black boxes. They marched to the far side of the room and smacked up against the distant walls that imprisoned them, frustrating their escape. When I bent down and squinted along the marching squares, I saw straight rows, but with a blink of my eyes, they shifted to diagonal rows and diamond shapes. With each blink, they changed from one to the other and back again, and after a while it made me dizzy and I had to stop staring.

The big floor was treacherous, unstable. How could you trust anything that could change its shape? I huddled tightly against Mom, warm, safe. She had a round, full face, soft and kind, and shining black hair pulled back into a neat bun. I leaned against her, embraced by her protective arm. Her summer dress reached to her ankles, almost touching the narrow straps of her shoes. The dress, like the floor, was decorated with flowers, but these were colorful and bright, rippling as in a summer breeze whenever Mom moved, dancing, it seemed, to silent music. Mom's black shoes rested solidly against the floor. Each shoe had a shiny little buckle that looked just like a regular belt buckle, as if it belonged to a doll.

My life began in that room, in those moments. I am not aware of anything having preceded that scene, or how or why we arrived there. We just were; it just was. I knew who I was, who Mom was, but all without a personal history, without preamble. As far as I knew, we had been created at that moment, in that corner of the oppressive turquoise room.

The opposite wall held a closed door, far across that uncertain desert. It was shadowy over there, so far from the small, dingy window. Muted sunlight seeped through and struggled across the floor trying to reach the door, but was forced to flow down and disappear into those black squares. I wondered where it went, that sunlight. Did that dark red stuff in the floor soak it all up? Perhaps it was spilling into some secret place down below us, the glorious opposite of this dark room—a place with a waterfall of sunlight. It must be a beautiful place, and someday I would go down there and explore and try to find those cascading rays. For now, I knew only this dingy room, and it was best to hold tightly to Mom and make sure my foot did not stray into the center of a black square.

That shadowy door was chipped and gray, matching the mood. I wanted to see what was on the other side, but that would require venturing onto the floor and maneuvering around the treacherous black squares, and possibly even stepping into them. I clung to Mom and stayed safe.

Mom sat still in the battered chair. I stood leaning my weight against her. She was quiet, subdued perhaps by the room, as I was. Or is my memory faulty? Was the turquoise room generating the oppressiveness and darkening our mood, or was Mom the source of the darkness, her shadowed emotions filling the room and dominating us? Is this what I was feeling—not the power of the room, but the power of Mom's emotions? She was uneasy, uncertain, sad.

2. Come to *l'America*

For Mom, emotion drove life, and what one felt at any moment was the essence of being alive. She had been taught to respect emotional honesty—one expresses what one feels; to suppress emotion is to tell a lie. Mom was an Italian 19th-century romantic trapped in this American 20th-century town. She was saddened at being miles from her home in Southern Italy, having joined my father in 1927 in this big, new country where she knew neither language nor custom. Coming to America for a better life for her family was a smart move, but the cost was great. Abandoned in that now distant warm and hilly region of Southern Italy were her mother and siblings, and everyone and everything else in the world that had mattered to her. She sighed and looked inward, seeing not only the distance of the great ocean, but also the fear that she would never see her family again.

Into that mix of emotion appeared a new anxiety. Not only had she come to an unfamiliar country, but just two years later she had found her family sliding into the worst economic depression that this huge and noisy new country had ever experienced. Mom had traded life in the European economic depression for life in the American economic depression. In Italy it had been said that America hummed with good jobs and fat pay envelopes, even more money than one family could use. Living would be good, children healthy, families happy, and life would have no economic cares. *La bell'America* offered a life brighter than any life possible in the many lovely but poor villages throughout Southern Italy, like her own Maida.

"Come to America," the voices urged. But the Great Depression had followed the stock market crash of 1929, and good living had danced away from them. Making one's way through life in a strange land with its unknown language, customs, and people, without the support of one's family, would be difficult enough. But trying to do so when men were being thrown out of work and sent wandering the country to beg in the streets was frightening. What was to become of them? One could pray and that always made her feel better, but prayers, no matter how passionately offered, were not always answered. Sometimes, it seemed, even God has other things to do.

Where was God? Throughout her long life Mom would maintain her religious devotion, but she would never understand God's vagueness and stark absences, often when He was most needed. My father had been made cynical by Godless poverty, a Godless war, and his family's Godless confrontations between 1927 and 1931 with soulless visitations of death, even for tiny babies. From such experience he concluded that God's absence was reality and God's existence was delusion.

I am aware of a shadowy sadness. At one time I had a sister and another brother, but they were not here any more. It was confusing—both were older than I, but neither succeeded in becoming as old as I. How could that be? I felt puzzled, disappointed, and sometimes even resentful that they were not here for me to know, and that I had not been there to know them. It would be years before I was able to understand those cloudy images of Mom and my unknown sister and brother and the feelings of loss. In time, I saw shadowed images of a baby who did not survive birth, a fat and happy 10-month-old who turned hot with raging fever, and a doctor whose instructions were too impatient for the immigrant woman who knew no English. I saw a church and priests who looked to heaven and thanked God even for this blasphemy, grim, silent men and sobbing women, and tiny white caskets.

If those were the realities that pressed hard on Mom, forcing her emotions, then those were what she expressed through her mood, dominating our world in the turquoise room. While I believed that life began in that room, at that moment Mom knew better. She, of course, had a past, and it was that past colliding with this present that generated the gloom of her distress. Mom sat in that dark room in the deep depression summer of 1935, filling the space with anxiety and sadness. I clung to her, a three-year-old, sensing the oppression, but blaming it all on the dark color of the walls.

3. The Red-and-Black Man

Shuffling footsteps approached from the other side of the gray door. I pressed closer to Mom, hiding my face so I wouldn't be seen. I was watcher and watched. She hugged and reassured me, but the gray door opened, and The Red-and-Black Man entered. I buried my face in the folds of Mom's dress, clutching the safety of its fabric, crushing the bright flowers. I turned just enough to peek out with the corner of my right eye. Only that would I allow. If I revealed no more than that, then perhaps he would not see me at all.

The Red-and-Black Man was huge, nearly to the ceiling, or so it seemed to me. His shoes were big, workingman's shoes, scuffed dull black and thick-soled, rising past his ankles like leather armor. They were powerful shoes, bringing him toward us with loud pounding steps that overwhelmed the dangerous black squares. With those shoes, he could never fall in. That was reassuring—the black squares, against those shoes, could do no harm. A powerful man, he strode across the linoleum and, with those armored shoes, had no fear of the black squares. I wanted shoes like that, big, strong, tough shoes, so that I too could stomp across the floor and not even worry about the black squares.

A round, flat leather cap with a narrow brim in front and stains around the edges topped his head. Black hair, rough-cut, escaped from under his cap and curled over his ears and collar. His broad, red face was wet and heavily peppered with black stubble. Tracks of sweat rolled down his face and disappeared under a large red-and-black bandana tied around his neck, the two ends hanging down at his open collar like a small, careless necktie. His shirt was checkered, red and black, not at all like the familiar blue shirts my father wore to work. His sleeves were rolled up. The muscles in his heavy arms bulged, and I could see a blue dragon sliding out from under his rolled-up sleeve and crawling down his arm. It had claws, wings, and a huge mouth with two tongues. Its eyes had not yet found me, but might at any moment. There were other things on his arms: a sword with words wrapped around it, an eagle with sharp talons, a flag, and a lady in a long dress holding up a torch; pictures in blue ink all over his arms. How did he do that, draw pictures on his arms?

A heavy brown leather apron was tied around his waist. My gaze was pulled to a matchstick in his mouth. When he talked, it moved up and down. Every now and then it skittered to a corner of his mouth, as if trying to escape, quivered for a while, like a frightened little mouse, and then scurried back into the other corner. The bobbing matchstick made you stare at it. How did it do that, march back and forth?

The Red-and-Black Man strode across the room, stopped at our corner, and looked down at us. "Ovah der?" he rumbled, as if accusing us of something, and pointed his thumb over his shoulder to the far wall.

I pressed closer to Mom, as far away from him as I could get. "Yeh," Mom said, nodding, pleased at her successful, if limited, conversation in *americano*.

The Red-and-Black Man leaned down and reached huge hands toward me. "Hey, yer a big boy," he thundered. The matchstick trembled in his mouth. "Ya gonna come in da truck and work wid me?"

I was terrified. I did not want to go in his truck! I squeezed against Mom. The Red-and-Black Man seemed surprised. Then he straightened up, smiled, and gently touched my hair with his rough hand.

"OK, big boy," he said, softly. "You stay here en' take care a' yer ma."

He smiled at me and left the room, and soon returned with another man, carrying a table. Six wooden chairs, a corner cabinet, and boxes of dishes, pots, and pans were also brought in. The men carried furniture to other rooms, stopping now and then to drink the cold water that Mom kept in a milk bottle in the icebox, up against the big block of ice.

4. *La Famiglia*

In time the turquoise was banished from the room. Over many years my parents transformed that old house. I had no understanding of how difficult it must have been to buy and maintain a house deep in those depression years, especially for penniless immigrants. It was a risky thing to do, with the economy as poor as it was, but they did it. All around us, Americans were losing their jobs and homes. On our street there were three abandoned houses, sad victims of the depression. One house was already decaying. Its dark and crumbling interior, where children once played and slept safely and mothers prepared family meals, had become a hollow husk of shadows and creaking floors where neighborhood boys dared to seek adventure, treasure, even ghosts. It is now, many years later, that I ask, How could my parents have possibly succeeded under those desperate economic conditions when so many other people, Americans who

cents and looked and behaved differently from the parents of my neighborhood friends, those "Real Americans" who, despite their Irish, German,
Dutch, or English origins, resided in one world only. In my earliest view
people were divided into two groups, Italians and Real Americans.

Years later I would learn that in the half-century from the 1880s to the
1920s, one-quarter of Southern Italy's population left for other places. It
was a massive migration; half of those people came to the United States,
and a pattern soon emerged of plying back and forth between countries,
of living in two worlds. They brought their Italian influence to their new
cultures and took new influences back to the old, weaving patterns that
bound one culture with the other.

Home was in both places. This was not the rootless wandering of dispos-
sessed people, but the enlargement of one's private world, the setting of
new roots by choice. They viewed crossing oceans as their natural right to
bind together and, in a sense, to conquer places and people through their
personal occupation of small spots on the globe.

Italy is approximately twice the size of New York State, a little larger
than Arizona. A long peninsula with a coastline of 7,600 kilometers, it is
nearly surrounded by the sea. Living in Italy means one cannot be too far
from an ocean. The peninsula is attached to the rest of Europe at its northern end with a mountainous border of 1,900 kilometers, separating it from
France on the west, Switzerland to the north, and Austria, Slovenia, and
Croatia on the east. Italy includes the peninsula, the major islands of Elba,
Sardinia, and Sicily, and another 70 smaller islands, adding still more coastline. Italians have historically been seafarers, and many traditional Italian
heroes were sailors.[1] Hundreds of years before the birth of Christ, Romans
voyaged to other lands and admitted others into their federation. They
journeyed across water and land, to England, Africa, and the East, conquering the world. They were among the world's earliest cosmopolitans,
and some of this has become part of the Italian character.

Southern Italians also held a conflicting parochial view, *campanilismo*, a
small-world attachment to a locale, a group, and codes of behavior. They
are contradictory attitudes, cosmopolitanism and *campanilismo*, both
linked to *la famiglia*, which is the core idea around which the others revolve. *La famiglia* was organized around the oldest blood relative in the
patronymic line, the matriarch or patriarch, in accord with the Italian traditions of respect for elders and primacy of the father's lineage. My father's
definition of our family was clear: his sister, Macrina, was the oldest family
member living in the United States. But she had married, thus losing the
primacy of their father's name. This made my father, the next oldest, our
family head.

---

1. For example: Giovanni Caboto, Alvise da Cadamosto, Cristoforo Colombo, Amerigo Ves-
pucci, Giovanni Verrazano.

For my father, the importance of the past had long ago evaporated in his passage to *l'America*. The past was of little importance for him in his New World in Nyack. My father's country was now the United States, not Italy; he now respected an elected president, not a king. *La famiglia* was still paramount, but *campanilismo* had faded. This was not his rejection of Italy but a new allegiance to the United States. As he defined himself in 1935, my father was an American, a naturalized citizen, having been in the country for 15 consecutive years, and for an earlier five years prior to World War I. His transition from Italian to American was complete, and he was at ease with it.

For Mom, however, past and present flowed together in a seamless stream of time, and she accepted without question the presence of the past. The matriarch of her family, *Nonna* Elisabetta, my maternal grandmother, lived in Italy, and the traditional age-based respect flowed from Nyack to Maida. Unlike my father, Mom still defined herself as Italian, with her identity still across the Atlantic, planted firmly in Southern Italy. Mom adjusted to Nyack, learned the language and customs, developed friendships, haggled with vendors, chatted with neighbors, consulted doctors, joined the Holy Name Society at St. Ann's Church, and successfully managed the family. Emotionally, however, Mom lived in Maida as much as she lived in Nyack.

It was not until my grandmother's death in Maida in 1969, at the age of 94, that our family center was transferred to Nyack. Mom became the family matriarch at the age of 67. It had taken her 40 years to make a full transition from Italian to American, to feel comfortable in her American identity and to feel that she lived in one world. In 1995, in her 95th year, Mom would explain to her grandchildren, "Italia is beautiful. I was born there and I grow up there. But Italy is no my country no more. Now, this is my country, the United States. America. I love this country."

I found considerable tension in self-definition. Are we Italian or are we American? The pressures were strong in each direction, and it would be many years, well into adulthood, before I resolved this. My definitional dilemma is a common experience of second-generation Italians born in the 1920s and 1930s who lived through World War II, in which Italy and the United States had become enemies.

Mom's world extended across continents and time. When I was a child, her reality reached back from the 1930s to the 1830s, through her grandparents, among the most important people in her life. "One hundred years," Mom explained. "*Cent'anni!*"

To me, a hundred of anything was an infinite amount. I was shown the carefully penned words at the close of letters from Italy: "*Cento baci*, Antonio (a hundred kisses, Anthony)"—probably the first written words that I learned to recognize. "*Per cent'anni* (for a hundred years)" was added to wishes for a happy birthday or anniversary. To offer "*buona fortuna per cent'anni* (good fortune for a hundred years)" was a sincere gift of good fortune and a long life.

"*Prego che trovi cento dollari in strada!* (May you find a hundred dollars in the street!)" was voiced when the immigrants learned the importance of the US dollar. Workingmen in the depression, those who had any jobs at all, might earn 12 cents an hour, so to have *cento dollari* was to be rich. I had never seen a hundred dollars. Indeed, I supposed that no one in the world had ever seen so much money. If such an amount existed, it must have been an enormous pile of green bills that would fill a room as large as our entire kitchen.

Such easy giving of things in the hundreds was not always benign. I remember *Zia* Angelina[2] sitting in our kitchen. With her powerful voice, her arms crossed defiantly, her face pulled into an impressive Italian scowl, she complained that an Italian butcher had tried to cheat her on the weight of some *bracciole*.[3] Had the butcher been German or Jewish, she would have been just as cheated, but not nearly as angry. For an Italian to do it—one whose own mother knelt and prayed so piously in St. Ann's Church right beside *Zia* Angelina—was intolerable. "But," she added, with a dismissive toss of her arm, "they're from Abruzzi, so what can you expect?" Still, that did not excuse him. He had insulted her. Shaking her fist, she declared "a hundred curses on him and on his whole store, too! *Cent'anni in Purgatorio!*"

It seemed a harsh penalty, a hundred years in Purgatory, for erring a few pennies on the price of *bracciole*. But some things, like everyday expressions of respect, are very important.

Another curse was so chilling that it froze in my memory, never to thaw. It created in me dark images so frightening that, with tightened fists, I had to hold my arms straight out in front of me, clench my teeth, and shake the images away.

"To him I send a hundred grinning demons to blacken his dreams and make him scream in the night for a hundred nights!"

I do not remember who said that or why. I do recall being frightened when I pictured those grinning demons flying on leathery wings through the black night and into the bedroom window, and I wondered what could have justified wishing such terror on anyone. Most frightening was the question that arose in my mind: What were they grinning about? What horrors had those demons in mind for their poor victim, shaking with the blankets pulled over his head? I was glad the lady had not been mad at me.

Such dark sentiments were accompanied by a gesture of no mercy—a gnashing of teeth on the side of the hand, accompanied by a menacing growl that would frighten anyone. That was the exclamation point of the curse, and it sealed the victim's fate. The wrong was righted and the world

2. "*Zia*" means "aunt." *Zia* Angelina was my aunt because she was my father's sister's husband's brother's wife. *La famiglia* could be extensive.
3. *Bracciole* or *bresaola* is thin-sliced beef

was again on its proper path. A curse was a useful way to settle accounts while safely stirring coffee. *Cento problemi* could be resolved in an afternoon's coffee session.

At that age I had no precise sense of numbers, but *cento* meant a very great amount. A family going back a hundred years was, to me, very old, and I did not consider who might have come before my great grandfather, Giuseppe Dattilo. One hundred years, or approximately three generations,[4] was the standard time span adopted by the people whom I knew. It included our own lifetime and our personal experiences with parents and grandparents.

This short-term view is understandable in a culture where written records, literacy, and a tradition of study from documents were not well developed. Well into Mom's generation, Southern Italian peasants were mostly illiterate, uneducated in any formal sense. The local church and municipalities had long kept records of births, deaths, and marriages, but most people lacked the skills to keep family diaries or other written records. The technology for creating a family record of photographs was not available to them until well into the 20th century, and even then, few people could afford cameras, film, or family portraits.

Family history was transmitted orally. When the elders died, their memories were only partly carried on. What remained was what the living remembered of what the recent dead had told them. Mom remembered her childhood, her parents, grandparents, and many of their stories about their own lives. Beyond that, the details of the everyday lives of real people in the early 19th century and before were impossible to maintain without written records.

One day in 1935, Mom sat with me on that old wooden chair in the turquoise room, silently asking, "How have we come to be here, struggling in a great depression in the midst of strangers, separated from our family?" Were Mom alive now to help answer that question, we would have to begin with her paternal grandfather, my great grandfather Giuseppe Dattilo, born in 1830. By my great grandfather's time, foreign invaders and popes had owned the peninsula for 1,000 years. Some were Italian kings, as in Sardinia. Some were the popes' minions in the Central states. Some were French, some Spanish, some Prussian. Mainly, there were the Austrians. They had stolen the Italians' homeland and the people grew angry. Whatever the origins of their rulers, the people said, "*U guvernu ladru!* (Government is a thief!)" and a powerful movement gathered to drive them out.

The 19th century was a time of European revolution, and my great grandfather's life was largely shaped by that turmoil. Living in the midst of it, he did not understand the scope of events rolling across Europe.

---

4. A generation, according to Webster's Dictionary, is the average span of time between the birth of parents and that of their offspring—approximately 32 years.

Like everyone else, he lived day to day in his small bit of the world. He had no formal education and knew little about the history that rushed at him and the millions, like my parents, who would leave their homes to cross the ocean to America. To understand those voyagers, we must review that history. As it unfolds in the succeeding chapters, I will introduce, in chronological sequence, the members of my family. They were ordinary people; no world shakers, no history makers, just people trying to live decent lives.

Chapter 2

Invaders and Popes (475–1700)
Napoleon's Italy (1792–1815)

1. Invaders and Popes

The Italian Peninsula, with its long coastline of 7,600 kilometers, had fine harbors, plains, a long mountain range, and, in the time of the Roman Empire, lush forests and gardens. The peninsula was a Mediterranean crossroads. People of many cultures and genetics came to trade, to live, to conquer or be conquered, and they acquired a rich and varied character.

A thousand years before Christ, the Etruscans—"intriguing, brilliant, charming, delightful, and highly humanistic people"[1]—had created a high civilization in the north before being nearly destroyed in the fifth century BC by invading Gauls. The Etruscans—it is not clear if they were indigenous or from another place—were absorbed by the powerful Roman State, one of hundreds in the peninsula. The Romans' humanistic philosophy, government, concepts of citizenship and liberty, art, science, and technology were drawn largely from the rich culture of the talented and peace-loving Etruscans. African, Byzantine, Etruscan, Greek, Phoenician, Saracen, and Roman civilization flowed together into the Roman Empire, further enriching the people's heritage. By 300 BC, the Roman Federation had incorporated the peninsula's 250 autonomous states into a unified Roman Empire that stood for the next 800 years.

Latin was the common language, and the right of Roman citizenship was extended throughout the Republic. Rome was the world, spreading westward to civilize Spain and the British Isles, southward into Africa, and eastward beyond Greece and Egypt. As explorers, travelers, traders, teachers, ambassadors, and conquerors, Romans ranged the world. Rome's language, laws, commerce, literature, arts, armies, and technology flowed along the Mediterranean Sea—the "Roman Lake"—connecting the world

---

1. di Franco (1988)

and shaping civilization. The Roman Empire was one of the contributions to civilization by the peoples of Italy. Another, the Italian Renaissance, would occur 1,000 years later.

Empires are not eternal. Rome fell in 475 AD, worn down after eight centuries and picked over by waves of invaders. Fractured, weak, and isolated, the cities that had been unified for a millennium under Rome were easy targets for the Austrian, Spanish, French, and German kings, and the Catholic popes. For the next 1,400 years the peninsula remained a feudal land, with a few lightly populated cities in constant rivalry. The popes and foreign monarchs, and their sycophantic hangers-on, owned everything and kept most people in poverty.

By the Roman Empire's end, Christianity had become the dominant religion. Roman popes fought and colluded with a succession of Germanic tribes—Astrogoths, Lombards, Franks, and Ottonians—for control over the Empire's remains. Invasions, alliances, intrigues, and rivalries fueled the centuries; feudal dynasties grew and collapsed. The peninsula was again a collection of separate small states. The Roman Church, however, remained a constant presence.

The Church provided a unifying sense of Italian identity and heritage. Even those who opposed the Church defined themselves with reference to it. The Roman Church preserved a rich Italian culture of art, scholarship, and science through the 1,400 years following Rome's collapse.[2,3]

In the 10th century, a political union of the papacy and the German king Otto I created the Holy Roman Empire. The Church and a succession of 50 royal dynasties, including the Habsburg, Hohenstaufen, Nassau, Luxemburg, and Wittelsbach families, owned the peninsula.[4]

By the 12th century, the European feudal order was changing. New commercial classes gained economic power in cities like Venice, Milan, Genoa, Florence, and Pisa. The rulers became dependent on the new bankers and businessmen. Italian city-states flourished as rich centers of business, arts, science, and politics, fueling the Renaissance, the outpouring of Italians' creative genius, from the 14th to the 17th centuries. The feudal societies of Northern and Central Italy were replaced by a resurrection of urbane, artistically brilliant cultures. Florence, the center of the Renaissance, was bathed in Etruscan heritage. Southern Italy, controlled by the Spanish Habsburgs and later by the Spanish Bourbons (*borboni*), remained a repressive feudal monarchy and contributed little to the Renaissance.[5]

---

2. Ibid., chapter 1.
3. Graziano and Raulin (2010), chapter 1.
4. By the 15th century, through their Spanish and Austrian branches, the Habsburgs had become the hereditary owners of much of Europe, including most of the Italian Peninsula. Through political marriages, intrigues, and wars, these families would maintain their wealth and power into the late 19th century.
5. This distinction between the urbane, developing north and the still-poor south continues in the economic conditions of the two regions, and is expressed in their mutual distrust and prejudice.

The Italian Renaissance flourished for nearly 300 years, after which Spain occupied much of the peninsula for two centuries. The Austrians drove the Spanish out in 1706, and began their 150-year occupation that lasted into the 19th century. The peninsula remained divided into small monarchies and dukedoms. The spoken dialects further separated one region from another. Nevertheless, by the mid-1700s, commerce and travel between the regions had grown. People began to realize that, despite the political separateness, their religion, literature, and history were shared. They grew resentful of the divisiveness that was forced on them by the foreigners and popes, preventing ordinary people from joining in common cause and threatening the rulers. From the gathering recognition of their common culture came a desire for national unity and freedom from foreign rule, fueling Italy's revolution.

By the end of the 18th century, Austrian monarchs had been in control of most of the peninsula for nearly 100 years, since they had ousted the Spanish. The Church, tied to the Austrians, owned the peninsula's center. The cultural mix, however, was churning—not only in Europe, but also in the American Colonies—and revolution against Europe's monarchies was under way.

By 1750, Europe's great powers, France and England, had reached into Africa, India, and North America, and soon after fought each other in the Seven Years' War to determine who would rule their world. One part of that war, known as the French and Indian War,[6] was over control of North America. From 1754 to 1763, some 30 battles were fought in Quebec, Newfoundland, Ontario, Nova Scotia, New York, Pennsylvania, and Virginia. With the aid of Prussia, England finally defeated the French navy and stripped away French colonies in India and Canada, gaining control over the Indian continent and also protecting the American Colonies from the French.

King George III then levied taxes on the American Colonies to help pay for the war that had "saved" them from the French. The Colonists objected. In the 15-year escalating controversy, the colonists demanded a greater voice in their own governance and the monarchy insisted on its right to control its colonies. By mid-1775, the American Revolutionary War was on.

On July 4, 1776, having had enough of King George and his taxes, the 13 American Colonies unanimously adopted the Declaration of Independence. The Declaration asserted that governments derive "their just powers from the consent of the governed," that all people have "unalienable rights," and that when a government destroys those rights "it is the right of the people to alter or to abolish it and to institute a new government." These were powerful revolutionary statements completely opposed to the European monarchs' assertion that they rule by "divine right." Those ideas

6. Anderson (2000).

of rights, revolution, and budding democracy guided the creation of the United States of America and flowed into the great antimonarchy, revolutionary wave that was to come in 19th-century Europe.

France saw an opportunity in the American Revolution (1760–1783) to strike back at England. Benjamin Franklin's years of diplomacy in Paris led to the colonists' 1778 alliance with France. It was an extraordinarily complicated business. France became the colonists' major ally, giving massive financial assistance, supplies, and troops, helping the Americans match the British military strength.

Here lay one of the great ironies of history: the French monarchy, driven by its hatred of England, helped to destroy itself by abetting the most severe threat against all monarchies—a successful democratic revolution. The court of Louis XVI—the time of Marie Antoinette[7]—was arguably the most corrupt, vain, foppish, egregiously selfish collection of royalty and useless hangers-on the world had ever seen. Franklin's pose as a simple "homespun" colonial (he was actually an urbane, brilliant, and sophisticated man), plus the Americans' revolutionary sentiments and later military successes, found a responsive antimonarchy dimension among the French people. The American Declaration of Independence fueled the brilliant French Declaration of the Rights of Man (1789), defining "the natural, unalienable and sacred rights of man." The American Revolution and its huge financial drain on France spurred the French Revolution (1789–1792) and the downfall of the monarchy that had supported the Americans.[8] The French Revolution transformed the government from an absolute monarchy to a constitutional republic, abolishing—at least in principle—feudalism and serfdom. It weakened the Roman Church and the hereditary privileges of the nobility, and established new freedoms for the people. With the sweeping popularity of its slogan "*Liberté, Egalité, Fraternité!*" it threatened Europe's monarchies and signaled the rise of formerly powerless subjects.

The revolution and the monarchies' attempts to stop the spread of seditious ideas about self-determination would dominate Europe for the next century. It was a stunning victory, a pivotal event in the world's move toward democratic governments. It deposed the French autocrats in a bloody and, as seen by revolutionaries in other countries, impressively effective manner. No wonder it caused such fear in other autocrats and emboldened revolutionaries throughout Europe. After the successes of the American and French revolutions, the Italians, like other Europeans, were caught up in the 19th-century flow of humanitarian, revolutionary, liberal ideas. The monarchies fought back, suppressing every liberal thrust, and Europe's next 100 years would be filled with the struggles of democratic liberals against the old order of conservative monarchists.[9]

7. Lever (2000).
8. Bowen (1948), pages 388–437.
9. This liberal-conservative struggle continues today, unabated.

The 18th- and 19th-century middle classes, growing larger, more educated, and prosperous, provided the revolutions' leadership and philosophies.[10] People were gaining knowledge of history, liberal ideas, and the concepts needed to create political philosophies. They realized the value of written constitutions and examined how states relate—or ought to relate—to their citizens.

In Italy, the early 19th-century revolutionaries were filled with American and French revolutionary enthusiasm. They fought against the autocratic rule of popes and kings, and demanded the separation of church and state in the tradition of the Roman Republic. Italians, they said, had too long been *un popolo senza patria,* a people without a country. Now, they urged, like America, like France, with the Roman Republic's political philosophy and law, it is time to overthrow the autocrats, unite the people, and create an independent nation of Italy.

Secret revolutionary societies spread throughout the peninsula. One, *i carbonari,* was named for the charcoal-makers who lived in the forests, hiding from the troops. The name symbolized coal (*carbone*), ". . . which, black and lifeless, burns brightly when it is kindled."[11] Members of *i carbonari* knew that, if caught, their next appointment would be with the hangman. But they persisted. The most influential group was Giuseppe Mazzini's *giovani italiani* (Young Italians).

In Italy, the middle class was small, northern, and urban, indebted to French culture. The leadership of the Italian Revolution, despite the southern men who fought and died in the campaigns, became primarily a Northern Italian undertaking. It is not surprising that its eventual benefits would be kept primarily by the northerners.

However, the *contadini* and *giornalieri*[12] of Southern Italy, like the peasants of all countries, had little time or energy to sustain revolutions. Repressed for generations by French and Spanish royalty, without the guidance of education and with little knowledge of history and political philosophies, they had few skills to understand relationships of people and their governments, or to create guiding constitutions. They knew that their lives were intolerable and their futures bleak, and that their rulers lived far better than they. These people rose periodically in rebellion over local issues and won some skirmishes, but lacked the intellectual and social tools to define complex issues and guide the long-term rebuilding of society.

The Italian Revolution had been gathering for decades, following much the same path as those of the American and French revolutions. By the early 1800s, many in Italy believed that their revolution was on the verge of destroying Austria's rule and the independence and unification of Italy were near, and that equal treatment of all Italians by a government of

10. Bowen (1948).
11. Hibbert (1985), page 246.
12. Farmers and laborers.

constitutional laws would soon begin. What happened next helped direct Italy's development over the next 150 years, through revolution, colonialism, militarism, world wars, Fascism, and national disaster.

2. The "Liberator" 1796–1815

Into the flood of the Italians' rising expectations in 1796 marched Napoleone Buonaparte[13] (1769–1821), who forced a complicated twist of history that still pervades Italian-French relations. Napoleon was a lieutenant at age 16, a captain at 23, and a brigadier general at 24. In 1796 he invaded the Italian Peninsula, defeated the Sardinians, drove out the Austrians, and became commander-in-chief of the French armies in Italy. For reasons of history and ties with French culture, Savoy and Nice at the northern French-Italian border were Napoleon's first targets. By 1799, he controlled nearly half of the peninsula, except for the kingdoms of Sardinia and the Spanish-Bourbon kingdom of Sicily-Naples. Sardinia had been conquered, but through treaties was allowed to retain its own monarchy, the Royal House of Savoy. In the south, Napoleon soon displaced the Spanish Bourbon monarchy.

Napoleon drove the Austrians from most of the peninsula, interrupted two centuries of Spanish Bourbon control of the south, and displaced the Church as the virtual monarchy of the peninsula's center. He was in control of the French government by 1801, and in 1804 he created the hereditary Empire of France, declaring himself "Emperor of France and King of All Italy." The French approved his transformation of their republic into a hereditary empire, and hailed Emperor Napoleon's family as the new ruling dynasty. He appointed his son king of Rome, a brother king of Spain, and two other brothers kings of Holland and Westphalia. One brother-in-law was made king of Naples and another king of Sweden, and his stepson became the viceroy of Italy.

By 1809, Napoleon's armies had overrun the peninsula and annexed Rome and the Papal States, and had briefly imprisoned the pope in order to reduce the Church's political power and replenish France's treasury. Napoleon's looters swarmed through the Roman galleries, cathedrals, and palaces, stripping them of their jewels and Renaissance paintings, sculptures and tapestries, even furniture. Masterpieces by Raphael, Caravaggio, and Bernini, hundreds of valuable manuscripts, and thousands of diamonds, emeralds, and rubies were loaded into wagons and trundled to Paris. It was said that one train included 500 wagons filled with stolen Roman treasure, protected by armed soldiers. Powerless citizens seethed as more than 1,500 Roman horses were led away to their new French owners.[14] Every hoofbeat

13. "Napoleone Buonaparte" is the Italian spelling, used for generations by the original Italian Buonaparte family. Napoleon I maintained his Italian name well into adulthood. The French and English form now commonly used is "Napoleon Bonaparte."
14. Hibbert (1985).

in that long procession on the cobbled streets was another stab of hatred for the French into Italians' hearts.

The French occupation of Rome (1796–1814) devastated the people. Not stopping at outright plunder, the French also imposed disastrous taxes, appropriated choice buildings for themselves, and paraded arrogantly in their plumed hats emblazoned with the French tricolor. The Roman economy was ruined, and the number of destitute citizens tripled in three years. Romans were routed from their homes and deported. Opposition was crushed by merciless French troops, whom the Romans named "the Assassins of Paris." Twice driven from Rome by Italian revolutionaries, the French armies regrouped, attacked, and reoccupied the city.

French rule was harsh. Soldiers and officials were arrogant and cruel looters of Italian treasures. They were dismissive of Italian people and their traditions and scornful of everything that was Italian, including the country's food and wine, even as they hungrily consumed both. When some men spoke of the French, they spat three times on the ground in contempt for "that race of dogs." The old men told the young, "*Se voi siete attaccati da un francese ed un lupo, spara prima il francese, perché lui è il più vizioso dei due.* (If you are attacked by a Frenchman and a wolf, shoot first the Frenchmen, for he is the more vicious of the two.)"

Napoleon the "liberator" had become the peninsula's despised new king, but many supported him. After all, some said, Napoleon had been Italian, not French, born into an Italian family on the island of Corsica just one year after France had annexed it from Genoa. His being a Frenchman by birth, they said, was but an accident of history that had robbed him of his true Italian heritage. And, they added, invader he may have been, but Napoleon was also a liberator, cleansing the peninsula of the Austrians, the "vermin Hun." Napoleon had spoken of his invasion as "liberation," just as our modern American imperialists in the 21st century define their encroachments into other countries.

"And where," some said, "do you think the Italian Revolution started? With Napoleon! He returned home, to his birthplace, liberated Italy, and brought to us the promise and excitement of the French Revolution!" In his first Italian campaign, Napoleon had introduced some of the enthusiasm of the American and French revolutions and helped stimulate hopes of freedom, democracy, and unification. By installing French-style republican governments, Napoleon created liberal codes and judicial reforms that would, half a century later, become bases for the new Italian nation. He introduced the long-divided Italians to a brief but important experience with the advantages of centralized government, and crafted the first unification of the peninsula in nearly 1,400 years. It was Napoleon, too, who determined the northern boundaries of what would later become Italy, identifying the line formed by the highest points of the Alps, Italy's "natural boundaries," as he called them. Napoleon predicted that Italy, with its unity of customs, language, and arts, would someday unite as a nation, with Rome as its capital.

Although powerful and prophetic, Napoleon had violated the liberal ideals of the American and French revolutions and become another oppressor. He had liberated the peninsula from the Austrians in order to dominate it himself, not to free it for the Italians. He parceled it out to his relatives and, when it was to his advantage, even gave Venetia back to the Austrians. The governments he created in France and Italy left little room for liberal revolutionary promises.[15] Napoleon had brought American and French ideas of liberty to the Italians and unified the country, but he did so under a French dictatorship, not an Italian democracy. He remade the peninsula into a French-style collection of "sister republics" operating on French rules and traditions. Some Italians supported the French, but most resented them and rebelled. With growing anger, Italians fought against French garrisons, but could not dislodge the powerful armies.

Italian revolutionaries had viewed the Americans and French in heroic terms—fellow revolutionaries in the liberal cause of freedom.[16] Napoleon had claimed to be Italy's liberator, but had become another oppressor whose greed derailed Italians' drive for independence. In the end, Napoleon, the French emperor, the Italian from Corsica, had little support in Italy.

Napoleon's exploits were not limited to the Italian Peninsula. In 1798, he attacked Egypt to weaken his major enemy, Great Britain, and to dominate North Africa. Napoleon attacked Syria to start his planned conquest of the Middle East. In 1800 he reached into the Americas and took back Spain's Louisiana territory, a million square miles that stretched from the Caribbean to the Canadian border.[17] He invaded the newly independent island of Haiti (then called Saint Domingue) to retake it as a French colony and restore slavery. Those former slaves, however, defeated the French army. With political problems at home he abandoned his plans for America and sold the Louisiana Territory to the United States, a country barely 20 years old.[18] By 1812, Napoleon controlled Western Europe and marched

15. In fact, according to the historian Simon Schama, Napoleon tried hard to dampen the memory of the French Revolution, proclaiming, on his rise to power in 1779, that the revolution was "dead." Schama (1989).

16. Such heroic regard was not shared by many Italians, particularly in the Papal States, who despised the French not only for their brutal revolution but for their decimation of the power of the Church in France.

17. The Louisiana Territory, stretching along the entire Mississippi Valley, had been claimed as a French possession in 1682 during the reign of Louis XIV—hence the name "Louisiana." In 1763, due to wars in Europe, the region was divided, and France ceded it to England and Spain. In 1800, France took major portions back from Spain, and in 1803 the entire territory was sold by France to the United States.

18. The Louisiana Purchase was completed in 1803. More than 800 million acres, stretching from the Gulf of Mexico to the Canadian border, were purchased from France for a total of $27,267,622 (about 4 cents an acre), doubling the size of the country. The territory included what is now much of Arkansas, Missouri, Iowa, Minnesota, North and South Dakota, Nebraska, Oklahoma, Kansas, Montana, Wyoming, Colorado, and Louisiana.

into Russia to punish Czar Alexander, his former ally against the British, for having reestablished trade with England. With nearly 700,000 men—French, Austrian, Spanish, Italian, Polish, Prussian—Napoleon marched to the edge of Moscow. The Russians, however, burned down their city, depriving Napoleon's armies of shelter and food, forcing them to retreat in the winter of 1812. When Napoleon saw that his war with Russia was lost, he abandoned his men and fled back to France to save his own life and protect his political future.[19] Napoleon's army had been beaten. Starving, freezing, depleted by desertions, injuries, and sickness, out of ammunition and supplies, his retreating armies were picked off in lightning rear-guard raids by Cossack cavalry. Fewer than 50,000 men—about 7 percent—survived,[20] struggling home long after their leader had safely returned. It was a degrading military defeat. His allies abandoned him and his European enemies renewed their plans to defeat him.

Uprisings against French occupation and other pressures fell on Napoleon. Austria again eyed the Northern Italian plains, preparing to oust the French and regain control over the peninsula. Although Napoleon's armies were decimated in their 1812 retreat from Moscow, this brilliant general was to win more battles. However, late in 1813, Austria, Great Britain, Sweden, Prussia, and Russia joined forces to defeat his armies in Central Europe, pursued him into France, and took Paris. Napoleon's hereditary empire collapsed, and France became a monarchy once again. Louis XVIII was installed as king,[21] reestablishing the royal line that had been interrupted when Louis XVI lost his head in the revolution.

Napoleon was not quite finished, however. In 1815 he escaped from exile at Elba, raised new armies of jubilant Frenchmen, and struck against the coalition forces in Europe. At first victorious, he was defeated by Belgian and British armies at Waterloo. In 1821, exiled to the small island of Santa Helena off the coast of Africa, Napoleon, at age 52, died of stomach cancer.[22]

"*Finalmente!*" the people of Italy said, ironically borrowing slogans from the French Revolution. "*Libertá! Equalitá! Unitá!*" The French and the Austrians were gone. Free of foreign control, Italians could now return to the task of unification. Liberty and democracy were surely near.

3. 1815, The Congress of Vienna: Kings Are Appointed by God!

But that was not yet to be. In 1814, anticipating Napoleon's final defeat, Austria brought together the European monarchs at the Congress of Vienna[23]

---

19. Napoleon seems to have done the same in 1798, when he abandoned his troops as his campaign in Egypt was about to be lost because of a defeat by the English navy.
20. Thus, nearly 650,000 men of the French armies were killed, maimed, or captured, or else deserted.
21. Louis XVII never reigned as king.
22. Napoleon died in 1821 at the age of 52 of a stomach ulcer, cancer, or their combined effects. See Flores (2007).
23. For a complete discussion, see Nicolson (1967).

to ensure that there would never be another Napoleon-like conqueror to threaten their monarchies. They would create a balance of power to ensure stability and peace.

The Congress of Vienna faced a whirlwind of demands for military protection, compensation, territory, trade, national pride, and countless other issues of self-interest. Its task was nothing less than the political reorganization of Europe. It was an extraordinary diplomatic effort, nine months of negotiations nearly overwhelming in their complexity and potential for failure, but the delegates succeeded. The Congress of Vienna was a diplomatic victory.

Peace and stability were major aims, but the Congress leaders also had other goals. The royal dynasties of Austria, Great Britain, Russia, and Prussia had been, with France, Europe's major powers before Napoleon's conquests, and were determined to restore their royal dominance. Reactionary conservatives, these people aimed to suppress the liberalism and democracy and the revolutionary ideals that had flowed through Europe.

When Talleyrand opened the Congress "in the name of the 'Public Right,'" the Prussians indignantly demanded, "What right have the public in any of the proceedings?" When England's representative timorously answered that his country was interested in the rights of the people, Austria's von Metternich arrogantly dismissed this idea. "The rights to be protected," he said, are the rights of royalty, the "rights of dynastic succession," the supremacy of "royalty over the public."[24]

The Congress of Vienna was a conservative counterrevolution to suppress democracy and liberalism and restore to power the monarchies, in particular the Royal House of Habsburg. The monarchs divided Europe amongst themselves, restored their pre-Napoleonic absolute powers, reestablished the principle of hereditary rule by "divine right," and suppressed the people's liberal democratic demands. They achieved a long run of relative peace, but also created a 100-year delay in the development of democracy in Europe.

The Congress of Vienna (October 1814–June 1815) was truly a royal affair, hosted by Francis I, Emperor of Austria, head of the Royal House of Habsburg. The Congress was a series of lavish banquets, balls, hunting parties, concerts, and other entertainments designed to keep its royal visitors and other delegates busy and satisfied. Beethoven's *Fidelio* and Seventh Symphony were performed. Although deaf by that time, the composer conducted a performance of his newest composition, his Opus 91, *Wellington's Victory*, to honor the win over Napoleon. Each royal leader brought an entourage of family, companions, servants, officials, physicians, and others. The logistics of accommodating so many royal personages in appropriate style, the provisions needed for the 1,400 horses and their carriages and tack, footmen and grooms, was a prodigious and enormously expensive undertaking, rather like that for a military engagement.

24. Page (1920).

Formal sessions of the Congress were never convened. All decisions were made during informal discussions among the four major countries, dominated by Austria. The restored French monarchy was added as the fifth power. The hundreds of other European delegates had little to do but enjoy the waltzes, champagne, and beautiful companions, and to agree with the decisions made by the major powers.

The political map of Europe was redrawn according to Austria's plans, and the Royal House of Habsburg emerged as the preeminent European power, followed by Prussia, Great Britain, and Russia. France was stripped of territories that had been conquered by Napoleon. Austria, Prussia, and Russia gained territory. Poland was given to Russia. The 300 German states of the Holy Roman Empire were coalesced into 39 new states of the German Confederation, to be controlled by Austria and Prussia. Norway was moved from Denmark to Sweden.

The "Italian question" was easily settled by regarding the peninsula as a problem of geography, with no complications such as democratic rights for the Italian people who were, after all, of no political importance to anyone. The Italian Peninsula and its islands were divided among the monarchies and the Church, given back to the same autocracies that had owned them before Napoleon's victories.

Austria appropriated the northern territories of Lombardy, Venezia, and Trentino.[25] The north-central areas—the Duchies of Tuscany, Modena, and Parma—were given to various Habsburgs, all related to the Austrian monarchy. The kingdom of Piedmont-Sardinia was expanded to include Genoa, Savoy, and Nice and was returned to the Royal House of Savoy, the only true Italian kingdom remaining on the peninsula. The southern kingdom of Sicily and Naples was returned to the Austrian-controlled Bourbon king Ferdinand, and Spanish feudalism, outlawed by Napoleon, returned to Southern Italy. Rome and the peninsula's center were taken by the Church, resurrecting the Papal States ruled by the pope, who was, in effect, another king.

The Congress of Vienna had restored Europe's absolute monarchies and the papacy and reaffirmed the pre-Napoleonic order of rule by divine right. It was a powerfully arrogant concept, asserting that God had given to a handful of families the right of absolute rule over everyone and everything. Charles Felix, the ruthless king of Sardinia who was restored to his throne by the Congress, was quoted as saying, "The king, as appointed by God, is the sole judge of what is best for the people, and the first duty of a loyal subject is not to complain."[26, 27]

25. One hundred years later, the Trentino would be a major factor in Italy's entry into World War I.
26. Page (1920)
27. I am reminded of President George W. Bush, who at a political rally in 2005 held up what was presumably a bible and announced something to the effect of, "I am loyal to a higher authority." His crowd of supporters cheered and stamped their feet in approval.

The Congress was a victory for the conservatives and a defeat of Europe's liberal, democratic drive. The idea, eloquently stated in the Americans' Declaration of Independence, that governments derive their "just powers from the consent of the governed," had been rejected by the monarchs at the Congress of Vienna.

After 1815, eight states remained in the Italian Peninsula, owned or influenced by Austria. By keeping the peninsula divided, Austria maintained control over the northern areas of Lombardy, Venetia, Tuscany, and Parma. The latter had been given to the Austrian archduke and the daughter of the Austrian emperor, respectively. Further, the restored Bourbon king of Naples (i.e., Sicily and Southern Italy) had an Austrian wife as his queen.

The House of Habsburg reached into every part of the peninsula, which was once again owned by the Austrians. The Italian people had not been consulted, had cast no votes, and had no part in those decisions, and their anger grew. The 1815 Congress of Vienna provided nourishment for the Italian underground to grow into revolution and wars against Austria over the next 100 years.

The Congress had created a long but restless peace in Europe. Political temperatures were rising, but the rulers ignored what was heating up below them. The Congress had renewed European monarchies and supported Prussia's domination of the reconstituted German states. In its various forms as Prussia, the German Empire, and a division of the German Reich, the German states would pull the world into wars stretching across another 100 years, into the mid 20th century.

Chapter 3

The Barn and the Castle
(Maida, 1815–1840)

1. "The World Is Turning!"

Following the 1815 Congress of Vienna, European royalty blossomed, enjoying a century-long golden age, growing in number, power, and extravagance. Europe seemed at peace, but beneath the surface anger grew. In the Italian Peninsula, people faced more Austrian rule and church domination, the same poverty and repression. Nothing had changed. The poor remained poor; unification and independence remained distant. The Congress had denied the Italians their liberal dreams of democracy, freedom, and unity.

Over the next half-century militant nationalism grew, not smoothly but in uneven jumps, with demands for independence and unification. Repression was the Austrians' response to any stirrings of liberal thought. To speak critically of the rulers was a crime. Newspapers were suppressed, all printing was government controlled, and any suspicion of radical thinking or even possession of an intelligent and questioning mind was enough to send men to the dungeons. When the young Giuseppe Mazzini, who later became a revolutionary leader, was jailed for the first time, the governor of Genoa commented: "What on earth has one to think of at his age? We do not like young people to think unless we know the subject of their thoughts."[1]

Dungeons overflowed with political prisoners, and executions filled the public squares. Families were forced to watch their men being hanged; women were beaten in the streets to intimidate their men; and mothers were billed for the cost of the rope used to hang their sons. Austria's long reign of terror against Italians is well illustrated by the Duke of Parma, who had been ousted in the first war of the revolution. After being returned to his throne by the Austrians, he wrote, ". . . now, send me the hangman!"[2]

For 800 years the history of the Italian Peninsula had swirled around the issue of who would rule—the Italian people or others. The Royal House

1. Page (1920).
2. Ibid.

of Habsburg, in its various forms as Austria, the Holy Roman Empire, the German Empire, and the Austro-Hungarian Empire, wanted the peninsula. The American Ambassador to Italy later wrote: ". . . however persistently the House of Habsburg claimed and invaded it, and fought for it, conquered parts of it, and established its provinces and its duchies, Italy was Italy and the Italians were Italians. Whatever the leaders may have thought, the people felt differently."[3]

Riots exploded in Naples in 1814, only to be put down by troops. In 1820, *i carbonari,* loosely organized groups of underground revolutionaries, invaded Naples and forced its Bourbon king—who had been installed by the Congress of Vienna—to accept a liberalizing constitution. A year later, Austria, aided by Prussia and Russia, put down the revolution. They restored all of Southern Italy to the Spanish-Bourbon king, commanded him to ignore the new constitution, and decreed execution for anyone who attended a meeting of *i carbonari.* The early uprisings failed to establish constitutional rule, but spurred the revolutionaries' determination and hatred of the Austrians.

The Italians and the French developed a cooperative antagonism that exists even today, but the Italians' dislike of the French was mild compared with their hatred of the Austrians, "the Huns." The passion to be free of the Austrians helped to drive Italy's 19th-century *rivoluzione* and *risorgimento.* For Italians, the century from 1820 to 1920 was a continuous war against Austria.

When my great grandfather Giuseppe Dattilo was born in 1830, Napoleon and the Congress of Vienna were long gone, Europe's royalty was again in control, the peninsula was still carved up by kings and popes, and the people struggled as much as ever.

Giuseppe knew that no one outside of the family was much concerned with their welfare. "Solamente *la famiglia se ne preoccupa!* (Only the family cares!)" *La famiglia* demanded respect and loyalty from each member, and in return protected them even from the law. *Omertà* (honor) is found in defense of family. *Disonore, disgrazia* (dishonor, disgrace) lie in failing to honor one's family, and the ultimate punishment is banishment from its circle. *La forza* (strength), like honor and respect, is rooted in the family— *la forza della famiglia.* Governments care only for themselves, and even the importance of the Church shrinks when it conflicts with family. Children learned the lesson early: "*la famiglia sopratutto,*" family above all.

Until Giuseppe was 30 years old, no one in his world had any experience of allegiance to a unified Italian nation. For that, they would have to reach back 50 generations, 1,500 years, to the Roman Empire. He felt no respect for his Austrian, Spanish, and French-derived rulers. Instead, he embraced the southerners' powerful sense of *campanilismo.* The term derives from

---

3. Ibid.

campanile (bell tower) and means an intense loyalty to one's specific locale and its traditions. Maida, like every southern town, had its *campanile* (tower) and *campana* (bell), proud symbols of the people's loyalties. All—*la famiglia, la campanile, la campana*, traditions, and loyalty—were enclosed within an imagined circle around the town. Friendship, respect, and affection reach from the family, decrease with distance, and disappear beyond the circle. The ringing bell called people not only to a place, but also to a code of morality and conduct, and to the security of being among one's own people. The returning traveler, hearing his town's *campana* in the distance, is reassured that his journey is nearly over and his town and family are within reach. In any town, the acquisition of a bell or replacement of one that had been melted down by the needs of war was a major event.

In Giuseppe's childhood (the 1830s), *la patria*, homeland, was within the circle of *campanilismo*. Loyalty was to *la famiglia*, then to *il paese* (the village) that circled the family, and next to *la regione* (the region) that circled the village. *Campanilismo* held people together but also kept regional groups apart. It was a narrow world view bound tightly by tradition, seeing the virtues of one's own kind, broadcasting distrust and suspicion of "outsiders," and keeping the people looking inward. Southern towns were no longer walled fortresses, but they remained separated as much by *campanilismo* as by the mountains and valleys that made travel difficult and dangerous.

During Giuseppe's first 40 years, from the 1830s to the 1870s, *campanilismo* was challenged as Italians were caught up in their long revolution. Their narrow view was pulled outward, toward the larger unity of a nation, and even the traditionally insular southerners flirted with the idea of a unified central government. Giuseppe remembered the angry men of the revolution who spoke fervently of "*Italia per gli italiani!* (Italy for Italians!)" They shook their fists at the Church, the "thieves" keeping people poor and powerless, at the ruling Spaniards and French and mainly the Austrians—the hated "Huns"—invaders who had carved up and feasted on the peninsula. They despised the northern Italians and the land-rich, greedy southerners who joined the foreigners.

The 19th-century Italian Revolution was primarily a fight against the Austrians. Riots in the early 1800s were beaten back by French and Austrian armies, but finally succeeded in Giuseppe's lifetime. Without formal schooling he knew little detailed history, but every child learned that Italians had achieved 3,000 years of civilization, that Rome had been established 750 years before the birth of Christ. Giuseppe had once heard a learned *gentiluomo* remark, "*Quando i francesi e gli austriaci erano ancora selvaggi, noi italiani già eravamo persone civilizate.* (When the French and the Austrians were still savages, we Italians were already civilized human beings)."

By Giuseppe's childhood in the 1830s, the French had been gone for nearly 20 years. He never saw a French soldier on Italian soil, although he heard that French troops remained in parts of the north and around Rome, to protect the pope. Old men's stories left Giuseppe with his own disdain for the French, which he would later pass on to his children.

All but the final eight years of Giuseppe Dattilo's long life—he would live to be 97—were scrolled out against the background of conflict with Austria. Not a literate man—only one in a hundred children in Southern Italy attended school[4]—he had not read liberal philosophies and revolutionary politics, but he knew of the failed uprisings against Austria. Ten years before Giuseppe's birth, travelers had brought exciting news of the 1820 revolution in Naples, defeat of the Bourbon king, and the promise of a new government for the south. But the Austrian army had been too powerful and nothing had come of it. By 1830, when Giuseppe was born, it seemed to the people as if their Bourbon king had always been in power.

In 1850, when Giuseppe was 20 years old, four revolutionaries arrived in Maida to enlist young men. They created more excitement and fear than the people had felt in years. The men, towering on huge horses, with their guns and belts of ammunition, excited the boys and caused mothers to hide with their children. The appearance of such large horses startled people in that hilly region, where horses were rare and sure-footed little donkeys were the rule. Some feared that the king's troops were in pursuit, just down the hill, advancing on Maida to rout the men and destroy the town. "Go away!" a courageous few raised their voices. "Leave us in peace!"

People came to the piazza to stare at these frightening men. Few recognized the bravery or perhaps the desperation of the men who dared to appear in public. One, about 50 years old but still vibrant and powerful, stood on a stone bench while his companions watched for any sign of the king's troops. He gave the people a history lesson filled with disturbing ideas.

"*Il mondo sta girando!* (The world is turning!)" he said, moving his arm in a circle. "Revolving, around and around. Turning from night to day; darkness to sunlight; yesterday to today; today to tomorrow! Turning, revolving. Without the world's revolution we huddle in darkness and cold, but each revolution brings us back into the sunlight! The world turns and we must turn with it! Revolution is as natural as it is necessary!"

Few understood his allusion to the world's turning successively through sunshine and shadow. The farmers knew it was the sun that journeyed across the sky, creating day and night, while the earth stood still. The man spoke impressively, but did he really know what he was talking about?

"Like the revolution of the world, we have our own revolution—the

---

4. As compared with 1/13 in Austrian-controlled Lombardy and 1/16 in England and Wales. Smith (1971).

revolution of the people, for the rights of all Italians from Calabria to il Trentino. *Siamo un popolo senza patria!* (We are a people without a country!) Right now, the poor are slaves of the rich who own the land, slaves of the Austrians, those hated devils who refuse to leave our land, slaves of the Church and the pope and the priests. The poor are tired of being poor, of having no work or work too meager to sustain their families. They are tired of having no freedoms, tired of whispering in the shadows to each other to talk of the injustice, thievery, and disrespect that falls on us constantly. They are rebelling. The rich of Austria, Spain, and France—not even Italians—claim our hills and valleys, our rivers, our fields and vineyards, our very sunshine as their own. Right now, the Church steals our land, steals our money, so the fat bishops and pope can live in riches while we starve, and they steal our souls to keep us frightened and quiet!"

The women, offended at his blasphemy against the Church, bowed their heads and made the sign of the cross. The men, being more cynical and less intimidated by the Church, agreed with the revolutionary, knowing that bishops, cardinals, and popes were only men like themselves, but more greedy. This revolutionary, they thought, spoke some truth, as long as he did not disparage *San Francesco di Paola*, the town's patron saint, or *La Madonna*. No man of Maida, but only the devil himself, would do that.

"All around us," he continued, "people are growing angry! They hear the words of our teacher, Giuseppe Mazzini, and are stirred by our general, Garibaldi, the soul and the sword of our revolution! Men now march, fight, die for *Libertà, Unità, Rivoluzione!*"

Giuseppe Dattilo looked around his quiet little town, at the hills and the clear skies. He saw Lupetto, the old brown dog, peacefully dozing in the shade, and signor Burgio's little donkey standing next to him with his head down, sleepily nodding, as if he, too, were praying. "What is this *patria* that he wants? *La patria* is here, under my feet. Where is this *rivoluzione*? Where are those angry fighting men and those fat and lazy priests?" His priest was a tall, wiry *prete* of constant energy and generous good will. What place was this man talking about?

"Our revolution," the man continued, "will destroy the Austrian devils and foreign thieves and the Italian traitors who support them. Revolution will free us, will create our united Italy, will put our lives into our own strong hands! Our revolution will break the grip of the Church, the kings, and the foreigners, and will give the land to the poor, to us, here in the south. When we own the land, all men will be paid their rightful respect. The land will belong to the Italian people, not to the pope, not to the rich, not to the foreign kings and their armies of devils!

"In our unity lies our freedom! We need brave men who will fight and who will one day return to their homes and say to their blessed parents, their wives and children, 'We are no longer owned by the Austrians! We are no longer serfs of the Huns! We are no longer slaves of the pope! *Non siamo un popolo senza patria*![5] Now we are citizens of our own republic! We are united; we are free; we have our respect once again! We are a people with a country!'"

For the man to give this speech was to risk his life and make himself vulnerable to the king's soldiers. His intensity was stunning, and he spoke with power and sincerity. Even those who did not like what he said agreed that he said it well, with passion and conviction. The sun was hot, but even there in *il mezzogiorno*,[6] it was rivaled by the fire of the revolutionary's speech.

Most of the people listened silently. The old men nodded, sadly agreeing, but were too worn out to participate. The women were frightened, seeing in his promises only more bleeding, tears, and dead sons. They knew that no good came from wars, but they remained quiet.

Cheering in approval, the young men raised their fists and pumped their arms in the air. The tall priest, however, was lividly angry and shouted his opposition, interrupting the speaker, unafraid of his men or their guns. In great agitation, his voice firm from years in the pulpit, he urged his people not to listen to those *disgraziati*. "*Vergogna!*" he shouted. "*Nulla di quello che loro dicono è vero! Loro sono peccatori, disgraziati, disgustosi. I lavoratori del diavolo!* (Shame! Nothing they say is true! They are sinners, disgraced, disgusting! They are the workers of the devil!)." The priest shouted at them, shaking his fist, stamping his feet, and turning so violently red in the face that some of the women rushed to his side, fearing he was about to collapse and writhe on the ground in his ecstasy of religious indignation.

Half a dozen young men, encouraging each other with back slaps and brave words, announced that they would join the revolution. After a night's sleep, however, and some cooling of intensity, only two went away with the revolutionaries, their mothers pleading that they stay with their families where they belonged. Months later, Giuseppe heard that both had joined a revolutionary group fighting in Naples. One had been killed in battle, the other captured and hanged. Most young men, however, remained in their towns, their peasant fatalism making them wary of easy promises. Too many times they had been promised a better life, but life, they knew, changes little. The fiery speech had heated them, but fire cools if not fed, and all was as it had always been. They remained to wage their own fight— the daily struggle against *la povert*à. *La rivoluzione* continued, but always, it seemed, somewhere else.

For all of Giuseppe's life, the revolution's promises had swirled in the background like fog. But commitment to revolution and to an Italy united under a single government meant pledging one's loyalty to distant people. While appealing to the more urbane northern Italians, this ran counter to

5. "We are no longer a people without a country!"
6. In the *mezzogiorno*. Because of its intensely hot weather in the summertime, Southern Italy was called *il mezzogiorno*, the noontime, of the peninsula.

the southerners' *campanilismo*. Like his neighbors, Giuseppe was not so much skeptical of the revolutionaries' convictions as he was distrustful of the distant *nordicani* (northerners) who seemed to be in control of the revolution. He was also doubtful that anything could improve their lives.

"But, then," he thought, "why not? If it is going to happen, as they say it will, then we will all be better off." Back and forth he went. "The revolution is good; it will help us. But why should I trust them, the northerners? The revolution is their fight. But if it helps us, then it is our fight. What to do? Pray, I suppose, and wait."

The people listened and waited. A few men left to join the fighting, but most did not. The poor do not make good revolutionaries. They are too cynical, too knotted up by daily reality to follow others' grand ideas. "Why should this be different?" they asked. They plodded on, too fatigued, too busy coping every day, not believing that the distant revolution could change their lives. As *il professore*, the schoolteacher, asked in the lofty style that he used to impress people, "Are we but wide-eyed children, beguiled by bright baubles dangled before us by seductive street vendors? No! We have work to do and families to feed, today, and not in some fantasy of the future."

2. Mazzini—"Monarchies Are the Enemies of Democracy"

As 19th-century industrialism grew, so did economic depression. Riots in Italy, Belgium, England, France, Greece, the Germanic Confederation, Poland, and Spain were quelled by soldiers and the "hangman's twine." Internal upheaval boiled beneath a light cover of international stability. The old conflict between liberal forces seeking power for more people and conservative forces fighting to keep power in the hands of the privileged few continued.

Il risorgimento was the 19th-century nationalistic drive for Italy's resurrection as a unified, independent nation. According to some, however, *risorgimento* was the bitter leavings of a betrayed, distorted, and usurped revolution. Either way, the people were drawing together, angered by the arrogance of the French, the thieving Austrians who had staged the Congress of Vienna, and the brutally repressive Austrian policies. Klemens Furst von Metternich had said that Italy was nothing but "*ein geographicher begriff* (a mere geographic expression)," referring to a peninsula that housed no nation of Italy. This was an insult, a haughty dismissal of the Italian people and their culture as being of no consequence, except as *servitore* of the Austrians. The Italians heard Austrian arrogance voiced by coarse people with inferior mentality and morality—but with powerful armies.

The 19th-century Italian Revolution (1820–1870) was an on-again, off-again war against foreign invaders. A hundred years later, Italy would fight her final battles against Austria in World War I, losing more than half a million young men and nearly becoming bankrupt.

For Giuseppe Dattilo, the revolutionary period was one of distant events of little immediate consequence. The ousting of the French in his father's time in 1815 had not improved their lives—they still had no land, no money, and no nation of Italy. The old monarchies, dominated by Austria, still controlled the peninsula and the people's lives. The distant revolution surged and ebbed as Italians fought against the Austrian-dominated monarchies and the church. *I carbonari, giovine italia*, and other secret societies spread underground, urging revolution. Bands of volunteers challenged the professional armies of kings and popes. Giuseppe Mazzini (1805–1872) emerged as the philosopher and intellectual leader of *la rivoluzione*.[7]

Widely read in European literature, philosophy, and poetry, and inspired by liberal ideas introduced by Napoleon, Mazzini joined the underground *i carbonari* in the 1820s in order to defeat the monarchies, end the pope's political rule, and merge the divided peninsula into a united Republic of Italy. He envisioned a broadly elected constitutional republic answerable to the people; a new, moral society throughout Europe; universal suffrage, freedom of the press, and a voice for the workers. Those goals, he believed, could be reached through education or, if necessary, armed revolution. He exhorted Italians to fight for a free and democratic Europe not only for themselves, but for all oppressed people. Italians, he said, could be the impelling power of a true European revolution.

Creating the radical organization *giovine italia* (young Italy), he argued that the monarchy must be defeated or Italians could never become an "independent, sovereign nation of free men and equals." A fiery revolutionist, Mazzini recruited activists, led uprisings, and gained so large a following that, in 1831, he was jailed and exiled. His writings were repressed and most were destroyed. From exile, Mazzini continued writing and organizing revolutionary groups in Europe (*giovine europa*). He became so influential that he was barred from Italy, France, and Switzerland, and was sentenced to death by the Austrians, who never caught him. His writing on liberalism, human rights, and revolution drew attention in Europe, and in America by those who saw in him reflections of their own American Revolution. Mazzini's supporters in England included Charles Dickens, Charles Swinburne, John Stuart Mill, and many others of note. In 1831, Mazzini wrote in his *Instructions for the Members of Giovine Italia*:[8] ". . . monarchies generate anarchy and despotism" and are the enemies of democracy. "Belief in the divine right of kings," he said, had long been the basis for monarchies. But that idea was no longer accepted, and a monarchy could not survive without the support of a powerful aristocracy, which is "the source of inequality and corruption to the whole nation" and must be destroyed.

7. For a discussion of this revolutionary period, see Lovett (1982).
8. Quoted and paraphrased from Mazzini (1831; 1945), pages 129–131.

The traditions of the Italian people, Mazzini said, are those of republicanism, a system whereby free citizens choose their leaders, who are guided by written agreement with the people—a constitution. Governments, he said, are responsible to those free citizens. Monarchies and other autocracies were inferior forms of government that were imposed by foreign invaders when the Roman Republic ended. He wrote: "The introduction of monarchy amongst us was coeval with our decay, and consummated our ruin by its constant servility to the foreigner, [its] antagonism to the people [and to] the unity of the nation."

Mazzini believed that the American and French revolutions had been incomplete. They had elevated to the highest priority the shallow and misleading idea that people have rights to liberty and happiness, but offered little definition of "responsibilities to the republic and for the greater good of all people." Emphasis on rights without demands for responsibilities, he argued, leads to selfishness and corruption, as it had in France following its Declaration of the Rights of Man. Modern Europe, he said, is as corrupted as the Roman Empire had become, leaving people no better off than if they were under autocratic control.

Mazzini spoke to the poor and the workers, to the realities of their lives. As mentioned in the preceding chapter, it is important to ask how so many Italians who felt little patriotism for an Italian nation became enthusiastic and patriotic citizens of the United States. Mazzini understood why, as indicated in his address to workingmen in 1844:[9] "You labor for ten or twelve hours of the day; how can you find time to educate yourselves? . . . You scarcely earn enough to maintain yourselves and your families; how can you find the means to educate yourselves? . . . The frequent interruption and uncertain duration of your work causes you to alternate excessive labor with periods of idleness; how can you acquire habits of order, regularity, and assiduity? . . . The scantiness of your earnings prevents all hope of saving . . . for your children . . . [or for] support of your old age; how can you acquire habits of economy? . . . You have no rights to citizenship, [no] participation either of election or vote [for] those laws which are to . . . govern your life . . . how can you feel the sentiment of citizenship, zeal for the welfare of the state, or sincere affection for its laws?" Mazzini believed that, while rights to liberty, the pursuit of happiness, and material comfort are important, perhaps even necessary, the highest level is duty to humanity. Each person, he wrote, ". . . is bound to live, not for himself, but for others. . . . The aim of existence is not to be more or less happy, but to make ourselves and others more virtuous. . . . To struggle against injustice and error . . . for the benefit of [our] brothers, is not only a right, but a duty; [it is] the duty of [one's] whole life."

In closing his *Essay on the Duties of Man* (1844), Mazzini emphasized a duty that he said was as important as the duty to one's country.

9. Mazzini (1844).

". . . in bidding you farewell, I will remind you [that] . . . your complete emancipation can only be founded and secured upon the triumph of . . . the principle of the <u>Unity of the Human Family</u>. [Today] one half of the human family is, by a singular contradiction, declared civilly, politically, and socially unequal and [is] excluded from the great Unity. [It is your duty] to protest on every occasion and by every means against this negation of unity. <u>The Emancipation of Women</u>, then, must be regarded as necessarily linked with the emancipation of the workingman. This will give to your endeavors the consecration of a universal truth."

In another presentation, Mazzini urged workingmen to "love and respect woman. Look to her not only for comfort, but for strength and inspiration and the doubling of your intellectual and moral powers. Blot out from your mind any idea of superiority; you have none."[10] Mazzini believed that through education and political action to remove autocratic obstacles, people would become free to enact those human duties. Only then would the full expression and satisfaction of human rights be possible.

He was a liberal idealist, aiming for a new, moral society in which all men and women understood and exercised their duties to each other, controlled their own lives, and were equal in all social, political, and moral respects. Universal suffrage, freedom of the press and religion, freedom of public congress, and development of labor unions were all goals of his social program. There was no room for kings or popes. Emancipation of the workingman and of all women was at the core of his campaign.

At the end of his life, he must have been disappointed, because while the revolution did bring about a united Italy, Mazzini's moral society in a true republic had not been achieved. His complex message had argued for revolution against the Austrians, national unification, a constitutional republic, and a new, moral society. However, it was only the first part of his message—revolution and unification—that was heard clearly and for which he is remembered. His major hope—for a democratic republic of free men and women, for full emancipation—was not achieved.

Among those influenced by Mazzini were Carlo Alberto (1798–1849), king of Sardinia; Giuseppe Garibaldi (1807–1882), the revolution's military leader; Camillo Benso di Cavour (1810–1861), the statesman of unification; and Vittorio Emanuele II (1820–1878), who became the first monarch of the United Kingdom of Italy. How ironic that Garibaldi, Cavour, and Vittorio Emanuele, three of the persons most credited for the revolution's success, would eventually be largely responsible for undermining the revolution and Mazzini's vision of a true republic.

---

10. Mazzini's ideas about women's status in society and his demands for true universal suffrage put him at least 100 years ahead of the United States, where women achieved the right to vote in August 1920 with ratification of the 19th Amendment to the Constitution.

The Kingdom of Sardinia under the House of Savoy[11] was one of the oldest and strongest in the peninsula. Sardinia had been left intact by Napoleon and enlarged by Austria's reconquest of Italy in the 1815 Congress of Vienna that had united Sardinia and Piedmonte into a single kingdom. Sardinia's monarchy and government were "reactionary and absolutist"[12] and dependent on Austria's continued protection. One of the eight Italian states created by Austria in 1815 to restore the absolute power of monarchy throughout the peninsula, Sardinia-Piedmonte would, within 50 years, usurp the democratic revolution, foist *il risorgimento* on the people, and turn all of Italy into a monarchy.

In 1831, just before being exiled, Mazzini appealed to Sardinia's new king, Carlo Alberto, to join the fight against the Austrians for a united Italy. Apparently incensed that a commoner would advise a king, Alberto refused. Ten years later he agreed, but with continued distrust of Mazzini. In 1848, Carlo Alberto committed Sardinia to fight the Austrians, agreed to a written constitution, and invited the other Italian states to join him. In fact the king was opposed to Mazzini's republicanism and had little love for the constitution, but agreed to it in order to cool the revolutionary threats to his monarchy.

3. Garibaldi—"Man Created God!"

The Italian Revolution continued through the 1840s, advancing and retreating as it won or lost skirmishes. In a failed 1834 uprising in Piedmonte, Giuseppe Garibaldi, influenced by Mazzini, began his flamboyant and heroic 40-year revolutionary career that stretched over two continents. Garibaldi was a sailor at 16 and a ship's captain at 26 who had battled pirates in the eastern Mediterranean. Unlike Mazzini, who was genuinely religious but antipapist, Garibaldi was fervently atheistic and opposed to the pope's rule, calling it "a cancer called popery." "Man created God, not God man," he once wrote to his followers.

Garibaldi's revolutionary career in Italy was aimed at defeating the Austrians and French in the north, the pope in the center, and the Bourbon monarchy in the south, unifying the peninsula and establishing Rome as the new nation's capital. He helped to achieve those goals, starting with a small volunteer army charged with Mazzini's and Garibaldi's fervor. They battled the armies of the pope, the French, the Bourbons, and the mighty Austrian-Hungarian Empire. Garibaldi fought, won, and lost, and twice escaped to the Americas, where he spent 22 years in exile, becoming a legendary revolutionary leader fighting against Brazilian and Argentinian repression.

---

11. Savoy is the royal house of Sardinia-Piedmonte, founded in 1032 by Humbert I, Count of Savoy.
12. Smith (1994), page 3.

He became a famous resident of the United States, living on Staten Island. Returning to Italy, he helped defeat Austria in the war of 1859, drove out the Bourbon king of Naples, and delivered all of Southern Italy and Sicily to the new Italian union in 1860. During his campaign, he was wounded two or three times in battle, sentenced to death and exiled several times, pursued by the French and the Austrians, branded an outlaw, shot and captured by his own king—but he returned later to fight for Italy.

Garibaldi helped maintain the revolutionary drive, raising *i camicie rosa* (the Red Shirts), his armies of laborers and shopkeepers. By 1860 he was a mythic figure, praised worldwide for the brilliance and bravery of his military campaigns in Italy and America.

In 1861, President Abraham Lincoln was so impressed by Garibaldi that he offered him a commission as a major general in the Union Army to lead troops against the South. However, after protests by the pope and influential American Catholics, Lincoln withdrew the offer. In 1864, Garibaldi was given a three-day welcome in London by half a million cheering people. The prince of Wales, the prime minister, and the foreign minister visited with him, and he was honored and named a "Freeman" of London (Smith, 1989). Vittorio Emanuele II, indignant that Garibaldi, not he, was honored as Italy's liberator, petulantly ordered the Italian ambassador to England to stay away from those celebrations for Garibaldi.

4. The Stone Barn

In the early 1850s, when Giuseppe was in his 20s, a small stone building, long empty, stood just outside of Maida. Perhaps it is still there. Its roof was caving in, and in the cold rainy season it was nearly as wet inside as out. No one mentioned "*i carbonari*" or "*giovine italia*" when speaking of the men who occasionally gathered there. Had either been voiced, the local police would no longer have kept their eyes averted, but would have been compelled to arrest the men for sedition.

When a few friends gathered at the old barn, one man stayed outside "to get the air" and watch the path. If someone came by he would be welcomed, offered a cup of wine, and told, "We come here to share a drop of wine and be away from our wives and the squalling little ones. You know how it is."

My great grandfather Giuseppe may have been part of those discussions. In their surreptitious meetings the men talked of politics, sharing news from other places. What they knew of the revolution was learned there. Their only newspaper was an occasional printed page and public notices posted in town, all controlled by the Bourbon king. Public discussions were never held for fear of arrest or worse. Jails, the wet and moldy ruins of Spanish Bourbon dungeons, were frightful places in which to rot and wait for "the king's necktie."

They talked of the gathering revolution, workers' riots throughout Italy,

Mazzini, Garibaldi, Sardinia-Piedmonte and its kings, Carlo Alberto and Vittorio Emanuele II. They understood the power of the Austrians, who, despite the appearance of separate kingdoms, were in control, marching troops everywhere to shoot down or hang insurrectionists. Mostly the men talked about their own repressive King Ferdinando, who had been restored to power in 1815 by the flourish of an Austrian pen at the Congress of Vienna. King Ferdinando's royal family was related to the Austrian Habsburgs, the Prussians, the French, and the Spanish throne. They lived luxuriously, having regained feudal privileges that had been interrupted by Napoleon, while the peasants continued to struggle in the soil and their few resources were taken by the wealthy.

I imagine their discussions might have gone something like this:

"I was in Naples," a young man reported, "and all the talk was of Carlo Alberto, that he is getting ready to fight *i borboni* and the Huns. They say he will soon sail with his Sardinian army down the west coast to invade Naples and destroy the Bourbons' garrison there."

Derisive snorts from the older men greeted that news. They had heard it all before.

"More men will join," he continued, not deterred by his companions' skepticism. "Thousands more. Alberto's army will grow, *i borboni* will be defeated. Southern Italy will be free. Then Alberto will march north, drive the French and Austrians from Rome and the whole peninsula."

Pietro was an old skeptic who had lived through the reign of the previous king, Napoleon's occupation, the Congress of Vienna, the restoration of the Bourbons in Southern Italy, the Austrians' political repression, and the reign of Ferdinando I. "Giorgio," the old man asked, "do you believe the Austrians will let Carlo Alberto do that? You think the Huns will stand by and watch *i borboni* get thrown out by the Sardinians and do nothing to stop it? And if they let Alberto reach Naples, do you think the Sardinians are strong enough to beat the Bourbon and Austrian armies?"

"Yes!" Giorgio replied. "Carlo Alberto, with his Sardinian army, could beat the Austrians, the French, and *i borboni* combined, if he had Garibaldi by his side!"

"Ah, but Garibaldi is not by his side. Carlo Alberto sent him away, and now Garibaldi is leading revolutions against the South American dictators, giving his best years to them. He's their revolutionary leader, their hero, when we need him over here!"

"Listen," another man added, "a few years ago Garibaldi almost beat the Austrians in Piedmonte. Their army was too strong for his few volunteers and he had to leave, go to South America, because the Austrians will kill him if they catch him. But he'll be back, stronger than ever, to join Mazzini. Then you'll see!"

"I think," young Arturo offered, "Carlo Alberto should bring his ships down the coast, march on Rome, and take it from the pope. Then, with the pope beaten, all the monarchies will give up and Italy will be united."

Were it not so serious, Pietro would have been amused by the young man's innocence. "Where do you get these fairy tales?" he asked. "First, the French army is garrisoned outside of Rome. They're all friends again: the French, the Huns, the pope. And don't forget the Sardinians are still friends with the Huns, even if they might want to take over the south of the peninsula. They all sleep in the same bed. They all have the same little bastards for children. If the Sardinians showed up, the French, the Austrians, *i borboni*, and probably the Spaniards, too, will all gang up on them. Who knows? Even the Prussians might jump in. And the Bourbon army with its 200,000 men will march up from Naples to help the pope. The pope's army alone has 150,000 men! They'd never let Rome be taken. And if Rome did fall, and if the pope was run off, what makes you think the rest of the kings in Italy would just quit and walk away?"

"What?" answered Arturo, who was now getting angry at this obstinate old man. "I'll tell you what. While they have their thumbs up their asses, they keep their noses in the air to sniff out how the wind blows. They'll know what's happening. We're on the way to unification. Look at all the riots in the cities. The kings will be thrown out, and they know that. They can see how the river flows, just like the rest of us can see it. They'll want to get out, save their own dirty necks. Then we'll have our republic!"

"Ah," the old man replied, "and right there is the next big problem."

"Revolution's always a big problem," Arturo said. "But we'll win. We can't go on forever like this. We'll win!"

"No," said Pietro. "I don't mean the revolution. I mean after the revolution."

"After? Why after? After the revolution is over, we'll be one country, united. The kings, the Huns, the French, all driven out. The pope locked up in his church. We'll get our land, like they promised. Our families, they can start living like human beings. We'll have our respect."

"You hope, my friend. Look," Pietro said, speaking with more firmness. "I'm telling you, if we win, then the next trouble starts, after the fighting is over. It's already started. Mazzini, he wants a democratic republic, no kings! You understand what that is? He wants the people to control the government, not the other way around. That's what a republic is. That's what he's been fighting for for 15 years. But Carlo Alberto, he's no dummy; he doesn't want a republic. He wants a strong monarchy for himself. He wants a kingdom, with his own army, so he can be king over all Italy, so his family, *la Casa Savoia*, can stay rich and rule everybody in the peninsula, not just in Sardinia-Piedmonte. Don't you see? The Sardinians will come down from the north, push Mazzini and his republicans out of the way, and conquer the whole peninsula, take it all over, turn it into one big monarchy with Alberto as king of everything! If we get unity that way it won't be unity for us; it will be invasion and conquest by the Sardinians, the northerners, over all of us. And where will we be? We will be the same ignorant *contadini*, powerless subjects of the king, and just as poor as always."

This pessimism made the others pause. After a while, the younger man answered. "Pietro, this takeover by the Sardinians, you call it 'invasion,' 'conquest'? What do you mean? It won't be invasion. It will be revolution, for unification. That's what we want, no?"

Pietro was saddened at how uninformed the enthusiastic youth could be. He answered, "Of course that's what we want. But Mazzini and Carlo Alberto have different ideas, and each has his followers. And Garibaldi, he says he wants a republic, like Mazzini does, but he'll fight for monarchy or republic, as long as Italy is united one way or the other. Even if we win the revolution, even if we drive out the Huns, then we have to fight ourselves. North against south, kings and popes against farmers and workers, like jealous brothers in a family, we will fight to see what wins—a monarchy with a king, or a republic with a president! If the king wins, then nothing changes. We'll just have a new king instead of the old king.

"That's the problem coming up! Right now, what they talk about is revolution and unification, and everybody agrees. That's what they're fighting for. But the problem is, what comes after? Which way will the new country go, monarchy or republic? A king or a president? If we choose Mazzini and his republic, we will be free, with honor and respect. But if we choose the Sardinian king and his monarchy, we will be conquered and forever be servants to the king."

Arturo was irritated at old Pietro's stubbornness. "Why is that a problem?" he asked. "What's the difference, kingdom or republic? Either way, it's good for us, as long as we're united, as long as we're all together, one country, that's what's important. That's what the revolution is about. Unification!"

"After all," another young man put in, "we're used to having a king. Maybe Alberto will be a better king for Italy than Ferdinando and his *borboni*. Maybe what we need is a strong king to hold us all together. This president they talk about, I don't know. Who would he be? Mazzini? Lots of people don't understand Mazzini and don't like him. I heard he even wants to make women equal to men; to let the women vote! My God, they don't even let us vote! And anyway, isn't a president just like a king? Don't they do the same thing, run the country? What's the difference, a king or a president?"

Pietro looked to heaven and slowly shook his head. "What's the difference? My boy, you don't know the difference between a king and a president, a monarchy and a democratic republic? Where have you been all your life, hiding in a Calabrian cave?

"I'm the old man here. You'd think I'd be the one to support the king, arguing to keep the old royalty, and you, the young ones, would be all fired up for the revolutionary republic, for Mazzini's new democratic world. That's the way it used to be. The old men want tradition, for things to stay the same; the young want everything new. But now it's all turned upside down, and this old man preaches revolution to the young, and the young preach monarchy to the old!

"You ask what's the difference? Kings and presidents? There's all the difference in the world! Don't you know what Mazzini's been talking about all these years? I will say it as many times as I have to: if we choose Mazzini, we will be free; if we choose the king, we will be but the king's subjects and nothing will be changed!"

The younger man, feeling insulted, thrust his arm over his head as if he were throwing away old Pietro's criticism. "I know about kings and presidents," he said. "You think I don't know?"

"Yes," Pietro said, sadness creeping into his voice. "That is what I think. You don't know."

Men learned from each other, but most lacked the sophistication to appreciate the struggle between Mazzini's republicans and Sardinia's royalists. Nor did they know much about the conflicting revolutionary and counterrevolutionary factions in the peninsula. They knew that poverty and oppression were growing; men were servile to the rich and could have little honor or respect even in the eyes of their own families, and some were rising in anger against their Austrian owners. However, until the rapid changes that began around 1860, the southerners were neither seriously involved nor well informed.

5. The Castle

At the other end of society lived Don Marino's [13] family, old and rich, the town's biggest landowners and employers. They were agreeable people, albeit aloof, abiding by the old rules of responsibility for the people who worked the land for them. Often the Don allowed the families of farmers who had been taken ill to remain, rent free, in one of the estate's huts. He showed kindness to tenants who were struggling with illness or other misfortune, and he made generous contributions to the Church.

For the most part, however, the gentry had little awareness of the struggles of the poor. It is not that they were uncaring but as people agreed, "*i ricchi non sono come noi, hanno altre cose a cui pensare* (the rich are not like us, they have other things to think about)."

The ladies of the Don's household had nothing to do with politics or business. They dressed beautifully, never worked, were aloof from the peasantry, and, although frequently driven through town in their carriages, never stepped down, but sent their servants to do their shopping. They attended religious services every day in their private chapels, where local priests went to them. Their social lives did not intersect with those of the townspeople. The Don's family sometimes traveled to Naples, a place few

---

13. This is not his actual name.

Maidese had ever seen. They even attended, by invitation of the king, some royal functions. They did, of course, interact with their own priests, servants, dressmakers, and tailors, and thus had some contact with the people of Maida. *Le donne* generally treated others with tempered, often kindly words, sometimes inquiring about a servant's health or that of a relative. Of course, in each generation there were one or two exceptions, distinctly haughty women who took their unearned status so seriously as to think they really were better than everyone else.

Don Marino walked his fields and orchards with his workers; when younger, he had often labored alongside them. He could discuss any topic with them—crops, livestock, markets, weather, health and illness, families and children, even God. But the political situation was one topic he and his workers avoided. On different sides of the issues, they still had to live and work together in the same town. They remained bound, each man dependent on and respectful of the others.

It was easy for young firebrands to revile the rich, as did those revolutionaries who had visited Maida. But when the issues were viewed in local terms, and "the rich" were the family of *Don Marino,* then the whole revolutionary drive was blunted. In that way, the local gentry served the king's purpose, forming a buffer between king and peasant.

Don Marino was careful with his words, especially in matters of politics. In those excited times, a casual remark on his part could cause a good deal of mischief. He was concerned about the uprisings, the growing demands for liberal political and social change and even for replacing the monarchy with a republic. But he would not voice those concerns to his farmers.

While the farmers and laborers met clandestinely in the old barn to share seditious political ideas, always alert for the police, *Don Marino* discussed his politics without fear of arrest. He did so only in the company of his family and close friends, taking care that no servants were present who might reveal his thoughts to others. The Don, too, was trapped: his political ideas were also clandestine, hidden not from the royal authorities, but from the farmers and laborers of his town.

Thus, secrecy prevailed. By tacit agreement, one side never challenged the other with open discussion of the revolution. Issues such as wages, crop payments to landlords, opportunities for farmers to buy land, political imprisonment and execution, suppression of free discussion, people's desire for active participation in government, and so on were never resolved. There were only two sides—the rich, with their Austrian and papal allies, and the poor, who had only themselves. Both sides maintained their feudal definitions of status, dignity, and mutual respect, and nothing ever changed. That was good for the Don and his family, but it frustrated the farmers and laborers, and inevitably would explode in revolution. It was said in Maida that *Don Marino* and his cousins Domenico and Gianni often relaxed after dinner, smoking and talking politics. *Don Marino* had no liking for cigars, but he did enjoy a good brandy after dinner, savoring its smooth warmth as he rolled each sip before swallowing.

Domenico was satisfied with his life. With large farms in a nearby province, his family lived quietly and well, untouched by the poverty that surrounded them. The Bourbon king, restored to Naples 25 years earlier by the Congress of Vienna, was good for the gentry. "The king is an amiable man," Domenico might have said one evening. "He maintains civil order and does not demand much from us, just some respect. Unlike those kings in the north, he makes little pretense of 'developing' his kingdom and wasting his treasury. He keeps our taxes low, leaves us alone to pursue our business, and everybody is happy about that."

However, Domenico was concerned about the northern revolutionaries, worried that things might change, even in the south. "The pressures are too great to resist forever," he said. "People are dissatisfied, rioting in the northern cities. The agitators are put down in one place and spring up in another. I wonder if those people understand what mischief they are letting loose, with all of their demands?"

"They are led by those two insane bandits," Gianni said. "Mazzini and the atheist Garibaldi. If they have their way, they will steal our land and tax us into the grave. They don't understand politics; they don't know the world. In their ignorance and greed, they dream of stupidities that will ruin us all if they win. But they'll never win with that ragged bunch following them around! And Garibaldi, he's nothing but a fisherman and probably can't even walk straight on solid ground."

"Don't be too sure," Domenico answered. "Just because you think they're insane doesn't mean they can't cause a great deal of mischief, and even win. They command thousands who are ready to follow them. And they have the new Sardinian king on their side, and maybe he's insane, too, but they begin to look like a real political force. I fear what they will be like in another few years."

"I'm not worried," Gianni said, with the dismissive certainty of rich young men who live well and have few responsibilities. "Garibaldi and his band of chicken thieves might be tough in the Argentine jungles against a bunch of savages, but they can't stand up against the Austrians, the French, and the pope. Throw in King Ferdinando's troops, and it's a force that the Garibaldini thieves cannot possibly beat."

"Hmm," *Don Marino* wondered, "and what about that new Sardinian king, Vittorio Emanuele II? How do you suppose he fits into all of this?"

"Ah! The Troglodyte." Gianni laughed. "He won't win any support based on his good looks! I've been thinking of joining his army just to see if he's as ugly as they say he is. And I heard he's so dense that he can't even compose one sentence in Italian or, for that matter, in his own French tongue."

They smiled at that.

"Still," Domenico suggested, "the Sardinian king might be a real problem for us, throwing in with Mazzini and Garibaldi, as he seems to be doing since his father's defeat by the Austrians. He's from an old military family, commands the strongest Italian army on the peninsula, and has no love for us here in the south. What do you think?"

"No," the Don answered. "I can't believe he's really in with Mazzini. It would be suicide. Look, they have different goals; Mazzini wants a republic, he has no love of royalty. If Mazzini prevails, then Vittorio Emanuele's head is on the block, and his monarchy is dead. I think he's more clever than he looks, that behind that doughy face lies a crafty brain. Or, more likely, Cavour is telling him what to think and do. He holds an uneasy alliance with Mazzini because they both want independence and unification of the peninsula under an Italian government. So they are both against the Austrians, and they both want Garibaldi's army help to drive out the Huns."

"So," Domenico said, "right now they need each other. Is that it?"

"I think so," the Don answered. "But what if they should succeed and take over the peninsula? They won't be able to live together. Mazzini wants his republic, and the king wants his own House of Savoy to rule the new country, to build a military empire, an even greater monarchy. Now they have the same goal, but reaching that goal will cause them to break apart and fight with each other."

Domenico was distressed by what *Don Marino* was saying. "What a disturbing picture you paint for our poor peninsula. If the revolutionists win, that means they will have beaten the Austrians, the French, the pope, and then come down here and defeat Ferdinando's army. That means bloody war all along the peninsula, including right here in our own fields and vineyards.

"And then, as you see it, Vittorio Emanuele is just using Mazzini, and when he no longer needs him, there will be even more bloody battles raging over the carcass of Italy. That's a picture of never-ending bloodletting, revolutions that will go on through generations and exhaust everybody. And if that happens, then Italy will become so weakened that in another ten years Austria will simply climb over the Alps, stroll southward through the peninsula, and take it over again, with hardly a shot to be fired!"

"I think that's not likely to happen," *Don Marino* said, "although the Austrian royal family would be happy if it did. No, I think the revolution might have a good chance of success, but there will be much bleeding. The real problem"—and here *Don Marino* began to sound very much like old Pietro in the ruined barn—"is the question of which faction of the revolutionaries will eventually take control—Mazzini and his revolutionary republicans, or Vittorio Emanuele and his monarchists. In either event, I am afraid that our own poor King Ferdinando is finished; the Bourbons are on their way out."

"But then, if the revolution succeeds, what will happen to us, to our lands? We'll be finished!"

"Perhaps not," *Don Marino* said. "There is still a small chance that King Ferdinando will survive in Naples. Then nothing much will change for us. His survival depends on how well the Austrians, French, and the pope deal with the revolution up north. They might be able to hold it off for another 20 or 30 years. So you and I, Domenico, might never see a real revolution in our lifetimes. But it will happen, eventually. Gianni, you're young, and I'm afraid things will change for you."

"Well," Domenico said, with an apologetic glance at Gianni, "a long delay is at least something to hope for. And if our king doesn't survive? What then?"

"Then it will all depend on which faction, republican or monarchist, ends up with the power. If Mazzini wins, we may be lost, our farms taken, the churches emptied, the peasants in control. If the Sardinian king wins, we will at least have some chance to keep what we own, although I can't find it in me to have much trust in that man. I think we won't like either of those two eventualities, though I suppose victory by the king would be the lesser of the evils."

"Ah, then we should do what we can to help our King Ferdinando," Domenico suggested. "And if that doesn't work, then we welcome the Troglodyte himself and accept a Sardinian monarchy. What do you suggest we do to help? What are you going to do, cousin?"

Don Marino pointed out the window to a field that was about two miles away, down the hill. "You can't see it from here," he said. "There is an old barn where my workers meet now and then, in secret they think, and talk about politics and about us. I don't want it voiced around that we are their enemies; discretion is our clear path. So, what will I do? Nothing at all. I intend to be quiet, to go about my business and see how it all comes out. I intend never to discuss politics outside of this room. I will be respectfully silent when others talk of politics, whatever side they take. Remember, if we show support for the monarchy, as our senses tell us to, then we will set the people's teeth on edge and maybe bared against us. We will run the risk of becoming their convenient targets in place of the king. Remember what the French peasants did to their royalty not too long ago. I don't say that will happen here. The French aristocrats were just as arrogant toward their own peasantry as they were toward Italians when they were here, and the peasants hated them. We have better feelings here, with our farmers, our workers. After all, we Italians are a great deal more civilized than the French. But let's not forget history.

"Only if we are careful and neutral can we reach over and take our share of the benefits from whichever faction wins. That's what I am going to do, or rather not do. And I advise the same for you." He looked pointedly at Gianni, his intemperate young cousin, who wanted action now.

While things remained quiet in Maida, Mazzini's demands for democratic reform stirred people elsewhere. Riots had exploded in 1820 and 1821 in Naples and Piedmonte, and in 1831 in Parma, Modena, Sicily, the Papal States, and again in Naples. Under the revolutionary pressures, several states, including Rome, adopted new social contracts with the people: constitutions. All the uprisings, however, were soon put down by Austrian, French, and papal troops, and the short-lived constitutions were rescinded or, as in the Kingdom of Naples, ignored. But a seething undercurrent for freedom persisted that would grow and break out again.

Some 15 years later, in 1847, Austria, already controlling most of Northern Italy from Trento eastward through the Kingdom of Lombardy-Venezia, marched into the papal state of Ferrara, an arrogant move that caused new rioting in every major Italian city. By 1848, liberal agitation and anger at Austria was at its peak, impelled in the south by continuing poverty and hopelessness, crop failures, famine, and increasingly violent oppression. To add to the misery, cholera epidemics swept up from India's Ganges and flowed into Russia, the Baltics, England, Europe, and even China. Those were not the best of times.

The men in the barn with their jug of wine and the men in the drawing room with their brandy and cigars shook their heads over the same issues, which they would not discuss with each other. Each confided with those they trusted, and everyone wondered where it would all lead.

Chapter 4
La rivoluzione (1840–1871)

1. The Pope's Liberal Errors

By the middle of the century, people's dissatisfaction, often starting with small, local issues, had become a surge of contradictory demands and uncoordinated rebellions. Stirred into this mix were Mazzini's revolutionary democratic ideas and antimonarchy sentiments, and the dramatic military actions of Garibaldi and other revolutionaries. More people criticized the conduct and legitimacy of their governments and began to recognize their shared concerns.

Liberal energy charged through Europe, seeking freedom, constitutions, and democracy. Repressive regimes in Austria, Denmark, Italy, Spain, the Netherlands, and the German states agreed to reforms. Europe briefly enjoyed a measure of freedom: public discussions were held without censorship or police reprisals; hundreds of newspapers were launched, and new journals devoted to sharp, critical caricatures of politicians flourished. Most people were illiterate, and the drawings—clever, biting, artistic, and entertaining—were openly enjoyed. Book publishing flourished for those who could read. Theater and opera enjoyed uncensored freedom to explore previously suppressed ideas. Europeans were variously rioting or celebrating, welcoming new constitutions and liberalized lives as the autocrats' repressive grasp weakened. Ordinary people glimpsed a brighter future.

In Lucca, Milan, Naples, Piedmont, Tuscany, Venezia, Sicily, and the Papal States, rebellion forced reforms. "This time," the people said, "we will keep our freedom." By 1849, the Italian Revolution finally seemed to be nearing victory.

Even the Church, much like a powerfully conservative monarchy, responded to the people's demands. Pope Gregory XVI had been viciously antiliberal, giving his roving band of counterrevolutionary terrorists, *i centurioni*, unlimited power to seek and destroy liberal activity anywhere in the Papal States. His successor in 1846, Pope Pius IX, was no liberal, but wanted to quell the revolutionary intensity. Influenced by a few liberal Vatican ministers, he promised a written constitution, amnesty for 1,000 of the Church's political prisoners, safe return for exiles, and freedom of the press. He even allowed the Jews to come out of their ghetto at night, lifting a restriction imposed long before by the inquisition.[1] He supported some liberal causes, such as construction of a railroad and creation of a peninsular customs league. Austria, Italian monarchies, most of the Vatican, and conservatives in general were opposed. They feared such reforms would increase contact in the divided peninsula, strengthen the drive for national unification, and overthrow the monarchies. It was in their self-interest to keep the peninsula divided.

The revolutionaries, heartened by the initial actions of Pius IX, mistakenly believed that his was a liberal papacy. They asked even more of their new, powerful "friend."

The pope, however, had expected his mild liberalizing to satisfy the Romans and dampen the uprisings. He became so irate when his reforms stimulated greater demands that, under pressure to take a more conservative stance, he renounced his "liberal errors" to assert his true conservatism and became a powerful opponent of liberalism and democracy. His Vatican scholars declared that liberalism was a product of Protestantism and was therefore antithetical to the true Church. Liberalism, like democracy, they said, was an abomination that would not be tolerated by this pope.

By 1847, Italian cities including *Torino* and Genoa were in open revolt. In 1848, under growing revolutionary pressure, Carlo Alberto, the peninsula's only Italian king, signed *uno statuto* (a constitution) transforming Sardinia's absolute monarchy into a constitutional monarchy. It imposed some constraints on the king's absolute rule for the first time in the long reign of the House of Savoy, but Carlo Alberto made sure that it was a conservative constitution. However, it was an improvement, and the citizens paraded jubilantly through *Torino*. *Lo statuto* did not describe Mazzini's democratic republic. Instead, it kept most of the power for the king. It reinforced the House of Savoy's hereditary rule, putting it in position for its final conquest of the peninsula that would come 23 years later. Old Pietro's prediction was coming true.

The Sardinian constitution's 81 articles defined the state as a "representative monarchial government" in which the "person of the king is sacred and inviolable." The king would rule as hereditary executive, working with a senate and a chamber of deputies. Senators and ministers would be appointed by and responsible to the king, who would make nearly all decisions and control the military. All citizens of the Sardinian Kingdom would be equal before the law and be guaranteed the rights of free speech, a free press, and peaceful assembly. Roman Catholicism would be the official state religion, but "existing forms of worship" (Judaism and Waldensian, the largest minority religions) would be "tolerated." Only 2 percent of the population, all men, would be allowed to vote, including all adult men of the royal family.

1. Smith (1971), page 12.

Giuseppe Dattilo was 18 when the Sardinian constitution was enacted in 1848. It was but another distant event and he had little understanding of its implications. Giuseppe lived under Southern Italy's Bourbon monarchy, within which he had no vote or influence on decisions outside of his own home. Had the constitution been in effect in his region of Calabria, it would have made not a ripple of difference for him.

The Sardinian constitutional monarchy became one of the two major visions that would drive the revolution over the next 20 years. Although carried by the wave of liberalism, it was a victory for conservatives, a poor compromise for liberals, and a sharp disappointment for Mazzini. He had envisioned a republic, an elected legislature and president, universal suffrage, freedom of the press, public assembly and religion, and equality of the sexes before the law. No king or pope was included. One of these two visions would survive to define Italy's future.

Mazzini had long insisted that to create a united Italy, the Austrians had to be driven out. Carlo Alberto agreed, but viewed Mazzini, Garibaldi, and all republicans and revolutionaries as Sardinia's enemies. However, he needed their help to defeat Austria and extend his monarchy over the northern peninsula. Thus, the king became warily allied with the republicans against Austria, their common enemy.

In 1848, Carlo Alberto's Sardinian army drove the Austrians from Lombardy. Seeing that success, Venetia, Parma, Modena, Tuscany, Naples, and even the pope pledged troops to fight Austria. Garibaldi, just returned from exile in America, offered to help, but Carlo Alberto, suspicious, of Garibaldi, rejected his offer. It was, perhaps, Alberto's greatest blunder.

Fighting Austria's powerful military was more difficult than Carlo Alberto had expected. Distracted by the continuing agitation in his northern cities, he made serious tactical errors, deploying too many troops against the radicals instead of fighting the Austrians. Also, his allies, the pope and the Kingdom of Naples, withdrew their support, having decided not to fight Austria.

While Sardinia fought Austria in 1848, the pope's political about-face caused anger and rioting in Rome. The papal prime minister, Count Pelegrino Rossi, was assassinated. Romans attacked the papal palace and forced Pope Pius IX to flee to Gaeta in the southern kingdom, protected by the Bourbon king of Naples, Ferdinando II. The following year, revolutionaries took over the holy city, abolished the pope's temporal powers, and established the Republic of Rome. Mazzini and the new Roman City Council drafted a liberal constitution. The pope, hearing of the plans to create a democratically elected assembly—it was rumored that even women would be allowed to vote—was outraged. It was, he said, "a monstrous act of unconcealed treason,"[2] and he threatened to excommunicate all who supported such "obscenity."

2. Hibbert (1985).

Giuseppe Mazzini, the revolution's philosopher, was a fiery, intense man who infected his followers with his powerful enthusiasm. To his enemies, he and his republicans were "degenerate Roman remnants."[3] Mazzini finally had the opportunity to craft a modern Roman Republic as the model for a new united Italy in contrast to Sardinia's constitutional monarchy. The constitution of the Roman Republic was the only one in the land created and adopted by publicly elected representatives of the people. Within a few months, Mazzini and his republicans drafted plans for land, labor, and trade reform. But they had no time to implement them.

At mid-century, contrasting visions of Italy's future stood before the people—Sardinia's conservative constitutional monarchy and Rome's liberal constitutional republic. One would prevail. The revolution was then at its highest point. Austrian troops were retreating from Carlo Alberto across the north. The pope had fled south, and the Roman Republic stood in the former Papal States.

2. The Monarchies' Counterrevolution

The papacy, Austria, France, the Kingdom of Naples and Sicily, other European monarchies, and Catholic groups around the world recovered from their surprised reactions to the revolutionaries' successes. They struck back with a powerful counterrevolution, and the liberal gains eroded. One of the first setbacks was Carlo Alberto's two defeats after his initial victories against Austria, forcing his abdication in 1849. His son, Vittorio Emanuele II, accepted a truce drafted by Austria; Sardinia would retain its kingdom while Austria solidified control of most of the north. Austria's field marshal, Joseph Radetzky, and its chancellor, Klemens von Metternich, wanted the Sardinian monarchy to survive as a defense against the still-active liberals and revolutionaries in the northern cities. Vittorio Emanuele, a committed monarchist like his father, agreed, and the Sardinian monarchy settled deeper into a conservative, antiliberal stance.

While Sardinia reinforced its monarchy, Pope Pius IX, no longer the "Liberal Pope," battled against democracy. From the safety of exile in Gaeta, he appealed to the world's Catholics for help. Ferdinando II of Naples sent an army to Rome, as did Austria. Louis Napoleon also dispatched troops, as much to keep an eye on the Austrians and Neopolitans as to protect Rome. The Republic of Rome and the entire revolution were now in peril, and the whole "Italian question" had become visible to the world. So much military activity was focused there that England, Spain, Prussia, and even the distant United States took notice, beginning to realize that Austria's continued subjugation of the Italians could cause serious problems for Europe.

After being rebuffed by Carlo Alberto, Garibaldi had joined Mazzini to

3. Ibid., page 254.

defend the Roman Republic. The French armies attacked in April 1849, expecting little resistance from the small defending force of Garibaldi's volunteers and Rome's ragtag crew of students and shopkeepers. But the French were surprised when the Italians made up in zeal and heroism what they lacked in armaments and training. The battles were ferocious, bloody attacks and counter-attacks by cavalry and foot soldiers, cannons, and hand-to-hand slashing and stabbing of sabers and bayonets. The revolutionaries drove the French army back 20 miles, leaving 500 French soldiers killed or wounded and another 500 captured. "Now, we finish them!" Garibaldi declared, marshaling his men for the final onslaught on the retreating, defeated French.

But here occurred a sharp conflict between the two leaders, one that would never be healed. Mazzini did not want a war with France and countermanded Garibaldi's order to pursue the French. He hoped to find peace with France to preserve the Roman Republic.

It was, Garibaldi thought, a colossal mistake, a decision that would lose the new Roman Republic to the French and the pope. "If Mazzini had been willing to understand that I might know something of war . . . how differently things would have turned out," he wrote later.

The French army, no longer pursued by Garibaldi, regrouped, rearmed, and struck back. After a long cannon bombardment of the city from the nearby hills and hand-to-hand fighting outside the city, they overpowered the defending republicans, and early in July 1849 marched into Rome, ending Mazzini's Roman Republic. Months later, when all was safe, Pope Pius IX returned to his Holy City, escorted by French troops.

Throughout the peninsula, French and Austrian armies put down the revolution and restored the former monarchs, who quickly revoked or ignored various short-lived constitutions. Garibaldi and Mazzini were again driven into exile. The French allowed Garibaldi to leave Rome with the remains of his army, but into the hands of the waiting Austrians. His troops fought their way to the sea, and Garibaldi escaped from the peninsula. The Italian revolution of 1849 was over, defeated by the Austrians, French, Bourbons, the pope, and Catholics around the world.

The monarchies' counterrevolutionary march across Europe in 1849 resulted in Sardinia's defeat, Mazzini's and Garibaldi's exile, destruction of the brief Roman Republic, and the revolution's general collapse throughout the peninsula. Conservative monarchies in Austria, Spain, France, the Germanys, the Italian Peninsula, and elsewhere in Europe had fought back against the liberals. The brief republics were crushed; constitutions were repealed; seditious newspapers, books, and journals were burned. Theater and opera were again heavily censored; labor unions were attacked and disbanded; and the people's rights to congregate, vote, and hold open discussions were abolished. Royal troops marched through cities and towns in every country, arresting thousands and executing many on the spot. In Southern Italy, King Ferdinando II ignored the constitution that he had so recently endorsed and locked 15,000 people in his dungeons. Three thousand were slaughtered in Paris after a workers' rebellion had been brought under control, and another 12,000 were imprisoned. The Austrians executed 1,000 political prisoners in Venezia and another 200 in Austria, and sentenced 5,000 more to long terms in the dungeons. The pope's hangmen in Rome were kept very busy.[4]

The mid-19th-century European revolutions were over. The pope and the monarchies again ruled, and liberalism, with its heady taste of freedom, had been brief. However, the people had glimpsed constitutional governments, and even the hangmen could not throttle that memory.

For the next five years, Garibaldi lived on Staten Island as a guest of Antonio Meucci[5] and became a naturalized U.S. citizen. Garibaldi maintained contact with his underground supporters in Italy to raise a new revolutionary army that would be ready to fight again when called. Mazzini, exiled in England, continued writing and teaching, and became a well-known radical democratic reformer. He urged Europeans to replace their monarchies with constitutional republics and to promote social reforms, including the emancipation of women.

In the 1850s, the Austrian, French, and papal repression of *la rivoluzione* kept the peninsula divided into eight states, much as it had been in 1815. Austria still owned Venice, Trieste, and much of the Trentino in the north. The pope, guarded by French troops, controlled the center. The Spanish Bourbon king, Francis II, successor to Ferdinando II, owned Sicily and all of Southern Italy, from Naples southward.

Despite Sardinia's military loss to Austria, the abdication of Carlo Alberto, and the defeated revolution, its role as a leader of the unification movement had been established. Sardinia had defied the Austrians in 1849, demonstrating its commitment to Italian freedom and national unity. Vittorio Emanuele II had inherited a Sardinia that was the battered—but still standing—challenger to Austria, readying for the next fight, calling the other states to join. That, at least, was the heroic picture that Vittorio Emanuele wanted to project, with himself as the military leader. Being a monarchy, and because its new king had agreed to oppose revolution, radicals, and republicans, Sardinia was spared further attacks by Austria. Had Sardinia been a republic or refused to serve as a buffer against radicals, Austria would probably have eliminated the smaller country.

With the fall of Mazzini's Roman Republic, the Sardinian monarchy became the leading model for unification, and the movement angled sharply away from Mazzini's vision of unifying under a liberal republic. Italians generally agreed on the major goal of independence from Austria and national unity, but differed over what form of government would best serve

4. Ibid.
5. Antonio Meucci was the inventor of the telephone. Many mistakenly believe that Alexander Graham Bell invented the telephone, but the true inventor was Meucci. Schiavo (1958).

the people. Many favored a democratic constitutional government, but many did not. Some wanted unification under a strong monarchy, continuing the old royalist traditions. Others supported a constitutional monarchy such as Sardinia's. A conservative clerical faction wanted a federation of states, with the pope as president. Others were opposed to unification, but were willing to accept a loose organization of independent states.

3. The King Is an Imbecile, Cavour Is a Master.

In the 1850s, Sardinia was the only peninsular government with a surviving constitution. Despite his father's loss to the Austrians, Vittorio Emanuele II wanted to unite the northern peninsula under his Sardinian monarchy. He was a boastful man, proud that his House of Savoy was Europe's longest-surviving monarchy. Apparently a man of little talent, he was nevertheless convinced that he had great military skill and a powerful army. As many in the government knew, that was more delusion than reality. From 1849 to his death in 1878, the king was absorbed in his dreams of military exploits. He squandered resources on enormous military expenditures and on hunting lodges, horses, and dogs, to the point that bankruptcy several times threatened the monarchy. He fantasized great military actions, fantasies that he inconsistently shared with some and kept secret from others. The king was known to shift suddenly from one scheme to another. He talked of invading the Balkans, defeating Turkey, taking back Trieste, and waging war on France, Austria, and England simultaneously. He proudly viewed militarism as his family heritage, believing it was the only honorable basis on which to build his monarchy's world stature—and he apparently believed that his tiny Sardinia was, indeed, a world power.

In 1867, the 19th year of Vittorio Emanuele's reign, the British foreign secretary said of the king:

"There is universal agreement that Vittorio Emanuele is an imbecile; he is a dishonest man who tells lies to everyone; at this rate he will end by losing his crown and ruining both Italy and his dynasty."[6]

It is doubtful that the king could have succeeded in Italy's unification without the skills of more able persons—Mazzini, Garibaldi, Napoleon III, and Sardinia's Count Camillo Benso di Cavour, an adroit master of politics. Cavour, a French-speaking Northern Italian nobleman, became Sardinia's prime minister in 1852. Originally a Mazzini republican, he assessed the realities of creating a union and concluded that a conservative constitutional monarchy rather than a democratic republic would be the best course at that time. The king agreed, of course, since that would preserve his monarchy and his family's power. The two men would lead the peninsula away from Mazzini's goal of a democratic republic and into a conservative constitutional monarchy. Their goals, although presented in

6. Smith (1989), page 42.

the context of a liberal revolution and Italian unification, were to strengthen the Royal House of Savoy and expand Sardinia across the northern peninsula.

Mazzini was the philosopher of the revolution, Garibaldi its military leader, and Cavour emerged in the 1850s as its statesman. In the pages of *Il Risorgimento*, the liberal newspaper he edited in 1847, Cavour helped to popularize Mazzini's cause and add his own strong advocacy for an alliance with their old enemy, France, to defeat the Austrians. Sardinia had economic and cultural ties with France and a positive view of Napoleon's impact on the Italians. Like other wealthy men, Cavour was French-educated, and wrote and spoke in French rather than in an Italian dialect. He soon rejected Mazzini's liberalism and came to view his old ally as his enemy.

Cavour, unlike Vittorio Emanuele, understood that Italian unification could not be achieved without the support of England, France, and Prussia. But how was he to convince those countries to oppose the mighty Austrians and support the tiny Kingdom of Sardinia, all to benefit Italy, which did not even exist? Those were the tasks to which Cavour applied his extraordinary diplomatic skills over the next decade.

Cavour's initial goals were to win freedom from Austria and expand Sardinia across the northern peninsula. The central states could remain with the pope, and the large southern kingdom would remain an independent monarchy and an ally of Sardinia. However, by 1860 he had developed more ambitious plans. He began working to gain powerful European allies in order to drive Austria from the peninsula, destroy the pope's secular power, and defeat Mazzini. The goal was to annex the north and central states into Sardinia and create the United Kingdom of Italy under the Royal House of Savoy. In essence, he was planning the Sardinian monarchy's conquest of the peninsula.

To achieve those goals, he needed support from the left—Mazzini and Garibaldi—and from the right—Vittorio Emanuele and other conservatives. Cavour saw these people more as obstacles than as allies, and skillfully played them as his political needs demanded. Into this mix he brought England, France, and Prussia, always moving toward the goal of defeating Austria.

Cavour knew that Mazzini despised all monarchies, Garibaldi was an independent-minded powerhouse who followed his own dictates, and Vittorio Emanuele II was shallow, thoughtless, and unpredictable. He understood that playing politics with powerful countries was a dangerous game, and his determination to defeat Austria, the most powerful country in Europe, could prove to be perilous for his small monarchy.

After becoming Sardinia's prime minister in 1852, Cavour began successful negotiations with England, Turkey, and France. He gained their support for unification and elevated the "Italian issue" from an internal affair to a world concern.

In 1858, the peninsula was still politically divided. In the northwest was Vittorio Emanuele's independent kingdom of Piedmonte-Sardinia. The Austrian-controlled territories of Lombardy and Venezia stretched across the top of the peninsula. The Church-controlled Papal States, with Rome protected by the French military, made up the peninsula's center. In the south, the Spanish Bourbon monarchy ruled Sicily, Naples, and all of the southern territory—nearly half of the peninsula. There were also a number of smaller kingdoms and duchies.

Cavour needed to counter Mazzini's liberal influence and shift the revolution's goals from a republic to a conservative constitutional monarchy. Ten years after the failed revolution of 1849, Cavour invited Garibaldi to return from exile in the United States and join Sardinia's fight against Austria, but this time as a Cavour-inspired monarchist rather than a Mazzini-inspired republican. Cavour was not at ease with Garibaldi's popularity and power, and realized the danger in bringing him back. Nevertheless, he needed Garibaldi's help, and it was a masterful political move.

Garibaldi, seeing another chance at Italian independence, accepted Cavour's invitation and prepared to fight in what became the Sardinian-Austrian War of 1859. Garibaldi gave up his original goals of an Italian Republic, joined Cavour's constitutional monarchists, and committed his loyalty to Vittorio Emanuele II. With his popularity, he brought prestige to Sardinia and strength to Cavour's plans.

The three most powerful men of the revolution were now joined in a common goal, to defeat Austria and strengthen Sardinia. Garibaldi remained popular, but some began to see him as abandoning his revolutionary principles and joining the monarchists. For Mazzini, whose offers of help had been rejected by Cavour, Garibaldi's complicity was a betrayal.

For seven years Cavour maneuvered the Italians, France, England, and Austria toward freeing the north from Austria. He redefined Italian unification as a drive toward a constitutional monarchy rather than a revolutionary republic. Knowing that Sardinia would need more help to defeat Austria, he negotiated secretly with Napoleon III, crafting an agreement to divide the Austrian-held north following a successful war. The events of 1859–1861 are Cavour's legacy.

4. *Grido di Dolore!*

With France as his ally, Cavour goaded Austria into declaring war. He drafted an inflammatory anti-Austria proclamation that was delivered by the king at the opening of Parliament in 1859. It promised Sardinia's support for Italian states that rose against Austria and sought unification. He called passionately for an end to the people's *"grido di dolore! (cry of pain!)"* It was a stirring speech, a call for revolution, freedom, and national unification, and it so infuriated the Austrians, who thought they had permanently subdued Sardinia in the 1849 revolution, that they demanded

Sardinia's immediate disarming. "Unarm in three days, or war!"[7] was Austria's ultimatum.

Cavour's new European allies refused to support Austria's demands, and with disrespectful insolence toward the royal Austrians, Cavour responded by ordering a significant increase in Sardinia's military force.

The Austrians, as Cavour predicted, declared war on the small kingdom, certain they would have no difficulty defeating it again. Thousands were killed in the bloody Austrian-Sardinian war of 1859, but for Cavour and other government leaders—who kept themselves safely far from the fighting—the gains were well worth the bloodshed of others. Garibaldi was appointed to the Sardinian rank of major-general and raised a mountaineer unit, which he named, with his usual flair, "*Cacciatori delle Alpi* (the Alpine Huntsmen)." His men scaled icy mountains, defeated Austria's mountain troops, captured Varese and Como, and advanced to the Austrian border, further ennobling Garibaldi's already mythic stature.[8]

The French and Italian armies drove the Austrians eastward to Venezia, suffering as many casualties as they inflicted. Then Louis-Napoleon III and Austria's Franz Joseph, without consulting Cavour, agreed to a truce. Napoleon III, concerned that Prussia might intervene to defend Austria, decided that a truce was prudent. Furious and politically weakened by Napoleon's duplicity, Cavour resigned as prime minister, but returned to the post the following year.

Austria gave up its northern holdings, except for Venice. Sardinia gained Lombardy, Tuscany, Parma, Modena, Reggio, Piacenza, Romagna, and Bologna. France would annex Nice and Savoy,[9] both on the French-Italian border. Many people were furious over Austria's ceding that prime territory to France. They denounced the agreement, the secrecy, and the hasty voting carried out under the eyes of the occupying French army to decide if Nice and Savoy would become French or remain Italian.

Nice was Garibaldi's birthplace, and he was so incensed that he resigned his commission and marched his army toward Nice, intending to burn the ballot boxes and rescue his home from the "French thieves." However, before reaching Nice, he turned his army to Sicily to aid the rebellion that had flared up there.

Piedmonte-Sardinia, under Cavour's leadership and with the help of Garibaldi and Louis-Napoleon III, had gained control of most of the northern peninsula and recognition by the European powers for having defeated the mighty Austrians. The liberal anti-monarchy revolution had been coopted by Cavour's conservatives and turned into a drive to enhance Sardinia's monarchy and achieve unification, at least in the north.

---

7. Page (1920).
8. Giuseppe Mazzini was, reportedly, in the ranks of Garibaldi's Mountaineers.
9. In return for its help, France was given Savoy and Nice, an arrangement that Italians still consider to have been too costly. They still harbor the hope that both might be returned to Italy.

Northern landowners, government officials, businessmen, and bankers fa-vored the monarchy's control of the future Italian nation. The thought that Mazzini and Garibaldi's "rabble" might gain control made the sweat pop out on their brows. By 1859, it was clear that the revolution had been split; Mazzini was near defeat, Sardinia's monarchy stood victorious in the north, and the southern revolution was about to surface.

Piedmonte-Sardinia was now a strong presence on the peninsula, but it had its problems. Of minor annoyance was the pope's excommunication of Cavour and Vittorio Emanuele for having weakened the Papal States by annexing Bologna. Further, the king's delusions of fighting any power in Europe, profligate spending for the military, and expensive amusements complicated Cavour's task. Most seriously, the agreement giving Savoy and Nice to France was causing a barrage of criticism and threatening Cavour's alliance with Garibaldi. The political infighting and intrigue among Sardin-ia's factions were relentless, and it took all of Cavour's enormous talents to maintain his course. Sardinia's expansion across the north had brought more people and factions into the Sardinian fold, each with grievances and demands. The high costs of the last two wars against Austria caused significant tax increases, with hardship and anger in all parts of society. In major cities, workers rioted against high taxes, unemployment, and food shortages. The monarchy, despite the constitution, reacted with harsh re-pression, stirring more anger and agitation.

In the final years of the 1850s, rebellion flared throughout the penin-sula. In the southern kingdom of Francesco II—nearly half of the penin-sula—riots flamed in Naples, Palermo, and Messina. Mazzini realized that Sardinia's successes had ended his hopes for a revolutionary liberal republic in the north. The southern riots, however, gave him an opportunity to continue his revolutionary drive for independence and national unification as a republic.

Mazzini believed that revolution of the people, an uprising from below, was essential for the establishment of a true republic. A people's revolution would be far different from what had occurred in the north—Sardinia's military invasion, occupation, and annexation of the northern areas. In the south, he thought, there was still a chance for a true people's revolution.

Mazzini's agents helped guide the Sicilian rebellion against King Fran-cesco II, who had succeeded his father, Ferdinando II, the previous year and was already hated by the southerners. Francesco sent reinforcements across the bay into Sicily to quell Mazzini's revolution.

Sicily was a large and strategic island. Cavour and Vittorio Emanuele feared that a successful revolution and independence there would strength-en their rival Mazzini, enhancing his drive toward a revolutionary demo-cratic republic. Any victory for Mazzini would be a defeat for the Sardinian monarchy. His success was unthinkable; the southern revolution had to be stopped.

However, Cavour did not want King Francesco to quell the southern revolution, because that would enhance the Bourbon monarchy, another potential rival for Sardinia. Cavour also knew that England, seeking to control the Mediterranean, had its own designs on the island. English warships patrolled Sicilian waters, and English troops might invade under the benevolent guise of restoring peace in a revolution-torn Sicily. Cavour knew that any of those outcomes—a successful Mazzini revolution, a strengthened Bourbon monarchy, or an English invasion of Sicily—would severely threaten the Sardinian monarchy's preeminence on the peninsula. It was Garibaldi who came to the Sardinians' aid. In perhaps the greatest irony of the Italians' 19th century, Garibaldi's magnificent revolutionary successes in the south choked off the liberal revolution, denied Mazzini's republic, and helped turn the entire peninsula into a Sardinian-controlled monarchy.

5. *"Obedisco"*

Garibaldi, furious over Nice and Savoy, resigned his Sardinian commission. Learning of the outbreaks in Sicily and urged by Mazzini, he led his 1,000 *camicie rosse* (Red Shirts)[10] to join the southern revolution. In April 1860, they left in two steamships from a port near Genoa and headed for Sicily. They landed at Marsala on the western shore despite the king's warships and 25,000 troops, a portion of the 150,000-man royal army. With only 1,000 men, Garibaldi was not intimidated by the king's army.

When Garibaldi landed in Sicily, Mazzini's uprising was already under way and included the Arberesh (Albanian-Italians). The Arberesh, living primarily in Sicily, Calabria, Basilicata, and Puglia, were a large linguistic minority, still speaking Albanian as their first language. Because of their cultural difference and independence, the Arberesh were particularly oppressed by the Bourbons.

Garibaldi moved his army into the Sicilian mountains, where they joined with the Arberesh and other bands of revolutionaries—like small streams flowing down the hillsides, merging into a great river. Advancing through the mountains, they battled royal troops, gaining volunteers. By the time they reached Palermo, Garibaldi's army had quadrupled.

The people of Palermo welcomed Garibaldi and hated their king, Francesco II. In 1848, fearing an overthrow of his monarchy, Francesco's father, Ferdinando, had granted his kingdom a weak constitution. When that did not quell the liberal demands, he sent his army into Sicily. From the surrounding hills, he viciously bombarded Messina (1848) and Palermo (1849). He destroyed the cities, inhumanely treated more than 15,000 political prisoners, and renounced the constitution. The Sicilians called Ferdinando *La Bomba* (The Bomb) and nourished a special hatred for

---

10. "Red Shirts"—called that because his volunteers retained the red tunics they had worn during Garibaldi's revolutionary leadership in 1834–1846 against Brazil and Argentina.

him.[11] When Francesco assumed the throne in 1859 after Ferdinando's abdication, he found he had inherited the people's hatred, their belief that he was but another "King Bomba," and their renewed drive to oust the Bourbon monarchy. It was no wonder the people rallied to Garibaldi when he landed on the island with his *camicie rosse* in the middle of 1860.

Garibaldi's forces, with the Arberesh and other Sicilian volunteers, defeated the royal army at the battle of Calatafama. The British, who had their own interests in Sicily, mediated an armistice. Francesco II withdrew to the mainland, abandoning Sicily, and the jubilant citizens named Garibaldi their new leader.

Cavour was pleased at the outcome—Sicily had been carved away from the Bourbon king, taken away from Mazzini and saved from the English, and was now controlled by Garibaldi. Now, Cavour knew, he must bring about Garibaldi's allegiance to the Sardinian king rather than to Mazzini's republic.

The Sicilians' victory over Francesco, and Garibaldi's soaring reputation, energized the southern revolution on the mainland. In desperation, Francesco promised to be a better king and even to honor the constitution that he had so arrogantly ignored. But it was too late. His own troops began to drop away.[12] Garibaldi crossed the straits and advanced through Southern Italy. Town by town, everywhere finding enthusiastic welcome, he moved northward winning one battle after another against the royal forces, including a major victory at the Volturno River.

In that summer of 1860, his army of 1,000 *camicie rosse* had grown to 30,000 volunteers. Well armed with captured weapons, they advanced against the king's diminishing forces. In September, barely five months after landing in Sicily, Garibaldi marched into Naples and was hailed as the popular new leader of the entire southern peninsula. The king withdrew to a position outside of Naples, still hoping to reassert his monarchy, but Francesco II had already become the last of the Bourbon kings of Southern Italy.

Garibaldi's triumphant march through the south excited the Italians and gained the admiration of Europeans and Americans. President Lincoln, impressed by Garibaldi's successes, had his own plans in America for the Italian soldier.[13]

In the southern campaign, Mazzini and Garibaldi had revived the revolutionary spirit and gained the southerners' enthusiastic support. They saw their victories as a true people's revolution, gaining the southerners' freedom from monarchy—a very different view from that held by Cavour and Vittorio Emanuele. Garibaldi was their hero who had delivered independence. Most

11. Columbia Encyclopedia (2004).
12. A large portion of Francesco II's royal army was composed of Swiss mercenaries. Shortly before the Sicilian uprisings, however, they were recalled to Switzerland, thus significantly reducing the king's army.
13. See Chapter Three.

southerners welcomed Garibaldi and hoped he would remain as the leader of their new, independent southern state.

While Garibaldi was advancing through the southern kingdom, Cavour and Vittorio Emanuele II, still savoring their victory over the Austrians in the war of 1859 (in which Sardinia had been aided by Garibaldi), were becoming concerned. Garibaldi had an international reputation, a growing following that no one else could match, and he moved his independent army wherever and whenever he pleased. The king feared Garibaldi was still a Mazzini republican at heart and might unleash his anger at Cavour and Vittorio Emanuele for having allowed the French to steal Nice. Garibaldi and Mazzini had revived the revolutionary spirit, and the king knew that an energized population demanding freedom from monarchies would be a severe threat.

Garibaldi had been declared *Dittatore* of Southern Italy in the name of King Vittorio Emanuele II. But, Cavour and the king wondered, would he continue to honor his earlier declaration of loyalty to the king, or would he take advantage of his popularity and strength to declare his own competing republic? Garibaldi could have done so, had he wanted.

The king now believed it would be necessary to annex the south in order to defeat Mazzini, control Garibaldi, and eliminate the threats of republicanism, democracy, and liberalism. Knowing his own ambitions, he misread Garibaldi's, believing that the general was propelled equally by motives of personal gain and power. But Garibaldi was not. He was an idealist, striving for independence and unification, a republic if possible, a constitutional monarchy if need be. His idealism would leave him open to ill treatment by his own king.

Adding to the king's concerns was Garibaldi's impatience with Cavour's complex diplomacy. Statesmanship takes time, and Garibaldi was a man of direct action. After liberating the southern kingdom, he was eager to march directly to Rome and seize the Papal States so he could destroy the secular power of the pope and declare the new United Kingdom of Italy and its rightful capital, Rome. Left on his own, he most probably would have done just that.

The pope was alarmed that this fearfully wild man, a proclaimed atheist and antipapist with an army of unkempt *briganti*, might return to Rome and destroy his political power. Protecting his own power, Pope Pius refused to grant the political reforms that Rome's citizens demanded, and again threatened to excommunicate Garibaldi and anyone else who opposed the Church's political control of Rome. As he had 10 years earlier, the pope appealed for help to build his holy army, and aid again poured in from Catholics around the world. Even some fragments of Francesco's defeated army joined the pope's military machine.

The pope's army gathered. Vittorio Emanuele's victorious Sardinian army moved southward, and Garibaldi's troops marched northward to

Rome. French troops were on their way to defend Rome against Garibaldi and the Sardinians. The Austrians, despite their recent defeat by the Italians in the north, were moving their armies to positions near Rome to take advantage of whatever might occur. The world, now taking seriously the "Italian question," watched to see what would happen when these forces collided at the Holy City, as they had in 1848.

Louis-Napoleon now feared that Sardinia, with Garibaldi's help, might take Rome and the Papal States. Sardinia would then extend to Naples, becoming a new European power large and strong enough to cause problems for France. It was important, then, for the French to protect Rome and the pope.

Vittorio Emanuele did not want Garibaldi to take Rome and have the honor of announcing the United Kingdom of Italy. He, Vittorio Emanuele II, must do that. Thus the Sardinian king readily accepted the offer made by Louis Napoleon: if the Sardinians stopped Garibaldi's march to Rome, the French would not intervene in Sardinia's annexation of the southern kingdom. Until then, Cavour's strategy had been not to annex the south but to forge an alliance with it. Here, however, was the opportunity to take over the southern half of the peninsula and add it to Sardinia. Vittorio Emanuele and Cavour understood the realities—France was more powerful than Sardinia and Garibaldi combined, and the still-powerful pope commanded the support of millions of people around the world. This was not yet the time to confront the power of the Catholic Church. It would be best to persuade Garibaldi to leave Rome alone, at least for now.

Out of his commitment to Italy's unification, Garibaldi renounced his leadership of the south and delivered it to the king. He dropped his plans to march on Rome and retired to the rocky island of Caprera after addressing a farewell to his troops.[14] His response to the king had been the single word "*obedisco* (I obey)" History reports that after Garibaldi's victory, the people of Sicily and Naples voted overwhelmingly to join Vittorio Emanuele and the Kingdom of Sardinia, but that was probably not true. The proportion of people allowed to vote was small, possibly less than 2 percent,[15] and no records were kept to verify the honesty of the count. It is not clear, then, that there was a resounding sentiment for annexation by Sardinia. Certainly there was strong support for Garibaldi as the south's new leader, but apparently not for Vittorio Emanuele.

Near the close of 1860, Francesco II was barricaded in the fortress at Gaeta with 4,000 loyal troops, still claiming that he was king of Naples. He held out for three months but eventually withdrew and was king no longer.

14. It was characteristic of Garibaldi that he took no compensation for his services to the new kingdom, although he could have been rewarded with a lucrative dukedom, tracts of land, and money.
15. Half the adult population (women) was not allowed to vote. For the other half, literacy was required. Since nearly all adults in the south, except for the upper class, were illiterate, only a very small percentage of men even qualified to vote. Williams (1938; 1969).

For a while he headquartered in Rome and launched several unsuccessful attempts at counterrevolution.[16]

6. The First Unification, 1861

Through plebiscites manipulated by Cavour, the peninsula (except for Austrian-controlled Venezia and the Papal States) joined Sardinia. The first united Italian parliament was convened in *Torino* on February 18, 1861, and the United Kingdom of Italy, with 22 million people,[17] was declared. In March, Vittorio Emanuele II was crowned the first *Re d'Italia* (King of Italy) "by grace of God and the will of the people." *Torino* remained Sardinia's capital, but Rome was declared the new nation's capital, even while still under the pope's control.

After 1,500 years, most Italians were united politically. Southerners, however, were unwilling new citizens, maintaining their allegiance to *campanilismo*. They did not welcome allegiance to the Sardinian king, or a national identity and new national laws. Further, Vittorio Emanuele turned out to be as repressive as any former king. His troops quelled the post-revolution riots that were to last for years, bringing the king's harsh martial law to the south. People protested heavy conscription of southern men into the military, high taxes, a continuing sharp difference between rich landowners and still-poor peasants, food shortages, unemployment, and confiscation of church property that was turned over to rich landowners.

The people had believed their revolution would bring them land, food, and respect, but it brought them none of those things. Their new king's oppression was in many ways worse than that of their old king. Again for the south, it seemed nothing had changed.

Unification was incomplete and unsatisfactory. Remaining outside of the kingdom were Venezia, owned by Austria, and the Papal States that had been left alone by the agreement between Sardinia and France. Cavour, having prevented Garibaldi from an "untimely" assault on Rome, planned his next moves aimed at bringing Rome and Venice into the kingdom. However, he died within four months, at the age of 51, and did not witness the final unification 10 years later.

7. The Duel in the Mountains

Two unfortunate events occurred near the end of the revolution: Garibaldi turned the southern kingdom over to the monarchy, and Mazzini died, an outlaw in hiding. After the unification in 1861, Garibaldi retired, to the relief of Pope Pius IX and Vittorio Emanuele. Only 54 years old, still vigorous and increasingly impatient because Rome and Venice were still not annexed, Garibaldi was influenced by Mazzini to complete

16. Acton (1961).
17. Smith (1997).

the unification. Mazzini knew by then there was no hope of a republic, but believed that at least the unification could be completed.

In 1862, a year after Cavour's death, Garibaldi and 2,000 volunteers marched toward Rome, believing that the king was in favor of their plan. Vittorio Emanuele, however, was not in favor. He did not want to antagonize Catholics, create an international furor, or fight the pope's mercenary army. Also, 6,000 French troops still guarded the pope. Garibaldi was not concerned about the world's outcry and never doubted that he could defeat the armies of the pope and France.

The king feared that another victory would increase Garibaldi's already high popularity, diminish his own status, and push the nation closer to Mazzini's demand to replace the monarchy with a republic. He, not Garibaldi, must have the acclaim of gathering Rome and Venice into a united peninsula. Garibaldi must be stopped. He pronounced Garibaldi to be *un proscritto* (an outlaw) and warned Italians not to cooperate with his assault on Rome, and he ordered the kingdom's armies to oppose him.

Blocked twice by the king's army from advancing on Rome, Garibaldi led his men into the mountains of Calabria. At the end of August, they collided with a division of the king's military at Aspromonte. Garibaldi, not wanting to fight his own king, ordered his men to hold their fire. From one side or the other, a shot was fired. The king's troops, tense and edgy at facing the fabled Garibaldi, opened up with a volley, killing several of Garibaldi's men. Standing at the head of his army, Garibaldi was shot, and his Roman campaign was over.

The king's troops summarily executed many of Garibaldi's men, and Vittorio Emanuele declared the outrageous incident to be a victory for the country.

The news spread quickly through the Calabrian mountains and into Maida, where Giuseppe Dattilo and all the townspeople heard the shouts. "Garibaldi has been killed, shot by order of the king!"[18]

People gathered in the piazza as they had 20 years earlier, when those fierce revolutionaries had come into town. Giuseppe, now a man of 32, could not believe such a tragic ending for the great hero, but could easily believe in the perfidy of the king. Had not the king given away Garibaldi's home, Nice, to the French? Now he was getting rid of Garibaldi himself! Rumors flowed down the mountainsides. "It was a duel," some claimed, adding a romantic Italian touch to the rumors. "And Vittorio Emanuele shot him."

"Never! How could that be? Garibaldi wouldn't miss; he would shoot the king right through the heart. One shot. He was a soldier! He knew how to shoot."

"No, Garibaldi is a man of honor, he would never shoot his king! He

---

18. This account of the rumored killing of Garibaldi was told to me by a 90-year-old family friend who claimed to remember it. I have no other source that there was such a rumor.

lowered his pistol and took his chances like a soldier, and the king, as cowardly as he is ugly, shot him!"

"Yes. That must be the way it was. The king knew that Garibaldi would never raise a gun to him, that he was fighting an unarmed man. It was murder; that's what it was! Murder!"

So the story was created and roared through the towns. Vittorio Emanuele, conqueror of Italy and vicious oppressor of the south, had murdered the noble Garibaldi in a cowardly and unfair ambush!

The facts—that the king had been nowhere near the event, that no duel had taken place, and that Garibaldi, while severely wounded, was still alive—took more time to circulate. The people's sympathies were with Garibaldi, and when all was done, there remained a seriously thickened residue of southern hatred for Vittorio Emanuele II.

The king had good reason to fear that if Garibaldi died, Mazzini and the republicans would gain popular support, leading to a new revolution, this time aimed at Vittorio Emanuele and his Royal House of Savoy. The doctors were told they had better save Garibaldi's life.

Garibaldi endured painful surgeries, and the country was for a time more intent on him than on the progress of unification. In Europe and the United States, people followed Garibaldi's ordeal. To everyone's relief, not least the king's, Garibaldi recovered and returned to his retirement on the island of Caprera.

At that time, President Lincoln offered Garibaldi a commission as general in the Union Army to assist in the Civil War. However, the pope and influential American Catholics so powerfully opposed Lincoln's invitation to this antipapist, atheistic, radical revolutionary that the offer was allowed to quietly fade away. At any rate, Garibaldi had already been wounded and was in no condition to accept.

8. Royal Arrogance

Ferdinando II had kept his national debt low by investing little in southern development and avoiding costly military entanglements. Prices and taxes were held down, but the lack of development helped perpetuate poverty. With the imposition of Vittorio Emanuele's new order throughout most of the peninsula, government spending soared. Military spending and northern development pushed up prices and taxes. The kingdom did not invest in the south, and the people there still could not acquire land or improve their economic conditions. As added insult, southerners began paying even higher taxes to finance northern economic development.

Taxes were traditionally levied on consumption, not on income or land ownership. To buy salt, bread, flour, and other necessities—often including water—one had to pay the consumption tax. The tax burden fell heavily on the poor, while those with high incomes and/or land holdings enjoyed light taxes.

Further, the Sardinians imposed severe anticlerical laws to weaken the political power of their remaining rival, the Church. However reactionary the Church may have been, in the south the clergy were the only friends the poor ever had. Thus, although many applauded, others were incensed when over the next five years more than 60 bishops were arrested for opposing the new regime and objecting to the unfair taxes on the poor. Tens of thousands of religious orders were suppressed, their properties confiscated and given to those who were already rich or had influence in the new government.

Continued poverty, unemployment, increased taxes, and the king's severe punishment of those who balked at harsh taxation caused southern hatred of the Sardinians. Many saw the king and Cavour as northern invaders rather than liberators, and not much better than the Austrians, French, or *i borboni* had been. Indeed in some ways life was worse. Garibaldi and most southerners had expected to join Sardinia as equal partners who would be consulted how to govern. Instead, they found that Cavour and the king had engineered a Sardinian invasion and annexation.

The king was now the ultimate representative of the new nation of Italy. How he behaved and the values he expressed were highly visible models for Italians. His personal treatment of the south was an important public statement of the values of the new country, and he was egregiously disrespectful and insulting. He voiced the ethnic and cultural prejudices held by many northerners—that southerners were not as civilized or intelligent, were incapable of understanding fine points of government, and were best handled as powerless subjects of the Savoy Monarchy. The king hated speaking Italian, preferring his native French. While visiting Naples he was ill mannered and arrogant, refusing sometimes even to speak to or acknowledge the presence of southerners. He refused to eat southern food that had been prepared for banquets in his honor.[19] The king was pointedly *irrespetoso* (disrespectful) of the southerners, communicating his disdain and sharply defining the south's lowly status within the new nation. His personal behavior toward the south provided a glimpse into how the northern government would treat *il mezzogiorno* over the next 100 years.

The abysmally poor remained so, and that did not endear Vittorio Emanuele to the people of the south. Add to this the mischief done by the false rumors of Garibaldi's murder, and we see why Vittorio Emanuele II, a hero of the unification, was no hero to the southerners. No wonder so many southerners spoke of secession from the union, as southerners did in the United States.

The final bitter medicine was the nature of the man they had lost compared with that of the man who now ruled them. Garibaldi, their hero, had given the south to the king, and the people did not understand why. The

19. Smith (1989).

two men could not be more different, even in their appearance. Garibaldi's rugged size and handsome bearing befitted his mythically heroic nature. Vittorio Emanuele was a short man with an unfortunately ugly face. "So ugly," some said, that "*quando il re è sul cavallo voi non potete discernere uno dall'altro* (when the king is on his horse, you can't tell one from the other)."

9. The Strange War for Venice, 1866

After 1861, the peninsula was a new reality. From a discordant collection of many smaller kingdoms a unified country had emerged. The king believed that he commanded a great army and navy, and that military might was the noblest expression of national honor. Despite the crushing financial burden, he continued building his armed forces, immersed in his delusions.

However, the unification of 1861 was incomplete. Mazzini and Garibaldi had urged military action to bring in Austrian-owned Venice and the Papal States. To avoid war, Austria actually offered to cede Venice to Italy, but, showing egregiously poor judgment, the Italians declined. The prime minister wanted not just Venice, but also the areas of Trentino and Trieste, preferring to win them through noble and glorious military action rather than receive them passively, without bloodshed. Several years of incompetent leadership and royal delusion followed, resulting in military defeat, dishonor, and, most amazingly, a significant success and final unification. This was the strange 1866 war for Venice, sometimes called the "Seven-Weeks' War," that involved Prussia, Italy, Austria, and France. England and other nations watched for the outcome of this small but ultimately important European struggle.

Since the Congress of Vienna in 1815, Prussia had consolidated power among the reorganized German states. Bismarck aimed to create a German Empire, and one of the obstacles was Austria. He saw an advantage in allying with Italy, Austria's long-time enemy, and together forcing a conflict.

Italy was not prepared for war. The king's armies were split between rival generals who had been selected for their political and family connections rather than their military expertise. Within a few hours of the start of the war for Venice, General Lamamora lost a minor battle at Custoza, which so demoralized other Italian units that they quickly retreated.

The only Italian military successes were Garibaldi's; he again drove the Austrians back across the Trentino to the Austrian border. While Garibaldi was defeating the Austrians, Bismarck's army won a decisive victory against Austria in the battle at Sadowa.

In contrast to Garibaldi's successes, the Italian navy was resoundingly defeated in the battle of the ironclads at Lissa, an island in the Adriatic Sea. In that humiliating defeat, the Austrian admiral Wilhelm von Tegetthoff surprised the Italians by aiming his fleet—which had been secretly converted into reinforced steel battering rams—at the Italian ships and ramming them at full speed.[20] More than 1,000 Italian sailors drowned in the sinking of two major Italian vessels,[21] and many more died as smaller ships were destroyed. It was Austria's only major victory in that war, but it gave the country control of the Adriatic for the next half-century, into World War I.

At the end of the war, Bismarck wanted to restore good relationships with Austria as part of his plans for a German Empire. Bolstered by his victory at Sadowa and Garibaldi's in the Trentino, he arranged a truce. As a result, Venice was ceded to Italy, and Austria officially recognized the new Italian nation. That was a momentous shift in the relationship between the Italians and the Austrians. Trentino, however, was to remain under Austria's domination, and Garibaldi had to give up all the territory that his troops had just won.

After Venice was added to the kingdom in 1867, only the Papal States remained to be annexed. Still protected by 6,000 French troops, the rabidly antiliberal and antidemocratic Pope Pius IX continued to oppose Italian unification. It was a meaningless opposition, since by then nearly the entire peninsula had been united. Earlier the pope had announced that his previous brief support for unification had been "in error," and that he would never accept "progress, liberalism, and modern civilization."

While the pope continued his defiance, Garibaldi, then the leader of the Society to Emancipate Italy, decided to make one more attempt on Rome. Rome was the last holdout, the center of Italian history, and thus of enormous symbolic importance. Italy would remain incomplete until Rome became its capital, but the armies of the pope and the French were still there. Garibaldi, now 61 years old, vowed that before he died he would see Rome become the true capital of Italy.

In 1867, following his victories against the Austrians in the Seven-Weeks' War of the previous year, Garibaldi led his aging, now poorly equipped army of volunteers against the combined French and papal troops that guarded Rome. It was not much of a contest. Garibaldi was defeated and captured, and, because of his popularity, set free to retire, again, on his island of Caprera.

10. Rome and Complete Unification, 1871

For the next four years, the pope and the French resisted all diplomatic attempts to bring the Papal States into the new nation, and French troops remained. Italy's opportunity finally came in 1871, when France, under Louis-Napoleon III, suffered a shattering defeat in the Franco-Prussian War of 1870–1871 and shifted its garrisons from Rome to France. Now faced only by the pope's army, the Italian national forces marched in and occupied the city. As he fled from Rome, Pope Pius IX declared that he

---

20. This encounter was the first major naval battle between iron-clad steamships.
21. The flagship, *Re d'Italia*, and the *Palestro*.

would never surrender and the invasion must be resisted. However, since neither the Italian nation nor the pope wanted Rome or the Vatican to be damaged, the assault and defense were perfunctory, more symbolic than real. Fighting lasted less than one day, mostly for a symbolic show of decisive action on one side and brave resistance on the other. Then they settled down to negotiate their truce.

In 1871, Rome was annexed into the Kingdom of Italy, and the city was declared the nation's capital, as it had been 1,500 years earlier. The ancient House of Savoy had triumphed and now ruled the peninsula. The pope was allowed to occupy the Vatican—the Holy City within the secular city—where he could reign over his Church. Angry at the loss of his temporal powers, the pope viewed his retreat into the Vatican as an imprisonment. The relations between the Italian government and the Vatican remained hostile until 1929, when Pope Pius XI recognized the existence of Italy 70 years after its founding.

Now the Italian Revolution was thought to be over. In fact, it would not be over until the middle of the 20th century. France was defeated, humiliated by its loss to Prussia. Reduced as a European power, France was forced to pay egregious monetary reparations as well as cede its prime territory of Alsace-Lorraine to Prussia.

The victorious Prussians, on the other hand, pulled together the German states that had been created at the Congress of Vienna in 1815 and formed the German Empire, the new military power of Europe. Headed by Bismarck, the German Empire set new standards of militarism that other Europeans, in self-defense, soon copied. German military ranks were filled by mandatory conscription instead of the traditional system of volunteers. New tactics emphasizing aggressive attack rather than defensive positions became the norm. Traditional 18th-century ideas of warfare were discarded, and armies were trained to use modern weapons and tactics. The great German military machine had been created and would dominate Europe and much of the world into the middle of the next century.

France's humiliation was impossible to contain, and a boiling anger at the new Germany brewed, causing the French Second Republic and Louis-Napoleon III to fall. The deep national bitterness against Germany became a smoldering demand for revenge and recovery of Alsace-Lorraine. The German Empire's strident militarism and France's seething need for revenge were among the factors that drove Europe into two massive world wars.

By 1871, just as Europe was being primed for a new level of militarism, the Italian Peninsula was finally merged into a unified, independent nation. There were jubilant celebrations, mostly in the north. Vittorio Emanuele II was embraced, but not by the southerners. *La rivoluzione* had succeeded. Italy, exhausted after two generations of revolution, hoped it could recoup its strength, enter the modern world of sovereign nations, and continue its cultural *risorgimento.*

The new nation, however, had entered a world that was at a new level of militarism and colonial expansion. Could this new, small, weak monarchy possibly survive in a world of such established power? Italy's next 75 years would be dominated by that central issue: survival.

Mazzini and Garibaldi had helped to create an independent, united Italy but had been deeply disappointed. Mazzini believed that the revolution had achieved only one of its goals, unification as an independent nation, but had failed in its most important goal of becoming a true republic. Instead, Cavour and Vittorio Emanuele II, with the aid of Garibaldi, had successfully defeated the drive toward a democratic republic and turned all of Italy into a monarchy. Mazzini's other great disappointment was his old compatriot Garibaldi, who unaccountably had abandoned the republican goals of the revolution.

In 1872, a year after the final unification, Mazzini died in Pisa, at the age of 67. Ironically, this hero of Italian independence was on Italian soil secretly and illegally when he died, declared by the king to be an outlaw. A revolutionary to the end, he had never given up his campaign for a democratic republic, social reforms, and women's rights.

Garibaldi's disappointment was more personal. Not only had Savoy and his home, Nice, been ceded to France, but he had been stopped twice by his own allies from taking Rome. Garibaldi died at the age of 75, on the island of Caprera, in the stone house he had built with his own hands.

Nineteenth-century Europe had seen a long struggle between the revolutionary liberal ideas and the old conservative power—those who wanted more democratic forms of government against those who wanted to maintain autocratic monarchies. It was, of course, more complicated than that, as the industrial and scientific revolutions rolled across the continent with profound impacts on all aspects of human life. For Italians, the main political outcome was the creation of a unified country.

A major political aim of the liberal revolutions had been to abolish monarchies and install democracies, but Italy emerged as a recast monarchy. It had missed an opportunity to enter the new century as a modern democratic state, where the people, not *la casa savoia*, reigned. Although born of the liberal revolution, its monarchy maintained much of the old aristocratic bearing, values, and autocratic power. It was not a victory for liberalism.

It was a victory of the north over the south, the middle and upper classes over the lower, cities over the countryside, militarism over peace. The revolution had been a northern, middle-class phenomenon. Its leaders were northerners. Sardinia, the triumphant peninsular monarchy, and its leaders, Garibaldi, Mazzini, Vittorio Emanuele II, and Cavour, were northern. Sardinia had defeated its peninsular rival, the southern kingdom of Naples and Sicily. It had defeated the pope and his European allies, France and Austria. It had been the political and military leader in the end phase of the revolution and had annexed the entire peninsula into its own domain, thereby establishing the new kingdom as a creation of the northern Italians. The peninsula had been united, but it had formed itself as a nation ruled by a monarchy and composed of dominant northerners and subordinate southerners. For many Italians, the northern revolution had subverted the dreams of a united republic. For the foreseeable future, this north-south dichotomy would prevail, reflected in the actions of the new central government, with its continuing hostility toward and rejection by many in the south.

Much unfinished business remained. A poor land to begin with, Italy had drained away resources during the long revolution and continued to do so under the delusional intensity of its king to create a great European military power. Additional problems included its many political rivalries and a dissatisfaction that would grow enormously. The Mazzini republicans wanted more rapid and extensive social reforms; the Church and its supporters saw the new government as waging social and economic war on them; the workers and farmers in the south saw that their lives were worse than before. The continuing distress and outright hatred would drive many of them into socialism, communism, and Fascism early in the 20th century. Among the southerners, there was little patriotic feeling for the new central government.

The problems of state-papacy relationships, poverty, and lack of development in the south and the north's growing antisouthern bigotry needed to be addressed. Italy, confronted by stronger countries that enjoyed age-old alliances, needed to strengthen itself in a Europe of growing military power.

Overriding all else was the unfinished business of Austria's two-centuries-old desire to conquer the peninsula. Italians knew that the Austrians might sweep down from the Alps, cross the Adriatic, and again march through Italy. In the closing of the 19th century and the opening of the 20th, that conviction would guide the Italians' diplomacy, wars, and colonial expansion. But Italy was not alone in its suspicion and rivalry. Europe was caught up in its own aggressive acts, opening moves to the world wars that would explode within the next half century. In 1871, at the time of Italy's unification, the revolution had touched the lives of my great grandfather Giuseppe Dattilo and great grandmother Anna Graziano only lightly, *come una promessa al vento* (like a promise in the wind). Indeed, it made things worse for many people, leaving them with a government that did not represent them.

Giuseppe was a quiet man, proud of his heritage that he traced to the early Romans. He wanted to own a farm, but that was not his lot in life. In good years, he rented a small plot as a sharecropper but owned virtually nothing. He struggled to dig the soil, gave his best crops to the landlord, paid the increasing taxes, and lived on Maida's economic edge.

On Sunday mornings, relieved briefly from farm work, Giuseppe walked along the road, murmuring to his first son, Michele,[22] who was born in

---

22. Michele Dattilo was to become my maternal grandfather.

1868, three years before the final unification. They were a frequent Sunday morning sight—the man walking slowly so the little boy's small steps could keep up, the boy chattering, picking up interesting pebbles. Giuseppe, puffing his pipe, was content with this moment. While they walked on Sunday morning, Anna attended church. She scolded him, "The boy should be in church, learning to pray, not roaming the roads *come u vagabondo* (like a tramp)!"

"Mmm," Giuseppe said. Then, as if she had not spoken at all, he took Michele's hand and began their walk, which further infuriated Anna. Giuseppe was more in touch with God while walking with his little boy in the sunshine than were all of the women piously stuffed inside the church.

He was particularly pleased at the revolution's victory over the Church, because now the pope would have to release good farmland to the people. The Church deserved its defeat. Giuseppe even considered visiting a church for the first time in years, to thank God for deliverance. Like most men in Maida, Giuseppe was deeply religious, believing in God and having a powerful devotion to La Madonna and to San Francesco. However, like many other men, he had little respect for the Church, the pope, or the priests, and he doubted that God had ever been a Roman Catholic.

Over the next few years, Giuseppe's views changed as he saw the government's continuing social and political war against the Church and the southerners. Like many, he came to support the Church. After all, as bad as it was, it was his church; far more, in fact, than the nation was his nation.

Much of the peninsula had been united, the Church tamed, and the Kingdom of Italy born. Giuseppe looked up at the bright sky as he and little Michele walked in the early morning. The heavens shimmered a beautiful, pale blue and the day was already hot. Even the birds were hiding in what little shade they could find. Giuseppe told his son about the new kingdom, that farmland would be given to the people and poverty would soon end. They walked by the stone barn where men once talked about politics. A phrase came floating back from the past. "I'll tell you again," old Pietro had said. "If we follow Mazzini, we will be free, but if we follow the king, we will be conquered."

"Hmmm," thought Giuseppe, in a silent question to San Francesco. "You know, Good Saint, we did follow the king. Was old Pietro right? Are we conquered instead of free?"

But the day was too beautiful, the path ahead bright.

For the little boy, the idea was planted that he would one day own his own farm. He was not sure how that would happen. Perhaps King Vittorio Emanuele II would come to Maida, knock on his door and say, "Michele, here is your farm!" That was a nice thought.

The shell of *campanilismo* had opened slightly, and some southerners began to look outward to their new government in Rome, although still with suspicion. Their primary allegiance remained with their locality, but they might hesitantly try a small portion of national patriotism. They looked to Rome, hoped, and waited.

Chapter 5

La rivoluzione mancata (1871–1900)

1. Waiting for Respect

Southern Italians waited for the promises of the revolution—one year, two, 10, 20. *La rivoluzione* had come and gone; *il risorgimento* had swept the peninsula. Foreigners had been defeated and expelled. Italy was united as a constitutional monarchy, but few benefits had reached the south. *Il mezzogiorno* remained poor, little developed beyond the old feudalism, with no better prospects for common people to be reliably employed, own property, or have greater voice in government. Unification had replaced one set of oppressors, the Bourbons, with another, the Sardinians. Government policies favored the north. Protective tariffs encouraged northern industrialization, weakened the south, and continued to drag the southerners into depression and poverty. Ruinous new taxes, the highest in Europe,[1] hit hardest in the south.

As if more ill fortune were needed, the south was devastated by droughts, volcanoes, earthquakes, erosion, and landslides. In the 1890s, fertile vineyards were destroyed by a plant parasite, phylloxera.[2] Italy's wine industry collapsed, its dominance of the world's wine markets crashed, and, like an insult from God, French wine seeped in and took over the market. Thousands of southern farm workers lost their already tenuous employment, and the rigid two-class society provided no alternatives.

The increasing wealth of the already rich contrasted with the economic decline of common people from 1870 into the 20th century. As promised, land taken from the Church had been made available, but was bought by landed families and northern speculators.[3] *La rivoluzione* had created a government of the northern middle and upper classes that sharply defined their distance from the southern peasantry and kept the power and profits for themselves.

1. Nelli (1983).
2. Phylloxera is a tiny, aphid-like insect that feeds on grapevine roots, destroying the plants. Native to the Eastern and Southern United States, the insect was introduced into Europe in the 1860s and spread within 20 years throughout Europe and into Africa and Australia, destroying nearly two-thirds of the European vineyards. Italy was particularly hard hit. Today, phylloxera continues to be a worldwide economic threat.
3. When land was made available by the new government, it was offered in very large, and therefore expensive, parcels. Nearly all was bought up by the already rich.

It is not surprising that the southerners' traditional distrust of government and hatred of the northern monarchy increased. It was a closed society with a few wealthy land-owning families, one with high-ranking clergy, government, and military people at the top. At the bottom were the majority, the laborers and tenant farmers, all poor, landless, and powerless. A great social distance stretched between the groups, and in that space lived a tiny knot of people, a small middle class to which one might aspire, but with little hope. Tenant farmers on poor land, faced with high taxes, weak markets, food shortages, low income, and high payments to the landlord, would never escape their condition.

The southern revolution of 1858–1860 had been intensely emotional and personal, bubbling up from the people. Southerners fought and died in their own provinces to free themselves from Bourbon oppression and willingly marched with Garibaldi toward an independent republic.

They fought for better lives, for political freedom and against lingering feudalism. Tenant farmers and laborers had for centuries been subservient to the small group of aristocrats, landowners, high Church officials, and the officer class of the military. Life was filled with class and status distinctions. For southerners, every encounter with *il padrone* or his family was another reminder of one's own lowly status—a repeated insult.

What fueled the change was half a century's spread of liberal democratic ideas of how governments should relate to their citizens. Since the American and French revolutions and Napoleon's influence, the idea of "revolutionary constitutionalism"[4] had spread—"a liberal nationalism . . . in which the nation is based on respect for liberal principles, including equal respect for basic human rights."[5] The southerners embraced this idea of 19th-century liberalism, not in those words, but in a desire to enjoy the same rights as the rich, to be treated equally, to be respected. They believed that their subservient, feudal-based, forced inferiority would be erased. That was the promise they heard in *la rivoluzione*: that the people would finally enjoy fair and equal treatment—in a word, *rispetto*.

"*Finché noi dobbiamo rimuovere i nostri cappelli al gentiluomo, noi non saremo né rispettati né liberati.* (As long as we must doff our hats to the gentleman, we will find neither respect nor freedom)."

More than a dream of farmland distributed to the poor, *la rivoluzione* was a promise that centuries-old degrading social arrangements would change. Mazzini's liberal democratic ideals had described a constitutional republic in which all people enjoyed equal treatment and respect by their government. Dignity and respect: that is what the southerners had expected from their revolution, and that is what they had waited for.

Can we imagine the depth of disappointment when their hero, Garibaldi,

4. See the discussion of "revolutionary constitutionalism" by Richards (1999).
5. Richards (1999).

after winning their revolution, gave the entire south to the Sardinians? Or the feeling of betrayal when the Sardinians treated them as defeated enemies and inferior people instead of equal partners? The new kingdom's soldiers continued the old kingdom's repression; the northern businessmen kept the south in poverty; even the king heaped on the disrespect and prejudice.[6] This was not what *rivoluzione* and *risorgimento* had promised them. Perhaps we begin to understand why so many Southern Italians had so little sense of a nation, so little allegiance to a country, so little of what Americans proudly embrace as "patriotism." The people's revolution had been usurped by Vittorio Emanuele and Cavour, with Garibaldi's help, and turned into an invasion and occupation by the new government. It was, simply, betrayal.

2. Education

Primary education on the Italian Peninsula had long been the province of the Church, which had traditionally opposed all but ecclesiastical teaching and fought against the radical democratic ideas of universal education. In 1877 the government took control of education away from the Church. In a radical, progressive move influenced by the legacy of Mazzini and the hostility between church and government, the Law of Compulsory Instruction was enacted. It required a minimum of four years of primary school for all children between the ages of six and nine. However, the reforms fell short because it left their implementation to local governments. Rome demanded universal education but provided little funding or leadership.

Calabria's school buildings were old, uncomfortable, and poorly maintained, and reeked of unsanitary conditions. The teachers, neither well trained nor well-paid, were not enthusiastic educators. Few girls were sent to school by their parents, and most boys were kept away whenever the needs of farm labor and family income arose.

Children of better-off families were favored by the teachers and kept aloof from the few lower-class boys who attended. Poor children were not welcomed in school. They were kept working in the fields and were further discouraged because their families could not afford appropriate clothing, especially shoes. When possible, they avoided school. When they did attend, many were disinterested and some created disruptions that were more entertaining than the lessons.

There were no games in school and friendships were not developed. The classroom atmosphere was grim. Punishment was common, and included hitting with knuckles or cane, or forcing boys to kneel for long periods on the floor until the position became unbearable. A particularly degrading punishment directed by the teacher was called "*sputtato al naso*," in which a favored pupil liberally licked his own fingers and then rubbed them over the offending child's nose.

---

6. See Chapter Four.

Il maestro professore was burdened with a demeaning system of few resources, disinterested boys, and uninvolved families. Adults were respectful, knowing that he labored alone in unappreciated frustration and with few rewards. Perhaps showing respect was their way of apologizing to him.

Frustrated over the unresponsive pupils, *il maestro* berated and ridiculed the boys as "*muto*," "*ostinato*," "*stupido*," "*pigro*," "*ignorante*," "*cieco*," "*assurdo*," "*lento*," "*ottuso*," "*imbarazzo*," "*inferiore*," "*vergognoso*," "*inadatto*," and "*un incidente di natura*." [7] He clapped them across the back of the head or rapped their knuckles or shins with his cane, called "*u fischio*" ("the whistler") for the slicing sound it made as it whipped through the air. The abuse did little to make boys better students, think positively about themselves, or become supporters of mandatory education.

Under such conditions, there was no enthusiasm for school in Southern Italy, and few boys were eager to sit in classrooms while more interesting things happened elsewhere. Schooled or not, most boys were destined to become *giornalieri* or *braccianti* in Maida or *immigranti* America. The honorable duty of boys was to grow into men, and the duty of men was to provide for their families. Boys had to learn how to work, not how to read. Of those who remained in school for the four-year minimum, many never advanced beyond the first level but simply aged out on their ninth birthday and became full-time laborers. The boys anticipated the freedom of adult life but did not appreciate that their fathers never had the luxury of a four-year postponement of full-time field labor.

The boys saw *il professore* as a temporary annoyance, irrelevant to real life, and they silently returned the same level of disrespect that he gave them. They knew that *il professore* misjudged them, failing to see that they were smart and resourceful outside of school. The lesson they learned was that school, books, and *il professore* contributed nothing of importance to their lives. One can understand why so few children and parents supported universal education and less than 3 percent of the children of Calabria attended school.[8] The school experience in the 1880s and 1890s would leave no misty-eyed memories of golden school days.

3. Michele Dattilo

By 1900, my great grandfather and his son Michele were disillusioned by the betrayal of the revolution and cynical about government. "*La rivoluzione mancata*," the people called it—the empty revolution, the missing revolution, the revolution that had never been.

Michele recalled his own grandfather's accounts of the time after Napoleon's withdrawal in 1815. People then had believed that unity, prosperity,

---

7. Mute, obstinate, stupid, lazy, ignorant, blind, absurd, slow, dull, an embarrassment, inferior, shameful, unfit, and an accident of nature.
8. Williams (1938).

dignity, and respect would follow, but they had not. Michele now shared his forbears' disappointments, which were to continue into his children's lives. "Four generations of poverty, of bowing to *il signore*, of searching for *rispetto*!" He shook his head. "Will it never change?"

"*La storia è la stessa*," the elders told the young. "*Non è mai finita.* (The tale is the same; it is never finished.)" Northern Italians regarded the southerners with disdain, made worse by the northerners' dominance in the new government. Michele could not understand this bigotry. "*Non simu tutti Italiani? Non simu ora una nazione unita?* (Aren't we all Italians? Aren't we now a nation united?) Isn't that what the long revolution was about? Of what use were Mazzini and Garibaldi if the very core of the revolution—unification—is being laughed at by the northerners?" Michele understood why some southerners spoke not of unification, but of separation. "We should go our own way," they said, "be independent from the north. Cut Italy in two, make our own country and tell *i nordicani*, '*va a lu diavulu!* (go to the devil!)'"

Northern Italians had a proprietary view of *la rivoluzione*: the important places and people of the revolution were north of Naples, Sardinia had been the unifying power, and the leaders—Carlo Alberto, Cavour, Vittorio Emanuele II, Mazzini, and Garibaldi—were northerners. Had they not liberated the south? Everything and everyone south of Rome, they believed, gave the country more problems than resources. *Il mezzogiorno* became Italy's "southern problem."

The accumulated disappointments, unending poverty, and demeaning status bred a growing sense of betrayal and the conviction that this new government could not be trusted. That was the lesson learned from *la rivoluzione mancata.* Southerners were driven into deeper allegiance to their families and regions, and redefined their relationship to the government and country. The new Italy, they realized, would never deal fairly with the south, and they concluded, "*in ritorno noi dobbiamo poco all'Italia* (in return, we owe little to Italy)." Given the opportunity, nine million Italians, mostly southerners, turned to migration in hope and desperation. *Il mezzogiorno* had become "*la terra di miseria* (the land of misery)," and it drove them out. The Italian emigration of 1880–1929 was due largely to Italy's failure to provide southerners with economic or personal opportunities. They were driven from Italy and drawn to the Americas. Such were the push-pull dynamics of migration.

Just as Italy came to represent the failure of the liberal revolutionary movement, the United States represented its success—in America, the liberal ideals of *la rivoluzione* were alive. America, they told each other, offered the best opportunities to earn respect and a good living. "*Loro ci aspettano in America* (They wait for us in America)." By 1890, 20 years after the unification, the southern peasants' embryonic national patriotism was dead. Their alienation drove them from the country to find better opportunities elsewhere.

Those who left were adventurers and risk-takers, seeking liberty, respect. Most were illiterate, despite the 1877 universal education law. School, in 19th-century Southern Italy, was not for those who had begun working the fields at age five. Coaxing plants and livestock to grow in the quasi-desert conditions of the south, learning to repair most everything and to maintain the already long lives of every tool, became the skills of boys by the age of 12. The lessons for girls included cooking, sewing, child care, washing clothes, tending livestock, and harvesting small crops like figs, chestnuts, oranges, and grapes. They also learned to preserve the flow of religion for their own generation.

The tasks for men were to work long, hard days, and on Sunday beg *il padrone*, hat in hand, head bowed, to pay the meager wages owed to them—knowing that he might or might not be inclined to do so. The women held each family together, using whatever their men provided. They bore and raised children, prepared nutritious meals using creative frugality, constantly revitalized aging clothes with their deft stitches, trained their daughters to maintain traditions, and practiced the ways of their religion, all when they were not also working the fields.

Upper-class life was different. Many could read because, unlike *i contadini* and *giornalieri* (farmers and laborers), these boys had the luxury to honor the mandatory school laws. Their futures were secure. They had little need to earn their own way, so only a few from the upper class joined the migrants' journeys to America.

Although retaining a streak of romanticism, Italian working men were hard realists, not like the women, who, at least until they were responsible for their own families, conjured silly ideas about life, ideas with no more substance than the silky weavings of the spider. But they, too, soon learned. Who among the poor could see what they saw, live as they lived, and then deny for very long their bleak lifetime prospects?

Every poor man faced the same task—providing for his family in the face of continuing poverty and the government's disinterest in his condition.

In 1900, small landowners survived and large landowners prospered. A small plot could provide a family with fresh vegetables, a few chickens, and eggs, and even have room for a goat for milk and cheese. But the poor had no money to buy even a small bit of land.

4. "*Oltremare!*"

Each man asked himself the self-defining question "How am I to protect, shelter, feed, and maintain the health and honor of my family? Stay here and cope with what I know or go elsewhere and cope with what I do not know?" In America, the risks were high, but so were the potential rewards. Either solution challenged the family's survival.

There have been three periods of large-scale migration from the Italian Peninsula. The first was during the Roman Empire, when "Italian colonists by the hundreds of thousands"[9] emigrated, spreading Italian culture throughout the world. After the fall of Rome in 476, foreign armies marched in, plundering the Empire's weakened remains, and Italians no longer emigrated and spread their culture. From the centralized order of the Roman Empire, the peninsula fell into eight dark centuries.

The second migration occurred during the Italian Renaissance, 1200 to late 1500. Northern city-states such as Genoa, Pisa, and Venice became Europe's dominant urban centers. Italians traveled as artists, merchants, teachers, and scholars, carriers of Italian culture. For hundreds of years, Italians taught the world.

By the end of the 16th century, Italy's energy was depleted. Other countries, tutored for centuries by the Italians, became the leaders. The students had become the masters.

In the earlier migrations, Italians had been colonizers of and teachers to the world, entering at the top of other societies with power and status. However, in their third wave of migration during the late 19th and early 20th centuries, they traveled as uneducated and poverty stricken migrants escaping their failed homeland. They entered America and other places not as conquerors and teachers at the top of society, but as powerless and poor laborers at the bottom. Neither welcomed nor feared, they were exploited and tolerated.

Italian migration to North America began with a few educated Northern Italians venturing to the American colonies in the 1700s. The numbers grew slowly for the next 100 years and increased sharply in the 1880s, impelled by *la rivoluzione mancata*. The Italian government estimated that from 1876–1926, of the 40 million people of Italy, seven million emigrated to Europe, six million to South America, four million to the United States, and a small number to Canada.[10] Seasonal migration to work in other countries was an old custom for Italians.

Italian men sorted themselves into those who chose to remain in Italy, those who became migrant workers and periodically returned home, and those who became true immigrants, remaining in their new countries. Migrants to America felt their insignificance against the size, power, and impersonality of that giant country. However, they stepped off the gangplanks in Boston, New York, New Orleans, and San Francisco willing to labor, learn, and earn what they could at the bottom of society.

Emigrating was a self-defining personal challenge, a test of strength to overcome forces that had held them in poverty, subjugation, and disrespect for generations. It was *un'avventura grande*, a great adventure. Men were driven by family responsibility and a striving for respect, independence, and liberty, as well as by the need to escape unremitting poverty and resentment.

9. Di Franco (1988), chapter four.
10. Mondello (1980); Smith (1997).

At first it was an adventure for young men, migrant workers intending to work in America temporarily and faithfully send their earnings home. They had no desire to learn the language and customs, establish permanent homes, raise families, and become citizens. They had no commitment to become *americani*. They had every reason to maintain their *campanilismo*, their dedication to their own town, people, and customs. With plans to return home soon, they had a strategy for survival and success: to keep their language and customs, live in the company of other Italians, and maintain their distance from the American society.[11]

Americans saw in those immigrants a clannishness and rejection of the American way of life. That suited the Americans who wanted the migrants to know their place as laborers. Nevertheless, in seeming contradiction, Americans were critical of the very insularity that they prized. "These Italians," they said, "don't appreciate America; they don't want to learn our ways." The Americans had tapped some truth, but they mistakenly attributed the "clannishness" to the Italians' selfishness and other character deficiencies. "They are closed, stubborn. They can't learn. They don't have the will or the intelligence to do so," was the Americans' explanation. "They are dull, stubborn types of low mentality and no ambition." From the start of this third Italian migration, Americans' views of Italians were sharply disparaging. Migrants were tolerated as temporary, unskilled laborers, to do the work that Americans refused to do.[12] They were paid little (although it seemed much by Italy's standards), housed cheaply, and abandoned when no longer needed.

The migrants, however, began to succeed and to discover reasons to remain. They sought permanent homes, learned the language and customs, attended school, and grew deeper roots in the American world. Their insularity—the "clannishness"—began to dissolve. Families were started, and the second-generation children became acculturated so quickly that it took their parents by surprise. Although 40 percent of the migrants returned permanently to Italy, the rest became true immigrants and, for the most part, return migration to Italy ceased.

The poor who left did so for good reasons; those who stayed, stayed for good reasons. Whichever path they chose, all agreed that living in Italy was hard and would remain so. The United States was a vibrant and growing country where work was plentiful. A man could earn four or five times as much each day as he could in Italy, and because work was year-round, his annual income could be 10 times that earned in Italy. "*Oltremare!* (Beyond the sea!)" That, they heard, was where one found a better life. "*Chi esce riesce* (who leaves, succeeds)," they were told.

11. Briggs (1978).
12. It is interesting that in 2008 the argument that we need immigrants to do the work that Americans refuse to do, for the low pay that Americans refuse to accept, is still very much alive. It now refers to our immigrants from Mexico. As a concept, it is just as demeaning and insulting now as it was more than a century ago.

"But," said others, "there are good reasons for staying in Italy. America is a dangerous place. If America devours me, what becomes of my family? How can I take them to such an uncivilized place? But how can I leave them alone, here, without my protection? In Italy, there is everything important to us. To leave is to abandon all of it."

Those who remained did not lack ambition. They stayed because, however difficult life in Italy might have been, each man depended on his ability to cope with whatever life presented. It was a statement of self-confidence. Living frugally in Italy, they believed, was better than living with money in the frenzied, dangerous, ugly, and uncivil world of *l'America*. Their lives in Italy, they concluded, held much of value despite the still-elusive *rispetto*. It was not to be found in *Italia*, but was *rispetto* guaranteed in America? The costs of leaving seemed too high; the benefits of staying seemed better. "Anyway," they told each other, "*È meglio giocare a carte col diavolo che conosci che col diavolo che non conosci* (it is better to gamble with the devil you know than with the devil you do not know)." So most men decided to remain in Italy with their families.

Those who left and those who stayed held the same view of Italy's unrewarding present and unpromising future. Perhaps one difference between them was the migrants' refusal to accept that future as necessarily being theirs. Perhaps, too, they felt an extra measure of anger and resentment toward their government and were more inclined to blame the politicians than to accept the idea that bad times were the workings of fate or God's will. The latter view tended to point men toward acceptance of the conditions and a willingness to use one's skills to continue coping with things as they were. The other view energized men to reject the conditions and use their skills to confront the risks of living in a new place. Most men chose not to take those particular risks. The migrants were the risk-takers, willing to gamble everything on the unknown chances of success, willing to play cards with "*u diavolu ignotu*," the unknown devil.

I think the difference, the tipping weight, was the emigrants' search for respect. They could survive in Italy, but their subservient status would bar them from the *rispetto* that, in Italy, only *i signori* enjoyed. Who knew if it could be found in America? But in America there was a chance at earning it. Those who left were willing to try for it. Perhaps we cannot now understand that deep need for respect, but we cannot minimize its importance to those immigrants. By the 1890s, young men commonly migrated to the Americas. My grandfather Michele heard the not-always-encouraging stories told by returned migrants. One man had told him in 1892, when he was 24:

"We go to America, to work. Why? Because here there's no work for us. In America we earn money; if we are smart and lucky, we save some of it. And for what? Soon we are back here, where there is still no work for us. We are like the poor boatman who can afford only one oar; we keep going around and around in circles and, after much sweat, maybe we get back only to where we started. *Giramu, giramu, e nu facimu nenti* (We go around and around, and we accomplish nothing)."

Two years later, the man wrote to his brother, who was about to emigrate. Michele did not remember the exact phrases, but the letter was a message of caution, a litany of bitterness:

"They make us work in mud all day, and then they call us 'Dirty.'
They make us stay together, and then they call us 'Clannish.'
They keep us from their schools, and then they call us 'Ignorant.'
They keep us from their churches, and then they call us 'Godless.'
They sell us wine and whiskey, and then they call us 'Drunkards.'
They wear us down, and when we rest they call us 'Lazy.'
They hear us sing to dull the pain, and then they call us 'Clowns.'
They pay us little, steal our money, and then they call us 'Thieves.'
And in the end they say *they* are civilized and *we* are *Selvaggi* (Savages)."

Such messages increased the young men's uneasiness about leaving but did not stem the exodus. Michele continued to struggle, earning enough from farm labor to support his aging parents and himself, and he listened to the men who returned.

Travel between the continents was commonplace, and those initially rustic men developed a traveler's sophistication, often meeting some of the same people on the ships on subsequent voyages. One young man[13] dubbed the circle of shipboard acquaintances "the steerage peerage." With each return home, the migrants had become more *americano*, and Michele saw the contrast between the vivid, modern life in America and the poor, limited existence in Maida. The money and gifts brought back proved that opportunities lay in *la bell'America*. Many had returned to Maida with the intention of staying, having remembered their homes in warm terms of beauty and civility. However, on meeting the realities, they quickly went back to America.

Each return visit and each new émigré was an indictment of Italy's continuing poverty and disillusion. Many of the older people resented the implicit criticism. The young, they saw, were losing proper *rispetto* for the old ways.

At first opposed to large-scale emigration, the Italian government soon began to subsidize some passages so men could funnel back their earnings. Going to America was a good economic move for individuals, and the $250 to $1,000 each brought back added hundreds of millions of U.S. dollars to the Italian economy. By 1910, more than $85 million a year was being sent home to Italy,[14] and by the start of the First World War that had skyrocketed to three-quarters of a billion dollars.[15]

13. Paolo Bellisone.
14. Margariti (1980).
15. Gallo (1981).

The exodus was a partial solution to the "southern problem," in effect exporting it elsewhere. Emigration helped to ease the population crisis and the government's burden of poverty and unemployment. Also, the growing number of Italian communities across America created a demand for imported Italian products—not only among Italians, but also among Americans who were being introduced to Italian foods and clothing, thus helping Italy's trade.[16]

In addition to their money, returnees introduced ideas of better sanitation and the value of education. Farm workers who remained in Southern Italy profited because the growing shortage of workers increased demand for their labor, resulting in higher wages and better treatment by employers. Also, as more returnees used their American dollars to buy farmland in Italy, real estate prices increased and the landowners profited enormously. There also occurred a small but important redistribution of land ownership.[17]

5. The White Widows

Emigration also had negative effects. Mondello[18] noted that the outflow of men made it difficult for Italy to meet military quotas and reduced the labor force, causing farm production and exports to fall and forcing large numbers of women into field labor. A particularly distressing effect was the introduction of *tubercolosi, la malattia americano*. Brought by returning migrants who had contracted it in the unhealthy American slums, tuberculosis spread throughout Italy, where it had not existed before.

On a personal level, emigration enhanced the returnees' personal status in the small towns. Young men viewed them with admiration, young women were attracted, and boys saw romantic adventurers and role models.

Some, however, criticized the emigrants for abandoning their homes, leaving wives and families for two or three years. The abandoned wives were called *vedove bianche* (white widows). Their widowhood was temporary, thus not requiring the traditional black dress of mourning. The *vedove bianche* were sometimes disdained by other women and made the targets of gossip. They were younger than most married women, had more money and fewer children. Without their husbands, they became more independent and self-assertive than good women ought to be, at least according to the old customs. Just as coping with a new country was a significant personal challenge for the men, remaining home and coping, alone, was a personal challenge for the wives. The challenges defeated some, but for others they brought about personal growth and permanent changes in the traditional roles of Italian women.

Some returnees displayed their American clothes and new status, presenting *la bella figura*. They defied traditional social customs, became

16. Ibid.
17. This point is discussed by Von Borosini (1912), pages 791–793.
18. Mondello (1980).

disrespectful of manners and of their superiors. Some were openly disdainful of the Church, and the priests and were seen laughing at the town's holy processions on saints' days. A few became too familiar in addressing their elders and even made unacceptable advances to young women, speaking directly to them in the streets instead of properly conferring with their parents and requesting permission to visit the young ladies at home. The old civilities were under attack.

One effect of the returnees was to increase dissatisfaction and to provoke even more criticism of the government. It was a self-fueling phenomenon: the more success the returnees displayed, the greater the contrast seen by the people and the more dissatisfaction felt. Even more young men would be convinced to emigrate.

Returnees also brought back their discovery that illiteracy was a handicap in America—"*L'uomo che sa leggere sta bene in America!* (The man who knows how to read does well in America!)" They became missionaries for education, bolstering the 1877 universal education law that had long been ignored by most southerners and increasing parents' willingness to send their sons to two or three years of school, enough to teach them how to read. Neither Giuseppe, who had grown up in the 1830s, nor his son Michele in the 1870s had attended school, but now some parents began to insist that their sons—not their daughters—do so. Italians had long respected the town's educated man, *u professore*. Until the 20th century, the poor held that education was "good for some people, but not for us." If boys were to spend their days in school to age eight or nine, then how could they work and help support their families? "Of what use is it to read and write? If I need to write a letter or know what this paper says, I ask *il professore* to do it for me. For two lire a year I have all the reading and writing I need. In the meantime, my sons will go to work, help feed the family, and not waste time in school!"

The ideas brought back from America helped to increase support for mandatory public education in Italy. For many immigrants, children's education became important, seen a major resource offered by America through the marvelous public school system available to them. Encouraged by Italian language newspapers such as *Il Progresso,* more Italian parents demanded that their American-born children remain in school and become educated—quite a difference from the views the same people had expressed while living in Italy.

Wearing American clothes, flashing American money, and raising their families to higher levels of comfort, the successful immigrants gained respect and brought excitement and hope. To Michele, they represented an opportunity to control his life, to escape the constraints of the poor economy and rigid society. The picture was mixed, but on balance, America offered opportunities far beyond those in Italy. Michele Dattilo was a realist. He knew the streets in America were not "paved in gold." That was only an expression for how rich the country was, and only the most foolish took it literally. They would find only dirty streets of mud and stones, and life would be demanding and risky. He would have agreed with an early observation: "Before I came to America, I thought that the streets were paved in gold. When I arrived, I learned three things: First, the streets were not paved with gold. Second, the streets were not paved at all. Finally, I was expected to pave them!"[19] Nevertheless, in Michele's mind, America was becoming "*la bell'America!*"

6. Onions and Coal

Michele continued to live with his parents, brothers, and sister in their small rented house on the farm of the rich *signore* Cinque, raising vegetables and a few chickens for eggs and bartering, a common practice of people with little money. The brothers had the task of taking onions or eggs to Salvatore Donadeo to be exchanged for charcoal to feed the copper brazier used for cooking. *Signore* Donadeo lived some distance down the hill, and this caused noisy arguments over who would carry the light onions down the hill and the heavier coal up the hill. Years later, with adult responsibilities, Michele sometimes thought about the simplicities of childhood, when important issues could revolve around onions and coal.

One day in 1895, when he was 27 years old, Michele mentioned this thought to his friend Paolo as they talked about the difficulties of making a living in Maida. Paolo, several years younger than Michele, had been among the few to complete five years of school, attending at night, after work, and against the objections of his father. Paolo was thoughtful, a rustic philosopher who pulled onions and hauled rocks. Whenever he could, Paolo read poetry, embarrassing his father and making him berate the boy for wasting his time when he should be working to help the family.

Paolo thought about Michele's observation. "Onions and coal," he mused. "You know, Michele, it really wasn't so easy then. It only seems like it now, when we look back. And, after all, isn't it now just the same?"

"What do you mean?" Michele asked, fearing that his friend was about to spin out some long explanation. "What's just the same?"

"Well, look. Here we are today, men, not boys, but our lives are still spent trying to see how many onions equal how many lumps of coal. Isn't that what our lives are about? Over and over trying to calculate the best values in this equation of onions and coal?"

Michele remained puzzled.

"See," Paolo went on, pointing at Michele with the stem of a green onion, "the problem is just the same. The difference is that now that we are grown men, we have many equations to solve: work in this farm or that farm; pay the shoemaker or pay the baker; make love to Maria or make love

19. Gallo (1982), page 44.

to Genevieve; stay here to find work or go someplace else. It's like when we were children, except then we had only a few problems, and our parents solved them. Now we have many problems, and we are the ones who must solve them. How quickly we have become the next generation! But the problems are no different than they ever were, there's only more of them. See? It's the same. Onions and coal; bakers and shoemakers; Maria and Genevieve."

"Hmm," Michele said, beginning to see his friend's point.

"That's what our lives have come to," Paolo continued, "in this hopeless land. Every day we try to balance the values of such little things, just like our fathers and grandfathers and their fathers, generation after generation! The centuries change, 1700 becomes 1800, 1800 becomes 1900, and we still don't have the luxury to think big ideas, only onions and coal! That's our life. You see? The question is, must it stay that way? Can't we make it better?"

Only six years later, Michele would recall that conversation, and the memory would bring on a deep sadness. "Ah, Paolo," he would think. "My poor, unfortunate young friend."

7. Elisabetta Bruni

Michele's life changed when he met Elisabetta Bruni, who lived in nearby Jacurso. In 1897, Elisabetta was a young lady of 22, and early in life she had known sorrow that children should not have to endure. She developed a tolerance, a stoic acceptance of what life might place at one's door, enabling her to restrain her response to distress, unlike many Southern Italian women, who had learned to express their emotions freely. The mature Elisabetta imparted an overall quality of quiet dignity, even in times of stress. Sometimes she seemed too old for her age.

Elisabetta was born in 1875. An only child, she lived happily and comfortably with her parents, who were from families of successful professionals, including lawyers, a priest, and a captain in the Bourbon Royal Army, members of Southern Italy's tiny middle class. Her father, Fortunato Bruni, was a sculptor. Her mother, Angela Ciliberti, was young and pretty, had brought money to the marriage, and was only 17 when she bore Elisabetta. Seven years later, in 1882, Elisabetta's lovely young mother died at the age of 24.

Death is inevitable, but the death of a young mother is a perversion, never to be reconciled by a grieving, frightened, and confused child. We have no details on how or why she died, perhaps from an infection that resisted all efforts of doctors and priests, a common scenario in those days. Death and illness are mysteries, the people said, tragic and devastating. "*Morte e patrune, no dumandare quandu vene* (You never know when death or the landlord will show up)." Nevertheless, they told the little girl, all are part of God's plan we cannot hope to understand. "We must have faith," the priest said. "Even in the midst of grief, we see the loving hand of God." None of that consoled the little girl. She was frightened, confused, devastated.

At the time of that first tragedy in Elisabetta's young life, her father disappeared. He had lived a more dissolute life than was expected of family men and was said to have squandered all of Angela's inheritance. Details have been lost and we do not know if the rumors were true. They hinted at late-night gambling, shouting, hot anger; two men leaping up, a table overturned; cards, drink, and coins scattered; one man sprawled dead and the sculptor gone. No one, of course, had seen anything and they had no idea where the sculptor was. But it was common knowledge that illegal passage to America could easily be arranged.

Elisabetta, with no siblings, now had no parents. How alone the little girl must have felt. Gently, she had been told, "Your mother was taken away by sickness. Now she is in God's hands." Elisabetta accepted her mother's death as a natural event, but she would never make peace with the abandonment by her father. That was not a natural event. It bore no hand of God. Her father had left no words of regret, love, or farewell; no explanations at all. Her aunts and uncles hinted at some knowledge but would not disclose the painful mystery.

The adults shook their heads in sympathy, perplexed that a just God would allow such punishment to fall on an innocent child. They asked, "Why should one little girl be forced to endure such tragedies?" At that point, the cosmic bureaucracy ruled that tragedy must be recorded in triplicate. The child would suffer still another assault.

Of her mother's small estate, only the modest house remained, now in trust for Elisabetta. Who was to care for this orphaned child? Unaccountably, it was left to the child to choose which family among her relatives was to take care of her. Two families were involved; one was well off and the other quite poor. We do not know how her choice was made, whether it was an independent choice or coerced, or how much a child of seven could understand of economic factors and the implications of her choice. She chose the poor family, and grew up in poverty instead of comfort, illiteracy instead of education, the unfortunate results of an immutable choice made by a child. Elisabetta would live to be 94 years old, and she always felt some regret for the choice she had made and the uncompromising refusal to allow her to change it.

She met Michele in Jacurso, and they were married in 1897, when Michele was 29 and Elisabetta was 22. She hoped that Michele would take her away from her sad life. The couple moved into his parents' small rented house on a farm just outside of Maida, a common arrangement for poor people who could not afford their own house. It had one small sleeping room and a cooking area that held a single bench and a charcoal brazier. There was no running water. For toilets, they used the natural facilities of the woods.

Several years earlier, when Giuseppe and Anna had been in their poorest state, they had lived in rented huts in the hills north of Maida. At those times Giuseppe felt humiliated and desperate, having fallen to the low level of the landless *contadini*, not even able to afford to lease a small plot of land to work. Instead, he had to rent a tiny hut made of a rough fieldstone foundation about a meter high, and the rest made of straw. Like his father, Giuseppe had previously leased a small plot and worked with dignity as a landed *contadino*. But under those terrible economic conditions of the 1880s, the Dattilo family had fallen to its poorest conditions. In the 1890s things improved a little, but with a son and new daughter-in-law moving in, their lives became even more strained.

Elisabetta found her new father-in-law, then 64 years old, to be kind, gentle, soft-voiced, shy, a pleasant listener. They often talked quietly, and the old man understood Elisabetta's sad childhood and her longing for a comforting future. Despite her past, she was a romantic at heart and believed that life would improve. After all, had not God brought to her Michele, a strong and capable man who was as gentle as his father? She did not know how he would manage it, but knew that he would make their lives better.

Giuseppe, too, was a romantic, different from the cynical, harshly realistic men of Maida at the turn of the 20th century. It was no wonder they found support in each other. "Of course things will be better," he assured her in his quiet way. "Maybe we stumble sometimes, but then we get up, brush off our knees, and we live, and things get better. *Il mondo non sarà triste per sempre. Il mondo migliora. Voi vedrete. Il mondo migliora.* (The world does not stay sad forever. The world gets better. You will see. The world gets better.)"

The comfort that Elisabetta found with Giuseppe was not repeated with her mother-in-law, Anna. The two families, crowded in the tiny house, faced daily struggles for a meager existence that eroded everyone's patience. There could be only one matriarch in a home, and *Nonna* Anna[20] played that role with a sharp and demanding edge that was mostly aimed at young Elisabetta.

Her friends, with their own mother-in-law problems, commiserated among themselves: "*e Miajju mu t'azzanna a vipara ca a socere perche' per vipara c'é l'antidoto* (the mother-in-law's bite is worse than that of the viper, because for the viper, there is an antidote)."

Such conflicts were not unusual at that time, when young families were forced to crowd themselves into the parents' already inadequate and stressed homes. Strong women, one mature, one young, each expecting to be mistress of her family, living every moment within inches of each other, constantly faced by threats of usurpation by the young and domination by the old, inevitably found themselves in disagreements and competition. Giuseppe, feeling pity for Elisabetta, recalled the adage "*Ricca maritata,*

20. Grandmother Anna.

senza donna né canata (Fortunate is the bride who has neither mother-in-law nor sister-in-law)."

Like most in Maida, Giuseppe and Anna lived simply. *Nonna* Anna's early romanticism had crumbled years ago, worn away in the eroding environment of poverty, marriage at 16, and the deaths of five of her 10 children. Losing children was common in the 1870s, but its banality did not reduce the pain. Each dying child dropped another veil of grief, like successive gray curtains over a window.

The dread of new catastrophes made it essential for Anna to control events in order to prevent such horrors and protect her family. She grew more determined to rule as the single matriarch of her house, a tyrannical extreme of the Southern Italian tradition. She was uncompromising in her control, and the tensions between Anna and Elisabetta wound tighter.

When available, farm labor paid a little over one lire for a 12-hour day, the equivalent of about 25 cents in American money. Adding to their difficulties, *i contadini* were often turned away by the padrone on Sunday morning, the traditional payday, because he simply was not ready to pay them. They could wait, he said, dismissing them. It was of little concern to him. The padrone's refusals were infuriating. Desperate for money, they could only wait submissively, seething, until he was ready to pay.

In 1900, Maida continued on the economic downside. As long as Michele could remember, life had been hard. In the best of times, tenant farm families lived fairly well. The padrone gave them use of a small hut, which they shared with one or more farm animals and allowed the farmer to raise crops and some livestock. In return, the tenant paid the padrone somewhat more than half of the annual crops and the money earned at market. As was the custom, at Christmas and Easter the tenant farmer was also expected to pay respect to his landlord by delivering gifts of vegetables and fruit, live chickens and rabbits, and perhaps some milk and cheese. Locked into those feudal traditions, each poor farmer gave most of his production to the landowner. Truly, it was said, "*i miajju frutti su do padrone* (the best fruit goes to the landlord)." In those difficult times, the tenant farmers barely maintained their families after paying the padrone. It was ironic that in this agricultural region some families went hungry and their children were sickly. Like the children, who had little fat on their bodies to see them through hard times, the economy of the new Italy had little fat, no margin, no cushion for families to fall back on.

As Michele knew, relatively good times could quickly degenerate to poverty. Bad weather, a poor harvest, illness or death of the father could devastate a family. That had happened to Emilio Corieri, who was mauled by a new farm machine being tried out by his padrone. His family, now with a father whose legs were so broken and twisted that he could hardly walk, was destitute. Two little girls and their mother now depended on relatives who were also poor. What was to become of them? It had been traditional in Maida that the padrone for whom one worked assumed some responsibility for providing shelter and food in such crises. Of late, however, that tradition was failing. It was hoped that Don Marino would respect it for the Corieri family.

Giuseppe and his sons labored when work was available, but they often found none. Each morning the hopeful laborers, *i braccianti*, gathered at the *piazza*. *U padronu* picked those he wanted and dismissed the rest to another penniless day. They felt the despair of being trapped in the growing economic depression. Anna, Elisabetta, and most of the other women also labored in the fields. The family worked as sharecroppers and paid their choicest crops to the padrone.

Nonna Anna insisted that she control the few lire they earned. This was the respectful way, as long as they lived in Anna's household, but Elisabetta grew frustrated at not being allowed the role of mother and mistress of her own family.

Giuseppe and Michele, quiet men, were caught in the middle. In his gentle way, Giuseppe tried to keep things smooth, but he had no solutions. Michele's main responsibility was to his wife and children, but he also respected his parents. Each man knew that to enter the arguments would make things worse, so they respected the advice "*la migliore parola è quella che non si dice* (the best word is the one left unspoken)." Michele worked and supported his parents and wife as best he could, but knew there could not be a sustained good life for them in Maida.

Elisabetta grew unhappy in the strained home and was distraught when their first child, a little girl, died after but a month of life. Infant death was common enough; God allowed it even if grieving young parents could neither understand nor prevent it. *Nonna* Anna had lost five children. Was this to be Elisabetta's future?

Their strained relationship was temporary, however. They adjusted and made peace with each other. *Nonna* Anna would live until 1918, help raise Elisabetta's six children, and be remembered as a warm and loving *nonna*.

By 1900, three generations of Michele's family depended on his labors. His parents were old, and Elisabetta was, after all, but a woman. His brothers would help, but Michele would have the major responsibility. The only way was to become a landowner, to buy a farm of his own. He did not remember how that dream had begun, long ago when his father had told him about the promises of land redistribution. But the king had not yet knocked on his door and said, "Michele, here is your farm!" In order to own a farm, he would have to buy it, and that was impossible when not only Maida, but all of Europe, was suffering in economic depression.

Each man must provide for and protect his family. No one else would do it for them—no government, agency, charity, god, or saint. The family's comfort, safety, and health were his responsibility. But how could he do that in Maida, where there was no steady work? It was time to make the choice that confronted all men of Maida—stay or leave. To save his family, he must leave them. The lure of America was doing to Italians what all the wars, the French, and the Austrians had never been able to do—break up the family.

Other than his family, what was holding him in Italy? He had a powerful sense of culture, of being Italian, but no commitment to the political entity. This was not surprising, for Italy had become a fully unified nation in his own lifetime. Michele was older than his government! What did he owe this government of barely 30 years? "I owe to Rome," he concluded, as had thousands of others, "as much as Rome has given me. Nothing!"

America enticed him, but it was a dangerous place where migrant workers were killed in mines and factories, at railroads, docks, and construction sites. Some had fallen in with criminals and been jailed by the police, or even killed by *i criminali americani*. Others had mysteriously disappeared. Suppose something happened to him? What, then, for his family?

There was another worry, but, of course, not one that affected his family. He had heard of men going away, generously sending money in good faith to their wives, who used it for amusements with other men. It was rumored that was how some of the young *vedove bianche*, angry at being abandoned and expecting to live virtuously in Italy while their husbands enjoyed freedom and good lives in America, struck back. People still talked about one woman and the man she was supporting with her husband's money, found murdered in a nearby town. At the time of the shooting, the husband had been far away in "*Filadelfia*," but it was reported in Italy that he had told friends in America, "*Nessuno mette le corni su di me* (Nobody puts the horns on me)."

Finally, Michele asked himself if he were too old for such adventure. At 32, he was no longer an exuberant young man with the energy needed to wrestle with a new country. He would not take his daughter and his wife, pregnant with their second child, across the ocean into that country where, he had heard, so much evil flourished. Elisabetta wanted to go with him but Michele said no. Reluctantly, she accepted that.

Once established, he would send money to both families. "It will not be long," he assured Elisabetta. "A three-week voyage, then I'll be working, earning money. Two months maybe, and you will rent a house in town, and every month I'll send money." He promised to return often for visits. "Later," he said, "we'll buy a house in town and a big farm up on the hill. No more will we be poor peasants. No more!"

Another option was to move to a northern Italian city. But that meant northern prejudice, low status, even scorn. At any rate, the economic picture in the north, in other European countries, and in South America was no longer so optimistic.

In 1900, Michele Dattilo, my grandfather, joined the migration to the

United States. Friends and relatives had already established themselves there and would help him find lodgings and a job. Michele made his decision, engaged *il signore maestro* to write a letter to friends in New Jersey, and soon received a reply. We do not have that letter, but it may have gone something like this:

1133 West Avenue
Ocean City, New Jersey[21]
March 18, 1900

Dear Michele,
    Come join us. Here is a job, money, and a place to live with us. The ocean journey will not be too bad. Some suffer *u mal di mare*, but maybe you will not. Tell us the name of your ship, when it sails and docks, so we know when to meet you. Be sure you have money with you, or they don't let you in. You need *dollari americani*, at least 25, more is better. Hide it in your clothes so nobody steals it. Be sure you bring our address in Ocean City, and tell them we will meet you. When they give you the shots in the arm, you wait so nobody is watching, then rub off the shot so you don't get sick from it.[22] Never trust any padrone—they will rob you even if they look like friendly men from Calabria, don't trust them! Write me a letter and tell me when you will come. When the ship comes to the harbor, they will put everybody on a barge, like sheep, but don't worry, it will be safe, just not nice. The barge will take you to a place called Castle Garden, where they will lift your eyelids and stick a spoon down your throat and poke your chest and check you over like everybody else, and then they take you where you wait for us and we come find you. We will show you New York City! Then the train takes us home to Ocean City.

Your friend,
Domenico

By the early 1900s, men traveling from Southern Italy had gained so much experience that they could guide new immigrants. This was "chain migration," in which those already settled in the country paved the way for newcomers.
    The trip would be expensive, taking funds from the family. A steamship

21. Michele would live at this address while in Ocean City.
22. Vaccination causes a mild form of infection, thereby building antibodies against the disease. However, this made people feel sick. By "rubbing off" the vaccination, they interfered with its function and sometimes avoided getting sick. Of course, they also destroyed the protective effects of the vaccination and left themselves susceptible to disease.

ticket to America equaled the wages of six months of farm labor. Elisabetta was still the legal owner of her mother's small house in Jacurso, all that was left of her family's earlier comfort. She sold the house. It did not bring much, but enough for Michele's first voyage to America. In 1900, he left Elisabetta and their infant daughter, Anna, his parents and siblings, and rode the train to Naples, where he boarded the ship *Regno d'Italia* to cross the ocean to *la bell'America*.

After the ship docked in New York, steerage passengers were made to wait while upper-deck passengers leisurely embarked directly from the ship. *Regno* then moved out into the harbor, where the 1,800 steerage passengers were loaded onto barges for the trip to Ellis Island, "*L'isola delle lacrime* (Isle of Tears)."[23] There, in the enormous Registry Room, Michele was processed through the immigration hurdles and, when no one was watching, dutifully rubbed off the vaccination.

Ellis Island's 700 employees processed an average of 5,000 people a day[24] and, on some days, 10,000. Michele had never seen so many people, and from all over the world. Expecting a long, difficult process, he was surprised when it took only three uncomplicated hours. Because he was an adult and alone, he had no delays, but he felt sorry for families with little children; they seemed to have a much more strained and lengthy time of it. Saddest were the 2 percent—about 100 people on that day—who, principally because of a highly contagious eye disease, trachoma, were rejected and sent back. Their families, too, had to return. Michele saw them huddled in little groups, mother, father, children, often an aged grandma, in despair, crying, praying, in all languages. "I can't imagine," he would later tell Elisabetta, "making all that sacrifice to come here, only to be sent back just a step from the shore."

When he stepped into New York in the fall of 1900, his friends were waiting. They had arranged for him to work with them in Ocean City. It was an unusual choice, when most migrants headed for the big cities, where they found large Italian populations and reminders of home. In 1900 Ocean City was a small community with few jobs and an Italian population of only 23 persons.[25] One would think that this socially and politically conservative city would not readily welcome impoverished and uneducated foreigners.[26] Perhaps it appealed to these men because the skies, beaches, and rolling ocean were reminiscent of the Italian coast. Michele's brothers, Antonio and Giuseppe, and a family friend, Giuseppe Graziano, would later join him and settle there with their wives and raise their families.

---

23. By then Ellis Island, not Castle Garden, was the immigration processing center.
24. The heaviest day on record was April 19, 1898, when 12,668 people were processed. With decreased immigration, it was closed in 1954, then the facility was rehabilitated and opened as a museum on September 9, 1965.
25. Regine (1999).
26. Gay Talese (1992) describes Ocean City in his retrospective *Unto the Sons*.

Migrant Italians were prodigious workers, their labor being what they had to offer this country. Michele worked the standard 10-to-12-hour days, six days a week at the city water plant, and in his off hours earned extra money at part-time work. His work schedule was grueling, but he supported himself and regularly sent generous amounts of money back to his family.

8. The Chef

Michele discovered an unexpected talent. Three men lived together in an apartment on West Avenue, and Michele joined them. They shared cooking duties, having decided that whatever else of home might have been lost, they would try to eat well. Each muddled through his turn at cooking and produced meals that were best forgotten. But when Michele's turn came, they had a real cook on their hands.

"Michele," they marveled, "this is wonderful! It's just like home! How do you know to cook like this?"

"Eh," he answered, with a shrug, "it's just *verde è fagioli* (greens and beans) with a little olive oil, a little tomato, a few *erbe* (herbs). That's all. Everybody knows how to make this."

"Ha," Domenico replied, poking his fork in his plate. "I know what's in here, but when I make it, it doesn't come out like this! Whatever you did to mix all the things in here, it's just right!"

Michele found that he liked to cook, and his skills grew as he tried to recreate the dishes he remembered from home. Presumably he had learned from his mother, Anna, but he had no recollection of having been tutored in cooking. Indeed, that would have violated the norms for training a growing boy in Maida. Michele had absorbed the tradition of creative cooking but had not been aware of his skills until he reached Ocean City. There, the meals that he prepared became known to other Italian men and created a demand for his good Southern Italian dishes. Michele soon turned his skills into additional income, cooking on weekends for parties, weddings, christenings, and other celebrations. "Mike Dattilo the Chef" became known among the group of immigrants.

Food—its growing, harvesting, preservation, preparation, and enjoyment—was central in the culture of *la famiglia*. Southern peasants were immersed in all phases of food, not simply as consumers. They were poor in Maida and, perhaps because of it, developed skills so that, according to my cousin Michael Bartolotti, "they could make five delicious meals out of one chicken, and waste nothing!" Out of necessity, the Italian peasants' basic diet consisted mainly of fresh greens, beans, olives, olive oil, peppers, squash, eggplant, scallions, onions, rice, figs, oranges, nuts, polenta, pasta, eggs, milk, and bread. Beef was not often served, but occasionally a chicken would be included. In some years, but only for the more fortunate who lived on farms, a fattened pig, shared by several families, would be converted to prosciutto, salami, pancetta, cappocolo, and other preserves that were hung from the ceilings for curing. Southern and central Italian cheeses such as ricotta, mozzarella, pecorino, and provolone also aged in the houses.

Meat and cheese were not abundant, because they were expensive. But fresh greens, grains, beans, squash, olive oil, pasta, fruits, and nuts were local products, forming the staples of the diet for the people of Maida. Those who owned or rented even a small plot grew much of their own food. One plentiful green-leafed weed with saw-toothed edges was given the fanciful name *dente di leone* (lion's teeth). Here, we call them dandelions. Those and other fresh greens were transformed into succulent dishes. The wild greens, free to all, were picked in the fields, briefly steamed or lightly boiled to remove some of their bitterness, then cooked *a saltato* (sautéd) in olive oil and garlic with nutritious white beans. Perhaps a fresh tomato was cut up and lightly cooked in. Seasoned with salt, a bit of fresh sweet basil, and a few red pepper seeds, the dish was enjoyed with a piece of warm, fresh-baked, hard-crusted bread and a glass of homemade red wine.

Thanks to the genius of the poor—despite their poverty, or perhaps because of it—Italian peasants could make meals out of weeds, meals that were delicious and, as we have recently realized, nutritious. This is the core of the touted Mediterranean diet, and it was the common food of the poor people of Southern Italy. No wonder that in Maida 100 years ago so many people lived well into their 90s.

Working long hours at the water plant and in his kitchen, Michele was able to send a good deal of money to Elisabetta. We have records showing that he opened a postal savings account in November 1912, making deposits ranging from $10 to $100 approximately every two months until September 1914, for an accumulated total of nearly $500. That was a sizeable amount, when immigrant laborers were paid 10 to 12 cents an hour, $7.20 for a 60-hour week. By Maida's standards, it was a fat pay envelope.

Michele did well in America, having achieved his three goals—he purchased a farm near Maida and a house in town and lifted his family from poverty. The farm was large by local standards, at least seven hectares (17.29 acres),[27] and it was to feed three generations before it passed out of our family. The Dattilos had not become rich, like the old landed gentry, but they now lived more comfortably as landowners of some status and, finally, they lived with *rispetto*.

Michele had no intention of immigrating, committing his life permanently to America, raising his children here. His brothers, Antonio and Giuseppe, were willing immigrants, neither having any desire to return to

---

27. Some of my relatives recall the farm's size to have been about seven hectare (17.29 acres) and others recall about 60 to 80 hectare (150–200 acres). In any event, it was a sizeable farm by Maidese standards.

Maida. (Anthony became a U.S. citizen in 1903.) But Michele had a mixed view of living here. *L'America,* he believed, was vulgar and corrupting; Americans were coarse people, interested in little beyond commercialism and a loud, rude culture of entertainment. He shook his head in disbelief at what the Italians called "*la pazzia americana*"—the Americans' craziness over sports—especially where two men battered each other bloody in a roped pen for money and entertainment! Could any culture be more crude? Money could be earned, certainly, in America, but the values and relationships of *la famiglia,* he believed, would be driven out of any children raised here. In most ways, his family was better off in Italy, where people were more civilized, more appreciative of substantial human values. He believed strongly that, even in poverty, life in Maida was personally and morally superior. If he could provide his family with the means to rise above poverty, then the quality of their lives in Maida would be preferable to that in America—and that was his aim.

Michele's views of America were not shared by his family. His brothers, cousins, and four of his six children would settle here, and his grandchildren would grow up as Americans. Elisabetta wanted to emigrate with him, but he refused to allow her to come to so vulgar a place. When her two sisters-in-law, Rosa and Bettina, left to join their husbands in America, Elisabetta said sadly, "Ah, they are the lucky ones."

In the years just before World War I, Michele was among the dwindling number of migrant workers from Italy, men who came here temporarily to work and then return home. True immigrants, who would become permanent citizens devoted to a new country, were replacing the migrants. He never intended his success in America to be an important precedent, easing the way for his own children to come to *la bell'America.*

By 1902, Michele was doing well in Ocean City, regularly sending money to Elisabetta and returning to Maida for several years each time. *La famiglia Dattilo* would thrive, but at the high cost of long separations and living on two continents, tied together by Michele's shuttling back and forth in search of work. It was, one might say, a long commute, but the rewards, he thought, made it worthwhile.

In order to protect and support his family, he had left them 3,000 miles away—the dilemma of an Italian father's responsibility in that time and place.

II

Coming to America

Chapter 6

Lady Liberty (1900)

1. A Poem for a Statue

My grandfather Michele Dattilo was fortunate settling into his new country, guided by friends who had preceded him. His friends, his job, and his extra work as "Mike the Chef" defined a new life. His first goal, earning money to send to his family, was met with surprising success, although with a workweek of some 80 hours. But then, hard work was not new to Italian men. His decision to emigrate had been a good one.

Michele knew that not all immigrants had been so fortunate. The 1880s and 1890s had seen horrendous events for many of his countrymen. Ocean City was a good place to settle, a happy accident for Michele. Here the immigrants seemed shielded from the worst of the prejudice and the outright attacks that he had heard were common elsewhere in *l'America*.

When Michele arrived in 1900, the Statue of Liberty was new, just four years in New York's harbor. Lady Liberty had become a symbol of freedom, drawing immigrants to America. The statue was new, but its inspiration dated from 2,000 years ago.

In 280 BC, the fabled Colossus of Rhodes, a gigantic bronze statue of Helios, the Sun God, stood 120 feet high, guiding travelers into the busy harbor of the Greek isle of Rhodes. Our "New Colossus," Lady Liberty, was sculpted by Frederic-Auguste Bartholdi,[1] who had been intrigued by tales of the ancient statue. The supporting steel frame was designed by Gustav Eiffel. The modern colossus stands on its star-shaped 27,000-ton concrete base on Liberty Island, holding its giant torch 305 feet high to guide travelers safely into New York's harbor. Dedicated in 1886, a gift from France to the United States, Lady Liberty was a powerful greeting for millions arriving from Europe and quickly became one of the world's best known landmarks.

---

1. Bartholdi's title for this monument is "Liberty Enlightening the World." Its inspiration was the fabled Colossus of Rhodes. Interestingly in light of our earlier discussions of *la rivoluzione*, Bartholdi served near Rome in 1870 in a French unit during the Franco-Prussian War. According to some, his unit's commander was Giuseppe Garibaldi, but I have not been able to verify that.

To Bartholdi's grand work of art was added another, "The New Colossus," a poem composed in 1883 by Emma Lazarus. Brought together, those two works express some of the noblest values of our country.

Come, they proclaim in their duet, leave behind your old world of autocracy and repression, and enjoy the liberty for all that was promised in the 18th-century American and French revolutions.

As the immigrants neared the statue, they strained to see the lines engraved across the base, lines penned expressly for them. In 1903, 40 years after the poet's death, the poem was engraved on a bronze plaque inside the hall. No reminiscence of European immigration to the United States can be complete without reprinting these lines.

The New Colossus
by Emma Lazarus

Not like the brazen giant of Greek fame,
With conquering limbs astride from land to land;
Here at our sea-washed, sunset gates shall stand
A mighty woman with a torch, whose flame
Is the imprisoned lightning, and her name
Mother of Exiles. From her beacon-hand
Glows world-wide welcome; her mild eyes command
The air-bridged harbor that twin cities frame.
"Keep, ancient lands, your storied pomp!" cries she
With silent lips. "Give me your tired, your poor,
Your huddled masses yearning to breathe free,
The wretched refuse of your teeming shore.
Send these, the homeless, tempest-tost to me,
I lift my lamp beside the golden door!"

I stood before those words during a recent visit to the monument, wrapped in its history and message. The plaque was not in place when my grandparents and parents filed through Castle Garden and Ellis Island 100 years ago. But Lady Liberty was there, welcoming each of them. Two families, mine and Sheila Ginsberg Graziano's,[2] came from different places in Europe, bringing different cultures and languages with them. What must they have thought as they looked up at that great copper-sheathed salute to freedom? Had they met, they could not have conversed with each other, with their tongues of mutual strangeness. But they could have stood together at the ship's rail and, looking up at Lady Liberty, easily communicated their gratitude for this welcome and their optimism for themselves, their children, and their grandchildren, without saying a word.

2. Sheila Ginsberg Graziano is the wife of the author.

Leaving the hall, I was pursued by a disturbing thought: today, we fear people who try to enter our country. We erect high border fences, write exclusionary laws, dispatch troops and private militia to keep them out.[3] We would all do well, I think, to visit that grand monument, read those lines, think about them, and be reminded of the nobility to which we once aspired.

However noble those ideals may have been, the reality of immigrants' lives was often grim. In 1900, Michele Dattilo was caught up in the surge of migration because Italy offered no future. Poverty was the product of a global depression that by 1930 would push more than 70 million migrants from Europe, Asia, and Africa. More than 40 million would go to the United States, five million of them from Italy, the largest immigrant group entering the country. That migration defined Europe as a net exporter of people, pushed by the 19th-century population explosion that had doubled Europe's inhabitants to 400 million. After World War I, 10 million persons wandered across Europe, having abandoned their homes because of poverty, politics, and the certainty of a hopeless future in their own countries.

2. The Lynching

Southern Italians were skilled farmers, but America needed men to work the docks and wield picks and shovels on road crews. With most clustered in large coastal cities, only 6 percent of the immigrants remained in agriculture, where their real skills could emerge.[4]

Their foreign language, manners, clannishness, and apparent unwillingness to adopt American ways brought Italians into view as foreign intruders who stole jobs from Americans, committed crimes, and created slums. By the 1890s, enmity against Italians had grown, stirred by the xenophobic drumbeat of the press and raised to murderous hatred. The press called Italians "Dagos." They reminded readers that each Dago concealed a "stiletto" with which he was skilled and which he was always ready to use.[5] On March 5, 1888, the *Buffalo Courier* reported that 42 "stalwart" Buffalo policemen "were ordered to bring in all the male Dago [sic] that looked as if they carried knives." More than 300 "swarthy foreigners" were rounded up. Two knives were found, proving that "Dagos" were dangerous.

In December 1890, *Popular Science Monthly* carried an article titled "What shall we do with the Dago?" "Stiletto-carrying Dagos," the author (Appleton Morgan) warned, would happily "lop off another Dago's finger or ear." The growing numbers of those rapidly breeding foreigners, such articles claimed, threatened the nation. Something must be done about them.

That same year, a construction boss testified before a congressional

3. This refers to our country's opposition to Mexican migrants—"illegal aliens."
4. Nelli (1983).
5. For more complete discussions of the prejudice stirred up and maintained by the American press, see Gallo (1981) and Mondello (1980).

committee investigating the influx of Italians. A congressman asked, "You don't call an Italian a white man?" Surprised at so naïve a question, the construction boss replied, "No, sir, an Italian is a Dago."[6]

As Italian immigration increased, so did the press barrage, and with it hatred and atrocities, including mob beatings of Italian workers and torchings of their homes. As described by Gallo,[7] several hundred Italians, mostly women and children, were driven out of New Orleans in 1894. Many were injured and their homes were burned down. In 1920, mobs raged for three days in West Frankfort, Illinois, stoning and clubbing Italian families, burning their homes and possessions, and driving hundreds out of town. From 1880 to 1910, mostly in the 1890s, violent mobs of Americans lynched more than three dozen Italians, primarily in the South (Florida, Louisiana, Mississippi, Virginia), but also in Colorado, Oklahoma, Pennsylvania, and Washington.

The New Orleans incident (1891–1892)[8] was the largest mass lynching in United States history. A mob dragged 11 Italian men from jail and murdered them. The background of this atrocity was an increasingly successful Italian population rivaling and angering many established Americans. Municipal corruption and competition between Italians and Irish formed an explosive mix. When Police Chief David Hennessy was murdered on October 15, 1890, New Orleans exploded. Shot in an ambush, Hennessy, who was suspected of being involved in prostitution and other illegal activities, gasped, "The Dagos shot me!"

"Arrest every Italian you come across!" Mayor Joseph Shakespeare ordered, and the police rounded up more than 150 men. When the courts began releasing them due to lack of evidence, the *New Orleans Times-Democrat* took action:

"All good citizens are invited to attend a mass meeting on Saturday, March 14, at 10 o'clock, a.m., at Clay's statue, to take steps to remedy the failure of justice in the Hennessy case. Come prepared for action!"

Can anyone deny that was a call for the lynch mob?

Some 8,000 enraged citizens smashed into the jail and dragged out and murdered every Italian they found. Two were hanged; nine were lined up against a wall and blasted with shotguns, rifles, and pistols. No one was ever prosecuted, and throughout the country Americans generally approved. Newspapers praised the New Orleans citizens for their justified action. *The New York Times* editorialized[9] about "those sneaking and cowardly Sicilians, the descendants of bandits and assassins . . . for whom the Lynch Law was the only course open. . . ."

6. Reported by Goldman (1952).
7. Gallo (1981).
8. This incident is described by many, including Nelli (1983) and Gallo (1981).
9. March 16 and 17, 1891, as discussed by Gallo (1981), page 116.

Theodore Roosevelt, who would become president 10 years later, reportedly commented that the lynching was "a rather good thing."[10]

Over the next 30 years, rule by arsonists and lynch mobs would be gradually replaced by more civilized expressions of prejudice, such as Congress' enactment of anti-immigration laws in the 1920s. The murderous hatred was muted over time, but a deep anti-Italian prejudice lingered into the 1950s, gradually decreasing in intensity. It continues today, but in quieter, more sophisticated ways.

As immigration continued to fill the cities in the early 20th century, established Americans—that is, earlier immigrants—abandoned their neighborhoods to the foreigners. Immigrants had little money to buy or maintain buildings, and the slum owners had no incentive to keep their properties in repair.[11] In 1905, prejudice was high. Americans, it was noted, continue to see each Italian as "a dirty, undersized individual who engages in degrading labor, is shunned by Americans, and who is often a member of the Mafia, and, as such, likely at any moment to draw a knife and stab you in the back."[12]

Italian immigrants continued to be viewed as a threatening swarm of jabbering, ignorant, uncivilized, unskilled, unwashed, near-barbarian thieves and louts invading the country. If allowed to intermarry, it was said, they would "weaken the American stock" and "destroy our moral fiber." In 1914, sociologist Edward Ross described Southern and Eastern European immigrants:

"Observe immigrants not as they come travel-wan up the gang-plank, nor as they issue, toil-begrimed from pit's mouth or mill-gate, but in their gatherings, washed, combed, and in their Sunday best. [They] are hirsute, low-browed, big-faced persons of obviously low mentality . . . out of place in black clothes and stiff collar, since clearly they belong in skins, in wattled huts at the close of the great ice age. These ox-like men are descendants of those who always stayed behind."[13]

Ross described the "dwarfishness" of Italians, their physical weakness that made them "unfit" for any real work. Italians, he noted, were also mentally inferior and unable to understand even simple commands or carry out anything more than uncomplicated, repetitive tasks.[14]

A young couple, sympathetic to the immigrants, traveled in steerage with a group of Italians. They wrote that the United States "assumes an enormous task when it undertakes to transform this grimy, stupid, riff-raff of Europe into intelligent, self-respecting American citizens."[15]

---

10. Krase and DeSena (1994).
11. Like slumlords everywhere, they found greater profits in collecting rents and allowing their properties to deteriorate than in spending money to maintain them.
12. Meade (1905).
13. Quoted by Kennedy (1966).
14. Mondello (1980), page 66.
15. Price (1917).

At times we become so troubled by "foreigners" that we create anti-immigration laws. The English, Irish, and Germans failed to remember that they had once been the foreign immigrants. The Chinese Exclusion Act (1882, 1892, and 1902) targeted the "Yellow Tide." In 1924, the Johnson-Reed Act (National Origins Act) restricted Italians and other Southern Europeans while encouraging the more desirable Northern Europeans and English. Italian immigration decreased from 283,738 in 1914, when immigration was suspended due to World War I, to 3,845, the new Italian quota in 1929, the year the new act went into effect—a greater than 98 percent reduction. Americans did not want more Italians.

Seasonal migrants were becoming permanent immigrants even as the nation moved toward the immigration-restriction laws of the 1920s. As discussed by D'Amico,[16] despite prejudice and other barriers, Italians created a record of reliability and value as workers, skilled tradesmen, business owners, and professionals. Americans might not have wanted Italians as friends, neighbors, and fellow parishioners, but they were willing to hire them at low wages, with no benefits.

The immigrants learned the language and ways of America and became more sophisticated and less vulnerable to the egregious scams, thievery, and physical abuse of earlier years. They established food markets and banks and Italian newspapers. Prosperous farms, vineyards, and wineries were created in upstate New York, and in San Francisco, Italians dominated the entire fishing industry. In New Orleans, where the horrific lynching had occurred, Italians owned more than half of all retail groceries, dominated other businesses, and gained political sophistication. They were becoming homeowners, businessmen, bankers, landlords, and politicians. Physicians and scholars came from Italy to serve Italian communities and to join the faculties of American universities.

3. Becoming Italian

Southern Italians achieved more than economic success. They also found a new identity and a new social organization, a hybrid formed from the traditional Italian *campanilismo* and the new American society.[17] *Campanilismo* meant allegiance to the family, town, and province. Each person took care of the family; each family took care of its own; every family was for itself, against a harsh world beyond the door. It was a remarkable stance, sharply independent of formal government and interdependent with family and friends. It served them well for 50 generations. There had been no powerful sense of community beyond the family and locale, and thus no magnification of power and influence that comes from socially cooperative action. The immigrants whom I knew in the 1930s, particularly

---

16. D'Amico (2005).
17. Nelli (1983).

the men, were so determinedly independent that, in their rejection of almost every government and social organization outside of the home, they maintained what my friend Murray Levine has called an implacable and irrational "counter-dependence." This was one source of the strength that they needed to cope with America's obstacles. It was also, however, a self-created hindrance that prevented the magnified social power that can come from collective action.

In American cities, Italians learned about social cooperation beyond the family. America, they found, was more complex than their towns in Italy. The urban immigrants in America were poor, but with a cosmopolitan flavor—German, Irish, Italian, Polish, Jewish, and other groups rubbed elbows. People of varying skin colors, languages, and cultures went about the common business of making a living. Human variety became visible to the traditionally isolated Southern Italians, forcing them to recognize that their little regions in Italy did not, after all, define the whole world.

They recognized, too, that despite the rigid distinctions made by their lingering *campanilismo*, all people from Italy were "*viaggiatori sullo stesso mare* (voyagers on the same sea)," and all shared the common task of finding their place in America. Although upon stepping into America they had viewed themselves as *Calabresi* or *Siciliani* or *Napolitani*, and so on, they learned that Americans did not make those distinctions but saw them as a single group, "Italians." That idea began to appeal to the immigrants. These people from separated regions, with distinctly different dialects and prejudices, had to come to America to learn that they shared not only a culture, but also a common situation. It is ironic, but the unity of Italians that the revolution had failed to bring about was finally found in America.

The hard, divisive lines drawn by traditional *campanilismo* began to melt. *La famiglia* remained supreme, but it was no longer the isolated and self-sufficient small world it had once been. In America, Italians learned how to magnify their social power through collective action such as by creating mutual aid societies to promote their common welfare. They formed social and political clubs; banking and business firms; educational, entertainment, religious, and artistic groups; and burial societies. This was a progressive shift of identity—first they accepted that they were all Italians; then they were ready to learn how to become Americans. They did it quickly, many in a single generation.

What was best for one's family could now be achieved through cooperation. I would see this many times in the 1930s, as members of my parents' small group in Nyack came together in mutual aid in times of need. Families blended together temporarily in various configurations, as one or more took over the responsibilities of another family that had fallen into health or economic crisis. Friends came, unbidden, into the homes of the bereaved or the ill, to cook and clean and care for children, to make necessary home repairs—to be there for the family in need.

I recall when my father bought our first washing machine to ease the labor of laundry. Mom was excited, but before he could install the new machine, Pop fell ill and was hospitalized. The big machine sat in our basement—gleaming white, impressive, and useless. One afternoon, Mom investigated noises in the basement and found *Zio*[18] Antonio Conace and his son, Joe, pouring a concrete base to anchor the machine, as was necessary then. They connected the plumbing and wiring, and Mom's new machine was ready to use. No one had asked them to do it; they just did.

4. *I Padroni*

L'America offered opportunities for success if one was willing to work hard and tolerate abuse while becoming established. Men brought families or were married in the United States, replacing their original goal of temporary migration with permanent immigration and citizenship. This was a major shift and a new experience—willingly giving allegiance to a nation. They were becoming Americans.

Through the collective genius of the United States, and despite the country's darker underside, even the junk dealer could, by his own hard work, become a substantial businessman, and his family could enjoy the comforts of America. Most never became rich, but *la bell'America* gave to all ambitious men and women the opportunity to achieve things far beyond the possibilities offered in Italy. The immigrants became grateful, patriotic American citizens. The people I knew in the 1930s were willing to forgive, or at least to tolerate, the insults, rejections, and prejudice, and to recognize and cherish the country for what it allowed them to achieve.

In the mid-1890s, before all that success would be realized, young men in Maida responded to America's mixed lure. Among the stories of goldpaved streets were also dark tales of failures, beatings, lynchings, sickness, and strange disappearances. Despite the growing success of the immigrants, living in the United States also meant crowding, disease, corruption, danger, and rampant prejudice that every day insulted each man. With their enthusiasm and sense of adventure, young men also recognized the peril. In the 1890s, they stepped into the most deadly period of Americans' hatred of Italians.

The migrants knew that on entering the United States they would have only their peasant clothes, a few dollars, the name of *il padrone*, and a willingness to work. These were meager buffers against the expenses of rent, food, and payment to the padrone for securing jobs and rooms, and the rampant prejudice that they had not yet experienced.

In America, where there is a need, enterprising persons will create a business to meet it. The *padroni* were intermediaries; they operated from about 1860, when Italian immigration began its sharp increase, until around

18. "*Zio*," meaning "uncle" is a term of respect for uncles or close family friends.

1910. By then, the acculturated Italians had become so well-established that new immigrants could depend upon their relatives and friends already here to help them adjust.

Il padrone in America was a creation of Southern Italian peasants and an important man in the early years of migration. From 1880 to 1920, more than four million Italians, 90 percent of them southerners, were recorded as having migrated to the United States.[19] That total is inflated, since many made several trips and were counted more than once. For years, there was a 40 percent repatriation rate—a "return migration" to Italy—the highest of any immigrant group. The anti-Italian prejudice probably contributed to that.

The immigrants climbed the gangplanks and spread into New York City, naive strangers in a confusing world filled with people who jabbered in the unknown American tongue. A system of intermediaries between the immigrants and the new culture was needed to help the newcomers survive and to help America gain all it could from so much willing labor. The padrone system[20] took on a uniquely American commercial character. In Italy, a literate person like *il professore* enjoyed the status of a scribe, translator, and general intermediary for illiterate townspeople. He was a trusted relative, neighbor, or friend and shared their values. In their homes, he translated documents and read and wrote letters, usually with the family clustered around, attentive to his skills.

For Southern Italians, knowing how to read and write was seldom necessary. They recognized no need for literacy or for children to stay in school, had no demand that local governments support compulsory education, as mandated by Rome in 1877. It was enough that a few trusted people in town could provide those skills when needed. After all, "*se c'è un buon calzolaio in città, nessun altro ha bisogno di sapere come fare le scarpe* (if there is one good shoemaker in town, then not everyone needs to know how to make shoes)."

Many *padroni* were concerned, helpful men, but there were some vicious exploiters of naive immigrants. No longer was the intermediary a trusted relative or friend; now he was a stranger who made his living at it. The immigrants were his clients, under the best of conditions, and his manipulated labor stock under the worst. When they landed in New York, the immigrants met a knowledgeable man who offered his help—a Southern Italian who spoke Italian and English and could interpret the culture. The new immigrant was ready to trust *il padrone*, not knowing, however, if he would be honest or deceitful.

---

19. According to Foerster (1919; 1968), in the 19th century, far more Italians migrated to Argentina than to the United States. In South America, the Italians' role was very different than it was in North America, being much like that of the earlier English, Dutch, and Germans in North America.

20. See the discussions of the padrone system by Foerster (1919) and Gallo (1981).

The padrone greeted new arrivals, arranged lodging and jobs, and guided them through the confusing cultural maze. He became their agent, teacher, counselor, banker, and translator in this overpowering new country. He showed them how to open savings accounts, mailed their money orders back home to their families, and warned them of pitfalls, of people and places to avoid. Without *il padrone*, many immigrants would not have survived.

I padroni were facile in English and Italian, skilled at negotiating and providing helpful services to the American and Italian communities. They were self-selected men who had the necessary intelligence, social facility, language skills, and, for some, willingness to exploit everyone, even their countrymen. They were businessmen, not friends. They collected a fee from the employer of each new worker, and a fee from each worker for having found the job. They collected a portion of the first rental payment from the migrant and from the landlord.

Some of the *padroni* made extravagant promises, lied, extorted money, and generally took advantage of the naive migrants. Among the worst were the labor bosses who assembled labor gangs for contractors and farmers and held the migrants in virtual slavery. They enlisted migrants into work gangs with promises of steady work and high pay—a promise might be for $1.25 a day, or five times the going rate back in Italy. Once enlisted, the immigrants were turned over to other bosses, who transported them to the work sites in open trucks or flatbed railroad cars, forced them to live in isolated work camps with hellish living conditions, and unmercifully victimized them. The bosses stole their money in countless ways—charging for transportation to the work site, food, lodgings in barely livable conditions, and even for the normal wear and breakage of tools. Under those conditions, a worker earning $1.25 a day might be able to keep 25 cents—essentially the going rate in Italy. Some bosses physically abused the laborers, made them work strenuously, and denied even minimum safety measures lest they slow the work. Some men were killed or injured, and none received compensation.

The migrants, even as they came to realize they were being victimized, continued to depend on their *padroni* until they had gained experience and joined social networks that guided newcomers to avoid being so easily and viciously exploited. The padrone system gradually disappeared.

Italian communities grew and produced political representatives who interacted with mayors' offices, schools, and city councils. Some *padroni*, with their social and bilingual skills, took on political roles, becoming ward representatives, city legislators, mayors, and governors. Italian immigrants were discovering American politics.

Chapter 7
Mario, Paolo, and Friends (1896–1902)

1. In Steerage

Late in 1902, while my grandfather Michele Dattilo worked in Ocean City, three young men returned to Italy. They and two others, Mario Gaitano and Paolo Bellisone,[1] had set out six years earlier to rescue their families from poverty and find adventure and employment in America. The friends grew up after the 1870 unification, while the new kingdom was supposedly abolishing oppression and subduing the avaricious church and rich families that had kept the southerners poor and powerless. However, continuing poverty and repression pushed them to leave Italy in search of better lives in *l'America*.

In 1895, those young men looked ahead and saw endless days of trudging through the mountains in predawn and evening blackness, and unending labor in the malarial lowlands. It was not the work that bothered them, but knowing that every day echoed every previous day, and unchanged years marched on to each man's final sundown. They were locked in a parade of fatigue and despair, traveling the same circular path daily, with no exit. Their only redemption was death.

"Death," thought Mario, a young man already turned cynical. "Here, in this place, death is the path to peace and the little fulfillment that might be possible. For Italians, *la morte è la vita; morire e vivere* (death is life; die and live). Dreadful ideas, he thought, preached by the priests—men of little worth who did no work themselves but only wormed into peoples' lives preaching death as fulfillment. Were the people celebrating life when they clogged the church or marched in their holy processions? No. They celebrated death. Such were his thoughts.

Mario was scornful of priests, peasants who had barely escaped their own poverty by donning the cloth and living off the toil and misery of others. Poor families were proud when a son became a priest, elevated a step above poverty to enjoy a life of some respect. Families sacrificed to support the boy who was diverted from a workingman's life and sent into the priesthood.

---

1. I do not know their true names. This is the only written account of the experiences of these five young men. It is a story that I heard in the 1930s, recounted by the older men.

They said it was their way of bringing God into their families. Cynics like Mario, however, saw it as a shrewd investment for future status, respect, and escape from the worst of poverty. Peasant priests were unsophisticated, insular men who knew no more about the world beyond Maida than did their parishioners.

The priests' status separated them from their simple origins and the people they helped to control. Expected to assist families with real problems, the priests had little to offer. Barred by the Church from marriage and parenthood, the priests were nevertheless expected to know what was best for man, woman, and child. Never soiling their hands with work, they pretended to understand the struggles of working people. Their job, Mario thought, was to serve the rich by keeping the poor focused on the myth of salvation through death, keeping the people from exploding in their poverty, frustration, and anger.

Perhaps most difficult for the village priest was his own imprisonment, something that Mario did not recognize. A priest enjoyed his parishioners' respect but was forever at the bottom of the church hierarchy. Elevated above his family, the village priest would never rise further, because advancement was reserved for the sons of the wealthy. He was a peasant torn from his roots and left in a narrow, low-ceilinged, lonely place from which he might fall but could never ascend. He had forsaken his own people and joined ranks with the rich to gain a marginally easier life, but he found himself left on the bottom step.

By the age of 20, Mario was one of Southern Italy's many cynical young men. At home, Mario no longer voiced his heretical ideas about the priesthood, because that set his mother crying and praying that God would make her son see his errors before they consumed him. His father, middle-aged and already worn down, admonished him for upsetting his mother and sisters but never disagreed with his feelings. It was only with his friends that Mario could find spoken agreement, although their ideas were not as intense as his.

According to Mario's grand uncle, who had known his own disappointments, the closed Southern Italian society offered young men two escapes from *la miseria della vita* (life's misery)—the priesthood and crime. His uncle told him:

"*Dintra sta vita ci suna due dirizioni per ogni giuvanu. Una va versu Dio, e l' altra va versu lu Diavulu.* (In this life, there are two directions for each young man. One path goes toward God, and the other goes toward the Devil.)"

He sighed and finished with the shrug of all people with little hope. "*E, nipute mio, pi ti diri la verita, su tutti li stessi!* (And, in truth, nephew, they are the same!)"

Men who had returned from America described a vibrant, brutal country, but its purpose was life, not death. Americans, he heard, did not worship death, did not parade death through the streets as did the villagers in holy processions here. They did not proclaim that death was the doorway to life, as did the priests and the old ladies of Maida.

Mario's feelings were strong. Living and dying were the pivotal issues of existence, and somewhere in this march toward death that we call life there must be room to take an independent path. One could not decide that he would never die, but one could decide not to embrace a life that led only to death. Mario knew, not by philosophical reasoning but by the guidance of intense feelings, that he must make a choice. He was no philosopher, no deep thinker like his friend Paolo, but he saw the realities of his poor town. His thoughts boiled with emotion and conflicting loyalties, with dissatisfaction and alarm over his future. "There must be more to life," he thought. "We do not live only to die."

For Mario, the unrelenting schedule of poverty wrapped in desperate religion was a trap as real as the net of the *cacciatore* (hunter) that snared poor animals in the field. If one allowed the entrapment, the binds would become tighter, until escape was impossible. The time to free himself, he knew, was now.

The priesthood was a mockery of life, a hurtful compromise. Crime was destructive and dangerous. There was no ready movement out of poverty and into a middle class. Unlike in the north, there was no middle class. Young people were not educated. There were no industries in the south of any merit, and jobs other than farm labor were impossible to find. The landowners hired and fired at will, paying only 1 to 1.5 lire a day (20 to 30 cents), a bit more during peak harvest time.[2] If a man protested, his job was given to the next man respectfully waiting in the long line, hat in hand.

Men returning from America in the early 1890s showed Mario a dramatically different future. Some strutted around town casually twirling elegantly tapered walking sticks. They wore the clothing of affluent American men: a white shirt and high starched collar holding the chin up in a haughty fashion, a wide cravat, and a tight, four-button jacket with elegantly thin vertical stripes. A two-pointed handkerchief splashing a bit of color from the slanted breast pocket, slim trousers tapering to polished black leather shoes, and, to top it off, a stylish derby or bowler. A golden watch chain crossed the vest, a shiny ring or two gleamed, smart gloves were casually carried in the hand, hair was worn short and neatly balanced by a carefully trimmed moustache. An overcoat was draped over the shoulders, European style. This was elegance.

The returnees flashed American money, making sure to point out the dollar's greater value over the lire. Some returned with money to buy homes and farms, immediately elevating their families' comfort and status. Their new wealth was impressive, but even more so was their new bearing.

2. Davenport (1904).

When young Giordano di Nunzio returned after five years in America and met his former padrone, he did not even doff his hat! He showed no respect, acting not as if he and the padrone were equals, but as if he held a superior status! The returnees had become men of the world, and they convinced younger men like Mario to aim for America.

In the summer of 1896, Mario, Paolo, and three friends began their journey to America. With common delays, it would take four to six weeks, with two at sea. First, they needed official permission to emigrate. They began the process by requesting the municipal secretary in Maida to forward copies of their birth certificates to the *questura*, the police headquarters for the Province of Catanzaro. There, records were checked for criminal activity. If none was found, the applications moved through the bureaucracy and, weeks later, passports were issued.

Now they could purchase steamship tickets from one of the agents who traveled the small towns. Tickets were expensive—125 to 180 lire, the earnings of four to six months of farm labor.[3] Each man had saved 80 to 100 lire for a ticket and would borrow the rest from relatives and friends, promising to repay the loan when he began earning money in America. The agent could have advanced the cost of the tickets, but that would commit the travelers to work for *il padrone* in America and pay his exorbitant interest. The friends had been warned that this was one of many snares waiting in America for unwary young travelers.

They bought their tickets—Naples to New York. Mario was excited, showing his ticket to everyone and announcing, "I am going to America, to New York City. *La bell'America!*"

There was still much to do—collect addresses of relatives in America, bid farewells. They needed lire for the train to Naples and for lodging while waiting for final clearance, and American dollars to show the authorities they were not destitute. The agent offered, for a 20 percent fee, to arrange lodgings in Naples and exchange their lire for dollars, but the friends decided to save the fees and make their own arrangements once they reached Naples.

"You'll be sorry!" the agent told them. "*Sono tutti banditi a Napoli* (They are all bandits in Naples)."

Excitement and sadness filled their final days in Maida. The little town was losing five young men whom everyone had known since birth. People who could not afford it gave them salami, provolone, mozzarella, bread, and jugs of wine. The jugs were too heavy to take, so for several days their friends helped drink the wine, and no one complained about that. Their mothers sewed their few clothes and put food into cloth sacks. On the day they left, their mothers wept and their fathers grew silent as the five young men boarded the train to Naples.

They had been warned to be wary in Naples, where swindlers saw the

3. Margariti (1980).

emigrants as "*polli sfortunati* (unfortunate chickens)" ready to be plucked. There were predators—men, women, even children would trick their money from them by offering fake services and documents. They promised wonderful jobs in America that paid more in a week than one could earn at home in a year. *Farmacisti* of dubious credentials touted "*medicine che sono assolutamente necessarie* (absolutely necessary medicines)" for their ocean voyage. Women in nuns' habits and men in clerical robes would bless them and offer, for a fee, prayers and holy relics to guarantee protection by God and the saints. Self-identified housing officials would offer nonexistent lodging that demanded advanced payment or would wave "official government permits" at them that had to be purchased before they boarded their ship.

Dignified bankers would promise dollars for lire, and then cheat them out of their money. Innkeepers would overcharge them, get them drunk, and steal their money and clothes. Girls selling flowers peddled other services. Official-looking men walked through the crowd to paste bogus "immigration clearance" stickers on bundles and suitcases, and then held out their hands for the "required municipal fee." And if the crooks could not scam their money from them, the pickpockets would simply reach in and steal it.

Forewarned, they stayed close together, protecting each other. If a convincing conniver swayed one of them, the others rescued him and laughed at his naivete. Each was tempted, each was rescued by the others, each took his turn being chided as "*un povero pollo* (a poor chicken)," each laughed at himself and his friends.

Young and enthusiastic, they enjoyed an exciting time. Being observant and bright young men, they learned to recognize scams and gained more big-city, self-protective savvy in a few days than most southerners learned in a lifetime.

On arriving in Naples, they were stunned. Naples was a madhouse. Thousands of people, mostly men, in clothing styles from all over Italy, were jammed at the ports. The babble of dialects was confusing and often not even understandable.

"Listen to the different languages!" Mario said, amazed. "These people must have come to Naples from all over the world!"

Another man, overhearing that, laughed. "Didn't you know?" he said. "We're all Italians here. We all speak Italian, different dialects!"

People huddled around their piles of cloth bundles and homemade suitcases. Some men had only the clothes they wore. Some families even had crates of live chickens! "Eh," said Paolo, pointing at the terrified chickens, "speaking of *polli sfortunati*."

A thousand peddlers wove through the crowd, shouting, selling everything, little of which was needed by any voyager. One man was selling rope. "Rope?" one of the friends asked. "Why rope? To tie up our bundles?"

"No," Paolo answered. "To hang ourselves when we suffer *u mal di mare*."

People were shouting, crying, praying, and several were frantically searching for children who had disappeared into the crowd. Men, weary from their long journeys to Naples, lay on the ground or on their bundles, trying to sleep. Government and steamship employees moved officiously through the crowd, trying to create order. Never before had the friends seen so many people, heard so much noise, or wondered at such confusion.

They remained in Naples for 11 days, sleeping most nights on the ground and a few in an overpriced, crowded, and filthy hotel. They endured questioning, medical examinations, inoculations, and a period of quarantine to rule out communicable disease such as cholera. Finally they were cleared to emigrate, and on the day of departure joined a huge throng waiting to board their ship.

"You! You there!" An important-looking man carrying a large folder and wearing a uniform cap with a badge on it approached them. "Where are your Municipal Embarkation Permits? Let me see them!"

"But what is that? We know nothing of that."

"You must have them or I cannot permit you to board the ship."

"But no one told us about this!"

"It is your responsibility to know what you need and to obtain all the necessary papers. If you don't have them, you must go to the office and apply for the permits."

"But where? What office? How long will it take? The ship is leaving today, in three hours!"

"The municipal office, back in your own province. If you send for them by mail, it will take six to eight weeks. It is best that you simply go back home and get them and then return here for another ship. Of course, you will lose the money you have already paid for your tickets." The man handed their papers back to them and began walking away.

"Wait!" they called. "Wait! Isn't there an office here, in Naples?"

"Yes," he said, pausing, "but that will take two or three weeks, because this office has a thousand applications that must go through the mail, too."

The prospect of returning to Maida, waiting many weeks for more paperwork, and repeating their journey to Naples, not to mention the loss of so much money for tickets and travel, was thoroughly discouraging.

"Is there anything you can do?" they pleaded. "Any way to help us?"

"Well," the official said, softening. "You seem like nice enough boys. Ah, well. I guess I could help you out, do a favor and take your applications for you now. But," he whispered, looking around, "I'm not supposed to do this, you know. It could mean my job. Here, you have to sign this form and pay the required municipal fee. Then I can issue an official permit."

He showed them a document—*Permesso d'Imbarco Temporaneo* (Temporary Embarkation Permit)—with spaces for their names and a golden seal stamped in the lower right-hand corner declaring "*L'Ufficio Municipale di Napoli* (Naples Municipal Office)."

"With that, I can allow you to board the ship. By the time your permits are finalized in the government office, you will already be in America. All the paperwork will be done right here, all legal and complete. The required municipal fee is 10 lire each, plus five lire each for the processing, and we can get this finished right now, if you want."

The men were grateful that he would help them out, but dismayed at the fee. At 15 lire each, they would have to part with 75 lire, a dozen weeks' work. While the others reluctantly reached into their pockets, Paolo was becoming suspicious.

"To me this smells like one of Nunzio's fish that he tries to sell at the end of the week. How do we know what he says is true? We gonna believe him? Give him our money? Fifteen lire each? Maybe first we better check with somebody else."

The man seemed insulted after having tried to help them. Rising on his toes, his hand high in the air, he pointed a finger upward.

"He's like a statue of San Francesco, pointing to heaven," Paolo thought, "waiting for the light of benediction."

Mario, too, thought it was a strange gesture to make.

"I," said the man, puffing his chest out with dignity, vigorously making circles in the air with his extended finger and tapping at his heart with his other hand, causing his papers to flutter like a caught white bird, "I am an official of the government. *Un funzionario del governo!* Do you understand? The government! I am not to be insulted!"

A sudden shouting and commotion came from behind them and they turned around. "Thief! Crook!" A small man, a poor emigrant just like them, was running toward them, angry, shouting, and waving his fists.

"You swindler, you crook! Liar! Cheat! I'll have you arrested! You stole my money! Thief! Crook!" With that loud diversion, the man with the shiny badge ran off and was quickly out of sight among the thousands of people.

The newcomer was agitated, and the friends had to calm him down. His name was Giovanni Riccola, he said, from Puglia, and he was on his way to America, where he was to join his beloved sister and her husband, who waited for him in the great city of *Filadelfia.* But the "thieves of Naples," he said with shaking voice and clenched fists, had stolen his money, belongings, and even his steamship ticket!

"And that one," he said, meaning the man who had run off, "was trying to steal from you. He cheated me of 15 lire for his phony papers! It's a good thing for you I came by and recognized him. He cheated me; he stole my money. But at least your money is safe!"

The friends thanked him and asked what he was going to do now, without money or ticket.

"Ah, *signore*," he said with sadness. "I am a proud man, reduced to begging. I hope the good will and generosity of my fellow travelers will bring me enough to buy another ticket. Many have helped, and now I need only another 25 lire, and I will be on my way to join my beloved mother, who right now waits for me in the great city of *Nuova Yorka*. But you gentlemen have your own concerns. I am happy to have helped you, so I bid you goodbye and *buon viaggio*."

He tipped his hat in a salute to the friends and began slowly walking away.

"The poor man," the friends said to each other. "He's stranded here. Maybe we could help him a little. After all, he saved us a lot of money by recognizing that thief."

"*Signore*!" they called. "Come back. We're grateful to you and want to help. We can't give 25 lire, but maybe one or two from each will bring you a bit closer to your ticket."

The little man gushed his appreciation, called down upon the young men the blessings of *il Buon Dio*, the saints, all the angels and good spirits, and the beautiful soul of his long-deceased mother in heaven. He accepted their 10 lire, bowed gratefully again, and walked into the crowd. The men felt good over their close call and virtuous over their generosity.

Later that day, Paolo suddenly burst into laughter and began to cluck like a chicken. The others stared at him.

"*Ma, che diavolo fai* (what the devil are you doing)?" they asked.

"We really are poor stupid chickens ready to be plucked. Cluck! Cluck! Cluck!" he said, turning in a circle and flapping his arms.

"*Ma, è diventato pazzo!* He's gone crazy!" one of the men observed, making circles around his ear. "If he flaps his arms like that any more, he'll fly right out there and splash in the bay."

Then they looked to where Paolo was pointing and saw the poor little migrant they had helped, and the crook, the man with his official hat. They were standing together, talking amiably, and seemed to be counting money between them.

"Crooks!" the friends shouted, now understanding the scam, running at the two men, shaking their fists. But the two men looked up and quickly ran off in opposite directions.

"See," said Paolo after they had lost the men in the crowd, "we are poorer but wiser. Those two, if the first one does not get us with his phony hat and papers, then he raises his hand like this, makes the circles for a signal, and calls in the other one. Then he comes running, just a poor traveler like us, and finishes the job. He's going to visit his sister in *Filadelfia*, he says, then it's his sainted mother in *Nuova Yorka*, who he tells us two minutes later is long departed in heaven. That's a good trick if she can do it, and we didn't see it, like dumb chickens. Ah, they were right, those who warned us: *sonno tutti banditi a Napoli*. Naples is full of thieves."

Hours later, it was their turn to show their papers a final time on Italian soil and then walk down the gangplank onto the huge ship, *Europa*. Elegantly dressed first- and second-class passengers leaned on the upper decks' railings, looking down on the steerage class with arched eyebrows. Imperious ship's officers in gold-braided uniforms stood with white-gloved hands clasped behind their backs, surveying their ship, while obsequious stewards ran here and there to assist the moneyed upper-class passengers.

Excited and anxious, the friends stood on the lower deck as the ship steamed south from Naples, down the Tyrrhenian Sea, and west through the Mediterranean. They were heading for the Strait of Gibraltar, their doorway to the great Atlantic Ocean and the long crossing to the fabled port of *Nuova Yorka*.

For the next two weeks, they would live in steerage, deep belowdecks, in a giant dormitory jammed with narrow wooden bunks stacked four high. Mario and his friends claimed five bunks and stowed their bundles on the thin padding.

"This is where we sleep?" Paolo asked, looking around. "Like chickens in a chicken coop?"

"It smells in here," added one of the friends. "Even a chicken coop smells better than this. And if you roll over in your sleep and fall off the top, you break your head on the floor!"

"And look, to get to my bed I have to crawl over five men! Five women, maybe. But five men?"

In truth, the accommodations offered some improvements for them. There was running water to drink and latrines instead of a bush in the woods to hide behind. The mattresses, however, were thin, coarse burlap bags of hay, and whatever crawled in there left them with stinging red welts on their skin.

The space was so crowded with bunks that there was little room even to sit together on the floor for the meals that were fed to them in buckets, six helpings per bucket. The men were fed twice a day in groups of six, one man being selected to stand on line to get food for all of them. Upon him was bestowed the impressive title "*il Capo di Rancio* (the Chief of Rations)." For these young men always looking for diversion, that bit of bureaucratic embellishment was too much to resist, and each day they carried out a ceremony. First, they selected one among them in a game, in which they stood in a circle and thrust their right hands into the center with one to three fingers extended, while loudly calling out their predicted total number of fingers: "*sette*," "*cinque*," "*dieci*," and so on. Those who called an incorrect total were eliminated, and the others contested again until there was only one left, who thus became *il Capo* for that day. Having made their selection, the others snapped smartly to attention, saluted the new

Capo di Rancio, and sent him on his way with their bucket and cup, reminding him to carry out his important duties with care and responsibility. They named their daily ceremony "*Assortimento del Capo* (Selection of the Chief)." Imitating bugles and drum rolls for a martial atmosphere, they marched smartly down the narrow aisles between the bunks while their fellow passengers applauded, enjoying this daily silliness. The new *Capo* stood on the food line, sometimes for an hour, eventually receiving the bucket of rations, pieces of bread, and cup of wine, which he distributed to his group.

Tin plates that had bits of dried food and rust from the previous users were issued. "Eh?" Paolo asked one of the stewards, scraping something dark and crusty from his tin dish. "We gotta pay extra for this crud, or do you throw it in free?" To avoid other people's crusted refuse, some of the men scraped down their plates and kept their tinware instead of dropping it into the cold, gray salt water of the wash-up barrels. Each man punched holes in the rim of his plate, ran string through the holes and the cup handle, and hung the jangling collection around his neck. The plates would remain dirty, but each thought, "at least it's my dirt."

Some had made the journey before and knew the power of well-aimed gratuity. They were prepared with extra money to be slipped to the stewards, so the stewards would bring food from the first- and second-class menus, served on real china. Mario saw that all sorts of amenities—blankets, clean thick mattresses, even bottles of wine—could be bought from the enterprising stewards, who paid nothing for their pilfered merchandise. Few steerage travelers could afford to buy such amenities, but they did not prevent others from doing so.

Down in steerage there were no windows to admit the sunlight or show how far underwater they were. Were they still floating? Was the ship sinking, slipping under the waves? One poor boy, barely 13 years old, upon descending to steerage far belowdecks, began to moan. He curled up with his arms covering his head and was convinced the sea was crushing the walls and they would be squeezed to death. "I know the walls are not shrinking," he said in his distress, his face pleading. "I know, I know. But I can't help it! It feels that way!" The only way to get him to stop moaning and give himself and everyone else some rest was to take him up on deck and stay there with him. However, in the dormitory, the boy moaned all night long.

Most distressing for the passengers, few of whom had ever been away from home and none on a tossing sea, was that their already uncomfortable and poorly ventilated quarters were unstable. The floor and walls shifted, swayed, rolled, lurched, rose up and dropped down, creaked, and groaned with alarming noises. Some were not affected, but many felt the wrenching, prolonged nausea of seasickness—*u mal di mare*. It was, they thought in their misery, as near to a torturous slow death as could be imagined. The shine and smell of vomit were everywhere.

The five friends, however, were enthusiastic and would not be dispirited. They stayed on deck as much as possible, even carrying their two meals a day there. They exulted in the swelling seas and laughed as they staggered and practiced keeping their balance (and their dinners). They developed a sailor's rolling gait while the ship lurched under them. "Ah!" Paolo shouted at the sea in one of his poetic moods, as he leaned into the bracing wind,

"Chi siamo?
E che vogliamo trovare?
Veramente siamo
I figli della mare!" [4]

"Be happy we're not married," they observed. During the daytime, families were allowed to be together, but after 7 p.m., the women and children were confined to their dormitory while the men and older boys were free to walk the lower deck. One must, after all, guard the virtues of womanhood from the dark desires of Southern European men.

In the 35 years before the First World War, transatlantic steamship companies, responding to the swelling emigration to the Americas, established lucrative ocean-crossing services. The passenger ships were models of society, stratified into the small numbers of first- and second-class passengers on the upper decks and the large numbers of steerage passengers crowded into the lower decks. Upper-class passengers paid more than double the steerage rates. For that, they had clean, ventilated, and comfortable cabins, ample deck space, and good food and drink. The amenities included entertainment, fine dining, medical attention, and, of course, fast and deferential service by the stewards.

It was not so for steerage, wherein lay the true business of the passenger ship. There the steamship companies made their profits, by crowding in as many people as possible at the lowest possible cost. Each steerage ticket brought in half as much money as did an upper-class ticket, but 12 steerage passengers could be jammed into the same space as one upper-deck voyager. Steerage passengers did not need expensive services—no laundry, sumptuous food, games, music, or doctor. Once sent down into steerage, these passengers were exploited, treated with contempt, or ignored.

The economics were clear: steerage brought in much money and cost the company very little. Steerage paid the ship's expenses and returned the profits to the owners. Steamship companies competed for steerage passengers, recruiting them with artful posters and brochures of magnificent ocean liners. Agents traveled the southern provinces, drumming up business and encouraging the exodus from Italy.

In time the Italian government, pressed by humanitarian organizations,

4. Who are we? / And for what do we search? / Truly, are we / The sons of the sea!

required improved steerage conditions. It would no longer be sufficient, for example, to have only a dozen toilets for 1,000 or more steerage passengers. Food had to be adequate and the preparation and serving conditions hygienic. A physician had to be available, the mattresses and quarters clean. Some reformers advocated Americanization classes during the voyages. When this was tried, the steerage passengers, eager for variation, responded with enthusiasm.[5]

2. Paper Flowers

Arriving in New York in 1896, the friends were awed by that grand lady, the just-completed Statue of Liberty. They were processed through the old facilities at Ellis Island, unaware that it would be all destroyed by fire within six months.[6] Federal inspectors checked their names, ages, marital status, work histories, and destination. Doctors examined them, particularly for signs of trachoma, a highly contagious eye disease. Any hint would send the hapless migrant back on the next boat home. The friends were surprised at how quickly and easily they were processed.

At first they were intimidated and bewildered by the onslaught of *l'America*: by its power and noise, and relentless activity; its overwhelming size and the impossible numbers of people who swarmed every which way on every confusing street. This was bigger than *Napoli*! "Battery thieves" were there, too—porters, cabbies, fake officials, and crooked police, ready to take advantage of new arrivals. Most dangerous were labor bosses, who abducted naïve men and packed them off in wagons to distant rural labor camps. There the men—the "new slaves," some called them—worked as unskilled laborers at low wages in mines, construction, and railroads. They were cheated by bosses, landlords, and the company stores that charged five times the going prices, and were even made to pay for the tools they used. The unfortunate men caught in that trap soon found that they were in so much debt, their wages could never buy their freedom. Eventually the immigrants learned not to step into *la bocca del leone* (the lion's mouth)—the employment agencies that trapped immigrants and sold them to labor bosses.[7]

"It's worse than Naples," the five friends told each other, looking around the Battery area. Fortunately, the lessons learned in Naples and their association with a particularly honest padrone helped them to avoid the many traps in *Nuova Yorka*.

Gino Talavere,[8] whose name had been given to them in Maida, was waiting for them. He wore stylish American clothes. Mario looked at his own

5. "Steerage" (1911).
6. New facilities would be designed, constructed, and, in 1900, opened. They remained in operation until 1954.
7. See also Chapter Six.
8. I was unable to determine this padrone's true name, so I have named him Gino Talavere.

rough clothing, soiled from the trip, and felt that everyone must be staring at him. He was, he realized, no longer an adventurer, a sailor on the seas, but a poor, ignorant immigrant wearing wrinkled old clothes, with all he owned wrapped in a small cloth bundle.

A man of two cultures, fluent in Italian and English, *Signor* Talavere, truly a gentleman, greeted them in their familiar Calabrese dialect. At ease after 16 years in America, *Signor* Talavere showered them with enthusiastic descriptions of the city, led them through crowded streets, pointed out sights, commented on the bustle around them, and switched easily to flowing English to speak with American acquaintances. With flair and self-assurance, this impressive man—a Calabrian immigrant just like them—guided them on a brief tour of the waterfront and took them to a corner restaurant where everyone seemed to know him. He bought their supper, *bucatini all' amatriciana,* a wonderfully flavorful dish of *pasta fresca.* It had lightly sauteed fresh tomatoes, onions, a touch of hot chili peppers, delicious chunks of *pancetta*, and a sprinkling of *pecorino romano.*[9] Never before had they tasted anything like this, for who in Maida could afford to put so much expensive *pancetta* in a single dish? If such opulence were not enough, there were bowls of minestrone, a loaf of fresh bread, and two bottles of rich *chianti.*

"It comes from near Rome, Amatrice," the chef explained. "The *pancetta* is from Parma, the best in the world!"

"We dine on fine Italian food from Roma," Paolo marveled, holding up his wine glass. "*A salute*, America! And we had to come 3,000 miles across the ocean to taste it."

This introduction to their new home, New York's Lower East Side, was a stunning contrast to steerage and their lives in Maida. The experience moved them from their intention of staying only three years to an enthusiastic acceptance of America as their permanent home.

"This is America?"

"Dinner in restaurants and wonderful Italian food and gracious *gentiluomini* who treat you with such kindness and respect? Ah! *L'America, l'America, veramente la bell'America!*"[10]

As they were about to find out, America was not often like that.

At first they worked on the docks with hundreds of men from all over the world—Irish and Polish, a few Swedish, and some with black skin such as they had never seen in Maida. They knew of Verdi's great opera *Aida*, that was all about black people, Africans fighting for their freedom, just as the Italians had done.

There were many Italians on the docks; their neighbors were nearly all

9. Pancetta is an Italian ham cured in salt and spices rather than smoked. Pecorino Romano is a tangy, hard cheese made of ewe's milk. It is considered to be the essential cheese to use in making basic pesto.
10. "America! America! Truly, beautiful America!"

Italian. Most of the people who lived in New York City were Italians, or so it seemed.[11] "Soon," they thought, "Italy will be emptied out, and all the *paisani* will be settled here, in *Nova Yorka.*"

In the Lower East Side neighborhood, where *Signore* Talavere had found their apartment, most families were from Calabria. Nearby were communities from *Sicilia, Basilicata, Puglia, Abruzzi,* and *Campania.* On Sundays, the five friends walked through the Italian settlements, marveling that in America one found Southern Italy in miniature. Despite the dominating presence of America, its massive concrete urban hardness and noise, the people managed to brew at least a light flavor of their homeland. In each regional enclave one found familiar foods, a traditional healer, an occasional Italian doctor, and an increasing number of priests from home. The priests celebrated each region's holidays, keeping a scheduled reverence for their particular saint. One could march in a different religious procession each week, it seemed, just by walking a few blocks from one neighborhood to another.

Each neighborhood had its own Italian dialect. The friends could communicate with people in each neighborhood if they spoke slowly and with much gesturing. But some, especially Sicilians, were almost impossible to understand. The five young men lived with two other men in a single room on the top floor of a five-story walk-up tenement. The Italian population had increased during the previous 15 years and the crowded, poor neighborhood was an abysmal slum. There were six rooms on each floor, originally two apartments. Each room was about 8 feet by 10 feet. On some floors, 40 or 50 men, women, and children were crowded together.

"This is worse," Mario thought, "than steerage!"

Here, however, the floor did not roll around, tossing one's stomach. When the crowding, heat, noise, and stench became too bad, the friends stepped carefully down the five flights of wooden stairs to join the world in the crowded, buzzing streets.

Negotiating those stairs was dangerous. Not only were they steep, but the stairway was as dark as a cave. Rubbish and people were often scattered there, invisible in the darkness, ready to trip you and send you careening the rest of the way down. There were no windows in the hallways to admit light and air; electricity had not yet arrived, and the gas jets were never lit, because no gas was piped into the building. Perhaps that was best. Imagine if a gas-fed fire had broken out and 40 or more panicked people raced from each floor, crammed into the narrow, dark stairway, pushing and screaming to get out?

These American tenements had no indoor plumbing, but the people were accustomed to that. The occupants shared a small, dirty, malodorous,

11. In just a few more years, before World War I, there would be more Italians living in New York City than in Rome; more in Philadelphia than in Florence. Over many years prior to the war, some 300,000 Southern Italians emigrated to the United States. Sartorio (1918; 1974).

fly-filled wooden outhouse located in the muddy yard behind the tenement. It was even worse for the families who lived in the cramped wooden addition that had been tacked onto the back of the building above the toilets. The building was cold in the winter, sweltering in the summer, always noisy, dirty, foul smelling, and writhing with flies, roaches, and rats.

Children died of infectious disease. Tiny bodies dressed in white, with pitiful garlands of bright little paper flowers, were laid out in wooden boxes and carried down the dark stairs to the street by somber men and sobbing women.

"Paper flowers," Paolo thought. "My God, paper flowers. In this country, is nothing real?"

Paper flowers, perhaps the same flowers that helped to kill the children, were used now for a sad spot of ironic color in their little coffins.

Coming in late at night and trudging up the five flights to their tenement, the men could see into the crowded rooms of their neighbors, the doors left open in the hope that some air would drift through. They saw women and young girls working long into the night, making paper flowers or sewing garments. If they worked hard every night, they might make an extra two dollars a week.

Those pale, sickly children born in these tenements made Paolo think. "Maybe they have never even seen a real flower. They don't even know what it is they try to imitate with their colored paper and glue. *Fiori di carta! Dio mio! Quello che è vero qui è una vergogna in Italia.* (Paper flowers! My God! What is real here is a disgrace in Italy.)" The men in those families, of course, did not help; making paper flowers was no work for a man.

The American tenements were so dismal, distressing, artificial, and unlike their homes in Maida that the men stayed away as much as possible, returning at night only to sleep. In good weather, they preferred sleeping on the docks, perhaps in an empty packing crate.

While their good pay envelopes made them feel rich by Maida's standards, the squalor reinforced their plans to leave. "Three years," they told each other. "Three years here, we save our money, and then go home to beautiful Maida."

The longer they stayed here, the better Maida seemed. They found themselves romanticizing their old town and its people, recalling blue skies, clean air, quiet countryside, family and lifelong friends—all the things, in fact, that were missing from New York City. The dismal images of Maida were fading.

Others had experienced the same transformation, constructing new, sanitized views of Italy, and longed to return. When they did return, they found their old town's poverty filled reality. Many then traveled back to the United States, willing to tolerate its ugliness and problems for the chance to work and to improve their future.

Mario, Paolo, and the others were still in the early process of creating romanticized images of Italy and firming up their intentions to return there. But while the squalor of the tenements helped to paint America in shades of black and gray, they were beginning to see some good things.

The streets surged with noise and activity. People were talking, shouting, singing, buying, selling—even fighting. Horses clattered along pulling wagons and leaving mounded trails of steaming, pungent droppings. Two-wheeled pushcarts threaded through the crowds, each with a row of jangling bells hanging from a wire stretched across the top. Men and women at tiny outdoor stalls sold everything. Religious processions wove by with skirted priests and altar boys waving incense. People carried painted plaster statues of the Virgin Mary and local saints draped in colorful garlands of paper flowers. Weaving through the tumult were children in their own parallel worlds, some playing, some working, some stealing.

There were, as yet, few Italian women for these single men, but they would come eventually. In the meantime, American women were available, for a price—women in bars and in some of the houses, or walking the evening streets. Each year, however, more families arrived from Italy.

The streets were dark, even in the daytime. Tall buildings cast long shadows like mountain peaks, leaving too little open space to admit the sun. In any event, the sun in America was a pale copy of the bright light that crossed Maida's heavens. "*Non c'è sole in America* (There is no sun in America)," they told each other. "We came here, but the sun stayed home." The blasting sunshine and heat they once cursed in *il mezzogiorno* were now longingly recalled.

Their thoughts about Americans came from their daily experiences. Americans were defined by the tough labor bosses, the saloon keepers, the corrupt policemen, judges, and politicians, the cheating and lying businessmen, the whores, and the outright crooks and thugs who preyed on naïve foreigners. The Catholic Church had little to offer. Priests spoke only English, and the pews were filled with the Irish who had immigrated earlier and did not welcome Italians into their churches. Stories circulated of Italian mothers wanting their babies baptized and being turned away by Irish priests who told them to "go to an Italian church."

To these Italian migrants, America was big, vibrant, and powerful, a social juggernaut that would one day dominate the world. It was noisy, dirty, crowded, and dangerous. There was money to be earned by those willing to work, but little refinement, culture, or morality. The migrants saw Americans as loud-mouthed, harsh, boorish, aggressive, vain, selfish, unforgiving, corrupt, and immoral people who would cheat you at every opportunity in order to gain another dollar. Unlike Italians, Americans had no social grace, no refinement, and no culture. As for the American women, their unbelievable immorality would never be tolerated in Italian villages.

Clearly, Americans were thought of as inferior to Italians in most of the ways that counted in life. But the Italians secretly admired the Americans' assertiveness and successes.

The advantage offered by America—and it was a major one—was the opportunity to work and do as well as one dared. And that may have been but an accident of history. After all, Italians had once owned the world and its wealth and power. Now it was the Americans' turn, but this, too, would pass.

Italian migrants in 1900 viewed America as a thriving place in which to earn enough money to return to Italy and live decent and refined lives. They also developed prejudices against Americans—which never outweighed their admiration—reinforcing their tendency to stay together in their ethnic enclaves, where they could at least imitate a small bit of their former lives. By banding together, they had some protection from the very American culture that they had chosen to join. Americans developed their own prejudices against Italians, and each group believed in its own superiority.

By the late 1920s, more than four million Italians had immigrated, most settled into the tightly packed slums of eastern seacoast cities. With their foreign customs, language, and behavior, they did not fit neatly into the American order. Americans' resentment and outright hostility grew, and the already deep prejudice against Italians intensified. As the Italian slums grew, so too did criticism of Italians' apparent willingness to live in squalor and crime, and they were blamed for the conditions that were forced upon them.

Such criticism was given high prominence throughout the country by the burgeoning press.[12] The picture of Italians incessantly offered by the press was that of slovenly, ignorant, physically and mentally inferior, lazy people who were natural criminals fit only for the simplest and dirtiest work.

It was the Italians who altered these views first, while the Americans maintained their anti-Italian prejudice for several more generations. By 1900, the Italian migrants—who had arrived with plans to earn money and return home—were already becoming true immigrants, planning to remain and commit themselves to America.

As they succeeded in their new culture, the immigrants gradually dulled the sharpest spikes of distrust of Americans. They began to move out from their insular enclaves and meet Americans on cordial, if not yet equal, terms. In the 1930s, Italians such as my parents and their countrymen could not yet be close friends with Americans, but they were discovering that Americans could be good neighbors, amiable acquaintances and co-workers, honest shopkeepers, and fair employers.

Some have characterized the Italian urban neighborhoods as recreated Italian cities and towns. But those neighborhoods were not reasonable

12. See Chapter Six. Also See Mondello (1980).

representations of Italian culture, and the name "Little Italy" is wrong. For those Southern Italians, American life in the crowded tenements of a concrete and asphalt world was not Italy. It was a caricature of Italy, like the paper flowers were caricatures of real flowers. At best, it was a transition, a makeover period from Italian to American culture. Unfortunately, the caricature is what many Americans saw and believed.

The urban neighborhoods grew and functioned much like medieval walled cities, to protect the people clustered within, fortified against the hostile and potentially marauding outside world. They had markets, rules, religion, recreation, rhythms, and styles of life. Strangers who breached the boundaries—police, social workers, reformers, and others—were easily identified, and the inhabitants' defenses raised. The Italians had constructed places of relative safety in which to live temporarily—at first only until enough money had been saved to return home to Italy, and later until enough social and economic success had been achieved to move into better American communities. Of course they wanted their language, family structure, food, and religion to reflect a little of what they had known back home. Those bits of old culture were lifelines in hostile seas. But however much the people created Italian imitations, they were submerged in and overpowered by the massive culture of *l'America*.

Those neighborhoods should more accurately have been named "Little Americas," areas of relative safety where people practiced being American as they understood it. They had to recreate and hang on to some of the safety of their past as they tried out their skills in their new country, much as a toddler holds on to his mother's leg with one hand while reaching out to a distant interesting toy.

It was in that transitional culture that Mario and his friends lived, worked, and practiced their growing skills in widening excursions into American life. They lived in a slum tenement, but that was only temporary. They had their plans.

In a short time, Italians had managed a good deal of success in America. Many were still pick-and-shovel laborers, but thousands had already climbed from the bottom of the working class and into skilled trades as carpenters and painters. Many had their own businesses—small contractors, barbers, tailors, bakers, and butchers. Some had developed large firms such as food-importing companies. There were stories of success in America such as that of Stefano Pasquale Molinare, who, much to the disdain of his relatives back in Italy, now called himself "Steven Moore." He had begun trimming his neighbors' hair in the evenings, after his work on the docks, sitting them on an old wooden chair in front of his tenement. Now he owned five barbershops, with fancy chairs and two or three barbers in each shop. It was said that he had brought to America a dozen uncles and cousins and their families, trained the men in barbering, and placed them all in his shops. Of course he had long since moved his family out of the tenement neighborhood, and now owned a fancy house somewhere else in the city. In fact, they said, he owned many houses and business properties, some of which were the homes of his relatives. Stefano Pasquale Molinare had not trimmed anyone's hair in years but had become a rich landlord instead.

Paolo was impressed by this tale, and he recited a rhyme:

> Old man Stefano,
>   The Barber from Milano
> He trims your hair
>   In a kitchen chair
> And makes you pay a dime.

"What the devil is that?" his friends asked. "'And makes you pay a dime'? It don't go. It don't rhyme!"

"Eh," replied Paolo with an unconcerned shrug. "So it needs a little work."

3. Her Majesty, Mary Powell

By 1900, the five friends were debt free. They had mailed dollars home to their parents, and each had established a postal savings account. While thousands of Italian men worked on road and railroad gangs, on farms in New Jersey, and in the coal mines of Pennsylvania and Ohio, the friends had worked on New York's docks, where they became tuned to the commerce and rhythm of the ports and the river.

Two of the friends had worked for a year on cargo launches plying the Hudson River—and that's where the idea for their business originated. They saw a need for small steam launches to deliver items quickly from the big city markets to buyers in towns like Nyack and Tarrytown, and as far north as Poughkeepsie, 70 miles away. Wholesalers would welcome rapid deliveries, particularly of perishable items such as seafood.

There were always old fishing boats for sale. They would buy one, repair, clean, and paint it—a bright red, white, and green (the Italian tricolor)—and set out in business. As business grew, a second boat would be added, and who knew how large their fleet could become? If Stefano the Barber could own five shops, they could own five boats, maybe more!

They had heard of good jobs in faraway Buffalo, in the construction of electric power plants, paying two or three dollars a week more than did jobs in New York City. That was 10 or 15 dollars a week extra for the five men, or nearly $800 in a year, more than enough to buy and refurbish a boat. In Buffalo, they would work at hard pick-and-shovel labor, digging ditches, laying pipes, mixing cement, clearing rocks, and grading hillsides. They would save their money, buy a boat, and take it through the Erie Canal down the Hudson to New York, to launch their new business.

They would begin their adventure by working their way up the Hudson River to Albany on cargo launches, stopping at towns on both sides of the river. With the stops and cargo handling, the trip would take a week or two. They would be paid two meals a day, and at Albany would transfer to one of the 240-ton barges that carried cargo on the Erie Canal to Buffalo. There, at the Black Rock harbor on the city's western outskirts, cargo was transferred to huge Lake Erie steamers and taken to western ports like Chicago, and even up to Canada. On arrival in Buffalo, the men were to contact another padrone, who would take them to their new employer to begin work at a construction site. The friends liked the plan. They would learn to navigate the Hudson and earn good money in Buffalo for their new shipping venture.

The Hudson River had long been part of the major waterway from New York City to Albany, and westward on the Erie Canal to Buffalo. The glory days of the elegant passenger steamships, huge paddle-wheelers journeying between New York City and Albany, were ending by the time the five friends began working on a cargo launch. One reason for the decline was the winter freeze-over, which lasted for as long as four months. Steam-powered trains running all year were taking over from the river traffic. The Hudson River Railroad ran from Chamber Street in New York to Albany, 145 miles of track. It ran mostly along the east bank of the river and passed through eight tunnels that had been blasted out of solid rock. Soon, new roads would be built, bringing new competition. By the 1920s, people would abandon the great river ships and take to the new automobiles, trucks, and trains.

The five friends could have taken the train to Albany, but by working their way on a cargo launch they would gain experience and save the train fare. Working on the river was more interesting, and suited the young men's sense of continuing *avventura*. Paolo in particular liked the idea of working their way up the river on a boat. Of the five, Paolo had most enjoyed their Atlantic voyage, fancying himself a sailor and poet, not just a laborer, and wishing he could sail away on a great ship. Paolo's shiny money clip with an engraved steamship was his prized token of that interest. His family and friends, each contributing a small amount, had presented it to him on the day he had left for Naples, to secure the many dollars he was surely going to earn in America. On it a local artisan had engraved a small scroll that read "*Italia—Paolo—America.*" He was eager to begin working on the cargo launch and to become a real sailor, if only for a short while, up the Hudson River and west on the Erie Canal.

In 1900, there were still about a hundred large steamships moving along the Hudson, plus smaller passenger and cargo boats, and the ferries moved east and west across the river, bouncing across the wakes of the big ships. The traffic was heavy, and the master of their small steam launch had to be alert not only for rocks in the shallows, but for ferries crossing his path and the heavy wakes of the big paddle-wheelers that raced by.

The paddle-wheelers' century of glory was almost over, but the friends did not know that. They were enthralled by the great river's bustling variety of steam and sailing ships and even small rowboats cutting through the water in every direction, seemingly intent on collision on all sides. Oars creaked in their locks, dipping in and out of the water; smoke poured from funnels; side-wheelers and stern-wheelers churned the river, their whistles blasting. Seagulls spiraled above, and elegant voyagers strolled the decks of the majestic passenger steamers.

Truly this was a vigorous country, seen right there on the river. As their cargo launch moved from one port to the next, the friends watched the passing traffic, marveling that so much could be happening all at once.

The most impressive sight was the famous side-wheeler, the elegant *Mary Powell*. They were fortunate to see that great ship several times on their journey. Paolo, the self-styled sailor, was so impressed each time that he stopped work to stare. "Hey!" the launch's captain would yell. "You! Goddammit, wake up! Get that forward line ready, we're gonna tie up in a minute."

Paolo kept calling the *Mary Powell* the *Maria Paolo* despite repeated corrections by his friends. "I don't care what you say," he told them. "That beautiful ship has my name. I know it, and she knows it! *Lei è veramente magnifica* (She is truly magnificent)!"

The *Mary Powell* steamed on the Hudson River from its launching in 1861 to its demolition 63 years later. When Paolo saw her in 1900, she was still glorious after 40 years of serving her passengers with the extravagance of a floating palace. The passengers were comfortably transported in ornate cabins, dining rooms, ballrooms, and promenade decks, the very best of Hudson River opulence. Her voyages from New York City to Albany were made in a single day, six to eight hours, covering the 145 miles at just over 20 miles an hour.[13]

Each trip on the *Mary Powell* was a pleasure cruise in the high style demanded by well-off people. The first time they saw the famous ship, the friends respectfully doffed their hats, recognizing that she was, after all, the Queen of the Hudson. It seemed the fitting thing to do.

Their trip up the Hudson was exciting. Paolo would not stop talking about the magnificent *Maria Paolo*, and his friends finally threatened to toss him overboard if he did not end his infatuation with *quella stupida barca a remi* (that stupid rowboat)! "Pah!" Paolo the poet responded with a superior expression, cupping his ear as if to listen to the wind. "*Penso di sentire la canzone della gelosia* (I think I hear the song of jealousy)."

---

13. The fastest speed was achieved by the paddle wheeler *Chauncey Vibbard* on April 8, 1876, when it covered the 145 miles from New York City to Albany in six hours and 20 minutes, for an average speed of 22.75 miles per hour. The travel time varied, depending upon river and weather conditions, the number of stops along the way, and the time spent at each port.

4. The Erie Canal

Their problems began soon after they landed in Albany for a one-night stopover. They were excited about the next phase of their voyage to Buffalo, traveling the Erie Canal, having heard about that great inland waterway, the major commercial link between the East Coast and western states. They had heard that Buffalo, the western terminus of the canal, was a rich, busy, and growing city. Now Buffalo was building electric power plants to provide long-distance transmission of alternating current through miles of electrical lines, and it was becoming an even greater city with its industry, commerce, and employment.

What they did not know was that the Erie Canal was no longer the great commercial waterway. Opened in 1825, the canal had thrived for half a century, but after about 1875 had dwindled in tonnage and importance. The number and size of the canal boats had grown from modest 60-footers of 30 tons in 1830 to 240-ton, 98-foot-long barges in the 1860s. By about 1875, however, the same factors that had reduced Hudson River commerce also reduced the canal's. The winter curtailment of shipping due to ice and snow was an even greater problem between Albany and Buffalo, where the winters were more severe than on the Hudson. Railroads captured increasing shares of cargo shipments, and traffic on the once-great canal declined. Optimistic plans for building 1,000-ton, 150-foot canal boats were scrapped. In 1900, when Mario and his friends arrived in Albany, canal commerce was down to a dwindling trickle.

The economic impact of the decline in canal commerce had been severe. Businesses in the string of small towns along the canal were decimated. Firms that had "shipped the Erie" for more than half a century were closing. Bargemen, dockworkers, and canal maintenance crews lost their jobs. Most people did not understand the economic forces that had brought an end to the canal's prominence, but true to the general views of the 1890s, the unemployed canal men knew exactly what the cause was. The country was awash with immigrants and foreigners, they told each other—"Wops, Dagos, Polacks, Hunkies, a few Spics, and even Niggers from the south." They came into New York City, they said, moved up the Hudson, and took jobs away from white men. The "ignorant immigrants" were willing to work for "practically nothing," and if there was any justice in the world, all of them would be "run out of the country and sent back to wherever the hell they came from."

Ironically, many of those angry men were themselves immigrants or sons of immigrants. They were the survivors and descendants of the thousands of illiterate Irish laborers who had been imported to dig the canal, virtually by hand, from 1812 to its opening 13 years later. Those Irish laborers had paid heavily in death, injury, and routine abuse, but they had persevered and built the canal and now had a proprietary sense that it was rightfully theirs. Now these jabbering newcomers, who had paid no price, who had no legitimate claim, were taking away their jobs, pushing their families into poverty. Their hatred of the new immigrants was intense.

That is what Mario, Paolo, and their friends stepped into when they landed at Albany in the summer of 1900.

After unloading the launch and loading it with new cargo for its return trip, they said goodbye to the captain, wandered around the dock area for a while, and had supper at a tavern frequented by canal and river workers. Looking around the tavern as they ate, Mario saw a dozen men drinking beer at tables near the back, glaring at the Italians. In a low voice, Mario advised his friends to finish their meals quickly and leave quietly before any trouble began.

Later, they camped on the bank of the canal for the night. Warmed by a campfire, they talked quietly of their plans and counted their remaining $90, more than enough to get them started in Buffalo. They talked of working another year, saving money, and returning to New York to start their business.

"I wonder what our boat will look like?"

"We'll paint it red, white, and green, for Italia."

"Or maybe blue and white for the skies of Maida."

"Hey, maybe we gonna get rich. Like the barber, Ol' Man Stefano!"

By 11 o'clock, it was dark and quiet; there was no canal traffic at that hour. The men slept, wrapped in their coats. An owl hooted nearby, and a dog barked in the distance—normal nighttime sounds. The campfire burned down to a glowing orange; its embers made crackling noises as they cooled. Mario, half asleep, heard a different sound and sat up. Looking around, he saw only shadows and silhouettes of trees, a few buildings, and boats tied to the canal banks. It was strange, he thought, seeing the boats so still. The wind was quiet and there were no waves or a strong tide to make the boats bob up and down as tethered boats usually do. Paolo sat up, having also heard something. They looked at the darkness and listened, but all was quiet.

"Nothing there," Paolo said, pulling his coat around his shoulders, preparing to go back to sleep. They settled. The night was still.

Then, with the suddenness of an artillery shell, the campfire exploded, spraying burning embers over the men, who scrambled to their feet and batted at their clothes, brushing away the searing coals. A heavy rock had been hurled into the fire, its force sending burning wood cascading over them. Paolo jumped up. "What's going on?" he started to say, but was stopped by a large stone hurled from the darkness, smashing into his face. Then all was noise and confusion; more rocks hit them. A dozen screaming, cursing men erupted from the darkness, swinging clubs and steel bars. The friends, half-asleep, tangled in their coats, tried to get up from the ground. They fought back, landing some good punches, but they had been unprepared for the attack, were outnumbered and overwhelmed by its suddenness. Knocked down and groggy from blows to his head, Mario could feel hands tearing through his pockets, taking his money, and he heard something thrown into the water. It was over quickly, and the attackers, laughing and shouting and waving their stolen money, ran off into the shadows.

Mario knelt on the ground, moaning in pain. He felt hot wetness on his skin and tasted the metallic tang of his own blood as it ran down his face. His upper lip had been cut nearly in half, one tooth had been broken out, and his left eye was swollen shut. The other men were also bloodied, and they shook their heads in pain and shock. Wiping blood from their eyes, they saw that Paolo was missing. "Paolo!" they shouted. "Where is Paolo?" Then Mario remembered the sound of something thrown into the water. "The canal. Hurry!" The water was dark, but they made out a floating shape at the edge of the canal. When they pulled him out, they could see the terrible wound in his head where the rock had struck. "He's still breathing. He's still alive! We have to get help."

Two of the men ran toward the nearest building, while Mario and another stayed with Paolo. It was nearly an hour before the police arrived, and another hour before the horse-drawn ambulance came and took Paolo to the hospital. Mario, still dazed and agitated, tried to tell the police about the attackers. His pronunciation of English, already heavily accented, was even more difficult to understand because of his smashed mouth. In response, the police arrested Mario and his friend.

"But why?" Mario protested, shocked that they, and not the attackers, were being arrested. "Those men. Whoever they were. They attacked us! We did nothing!"

"Sure," one of the policemen said. "Sure. You Dagos never do nothin'! You're under arrest for disturbing the peace, inciting a public brawl, assaulting peaceful citizens, vagrancy, litterin' the canal banks, and public drunkenness. And maybe I'll think of a few more things! Now get your asses in the wagon or we'll give you more to worry about!"

"Drunk? We no drunk! We drink nothing! Nothing! We just have some supper!" Mario said in growing anger, but seeing the looks that passed among the police and their hands tightening on the nightsticks, he stopped talking and quietly submitted. At the police station they were locked into a cell where they found their two friends, jailed when they had gone for help. The men were searched and $40—money the attackers had overlooked in their haste—was taken away for "safekeeping."

The four men needed medical attention, but none was given. Hours later, they were taken to a room where there was a bucket of cold, dirty water and told to wash up, because they would soon be seeing the judge. They had to use their soiled shirts as towels, but the cold water, even though it stung in their open wounds, refreshed them somewhat.

"Where's Paolo? Our friend Paolo. Where is he? What happened to him?" Mario asked, talking with great difficulty through his injuries and his stiffening lips.

"You don't have to worry about him any more," one of the policemen said, laughing. "He's dead. Died on the way to the hospital."

"Yeah," added another. "I guess he didn't like the accommodations in the wagon. Wasn't comfortable enough for him."

Later that morning the four men, dazed, confused, in pain, and despondent over Paolo's death, faced the judge in his courtroom. A man dressed in a black suit was pointing at them, talking to the judge, saying things that Mario and his friends could not easily understand. Two men in workman's clothes were brought in, and they glared at the four defendants. One carried a heavy iron wrecking bar. Mario was glad to see that both of them had swollen faces. They were the accusers, the plaintiffs.

"Judge, we're good citizens. Jus' workin' men. Famb'ly men. We been livin' here all our life. Lately been havin' a hard time for the wife 'n' kids 'cause the canal, it ain't running so good no more. We was jus' peaceful-like, the two o' us. Jus' sittin' there on the canal bank, jus' talkin', an' the five Dagos, they snook up behind our backs in the dark, came out o' nowhere, jumped us from behind our backs, swingin' them eyron bars, en' before we knowed nothin', they knocked us down en' stold our money!"

"How did those men get their injuries?" The judge asked, pointing to Mario and his friends.

"We fought back, Judge, your honor. They was five, six, seven, maybe more o' them, en' on'y two o' us. But two white men against six, seven Dagos is pretty even odds. We give 'em some good licks, we did!"

"And here," he added, holding up the steel bar. "Here's one o' them eyron bars they used. I brung it to show you."

"Move to place the iron bar in evidence," said the man in the black suit.

"Any objections from the defense?" the judge asked, looking at Mario, who had no idea what to say.

"No?" the judge continued. Then, looking at the clerk, "Go ahead. Label it for evidence."[14]

"Now," he asked the witnesses, "how much did they steal?"

"I don't know, Judge," the witness said. "I don't know exactly how much we had between us."

"Fifteen dollars, your honor," the arresting officer spoke up. "We found the money on the eye-talians after we arrested them. Fifteen dollars they stole."

"Return the money to the plaintiffs," the judge ordered, pointing his gavel. "At least they'll get something back."

His honor then found Mario and his friends guilty as charged, pronounced a sentence, and banged his gavel in finality.

Although the four Italians could not understand everything that was being said, they knew what was happening to them. The two men were

14. In those days, maintaining the integrity of the chain of evidence was apparently not a commonly exercised priority.

liars! In just a few minutes in court, the friends had been robbed of their remaining money, convicted of attacking, injuring, and robbing two men who had been among the gang of attackers, and convicted of vagrancy because they had no money or visible means of support. Worst of all, poor Paolo's murder was being ignored! To add insult to injury, their remaining few dollars were given to their attackers! Not until much later did Mario realize that while the police had taken $40 from them, they admitted to the judge that they had "found" only $15, which was turned over to the attackers. What had happened, he wondered, to the other $25?

"You broke the law," the judge said, as he pronounced the sentence. "You people are animals. But by the condition of your faces, you were the ones hurt most by your own actions, so you've already been punished. Putting you in jail would only cost the county more good money."

Confused, in shock, they were led from the courtroom and taken outside, onto the street.

"Go on!" the policeman told the perplexed men, prodding them away with his nightstick. "You're free to go."

"But," Mario began to ask, "what about our money? And Paolo. What about our poor friend Paolo?"

"Don't ask so many goddamn questions. You're lucky the judge was in a good mood, or you Dagos would be in jail for the next five years. The judge suspended your sentences, and be glad for that. Just get your asses the hell outta here and don't never come back!"

"Here," one of the policemen said, reaching into his pocket and pulling out some dollar bills. "We can't let you go with no money, or we'd just have to arrest you for vagrancy all over again."

He counted out four dollar bills and handed them to Mario.

"That should get you to Buffalo. Let 'em take care of you up there. Now go on, beat it, get the hell outta here!"

The policeman returned the rest of the money to his pocket. The bills, Mario saw, were secured with a wide, shiny money clip engraved with a little scroll that read "*Italia—Paolo—America.*"

The four men, injured and despondent, found work on a barge. They would be paid one meal each day and were thankful for that. They reached Buffalo and contacted a padrone whose name had been given to them in New York City, and their construction jobs were arranged. They agreed to pay the padrone, the employer, and the crew boss the standard tribute, a portion of their combined wages for the first three months. After that, the money they earned would be theirs.

The work was hard, especially for Mario, whose face and jaw often flamed up in pain. His lip was mending together in a twisted way that marred his once handsome face. One week later, while moving some shipping pallets as ordered by the boss, Mario stepped into a puddle left by a rainstorm. Because he still could not see well with his injured left eye, he inadvertently brushed against an exposed coupling that secured two thick electrical cables and was instantly electrocuted.[15]

Mario was buried in the poorest section of a Niagara County cemetery. A priest, Mario's three friends, and a few other Italian workers stood at the graveside. Two gravediggers waited with shovels. Mario had not reached his 24th birthday.

The decade of the 1890s was a violent one. Italians, among the many victims of American bigotry, were caught up in it. But America's violence was not limited to immigrants. On Friday, September 6, 1901, President William McKinley was shot while visiting the Pan-American Exposition in Buffalo. He lingered painfully for eight days and died in the early morning of September 14, of "gangrene of both walls of [the] stomach and pancreas following [a] gunshot wound."[16] That afternoon in the Delaware Avenue mansion of his friend Ansley Wilcox, Vice President Theodore Roosevelt, the man who had not long before declared that the lynching of 11 Italians in New Orleans "was a rather good thing," was sworn in as the new president.

America was in mourning; people were enraged that violence had turned against their president. Mario and Paolo's three friends, still distraught over what had happened to them, were also shocked by the president's assassination, in the very city where they lived. "What kind of country is this?" they asked each other. "Wherever we go, we are stalked by violence."

Early in 1902, only a few months after McKinley's murder, the three young men, grieving, defeated, disillusioned, their cargo business forgotten, returned to Italy, determined never to come back to *la bell'America*.

Paolo, despite the Albany policeman's report of his death, had survived the attack—if "survived" is the right word. Brain damage from the head injury or lack of oxygen while he remained submerged, or both, had left him disabled. His speech was stumbling and slurred, his eyesight faulty, and he had trouble concentrating and remembering things. Paolo no longer read books, recited poetry, made jokes, argued about philosophy, or spoke of beautiful ships and women. His padrone, Signore Talavere, who would later become a powerful politician and representative of the Italian community in New York City, learned of Paolo's injuries. At his own expense, he arranged through a Catholic priest in Albany to have the injured man moved back to New York City by train, and eventually to Ambler, Pennsylvania. There, Paolo lived out his life, unmarried, working sporadically at simple, odd jobs, protected by his younger brother, who had arrived in 1900 to join Ambler's growing Italian community. Paolo's only amusement was carving small boats from scrap wood, which he gave to the

---

15. There was no OSHA (Occupational Safety and Health Administration) in those days. Work sites were extremely dangerous, and deaths and injuries were common.
16. From the Erie County coroner's report, September 14, 1901.

neighborhood children. Always in poor health, Paolo died of pneumonia in 1920, just over 40 years of age. In his small room behind the kitchen of his brother's house, a beautifully carved little model of a paddle wheeler was found.

The story of Mario, Paolo, and their friends circulated back to Maida and became a warning to adventurers that *la bell'America*, for all its opportunities, also held hidden dangers. Romanticism is never far away in Italian stories, and the appeal to mystery could not be denied. "Did you know," it was said, whenever the story was told, "that poor Paolo took his final breath on the very day in 1920 that the *Mary Powell* was towed into the wrecking dock to be cut up into scrap?" One wonders if that was true. But as the Italians say, "*Se non è vero, è, una buona trovata.*"[17]

---

17. "If it isn't true, it is well invented."

Chapter 8
Views of Maida: Teresa (1901–1909)

1. A Muscular Religion

Maida, a village of about 3,500 people, had grown on the mountain range that ripples like a giant's spine along the length of the peninsula. As the 20th century opened, the rhythms of Maida were much the same as they had been 100 years earlier. The houses were close together, many attached in long rows, some perched on steep slopes, a few leaning almost to the point of toppling over. They were small and old, thick-walled stone and stucco, still inhabited after 200 years. The walls were whitewashed, presenting a clean, modern appearance of rectangular planes, light and shadow, gleaming in the sun like clean canvas ready for the artist's brush. Whitewashing helped to keep the interior cool by reflecting the heat of the sun, and destroyed insects and other little creatures lodged in tiny cracks and crevices. Some homes were the vestiges of outbuildings that had once belonged to feudal barons. A thick-walled Norman castle stood at the top of a hill, having protected well its wealthy families of long ago.

Down the hill was a convent and, next to it, the church of *San Francesco*, the patron saint of Maida.[1] A long-abandoned tunnel ran from castle to convent, having served in past times as the families' escape route. Some cynical men smirked that the dukes may have had other purposes for their hidden connection between home and convent. Most people discounted such disrespectful stories.

"Stay away from that tunnel!" children were told. Girls, frightened of ghosts and demons, never ventured there. Boys were just as frightened, but dared each other to explore and, in each generation, told of skeletons chained to walls, poisonous creatures slithering among wet rocks, and frightful, moaning spirits flying at them through the gloom. Everyone had heard the delicious story of two disobedient boys who went into the tunnel despite warnings and were never again seen alive. Children never doubted the story, but no one seemed to know who those boys had been.

The castle was in ruins, but its dungeons still served as the town's jail.

---

1. San Francesco di Paola (celebrated also as the fire handler) was a 15th-century Calabrian-born friar and the *Santo Patrono* of Maida.

Such dungeons lay in old castles throughout Southern Italy, filled during *la rivoluzione* with the Bourbon kings' political prisoners until they were hauled away to the hangman.

Like other small Southern Italian towns in 1900, Maida was a place of churches. Three large, old churches were in use, while the 30 smaller churches and private chapels were seldom used. Daily mass, holy days, processions, and celebrations were so evident that one would think religion dominated life. The Maidese appeared unified in their devotion to God, saints, church, pope, priests, and the entire religious framework of belief and myth, but that was only partly true. The women were devout, but the men harbored a good amount of cynicism toward the Church and its ministers, from pope to priest. Of 100 people attending mass, it was said, one might find two old men, both probably asleep, and 98 women who either prayed to God for personal favors or complained about their sons' wives, their children, and their neighbors.

The 200 days a year of religious observances[2] kept the priests busy. The three major feast days were those of *San Francesco* in July, *Santa Maria* in the final week of August, and *la Madonna di Rosario* in the first week of October.[3] Even ordinarily cynical men participated. "Those men might not think much of God and the Church," my cousins Bebè and Nina once told me, "but you better not criticize their saint."

Preparations for *le feste*, the days of celebration, began days in advance—cleaning homes, sweeping streets, preparing special food. Excitement and devotion burgeoned, and some *feste* continued for several days. Here was religion as a social spectacular, a huge party complete with praying, chanting, marching, crying, cooking, feasting, drinking, and singing. All of it, as one priest suggested, was a "joyous way of praying." Brightly colored fabrics rippled in the wind. Children and dogs, equally excited, threaded through it all. People were united more profoundly than any *rivoluzione* or *guverno a Roma* could bring about. The villagers and vendors shared the streets, the little bands played in friendly competition, and food was everywhere. The people dressed up, sang, laughed, and prayed—and some even scourged themselves in their ecstasy of pain and devotion.

My cousins recalled *la cecciaratta*, the all-day *festa* in April, when men cooked *pasta e ceci* (pasta and chickpeas), a tasty and much enjoyed dish stirred in huge pots over outdoor fires. Although this was not the main celebration for *San Francesco*, everyone was aware of the Good Saint's presence. I asked my cousins, "Why *pasta e ceci*, why not cook something else?"

"Eh," Bebe answered, with a little shrug and a smile, "maybe *San Francesco*, he likes *pasta e ceci*?"

2. Williams (1938; 1969).
3. These feasts are still celebrated today, although perhaps not with the same fervor as in earlier times. In a fascinating book, Orsi (2002) describes similar celebrations transplanted to the United States.

Weaving throughout was *San Francesco*'s beautifully painted statue,[4] carved from dense wood so heavy that it required many men to hoist it on beams and bear the Good Saint high on their shoulders. They performed their muscular task with a powerful sense of manhood, pride, and piety. In sanctified choreography, two sweating men stepped out from under and two others stepped in to take their places without disturbing the saint, as the bearers struggled up and down stony pathways. When a young lad first took his place under the timbers, he knew he had reached manhood.

The floating saint traveled every street and paused at every house, lingering where illness dwelled. People tied strings of paper lire around the statue, and by evening *San Francesco* was garbed in money. The saint was elevated, as saints should be, high above the marchers, who wore the expressions of joyfully grim fervor mastered by the very religious. From a distance, the saint, resplendent in flowing ribbons of money, could be seen floating above the marchers. With hand upraised in blessing, he dipped and bobbed up and down the hills in an all-day journey that ended late at night at the doors of the church with the bang and brilliance of a fireworks display. It was a holy levitation, the Good Saint in spiritual motion, sweeping through the air of Maida.

Flowers, veils, and ribbons were draped on various statues, particularly that of *la Madonna*, and the devout pinned on them what few paper lire they could afford. The story is told that early in the century the bishop, apparently passing through Calabria, decreed that the practice of coating holy statues with money was unseemly and would no longer be allowed. "Give your lire to the Church," he ordered, "but do not desecrate our holy images!"

"Who is he, this bishop who does not even live in Maida, telling us what to do? This is our *madonna*, our *San Francesco*, our town, our money, our people!" Here was *campanilismo* stirred up! Some adolescent boys decided, as much in the service of mischief as in religious indignation, to show their independence. They sneaked into church, abducted a small statue of *San Francesco*, and paraded him around town, inviting people to drape on their ribbons and money. Many did, a clear insult to the bishop. We wonder if that holy man fumed, smiled, or just raised his eyes to heaven when he heard of the escapade.

Unfortunately, church and town officials were "*dita di una mano* (fingers on one hand)," and the young men soon found themselves brooding in the castle's damp dungeon, awaiting their trial. They were charged with blasphemy, theft of church property, running a confidence game, gambling, and illegal assembly. The saint, in the meantime, was restored to his comfortable pedestal in church, a votive candle was lighted in penance, and

---

4. More recently, a local artist, Tomasso Gallo, had the honor of revitalizing the statue. He came to the United States in the 1960s hoping to earn a living with his art. After several years of an indifferent American reception, he returned, sadly, to Maida.

the money that had been collected by the boys dropped into the church coffers. We do not know how *il magistrato* dealt with those young *malefattosi* (malefactors), but apparently theirs was not considered to have been a capital crime. The people were on the lads' side; even the officials saw some humor and youthful exuberance in it, and the youngsters survived their brief stay in the dungeon. Years later two of them, the suspected ringleader Michele Graziano and his young friend Giuseppe Bartolotti, would marry into the Dattilo family and become, respectively, my father and my uncle.

Processions were both solemn and joyous, accepting death and celebrating life. Religious intensity was in the air, but so too was cultural tradition. *La festa* was not only a celebration of faith, but was also a vigorous assertion of *la famiglia, le relazioni,* and *la comunitá.* It was a people's celebration of who they were and what they valued. It passed traditions to the children, who were included not as well-behaved little washed and combed onlookers, but as vigorously active and necessary participants, learning for their generation.

This was a lively, hearty, vigorous, even muscular religion of faith and the senses. It retained, it seemed, some pagan character, an emotional celebration, more natural and invigorating than the constricting, gray-toned Protestantism of America that was waiting to civilize all those boisterous Italian immigrants who insisted on going to *l'America.*

Here was religion for everyone. Women prayed, some sedately, some fervently; and, with no sense of irony, men could pray sincerely to *San Francesco* for protection from popes, bishops, and priests.

2. *I Dollari Americani*

In 1902, Mario and Paolo's friends, defeated by *l'America,* returned to Italy. Michele Dattilo had gone to America and was sending postal money orders to his family. Elisabetta and their daughters, Anna and Teresa, continued to live with Michele's parents in their crowded rented house dominated by *Nonna* Anna. Now, with Michele's money orders, their lives were beginning to improve.

Giuseppe, now "*Nonno* Peppe" in honor of his grandfatherly status, was 72 years old and had crossed into the new century. With so many young men leaving for America, he and other elderly men were occasionally hired for farm labor. In that respect, he thought, life had not much improved. *La terra di miseria*[5] lived on. Each season, the work was more demanding and tiring. Giuseppe's clothes, like him, he thought, grew older and more worn out as Anna, aging with him, could no longer keep up with the mending. The soil of the farm penetrated more deeply into his wrinkled skin, which had become like the valleys and hills between Maida and the sea. The grime

5. The land of misery.

on his hands threatened to become permanent. Too old now to work every day, Giuseppe worked a day or two a week, and then only during the season's busiest times. He seldom complained. After all, "*Così è la vita. Dovete cenare alla tavola che natura e destino hanno messo per voi* (That's life. You must dine at the table that nature and fate set out for you)."

Giuseppe, a small, shy man, spoke softly, and rarely to anyone outside of his family. However, he liked to talk quietly to *San Francesco*, "*u Santo Patrono di Maida.*" Like other Maidese, Giuseppe thought of his saint as a friend; indeed, as a member of his extended family. Saints were welcomed with affection into Southern Italian homes, their pictures tacked onto walls, just as people would later display photographs of other family members. Saints were like family, and a respectful familiarity grew when one was talking with a saint, as one might speak with an older, wiser uncle.

San Francesco seldom answered in words. One had to search for signs that the Good Saint had heard, such as a good harvest or healthy children. Often, the signs were hard to read or there were none at all. But, Giuseppe knew, such are the ways of saints.

Giuseppe seldom asked for favors, but just visited with the Good Saint, sharing his thoughts. When he did occasionally make a request, always modest and usually to benefit someone else, it was with hesitation and respect, more an observation or suggestion. Of course, *San Francesco* was capable of seeing everything in Maida, but Giuseppe knew that sometimes a saint just might be busy with other things. At such times it might help to try gently to redirect the Good Saint's attention. "Have you noticed," Giuseppe might say to *San Francesco*, "how sad Elisabetta has become now that her husband is away, and Anna is bossing her around more than ever? It would be nice if Elisabetta could be cheered up, don't you think?"

Giuseppe held his longest conversations with *San Francesco* while walking. Warm days with clear skies, when Giuseppe felt most thankful and at peace, were the best times to talk, because *San Francesco*, too, must enjoy such splendid days and be in a good mood. It would be a great insult to approach the Good Saint while feeling angry or greedy. Too many people, Giuseppe knew, asked *San Francesco* to satisfy their selfish desires—"grant me this or grant me that." Saints should not be bothered with such things.

"My Good Saint," Giuseppe addressed him. There was no need to refer to *San Francesco* by name, since the Good Saint certainly knew who was being addressed. "Thank you, my Good Saint," Giuseppe would offer, "for this work that you give me. Even as little as it pays," he would add, but apologetically, so as not to cause the Good Saint to think he was not appreciative.

"And thank you, too, for giving me only two days of work this week. Anna wants you to send more, but if you do, I will soon be knocking on your door. 'Anna,' I tell her, 'this work is hard. Just walking up the mountain to come home at night is hard. I'm not a young man anymore. If *San*

Francesco sends more days to work, I will have not so many days left to be with you, and where will that leave you?'

"And then, my Good Saint, what am I going to do in heaven, worn out and 73 years old? Is there a place in heaven for such as me? Is it true, as I have heard, that in heaven we all become young again? What a nice idea, if it's true. I would like that, I think. That is, if my path really is destined for heaven. And if it is not, *cosa posso fare* (what can I do)?"

"And, Good Saint, as long as we speak of paths, have you noticed how steep the path up the hill has become after a long day's work in the fields? It would be nice if maybe the path could be a little less steep, don't you think?"

San Francesco never did make the hill less steep or a day's work less tiring for Giuseppe. Although he listened to all that one had to say, *San Francesco* thought carefully about the flood of suggestions and requests rising up from Maida to determine which he would act upon. And, Giuseppe knew, one could never fathom the basis on which the Good Saint made his decisions.

Giuseppe knew that *San Francesco* had listened to him and had chosen to help the family by seeing Michele safely to America. Michele was now earning *i dollari americani* to send home, more money than they had ever had before. His family now could enjoy a little more comfort.

Life had improved for Giuseppe and Anna in just the few years since their three sons had gone to America and began sending money home. Anna, of course, took possession of the postal money orders sent to them by Antonio and Giuseppe. She cashed them and used the money to rent a nicer place to live and to buy more and better food. It was a big help, too, that Giuseppe no longer needed to support Elisabetta and her children, given the substantial amount of money that Michele sent to them each month. Now, with Giuseppe's own small earnings from occasional farm labor and the money sent by their sons, the aging couple lived better than ever before.

Years later, after Anna died (in 1918), Giuseppe continued receiving money orders from America, but as he confided to *San Francesco*, "Why do I need so much money? Alone, without Anna, with no children to raise, I spend little, and Elisabetta feeds me, she takes good care of me. So what do I need that costs so much? Wouldn't it be better," he asked the Good Saint, "for me to put these pieces of paper away, to use when someday, maybe, I will need them?"

"Hmm," the Good Saint answered.

"So," the old man decided, "I will put them here, safely inside my mattress, through this little tear in the side. This," Giuseppe whispered to the Good Saint, "will be our secret."

Over the years, Giuseppe would cash some of the money orders to meet his modest needs, but he also carefully saved many of them, inside the secret place that only he and the good *San Francesco* knew about. Giuseppe went to bed at night knowing that those little promises of *dollari Americani* were safely with him, and he felt secure, thankful, and quite independent.

Michele Dattilo continued to work in Ocean City and regularly returned to Maida to visit. By 1910, he had achieved one of his major goals—from the family of *il signore* Votea, "rich people," he purchased a large farm.[6] Now he could grow more food for the table, sell some in the market, and lease garden plots to others. By 1909, three more children, Caterina, Angela, and Giuseppe, who was called "Peppino," had been born to Elisabetta and Michele. In 1916, Francesca, their last child, arrived.

Michele had become a landowner. "Now," he thought, "my family is secure and people show us more respect." They had been elevated from landless *giornalieri* (day laborers) to land-owning *contadini* (farmers). The Dattilos had not become rich, like the old, landed families, but they now enjoyed much more security and comfort.

"Finally, the clouds break, the air clears," he told Elisabetta during a long visit in 1910. "After generations of being poor, now we can breathe, live in some comfort."

"Yes," she smiled. "*Grazie a Dio*. Yes."

Nonno Peppe, by then 80 years old, quietly added, "*Grazie a Dio, sì. Ma, anche, grazie a San Francesco* (Thank God, yes. But, also, thanks to *San Francesco*)."

Through his hard work, Michele had made Elisabetta's life better. The Dattilos' step up to land ownership was considerable, and the family now held some status in the little town. The power of *l'America* had crossed the ocean and entered their lives.

In Italian tradition, the family elders were the respected family heads, much to Elisabetta's discomfort. Now, however, responsibility for the family had shifted to the next generation, to Michele, whose success—as measured by the money he was sending from America—was far greater than what Giuseppe had ever managed. The family acknowledged this with new respect for Michele and growing dependency on him.

That respect reflected onto Elisabetta, who had become a person of importance to the family. Like other wives whose husbands had emigrated, Elisabetta was maturing into a more assertive, self-determined woman. In Michele's absence, Elisabetta, not Anna, was becoming the decision maker. The money orders from Michele were addressed to Elisabetta, who determined how to spend them. It was as if Michele had promoted her to the rank of first lieutenant, and the family, including Anna, was bound to abide by her decisions while he was away.

Nonna Anna, now 70 years old, knew what was happening, could feel it in her heart. She resented the changes and increased her efforts to dominate

---

6. There is considerable variation in my relatives' reports of the farm's size, some recalling about 7 hectare (17.29 acres) and others reporting about 60 to 80 hectare (150 to 200 acres). Either way, it was a sizeable farm by Maidese standards. See Chapter Five.

her daughter-in-law, and for a short while there was even more friction between them. But whoever controlled the purse would prevail, and that person now was Elisabetta.

With fathers gone to America, older male relatives took on active roles with the children. Giuseppe was a kind, patient, good-humored, and nurturing man, and now his quiet paternalism gained a longer life, extending into the next generation. This delighted him, having little children again, and it drew him closer to Elisabetta. The girls, in particular, loved his gentle presence. He told them funny stories of his childhood in the "old days," carved whistles and tiny doll furniture, and took them on walks up to the farm. There the girls helped him with light chores, such as gathering *castagne* and *fichi* (chestnuts, figs) that had fallen to the ground. Mostly, however, they played in the sunshine while their grandfather, *Nonna* Anna, and their mother worked. When they were older, the girls became part of the farm's work force, particularly during harvest times. *Nonno* Peppe found time for the children, to talk with them, listen to them, teach and entertain them. Any family with young children whose father was away in America and whose grandfather was still living recognized their good fortune.

Now Giuseppe had the children to talk with. They were not as grand as *San Francesco*, but they were marvelously endearing and a good deal more fun. "Forgive me, Good Saint," he would remember to say every once in a while with an apologetic shrug, "for not visiting with you so much lately, but as you see, I have been busy."

Nonno Peppe lived to be 97, a sweet influence in the children's lives. Grandmothers, while deeply respected and loved by the children, enjoyed little enhancement from the fathers' absences—young families needed surrogate fathers, not surrogate mothers.

Giuseppe enjoyed his enhanced role. By 1910, at 80 years old, he felt rejuvenated. Was this *San Francesco*'s answer to his question of whether one grows younger in heaven? Was it the Good Saint's gift of an extension and a little grace in this life? He felt younger, happier than he had in years. "*Grazie a San Francesco*," he offered, happily and silently.

Giuseppe was not a tall man, and perhaps that helped to make him so markedly shy. Every day he lived the metaphor of "looking up" to people. Many men were taller than he, making it necessary for him to look upward. That tightened his neck and shoulders and made him feel tense, like a poor supplicant before men of higher status.

"They give me a pain in the neck," he told *San Francesco*. "Really. A pain in the neck.

"Have you noticed," he asked the Good Saint, "that so many people are made stretched out so they might be a few inches closer to heaven, but does that make them holier? What do you think, Good Saint?"

San Francesco would not make Giuseppe taller or others shorter, and

Giuseppe knew that whatever was, was because God made it so. "But," he admitted to the Good Saint, "they still give me a pain in the neck!"

When approaching others on the road, Giuseppe often changed his direction in order to avoid face-to-face meetings. It was customary when meeting *il signore* or *la signora*—people of higher social status—to remove one's hat, bow the head, and respectfully acknowledge their presence. Giuseppe hated to do that and tried to avoid those fine people whenever possible. When he could not, he gazed at the ground, because looking up at the other person emphasized the difference in height, and that intimated a reduced status, which made him feel even smaller and more insignificant.

With children he was quiet, gentle, always pleasant, never admonishing. When his sons left for America, Giuseppe gratefully became the family's surrogate father and again the man of the family. Similar changes were occurring in other families whose fathers had gone away to work and the grandfather and mother gained status, at some cost to the grandmother. *Nonna* Anna was aware of Giuseppe's enhanced status and ordinarily would have been quite happy about it, but she also saw a decrease in her own status, and that made her unhappy. Certainly life was improving, but on balance, Anna was growing discontented. Grandmothers felt the encroachment of their daughters-in-law, the erosion of *la nonna's* authority, and they complained to each other how *l'America* was destroying the traditional respect of the young for their elders, weakening the old family values.

Anna's neighbor Genoveva was particularly distressed by the changes and made her feelings known to other grandmothers as they sat in the shade of her house.

"You hear how my daughter-in-law talks to me, now that she gets money from America? She has all the answers! She wants all the say in the house. She thinks I don't know what's good for the children, and after I raised seven myself—seven, thank God they're all healthy. What can I do? I try to explain, to keep her straight, tell her what is right, what is wrong. *Ma, non è più possibile* (but it is not possible any more). I tell you, America is ruining our young women!"

"But, Genoveva," another answered, her hands together as in prayer, in the gesture that said "be reasonable." "You like the money, no? Your son, he sends home *I dollari americani* for you, too, not just for your daughter-in-law, and now you live better, too. All of us do better when the men go to America to work. Now we have a little money to buy the coffee so we can sit here and rest for a few minutes, and talk a little bit. This is our good fortune. God has decided to help us in this way. It's worth it, no?"

"No!" Genoveva was irritated. "What's the matter with you? We lose the respect of our young. We lose our sons to another country. Our husbands are gone, our beds are cold at night. They leave us here to do the work and take care of everything by ourselves. They tell us we have to stay the same as always—raise their children, go to church, pray, never step from the path laid out for good women, never bring disrespect to the men. You hear? To the men, who are not even here. And we don't even know what they do over there! *A gajina fa l'uavu ma o gaju fa lu doglie* (The hen lays the eggs, but the rooster has the fun)!

"For all we have to put up with, they toss at us a handful of coins. What does a few more lire mean? *Una tazza di caffè? Un altro biscotto?* (A cup of coffee? Another sweetcake?) We were poor before, and we're still poor now. A little better in some ways, maybe, but our houses are empty of our sons and husbands, and we are still poor, so we are worse, not better. At least before, our families were around us, we had respect. Now, we sell our sons to foreign bosses for a few lire. Is this what God wants for us? I don't believe it. No! This is what the devil wants. *Questo è lavoro du diavolu!* (This is the work of the devil!) and I pray to God to help us, to deliver us from the devil and from the devil's own country, America!"

"Ahh, Genoveva, you complain too much," said the other woman. "Be careful, or God will hear you! Did you forget what it was like to be so poor? You, me, our parents, their parents? Did you forget? Italy is changing. Some good, some not so good. We all want the good things that God gives us. So we have to take the bad that He sends, too. It's like two ends of the sausage—you can't have one end without the other. They go together, always. Be thankful, Genoveva. Be thankful for whatever God sends us, good and bad! You keep complaining like that and then, *pas u angelo* (an angel will pass by) and he will say, 'So, you think all is bad, eh? Well, *here* is bad,' and then, *cara Genoveva mia*, you will be sorry!"

"Yes," agreed another. "We thank God for all of it, what we like and don't like. We have to pray and thank Him for all that He sends, What else can we do? We live, we go on, we pray, that's what."

Genoveva looked up to heaven. "Why can't these women see what's going on?" she asked. "They think I'm just a complaining old woman. They don't know what's happening to them, their sons, their sons' wives."

Aloud, she said, "Sausages? These are not strings of sausages spoiling; these are our lives going bad! And if these young wives don't know it, at least they should show some respect to us. I tell my daughter-in-law, 'If you don't respect me now, you think your own children will respect you when you get old? Then you'll see.' I tell her, 'Then you'll know what we know.' *Quello che seminate in primavera, raccogliette in autunno* (What you sow in the spring, you reap in the fall)! I tell her. But she don't listen. These young women today, they don't listen!"

"Maybe you're right," offered Adriana. "The young wives, they don't listen, that's true, not like they used to. Not like we did with our mothers."

"So," Genoveva suggested, "when we pray, we should ask God to put some respect in the heads of those young wives before it's too late; too late for them, too late for us."

"Listen, Genoveva, it's never too late for God to put things right."

"I don't know," Genoveva answered, more quietly now, and sadly. "I think maybe it's already too late. Maybe even God can't fix it no more!"

The other ladies hurriedly made the sign of the cross at such fearful blasphemy. God, they knew, had no such limitations.

The power of America was changing the lives of the people who did not migrate. Young men were leaving to find adventure, danger, and good incomes. Too many of the young wives, left behind, were becoming assertive and troublesome sorts of people. Even the young boys were changing, dreaming of going to America as soon as they could instead of staying home, marrying, and meeting their traditional responsibilities to their families and regions. The young ladies were blinded by the glamour of young men's visits and their American ways and clothes, and pockets filled with money, and were susceptible to all their suggestions. The elders were left behind to hold together the broken pieces of the old ways, even while they knew it was no longer possible to do so. The world was changing. Much was for the better, but too much was not.

The grandmothers begged the young men not to leave but had no power to stop them. Sons and husbands expressed sorrow at leaving their mothers, sisters, and wives, but leave they did. The women might agree or not, accompany them or remain behind, but the decision was up to the men. The grandmothers could try to slow the changes, maintain as much dignity as possible, and carry on a continuing and ultimately failed struggle with the younger women. Religion and prayer were still open to them. They could pray to the saints, to the Virgin Mother, to God, asking for their help in maintaining the old values and slowing the rushing decay. This role of the family's religious sentinel, the protector of morality, the mediator between God and the family, became the grandmothers' province, undisputed by the young.

Le Nonne intensified their already intense religious lives. As their directive roles in the everyday affairs of the family diminished, their roles as acknowledged stewards of religious life expanded. They had prayed before, but they prayed even more fervently now. Their influence fell most heavily on their granddaughters, who, being young and available, were most susceptible to persuasion into intense religious feelings.

3. The Mountain Stream

Men were leaving Italy in droves. Their poverty, frustration, cynicism, and rejection of Italy's government, economics, rigid class system, priests, and religion were at their highest. Italy had failed them for generations. It was time to go elsewhere, and they entered America and other countries as religious cynics. They prayed little; had no time, patience, or enthusiasm for priests or churches. In Italy, however, the grandmothers were preparing the next generation of young girls to be the carriers of their enhanced religiosity. Years later, when those girls joined their men overseas, they made up for the men's lack of religious commitment. They created a strong religious dimension for their families in their new countries, passing on to their children the religion of their grandmothers. This was an accomplishment of women, a powerful assertion of values and beliefs, planted successfully with firmness and care into each family, and it would help to define this ethnic group in America for generations.

Southern Italian society was a well-defined class system, a remnant of 1,000-year-old land-based feudalism.[7] At the bottom was the largest group, *i giornalieri,* the day laborers, poor men who headed poor families. They sought work day by day, mostly as farm laborers, waiting in the piazza at dawn for an offer of a day's work, accepting whatever was available, whenever and wherever it was available. They did not earn much, did not own much, and lived cramped together in small, crowded, rented huts.

Given the rigidity of the class system despite *la rivoluzione,* these families were destined to remain at that level, struggling for generation after generation. Worn down by long-standing poverty, they developed a fatalistic acceptance of the world as it was. This is God's order of things. It could not be changed, and a finer existence must wait until the next life. There was little hope for this world, but much praying, mostly by the women, for their families' salvation in heaven. These people had nearly given up on this earth as a place to dream and plan. For them, work was their lot and their virtue. The virtuous person worked hard, never rebelled against the system, accepted God's order by working within it all of his or her life, and hoped to find heavenly rewards.

I giornalieri were the workforce of the feudal system. As long as they labored, produced the next generation of workers, and accepted the system with proper docility, then the system would remain stable. It is no surprise that wealthy families were solidly opposed to education for the masses, for with education comes questioning. It is unfortunate, though, that laborers and farmers were also opposed, and thus perpetuated the very system that bore down so heavily upon them.

The local priests helped to maintain the people's fatalistic docility, reminding them that God's rewards lay in the next world. Believing their own sermons, the priests knew they carried out the most important work of all, saving souls.

In the feudal system, the holdover of Spanish Bourbon reign, land ownership was the measure of wealth. Rich families owned the land and kept it through inheritance. Thus, there was little land, and therefore little wealth, for anyone else. *I giornalieri* tilled the soil of *i padroni* but could not own it.

7. Teresa, who would become my mother, would never have accepted this description of the social organization of her little town or of the function of the priests. Her view was much more idealistic. The description given here is based on the somewhat more cynical views of my father, Michele, who lived in the same town but experienced and remembered it very differently.

In the late 19th and early 20th centuries' depression and poverty, *i gior-nalieri* could only continue to labor, day by day, knowing there was no so-cial ladder on which to climb higher. Only God could make things better. Of course, God might make things worse, as He seemed to have done with His floods, droughts, and disease. God was in control.

After purchasing the farm, Teresa's family lived at the next economic level, that of the *contadini* (farmers), who owned or leased. Rather than seeking work, *il contadino* hired *i giornalieri*. However small their farms might be, *i contadini*, compared with *i giornalieri*, enjoyed better food and higher social status. Among the *contadini*, those who owned their land were of a higher status than those who leased from large landowners. Together *i giornalieri*, the largest group, and *i contadini* were the laborers and farmers of Southern Italy.

In the United States, farm families were isolated, living on large farms far from neighbors, meeting others at church or on shopping trips. That was not the case in Southern Italy, where farm families lived in town, their homes close to or even attached to one another. They worked distant fields, but returned nightly to their homes and close neighbors. The group of im-migrants in Nyack maintained that closeness, and it helped to define them.

A step above *i contadini* were the town's minor officials, merchants, and artisans. Known collectively as *artigiani*, they were respected but had little money. Merchants, although successful by local standards, were limited by local economics. Their families lived better than most. Their sons or daughters were good catches but stayed in their own class, allowing little opportunity for children of *i contadini or I giornalieri* to move up by mar-riage. Occasionally the son of *un' contadino* might be fortunate enough to be appointed to a minor official position. Although he did not earn much money, he had a steady income. He would adopt the manners of the higher class, walk with dignity in the piazza, and, no matter how insignificant his position, enjoy the respect due to his status. The needs of each small town for merchants, artisans, and minor officials were modest, so it was a small group. At the top of society were the gentry, *i signori* and *le signore* (gentlemen and ladies), and some professionals such as lawyers, military officers, and doctors. They owned land, controlled commerce, and ran the government. Church authorities, from the pope to cardinals and bishops, were virtual nobility. In small towns, the local priest and the schoolteacher *(il professore)* could be included in the upper class, but only at the bottom-most rung—they had respect, but little money or power.

Life was good for the few at the top. They lived comfortably, whatever might be happening in the economy. Their land-based wealth gave these families leisure and luxury. For the *artigiani* and the land-owning *conta-dini*, life could be comfortable, too, but was dependent on shifts in the economic picture. Most worked continuously in order to maintain their status, and work gave them some control over the quality of their lives. For the *giornalieri*, life remained on the economic edge. Within their homes they controlled their lives, but once they stepped outside they fell to the mercy of economics and the class system.

The rigidity of this still-feudal system was a barrier, allowing little upward movement. When economic times were bad, as they were for Teresa's generation, men could do little to improve their family's condition. They might dream of someday owning a small patch of land, but if land was already owned by others, and if there was too little employment and money to purchase any if it became available, then there was no chance to move up economically. It was a closed system.

Teresa, however, born in 1901, had no recognition of living in poverty, as her parents and grandparents had. Even her older sister, Anna, remembered only the family's better times. By the time Teresa was nine years old, her father, working in America, had purchased their farm and rented a house in town. No more would they live in little straw huts. Safe within *la famiglia*, Teresa thought she must be rich, because she could claim three homes as her own, as well as their beautiful farm up the hill. Two of the houses, small, two-storied, with no indoor plumbing, were in town next to each other, around an open *terrazzo* where the children played. In one, Teresa lived with her mother, sisters, and brother.[8] The upper floor held two rooms, one for cooking and one for sleeping. The ground floor was typical: an entrance, a storage room, and nighttime shelter for their donkey. The small house was crowded with energetic children who demanded more space than their size required, but it was warm and happily noisy, and Teresa felt enveloped in safety.

One wall held a two-tiered shelf that, in Teresa's imagination, became a two-storied doll's house, a little model of her own home. It held doll-sized furniture—a bed, a table, and a tiny altar for the Virgin Mother. *Nonno* Peppe had carved some, but the pieces that looked most real were made for her by Piti Scalese, the cabinetmaker's young son. Cloth dolls made by her sister Anna did their cooking over the make-believe coal brazier, entertained doll visitors, and washed doll clothes in a make-believe stream. The dolls shopped in a make-believe market and were dressed up for church on Sundays. Saints' days were special: the dolls wore bits of white lace and colored ribbons and marched in processions, accompanied by the imagined music of a make-believe band.

While boys worked in fields and orchards, girls learned to cook, sew, and care for younger children, early training for maternal responsibilities. Life for Teresa and her sisters was intensely social, filled with family and visitors. Even work was an opportunity for socializing. Sewing and knitting were social activities. Women sat outside, shaded by a white-washed wall, working, laughing, and sharing gossip.

8. In their order of birth, the children were as follows: Anna, Teresa, Caterina, Giuseppe, Angela, and Francesca.

When new clothes were needed, the dressmaker came by—*la donna*, they called her. She was a true artisan, measuring the girls, marking and cutting patterns exactly right. The women and girls then stitched together what *la donna* had designed. Most people had little money for *la donna*, and Teresa would recall only a few special times when the dressmaker visited. They were happy moments in her young life, her memory multiplying the true number of visits and magnifying the excitement.

The girls enjoyed going to the stream with their mother to wash clothes. It was a happy chance to splash in the stream and cool off from the hot sun. The little girls were given small bits of laundry to wash, wring out, and lay smooth on the flat, hot stones to dry, carefully imitating their mother. However, once they were older and the work was real, it was not so enjoyable. "Oh, my back!" Anna complained after carrying the big bundles of laundry to the stream, scrubbing and beating them on the rocks, rinsing and twisting them to free the soap and water from the fabric. "I can feel my arms falling off. There! See? There goes one in the water. It's floating away! Ai, my arm, my arm! What am I going to do with only one arm?" she shouted, hopping around, hiding her left arm behind her back, waving the other in the air.

Teresa laughed. Her sister's antics made the hard work a little less burdensome.

"Anna!" a neighbor scolded, shaking her finger. "*Non fare cosi! Pas u angelu, eh, poi?* . . . (Don't do that! An angel passes by, and then? . . .)"

Reminded of the punishment for mocking God, Anna looked up at the sky and made the sign of the cross in apology, in case an angel did happen to pass by and decide to teach her a lesson and make her mockery come true. "Ooh," she shuddered. "One arm. Ugh."

On this wash day, several women and their young daughters had gathered. It was another social event, a sharing, an easing of the burdens of work. While they worked, the women talked and laughed about their men, watched and scolded each other's children, caught up on news of the church and the town, and giggled over gossip, while the little ones played.

The small stream, only a few feet across and half a foot deep, bounced over the rocks. Here it had been widened into a slightly deeper pool, where the youngsters and some of the women waded, their skirts rolled up to midshin while they washed the clothes. During the summers, however, the meager stream dried up and water became scarce. Washing clothes was then so infrequent that piles of soiled clothing accumulated, and the men wore the same unwashed trousers and shirts to work for weeks. The tough fabric became so stiffly encrusted with grime that they could, it was joked, "stand up and walk by themselves to the fields. Hand them a hoe, they'll even do the work for you. And," it was added, "if they do the work too good, *u padronu* will fire you and hire your *pantaloni* for half the wages."

Older women told stories about this little stream as it had been in their great grandmothers' time, 150 years earlier (in the mid-1700s). "If we could go back now," they said, "we'd find our stream bigger. We'd be wading in a real stream, cool and clear, not muddy like now, and it bubbled all year, even in the summer. We'd find trees, too, all around, and we would work in the cool shade with the little birds hopping and singing in the branches. On the hills we'd see many trees and everything greener and cooler, with good, clean water for everybody."

"How nice," Teresa thought, "to have the trees with their cool shade, and the little birds singing, and lots of water. I wonder where they all went?"

In Teresa's time, summers in Southern Italy were hot and dry, a perpetual drought. Normal weather seemed out of phase with people's needs—the rains came in the wintertime, but not in the summer when the growing crops needed it most. When rain fell, it was sparse compared with that in Northern Italy—another difference between the north and the south.

The great Sahara Desert was just across the Mediterranean, and desert winds blew over Southern Italy, bringing hot, desiccated air. The climate had changed over hundreds of years. The southern peninsula's lush gardens and forests that had served Mediterranean cultures in antiquity—the "Roman granary" and "Roman lumberjack" they had been called—decayed into the dry, stony conditions of the 19th century.

The Romans had started Italy's unfortunate history of exploitation by cutting down the forests to build ships. The resulting erosion caused more drought, slowing new growth of forests and grass. There was no coal for fuel, and *i carbonari* (the charcoal makers) and absentee owners continued to destroy the remaining trees. Generations of overgrazing in the cleared forests continued killing the vegetation. The topsoil, with fewer and weaker roots to hold it, eroded down the hillsides, leaving dry, rocky slopes that could no longer be farmed, and choked the valleys, blocking their natural drainage. Silt and mud built up in the lowlands; swamps developed in the valleys and became mosquito breeding grounds that soon released devastating attacks of malaria. With fewer trees and grass, the hillsides grew dry and hot, and the summer sun beat down without the umbrella of leaves to cast cooling shade.

The people adapted. They began moving out of the valleys and up the hills to escape the swamps with their lurking *mal aria* (bad air). They built their villages high on the rocky hillsides, but the fertile soil for farming had eroded to the bottom. Now, with homes and farms separated, people walked, often three or more miles, down to the fields and back up again at night. Walking hours each day helped make them so fatigued that at night they could only fall into bed, exhausted.

To Teresa, however, her little town was beautiful and her life was full and rich. She knew that men, boys, and often women went early in the morning to work in the fields, and returned late at night after she had gone to sleep. But that was normal, as it was that adults were grimy and exhausted each day.

She had been taught not to waste water but never appreciated that they lived in perpetual drought. No fountains or private wells served the families. Water was scarce, carried home from a stream or town pump in clay pots, one under each arm and one balanced on the head. It was a quaint and lovely picture if one were a man or woman of a noble family who did not need to do the carrying. But it was a hard chore each day over hard, rocky ground for the barefoot women and girls.

For centuries, Southern Italians produced bountiful crops and superb grapes, figs, and olives prized by the world, and did so in spite of the perverse growing conditions that would have defeated a less determined people. Their agricultural successes were testaments to these farmers' extraordinary skills.

In Teresa's time, people did not drink much water, fearing with justification that it was not safe. They used it sparingly in cooking, preferring to bake or grill their foods. For those who could afford it, *l'aqua potabile* (drinking water) was purchased in small amounts from *l'equipaggio di barile*, the barrel men and women. They climbed the hills early in the morning to find clean, cool water, snow, or ice to bring to town. Bathing was a rare event, because it consumed so much water. In some towns, guards were posted at the village pump to prevent waste, and sometimes to collect the municipal water tax.

How nice, Teresa thought, to find the barrel man, who sold fresh, cool water by the glass from his little table in the piazza. For an extra charge, he added a dash of anise for flavoring. A few times, during visits by her father, Teresa had been treated to such wonderful delights, and she remembered them for years. What a fortunate town, she thought, to have such luxuries and little bits of elegance.

The women labored over their washing for most of the day, not concerned that the grime and hard homemade soap polluted the little stream and flowed away to the next town. The work was hard, their muscles ached, and they were soaked from the splashing, but the socializing made it a shared burden, and it became, like life itself, a mix of common duty, exhaustion, and pleasure.

They finished, folded the clothing that had partially dried on the rocks, and rolled down their sleeves. Gathering their children, they carried the heavy laundry up the hill, glad that this job was over for another month or so.

People worked hard in Maida, but poverty was the norm. Nevertheless, royalty continued to enjoy their extravagant lives, while the Dattilos and Grazianos and their neighbors chopped into the dry ground and struggled to live day by day. The world of king and government was far from the daily reality of the southerners, like a faraway mountain in the clouds. Distant "others" ruled the land, and what the people of the south did or desired was irrelevant to the rulers. Most southerners had no part in decisions, cast no votes, selected no representatives. They just struggled.

For Teresa and her sisters, in the home rented by her father with his American wages, life was comfortable. Even their work was filled with love, laughter, and close relationships, including many cherished elders in their 90s. For Teresa, her town was beautiful, the people happy and long-lived, and "*la terra di miseria*" that she had heard about must have been somewhere else. Years later, she would tell her grandchildren that Maida must have been a very healthy place in which to live.[9]

Teresa's second home was next door, and each evening she skipped over to stay with her aunt, who believed in ghosts and was afraid to be alone at night while her husband was away in America. While keeping her aunt company, the little girl often sat at a window on warm evenings[10] to sing and talk with her sisters, just a few yards away at their own window. Family, neighbors, friends swirled about, filling her busy world with loving people of all ages, from venerable grandparents to tiny infant cousins.

Every day, Teresa ran eagerly up the hill to her third home, to visit her grandparents, *Nonno* Peppe and *Nonna* Anna, who embraced her each time as if they had not seen her in years. There she floated in a warm sea of stories—sad, sweet, funny stories about Maida, its people and events of long ago. With those stories, her world stretched into the past, where things of long ago still existed, now, as long as her grandparents were there to make them real. For Teresa, what once was, remained.

Early in the 20th century, girls growing up in Maida learned many roles, shifting between child and adult behavior as needed. They were children and little sisters to parents and older siblings; playmates and friends to peers; and responsible and authoritative big sisters to their younger siblings and cousins. At a moment's need, a young girl set aside her dolls and assumed adult responsibility, such as taking care of a younger child. The girls practiced adult things—making bread and preparing family meals—while the adults worked in the fields, and, once their tasks were completed, returned to their dolls. Almost 90 years later, Teresa would tell her grandchildren of her determination one day to surprise her family. She had prepared dough as she had seen her mother do, set the fire, and baked bread in the stone hearth her father had built outside the house. When the family returned, they found a mess of flour and dough,

9. Of course, Teresa had no objective data on longevity, and her account is based on her subjective recall. Her grandfather *Nonno* Peppe would live to be 97, and her mother, Elisabetta, to 95. Ferdinando Graziano, her future father-in-law, lived into his 80s or early 90s. Teresa would live to 95 and two of her closest friends in Maida, Caterina (Cuci) Serratore and Angelina (Pileggi) Conace, would live to 100 and 94. The friendship of those three ladies spanned two continents and 100 years, sharing virtually the entire 20th century!

10. Glass was expensive, so there were only small openings in the wall and wooden shutters to close them for the night.

a self-satisfied six-year-old, and three or four tiny but—at least according to her mother—perfect little loaves of fresh-baked bread.

Boys began training at a young age for their adult role of family provider and protector. A man must be hard, tough, strong, bound by reality and not fantasy, and focused on responsibility to the family over all else. Boys of five or six were sent to work in the fields or the local shops, and some became apprentices to craftsmen in town. Boys were ordered about by virtually any adult and were frequently cuffed by parents, older brothers, employers, and priests, needing to be taught that the world was a hard and unforgiving place. Such discipline was seldom used on girls. For boys, however, it was expected that in their training they must be made to suffer some pain and disappointment and learn about the world's realities.

In 1900, no girls and few boys in Maida attended school, although 20 years earlier Rome had mandated school for six-to-nine-year-olds and had left the details to the localities.

Primary and secondary education improved in the north, and many youth went on to technical schools or universities. In the south, however, more than two-thirds of the adults were illiterate, few teachers and little funds were available, and there was no monitoring of the law by the Roman government. The few boys who attended primary school, like Paolo, did so at night, after long days of farm work, and few continued beyond a year or two. Formal education was of little importance, literacy in that still-feudal society unnecessary, and time in school was wasted.

La famiglia was life's center, organizing, guiding, providing affection and values, demanding loyalty and responsibility. Nothing was more important than *la famiglia*. Religion was important as a system that served the interests of *la famiglia*, helping to keep the family together. The family—not religion—was primary.

Physical labor was the consuming activity of life for everyone, leaving little time or energy for much else. Hard work was not only necessary in *la terra di miseria*, but it also provided its own virtue because, it was said, "*u fatiga amazza u miseria* (work kills misery)."

For Teresa, *la famiglia* extended through time to include three generations—Teresa's, her parents', and her grandparents'.[11] Teresa's world in the early 20th century was bound as if by a 100-year circle drawn on a calendar. What was real for Teresa included more than the events and people of her present reality. Years later, Teresa, my mother, would try to communicate to me the puzzling notion that there is no past, that all is present; everything is still alive, still real, as long as we can feel it, remember it, imagine it.

"It is still here," she would tell me, touching my forehead. "And here," tapping my chest. "In your mind, in your heart. It's all still here. Nothing

11. Years later Teresa's real world would encompass four living generations, when her first child, Ferdinando, was born in 1921.

dies, nothing goes away, as long as your heart and your head remember. They go away only if you let them go away. Otherwise, everything is all still here, with you, with us. Always. You see?"

I accepted it, but it would be many years before it made sense to me.

4. *Il Professore's Aeroplano*

Teresa and three of her sisters were close in age, but the youngest, Francesca, was born in 1916, when Teresa was 15. The girls enjoyed each other's company and played together in their largely feminine world. Giuseppe, the only boy, was seven years younger than Teresa, and was outnumbered by five sisters. Peppino, as they called him, looked outside the family for companionship. The young girls shared a home-centered life, surrounded by women, learning household skills, playing with dolls, and practicing religious devotions. Peppino went off with other boys to work the fields, climb the hills, throw stones, and play soldiers.

In 1913, when Peppino was six, his mother sent him to school. *Nonna* Anna was not pleased with this waste of the young boy's time, but *Nonno* Peppe was in favor. "How nice it would be," he confided one day to *San Francesco,* "if I could read and write."

Elisabetta's decision had been influenced by Michele, who had learned how disadvantaged by illiteracy the immigrants were in America. A new idea was circulating: *"L'uomo che sa leggere sta bene in America* (The man who reads does well in America)." Originally referring to migrants in America, it came to mean that the literate man does well anywhere. Whatever her reasons, Elisabetta saw to it that her son would become *un uomo che sa leggere.*

Peppino completed three years of school, the first in the family to do so. Anna, Teresa, and Caterina were 14, 12, and 10 years old when their little brother started school, and were curious about it. "What do you do in school?" they asked him. "What does *il maestro professore* teach you?" Teresa was particularly interested, thinking that school must be a special place where children and *il professore* looked out at the world and learned things that no one else in Maida knew about. She liked to page through Peppino's few books, although she could not read them.

Teresa's enthusiasm for school was not dampened by Peppino's disinterest. He was learning to read and write and went to school on most school days, but was happy when he was finally finished with it.

"We want to go to school, too, like Peppino," the girls told their mother.

"Ah," Elisabetta replied. "But girls don't go to school."

"Some do, Mamma. Peppino says there are some girls who go to school. So why can't we?"

"But they are girls from rich families. They go to girls' schools, rich schools. They have nothing better to do. If you go to school, who will help us in the house?"

"But we don't have to go to school every day," they pleaded. "Maybe just some days? Then we can still work in the house!"

Nonna Anna was becoming annoyed at this conversation. "School is no place for girls!" she said. "Girls are ruined by school. They are no good after they go to school. Look what happened to the Perrillo sisters. They went to school, and look what happened to them!"

The girls knew that one of the sisters had given birth to a baby boy, but what that Perrillo girl's maternity had to do with going to school was not obvious to them. "And anyway," the girls thought to themselves, "sooner or later everybody has babies, a new one each year for some girls." Of course, they would not voice that argument to their mother and grandmother because it would be *scustumatu,* insolent and disrespectful, to contradict their elders. Nice girls, they knew, did not do that.

The women knew why girls of their social class did not attend school, but they could not easily tell their girls for fear of causing the very problem they were trying to prevent. *Nonna* Anna had lived a long time and was wise to the ways of boys and girls. She knew with certainty that if girls learned to read and write, they would soon be sneaking love letters from boys and composing their own increasingly lurid replies. That would inflame their youthful passions, leading to clandestine, breathless, and turbulent trysts in distant haystacks. "And we know what happens then. Ruination, that's what!" That's the way it had always been with girls and boys who had the bodies of women and men but the foolish sense of children. Girls belonged at home, where they were safe and protected from the temptations of provocative words and acts of passion. School was no place for girls. With adamant certainty, she advised Elisabetta to keep the girls away from school. "*Prima le parole dolci,*" Anna warned her, shaking her finger for emphasis, "*e poi mani veloci!*" [12]

Elisabetta had some understanding of the traditional social control value in keeping girls and women unlettered. She knew that most men favored keeping their wives and daughters at home and ignorant or, perhaps, *innocente* about the ways of the world, but she felt that it was somehow not right.

"Why do you girls think you need school?" Elisabetta asked.

"Because we want to read books, too, like Peppino."

"Girls don't have to read books," *Nonna* Anna broke in, now sorely irritated, because her earlier declarations had not put an end to this discussion. "Whatever you need to know, we can teach you right here, in your own kitchen. Right here!" She gave the table a hard slap with her hand and added, "*A prima ducazione vene du focularu!*" [13]

12. "First the sweet words, and then (will come) the fast hands!"
13. "The most important education comes at the mother's knee" (literally, at the hearth or fireside).

The girls were dismayed at their grandmother's absolute opposition.

"You don't need school!" *Nonna* Anna continued. "Get that silly idea out of your heads. School is not for girls. Even Peppino wastes his time in school when he could be out working, learning some good trade, bringing home some money for the family. School is not for us!"

Elisabetta agreed about the girls and school, but not about Peppino. "Peppino is a boy, and he must learn to read and write, not like it was years ago. I don't want him growing up ignorant, like the men around here. Your own son, Michele, says so. He sent a letter. *Il signore professore* [14] read it to us, about how in Italy it will soon be just like in America. A man must read and write. And remember what *il professore* told us: "*No pane vuajju, ne scola vaju* (The man who does not want to eat does not go to school)."

Universal education, while mandated by law after independence, was not yet generally available in Southern Italy. Farmers needed their sons to work in the fields. "One or two years is already too much schooling for anybody," they said. Providing school for all was difficult for small towns, because Rome was not generous with education funds. Indeed, education was a casualty of the northern-dominated government's 40 years of spending the country's resources on the military while ignoring civilian needs, particularly in the south. It was one of the new country's greatest errors.

In her demand that Peppino attend school, Elisabetta was ahead of the times. That would change soon after the First World War, but in 1912 they knew nothing of those future events.

"So," she continued, speaking to the girls, "Peppino will go to school, but you are too old to start now. Would you want to be with the five-year-olds? Sitting on the tiny benches and the little tables? I don't think so." (Actually, it sounded rather nice to Teresa.) "And Francesca is still a baby, she's too young to go to school. Maybe someday, somebody will teach you to read. Then you can read nice books. All you want. But go to school? No, sweethearts. I'm sorry. No school."

Her sisters were not disappointed, since they had not been eager for school, but Teresa was. She knew, however, that children must accept their parents' decisions. Anna, Teresa, and Caterina never would attend school, but their younger sisters, Angela and Francesca, would. By 1918, after Angela had reached school age, attitudes toward education were already changing. More boys began attending school, with the blessing of their parents, if not always enthusiasm of their own. Girls were still neither expected nor encouraged to go to school, but some did. Angela, however, had declared her determination to seek holy orders, to become a nun, and literacy was a requirement to enter her chosen order. She began her education, the second person in the family to do so, and in 1922 Francesca followed. Angela would go on to higher levels of education, and, as *Suor*

14. The schoolteacher.

Eugenia, would enjoy a long and dedicated career in a large children's hospital in the Province of Cuneo.

Teresa's interest in school was also encouraged by *il professore*, a retired schoolteacher, his name lost to me now, who enjoyed that respected title. A literate man, he had journeyed by train to big cities like Napoli, Roma, Milano, Venezia, and some said even to Paris and Vienna. *Il professore* had spoken with world travelers and had read French, German, and Italian newspapers. Now elderly, clean-shaven, and bald, he had impressively bushy white eyebrows that jumped up and down when he spoke like two fat caterpillars wiggling across the top of his prodigious Italian nose.

In that first decade of the 20th century, *il professore* sat in the piazza on most warm days, always ready to tell about the wondrous things that were coming to Italy. He spoke of machines powered by great, roaring engines, flying through the air, carrying people 100 meters above the ground, taking them to Rome and, someday, even across the ocean to *la bell'America*. He kept watch on the skies, hoping to see a dirigible or a new *aeroplano* like that of the American Wright brothers or the Brazilian Santos-Dumont or France's Voisin brothers flying right over Maida's piazza. In 1908, people in Maida knew about balloons that carried men through the air, but news of the Wright brothers' 1903 success with their *aeroplano* had not yet reached most of Europe. *Il professore* knew about these aeronautical pioneers, but found only skepticism in his neighbors when he tried to tell them.

Another machine, he said, *l'automobile*, a carriage that needed no horses, would transport people the entire length of Italy. Smaller and quieter than the loud, puffing *treno*, it needed no tracks, could go anywhere, and provided private transportation just for one's own family. Up north in *Torino*, he said, such an automobile had been running for years, and it would soon come into Maida. Long accustomed to *il treno* that linked Calabria with Naples, Rome, and the northern cities, people found it easy to believe that a smaller version, *l'automobile*, was possible. They envisioned contrivances that looked like small-scale railroad coaches, steam-driven and puffing clouds through tall smokestacks, chugging through the piazza. But a giant machine hurtling 100 meters up in the air carrying people to America? That was too much to believe.

"But there is even more!" *il professore* continued. "With a marvelous little machine invented by Giuseppe Meucci, you speak with people two, three hundred kilometers away. This machine is already in every city in the United States! The Vatican has Meucci's *telefono* in use! It will take your voice, in Maida, and hurl it up and down and across the country to anyone you choose. Not like *il telegrafo*, just metallic clicks of a machine. No, it is your voice traveling the distance, carried by Meucci's marvelous invention. And," he promised, "there will someday be one in every town!"

That was not all, he told them. "Voices from *La Scala* and other great opera houses can be captured anywhere in the world. Then they can be released wherever you want, and as often as you wish, to be heard again, as if the performers stood right next to you. Great opera and symphonies performed far away can be heard, through *il fonografo*, right here in Maida!"

Most people had already heard about *l'automobile, il telefono*, and *il fonografo*, and a few had even seen them. What was exciting about *il professore's* account was his prediction that they would soon be in common use, that every town would have *un telefono*. I suppose the older or more cynical people must have said something equivalent to "don't hold your breath."

He spoke, too, of *candele elettriche* (electric candles) in every home so people could discard their murky oil lanterns and turn night into day. The strange new force, *l'elettricità,* the discovery of our own Count Allesandro Volta, he said, was already powering industry and lighting the cities in the United States and in Milano, Firenze, and Roma. Some people in America had their homes filled with *candele elettriche*, and the shadows in the corners had all been banished. He smiled, enjoying his own story, sending the fat white caterpillars dancing. "And," he said mischievously, "*i diavoli e demoni hanno tutti abbandonato l'America perché loro non hanno più angoli scuri in cui nascondere. Allora,*" he continued, with a well-practiced shrug, "*ora, il diavolo è solamente qui, con noi, in Italia.* (The devils and demons have all fled America, because they have no more dark corners in which to hide. And so, now, the Devil is only here, with us, in Italy.)"

These seemed wild tales in Maida at the turn of the 20th century. Who could believe there existed people-carrying machines racing through the skies, lanterns glowing from a strange power, and places without demons? People showed the old man respect due to his age and his former status as a teacher, but shook their heads and smiled indulgently at his enthusiasm for such fanciful nonsense. Sometimes young men, who had not known him when he was an active *professore* and were looking for amusement, would ask him how this *elettricittà* was made. "*D' aqua!*" he would say. "From water!" And he would try to explain about high waterfalls turning giant turbines to produce *l'elettricitá*. But that was too much for these disrespectful young men. "*Per favore*," one might call out. "*Portatemi un bicchiere d'acqua. Io voglio accendermi.* (Please, bring me a glass of water. I want to light myself up.)"

The old schoolteacher's vision of the 20th century was prophetic but not taken seriously by most people. Their reality at the turn of the century was that of donkeys carrying bundles and women skillfully balancing jugs of water on their heads. Devils and demons certainly existed, hiding in the darkness and riding on the chilling drafts of nighttime winds. In this Italian Peninsula, Leonardo da Vinci had designed flying machines 400 years before. The internal combustion engine had been in use since the 1830s, Allesandro Volta had created the first storage batteries a hundred years earlier, electricity had been running streetcars for 20 years, and here the inventors of the telephone and telegraph had been born. But in Maida, the impossibility of human flight through the air was uncontested. Although Marconi was the first to send a wireless telegraphic message across the ocean in 1901, and *il professore* might scan the skies for his *aeroplani*, the citizens knew it was fantasy. It was not until the First World War in 1914-1918 that his prophesy of flying machines was taken seriously by the Maidese. Even so, the military *aeroplano* was not the same as the giant machines that he said would carry people across the ocean.

Teresa believed him—after all, he was *il professore*. Everything he described was exciting and would be nice to see someday. Indeed, in the first decade of the new century, men who returned after working in the United States and in Northern Italian cities reported that *il professore* had been right! In the greatest cities, they said, like Buffalo, New York, Chicago, and Atlantic City, *l'ettricità* was running factories and trains and lighting up shops and the homes of the rich.

"How do you know all this?" Teresa once asked *il professore*.

"From books," he said. "You must read. Read everything."

"Ah," *Nonna* Anna would say whenever Teresa excitedly recounted *il professore's* stories and wished she were able to read his books. "*Ma perché ne abbiamo bisogno? De libri? Noi abbiamo in Maida la maggior parte di tutto quello di cui abbiamo bisogno.* (But why do we need them? The books? In Maida we have most everything we need.)"

For *Nonna* Anna, none of those wonders was essential for a good life. Turn-of-the-century Maida, she knew, needed more employment, more rain, better crops, and more respectful daughters-in-law, but not *aeroplani* or *automobile*.

Years later, Teresa would tell her own little boy about *il professore*, that old teacher back in Maida who so clearly read the future but whom no one would believe. "*Il professore* was right," she would one day tell me, "about everything."

In Teresa's childhood, men were constantly departing for or returning from America. They moved back and forth across the ocean, interlacing the fabric of two lands. America was becoming an Italian outpost, a part of Italy, even for those who had never been there. Returning men brought news from America, usually good news, though sometimes not, of jobs and success.

The Dattilo children enjoyed their close family. Whatever problems the adults faced were not evident to the girls. They had their home, their family, and, as far they knew, everything necessary for a good life. In the background was always America: huge but accessible, mysterious but familiar, distant but near. It was far across the ocean, but never having seen the ocean, they had only a vague idea of how far it really was.

Peppino, however, was growing restless. Unlike the girls, he had freedom to explore and have experiences outside of the family. Peppino felt the allure of America that had enticed his father and planned to leave the farm to find a more rewarding and adventurous life. His father had been the transitional migrant for the family, journeying to America seeking work to secure a good life for his family in Maida. Peppino was of the next generation, those who wanted to leave permanently. Unfortunately, by the time he was old enough in the late 1920s, the United States had passed restrictive, anti-Italian immigration laws and the waiting lists had become impossibly long. By then, the Italian dictator, Mussolini, was pressing men into the African colonies, extending his dream of a modern Italian Empire and dealing with the southerners' "unemployment problem" by shipping young men out of the country. "*Allunghiamo lo stivale fino all'africa orientale!* (We will stretch the boot until it reaches East Africa!)" he proclaimed. Peppino would have to wait another 35 years, until after the Second World War, to finally reach America.

From 1900 to 1914, Michele Dattilo was away in America much of the time, but *Nonno* Peppe was still there, filling the paternal space. He was the family patriarch, the main figure of family stability. The first sadness of Teresa's life was the lack of contact with her father. She knew he was far away in America, working to send money home. They spoke of him every day, and he sent frequent letters. "Papa is away for a while," their mother told them. "But he is with us always." Teresa learned early in life that a person's existence and influence can be strong in mind, love, and spirit, even if not present in body. Still, she was sad over his absence.

Teresa recalled an anxiously happy day in 1905 when she was four years old—her father was coming home from America and was going to stay for several years. Three years earlier he had come home, but Teresa had been an infant and did not remember.

On the day he was to arrive, Teresa ran outside at every clacking sound of donkey's hooves. Finally she heard the rattling and kicking of stones, the grating of wooden wheels moving up the hill, and the shouted greetings, "*Buon giorno, Michele. Benvenuto!*"[15] moving ever closer to their house.

The wagon stopped and the little donkey bobbed her head up and down, asking for a drink of water, Teresa thought. A big, smiling man gathered his bundles and jumped down from the wagon. He stood there with his arms out, ready to sweep up his family. Teresa hesitated. He was a stranger but he looked like *Nonno* Peppe, only younger and taller. His smile was the same, and he seemed to have the same gentle patience. Michele was 37, a vigorous man, his pockets filled with American money and his head with ideas for his family. Michele smiled and waited. "*Teresina mia,*" he said.

Still, Teresa hesitated. *Nonno* Peppe, who was then 75 years old, stood beside her. She felt his hand on her shoulder and she pressed into him for reassurance. "Go to your father," he urged gently. Teresa looked up at her grandfather, still clinging to his familiar safety. He smiled and nodded.

15. "Hello, Michele! Welcome! Welcome!"

Standing beside the wagon, her father waited, smiling, holding his arms out for her.

Then, all was as it should be. She looked again at her grandfather and, without knowing why, hugged him and cried. After a moment Teresa pulled herself away and ran the few steps to her waiting father. He whirled her into the air, both of them laughing and crying, caught up in their swirling emotions, and he hugged his little girl with the ferocious strength of his sheer happiness.

For the next decade, until 1914, life was pleasant, comfortable, and safe but punctuated by sadder periods when her father was away in America. When he was in Maida the family was complete, and under her father's protection the family lived in their rented house in town and worked their big farm up the hill, thriving on what it produced. Teresa knew nothing of poverty and would remember those years as the happiest time of her childhood. Her Maida was defined by those years—a sweet, comfortable town of beauty, security, and happiness.

The farm was just a mile or two north of town, some of it on a rocky slope that could not be cultivated easily. It included a small wooded area, a stream, and fields. Everyone in the family worked there, even the children. Peppino had no love for farm work and preferred being with his friends, exploring other places and ideas. Each day he went to school and dreamed of one day leaving Maida.

Teresa recalled olive groves, fig trees, oranges, lemons, chestnuts, grapes, onions, tomatoes, peppers, eggplant, scallions, squash, beans, peas, and *ghiande*, an acorn for livestock feed. There were chickens, two milking cows, and a fattening pig that made Teresa feel sad because of its unfortunate destiny. At least the poor thing had no idea what was coming.

The best times, Teresa thought, were the harvests. Peas and sweet red strawberries were picked early in the season. Because the strawberries were so small, it took a great deal of picking to fill even one pail. The peas, however, were bountiful. Several families with no land of their own rented plots on the Dattilos' farm. The fall harvests stretched over several weeks and, despite the hard work, were festive.

Teresa loved the figs best. She would never forget how *Nonno* Peppe reminded everyone, "Nothing that God makes in this world is so perfect as the sweet, ripe fig, so ready that it drops happily from the tree right into your hand." That, the family joked, was the longest speech that *Nonno* Peppe had ever made. Many years later, in another country, Teresa would hear an echo of *Nonno* Peppe's sentiment, this time voiced by our family doctor. "Here," Dr. Relland, who had immigrated from France, would say, smiling and holding in his hand a fresh, ripe fig from my father's tree in Nyack, "is God's perfection."

Teresa remembers how olives were squeezed for their golden oil and the fragrant grapes yielded rich, red wine. Wooden barrels, including one that the little girl thought was as big as a house, took in the juice of the grapes and, by magic, poured out smooth, finished wine.

One day in 1909, Teresa insisted, despite her father's concerns, that she could balance the earthen jug of wine on her head, the way some of the women did, and safely carry it down the hill to their house. All went well until she tripped. Teresa and the jug fell, it broke, the wine seeped into the ground, and Teresa cried, not in pain, for she was not injured, but in humiliation and remorse for wasting her father's wine. He knelt by her and wiped her tears. "Look," he said gently, pointing back up the hill. She looked.

"Up there is the barrel. See how big it is?[16] In there we have lots more wine—many, many gallons. So don't worry if a little spills. Anyway, maybe it will make the ground sweeter, eh?"

Michele picked her up, tenderly, and carried her home.

Sixty-five years later, when my cousin Michael Bartolotti visited Maida, he was shown a huge barrel on the hill. Unused for well over a generation, it had survived the years and the enthusiastic destructiveness of soldiers in two World Wars. The barrel was no longer tight, some staves were dried and cracked, but it was still there, weakened but still standing, silent, a faithful old sentinel. Was it the same barrel that Teresa had seen, so long ago? Perhaps.

The years rolled on to 1914. Teresa grew into adolescence. The harvests came each year, bringing the vivid colors of early fall—green, orange, yellow, purple, and brown. They brought voices calling, laughing, singing; the sounds of labor, of tools chopping, digging, working the earth, chinking on stones, the snip of clippers through stems, and the soft sounds of fruit dropping into pails. With each harvest came the juicy, sweet taste of ripe figs, the aromas of crushed grapes, pressed olives, golden oil, and foods being cooked, smoked, and preserved. They brought, too, the palette of wondrous tastes that children sneaked when no one was watching. At the end was the big, happily noisy harvest feast. For Teresa, it was all a grand symphony from long ago. No matter how many years were to separate her from those events, she could close her eyes at any time and there it was, the symphony, vividly performed again.

There is no past; all is present; whatever was lived, is lived.

16. As reported by relatives who remember the barrel, it held 5,000 gallons (18,900 liters). The largest wine barrel today is in Heidelberg, Germany, with a capacity of 55,000 gallons, or 221,700 liters.

Chapter 9

The Giant at the Top of the Stairs (1909–1914)

1. On the Eve of War

It was 1914, the eve of World War I. Teresa's father, Michele Dattilo, was again on the ocean, returning to Italy. With him were his cousins Giuseppe and Michele Graziano, young men who would soon marry Michele Dattilo's daughters Anna and Teresa.

Michele Graziano was one of the few who had completed the mandatory four years of primary school before starting full-time farm labor at the age of eight or nine. Despite the government's progressive universal education law passed in 1877 over the Church's opposition, there had been little improvement at the local level. When Michele attended school from 1898 to 1902, the experience for boys from poor families was too often degrading and generally negative.[1,2]

However, Michele enjoyed school despite its harshness. He especially liked the arithmetic problems that were introduced in the third year and was intrigued when he caught glimpses of proportionality, volume, and area. Those were advanced topics for such early schooling, and *il professore* was genuinely happy to find a responsive pupil. Michele also liked to handle tools and build and repair things, and knew the use of any tool from its form and feel. Now that he was in school and learning about measurement, he drew diagrams of buildings, determining the dimensions needed to house a family or a given number of animals or volume of crops. His family recognized his interest and encouraged him, but they also knew it was of little value. After all, farmers had always constructed buildings without first drawing plans—a wall starts *here* and ends *there* and should be *this* high and *this* thick. Women needed no formal measurements beyond "some of this" and "a little of that," whether they were cooking or giving advice to their children. Tailors and dressmakers, specialists in the use of careful measurement, were the most precise workers in town.

Michele was promoted each year despite his many absences due to farm work, and on reaching his ninth birthday had mixed feelings about leaving

---

1. See Chapter Five.
2. Williams (1938).

school. He was one of the few boys who gained some academic skills and respect for *il professore*. His friends looked to him to read and interpret letters, public notices, and accounts of life in Naples, America, and other thriving places. Reading to his friends was an example, Michele later admitted, of "the near-sighted leading the non-sighted."

Years later he realized that some of the boys who had learned so little in school nevertheless conducted their adult affairs competently. Some learned to read and a few became literate in two languages, Italian and English, French, or Spanish, after spending time in other countries. One young man who was later killed in the Great War had learned all four languages. Apparently *il professore* had managed to squeeze some lasting ideas into their resistant heads and he would have been pleased.

For Michele, full-time work began in 1900, the turn of the new century. A boy of eight could not match a man's labor, but five or six boys made a good contribution to a day's work and cost *u padronu* very little. Matching the men's working hours, the boys descended the hill to the farm in the early morning and returned in the dark evening, too tired to do anything but fall into bed after a quick supper. During the summer's hot *mezzogiorno*,[3] the workers found shady places for their *pranzo e riposo* (lunch and rest), waiting for the less intense slanting afternoon rays before resuming their labors.

The boys ran errands, carried tools and drinking water, fed livestock, and did other tasks that required little skill. A few boys became unofficial apprentices to masons and other skilled workers. They learned to use tools, to plant, prune, and harvest, to repair most everything, to measure and calculate dimensions, angles, and areas. The barns, workshops, fields, vineyards, and slaughterhouses were their classrooms, and the workers were their teachers. In his five years of farm work, Michele, with his aptitude for using tools, learned a wide range of practical skills.

2. *Rispetto*

Harvest time was particularly busy. Even the air became excited as young women and men in the healthy roundness of late adolescence worked side by side in the fields—the girls watched closely by their parents. It was 1902, and one young lady, Marianna Renella,[4] had "ripened" suddenly, as the young men said, "*proprio a perfezione* (to perfection)." To the appreciative young men, she had become the most beautiful, desirable, and unapproachable young lady in Maida. "*La Bella Renella*" they named her, and the young men rolled their eyes to heaven and kissed their fingertips in thankful appreciation whenever they saw or thought of her.

Unfortunately for them, so valued a prize as *La Bella Renella*, the acknowledged princess of Maida, was not to be easily won. Her parents were

3. Midday, noontime.
4. This is not her real name.

concerned, knowing that Marianna, now nearly 16, must soon be married or risk sliding into lifelong spinsterhood. They also knew that a young lady of such beauty would attract the finest young men, like the son of the rich tailor or perhaps a son of the local gentry. They had to be careful about that, because rich sons, with their sense of entitlement, might use and abandon her. Her parents needed to make their choice with care, and they dutifully protected Marianna from undesirable young men. She was not cloistered, but was carefully protected while being kept in the town's eye to remind others she was there but interested only in the best young men.

Marianna was seen walking to church with her mother, shopping or strolling arm in arm with her four cousins, always watched closely by a pair of formidable aunts. The cousins were dark-haired beauties, but in the presence of Marianna even those attractive girls faded to ordinary prettiness. They were a little envious, but also knew they gained a good deal of admiring attention by associating with Marianna, who was held aloof from most everyone else. They were an exclusive group of five attractive young ladies. The cousins bloomed in Marianna's reflected beauty, and they were quite happy to accept that.

Marianna was aware of her effect on young men. Admiring attention was flattering, but the past year had been too accelerated. The playtimes and easy friendships of childhood were rapidly falling behind. Pleased with many of the changes that she saw in herself, she also sometimes longed to once again be just a little girl. How nice it would be to play and laugh with her cousins and not be burdened by everyone's changing expectations of her. A child growing into in a woman's body, Marianna was no longer sure how to behave with her cousins and friends, who she realized had similar uncertainties.

"I will become a nun," she solemnly announced one day, hand over heart, her face radiantly turned to heaven. "I will give my life to God and the Church in love and virtue."

Through her cousins' gossip, this became known to the town's young men, who tortured themselves with distressful images of Marianna's beauty forever hidden by the nun's black habit.

However, that was not to be. Marianna gave herself up to the control of her parents, who, being sensible people, were more intent on a good marriage for their daughter and many fat grandchildren than they were on service to the Church. As the harvest of 1900 approached, she followed the guidance of her parents and tolerated the admiring gazes of the young men who were kept at a safe distance all around her.

Her presence in the fields excited the young men as nothing else could. Her mother and aunts surrounded her, and the admirers could but look, whisper among themselves, and pray to heaven to grant at least one little fantasy. Such intense thoughts and images would have to be admitted to the good *prete* at the next confessional, but of course they never were.

Despite the festive air, the boys were fatigued and grimed by the hard work, just as on any other days of labor. They learned to modulate their efforts, because there were always some men who, for amusement, sent them on foolish errands or ordered them to carry out tasks that were too menial for men and often too hard for the boys. In their own defense, the youngsters learned to find a distant shady tree under which to stop unseen and rest for a moment. When chided for taking too long, they claimed that, while dutifully on their way to carry out the errand, they had been interrupted by *il padrone* himself and ordered to do something else.

"If you don't believe me, go ask *u padrone*," the boy would say, "and you tell him to stop interfering like that with your orders."

Of course, no *giornaliere* would question *u padronu*, and the boys always got away with it.

Like most boys, they were ebullient, with endless energy and deep pools of mischief. They were a vocal young group, talking and joking with each other and unafraid to speak out, and they practiced the skills of insult. With the directness of children with little concern for others' feelings, they zeroed in on a person's weaknesses and wove them into a custom-designed insult.

The art of insult depended on one's creativity and on knowing which class of insult to use each time. Finesse came with maturity and practice. When an insult was meant only as a humorous tap rather than an injurious attack, it would not be built around a person's real weaknesses. Those were friendly insults, accepted and responded to with humor. When, however, the insult was impelled by anger, it was meant to hurt. Those insults were built on the targeted person's weaknesses that were sharply perceived by the boys. Their intent was to cause hurt, and it was truly insulting because it spoke the truth.

The boys' insults were crude, not yet smoothed by maturity. Sometimes they required the creative cooperation of several boys, who ganged up on a victim such as Tito Bucconese. Tito was a slightly stout man in his 40s, with a right leg that was shorter than the left, causing a limping walk and making it difficult for him to run. He also had some difficulty seeing things clearly at a distance, but that did not impede his work, which was never farther away than the length of a shovel. Tito's two sons had gone to America and his daughters had married and moved to Abruzzi. Life in his one-room rented house was strained. His wife, an unhappy lady, berated him for one thing or another, and he had no place to hide from her.

Tito had been *un bracciante*, a farm laborer, since the age of five. Despite 40 years of farm experience, he did not have the ambition or skills to become an overseer, and younger workers soon rose above him. Life had been disappointing, withholding the respect that a man should be given. Neither his wife nor his fellow workers respected him, and he no longer had children at home to force into a feigned respect.

Tito was an earthy man, openly expressing his bodily functions whenever the need arose. Thus dignity, a necessary characteristic if one wanted respect from others, was not in Tito's makeup. The boys came to know him well, a man of middling skill and not much ambition. He was the first to stop work at lunchtime and the last to return to work afterward. His one skill, it seemed, was getting others to do his work for him. He thought he was clever in this regard, but his maneuvers were so clumsy and transparent that other men simply ignored them. The youngest boys, however, were naive and easily manipulated.

"*Vincenzo, vieni qui* (come here)!" he would call to the youngest boy. "Give me a hand."

Soon Vincenzo was working while Tito pretended. When the overseer came by, Tito, with an innocence that could fool a saint, claimed that he was teaching the boy some important skill. He never stopped trying to ease his own burden, to impress the youngsters and earn their respect.

Tito also liked to play demeaning tricks on the youngsters, jokes that were not at all funny to the boys. He believed he had a fine sense of humor and enjoyed laughing each time he showed his superiority over a gullible boy. If a new boy joined the crew, Tito would order him to bring some heavy tool to him. After struggling barefoot across the rough fields, carrying the heavy burden and banging his shins in his bumpy progress, the youngster would find Tito already in possession of a similar tool, laughing at the boy for his foolishness in not having been more observant.

Tito was a bully and became a target for the resentful and resourceful boys. Ten-year-old Angelino—a misapplied name if ever there was one—usually led those attacks. Angelino, it was said, had been "*nominato dei angeli, guidare di diavoli* (named for the angels, but guided by the devils)." He was a bright, outspoken, irrepressibly energetic youngster with a strong theatrical flair. Angelino was always embroiled in some mischief or other, but with such infectious good humor and an impish, wide-eyed smile that even his victims, except Tito, tolerated most everything he did.

Angelino truly did not like Tito, and what he aimed at that man was decidedly more than impish pranks. Fully intending to insult and offend him, he derisively called Tito *Santo Tito lo Zoppo* (Saint Tito the Lame). "Hey, *Santo Tito!*" Angelino would shout, keeping a safe distance. "You don't know your *culo* from your face!"

While Tito, hampered by his shorter right leg, lunged at the agile Angelino, another boy shouted, "And then you blow farts in church 'cause you're too dumb to know it's your nose and not your *culo* that needs blowin'!"

The whooping boys then ran in opposite directions, shouting, "Santo Tito blows farts in church!" leaving the incensed Tito turning back and forth from one to the other, cursing and shaking his fist.

This was egregiously bad behavior and would never have been allowed by adults of more dignity or authority. Tito, for obvious reasons, refused to call Angelino by his given name, instead calling him *Diavolino* (Little Devil). The two worked themselves into a continuous struggle, Santo Tito versus *Diavolino*. Given Tito's greater reach and strength and the boy's greater wit and agility, the contests were evenly matched, but that was about to change.

It may be that some men's toleration of the boys' disrespect helped to sharpen the differences in status among them, thus emphasizing the importance of paying true respect to those who deserved it. *Rispetto* was important in that society, and this was, in effect, the other side of the coin. To learn to be respectful, the boys practiced also how to be disrespectful, and to do so appropriately. An example is the seemingly contradictory set of attitudes many Italian men have toward their religion—they could be deeply respectful of God, the saints, and the nuns, but acidly disrespectful of the Church, its priests, and the pope. Also, Southern Italians held a passionate commitment to their cultural heritage but a hotly disrespectful contempt for the government in Rome or the provinces.

One noontime at harvest season, while the workers were enjoying their *pranzo e riposo*, Angelino and several other boys suddenly appeared. With wide grins and bright eyes, they ran noisily and in great excitement past the shady spot where Tito sat against a tree enjoying bread and a piece of provolone. He could see that they were highly excited, far beyond their usual liveliness.

"Hey!" Tito shouted, "Hey, *Diavolino*! What's going on?"

"Nothing!" Angelino answered as he ran close by, adroitly eluding Tito, obviously bursting with some secret. "It's none of your business!"

The boys were hopping with suppressed excitement, and Tito was determined to learn why. As the boys ran past him, he jumped up and caught Gianni and Vito by the arms. They twisted and pulled and tried to escape, but he held them tightly with his big hands. Had he been a little more reflective, Tito would have wondered why it had been so easy to catch these usually elusive boys.

"Now, you little animals, tell me what's going on!"

"No! We don't want you to see. . . ."

"Be quiet," said Gianni. "Don't tell him!"

"Don't tell me what?" demanded Tito, squeezing their arms tighter. "What don't you want me to see? Come on, tell me!"

"Ow! Stop! I'll tell you. Over there," Vito pointed, "she's in the stream, and she thinks nobody can see her 'cause everybody's supposed to be resting up by the barns, and she's all naked. *Tutta nuda! Tutta, tutta nuda* (All naked! All, all naked), and you can see everything. Everything!"

"So you want to keep it all to yourself, eh? And not let Tito go and see, eh? Who's in the stream? Some old woman nobody but little animals like you want to see anyway? Who?"

The boys looked at each other. Vito shrugged and said, "Marianna, that's who. *La Bella Renella*!"

This news almost knocked Tito over. "Aiii!" he moaned. "*La Bella Renella? Nuda? Tutta nuda?*" A picture began to form in his mind: *La Bella Renella* standing in the ankle-high water, her long legs and glorious body totally bare, her golden hair rippling down her back like a lustrous waterfall, and all of her wondrous gifts right there, right there for his viewing! What an opportunity! What a gift from heaven!

Grasping the boys' arms even harder, he demanded, "Did you tell anybody else? Did you? Does anybody else know? Eh?"

"No. No, sir. Nobody else."

"Good. Don't say anything to anybody else. You hear? Nothing!"

"Oh, yes, sir. We hear."

Tito pushed them away. "You stay here. Don't go over there. If I catch you over there, I'll wallop you! You hear me?"

"Yes, sir. We'll stay here. We won't go there."

Convinced that he had intimidated them, Tito headed toward the stream, planning to keep the wonderful vision to himself. As he approached the slope that rose by the side of the stream, Tito began to walk quietly, so as not to alarm Marianna and perhaps force her to cover up.

There! There she was! Because of his poor eyesight her image was blurry, but Tito could make out the back of her head as she leaned against the stream bank. Her golden hair cascaded below her shoulders and out of sight behind the rise of the little hill.

"*Ah, Dio mio!*" he thought. "There she is. She must be resting now." A new image formed in Tito's mind: *La Bella Renella*, naked, leaning back against the bank, her eyes closed, her back arched, her beautiful body pressing up toward the warm, caressing sun. "*Ah, Dio mio, Dio mio, Dio mio,*" he said, over and over, not quite believing his good fortune. "I have to get closer. I have to see her better."

As he crept silently a few more feet toward the bank, Marianna began to stand up, her back still toward Tito, still not aware that he was just a short distance away, watching. Slowly her shoulders rose into view, those beautiful bare shoulders; and then her back, so smooth, so lovely, with that golden hair all the way down to her waist. Tito was still too far away for a clear view, but there was no doubt that he now could see her beautiful, rounded buttocks, her thighs, and the lovely, dimpled backs of her knees. "*Dio mio, Dio mio, Dio mio,*" he kept mumbling, as if he had lost all other words. "I must get closer!"

"Please," he prayed silently. "Please make her turn around so I can see. Please." He was breathing hard, now, excited. "Please, make her turn around."

And she did. As if she knew what he wanted, as if answering his prayer, Marianna, *La Bella Renella*, the one with the glorious body, slowly, languidly, provocatively turned toward him. With her arms spread out, she stepped up onto the bank until she was completely and magnificently revealed in all her naked perfection, just for Tito.

He gasped and staggered, stumbling in his confusion, frustration, rage, and finally his terrible understanding. After a moment of staring and adjusting his poor, weak eyes, he screamed. It was a sound of such ferocious and deeply anguished disappointment that, on hearing it, anyone must have felt terribly sorry for the poor man. In his rocketing desperation, Tito convulsively reached out his hands, fingers curved, and clawed at the air as if he wanted to grab the apparition by the throat and kill it, but he was still too far away for that.

"No! No! No!" he screamed. "You devil! What did you do? I will kill you!"

Then, exploding from behind trees and shrubs came all of the boys, laughing at Tito's frustration, while 10-year-old Angelino, the Little Angel, wearing only a wig of golden hay that reached down his back, pranced on top of the little stream bank to the boys' applause. Like a performer on stage, Angelino swept off his golden wig and bowed grandly, with a dramatic flourish, toward Tito.

That Angelino had stood in complete nudity was so shocking a breach of the Southern Italians' sense of morality that it made the insult an even more humiliating and disrespectful attack on Tito. After that day, Tito was no longer so quick to take advantage of the boys. Even years later, a fellow worker might casually wave a long stem of golden hay and ask, "Eh, Tito, how's that girlfriend of yours? You know, the one with the long blonde hair?"

Michele Graziano, even at age eight, was a good observer. He was not loquacious and outgoing, like the misnamed Angelino, nor was he a leader, or even much of a follower. Instead, he typically watched what was going on, and then, on some basis known only to himself, decided whether to join in, observe, or walk away. Michele was sometimes criticized for his unwillingness to join the other boys in their mischief, but being wiry and tough enough, he could defend himself as long as he and his accuser were about the same size. It was the older, bigger boys who gave him trouble. Being degraded by others just because they used their greater size was infuriating. Michele developed a dimension to his personality that stayed with him his entire life—he delighted in challenging and besting anyone bigger or in some ways more powerful than himself. Any type of contest would do—arm-wrestling, foot racing, lifting heavy rocks, verbal arguments, and occasionally even fighting. When he won, he was vindicated; when he lost, he explained to himself that, after all, this adversary had been bigger or stronger, or older, and there would be another day to try again. This personal testing against the odds became a lifelong characteristic that sometimes brought him trouble but, most important, helped him to define his goals. For example, he determined that someday he would have a bigger, grander house for his family than any house in Maida.

When Michele began his working life in 1900, Italy was still struggling in post-revolutionary turmoil and the world was losing control in its long slide to *la grande guerra* (the Great War) of 1914. Unremitting poverty and political rivalries exploded in labor revolts in northern cities. Angry anarchists and idealistic socialists demanded political and social change. King Umberto I, who had succeeded Vittorio Emanuele II, launched Italy's grandiose but ultimately failed 45-year colonial expansion into Africa and the continued wasting of its shallow resources on a modern military. In 1900, Umberto I was assassinated by an anarchist. Then Vittorio Emanuele III, in the tradition of *la casa savoia*, continued building the military and ignoring the needs of his people.

In 1900, eight-year-old Michele was little affected by explosive world affairs, being caught up in his own adventure—becoming a full-time working man. What did the death of a king have to do with him? In any event, there was a new king. The king is dead! Long live the king! Life goes on.

Among the lessons he learned in farm work from 1900 to 1906 was the importance of dignity and the respect it created. He watched 70-year-old Emilio. Emilio was skilled in many tasks and worked hard, doing more than his share, neither complaining nor boasting. A quiet man, Emilio said little while others talked too much. He smoked his pipe with its long, curved stem and quietly observed. When he did speak, always briefly, to the point, and quietly, others listened.

Everything Emilio did suggested dignity. Even walking across a field with a shovel over his shoulder was accomplished with an unhurried stateliness. The others respected Emilio. This, Michele thought, must be real respect, based on the nature of the man rather than on social position. Respect was paid to the padrone, but that was because he was rich and owned the farm. Emilio, however, was respected even by the padrone, because of what he was, what he knew, what he did. Without realizing it, Michele began to emulate Emilio.

Through years of farm work, Michele accumulated many practical skills. By the age of 14, he had acquired so many skills and such familiarity with tools that he would be able to make his way anywhere in the world. He also learned that a man without respect and dignity had no substance. Tito Bucconese was such a man—he craved respect but did not know how to earn it. Tito had no dignity and therefore no substance, and thus deserved no respect. Michele learned that whatever a man does in his life must be achieved in a manner to earn the respect of others—family, coworkers, friends. To gain respect, one must act with dignity. And what, according to Emilio, was dignity? It was a certain reserve in one's manner, a quiet approach to life suggesting a careful and thoughtful view of things, and respect for others, when deserved. A person born into high status was handed a dignified existence and went through life being grudgingly respected without ever earning it. Men like old Emilio and young Michele, born into poor conditions, would have to earn it.

Emilio had made a strong impression on him, and Michele had impressed Emilio as well. Here, the man thought, was a lad who, like Angelino, was different from the others. Angelino was flamboyant and assertive, and Emilio was sure he would have an interesting and successful life. Michele, on the other hand, was reserved, an observer, a quiet learner. He too, Emilio thought, would succeed, but by following a path different from Angelino's. Both boys, Emilio knew, searched for something that neither would find easily, if at all, in Maida.

It was Michele's quiet appraisal of things, and the clear respect that he extended to older men in general and to Emilio in particular, that first caught the old man's attention. "Here," he thought, "is a lad who already has some understanding of *rispetto*."

"Michele," he called on day, "come, I want you to help me tie up the vines."

This was an honor. While the other boys were running errands and generally taking orders from all the men, Michelle was being singled out to help Emilio! Michele knew that if he did well, Emilio would become his mentor. He would learn a great deal and others, like the bully Tito Bucconese, would never dare to bother him. Michele was pleased but also anxious, because working with Emilio meant meeting Emilio's high standards. He followed the old man to the vineyard. "Here," Emilio told him. "You carry this twine, and I'll carry the shears, because the blades are a little too sharp for you yet. And bring *la zappa* (the hoe)."

At the first post, the anchor of a long line of vines, Emilio began to trim with practiced precision while Michele watched. "How does he know," Michele thought, "which to cut off, with so many vines all tangled up?"

As if he had heard the question, Emilio asked, "Michele, point to the main trunks of this vine."

"There, the two thick ones, the ones growing straight up in the middle."

"Yes. And look how many branches there are. Too many. See, with all the branches, the life of the vine goes off in too many directions. It does not know what it wants. It grows because it is full of enthusiasm to grow, full of life. But with no plan, no reason."

Michele nodded.

"So," continued the old man, "we help it a little. We are teachers to the vines, we guide them, give them a plan, a direction. We teach them to grow strong. That way, the life of the vine goes surely to its best growth, to its strength. When the vine grows strong, the grapes are good. Now watch. We want to encourage four good branches off this trunk; always four, two on each side. Everything else we trim off. See? This one is already brittle and dead; we snip it off. This one is broken, and off it comes. This one here, it is too thin. Snip, it goes. Now we have five branches and have to take off one more. Which one do you think should be trimmed off?"

"That one." Michele pointed without hesitation. "It looks funny, maybe too pinched there, skinny, and it looks too close to that bigger one that maybe we should save."

"Yes, very good. That's the one we trim off."

When the vine was trimmed to his satisfaction, Emilio showed Michele how to tie the branches with twine, which he cut with his small knife carried in a leather sheath on his belt. "We tie them up so they don't fall on the ground, but not too tight; we don't want to choke them. The twine holds them up just until the vines can hold on by themselves. Then they don't need the twine no more. See?

"Now, this next one. I'll hold it up here, you cut the twine and tie up the branch. Go ahead."

Michele looked at the old man. "I don't have a knife."

"Ah," Emilio said. "Here, use mine. But be careful, it's very sharp."

By the time Michele was 14, he had completed nearly six years of farm work, and although he had learned much and liked the work and the men, that had been enough. Farm labor was not going to be his life. Angelino, who was two years older, agreed.

"I," Angelino announced, with his usual flourish, dramatically placing his hand over his heart, "am going to be a great actor."

The two boys, 14 and 16, pooled their few lire and, in 1906, despite their parents' warnings, left the farm and went off to Naples to find a more exciting life. An important responsibility went with them: as dutiful young laborers, they had contributed their earnings to their families. Now, wherever they worked, they would have to continue to provide at least some support. We have no details on how they fared in Naples or if they journeyed to other places. They must have had some success, because they lived there for three years, returning periodically to Maida, grandly wearing city clothes and bringing their wages and gifts. Certainly they gained experience in the big city and learned more about their country and the world.

By 1906, when the boys arrived in Naples, conflicts were sparking all over Europe and there was a growing fear of Kaiser Wilhelm's new Germany, with its burgeoning military and aims of empire. The continent was moving closer to total war.

Emigration had increased over the last 25 years, and desperate men talked of going to America or becoming government laborers in Italy's new African colonies, to find relief from poverty.

Back home, the two friends had seen a few soldiers, young men home on leave. People knew something of the world situation, but growing tensions and Europe's march to war were distant events. The poor attributed their continued poverty to "the way things have always been," not recognizing how much Rome's military expenditures drained resources from civil society. In another 10 years they would realize how blind they had been.

The boys saw massive battleships steaming by Naples, beyond the edge of the harbor, black smoke pouring from their funnels. Their menacing beauty was impressive and frightening. They saw marching soldiers and suspected that they would someday be in the army—not a prospect they cherished. The military presence, the newspapers, and the rumors running in the streets of Naples told the boys that events far beyond their control were changing the country. They heard talk of war, of joining with France, their old enemy, and again beating the Austrians, who were building fortifications on the border. Maybe they would invade Africa or Austria, take back Trieste and the Trentino. Italy, they learned, was building a fleet of giant battleships in competition with France and Austria, and might very well again fight the Austrians, who were just to the east, right across the narrow Adriatic Sea.

"We beat the Austrians before," people said, recalling, selectively of course, the 1866 triumphs of Garibaldi's army that had helped to defeat the Austrians in the Seven Weeks' War.[5] "We drove them out then, and now maybe we have to go to sea and beat them again!" They did not speak of the humiliating defeat of the Italian navy by the Austrians in that war.

As the calendar unrolled toward still-distant 1914, the country's military battles seemed to be of little importance to daily life. Until, that is, grieving families whose homes had once held living sons and husbands began to receive the slim, sad letters from Rome.

Young men were conscripted unless they were in university or the priesthood or their families were rich and well connected. There were growing rumblings about Rome's demands that the young fight wars they had not created and did not understand, need, or want. Uprisings against conscription flared in some southern provinces, but soldiers soon dampened those.

Most of the conscripted men were from the south, poor and uneducated, resentful of an aloof government on which they had no influence. Many were so undernourished and ill from poverty and malaria that they were not fit for conscription, but they were taken anyway. They went into the army without enthusiasm for or commitment to a government they hardly recognized as their own—unwilling soldiers, more resentful than patriotic.

That was the climate in which Michele and Angelino grew up—poverty, powerlessness, resentment, turmoil, low morale, and war preparations. They returned to Maida several times between 1906 and 1909, each time a bit more urbane. Michele, who had always been particular about his appearance, had become even more attentive, having accepted the advice, "*Come ti vedonu, ti tratonu.* (They treat you the way they see you.)" He bought his one suit in Naples, to wear when he visited Maida.

Michele was slim and wiry, and dressed with careful neatness. When visiting home, he drew admiring glances from girls and disdainful remarks

5. See Chapter Four.

from some of the elders. This good lad, they said, who had worked so well on the farms, whom old Emilio had taught, had become *un grandioso,* losing sight of his proper position, just like those insolent young men who had returned from America. "That's what becomes of boys going off to the big cities," they said.

3. Giuseppe Conace

Michele's life changed again in 1909, when he was 17. He and Angelino suddenly returned to Maida. They were anxious and seemed always to be looking over a shoulder. Their friends asked what was wrong, but the boys only looked at each other, shrugged, and said nothing. Macrina, Michele's older sister, wondered, "Now what has he done?"

Macrina was pledged to marry Giuseppe Conace, a man of 24 who had gone to *l'America* in 1903 with his younger brother, Antonio. Giuseppe was determined to become rich, at least by Maidese standards, and to build a fine house for his future family. The friendship between the Conace and Graziano families reached back a long time, and it was expected that Giuseppe and Macrina would marry.

Unlike most Italian immigrants, Giuseppe Conace did not settle in a large American city—crowded tenements in urban slums were not for him. He profited from the practice of chain migration and made contact with the Fiola family, who had been in America for some time. They helped him settle in and find work and guided him in his new country.

His family had always been farmers, and Giuseppe was good at it. Arriving in America, he applied his agricultural skills and settled in Rockland County, a farming district some 25 miles north of New York City. Working at whatever jobs he could find, Giuseppe saved money for several years and bought a few farm acres on a hill in Central Nyack. He purchased a horse and secondhand farm equipment, hired two other Italian immigrants to work for him, and started cultivating his new fields.

The next year, when his first crop came in, Giuseppe hitched up his horse and drove down into Nyack. He hired a sign painter and watched proudly as golden Edwardian script flowed onto both sides of the wagon:

G. Conace · Eggs, Vegetables & Flowers

Giuseppe began selling fresh produce from his wagon, establishing a successful route through the streets of Upper Nyack, where his customers appreciated the crisp, freshly harvested produce. In just six years, he was able to expand his farm and send for Macrina so they could be married. Giuseppe was eager to meet her in New York City and escort her to the single room that was to be their home on the top floor of his barn. It was not elegant, and he planned to build a house for her, one far superior to anything found in Maida, even those of the rich landowners.

Macrina was excited and anxious when, in the summer of 1909, his letter arrived, inviting her to come to *la bell'America*. Like all emigrants, she had mixed feelings about leaving her home. At 21 she knew only Maida, the rest of the world being only secondhand images. Macrina was illiterate ("girls don't go to school," she had been taught) and felt ignorant and poorly prepared to take so large a step. She was competent in all that was demanded by her family. "I can work the fields," she told her young brother, Michele, "as good as anybody. I can raise animals and milk goats and make bread and pasta. I can cook and I can mend clothes and I can even make the clothes, if I have to."

As the oldest daughter in her family, Macrina bore much responsibility, and her family would miss her hard work and maturity. "But what do I know about America? What do I know about New York? I know nothing about what I'll have to do there. They say everybody there must know how to read in *americano*. I don't even know how to read in *italiano*!"

Macrina was not one to panic, but she began to feel overwhelmed. Michele, seeing her growing anxiety, joked, "Don't worry, Macri, I hear they don't even have goats in America."

"You!" she said, laughing, her anxiety dissolving. "What's goats in America got to do with it? That's not what worries me."

Michele just smiled at her, his little, quiet smile. He was younger by four years, and Macrina, the big sister, had taken care of him as he grew up. "Not that he's all grown up yet," she thought. "He still gets into too much trouble. Like now, in Naples with Angelino, whatever it is they don't tell nobody about."

"Michele!" she said with a sudden, new thought, putting an arm around his shoulder. "You will come with me!"

As competent as she knew herself to be in Maida, Macrina was anxious about the challenges in America, that giant country of which she knew virtually nothing. However, Macrina's sturdy, peasant competence went beyond physical work. She did not yet know it, but within her were intellectual and creative resources that would later emerge and carry her successfully through heavy hardships in America. Had she known that, Macrina would have felt more reassured and not so anxious and inadequate. "Michele," she said, "we are really going to America!"

There was a great deal to do: obtain visas and steamship tickets, pack clothes, change lire to dollars, say their tearfully happy goodbyes, and travel to the Port of Naples. Michele had thought often about emigrating, and this was a good time for him to get away from Italy for a while. He said goodbye to his friend Angelino, not knowing that 26 years would pass before they would meet again. On November 26, 1909, Macrina, 21, and Michele, 17, embarked from Naples on the new German ship *Berlin*.

Macrina had never seen so many people in one place—2,700 steerage passengers, another 500 in first and second class, plus the crew. That a single ship could hold 3,500 people, as many as lived in all of Maida, was astounding. Michele, too, was impressed, but he had lived in Naples and crowds of people no longer astonished him.

The *Berlin* was new and efficiently German. Steerage was crowded but clean and comfortable. The bunks were stacked only three high and were glossy, white-painted steel, not like the four- or five-tiered wooden bunks that earlier migrants had used. The food was plentiful; some dishes were strange but could be tolerated for the nearly two-week ocean journey.

In the daytime, Macrina and Michele were together. They walked the lower deck when the December winds were not too biting, marveled at the sea that never stopped rolling, and met people from all over Italy. Strong friendships developed, and promises were made to stay in contact after reaching *l'America*. They took their meals together and attended classes that taught them about America. Only one doctor was available for the 2,700 steerage passengers, but it was good to have him, especially for the children, even if one had to wait in line for hours.

Each evening at 7:00, the women and children were confined to their section while the men and older boys enjoyed their freedom in the rest of steerage.

It was a smooth, surprisingly enjoyable trip, not the rough winter crossing they had been warned about. Macrina, being older, assumed that she was in charge, responsible for the welfare of her young brother. She watched over him, at least during the day, and fussed over him to make sure that he was dressed warmly enough for the voyage and ate properly and had enough sleep. Macrina insisted on holding their money, sure that he would be tempted to play cards, *scopa* or *briscola*, at night, and lose it all. Michele, however, asserted that he, as the man of the family, held the responsibility of protecting his sister and bringing her safely to Giuseppe. After all, he was experienced in the ways of the world. Had not he and Angelino survived three years in Naples, while Macrina had never before even left the safety of her doorstep in Maida?

Michele enjoyed the daytime hours with Macrina and cherished his self-determined role as her protector. He also liked the evenings, when, for long hours, not hampered by the women and children, the men joked, complained, and shared tall stories. They talked about America, its promises and dangers, and, most interesting, told stories about the scandalous behavior of American women, leaving Michele wide-eyed and even more vigilant about his sister.

Michele was pleased to be accepted as one of the men. They talked, smoked, played cards, and drank wine and American whiskey, although most of the Italian men had little taste for the latter. On most nights, the more experienced travelers collected coins from each man in a small group of six or so and tipped Max, one of the stewards, to raid the ship's wine stores and bring them three or four bottles. This arrangement was a bargain for the men. Everyone was pleased with it. Max pocketed the tip for his service and a share of the small charge for the wine. It was a clandestine shipboard commerce in which stewards and steerage passengers all gained something. The ship's owners unknowingly supported the little business. Of course it was only German wine, but after a glass or two, even that no longer mattered.

At Macrina's insistence, Michele had grudgingly given his money to her for safekeeping. Actually he had given her only half, telling her that was all he had. Some of his remaining money went for the nightly wine purchases from Max and to buy tobacco. He had never liked smoking, even though he thought it made him look older and sophisticated while he was on his own in Naples. However, here in steerage, casually choking on harsh cigarettes while drinking wine and gambling was part of his initiation into the circle of men, paying his dues, so to speak. Most of his money was soon lost at the card table. The older men were sympathetic about the boy's losses and patted his back with consoling gestures. But that never stopped them from letting him into the games. For young Michele, it was distressing to see his money drain away each night, but it was far worse to know that Macrina had been right! She must never find out!

In their second week at sea, when he had been reduced to nearly his last coin, he had a wonderfully successful night at cards, winning back almost everything he had lost. True, he was still short of his original amount, but it felt like a great windfall, a sudden increase in wealth. And what does an unfettered 17-year-old do with such sudden wealth? He spends it! The next day he did what he had seen the seasoned travelers do. Michele spoke quietly to the steward, Max, and flashed his winnings. Max nodded in understanding as he pocketed the bills. Later, before the regular dinnertime, Michele put on his white shirt and his suit from Naples, although by then they were wrinkled from being rolled up in his bundle. Guiding his sister by the arm, he led her astern, almost to the very end of the deck.

"Where are we going, and why are you so dressed up?" Macrina asked, with some suspicion.

"Shh, Macri," he said. "You'll see. Come with me."

Puzzled, she followed, and found Max waiting for them, standing next to a wooden crate and two folding chairs that he had arranged cozily behind a wide bulkhead, in front of a fire hose and between two canvas-covered lifeboats. Neatly covering the crate was a white cloth, and arrayed on that was the most elegant setting of plates, silverware, and food she had ever seen. There was even a chilled bottle of crisp German Riesling and two long-stemmed glasses.

"For you, Macrina," Michele said, lifting a glass. "For you and Giuseppe: my gift for your wedding. "*Salute!*" It was, she thought, the finest dinner of her life.

They enjoyed their dinner in the private little dining room on the steer- ·

age deck. Max had to return to his official duties, and Michele kept anxious watch lest anyone see them—steerage passengers were not supposed to enjoy first-class food and purloined wine.

Perhaps it was the opulence of the clandestine first-class meal hidden between the lifeboats that did it—this must have been the way first-class passengers were treated all the time! Steerage was bearable, but first class was better. What separated Michele from the upper classes was a single steep steel staircase. Each day he walked past the bottom of that staircase and looked up. "Certainly," he told himself, "if I climb those stairs, I will become one of them."

As an adolescent, Michele had displayed a lifelong characteristic—a quick anger and a rush to assert his own dignity whenever he was disrespected and insulted. A person bigger, richer, or of higher status who even hinted at a patronizing superiority was insulting. He had no problems with those who had earned their higher status and behaved with dignity and honor, like Emilio. Indeed, he admired them, and they deserved his respect. But he could not accept even a suggestion of disdain. Outright arrogance or unfair presumptiveness infuriated him and, as Macrina knew, had often caused him sharp troubles. Maybe, she thought, something like that had happened to him and Angelino in Naples? She would never know. Even milder affronts, such as the presence of the first-class passengers, implied disrespect, creating in him annoyance, anger, and a need to erase the differences between them.

Squaring his shoulders, puffing out his chest, and lifting his chin, he silently announced to the upper deck, "I am a man of dignity, as good as you are, and I deserve at least the respect that you want for yourself." That is what he felt as he considered the first-class passengers up there, the steerage passengers down here, and that damnable steel stairway between them. To others, that staircase was a barrier. To Michele, it was a challenge.

One afternoon, with a few days left in the voyage, Michele again put on his white shirt and wrinkled suit from Napoli, carefully tied his scarf around his neck, and adjusted a white handkerchief in his breast pocket. He tugged at his sleeves, trying without success to straighten some of the wrinkles, ran his fingers through his hair, wiped the dust from his shoes, dangled a cigarette in his mouth, and, properly first class, he thought, made his way to that staircase.

As he climbed the steel steps, the 17-year-old practiced the mildly bored expression that he imagined would be carried by a first-class *gentiluomo*—eyes half closed, nose tilted up, lips slightly pursed, a hint of patronizing haughtiness playing over his face. His left hand was casually slipped into his jacket pocket, the thumb carelessly hooked over the top. With his back straight, chin up, and right hand sliding up the railing with an easy certainty of where it was going, he ascended, dignified and handsome, toward the upper world of first class.

When he was halfway up, the biggest man he had ever seen appeared at the top of the stairs, and Michele's view from below made him seem even bigger, turning the man, truly, into a giant. He was radiant in a white uniform with enough gold decorations, Michele thought, to pay for his and his sister's passages to America and back again, had it been real gold. The giant wore a peaked cap with a riot of gold stitching on its high front. A double line of brass buttons marched down the front of his jacket, glittering like so many suns, and other suns gleamed at the ends of his sleeves. His shoulders were so wide they stretched across the width of the stairs, and his crossed arms were as thick as tree trunks.

"This man," Michele thought, looking up, "must be the king of a great country, or the admiral of the whole German navy, or at least captain of this ship." In truth, he was only one of the lesser ship's officers, but even a man in that lower position wore an impressive German uniform.

The giant at the top of the stairs barred the way. His only movements were a narrowing of his eyes and the slow rise and fall of his chest. His lips tightly pressed together, he stared down at the approaching youngster. Michele did not hesitate in his march up the stairs, nor flinch from the resplendent giant with his unwavering expression, which gave a warning that Michele chose to ignore. The two stared into each other's eyes. The boy rose higher. The man stood, rooted. Neither spoke. Michele continued to climb.

"I," Michele told himself, "am a man of dignity, as good as any first-class passenger. He will see that and will move out of my way when I reach the top of the stairs." Michele concentrated on those thoughts and he radiated confidence (and the naïve arrogance of a boy who did not recognize his own foolishness).

When four steps separated them, the giant's mouth angled up in one corner, so slightly that one had to be as near as Michele to see it. It was the most chilling smile that he had ever seen.

Slowly, silently, deliberately, with slow-motion choreography and still staring into Michele's eyes, the giant lifted his right foot and, with his leg bent at the knee, placed the sole of his huge shoe in the middle of Michele's chest. The boy's progress was stopped and he felt the hard, flat sole, an armored barrier so large that its toe pressed his chin upward while its heel was almost at his belt. They stood unmoving for a fractional moment that seemed endless, while the silent giant's eyes drilled into Michele's. Stored in the muscles of the giant's leg was potential energy that could turn into 500 pounds of force, waiting for release, like the power in an archer's bow. Then, with no palpable effort or further warning, still not moving any other part of his body and not uttering a sound or changing his expression, the giant snapped his leg straight out. The stored energy was released into Michele's chest, sending the boy bouncing, rolling, sliding, and clanging down the steel stairs, head over heels, all the way to steerage, where he belonged.

Although he would ache miserably, walk painfully, and carry visible bruises that turned richly colorful over the next few days, Michele was not seriously hurt, not physically at least. One of his new friends in steerage told him that his green, yellow, and purple face made him look very festive, "*come un biscotto di natale* (like a Christmas cookie)."

Michele had learned something: whatever dignity he had affected while ascending those stairs had been lost in his demeaning slide back down. If he wanted to be respected, then he would have to learn to take the measure of whomever he was facing and not go bumbling into unknown places without adequate preparation. The giant at the top of the stairs had seen "steerage" stamped upon Michele and had treated him with contempt, not respect. Michele learned that he could not be "first class" simply by trying to act the part. Like dignified old Emilio, one had to be able to present something of worth: strength, achievement, skills that justify respect. What would be the nature of those strengths in America, and how was he to identify and achieve them? That, he knew, was a question he must answer if he was to survive and prosper as a man in a new country, a man with respect.

4. Under the River and to the Farm

On December 7, 1909, after stepping from the Ellis Island ferry and into New York City, Macrina and Michele were met by her betrothed, Giuseppe Conace. He led Macrina and his young soon-to-be brother-in-law by way of trolley cars, a long train ride, and a horse-drawn wagon to his hillside farm in Central Nyack. "My God!" he asked, staring at Michele's colorfully bruised face. "Did you fall under a horse?"

"No," said Michele, quietly, head down, too embarrassed to explain. "I tripped. On the boat."

Giuseppe stared for a moment but, seeing the boy's discomfort, did not pursue it. Macrina, who by then knew the story and had satisfied herself that her brother was not seriously injured, sighed and shook her head. To herself, she thought, "How does one quiet boy get into so much trouble?" It was neither the first nor the last time she would ask that question.

Their introduction to *la bell'America* in 1909 was stunning. The impossibly huge buildings and the wide streets went on forever. The masses of people going every which way were a total confusion. The trolleys and wagons, horses and occasional motor vehicles, the bustle and noise were hard to believe. Giuseppe took them to a marvelous train station, the biggest and most beautiful building they had ever seen. This was Pennsylvania Station, under construction from 1905 to 1910. Its beaux arts magnificence was unmatched anywhere in the world. (It would be torn down in 1964 to make room for a parking lot.) For Macrina and Michele, it was truly *un palazzo dalla fantasia*, a palace from one's fantasies. The huge structure of pink marble was as grand as the ancient Roman baths—bigger than Saint Peter's in Rome. Its marble colonnades reached to the sky, its ceilings were of glass, and the trains rolled right inside the building! And what trains they were, gliding silently, with no choking smoke or snaky hissing and chugging of steam.

"*L'elettricità*," Giuseppe told them. "These trains are run by electricity. No more fire and dirty coal-burning like the old steam engines!"

"It's just like the old *professore*[6] told us all those years," Macrina said. "*L'elettricità*. And we always thought he was just telling us crazy things! He was right. Look, Michele, he was right, the old *professore!*"

When the marvelous train took them into a black tunnel—to them it seemed an archway to the underworld—Macrina became so alarmed that she sat like a turtle with her neck pulled into her shoulders. Michele was equally alarmed but was not about to show it. The train, Giuseppe said, was taking them right under the Hudson River! "Under the river? How is that possible? Will the water rush down on top of us and we drown?" They marveled, too, at Giuseppe, who was unafraid, his hands relaxed in his lap, a little smile on his face, not at all worried about the river flowing above their heads. He had become a man of the world, they saw, while they were still only country people from Maida. "Ah," thought Michele, "so much for my worldly experience in Napoli."

They reached the train station in Nyack and climbed onto the open wagon, the taxi that would carry them the final four miles of their journey to the Conace farm. They were so overcome with the cold that they noticed nothing of the town. It was nearly Christmas, and neither Macrina nor Michele had ever before experienced such chilling air and biting wind, which cut right through the heavy wool blanket that Giuseppe had wrapped around them. Glistening frozen snow crackled on the ground, sharp and sparkling, marvelous, magical, and wondrously new to them, but they were too cold to appreciate the experience. "Take me back to Maida," Macrina said, shivering.

Macrina and Giuseppe married in Nyack and settled on the farm. Their wedding celebration must have been as much like those in Maida as they could make it. Their guests were the dozen Italian families living in Nyack and nearby Piermont. In every happy gathering of Italians were men who played *u mandolino* and *la tromba* (mandolin and trumpet) and several older gentlemen who insisted on singing to the couple in wavering voices that at one time had been quite good, while everyone else enjoyed what should have been their embarrassment. The women brought trays of home-baked *pasticcini* (pastries), and each man a few bottles of home-pressed wine. Everyone, even the Irish priest who had made the sign of the cross and pronounced them "man and wife," enjoyed the food, drink, music, laughter, off-color wedding-night jokes, and even the high-energy

6. See Chapter Eight.

antics of the children who swirled among the grown-ups' feet. For a few hours, they lived a little bit of Maida.

Michele was fortunate in having the security and guidance of his hard-working brother-in-law, profiting from the tough lessons that Giuseppe had learned in America. He worked on the farm, living for a time with Macrina and Giuseppe in their crowded little apartment above the barn. With Michele's help, Giuseppe expanded it to three rooms.

Winter was busy with repairs and preparation for next year. Giuseppe found his young brother-in-law to be hard working, surprisingly skilled for one so young, and ready to learn new skills. In Maida Michele had learned to build with fieldstones carefully selected and set to make strong walls, even without mortar. In America, he was learning, men built with wood, because trees were as plentiful here as stones were in Maida. Within a few months, he had become a credible carpenter.

With Michele's help, the farm prospered. Giuseppe, always alert to business opportunities, saw a potential wholesale market for flowers. His business expanded; more laborers were hired and he made plans to construct five greenhouses to grow spring flowers for the Easter trade. Macrina worked beside him, digging, trundling the wheelbarrow, spreading manure, sowing, planting, weeding, harvesting, packing and shipping flowers, and mastering the paperwork. The fact that Macrina learned to handle finances and bookkeeping was remarkable, considering that she had never attended school and was learning it all on the job, and in a foreign language.

At first she thought that the long days and hard physical labor were not different from her life back in Maida. "But," she thought, "here we are the *padroni* instead of the hired laborers!" This idea astounded and delighted Macrina. It was hard to believe that, in a handful of years, they had stepped from penniless field laborers in one country to landowners, employers, and business partners in another. Truly, this was *la bell'America*!

The farm prospered and the family grew. By 1914 their three sons, Joseph, Frederick, and Frank, had been born, and a few years later their daughter, Maria. Michele had become an uncle before he was 19, and life began to look different. The family grew in yet another way—Giuseppe's younger brother, Antonio, worked on the farm for several years before he married Angelina Pileggi and settled in Nyack, where they would raise their large family. The Conace brothers and their families were the beginnings of my own extended family, which was to grow in Nyack 15 years later.

Michele worked on the farm from 1909 through 1912. Like his sister, he learned English and the ways of America and grew self-reliant. He respected Giuseppe's skills, ambition, and success, was pleased at Macrina's happiness, and was grateful for their help. He was pleased, too, to have contributed to the farm's success. However, with Macrina's family growing and her apartment over the barn becoming as crowded as those in Maida, it was time for him to move out. Anyway, Michele had long ago determined he would not remain a farmer.

In 1913, he moved to Nyack, rooming with other newly arrived Italian men. The Italian community in Nyack was small and growing, and already there were Italian-owned businesses—Giuseppe's farm and that of the nearby Gallo brothers, and a grocery store owned by the Rasso family. The young men were settling in, migrants becoming immigrants, preparing to raise families. Italians in Nyack were becoming established and offered support and friendship to each new arrival. The Conace farm would provide employment for many as they adjusted to America. Those families were a close group that would grow, but never very large, into the community of lively people I would know in the 1930s and 1940s.

Most found work on farms or doing road maintenance, wielding the picks and shovels that had become associated with Italian men as if they were natural extensions of their arms. Except during his brief stay with Angelino in Napoli, Michele's work had been outdoor labor, digging in the ground, planting and harvesting, wielding pick and shovel. His working life had been seasonal, working "out-of-doors and in the dirt," where, he was told by an American boss, "you Italians belong."

Better jobs existed indoors, in factories protected from the weather; reliable, year-around employment that did not end when the seasons changed. Those jobs would be a substantial improvement and an important goal, a measure of success, but they were not usually offered to Italians. Another example of American disrespect, Michele thought.

It was a 45-minute walk or a quarter-hour wagon ride over the three or four miles from the farm to the center of Nyack—not far, but distant enough to put Michele just beyond the reach of his sister's watchful concern.

"Michele, please be careful down there in Nyack," Macrina told him. "There are bad people there, and bad places, especially on Saturday night. Be careful. For a quiet boy, you always seem to get yourself into some kind of trouble. You watch out, OK?"

To herself, she thought, "I know he'll get into trouble. He always does."

Michele was 20 by then, hardly a boy, but his sister still worried about him and he was a little embarrassed by her concern. After all, he was the family's world traveler, the one with experience. But in truth, he was pleased and warmed by her concern and their closeness. "*La famiglia,*" he sighed, with a resigned smile.

We do not know the details of what happened during his short stay in Nyack. Michele's problems appear to have involved the alleged unfair treatment of Italian men who were working or wanted to work in one of the local factories, the sewing machine plant down at the railroad tracks, at Cedar Hill and Franklin Streets.

"Why do they pay us less than the others?" Michele complained to his friends. "We work just as hard, but they get two dollars a day, and we get a dollar and a quarter! And why do they give us all the dirty jobs and never give us a chance for the good jobs?"

"Listen," older men advised. "Be grateful we got these jobs. We work here, we don't get rained on and snowed on and freeze our asses off outside in the cold and we don't break our backs choppin' the hard ground and movin' rocks. Don't be so quick to complain. Have patience. Someday we'll have our chance, too. Just like *gli irlandesi* (the Irish) do now."

But to Michele, the youngest of the workers, this was a personal dishonoring, unfair and insulting, still another instance of the steel staircase that separated steerage and first class, an infuriating barrier to keep him subordinate to those who were no better than he. With the certainty or perhaps the foolish arrogance of youth, he confronted the employer, made demands, and became embroiled in a dispute until one day anger exploded on all sides, and that derisive word was spat out: "Wops!"

What Michele did then brought him a great deal of trouble. Facing down employers in those days with no labor unions for support, while perhaps an act of bravery, was also foolhardy.

"Giuseppe, I have to leave, right away; tonight, after dark!" he urgently told his brother-in-law later that day. "Can you take me in the wagon to the train station? Not the one in Nyack, but a station over in Jersey? Do they have a station in Norwood?"

"Oh my God! Michele, now what did you do?" Macrina asked, alarmed.

"They asked for it!" Michele told her. "And remember, you don't know anything about it, if they come here looking for me!"

"Looking for you? Who? Who will come looking for you?"

"The police."

"Oh my God!"

Michele left immediately, driven through the midnight darkness by his brother-in-law, in the old farm wagon with G. Conace—Eggs, Vegetables & Flowers painted in big golden letters on the side, to a New Jersey train station. He tried to sleep on one of the hard benches on the station platform, but jumped up at every sound that he imagined was a stealthy Nyack detective sneaking up on him. In the morning, tired, worried, and disheveled, he boarded a train to Ocean City, where he joined his cousin Giuseppe Graziano and the three Dattilo brothers. He worked with them at the city water and gas company for the next several months.

By then it was early 1914. War was about to explode in Europe. Italy had depleted its resources in its 1912 victory over Turkey and had not yet recovered. The pressures toward an even greater war were growing, and Italy had called for its expatriate men to return for military service. Michele, then 21, knew that the army was in his immediate future. The two young cousins decided to return to Italy and join the army. Michele Dattilo (Teresa's father), at 46, was beyond military age but returned with the young men to be with his family during the war. His younger brother, Giuseppe Dattilo, who wanted no part of Italian politics, enlisted in the U.S. Army and would later serve in France in 1918. In Nyack, Antonio Conace and Jimmie Fiola, who had worked on the farm, also decided to join the American Army and served during the war. An estimated 400,000 Italian immigrants enlisted in the American military during World War I.[7] Because of their military service, they were later allowed to bring their wives from Italy as citizens.

In 1914, on the eve of World War I, a worried Michele Dattilo was on his way back to Maida, accompanied by his young friends, the two Graziano cousins, who were about to become small pawns in *la grande guerra*.

7. Belmonte (2001).

Chapter 10
La Grande Guerra (1914–1919)

1. A Family Affair

Long accustomed to absolute power, European kings controlled both policymaking and ceremonial functions. The 19th-century revolutions had forced some monarchs to accept constitutions that limited their autocratic power. Royalty, skilled at self-preservation, managed a compromise. In return for giving some policymaking power to prime ministers and parliaments, they continued as ceremonial heads of state, thus preserving their families' public-supported wealth and lifestyle. Some, including Vittorio Emanuele II, kept most of their power. For the Italian king, the new constitution was a minor inconvenience. In truth, his power had expanded enormously, and now he ruled an entire peninsula. The revolution had been very good for *la casa Savoia*.

So successful was royalty's survival that by 1910 the number of reigning European kings had grown to 20 and every nation in Europe except France and Switzerland had a crowned sovereign guaranteed by hereditary succession. Royalty flourished. The royals filled their roles enthusiastically, and some believed their ceremonial functions were more important than the policy decisions of prime ministers and parliaments. The period from 1860 to World War I was a golden period of privilege and indulgence enjoyed by a handful of royal families who believed in their supreme importance and thought they would reign forever.

In 1914, Europe was a family affair. Kaiser Wilhelm II of Germany, England's King Edward V, and Czar Nicholas II of Russia were first cousins, grandchildren of the late Queen Victoria (1819–1901). Seven of the 20 kings in Europe were direct descendants of the estimable queen, and two others were close descendents.

Whatever the 19th-century revolutions had achieved, royalty remained wealthy and self-indulgent, exerting little effort in life other than ordering servants about. Immersed in luxury, surrounded by bowing, scraping, and scurrying lackeys, they believed in their glorious superiority, magnificence, and invincibility. No opulence, however outrageous, could be faulted. They lived in a fairy tale world of palaces and delusion, viewing their amusements as virtues while real people struggled to survive. Cousin Nikki (Nicholas II) continued his autocratic, corrupt, incompetent, and, some would say, insane mismanagement of Russia while revolution boiled around him. Archduke Francis Ferdinand, the heir to the throne of Austria, attained his greatest life achievement—shooting his 5,000th deer. While royal men stalked terrified animals in tamed game preserves, their women lived in order to dress prettily for dinner.

The royals believed that their subjects demanded more extravagant and magnificent noble displays than those of other countries. After about 1860, a half-century of pompous, luxuriously expensive, and vainglorious competition resulted; royals played royal games.

They believed their privileges were morally justified, ordained by God. They felt secure in their extraordinary positions. They owned the world; it was their families' playground. Three powerful countries—Germany, England, and Russia—were virtually owned by Cousin Willie, Cousin Eddie, and Cousin Nikki. Seen through their delusional grandeur, the world was a family extension. Why should it not continue forever?

In their complacency, they believed that the royal families would maintain world order despite occasional family squabbles. They did not see that Cousin Nikki and Russia's royalty were already lost, the country awash in revolution; that resentment over royalty's extravagant lives and the deep social inequities were growing to an explosive level. Neither did they see that socialism and bolshevism were already gathering up the people's frustrations, and that Fascism and Nazism were just around the corner. They dismissed the Balkans' skirmishes as nuisances. They did not see that the military buildup of Cousin Willie's new Germany threatened peace, or that a small, weak, impoverished, infant nation like Italy could possibly rise up and challenge mighty Austria and actually win. What they saw was their own magnificence, in perpetuity.

There were three European worlds in that half-century beginning in 1860: poverty, militarism, and the gilded ceremonial world of royalty floating in unapologetic luxury, oblivious to the truth boiling below them. The first was reality, the second was truculent stupidity, and the third was delusion.

Those decades might be named the Age of Royal Delusion. As important as the royals thought themselves to be, they were in fact not needed by the world. But by 1914, they had built powerful military forces controlled by the whims of but a few men.

With all its passionate 19th-century drive for freedom, liberty, and democratic ideals, Italy had emerged from revolution not as a democratic republic but as a constitutional monarchy. Vittorio Emanuele II, with the help of Cavour and Garibaldi, had distorted the revolution in order to expand his monarchy. The new Italian rulers were authoritarian, militaristic, rigidly and truculently nationalistic in the tradition of the old Sardinian monarchy, believing that national pride and success lay in military power. The peninsula had been united, the foreign occupiers driven out, and the monarch was Italian and not foreign. The people, however, remained subjects of the king, and the decision makers were a few men chosen by the king to help him rule. By the 1880s, Italians had made two major national decisions: The first was to choose a monarchy over a democratic republic, and the second was to choose military over civilian development. Would the new leaders focus on building a civilian economy? Would they create an environment to support human dignity and success and to raise educational, health, and economic levels, to reduce the old regional barriers? Or would they buy armies and navies instead? The decision was made. Nationalism, militarism, and colonialism were chosen. Civilian needs, especially in the southern half of the nation, would be ignored. Those were disastrous decisions made collectively by Italians, step by step, in their long revolutionary struggle. The Italian people did not own their government. Mazzini's dreams of republic, reforms, freedoms, and rights were gone, buried under 50 years of royal rule. "In our homes," men said, "we make believe we are kings, we make the rules and enjoy our little circle of respect. But when we leave our miserable huts to go work for *i signore*, we go hat in hand, with our heads bowed down. We say, '*sì signore,*' '*No signore,*' '*bene, signore,*' '*tutto quello che volete, signore.*'[1] The priests tell us we must respect God, the pope, and our padrone, because that is God's way. *Il governo* tells us to go fight in wars that we don't make, don't understand, and don't want. They all tell us our 'place' is to be servants to the masters, marionettes on strings, make-believe men. Where is the honor, the respect, for us?" "What do we own?" the southern peasants asked. "We don't own the country, the province, the town, the cities, the mountains. We don't even own this miserable clod of soil that we dig or, finally, our own graves. We don't own ourselves; they throw our bodies in the dungeon whenever they want, for as long as they want. "And what of our souls? The priests say that our souls belong to God and we are only caretakers for a few miserable years. We must keep our souls and feed our bodies until the pope, God, or the king decides to take them back. Where does that leave us? We are subjects of the king, subjects of the pope, subjects of God, masters of nothing." "So," many concluded, "If we are ever to be free, we must do away not only with the king, but also with God." In the 1880s, Italy was a young, small, still-fragile constitutional monarchy. In 1882, the right to vote was extended to men who were at least 25 years old, were taxpayers, and were literate (about 7 percent of the population). The vote was denied to all women, most northern men, and nearly everyone in the south. With few natural resources, little industry, a budget-draining military, and pervasive poverty, Italy struggled for survival. Internal problems were not the only concerns. Italy might be taken over by France, Germany, or another powerful country and would soon be fighting

1. "Yes, Sir, no, Sir, whatever you want, Sir, very well, Sir."

with Turkey over Libya. The Austro-Hungarian Empire, still Italy's greatest threat and a powerful European monarchy, was just over the Alps and across the narrow Adriatic. Austria's armies and navy bracketed Italy's northeast border and eastern coast from Venice nearly to the Mediterranean. In 1871 Prussia had consolidated the Germanic states into the German Empire.[2] Under its monarch, Kaiser Wilhelm II, and its ultraconservative chancellor, Otto von Bismarck, the new Germany was an aggressive militaristic state. Rivaling Austria, it pursued colonial expansion into South Africa, the Pacific, and China and fed the tensions leading to the Great War of 1914.To the east loomed czarist Russia, gigantic and largely unknown, building the largest army in the world, pushing to the Black Sea and into the Balkans and seeking a footing in Europe. These powers crowded the Italians and their small peninsula, threatening to engulf them. Having created their independent nation, the Italians now had to protect it in the threatening militaristic world, and they began to strengthen their military. In 1885, following the examples of France, England, and the new Germany, Italy began a six-decade colonial foray into Africa. This conflicted with the interests of Austria, Turkey, France, Germany, and England, each of which viewed itself as the rightful colonizer of the African continent. Apparently the peoples of Africa had nothing to say about it. In the 1890s, France and Italy waged a warship-building contest for control of the Mediterranean and access to Africa, with Austria soon joining in. Italy's eastern coast lies on the Adriatic Sea, and just across that narrow water was the Austro-Hungarian Empire, with one of the most powerful monarchies remaining in Europe, the House of Habsburg. The Italians were concerned that both coastlines, totaling some 2,500 miles, were vulnerable to French and Austrian attack; this concern kept the ship-building competition going with Austria-Hungary and France. All three countries strained their economies building bigger warships; the costly race continued from the 1880s to the Great War of 1914–1918. It was those Italian battleships steaming past Naples that had so impressed Michele and Angelino in 1907. In the closing years of the 19th century, control of the Mediterranean was one of many issues in the buildup to *la grande guerra*, the Great War. Russia planned to move its navy through the Black Sea into the Mediterranean. Austria, still angered over its loss of the Italian Peninsula, set out to regain it. Great Britain needed to protect the Suez Canal; bolster its influence in North Africa, Arabia, Palestine, and the Balkans; and maintain its Middle-Eastern sources of crude oil. France had to protect its North African colonies and Italy its long, vulnerable coasts. Germany aimed to expand into Africa and the Pacific, displacing the English navy. Spain dreamed of regaining its old colonial grandeur. Turkey, with

2. The peoples of the Germanic states had occupied the same Central European area for nearly 2,000 years. They shared common language, customs, and religion, but remained a collection of politically separate states. In 1870, Bismarck consolidated the states into the German Empire, militarizing and launching the new Germany into world power.

its access to the Mediterranean through the Dardanelle Straits, dreamed of restoring the Ottoman Empire that had once ruled the Balkans, North Africa, and parts of Europe. All the while, Italy and Austria, the two old enemies, glared with suspicion at each other across the slim Adriatic. From 1880 to 1914, Europe smoldered with shifting alliances, secret pacts, colonial expansion, military buildups, threats, blusters, and small wars. The royalty lived their pleasantly deluded lives while millions of young men in armies and navies were shuffled across Europe like dumb tokens on a great board game. A partial list of events suggests the tensions that led to *la grande guerra*: Czarist Russia pushed closer to the Mediterranean, generating a warning from Austria. Turkey invaded Albania and fought a war with Greece. France, England, and Germany battled in North Africa. Russia and Japan went to war. England fought the Boer Wars in South Africa for gold and control of the southern continent. The United States declared war on Spain and seized Cuba, Puerto Rico, the Philippine Islands, Guam, and the remaining Spanish Empire in the Pacific. A few years later, the United States warred with Mexico. In 1906, England, France, and Italy agreed to divide North and East Africa among themselves, doing to Africa what the Italian Revolution had battled against on its own peninsula. Germany seized African territories. The Bulgarians and Serbians fought the Turks. Albania, with its opening to the Adriatic, was eyed covetously by Montenegro and Bulgaria. Austria-Hungary contested territory with Serbia and annexed the Turkish provinces of Bosnia and Herzegovena in 1908, extending Austria southward along the Adriatic coast. Italy won its 1912 war with Turkey over control of Libya and access to the Mediterranean. Austria then threatened Italy with coastal bombardment and invasion if its navies did not end their actions against Turkish interests in the Adriatic. Bulgaria lost the war it had started against Serbia and Greece. Romania declared war on Bulgaria. Germany and Austria-Hungary formed Europe's most powerful military alliance. Defining themselves as "The Greater Germany, Which Knows No Frontiers," they stood together in 1914, ready to take over Europe. Italy had become a modern nation, but at a high cost. The country was too young, too small, and too poor to compete for world power. It struggled to complete its unification and solve its internal problems—healing the continuing differences among monarchists, republicans, and papists—while dealing with the poor economy, the south, the growing labor unrest, and an increasing number of warring political factions all going in different directions. The antidemocratic papists and monarchists continued to press for a more autocratic government, for dissolving parliament, for giving full control to the king or the pope, and for forging Italy into a militaristic state. Building its military and going to war would wear Italy down economically, but it feared that not doing so would leave the peninsula open to Austrian invasion. In either event, Italy's future was dark. The military route, the conservatives believed, would protect them from Austria, bolster national pride, and help the country to survive into the 20th century. It also meant great profits for Italian industrialists and the German financiers who continued their heavy investments in Italy. By the time the war erupted in 1914, Italy and Germany were so economically intertwined that Italy would have great difficulty divesting itself of German finances and joining the Allies. It was too soon to test the young country in a World War. Italy had to balance its meager resources between the needs of internal development and the need to protect itself from an increasingly hostile and unforgiving world. It competed in a rich league, beyond its means, and diverted its limited resources from civilian needs to the military. Steel, coal, and much of the food had to be imported at high cost, which meant increased taxes. It was a mixed achievement—gaining world attention and national pride but deepening poverty and internal stress. The national debt, taxes, and the military grew, while everyday life, particularly in the south, worsened. Northern cities roiled with labor protests. Socialists and anarchists gained political power and, in 1900, King Umberto I, successor to Vittorio Emanuele II, was assassinated. Millions of Southern Italians emigrated from 1880 through 1914 because the country offered them only poverty and the government spent the people's resources on armies and warships. Ironically, the great warships built in the 1890s by France, Italy, and Austria were made obsolete just 10 years later by the 20th century's rapid improvements in design.

To maintain a pose of world power, Italy would consume itself. The leaders, caught up in strident militarism, did not see the depths of the people's struggles and the strain on the country. From 1900 to 1914, as Michele Graziano attended school, labored on farms, lived in Naples, and worked in America, the leaders pauperized the country. Political decisions made in Rome were distant events for people of the south. Even the assassination of King Umberto in 1900 had little effect on Michele and the people of Maida. Everyone, however, felt the impact of migration.

The government of northerners had hijacked Italy's promise of democracy. It had squandered the country's resources, bound southerners more tightly to their poverty, and allowed them little control over their lives. Southerners long ago realized that their grandfathers' *rivoluzione* had brought few rewards. Now, they were about to learn, not only would they sacrifice their young men in wars they neither understood nor wanted, but they would be obligated to pay the high taxes for the military machine that was to kill them.

Among the revolution's unfinished political tasks was the reclaiming of disputed areas that were still controlled by Austria. The most important were the Trentino in the north, Istria, a small peninsula in the Adriatic, and the seaport city of Trieste in the northeastern corner, just beyond Venice. Known as *Italia irredenta* (unredeemed Italy),[3] these areas were considered

---

3. Some areas in the Baltic and in North and East Africa were also considered to be part of *Italia irredenta* and became important in the coming colonial and military struggles.

by the Italians to be theirs by history, ethnicity, language, and religion but had been stolen from them by Austria. *Irredentismo* became a passionately popular cause, an unfinished leftover of *il risorgimento*, a necessary final adjustment to complete the revolution and national unity. "We will not be whole until Trento, Trieste, and Istria are brought home!" the *irredentiste* shouted. Patriotic fervor deepened when Austria launched its anti-irredentism policy that was designed to "Austrianize" and "de-Italianize" those provinces. Italian schools were prohibited, use of the Italian language was attacked, and Italian newspapers were sacked. The anger of the Italian people against Austria grew even deeper.

According to Thomas Page,[4] the American ambassador to Italy (1913–1919), Austria was the "premier power" in Europe and it wanted to reclaim Italy. The Italians' 100-year *rivoluzione* had been primarily a war against Austria. Their powerful dislike of the French was mild compared with their still-growing hatred of the Austrians.

In the long buildup to *la grande guerra*, tens of thousands of Austro-Hungarian troops dug into the mountains on the Italian-Austrian border, anchoring their heavy artillery and aiming their guns down on the Italians' lush plains and cities. The military line was designed to be impregnable because of its strategic position up in the mountains and the size and power of its army and weaponry. Austria's line of steel grew year by year, blocking Italy's land routes to Northern and Eastern Europe. Austria-Hungary was preparing for its coming invasion of Italy's rich northern plains, from which it had been driven by the Italian Revolution not so long before. Austria-Hungary would also soon control the Adriatic Sea, threatening Italy's entire eastern coast. Austria's Adriatic coast, unlike Italy's, had protective islands and deep harbors to shield its navy. With its mountain fortifications in the north and its navy and protected coast on the Adriatic, Austria-Hungary's military bracketed more than half of Italy's land and sea borders, from which it aimed its growing arsenal at the peninsula. Poised for war, Austria-Hungary was the greatest threat to Italy's brief autonomy.

Austria and Germany tried to persuade the Italians to join them, or at least to remain neutral in the coming war against England and France. When it became clear that Italy would do neither, Austria released her armies down the mountains into Northern Italy and launched her navy across the Adriatic. Italy was soon in a fight for its life, and the freedom won from Austria just a generation earlier was at risk of being lost in a few months of all-out modern war.

2. The Archduke

Europe had reached a point of high tension. A single event then occurred

4. Page (1920).

in the Balkans, Eastern Europe's high-pressure area of frustrated revolution, causing Europe to explode. In June 1914, a Bosnian-Serb nationalist, Gavrilo Princip, shot and killed Archduke Franz Ferdinand, heir to the Austro-Hungarian throne, as he and his wife rode by in an open automobile. The archduke had not been a particularly important person, but the event was enough for Austria to launch the war that became the First World War, the "War to End all Wars," the "Great War," *la grande guerra.*

Austria's leaders, in their royal righteousness, conservative opposition to democracy, and delusions of invincibility, did not predict that in the first 25 days of the war, August 4 to August 29, half a million French and German soldiers would be killed. They did not know that the war would last four and a half years, kill 10 million civilians, and leave 40 million soldiers dead, wounded, missing, or imprisoned.[5] They did not know that Austria-Hungary would be destroyed and its House of Habsburg dethroned after more than 600 years of rule. Nor did they know that Europe would sink and anarchy would spawn murderous psychopaths who would take over Italy, Spain, Russia, and Germany. They did not know that, in the postwar chaos, Communism, Fascism, and Nazism would, in less than 20 years, pull the world into the next, even more massive, World War.

A few weeks after the archduke's assassination, Austria declared war on Serbia—not surprising, given Austria's long-brewing plans to annex the nation. Diplomacy was possible, but Austria wanted war, believing that it could control events. The Austrian war declaration activated complex alliances; 50 countries were at war by 1915. In 1914 Russia mobilized to protect its ally Serbia. Germany, Austria's ally, declared war on Russia. France, treaty-bound to Russia, declared war on Germany and Austria. Germany invaded Luxembourg. Britain, a treaty partner of France, was then obliged to declare war. Her colonies and dominions (Australia, Canada, India, New Zealand, and South Africa) pledged their assistance. Japan, bound by treaties with Britain, declared war on Germany. Austria-Hungary then declared war on Japan. Italy abandoned its neutrality in 1915 and declared war on Austria-Hungary and, in 1916, on its economic partner, Germany. A year later, the United States, under continued heavy losses of commercial shipping to German and Austrian submarines, entered the war against Germany.[6] Bit by bit, the world fell into the fire.

---

5. The number of troops killed, wounded, missing, or taken prisoner were as follows: Russia, 9,150,000; France, 6,150,000; Great Britain, 3,200,000; Italy, 2,197,000; Romania, 535,000; the United States, 365,000; Serbia, 331,000; other allies, 170,000. From the Central Powers: Germany, 7,142,558; Austria-Hungary, 7,020,000; Turkey, 975,000; Bulgaria, 267,000. The grand total is well over 37,000,000. Austria-Hungary lost 90 percent of the troops it had mobilized, while the United States lost 8 percent of its troops.
6. The enemies in World War I were the Western and Eastern Allies—England, France, Belgium, Luxembourg, Russia, and Serbia (1914); Italy (1915); Portugal, Albania, Montenegro, and Romania (1916); Greece and the United States (1917); and the Central Powers—Austria-Hungary, Germany, and Turkey (1914); Bulgaria (1915).

3. Maida, 1914

For Teresa and Anna Dattilo, now 13 and 16, respectively, 1914 was an emotional mix. Their father and their future husbands, Giuseppe and Michele, had returned from America, but the war had begun. The young men became soldiers, returning briefly to Maida before being shipped to the battlefront. While on leave, the two young men were drawn to the Dattilo family, where Anna and Teresa were no longer little girls with dolls. The young ladies saw with interest that the boys were now young men in uniform. Anna agreed to marry Giuseppe, but Teresa maintained that she was too young to consider marriage, preferring to remain single, at least for the time being. The families had long known that the lifelong friends would eventually be married—the two sisters to the two cousins.

Hearing about America from their father, Teresa and Anna began to view it not as a distant and strange place across the ocean, but as an extension of Italy that was only a few weeks' journey away. America, they learned, was inhabited by strangers who spoke a foreign language but, more important, by relatives and friends who welcomed new arrivals from Maida. America was becoming a familiar place for the Maidese, and many young people would emigrate to America after the Great War. But that did not appeal to Teresa. Going to America was good choice for those who were dissatisfied with Maida. But Teresa's father had returned; they now owned a nice farm; her family was intact. Teresa was satisfied, and knew she would never leave her family.

The boys, however, absorbed the adventurous idea of America. Girls, kept close to home, were not encouraged to have free-ranging thoughts of world travel. The allure of crossing the Atlantic pulled the men; the decision to go to America was a man's decision. Young men were swayed by travelers who told stories of great American cities, thick pay envelopes, and wonderfully independent lives. They knew that when the war was over they would still face the bleak economic conditions in Italy that had confronted their fathers. Going to America was their major route to success. But, for now, *la grande guerra* overshadowed all else.

4. The War

The major battlefronts[7] ranged across the globe: France, Northern Italy, Russia Turkey, Gallipoli, the Dardanelles, North Africa, and the Middle East. Naval battles were fought in the Pacific and Atlantic oceans, and the Mediterranean, Adriatic, and North seas. Most of Italy's involvement was along its own border with Austria and in the Adriatic Sea, with additional fighting in France, Africa, Greece, Turkey, and the Baltic. England, France, and the United States fought Germany primarily in France, while England,

7. The Western Front (France); Italian Front (Italy); Eastern Front (Russia); the Balkan, African, and North Sea Fronts.

France, and Italy were also combatants in ground and naval operations on the Baltic front against Austria, Bulgaria, and Turkey. Germany fought major wars on the Western and Russian fronts and smaller battles elsewhere.

The Western Front, the ground and air war across France, had a 475-mile battle line. That is what Americans know as World War I, where most American soldiers died in 1918. That was the stage for gray images of men huddled in trenches, rolling clouds of gas, the slash of bayonets, and the dead and dying hanging tangled in barbed wire or sprawled in blood-soaked mud. For the millions who fell on other fronts and drowned in the seas, the Great War meant death in Northern Italy, the Adriatic, the Dardanelles, Gallipoli, Mesopotamia, the North Sea, Palestine, Greece, Russia, and Africa; but we in the United States know little of such places and events.

Over the centuries, invaders had poured into Italy across the Alps. In 1915, the mountainous 300-mile Italian-Austrian border, from Switzerland to the Adriatic, bristled with Austrian artillery, dominating Italy's northeast and threatening her northern cities and plains. With only Switzerland between them, Germany dominated the center of Italy's northern border. The remaining northwest border with France was controlled by the German occupation. Thus, Germany and Austria-Hungary sealed off most of Italy's northern borders and land routes to Europe. At the same time, Italy's entire Adriatic coast was threatened by Austria, whose warships steamed out of hiding long enough to bombard Italy's coast and railroads and then raced back across the narrow sea into their protected harbors.

It is understandable that Italy, in spite of 30 years of economic ties with Germany, joined England and France in the war. Italy made its first military moves in mid-1915 on two fronts against her old tormenter, Austria: in the Adriatic Sea to combat Austria's navy, and in the northeast area of the Isonzo River. Hinged between the two battle zones was the port city of Trieste, for which the *irredentiste* clamored.

The young, ill-equipped Italian army was thought to be no match for the powerful, disciplined, well-equipped Austro-Hungarians and their German, Turkish, and Bulgarian allies. The Italians were in vulnerable positions down on the plains, while the Austrians were solidly entrenched up in the mountains. Italian troops would need to fight up the mountains, scaling ice-covered peaks and building bridges and cable-car machinery across the deep valleys, while the Austro-Hungarians, in their protected mountain barricades, fired down on them. Austrian victory seemed certain. However, there was an important factor: while Austria fought to expand its territory, Italy fought to save its life.

In 1915, a few months before the start of the northern ground war, the Italian navy began operations against Austria-Hungary in the Adriatic, joining the French and British warships already there. The joint navies drove the Austrian fleet into its harbors, keeping it largely contained in the Adriatic. This was an enormously important operation that prevented the Austro-Hungarian surface navy from attacking allied shipping in the Mediterranean and transporting reinforcements to the Germans in France. After the war, however, Italy's allies would dismiss her achievements in helping to contain the Austro-Hungarian navy as being of little importance compared with their own efforts on the Western Front.

The Allies could not, however, readily control the German and Austrian submarines that were based in the protected Austrian harbors and that roamed invisibly under the surface, causing massive Allied losses.

At first, the English and Americans were optimistic, even enthusiastic, about the war, believing it would be over quickly, singing, "The boys will all be home by Christmas!" Few anticipated what would happen—a long, vicious celebration of blood-letting on all sides, with brief advantage passing back and forth. Massive artillery bombardments on a scale never before seen devastated armies and cities. Trench warfare was a bloody slaughter; men advanced a few hundred yards then fell back, leaving thousands dead on each side. It was said that in the Battle of the Somme on September 15, 1916, five or six men died for each inch of land captured.

Lumbering armored behemoths called tanks,[8] a British invention, appeared on the Western Front in 1917. They were murderous against foot soldiers and horse cavalry, despite their frequent mechanical breakdowns. Of greatest impact were the new machine guns, first used in large numbers by Germany. They fired 600 rounds a minute,[9] compared with the eight to 12 rounds per minute of the best rifles. One machine gun with its four-man crew was equal to 80 riflemen and could kill a hundred men in 10 seconds.

Submarines were used extensively for the first time,[10] and, with their new torpedoes, Germany and Austria caused heavy Allied losses. For the first time, too, men fought in the air, shooting each other out of the skies,[11] machine-gunning troops on the ground, and, from huge biplane bombers and German zeppelins, raining bombs from the clouds. The Germans introduced refinements in killing—rolling clouds of poison gas that silently sickened and killed, and searing waves of "liquid fire" to burn the Allied soldiers alive.

An Italian naval innovation was the small, fast torpedo boat, hard to see because it was low in the water. Called "mosquitoes" for their quick sting, they darted in and out of heavily protected Austrian harbors, attacking and sinking anchored warships. Captain Luigi Rizzo destroyed Austria's mas-

8. In the first shipments from England, these new battle vehicles were enclosed in large containers labeled "water tanks."
9. This rate would double by the end of the war.
10. Primitive submarines had been tried out in the American Civil War half a century earlier.
11. The Wright brothers' first successful flight was in 1903, only 11 years before the war. Prior to 1914, most Europeans had never heard of airplanes or even seen one, and just five years before the war, few Europeans had flown in one.

sive battleship *Wien* in harbor and Austria's powerful new dreadnought *Szent Istvan* in an open-sea battle. The *Szent Istvan,* another dreadnought, and 10 Austrian destroyers had been en route to the Mediterranean to fight the Allies. Captain Rizzo's naval victory early in 1918 ended Austria's plans to dominate the Adriatic and Mediterranean. The mosquitoes were so successful that Italy produced 400, and other nations continued to develop and employ them in later wars.

On the Western Front, England, France, and Germany fought a long stalemated war of 15 million casualties. The battles across Northern Italy were the same: advance, retreat, slaughter, and stalemate. Gains measured in a few yards came at the cost of lives measured in thousands.

Russia's army, the world's largest in 1914, at first succeeded in going to Serbia's aid, but Russia was in turmoil. The czar dropped deeper into insanity and the "Mad Monk," Rasputin, tightened his control over the czar's wife, the government, and the military. Corruption and suppression of liberties continued to stir revolutionary fervor. Incompetent leadership, insufficient materials, and limited transportation plagued the military. Russia suffered major losses to Germany in 1915, achieved brief victories in mid-1916, and then saw a series of severe defeats. That year, Russian aristocrats murdered Rasputin, and the country, still fighting Germany and Austria, was in tatters. Revolutionary agitation, growing for years, increased and riots again erupted. Czar Nicholas II—soon to be murdered with his family—abdicated, ending the House of Romanov and the czarist Russian Empire. The provisional government soon fell in the Bolshevik revolution. By the end of 1917, Russia, deep into revolution and chaos, was defeated in the field and forced into a humiliating and costly surrender to Germany.

5. Isonzo and Caporetto

In 1915, mindful of his country's vulnerable strategic position and paucity of equipment, the Italian chief of staff, Luigi Cadorna, decided on a quick, massive offensive along the 60-mile Isonzo River. Flanked by mountains, the Isonzo lay in a valley just inside Austria. The coastal plain at the southern end of the Isonzo would give the best chance of advancing around the Austrians' superior positions in the mountains and of driving through to Trieste. Cadorna readied his troops to fight up the mountains against Austria's protected positions.

Moving quickly, he launched the first of 12 battles of the Isonzo,[12] which took place from mid-1915 to late 1918. Italian troops drove back the astonished Austrians with brilliant and surprising victories—the Italian David besting the Austrian Goliath. The exultant Italians began to hope they would quickly regain Trentino, Venice, and Trieste, control the Adri-

12. Some of the battles merged into one another and historians do not agree on the number of battles but put them at 10 to 15.

atic, and see the end of a brief war. But that was not to be.

By the autumn of 1915, the Italian advance was stopped at the foot of Austria's mountain fortifications. Cadorna threw waves of exhausted and ill-equipped men into a dreadful carnage, but, protected by the mountains, the Austrians held the line. From both sides, trapped in a hellish stalemate, blood flowed down the mountain.

In mid-1916, the war looked bleak for the Allies. The Italian advance had been stopped. Italy was drained, lacking coal, steel, fuel, and grain. Unable to resupply its armies, Italy appealed to its allies for munitions and raw materials, but none were sent. The Western Front was also in a bloody stalemate. England and France were running out of resources. The Russian army was in tatters, retreating from the Germans and Austrians.[13] Turkey and Bulgaria increased their military support for Austria. The West's allies, Albania, Lithuania, Montenegro, and Serbia, had been defeated.

In 1915, England's First Lord of the Admiralty, Winston Churchill, launched the English navy in a preemptive attack on the Turkish-held Dardanelle Straits,[14] a strategically important passageway in Mesopotamia for the shipping of arms from the Mediterranean to Russia. Churchill's plan was to open this Eastern Front by attacking the Ottoman Empire, which had joined the Central Powers in late 1914. A quick victory to capture the Dardanelles and Istanbul would weaken Germany. However, the Turks' shoreline batteries, floating mines, and torpedoes roundly defeated the English. Pushed by Churchill, England and her allies (Australia, New Zealand, and the French colonies) then launched a series of invasions on the Gallipoli peninsula to seize the area adjoining the Dardanelles. Again defeated by the Turks and sustaining 285,000 casualties, the English surrendered in January 1916 after a year of brutal sea and land battles. The humiliating defeats nearly ended Churchill's career and remained expensive lessons for England 25 years later, in World War II.[15]

German and Austrian submarines, pursuing a "policy of frightfulness," continued to sink Allied passenger, hospital, and war ships. In May, the great naval battle of Jutland in the North Sea off the Danish coast was a disaster for the Allies. England lost 14 major ships and 7,000 men, while Germany lost nine ships and 2,500 men. Germany celebrated its naval victory while its giant zeppelins roamed the skies, bombing Allied cities and armies.[16]

Having smashed Serbia and Romania, Germany's General Ludendorff

13. The Russians would recover later and fight tenaciously with some success. But by 1917, they would collapse in political disorganization and give up their fight against Germany and Austria.

14. The Dardanelles: a strategically important passage connecting Turkey with the Aegean and, ultimately, the Mediterranean Sea.

15. See Hart and Steel (2002) and Travers (2001).

16. Germany's fleet was considerably smaller than England's. At first seen as a great German victory, this battle was ultimately understood to have been the effective end of the German navy, because its losses, relative to its fleet size, were actually crippling.

planned a similar assault to annihilate Italy, even though the two countries were not then officially at war. In the 1915–1916 winter and spring, while the Italian advance was stalled, the Austrians and Germans prepared a major "punitive expedition"[17] to bring the Italians to total defeat. The assault on Italy opened along the front in May 1916 with an immense hail of artillery by German and Austrian heavy guns. Eighteen divisions (400,000 troops) poured down onto the Italian plains following the path of their continuous artillery bombardment. This tactic was called a "creeping barrage," a heavy hail of shells that kept moving toward the enemy just ahead of one's own advancing troops. The Austrians swept away the Italian defenders and advanced west and south, destroying farms and villages. Panicked refugees, trying to save their children and livestock, were forced into the cauldron of tragedy, terror, and confusion.

General Cadorna pulled the center of his line back from the advancing Austrians, fighting at every step but losing an immense number of men and almost all the territory they had won the previous year. Austrian troops advanced down the mountains into the northern plains and were ready for a southward turn to invade all of Italy. They saw victory near and anticipated that Venice, Turin, Florence, Pisa, Rome, and Naples would fall, one by one, as they advanced down the peninsula.

Italy's defeat would leave France unprotected from Austrian invasion. By taking Northern Italy, Austria would gain control of both shores of the North Adriatic, the northern Italian ports facing France, the northern Tyrrhenian and the Ligurian seas, and Italy's entire northern border. Austria could then ship troops and supplies to France by sea and land. More than half a million Austrian, Hungarian, Turkish, and Bulgarian troops would march across the French-Italian border to join the German armies on the Western Front.[18] The Allies would be overwhelmed and would quickly lose the war. Italy's defeat would be disastrous for the Allies.

The Italian armies had been routed, and the Austrians threatened a full invasion of Italy. Young men were being thrown into the fire by the tens of thousands, and the people's grief and deprivations were taking their toll. Austria—the hated "Hun"—was again on their doorstep, ready to reclaim the peninsula.

Keeping his retreat under control, Cadorna made plans to mobilize another army of 400,000 men. In an extraordinary display of speed and efficiency—traits not often associated with Italian bureaucracy—this massive army was assembled, outfitted, transported, and in fighting position within just a few weeks.

17. General Conrad von Hoetzendorf, Austria's chief of staff for this operation, was known to harbor a seething hatred of Italians, because he believed they posed the greatest threat to Austria and because of their "treachery" in having refused to join Austria. This massive offensive was to be Italy's punishment.
18. Those troops would be redeployed from the Central Powers' victorious Russian and Italian campaigns.

In early August 1916, Cadorna was ready. His new troops were in position, waiting, while he stabilized the center of his army. Drawing a line beyond which he would not retreat, Cadorna began his counterattack, the sixth battle of the Isonzo. Again the Austrians were astonished at the Italians' ferocity, and they responded with their own intense fighting. The casualties on both sides were horrific. The Italians' center held no matter what the Austrians threw at them. Austrian casualties piled higher; Cadorna sensed a weakening in their lines. Maintaining his attack on the center of the line, he ordered simultaneous attacks on Austria's right and left flanks by the newly mobilized army, which he had held back for this maneuver. This three-sided assault collapsed the Austrians' offensive, and they were driven back eastward, once again retreating into the mountains beyond the Isonzo River.

Austria's imminent invasion of Italy and potential attack on France had been held off. Cadorna, Italy's new hero, had saved Italy, France, and the war for the Allies.

The intense fighting continued through the ninth battle of the Isonzo. The November snows settled in, the fighting slowed to deadly stalemate, and hospitals filled with the wounded and dying. Trains of cattle cars jammed with frightened 17-year-olds rushed to the front. The horror of unimaginable carnage seeped back into Italy as generals on both sides continued throwing their troops into the great death machine that roared at the base of the mountains and boys were ground up by the hundreds of thousands. A few blood-saturated meters would be gained one day and lost the next.

Forlorn soldiers on both sides, fatigued beyond endurance, became so thoroughly demoralized that desertions nearly equaled the number of deaths. The generals—who were safely far from the lines of combat—were so enraged that they began to publicly execute their own soldiers. Many were but frightened adolescents.[19] Cadorna raised even that level of horror by ordering the execution soldiers from his own troops who were *randomly selected,* as examples, to control the "cowards."

People knew little of those events and were grateful to Cadorna and his heroic soldiers who had saved the country. But the war continued, and questions were raised: had the generals planned better, might the retreat and massive sacrifice of soldiers have been prevented? Public anger grew with the mounting deaths and shortages. Long bread lines snaked around corners, only to end up at empty bakeries. "When will the killing and our starvation end?" the people asked. "What is happening at the front? When will this war be finished and our boys returned to us?"

But Cadorna, an old-line authoritarian conservative, believed that civilians—including government officials—had no right to question his military

19. The war was so brutally demoralizing that desertions were high on both sides. More than 600 executions of deserters occurred across all armies except that of the United States, which refused to execute its own soldiers for desertion.

decisions, and he refused to give information. He would not tell them of the terrible and mounting casualties, the growing desertions, or the executions of his own men, the people's sons, fathers, and husbands. Nor would he disclose that his armies, after the ferocity of so much fighting, were locked in a bloody stalemate. Cadorna reportedly issued false reports claiming victories and advances that never happened. He jailed or dismissed hundreds of officers who criticized him and, when his strategies failed, blamed the troops.[20] The people began learning the truth through rumors and the horrific accounts of the returning wounded and dying. People had been told of Italy's victory but now began to learn of the costs. Count Luigi Cadorna, northern aristocrat, firm monarchist, and hero of the war, was beginning to be doubted.

Following the successes of Italy's 1916 counteroffensive, 1917 opened to stalemate on the Isonzo. Urged by her allies, Italy had finally declared war on Germany. A year later (April 1917), the United States, with growing losses to German submarines,[21] also declared war. It would be another year before significant numbers of American troops arrived at the Western Front, but the Allies were encouraged by that prospect.

In 1917, despite Russia's defeat, the Western Front began to improve for the Allies, although the fighting remained fierce and costly. In the east, England made progress, taking Baghdad and Jerusalem. Germany hinted at peace talks, but the Allies wanted a decisive victory rather than a halt to hostilities that would leave the Central Powers in control of too much territory. The war raged on.

In the spring of 1917, fighting resumed on the Isonzo. Despite the victories of the previous year, Italy was growing weaker because of the bleeding away of troops and the worsening shortages of steel, food, ammunition, and fuel. How could the country sustain its drive without the resources to resupply the army? Again, Cadorna appealed to his allies for munitions, supplies, and men. David Lloyd George, England's new prime minister, was in favor, arguing that the war could not be won without resources being shifted from the Western Front to the Italian front. Douglas Haig, the British field marshal, was opposed. He wanted, instead, to press the offensive on the Western Front, asserting that the best strategy was to focus on France and let the Italians protect the Allies' east flank by continuing to hold off the Austrians as long as possible.[22]

20. Smith (1989).
21. There were many reasons for the United States' entry into the war, the German submarine attacks being one. Another was Germany's effrontery in urging Mexico to declare war on the United States, with the promise to return the American Southwest to Mexico after Germany's victory. The United States was already in armed conflict against the Mexican revolutionary who called himself Pancho Villa, and the German attempt to escalate that conflict to a full war was not appreciated.
22. One of the Allies' suspicions was that supplies shipped into Italy might fall into the black market to be shipped across the Swiss border, into Germany. There was little truth in this idea.

Italy would not receive aid from her allies, but Austria was about to receive aid from Germany. With the defeat of Russia in 1917, German troops were freed up and moved to the Italian front. Ten German divisions would soon join the battle against the Italians, who were about to face, alone, the reinforced armies of Austria, Hungary, Germany, Turkey, Bulgaria, and Yugoslavia.

Cadorna, urged by his allies, who wanted to relieve the pressure on France, launched two more offensives (June and August 1917), the 10th and 11th battles of the Isonzo. Both were costly for the two sides, but included victories by Commander Luigi Capello, whose army on the northern end of the front had driven the Austrians back more than 10 kilometers. Capello, unlike Cadorna, sought public attention, inviting reporters and politicians to tour the front. Appreciative reporters wrote glowing accounts, hailing Capello and inflating the importance of his victories.

The Austrians were weakening, and Cadorna's advancing armies were on the verge of a breakthrough, possibly a final victory. He wanted to launch a major offensive but had two concerns: first, his troops were exhausted, nearly out of munitions and supplies, and the Allies continued to ignore his requests for aid; second, Germany, seeing Austria's imminent defeat, might send reinforcements to the Italian front. Accordingly, Cadorna halted his attacks and ordered his armies to reorganize into defensive positions along the front. If Austria attacked, even with German reinforcements, he reasoned, his defense would hold, and later he would resume the offense.

Germany moved 10 divisions to the Italian front[23] just as Cadorna had foreseen. In October 1917, the Central Powers' combined armies launched a powerful counterattack on a weak portion of the Italian line near the town of Caporetto, where Capello was headquartered.

Had they attacked anywhere else, the disaster for the Italians would not have occurred, because Cadorna was ready with his defensive positions. Capello, however, had ignored Cadorna's order to prepare a defensive line. Instead, not knowing of the imminent German-Austrian counterattack, he decided to proceed with his own attack, hoping to continue his recent victories. Thus, when the German-Austrian attack began near Caporetto, Capello's forces were not there; they were far away, deployed to launch their own offensive.

Starting with heavy artillery and poison gas, the combined German and Austro-Hungarian forces, bolstered by reinforcements from Turkey, Bulgaria, and Yugoslavia, drove the Italian line nearly 25 kilometers in only one day. The Battle of Caporetto caused massive Italian losses—an estimated 30,000 dead or wounded, 270,000 captured, and nearly a third of their artillery lost. The Italians fought desperate rear-guard actions to

---

23. An army division is a major unit that contains all the troops, tactical and administrative groups, weapons, and supplies necessary for it to function as a self-contained unit capable of independent action.

slow the enemy and allow most of their own troops and thousands of fleeing civilians to retreat to safety. Seventeen days later, the retreating troops
reached the Piave River and regrouped to stand against the advancing enemy coalition.

The battle of Caporetto—the 12th battle of the Isonzo—was a major
victory for Germany and Austria-Hungary and a colossal defeat for Italy, a
catastrophic loss of men, equipment, territory, and prestige. Those three
weeks of retreat were Italy's lowest point in the war. Shock, anger, and
intensified fears of an Austrian-German invasion of Italy raced among the
people, who began to realize what had been lost—nearly all of the territory
gained in the previous two and a half years, gains that had cost the lives of
more than a quarter of a million soldiers.

Several northern provinces were again under Austrian control and Venice was imperiled, only a few kilometers from the advancing enemy. Austria
was poised to overrun the northern cities, and once again all Italy might
be just months away from falling under Austrian rule, just as it had been
before the revolution.

Public alarm, humiliation, and outrage forced the prime minister to re-
sign and a new government to form. General Cadorna, so recently a hero,
was relieved of command and replaced by General Armando Diaz. General
Capello was disgraced but unaccountably was retained in the military.

The German-Austrian victory threatened not only Italy, but also the outcome of the entire war. If the enemy continued to advance across Northern
Italy, the way would be open for Austria-Hungary to march into France,
strengthen the German forces, and defeat the Allies. The Allies, distant
onlookers of the whole Caporetto debacle, were scornfully critical of the
Italians' retreat, apparently forgetting their own many retreats before the
Germans and the Turks. Such blatant insubordination as Capello's action
and the incompetence of Cadorna could never occur in properly disciplined armies such as their own, they thought. The scorn was sharp, and
Italy was humiliated and devalued in the eyes of the Allies.

The French and English were scornful, but were so alarmed at the defeat of their main defense against Austrian invasions into France that they
finally pledged to the new prime minister, Vittorio Orlando, to send aid
to Italy.

The 19th-century revolution, long thought to be over, was not. In 1917,
Italy still fought its old oppressor, Austria. Its response to the Caporetto
disaster would be enormously important, either protecting its freedom or
dragging it back under Austrian control.

With ammunition and supplies promised by the Allies but not yet delivered, General Diaz set out to raise his troops' morale and organize them
into strong defensive positions along the Piave. In November the Austrians
launched another attack, aiming for a final, crippling defeat, but as the
winter of 1917 drew around them, Diaz's armies held the line. Despite the

ferocity of the fighting and hundreds of thousands of casualties, another winter found the stalemated armies in almost the same positions they had held a year and a half earlier. There was no victor, no vanquished, no territory seized by one or the other. However, the invasion had again been stopped, and the Italians had shown they were equal to the combined German-Austrian-Hungarian armies.

As 1918 opened, the armies continued to hold at the Piave River but conditions in Italy had worsened. Italy was nearly out of war material, starvation plagued many areas, the casualties continued, and the people's morale eroded. German and Austrian submarines intensified their blockade of the peninsula, sinking so many relief ships that even more starvation was feared. To further erode civilian morale, Austrian aircraft began bombing the northern cities of Verona, Padua, and Venice. Thousands of desperate refugees fleeing the Austrians poured from the north into the already overburdened central Italian cities.

In the spring of 1918, having withdrawn their victorious troops from defeated Russia and from the Italian front after the Battle of Caporetto, Germany launched another major offensive in France with five successive assaults, sending French and British troops into massive retreat. It seemed almost a replay of the Caporetto disaster; this time it was British and French troops running in defeat from the Germans. Italy continued to hold at the Piave River and even sent two divisions of reinforcements to fight in France, plus 50,000 labor troops.

Coordinating with the German drive in France, Austria-Hungary prepared another major offensive against Italy. Its intent was to attack with massive force, finally defeat Italy, and march into France to aid the Germans. For three years the Italians had kept Austria away from France and it was time, Austria decided, to defeat them. The Austro-Hungarians attacked in June 1918, and the Battle of the Piave River began.

6. The Battle of the Piave River

In 1918 supplies finally began reaching Italy from the Allies. When the Austrians attacked, they were met by a partially resupplied Italian army and troops with renewed morale. In eight days of fighting, Diaz's armies drove back the 70 enemy divisions, inflicting 200,000 casualties and sustaining 90,000 losses. This crucial Italian victory at the Battle of the Piave River was a complete reversal of the Caporetto disaster. Decisively defeated and demoralized, the beaten Austrians retreated across the Piave.

Although defeated at the Piave, Austria still occupied territory 100 kilometers inside Italy. Had the Allies provided aid earlier, General Diaz believed, Italy could have continued the momentum from the Piave victory and defeated Austria. With her major ally defeated, he said, Germany would have come to terms and the war could have been over before the end of that summer. However, the Italians did not have the depth of troops needed for the continued advance, which would have required spreading the army all along the river. They had to stop after driving the Austrians across the Piave. This pause gave the Austrians time to recover and reorganize for the next battle.

Diaz's assessment was consistent with that of the Italian government throughout the war—the way to victory would be best pursued, they believed, by focusing first on the defeat of Austria to the east, rather than the defeat of Germany in the west. The Allies could have defeated Austria early in the war by aiding Italy to Austria's west and Russia to her east. As it was, Italy, virtually alone, especially after Russia's total defeat, had held off the Austrians for three years. With a focused Allied effort, Austria could have been defeated rather than stalemated; Turkey and Bulgaria would have surrendered, and "the whole Balkan peninsula would fall away from Germany."[24] Germany, with its entire eastern flank crumbled, would be left open to attack from all sides by land and from the north and west by sea, and would quickly give up. The Allies, however, had rejected that argument and until the Caporetto disaster had continued to ignore Italy's efforts in the north and her repeated requests for supplies.

In 1918 the war turned in the Allies' favor. In June, Italy decisively defeated the Austro-Hungarian armies at the Battle of the Piave. That stopped Austria's advance and kept it from France. In July, Allied armies began to halt the German offensive on the Western Front. By September, the Germans were retreating in France, although the fighting continued at a ferocious level. By October, the Turks had been defeated in Palestine, Beirut was taken, and Constantinople was threatened by the Allies. By the end of the month, Turkey called for an armistice, gave up control of the Dardanelles, surrendered her warships, and returned all prisoners. In early October, Germany's call for a cease-fire was rejected by the advancing Allies because Germany still occupied some parts of France. That month, too, Bulgaria surrendered to the Allies.

Austria still held territory in Italy, an advantage in peace talks. It was important, then, for Italy to follow up its June victory at the Piave and drive out the Austro-Hungarians before the war ended in order to establish Italian control and claims over northeastern Italy (Trieste and Istria). In the last weeks of the war, Italy and Austria would fight their final battles to establish their bargaining positions in future armistice negotiations.

General Diaz drew up a plan of defense to be followed by his simultaneous attacks along the Piave and the mountain borders, a 60-kilometer front. The Allies had finally sent three British and two French divisions, but only one U.S. regiment,[25] to augment the 51 Italian divisions. Nevertheless,

---

24. Page (1920).
25. After Caporetto, the United States had promised a division but sent only a regiment. The Americans' arrival was a great morale booster but contributed little to the actual fighting in the final battle.

Italy was still at a disadvantage compared with Austria's mountain fortifications, troop strength, and munitions.

Austria had the positional advantage, 64 divisions to Italy's combined 56, and superiority in armament. However, her troops were disheartened after their June defeat at the Piave. At the same time, conditions were deteriorating in Vienna and Budapest, where protests were growing against the government's continuation of the war.

The Italian soldiers, with their new general staff, a recent influx of supplies, and the psychologically important presence of some Allied forces, particularly the token American contribution, were more optimistic, anticipating the hated Austrians' final defeat. Most important, they were energized by their recent victories on the Piave and were eager to defeat their old enemy and finish the war in a strong position.

Another issue burned in the Italians' determination to win the final battles. Italy had felt a growing isolation, being ignored by the Allies and seeing their stand against Austria-Hungary devalued. England supported France with massive resources, as did the United States, particularly in the final year of the war. In contrast, Italy's repeated requests for aid had been denied so consistently and for so long that the Italians began to believe it reflected an anti-Italian policy rather than limited resources.

Hard pressed for three years by the Central Powers' superior military, mourning so many young soldiers, and suffering the civilian privations of a destitute economy, Italy became suspicious of her allies, France in particular. Earlier, the British High Command had barred aid to Italy, but now it was Ferdinand Foch, grand marshal of France and Allied supreme commander, who determined that resources would remain in France while Italy fought on, virtually alone.

The massive aid that poured into France from England and the United States bolstered the military and the French economy. But Italy had no great infusion of English pounds and U.S. dollars, and her economy continued to deteriorate under the assaults of war. When in 1918 Italy was pressured to place all her troops under the single Allied command of Ferdinand Foch, the Italians refused. They were by then highly suspicious of Foch and the French, believing that if he were allowed command of Italian troops, he would withdraw most of them from the Italian front and send them to help save France, leaving Italy defenseless against Austria-Hungary. Italy's refusal, justified or not, was deplored by her allies as a "lack of cooperation," and that would be brought up again in the postwar negotiations.

Events moved rapidly in the final three months of 1918. Allied troops pursued the retreating Germans across France in furious fighting, leaving terrible casualties on all sides. Diaz launched his coordinated offensive in October, in the Battle of Vittorio Veneto, the final battle of Italy's war. The start of the offensive was set for October 16, but severe flooding of the

Piave delayed it until the next opportune date, October 24, the anniversary of the Italians' terrible defeat at Caporetto. It had not been planned that way, but the coincidence was not lost on the troops and they were determined to avenge that national humiliation.

Diaz coordinated his attacks at several points along the river. Bridges were constructed, washed away by violent floods, blown up by Austrian artillery, and rebuilt, and the river was crossed. From October 24 to November 4, Diaz's troops again pushed back the Austro-Hungarian armies, fighting at the rivers, through the mountain passes, and on the plains. By November 1, Diaz had driven the enemy to the Austrian border, inflicting severe casualties and capturing more than 300,000 Austrian prisoners and nearly all of her heavy artillery. Ambassador Page wrote, "The unbroken, murderous battle . . . raged for days along the entire northern and northeastern border of Italy."[26]

By November 3, under continued hammering by the Italian troops, the Austrians were in full retreat, their discipline in complete dissolution. Some of Diaz's army units fought their way through the Trentino to Venice and took back the city. There, an invasion force was assembled to attack the Istrian coast and take Trieste from the east. Venice, along with Trento, Istria, Trieste—*Italia irredente*—was redeemed, and Italy finally had the unity it had sought during the revolution.

While the ground war raced on toward Austria's final defeat, Austria's navy was also under attack. It had been in June 1918, about the time of the Italian victory on the Piave River, that Captain Rizzo steered his mosquito boats into battle and, evading the 10 protective destroyers, sunk the new Austrian dreadnought *Szent Istvan*. At the time that the Battle of Vittorio Venetto was raging, the Austrian flagship, *Viribus Unitas*, was destroyed by Italian torpedoes and mines. Those victories ended the Austrian navy's plans of fighting in the Mediterranean and nullified their fleet in the Adriatric.

By November 3, the Italian forces had destroyed Austria's military, and a flag of truce was sent to General Diaz. However, proper protocol had to be observed. Because the flag was borne by a low-ranking officer, Diaz refused it. Soon, an appropriately high-ranking officer returned, bearing the flag of Austria's surrender to Italy. The Italian-Austrian armistice began at 3:00 p.m. on November 4, 1918.

In the final battles there were no humiliations for Italy—only bravery, determination, and victory. Against all odds, the Italians had thoroughly defeated their old tormenter and enemy. Mighty Austria, the last great monarchy on the Western European mainland, had been humbled, reduced to a minor state, its military destroyed, its world influence crumbled. Austria would never again menace the world as it had for so many centuries,

26. Page (1920).

nor again threaten Italy. The Italians could now look to their northeastern border and see grand mountains and access to Europe rather than a menacing, impenetrable Austrian military line.

Italy had won its war and redeemed itself. At that moment of victory Italy stood high, the people proud. They were right to savor the moment, for it was not to last.

German troops continued to retreat on the Western Front. On the day that Austria surrendered to Italy, the German navy mutinied, refusing orders to go to sea. The mutiny spread rapidly, the navy collapsed, and the naval high commander, Prince Henry, ran for his life. The mutineers poured out of their docked ships, commandeered trains, and rushed to Berlin, where they joined Russian-inspired Bolshevists and other radicals and revolutionaries to attack the government. Hamburg, Frankfort, Leipzig, Cologne, and Essen all exploded in mutiny and revolution as the Allied armies pressed toward the Rhine.

Germany was alone; Austria-Hungary, Bulgaria, and Turkey had been defeated. Kaiser Wilhelm II, who had made military might, bravery, and manly honor the center of his rule over Germany, ran off to hide somewhere in Holland, followed by the crown prince.

Five days after Austria's surrender, Germany signed the armistice. Then, at the 11th hour, on the 11th day of the 11th month, The Great War was officially over.

"La grande guerra è finita!"

Chapter 11
Views of Maida: Teresa and Michele (1919–1927)

1. Emilio's Gift

General Cadorna had thrown his armies against the Austrians in suicidal campaigns. In the end, Italy won and Austria was decisively defeated, but it was a costly victory—300,000 Italian soldiers were killed on the Northern Front alone, nearly half of Italy's losses for the entire war.[1] The government fell, distress and chaos grew, and within three years the country would turn to a fascist dictator.[2] Adding to the postwar misfortunes, Italy suffered its share of the 40 million deaths in the world's influenza epidemic, in 1918–1919.[3]

Priests had celebrated masses for soldiers, those who were dead and those not yet dead. Eighty years later, Teresa would recall how she "ran home and cried" in distress after hearing a neighbor lament, sobbing and holding a tear-sodden official letter up to heaven so God might read it, "*Mai più, mai più* (never again, never again)! Never again will I see my Gennarino. *Gennarino, figlio mio, dove sei, ora?* (Gennarino, my son, where are you now?)"

Hundreds of thousands of men and boys from the southern provinces had been thrown into the flames at the base of the mountains. Many northerners, it was rumored, because of family influence, had been exempted from service or, with their better literacy, assigned to safe desk duties far behind the killing zones. Soldiers hated the war, and southerners grew also to despise the commanders, the government, and the northerners. They would fight passionately to protect their families, but General Cadorna's campaigns brutalized even his own men. Soldiers, raised in the disillusionment of *la rivoluzione mancata*, grew more cynical and felt little allegiance to the northern-dominated government that continued to betray them.

In 1918, the war ended. Spared direct destruction in the war, the south had lost its young men, crops, and livestock. Heavy consumption taxes were levied on basic items like flour, salt, and, in some places, water, but

---

1. In the war, 689,000 Italian soldiers were killed and 959,000 injured, totaling more than 1.6 million losses, plus those missing or taken prisoner.
2. Benito Mussolini, the Fascist dictator from 1922 to 1943.
3. Taubenberger, Reid, and Fanning (2005).

not on income or property. Soldiers guarded town pumps to collect water taxes! While the poor paid the bulk of the taxes and continued to spiral downward, rich, propertied families paid relatively little tax and maintained their comfortable lives. It was a blatant system designed to keep the burden on the poor in order to maintain comfort for those who made the rules.

More than 100 years, *cent anni*, of revolution and war had left them deep in poverty. A sense of oppression and betrayal wormed its way among the people. In the northern cities, unemployed, frustrated men became socialists and anarchists, demanding an end to the monarchy. The old stone barn once again heard angry men saying much the same things that their fathers and grandfathers had said so long ago.

"The war is over, and we won the honor of letting Rome take away our boys to be killed. And now they grant us the honor of paying the bill."

Although victorious, Italy did not fare well after the war. Despite her heavy casualties, her victory in the north that helped save France, and her battles that neutralized Austria's navy, Italy was not thought by the Allies to have been an important force in the winning of the war. The Allies could not forget Caporetto, although England's disasters at the hands of the Turks and its defeat in the North Sea battle and the Allies' retreat before the German counteroffensive late in the war were viewed as normal and heroic tides of war.

Despite its fierce sadness in presaging the war, 1914 had brought some happiness to Teresa and Anna—their father had returned from America, making the family complete. Through the war years, the Dattilos rented a home in town and walked up the hill to work their farm. They were more fortunate than most, as the farm provided food and income.

For five years the war had defined Michele's and Giuseppe's lives. In 1919, Michele returned with corporal's stripes, three medals, and, coursing silently through his bloodstream, a million malaria spirochetes that were to savage him later in life. He was thankful to have returned at all and to be about to marry Teresa Dattilo. A year earlier, Giuseppe, carrying his own war decoration—a disfigured jaw smashed by an Austrian bullet—had married Anna, and they were already planning to go to America.

In 1904, while three-year-old Teresa had been playing with her dolls, 12-year-old Michele had already been a full-time child laborer for six years. When Michele became a soldier, Teresa turned 13. Now Teresa was a young lady of 18 and Michele was 27, respectable ages for marriage. "How nice how that works," Michele thought. "With no change in the number of years between us, we have caught up with each other." Their age disparity was resolved.

Their wedding in 1919 was a happy event, set against the gloom of the little town's poverty and its mourning for lost sons. It was a typical wedding—a procession to the church, tears and kisses, an enthusiastic little orchestra, family, friends, neighbors, singing, dancing, and feasting.

The photographer set up his big wooden camera and stooped under the black hood, and the couple posed for their wedding portrait. Had that photograph survived, we could see them now, standing too seriously for our modern taste, as was the custom in such formal pictures. Bride and groom were dressed beautifully, as poverty was suspended for that moment, a wonderful act of magic that even poor families could conjure up. The dressmaker, respectfully called "*la maestra*," "*la padrona*," or "*la donna*," had come to the Dattilos' house weeks before with the fabric, and had measured, laid out patterns, and cut the cloth. Teresa's mother, sisters, and aunts, as was the practice at the time, did the meticulous sewing, as instructed by *la maestra*, who returned later to carry out the final fitting.

Returning soldiers were told they would find their families changed by the war and their lives more strained than ever. However, their problem was not that things had changed, but that they had not. *Il re di povertà* (the king of poverty) continued his reign even more autocratically. The cousins, Michele and Giuseppe, had hoped that the war might shake loose better times, but it had not. The treasury was depleted, the economy was ruined, and the south was still deep in *la povertà*. They found the same poverty, taxes, and fatiguing farm work that allowed their families little more than subsistence.

On their return they confronted the absence of young relatives and friends, soldiers who would never come back. Even their names would someday fade from the monument in the piazza. Some of the old folks had died. Emilio, Michele's mentor in his farm days, had died in his 93rd year. Michele visited Emilio's widow, *una signora* as dignified as Emilio had been. They talked of Emilio. He had died peacefully, she said. *U vecchiaia* (old age) had slowly crept up the hill, hidden in the wind, and carried his soul over the mountains. Opening a small, carved wooden box, she drew out a slim leather case and handed it to Michele. It was old, worn, and well oiled.

"He said you must have this," she told Michele, with a sweet-sad smile. "That I must be sure to give it to you, and to no one else, when you come home from the war."

Michele knew it was Emilio's knife, the one his old teacher had used for so many years to cut twine and tie grapevines.[4] He held the soft leather and thought of the dignified man who had helped him gain so much value from his years of child labor.

Walking home from his visit, Michele met three boys, six or seven years old, ragged, dirty, and playing at war. They were shooting invisible guns at an invisible enemy, making explosive sounds and throwing clumps of dry dirt at a stone wall to create satisfying clouds of dust, like exploding artillery shells.

4. I still have that small knife, given to me by my father, Michele. One blade had long ago broken off and the other is now but a thin, curved sliver, worn down by years of work. At this writing (2007), Emilio's knife must be over 120 years old.

"Over there!" they shouted, turning their make-believe guns on Michele. "Get him. It's a sneak attack."

"Whoa," Michele pleaded, raising his hands in surrender. "Don't shoot. I'm on your side."

"No, you're not!" they said. "You're a Hun! We gonna shoot you!"

"But I don't see any Huns," Michele told them, looking around. "Where are the Huns?"

"Ha!" a grimy boy said, apparently the sergeant of the platoon. "You don't see 'em 'cause we already beat 'em, and they run off, over the hills, back to Austria where they belong."

"Yes!" another urchin added, strutting around, his skinny little chest puffed up. "And they'll never come back! We really beat the lousy Huns. *I mascalzoni!* (The bastards)!"

"Belligerent little monkeys," Michele thought, suddenly irritated with these children, this example of the next generation, urchins who had learned nothing from Italy's terrible wartime experiences. "They play at war; they think it's noble. I hope they never need to for real."

"Shouldn't you be in school?" he said, in a suddenly stern voice that surprised him and startled the boys. "What are you doing out here, anyway?"

The boys heard the irritation and threat in his voice. Knowing that they were supposed to be in school, they looked at each other, alarmed. "Let's go, men!" their leader commanded. "Over there! Follow me!" They ran up the hill, turning once from a safe distance to point their fingers and shoot "the Hun" before moving on to their next battle.

Michele shook his head, feeling bad for his harshness toward the boys. What did they know, after all? They were just children.

"At their age," he thought, "I was already working on the farm. I wonder how they would like that, these ragged children of today. Now the government says they must be in school for their benefit. And what are they doing? Wallowing in the dirt, hiding from *il maestro professore*, killing their own futures, playing at things that are best forgotten. If this generation doesn't learn from what we've been through, then no one will." It was a despairing thought.

2. Our Own School

Michele had completed only three years of school but recognized the value of education, seeing the weakness of its lack in himself, his town, and even in the next generation, as suggested by those boys. Shortly after his marriage in 1919, he brought home an old schoolbook. "Look," he told Teresa, handing it to her, "if we're going to live in America, you have to learn to read and write." With his third-grade education from 20 years earlier, Michele offered to be Teresa's personal *professore*. She had already taught herself to read a little, following her disappointment years before at not having been allowed to attend school because girls of her station did not do that.

"*Bene, Teresa, bene,*" her mother encouraged her. "We didn't send you to school, but now you have your own special teacher."

Teresa was eager to learn. "But," she thought, "is it too late? The children in school, they can read and write better than me. Am I too old, now, 19? A grown woman, already married?"

"*Bravo, Michele!*" her father said, clapping his new son-in-law on the shoulder. He told his daughter, "*Teresa, non e mai troppo tardi* (it is never too late)!"

Nonno Peppe, who was by then 87 and had been in favor of Teresa's education, also encouraged her. "*Finalmente* (finally)!" he said. "You should learn, like Michele says, if you're going to America. There, everybody reads and writes. Then you can write letters, so we'll know you and Michele and your children are healthy and happy."

"*Non e' mai troppo tardi!*" were welcome words for Teresa; in the past, they had been reserved for men, never for girls and women. Teresa was elated, grateful to Michele for his modern ideas and her family for their support. Times had changed, and this was not like the discouraging discussions years earlier with her mother and *Nonna* Anna, who had died the previous year, about what is proper for girls. This was 1919, the modern world!

"We'll have our own school," Teresa announced happily, and urged her sisters, Anna, Caterina, and Angela, to join her. "Come, we'll move the bench over here." Anna, the oldest, cooperated, but with little enthusiasm, having other things to think about—her husband, Giuseppe, and the new life that was growing inside her. Three-year-old Francesca also wanted to be in school. She climbed onto the bench and clapped her hands enthusiastically, but soon fell asleep in Caterina's lap. "I'll learn, too," added *Nonno* Peppe, having heard the words "*non e mai troppo tardi.*" He had often wished he could read. Now, he would learn. The girls and the grandfather sat crowded on the bench, the four older sisters tussling in good humor over their single book. *Nonno* Peppe smiled at their exuberance. They turned attentively to Michele. He stood before his class holding a small slate and piece of chalk, ready to teach them how to read and write.

"*Nonno* Peppe," Angela giggled, fanning her hand in front of her face, her hair circled with smoke like a saint's halo. "You can't smoke your old pipe in school!"

"No?" *Nonno* Peppe said, innocently. "Is that true?" he asked, looking up to *San Francesco.* Apparently, the Good Saint agreed that it was so, and with a sigh and a final puff, *Nonno* Peppe set his pipe on the floor under the bench, where it soon went out.

Michele looked at his little class: two young wives, one of them pregnant; an adolescent; a baby; and an old grandfather. This was not exactly what he had in mind when he had offered to teach Teresa, and he suspected that it was getting out of hand. What did he know about teaching? Well, he was willing to try.

"Look," he said, writing on the slate. "These are letters. See? The alphabet."

"My God, Michele!" Anna broke in, irritated and insulted. "We know what letters are! What do you think? *Non siamo ignoranti* (We are not ignorant)!"

"I know you know what letters are, Anna. But you have to know which letters they are. You have to know their names and the sounds they make before you can read the words! You have to know how the letters make the words. How they come together. Now, listen. I'll say the letters and make the sounds and then you say each one."

The class settled, ready. "*Ah, bi, ci, di, e, effe,*" he pronounced the letters and carefully wrote each one. The class dutifully repeated them in unison.

The drill continued as Michele wrote and sounded out the Italian alphabet, carefully matching each letter to its sound. The little class had no difficulty imitating the sounds—after all, they had been speaking quite adequately all their lives. But they had more trouble when Michele asked them to identify and pronounce the printed letters and to read words from his book. *Nonno* Peppe was having great fun, enjoying the lesson, but his old eyes did not let him see the letters clearly, and Michele had to write them very large for him. After 20 minutes of struggle, Anna complained that they still could not read and write.

Michele was patient. "Anna, did you think you would learn in a few minutes, that I could just tell you how to read and then you could go off and read everything? You have to study! To practice every day if you want to learn."

Frustration darkened Anna's face. She stood up, hands on hips, defiantly.

"Eh, *Signore Professore* Michele Graziano," she challenged. "Can you write '*fagioli*' on that slate?"

"Beans?"

"Yes, beans."

"*Fagioli,*" he wrote carefully, being sure to spell it correctly. "There," he said, holding up the slate. "Beans."

"That's 'beans'?"

"Yes. I said that's 'beans.'"

"So," said Anna, standing and pointing to the word. "Beans. I am going to clean the beans for supper." And she left.

"Me, too," added Caterina, with an emphatic nod. "The beans, they need two people." And she, too, left, carrying the still-sleeping Francesca.

Michele's new career as classroom teacher was over as quickly as that. He felt relieved at no longer being responsible for so many students, however small or informal his class might have been. He and Teresa continued working nearly every day with the old schoolbook, sitting close together on a shady bench. Teresa practiced reading and writing words and, soon, sentences. She enjoyed her solitary moments when she held her book or a letter from America and slowly deciphered the writing. "How wonderful!" she told herself one day, when she realized that she had discovered a secret that most people did not understand. "This paper," she marveled, tracing the words with her finger, "it talks to me!"

One of the priests, noting Teresa's interest in reading, gave her a book about the lives of the saints. A drawing of Saint Teresa was on its cover, and it became Teresa's textbook. With Michele's often uncertain help, she deciphered the text, letter by letter, word by word, line by line. Michele had no interest in the lives of the saints, but enjoyed Teresa's progress and her delight as she came to understand each phrase. Teresa sharpened her reading skills and became the family's expert on saints.

"Did you know," she told the family, "that *San Francesco's* father was French? But not a nice man, and poor *San Francesco* had to run away from home when he was very young! And his poor *madre* was so sad."[5]

Nonno Peppe, recalling his father's stories of the French occupation in the early 1800s, knew that his saint, *San Francesco di Paolo*, had no French blood in him. It was easy, however, to believe that if the earlier saint's father had indeed been a Frenchman, then certainly he had not been a "nice man."

Anna eventually learned to read and write, taking private lessons in town, and enjoyed not only religious books but also romantic novels about adventurous Italian heroines.[6] Caterina never did learn, but managed her life quite well without it. *Nonno* Peppe gave up after that first day of class, reluctantly accepting that, approaching 90 years of age, he was probably not going to learn much about reading and writing.

"It's better," he said to *San Francesco*, "to leave the reading to the young people. Don't you think?"

But he still liked to listen to Teresa working on her studies with Michele.

Giuseppe Bartolotti, a 14-year-old neighbor, joined Teresa and Michele in their reading. His parents had moved to Maida years before, appointed as superintendents of the town's jail in the old castle's dungeons. His mother was in charge of the women's section and his father, the men's. Their official positions imparted some status to the Bartolottis. Teresa's parents, by then landowners, also enjoyed an enhanced status, and the two families, neighbors and old friends, shared what Teresa would later describe as a "middle class" lifestyle. "Of course," Teresa explained, "middle class in Maida in 1920 was not like middle class here [the United States in the 1960s]. Then, we had no water, no toilet, no electricity, and the houses was very small."

5. *San Francesco di Assisi* (1182–1226) lived long before *Nonno* Peppe's *San Francesco di Paola* (1416–1507), and Teresa may have briefly confused one for the other.
6. We have a photograph from the 1940s of the two sisters, Anna and Teresa, relaxing under an umbrella on the beach in Ocean City, each one absorbed in a paperback book.

Just a few years earlier, young Giuseppe Bartolotti had completed four years of school, and with his more updated education volunteered to help the girls with their reading.

"I have newer books," he told them, pointing out that Teresa's textbook, printed in 1901, was almost 20 years old. With her romantic view of the world, this information transformed the volume to an endearing old companion, like her book about the saints.

"Look," she said. "We were born in the same year! Me and this little book that my Michele gave me; we're like twin sisters."

Michele was happy to have help in his role of *professore*, because Teresa was reaching beyond his own level, asking questions that he had difficulty answering. She was a willing student and progressed well. Her young brother Peppino had also recently completed four years of school and was the best-educated member of the family, but had little interest in assisting with the lessons for his sister. Anna stayed away from the lessons, saying that she was too busy taking care of her new husband, Giuseppe.

Caterina, possibly more interested in the young Giuseppe Bartolotti than in the lessons, joined them now and again but never did learn to read. Francesca, three years old, liked to pretend that she, too, was in school. Just a few years later, she would attend school. Ten-year-old Angela eventually learned to read when she prepared to become a nun, but was not yet interested in the lessons. Teresa, however, was fast becoming the family's reader and scribe.

In 1921, disheartened at the dismal postwar conditions, Teresa's father announced his decision to rejoin his brothers Giuseppe and Antonio in Ocean City and again earn money to send home. When he had returned to Maida in 1914, just before the war, his brothers had remained in America. Giuseppe had joined the American Army and served in France. Both became naturalized U.S. citizens in the 1920s and never returned to live in Italy.

Michele's brothers married two sisters, Rosa and Elisabetta (Bettina) Paone, in family-arranged weddings, brought them to America, and settled in Ocean City. Some years later, Antonio and Rosa bought a house on West Avenue and converted the front to a grocery store—the first Italian-owned grocery in the city. They operated it into the 1940s or 1950s, living with their six children in the rear apartment. Along with their success they also knew grief; in 1928, their youngest child, Sam, was killed by an automobile near their home.

Giuseppe and Bettina had one child, Joseph, born in Italy and brought to America in 1927. As his father had done in World War I, Joseph would join the U.S. Army in 1942. He would serve in the Pacific against Japan. Joseph would go on to complete college and become a high school guidance counselor.

In 1920, while his brothers were building their new lives in America,

Michele Dattilo was preparing to leave Maida again. "The work in Maida is worse," he told his wife, Elisabetta. "I have never seen it so bad. I'll stay in America only two, three years, earn money, and come home." Anna and her new husband, Giuseppe Graziano, would soon join him. By 1921, when Michele Dattilo returned to Ocean City, a good portion of the Dattilo family had moved from Maida to America. The Dattilos had become a family on two continents, a family in transition, from Italian to American.

3. *La Zappa* [7]

Giuseppe Graziano had returned from the war missing a piece of his jaw and a number of teeth, but also with a government pension that allowed him to buy a house in Maida. Hoping to return to America, he applied for emigration. While waiting, he and his bride, Anna, would cultivate the land that had been given to them by Anna's father from his large farm. The work, never easy, was especially hard for Giuseppe, who was still recovering from his war wound and the primitive surgery on his jaw.

One afternoon while clearing a field, Giuseppe saw a friend running up the hill waving papers and shouting, "Giuseppe, look! Your papers are here. You are going to America, *la bell'America!*"

With a "Whoop!" that drowned out his friend, Giuseppe threw *la zappa* into the air, and it lodged in a tree. Never looking back, he ran down the hill, leaving his home and his plot of land to whomever wanted it. His thoughts were already in America.

Anna and Giuseppe crossed the Atlantic to Ocean City—a fitting name, he thought. With her father's help they bought a house on West Avenue, in which they raised their daughter, Rosina. They renovated a small bungalow on the property to generate rental income, which proved to be a great help during the 1930s depression. Giuseppe worked at the city gas plant, maintained his property, cultivated a small garden and a fine fig tree in the sandy southern New Jersey soil, and kept his family in health and comfort far beyond anything possible in Maida.

Giuseppe and Anna Graziano—my Uncle Joe and Aunt Annie—would live in their house on West Avenue for more than 50 years. We visited them frequently in the 1930s and 1940s, driving the 100 or so hazardous miles in Pop's 1929 Packard and enjoying Ocean City's beach and boardwalk. After retirement, they would build, with their daughter, Rose, and son-in-law, Nicholas, a second home in Florida, dividing their time between Florida and Ocean City. For them, *la bell'America* had been the right choice.

Teresa felt her father and sister's absence—the girls had been close. The family was breaking up, and she knew that she, too, now married to Michele, would soon head for America.

Like other young men who had returned from the war, Michele had poor

---

7. The hoe.

prospects in Italy. His parents, younger sister, and brother, who still lived in a two-room rented house outside of town, worked for *u padronu* and managed to survive day by day. Michele's memories of childhood would be of poverty. Teresa's, however, were idealized images of comfort enjoyed by the Dattilos and the Bartolottis. Years later, as I listened to my mother and father describing the same little town of Maida, one would think they had lived in two different places—one prosperous and comfortable, the other its dark and squalid underside.

However, in spite of the economic and social distance between them, their families were close, laboring under similar conditions and struggling with the same problems.

Michele thought often of Macrina, living in America for 10 years with her husband, Giuseppe Conace, prospering on their farm. "What a world of difference," he thought, as he compared his earlier years in America with his future in Maida. It was an easy decision—he would return to America just as Teresa's father had done, but he would be a true immigrant, not a migrant. He and Teresa would settle there; their future was an American future.

Teresa was reluctant to leave her family. "Come with us, Mamma," she pleaded. "Bring the whole family and live in America, so we'll be all together."

Moving a whole family to another country was not that easy. Even if they could afford passage for everyone, the waiting lists for visas were long. In any event, although Elisabetta wanted to emigrate, Teresa's father opposed it. America was too uncivil, he said, and anti-Italian prejudice was rampant. He believed that without her relatives and friends, Elisabetta would be lonely and unhappy. Elisabetta had to remain in Maida. With her husband's refusal, she would never receive official permission to leave Italy.

Elisabetta had become an independent, strong-willed person from the years that her husband had been away in America, and she had assumed responsibility for her family. However, the family's relatively comfortable life notwithstanding, Elisabetta's continued separation from her husband was a major source of unhappiness.

"Michele," Teresa asked, "why can't we stay here, where we belong, in our home? We can have Papa's farm. Peppino doesn't want it; he wants to go in the army, to see the world. We can live right here, in Maida, and never have to go to America. Let's stay here."

4. The Sun in Every Room

Michele's reasons for leaving were clear, and he had made his decision long before.

"Teresa," he said, "I know it's hard for you to leave, but I promise you a big, beautiful house in America, with many rooms, like none in Maida!"

Teresa could not believe they would be able to own so grand a house.

"But, Michele," she asked, her hands together as in prayer, swiveling up and down at the wrists, "how? You don't even have enough money saved for your steamship ticket! How will you buy a house?"

"It's not possible here," Michele said. "Only in America can I make enough money. And you know, I've had enough of farming. Up to here," he added, touching his eyebrows. Then, thinking of his parents' crowded two-room rented house on the hill where he had grown up, he said, "No, I won't be a poor farmer for the rest of my life."

Teresa thought of her father, her family and their farm. Poor? They were not poor! They lived well enough right in Maida.

Teresa's sheltered home was the source of her rosy views of Maida. What Michele saw, however, was a darkening poverty that he could not long keep at bay. Staying in Italy, he feared, would bring that dark beast crashing through the door, stamping grief on everyone. Then Teresa would see it, but too late. He would not let that happen to his family.

"There's no work here. It's worse than ever. That's why your father went back to America, to earn enough so you don't lose the farm that he worked so hard to buy for you."

"I know," Teresa admitted. "Papa sacrifices so much for us," she began to say, as she had so many times before. Then a new thought surged up, one never before allowed to take form—her father had left them! He had gone off to America for years at a time, leaving her mother and the children alone. Shocked at this new image of her gentle father, she fought to suppress it as guilt washed through her. She shuddered, mentally crossed herself, and asked God's forgiveness for such disgracefully disloyal thoughts.

Michele saw the emotion on her face. "Teresa," he asked, gently, "what's wrong?"

"Why?" she started to ask, but began to cry and hid her face on Michele's shoulder. He embraced and comforted her. What had he said? Had he frightened her with his talk of everything being so new for them in America?

"I don't know why Papa's so unhappy," Teresa sobbed. "We have our farm, our family. Maybe if we all prayed, then God would make things better after a time. But why, . . ." and here the terrible thought fought its way back, "why does Papa or you want to give up the family and everything in our beautiful town, to leave us here, all alone, so you can go someplace else?" She looked at him. "Michele," she asked, now in a very small voice, having finally arrived at the core of her dismay. "If we go, will we be the same, just as terrible, leaving the families here, all alone?"

Now Michele began to understand. It was different for the women. While he felt excited and eager to be off, Teresa felt sadness and loss. When a woman went to America, she was taken away by her husband's decision, pulled from her home, her family. For her, it was a loving life lost; for the man, it was an exciting life gained. For Michele it was a challenge, a high-stakes and, hopefully, high-reward adventure. For Teresa, no matter how well it might go, it meant abandoning people who loved her. That's why she cried; for her father, for the new, disturbing thought that he had abandoned the family, and for her awful guilt that she was about to do the same.

Michele defended his father-in-law. "He has to go where there is work. What else can he do? The farm is good, it feeds the family, but that's getting harder to do. People have no money. We barter, but how long can that go on? Everybody keeps trading, and soon you get your own things back, and what gain is that? We try to save enough to pay *il calzolaio* once a year, but how can he live like that for long? Can we keep trading figs for shoes?"

Teresa knew he was right, but it was so hard to accept.

"It's much better in America," Michele went on. "You'll like America. Each year more Italian families go there, and your father and Anna, and Macrina and her husband, and all their children. And *Zio* Giuseppe and Antonio are there too, in Ocean City, with their families. My brother talks of going there. Who'll be left in Maida? Soon there will be more Italians in America than in Italy! You'll see; we won't be alone. We'll be happy there."

Teresa wanted to believe him.

He told her of America's rich economy, jobs, and good pay. "Nyack," he said, "is a little city with paved streets, not just dirt, like here. Electric trolleys with ringing bells run on the streets, people hopping on and off. The houses are two, three floors, and each house has its own garden, and you grow whatever you want. I will grow tomatoes for you, and beans, and grapes, and even figs! We'll take some cuttings from our trees with us, on the boat, nobody will know, and we'll plant them in our own garden, figs from Maida. Your father's trees will come with us! I will give you a house with two floors and glass windows, real glass, not just a hole chopped in the wall. It will have a sink and running water just from twisting a little knob, and toilets, all inside the houses, so we don't have to be like here, like animals in the woods. And when you push a little black button on the wall, the house is filled with light like the sun, in every room!"

Teresa was dazzled. "So many rooms and the sun in every one!"

Michele's enthusiasm was running high. He had no house for Teresa and did not know where he would find one. And if he did, how in the world would he afford it? Even Macrina and Giuseppe, as successful as they were, had until recently lived in the rough rooms above their barn. Doubts tugged at him. "What if I can't give her that grand house?" he thought. What if all this was just the fluff of imagination and he was but a pretender, *un bragadoccio*, with words that had no reality? There were plenty of poor in America, and many were Italian immigrants. What made him think he could do what so many could not?

But, having turned loose those crazy ideas, he became even more determined that their house would be just as he described.

"You will have *una cucina grande* to cook in, like you've never seen, with a big stove like you can't imagine, and no more cooking outside over a handful of charcoal, like here. You will have a whole room with a beautiful, big table so shiny you can see your face in it, like a mirror. And you'll have another whole room with cushions on the chairs and couches so soft you sink in and talk with your visitors. And on the floor will be *un tappeto grande* (a grand carpet), red and gold, like only the rich have here in their villas, and a bedroom just for you and me, and one for each of our children! Your house will have two, three floors and seven, eight, maybe more rooms! Our friends will come to visit. We'll sit in your cushioned sofas and every day we'll sip espresso from tiny cups that we'll hold like this, see, with the little finger sticking out, like only the rich do here."

Teresa laughed at Michele pretending to sip espresso properly from a little *demitasse*. She put her hands against her face and shook her head in wonderment. "Can all that be true?" She looked around her small two rooms, home to the crowded family, and thought of the pig and goat below, and could not imagine owning anything as grand as a house with seven rooms! Teresa imagined herself lost in endless halls as in a giant castle. "Who can take care of such a place?

"And the shops, Teresa. Not just on one little street, but three, four long streets with stores that have everything. And the beautiful Hudson River, the one I told you about, when Giuseppe took me and Macrina on that train 10 years ago and we went right under the river, right through a black tunnel. Macrina was scared and Giuseppe laughed. Now I can laugh, too.

"And, Teresa, in Nyack the trains come in and out of the station, and you can hear them at night, coming from far away. And the church, you'll like the church. *Chiesa di Sant'Anna* (Saint Ann's Church). You saw Macrina's letter. They were married there. The priest, not Italian, only Irish, but over there that's all right."

"Can it really be like that, Michele? You lived there five years before the war and saw so many wonderful houses in America. But can it really be so rich, like you say? How can they be so rich? And even if it's true for them, how can people like us afford such grand living? Are you just making up stories to fool me? Are you, Michele? I can't imagine what you say!"

"It's all true, Teresa! Everything. Some people don't have a fine house. A lot of people over there are poor, too, just like here. But we won't be poor, I promise you. You and me, we know how to work, we know it all our lives. Here in Maida, we work like donkeys and we just get older and poorer. In America, we will still work like donkeys, but we'll get paid real money and live in a palace! I will work in a good job, in a factory, and you in our fine house. You and me, together, we will do it all, just like I say!"

"But then, is it true," Teresa asked, "that the streets in America are all gold? Papa told us so many times that's only a story, a fairy tale for silly people, and it's not true at all. Now you make it sound like everything will be so easy!"

"No, the streets are black, paved *con catrame* (with tar), or mostly not paved at all. The gold, it's not in the streets; it's in our hands, in our backs. Here's what I learned when I lived in America for five years." He held out his hands, cupping them together as if in his palms he held a whole world for her. "I learned in America that if you work hard you can get anything you want!"

She looked at his hands, her eyes following the curves of his palms, and she could almost see a glowing globe, a new world nestled there, Michele's gift.

His voice grew softer, not in weakness but in certainty.

"Anything, Teresa. Anything," he continued. "A lot of people in America, they don't know how to work, they don't have fine houses, they don't get what they want. But we know how to work. That's our secret. And those others, the puzzled ones, the lazy ones, the stupid ones, sometimes they get mad at Italians, because we know how to work and they don't. But we don't have to worry about them; what they do is their business, and what we do is our business."

Teresa's mind lingered on the images of an impossible seven-room house. How could they live in anything so big? How would she be able to work in the fields, as the women did in Maida, and still manage a seven-room house? How far would she have to carry clothes to the river for washing?

"And what of the sons we will have?" Teresa asked. "Do they have jobs in America for children, too, so they can help the family? Can they be apprenticed to *il calzolaio* (the shoemaker) or *il barbiere*? Can they work on the farms? How far will they have to walk to the farms?"

"No, no children's jobs!" Michele laughed. "The children all go to school in America, and they don't have to work on the farms and dig in the dirt like I did, like we make the children do here. When they walk, they walk to school, not to the farm. Our children will grow up to be educated men and women. Educated! Not like us, struggling to read two words on a paper nailed up in the piazza! They can be *giuristi* (lawyers), or *dottori*, or maybe even *professori* if they want. And if they don't, they will still be educated and will work in good jobs in the factories, and will bring money home to help the family. But first, they will all go to school."

"Educated," she marveled. "And they will read books? And the girls? Even the girls, too?"

"Yes, even the girls. All will be educated."

That was probably the longest and most animated declaration that Michele, normally a quiet young man who preferred to let others talk, had ever made. Teresa had to admit that she was impressed and was growing excited, but in truth she was still a little frightened.

Although warming to the idea, she remained resistant, not wanting to leave her mother and *Nonno* Peppe, who was then 90 years old. The ties were strong, perhaps too strong to overcome, and Teresa's responsibility to her family was the major barrier against Michele's arguments.

America was booming, Michele knew, while poor Maida continued its downward struggle. *Una casa grande*, he promised Teresa, and a fine life for their family, and education for their children. Michele's reasons for leaving in 1920 were clear enough. He did not then know he would soon have another reason to move his family to America. Even as he spoke, the rise of Mussolini's Fascism[8] had already begun.

For Michele, the young man who bristled at any suggestion of demeaned status, of invidious comparisons with others, this was a challenge. Although he was now a man of 28, a bit of Michele was still the 17-year-old who had foolishly marched up those ship's stairs to face the giant at the top.

5. A Subject of the King

Michele left Maida in 1920 with his 16-year-old brother, Giuseppe. They traveled with 1,847 third-class passengers on the French ship *Providence*, arriving at New York's harbor on August 25, 1920.[9] They were eager to join their sister, Macrina, who had been in America for 10 years working with her husband on their farm. In spite of their age difference, the brothers were close, crossing the ocean together, working for a while on Macrina's farm, and then sharing an apartment in Nyack. Protectively, Michele guided his young brother to adjust to America.

Michele worried about leaving Teresa, who was pregnant with their first child, but he was eager to work again on Giuseppe's farm, helping them as he had before the war. Macrina welcomed her younger brothers. They worked on the farm for a year, and then began work at Gair's factory in Piermont, known locally as "The Mill." Michele planned to save money, buy a house, and in a year or two bring Teresa to America, where their new lives would begin.

Seven years would pass before Teresa joined Michele, not because of her reluctance to leave, but because of delays due to the increasing number of Southern Italians waiting to emigrate. Whenever Michele inquired about her status, dismissive officials said that she was "on the waiting list." In order to see his family, Michele made the long, expensive voyage to Italy several times between 1922 and 1927.

Even more troubling was America's growing anti-immigrant sentiment. Southern Europeans, and Italians in particular, were no longer welcomed. The Johnson-Reed National Origins Act was borne on a long-growing

---

8. See Chapter Twenty-Three.
9. The *Providence* continued its Mediterranean to New York service from 1915 until it was scrapped in 1951.

anti-Italian wave. Passed by Congress in 1924, it went into effect in 1929, resulting in a 98 percent decrease in Southern Italian immigration.[10] By 1925, Italians' anticipation of the law stimulated more visa applications and delays. Teresa began to fear that if she did not soon get her visa, she would not be allowed to go at all.

While Michele worked in America, Teresa, their infant son Ferdinando (called 'Nando), and Teresa's mother and siblings lived in the small house in Maida that Michele had bought for them with money earned in America.

With improving literacy, Teresa wrote to Michele often, telling him of the wonderful things 'Nando was learning. When he read her letters, Michele felt so lonely that he wanted to give up *la bell'America* and return to his family. Her letters, at first brief and laboriously composed, became more fluent, and she needed less help to write them. Michele answered from America, but not as frequently, since writing was now more of a challenge for him than for Teresa. The student had outpaced her teacher.

Teresa discovered how much she enjoyed writing letters. Relatives and neighbors brought letters they had received from America, asking her to read them aloud and write their answers. For the rest of her life, first in Maida and then in Nyack, Teresa would be the communicator and scribe for family and friends across the ocean.

While Teresa waited in Maida, Michele became reacquainted with Nyack, improving his English and learning the ways of America. Nyack had changed since his first stay, before the Great War. It was bigger, more crowded and active. People were dressed better, had money to spend, and were pleased with their good fortune. There were cars and trucks now; Model T Fords demanded space on the streets, displacing horses and wagons. The terrible destruction, the sickness, rubble, and dust of war that he had known in Europe, followed by the poverty of Maida, were not to be seen here. There were some places in Nyack that looked much like the poor hovels he remembered in Maida, and some families here were in a similarly sad way. But the people whom he knew in Nyack were living more comfortably than they had before the war, and certainly far better than in Maida.

In the 1920s, before the restrictive immigration law, more families from Southern Italy moved into Rockland County, most of which was still farmland. A few, including Macrina and Giuseppe and friends such as the Asaro, Conace, Fiola, Paone, and Serratore families, formed Michele's closest group. In 1925 the second Graziano family wedding in America was held—Michele's brother, Giuseppe, 21 years old, married Nunziatta Milazzo. They settled into a large stone house with beautifully finished wood interiors on her father's farm in Central Nyack, not far from Macrina.

---

10. Italian immigration to the United States decreased from 283,738 in 1914, the year before the war, to 3,845, the new quota in 1929, the year the act went into effect. See Chapter Six.

Giuseppe's father-in-law,[11] a stone mason, had built the house and two others in the mid-1920s.

By 1926, Michele had learned the language and customs and had steady employment, a small bank account, and a settled group of relatives and friends. As 1927 neared, he rented an apartment at 118 Washington Avenue in South Nyack and readied it for Teresa. It was not the fine house he had promised her, but was more spacious than anything they had known in Maida. It would be a good start, and he knew she would like it.

The next step was to become a citizen of the United States. He hoped that would allow some advantage over other immigrants in bringing his family into the country. However, the new law after 1924 meant that being a naturalized citizen gave no advantage to spouses and families for immigration.

For Michele, Italy was far behind. He had strong family ties there—his parents and one sister, Josephina, had remained—but felt no obligation to his old country. "I gave *Italia* most of my life," he told himself. "My youth, my labor, five years in the army. Now the rest of my life belongs to my new family, here in America." He had no hesitation in signing the application for citizenship:

"*United States of America Declaration of Intent.*

"*It is my bona fide intention to renounce forever all allegiance and fidelity to any foreign prince, potentate, state, or sovereignty, and particularly to Victor Emanuel III, King of Italy, of whom I am now a subject. . . . I am not an anarchist; I am not a polygamist nor a believer in the practice of polygamy; and it is my intention in good faith to become a citizen of the United States of America and to permanently reside therein; so help me, God.*"[12]

Michele studied citizenship booklets and attended night classes in the Nyack library on Broadway. It seemed strange, being inside a classroom again for the first time since he was eight years old! His teacher's name was Miss Scrive, and he thought that was a fine name for a teacher. With some pride, Michele told Miss Scrive that in her own civil war, President Abraham Lincoln had invited the great Italian general, Giuseppe Garibaldi, to lead the United States Army against the confederacy. "Oh, how interesting," she answered but, to his disappointment, had not pursued it with the class.

On Saturday, November 27, 1926, with a dozen other people at the county courthouse, 34-year-old Michele held his Certificate of Naturalization. Not a romantic like Teresa, he nonetheless felt a little misty-eyed as he signed the document where the smiling clerk pointed. Michele's wavering, fourth-grade signature was now officially and indelibly on paper. Although he had learned to read some English, his skills were not enough to easily

11. Vincenzo Milazzo had immigrated in 1908 from Bisceglia, Southern Italy, with his wife, Deloyal Logretz, and their three-year-old daughter, Nunziatta, who would become my Aunt Nancy. Vincenzo built three large houses near each other, and one of them became their family home.
12. Quoted from Michele Graziano's Certificate of Intent for Naturalization (1926).

decipher the printed words. No matter; the judge had read them aloud to the dozen persons granted citizenship that day:

"...*the Court, having found that the petitioner, [Michele Graziano], intends to reside permanently in the United States, and that he has in all respects complied with the Naturalization Laws of the United States, and that he was entitled to be so admitted, it is thereupon ordered by the said court that he be admitted as a citizen of the United States of America.*"

Michele carefully folded the document and slid it into its stiff paper envelope. He would read it frequently over the next few months, and eventually decipher all the words. One phrase in particular, at the end of the document, spoke to him. He read it many times, smiling.

"*Michele Graziano, who previous to his naturalization was a subject of Victor Emanuel III, King of Italy, [is] admitted as a citizen of the United States of America.*"

"Here," he thought, tapping the document, "is the whole story. Michele the Subject is now Michele the Citizen!" He had completed a long journey from poverty through a World War, across an ocean, to a new land and new life. Most of all, he had traveled from king's subject to free citizen, a journey of which to be proud.

I like to think that on that November Saturday in 1926 Michele, my father, may have glimpsed another meaning in his accomplishment. He had succeeded where, sadly, his country had failed. Michele was no longer beholden to a monarch, but his old country was. Italy's struggles for independence and unity through its long *rivoluzione* and *risorgimento* had resulted not in democracy, but in the perpetuation of a monarchy. I do not think that Michele would have allowed himself any self-congratulation for his success where Italy had failed. Rather, I hope that he viewed his own journey, like the journeys of so many Italians, as a model, a promise, of what Italy might accomplish in the future—to become, someday, a true democratic republic.

As 1926 closed, Michele was ready to journey again to Italy—this time as a citizen of the United States—to claim his wife and son and bring them to their new home in America. However, there was to be another delay. While 1926 had started as a year of accomplishment for the family, it would turn to tragedy, sorrow, and crisis.

6. The Greenhouse

Giuseppe Conace's farm on the hill in Central Nyack prospered, and by 1926, he and Macrina were successfully growing flowers for the wholesale market. They talked of opening a retail flower shop in Nyack, perhaps in another few years. It was exciting, this new adventure, and a little unbelievable, its success surprising even for someone as optimistic and ambitious as Giuseppe. In Italy there had been no prospects of owning land or developing a successful business. Here in America, however, anything was possible.

Giuseppe designed and built the first of five greenhouses, and the first year's crop was already being harvested, ready for the Easter trade, so people could enjoy the spring flowers. The big greenhouse was bursting with color and fragrance. Long stems of snapdragons with crisp, fat blossoms, white, yellow, blue, red, and pink sprouting along the stems, were harvested, trimmed, arranged into bundles, and gently wrapped in cones of green tissue paper. They carefully packed the flowers in ventilated cardboard boxes, loaded them onto the truck, and delivered them to stores and the railroad station.

Michele, his brother, Giuseppe, Antonio Conace, and Macrina and her teenaged sons, Joseph and Fred, worked those frantic weeks with Macrina's husband to bring the spring harvest to market. They perspired torrents in the tropical heat of the sun-filled glass house, wiping their faces and succeeding only in spreading layers of mud on their already sun-darkened skin, making their eyes and teeth shine in ivory-like contrast.

"Ay, Macrina!" someone shouted. "Who is that black man over there?"

"That's no black man!" she laughed. "That's my Giuseppe. If he looks like that, it means he's workin' hard, like he's suppose' to."

The streaming sunshine, trapped under the glass roof and walls, drove up the temperature as the day wore on. Every hour a bucket of cool water was carried along the flower beds and into the packing shed, and thirsty workers eagerly dipped into it with a shared ladle. They gathered around the hose to soak their hair, hats, and red bandanas to help keep cool for a few minutes. As the temperature climbed, Giuseppe moved along the high rows of wooden flower beds and turned iron wheels like the steering wheel of their Model T. Toothed gears were brought together, meshed, and rotated and, with metallic groans and rusty squeals, set into motion long vertical rods and pivots that operated the banks of hinged ventilation windows high up in the glass roof. A long row of windows swiveled upward as he turned each wheel, and the trapped heat rushed out in wavy lines that climbed and danced up into the sky, as if elated at their escape.

Giuseppe Conace was an ambitious man with vast energy, a booming voice, and bubbling ideas for the future. Everything was working in their favor. He and Macrina now owned the farm and three additional houses for rental income. That year the family moved out of their rough rooms above the barn and temporarily into one of their houses, anticipating construction of the beautiful new house on top of the hill that Giuseppe had promised to Macrina.

The farm now included more equipment. The horse, old now, was comfortably retired in the fenced field, his labors taken over by the secondhand 1919 Model T Ford truck that Giuseppe had bought for $35. The old wagon, with its proud but faded golden words, "G. Conace—eggs, vegetables, and flowers," now rested at one end of the barn, its wooden wheels sinking into the soft earth, having become another place to store boxes and tools.

That year, recognizing that he now had a large family and more assets to protect, Giuseppe arranged for a substantial life insurance policy.

"Macrina," he declared, "I'm going to get insurance."

"What's that?" she asked.

"Insurance, *assicurazione sulla vita*. Life insurance. For me, so you'll have money to live on. You know, in case I die."

"You're no gonna die! Don' talk like that! I don' want to hear that!"

Macrina put her hands up, palms out, to signal him to be quiet and backed out of the room, shaking her head, refusing to listen to any more unsettling talk. A few months later Giuseppe became ill and, in one week, inflamed with fever and desperate for breath, died. He was 39 years old. Macrina and her children were now on their own.

"I'm sorry," Dr. Monteith said gently. "Pneumonia. There's nothing we can do. I'm sorry."

Macrina, clouded with grief, was left to care for four youngsters, the farm, and the business. The world had dropped onto her shoulders.

After the funeral, Macrina, dressed in mourning black, sat at Giuseppe's rolltop desk staring at the mail that had piled up unanswered during his illness. Bills, orders, and letters from advertisers, customers, creditors, banks, and government agencies spilled across the desk. Bills and taxes were due, and dates for flower shipments had to be met or customers and income would be lost. That river of communication carried the business, and Giuseppe had always managed it. To Macrina, who had never attended school, it was an opaque mass of tangled words and numbers. She knew that loan payments were due to avoid foreclosure, but did not know how to make the payments, how much to pay or to whom, or even how to access their bank account.

Having worked at Giuseppe's side, Macrina had learned how to grow, harvest, and ship the flowers, and she could match any man, hour for hour, in physical work. She had watched him maintain the business records, and she learned to keep production and shipment records under Giuseppe's supervision. These were considerable achievements. With no formal education, she had learned in her mid-20s to read, write, and calculate on the job, and all in a foreign language. However, Macrina had never been responsible for records, paperwork, or correspondence, or interactions with banks, customers, and suppliers. All had been mysteries to her, attended by Giuseppe. How was she to decipher and untangle these accumulated demands? Even if she could, where was the flow of money to keep it going?

She gazed through the window at the big greenhouse. In the next few weeks, the flower beds had to be emptied, cleaned, and whitewashed with lime to keep down the growth of pests. The soil had to be changed, fertilized, prepared for the spring growing season, a big job for half a dozen men that Giuseppe, with his knowledge and extraordinary energy, had always directed. Winter repairs of machinery and buildings waited, workers had to be supervised and paid, and payments made to suppliers. The rhythms of the growing season and the commercial calendar had to be respected, or they would leave her and the children behind.

Macrina was deep in grief over Giuseppe's death. She stared at the mass of papers, heard the demands of the marketplace, and felt the heavy dependency of her four children. It was too much, too heavy a burden for one person, too complicated, too constantly demanding and unforgiving, and Macrina knew she would soon lose their business, their farm, and their home.

Chapter 12

The Move to America (1927–1930)

1. The Greenhouse Revolution

Six men armed with shovels, hoes, and rakes carried over their shoulders like rifles marched westward along Route 59 like a small brigade in a peasants' revolt. Only a ragged tricolor waving above them was missing from the tableau. They marched from their homes, three or four miles, depending upon where they lived. "What's this?" Macrina thought when she saw them coming up the hill toward her farm.

"Hey, Mom," said her oldest son, Fred, laughing, his first smile in weeks. "We're gettin' invaded. Look!"

She went out to meet them—her two brothers, Michele and Giuseppe; her brother-in-law, Antonio Conace; and Jimmie Fiola, Antonio Asaro, and Jimmie Milazzo, men who had worked on the farm and knew what was needed to keep it going.

"Why are you marching around like you're starting a revolution?" she asked.

"But we are!" they said. "The revolution is here, on the farm! The soil, it gotta be loosened. The seeds, they gotta be picked through and planted. The greenhouse, the flower beds, the packing shed, they all gotta be fixed. Gotta do lotta work, Macri, if we gonna get this place runnin' again."

Fred and Joe, Macrina's teenagers, ran out to join the men in the big greenhouse to begin the work of reviving the farm. Macrina, still in widow's black weeks after the funeral, had remained stunned, grieving, only slowly rousing herself to reach for the loose ends that had unraveled after Giuseppe's death, but she had not been able to knit them back together to save the farm and business from certain failure.

"Come, Macri," Michele urged in his quiet way, gently taking her hand. "Time to get to work. *Andiamo.* Let's go."

And she did. Moved by their kindness and enthusiasm, shedding tears of sorrow and gratitude, Macrina packed away forever her widow's veil and long black dress. "Done," she told herself, closing the curved lid of the big trunk that Giuseppe had bought for her during their happy first year of marriage. "That was another life," she thought, wiping her eyes with the heel of her hand. "That's over. No more tears. Now to work, like Giuseppe would want."

Macrina again became the competent, hardworking businesswoman, this time, however, bearing full responsibility for everything. With her young sons to help read the letters, notices, and forms, she dove into the pile of paperwork and, after hours of struggle, they sorted it all out. She felt better now that she was gaining some control over what had seemed impossible chaos.

While Macrina and Fred made sense of the paperwork, the men worked in the greenhouse, determined to plant, grow, and harvest a good spring crop. Every afternoon and evening after their factory or road construction jobs, and all day Sunday, they trooped up to the farm to work, to bring it back to life. "Makes me think of the old days in Maida," they told each other. "Walkin' miles to the farm, carryin' shovels on our shoulders. But now we do it to help Macrina and not because we gotta scrabble in the dirt just to live another day. It's good this way. No?"

"Let's get this thing running again!" Joe said, pulling his older brother outside to poke under the hood of the old truck. Neither brother was old enough for a driver's license, but they had moved the truck around the farm between the barn and the greenhouse under their father's supervision and therefore knew they were experienced drivers. While Fred manipulated the levers to control spark and choke, Joe labored to turn the crank. Finally, with a roar and a loud, pipe-cleansing belch of black smoke, the old Model T started, shaking violently for a while before settling into a rattling steadiness, and the boys added their whoops to the noise. After dark, when the tired men were ready to return home, Fred drove through the night, quite illegally, saving them the long walk after their exhausting day, but in the process putting them all at considerable risk of life and limb, as well as the threat of arrest.

In those months of 1926 and 1927, the group labored together in good spirits to save Macrina's farm. It was exhausting, working self-imposed double shifts—their willing labor for *la famiglia*—and Giuseppe's customers would have their Easter flowers after all. Macrina, pulled out of her gloom, reentered the world.

But Macrina still had a problem—money. Where was it to come from to pay for seeds, fertilizer, lime, glass, roofing tar, boxes, tissue paper, gasoline, heating fuel, the continuing demands of taxes, loan payments, groceries, clothes, doctor bills, and the labor that was, for now, being freely given by those good-hearted men?

Giuseppe had not been a religious man, and Macrina, unlike most Southern Italian women, had always been more of a peasant realist than a religious romantic. Later, when people praised God for His mercy and said that it was "a miracle" that He had sent such good fortune, Macrina understood that there had been no miracle. It had been, she knew, Giuseppe's thoughtful planning and the convincing sales pitch of an eager young Metropolitan Life insurance salesman from Nyack. The policy had been written for a considerable amount, and weeks after the funeral Mr. Moffit, the agent, surprised Macrina with a large and most appreciated check.

2. The Banker

On a Thursday morning, Fred helped his mother climb into the high old truck with its open cab, battered fenders, broken headlight, and missing windshield. Not at all concerned that he lacked New York State's official permission to operate a motor vehicle, Fred chauffeured Macrina into Nyack and parked right in front of the bank.

The small Italian lady with the dark, work-roughened hands and uncertain language, wearing her best little hat and ankle-length flowered dress, walked hesitantly into the bank, holding her son's arm more for psychological than physical support.

"Like a cathedral," she thought, stepping gingerly amongst the great columns that rose like tree trunks from the vast marble floor. Three dark-suited men sat at desks on the other side of a waist-high balustrade that looked, she thought, "like an altar rail in church." They spoke authoritatively into telephones and with each other. She noticed the tellers, unfortunate prisoners, they seemed, peering at her from behind rows of barred windows. This was a new world for Macrina, opulent and intimidating.

Fred spoke to a teller, who wrote Macrina's name on a card and led them to the balustrade, where she handed the card to a man at one of the desks. They were ushered through a low swinging gate, and Macrina noticed that the man's domain on this more private side of the balustrade was set on soft, red carpet. "*Che lusso* (such luxury)," she whispered to Fred.

The man read the card and looked up as they stood before his desk, taking in their plain clothing and Macrina's work-soiled hands. He did not rise for them. "I am Mr. Franklyn McKay,"[1] he said, grandly, emphasizing the "Mr.," as befit his position "And what might we do for you, ah. . . ." He looked again at the card. "Macrina, is it?"

At first he directed his question to the peasant woman, but quickly swung his gaze to the tall adolescent at her side. "We're here," Fred began, in his most determined voice, which cracked without warning in its struggle with puberty, making him feel embarrassed and angry. He recovered quickly. Leaning forward presumptuously with one hand on Mr. Franklyn McKay's desk and staring right into the man's eyes, he continued, "To negotiate a business loan."

The surprised man, eyebrows raised, listened as the youngster introduced himself and his mother. Fred felt nervous facing this banker, who was undoubtedly a rich and important man of substance in this intimidating

1. This was not his real name.

domain. Then a reassuring thought rose up, and Fred almost laughed.

"He's just a little man," Fred told himself, looking down at Mr. McKay. "I'm bigger than he is! And he has a bald spot, right on the top of his head."

Although Fred knew that the man's height and hair—or lack of either—had nothing to do with the task at hand, he felt better, somehow reassured.

"My name," he said, standing taller, squaring his already broad shoulders and venturing a hint of a smile, "is Frederick Conace." He gave his family name the American rather than the Italian pronunciation. "This lady is my mother, Mrs. Joseph Conace." He emphasized "lady" and "Mrs.," having been sharply offended at the man's patronizing use of his mother's first name.

Fred put the impressive insurance check on the desk for deposit into their business account. The amount grabbed Mr. McKay's attention. As Fred spoke, he brought out the documents that he had organized and placed them on the desk as he came to each point. He talked about the assessed value of the farm and business, its past and anticipated net income, and the increased value of the property once their planned expansions were completed. Fred presented receipts for payment of bills, taxes, and the monthly mortgage payments, all made on time. He showed the banker the orders for flowers to be delivered for the Easter season next spring, and the expected income and profit. With his late father's insurance settlement, Fred explained, expenses would be met and the business maintained for another two years.

But, he said, in order to expand the business as his father had planned, to build the remaining four greenhouses and resume construction of their new house, they would need an additional loan. He explained exactly how much they would need, how it was to be used, and how they planned to repay it.

In 1927, single women, even mature widows, were not granted loans by banks. Indeed, it had been only seven years since women had finally won the right to vote in the United States! Neither were 13-year-old boys granted bank loans. But the banker listened, increasingly impressed by this youngster who spoke knowingly of business, loans, and collateral.

With the banker's help, Fred filled out a loan application, carefully reading and explaining each item to his mother. Macrina, speaking in Italian although she could very well have used English, asked questions about interest rates, payments, and insurance. Fred translated between McKay and Macrina. Finally satisfied, Macrina nodded and signed the application.

Fred's presentation of business matters was so convincing that the banker, thoroughly impressed, had interrupted only once, calling another man to come and listen to the youngster.

"That was an excellent presentation, young man," he complimented Fred, standing up and reaching out his hand. "We'll review your loan application Macrin . . . er, I mean Mrs. Conace, and will let you know by this time next week."

A week later, the bank's letter arrived; her loan application had been approved. In his remaining years at the bank, Franklyn McKay often recalled that day in 1927 when an eighth grader had walked in and successfully negotiated a large business loan.

By the middle of 1927, the farm was reviving. Macrina was in charge now, managing the farm and wholesale business as Giuseppe had taught her. All was going well, but what no one knew was that within another few years they would again be pushed to the edge of bankruptcy. For now, however, the immediate crisis had been calmed.

3. *Nonno* Peppe's Secret

Michele, now free from the consuming concern and labor for Macrina's farm, resumed his efforts to bring his family to Nyack. Teresa's visa had finally been granted, and she began preparations for her journey to America. In July, Michele paid two months' rent in advance on his Washington Avenue apartment and returned to Maida to escort his family to their new home.

Everyone was happy to see Michele again after his six years in America, but they were saddened, too, because Teresa and little 'Nando would be leaving. Michele was now a citizen of the United States, and they understood what that meant—a permanent break with his old home.

Michele knew this would be his final time in Maida, for he had no intention of ever returning. He had made his decision—America, not Italy, was his future. His happiness at being back was dampened by sadness and some guilt. On this, his final visit to his parents and younger sister, Josephina, Michele carried the news of how well his young brother Giuseppe fared in America. He spoke of his sister, Macrina—his parents had not seen her in 17 years, since she had left in 1909. Michele told them of her farm and business, and how well her four children were growing. "In America, they all go to school," he told them. "They read and write like *i professore*."

But he also carried details of the sad news they had already learned in letters of the sudden *polmonite* (pneumonia), that terrible disease with no cure, that had ended Giuseppe's vigorous and successful life. For the saddened family, hearing it from Michele made it real.

"Here they are," he said, handing his mother three photographs. Because his father, Ferdinando, was by then nearly blind, Michele described the photos. Here was their son Giuseppe with his wife, Nunziatta (Nancy), and two-year-old Fred, standing before the splendid stone house that had been built by her father. "See, here's your littlest grandson," Michele said. In another photo, Macrina, Giuseppe, and their four children smiled, standing in the sunshine by their big barn, just a few months before Giuseppe's death.

"Here are your other grandsons," Michele said, pointing. "Look how big they are, and strong. Ferdinando, Giuseppe, and Francesco. They are going to be the biggest men in the family! Ferdinando's 13 now, Fred they call him in America, and his brothers they call Joe and Frank, and already Fred towers over everybody. They know how to work, those boys. You'd be proud of them, three grown men in the family. And here, here's the little one. See? Your granddaughter, Maria. She's only five and already talks more than anybody else, tells everybody what to do, and her smile is so bright nobody can refuse her. You should see the way her big brothers take care of her and protect her, their little baby sister.

"And look, in this picture, here's Giuseppe's barn, bigger than any barn here. And that's their horse, Gisella, they call him. I don't know why they call him that, after all, he is *un' maschio, un stallone* (a male, a stallion). I guess," he said, smiling, "Giuseppe was making a joke. And over there is the greenhouse Giuseppe built the year before he died. All glass! Hundreds of windows, enough for all the houses in Maida! To grow his flowers. He wanted to build four more, that poor man, but. . . ."

"Michele," his father said, "when you go back, be sure you help take care of your sister and the children. Promise us you will."

"Of course I will, don't worry. I'll always be there to help Macrina, always, and so will Antonio and Giuseppe.[2] The family will be fine."

Teresa felt weighted by sadness mixed with excitement. At 26, she had never been away from Maida. Now she was about to leave her family, most poignantly her mother and grandfather. *Nonna* Anna, her grandmother, had died 10 years before, leaving a deep sadness in Teresa. Now *Nonno* Pepp*e*, born in 1830 and in his 98th year, her virtual father for much of her life. *Nonno* Peppe had been there, reassuring and loving, for his children, his grandchildren, and now his great grandchildren. How 'Nando would miss this steady man who had been part of the little boy's world for all of his six years. Teresa could not think of life without *Nonno* Peppe.

Nonno Peppe, too, was saddened over Teresa's departure, but he was also beginning to feel a sense of completion for himself, of having successfully made his way through a long life that was approaching *cent'anni*. He asked *San Francesco*, "Maybe I've stayed long enough? Teresa is going to America; my sons are there and my granddaughter, Anna, and her husband, and maybe Caterina too will go someday. They are *americani* now. My great grandchildren will grow up *stranieri* (strangers) to me, so far away. What is left for me here? Maybe I should go to America, too, but do they need another old man over there? No. I don't think so."

"Hmm," said the saint, quietly, in *Nonno Peppe's* ear.

"What will they be like," continued the old man, "my great grandchildren? What will they know of me, of Anna, their *bisnonna* (great grandmother)? Anna waits for me up there with you, no?"

---

2. Antonio Conace was Macrina's brother-in-law; Giuseppe Graziano was Macrina and Michele's younger brother.

"Yes," the saint told him. "Anna is here, waiting."

"So, maybe it's time for me, too. Don't you think?" he asked the Good Saint.

"Hmm," the Good Saint replied.

On Wednesday, as Teresa entered her final week in Maida, *Nonno* Peppe felt comfortable with his "journey," as he called it. "Teresina," he told her that morning, "*anche io farò un viaggio; giovedì, venerdì, sabato, domenica, lunedì. Sì lunedì farò il mio viaggio. Sì. Lunedì.* (I, too, will make a journey; Thursday, Friday, Saturday, Sunday, Monday. Yes. Monday.)" The old man held up his fingers and counted off again, "*Giovedì, venerdì, sabato, domenica, lunedì.*" The family was alarmed at what he was suggesting. But *Nonno* Peppe, at 97, was a healthy man who still enjoyed a glass or two of red wine with each day's supper. "*Questo,*" the old men of Maida said, holding up their glasses in salute, "*è quello che ci mantiene giovani.* (This is what keeps us young.)"

"*Sì, lunedì farò il mio viaggio.* (Yes, on Monday I will make my journey.)" And he did, and everyone knew it was just as he had planned, with the help, of course, of his Good Saint.

The following week, grieving over *Nonno* Peppe's death, Teresa and Michele, with little 'Nando in hand, boarded the train for the port of Naples, to sail to *la bell'America.*

Just before Teresa and her family left, the strange event of *u materazza* (the mattress) occurred. Out of hygienic concern, and perhaps respect for death's recent presence, *Nonno* Peppe's mattress had to be disposed of. It was decided to follow a common practice and burn the old bedding.

The straw-stuffed mattress was carried outside and placed on a small pile of dried twigs. Some blessed holy water was sprinkled to help it into the next world, and a little candle oil was added to help it out of this one. A match was struck, and the flames acknowledged *Nonno* Peppe's long life. As the family watched, the fire consumed the old mattress, the smoke rising. They imagined *Nonno* Peppe's soul floating up to heaven, and they said a prayer for him.

But *Nonno* Peppe, it seemed, was taking more than his soul with him.

"Look," Teresa said, pointing. "What's that? Those black things flying up? See? They're coming out of the mattress!"

Black wisps, like small, winged creatures, charred and crinkled, were silently emerging from the burning mattress, so light that they floated easily in the warmed air, up and up, toward heaven. A shudder of superstition passed briefly through the family as they tried to understand the mysterious black shapes.

"Oh, no!" Peppino shouted, realizing what they were. He ran to the burning mattress and beat it with a shovel, trying to smother the flames. It was too late. What was done was done.

They tried to catch some of the floating ashes, plucking them out of the air only to have them crumble in their fingers and drift to the ground like black snow, leaving their hands streaked with carbon. One, not completely burned, still had some printing on it, and they could just make out the words in English: ". . . ted States of Amer . . . ostal Money Order . . . enty dollars and 00 cen. . . ."

How many of those bits of paper, sent for so many years by his sons in America, had *Nonno* Peppe stuffed into his mattress? For what had he been saving? And how much American money had gone up in flames? No one would ever know.

4. Teresa's Nyack

Michele led them to Naples, onto the Italian liner *Roma*, across the ocean, and, on August 22, 1927, into *la bell'America*. He took them to their new home in Nyack, the second-floor apartment at 118 Washington Avenue that he had prepared for them. They climbed the steps to the front porch and were welcomed by the landlord, a smiling, elderly man who had come from Germany many years ago. "He's like *Nonno* Peppe," Teresa thought. Michele led them up the narrow inner stairs, opened the door, and with a courtly flourish ushered in his little family.

'Nando ran through the rooms, excitedly touching everything and peering through the windows at the neighbors' houses and asking, "Is this our house? Is this our house?" Teresa marveled at the four rooms, each almost as large as her entire house in Maida. Michele had been right; here were glass windows, not just holes in the wall, through which the sun streamed, warm and bright. In the kitchen she found a large metal-lined wooden sink with a single faucet protruding from the high back panel. With a twist of her hand, cool water flowed out. Some people, she would soon learn, had sinks with two faucets, from one of which magically flowed hot water.

"In Maida," Teresa said, "I carried water in jugs to the house, even on my head." She laughed, remembering her struggles to balance the heavy jugs. "And now I just turn this little handle, in my own kitchen, and out comes the water, fresh and clean and as much as I want."

She kept turning the water on and off, suspicious that it might not work the next time. The faucet gave a small squeak at each turn. "*Come un piccolo topo* (like a little mouse)," she thought. 'Nando climbed onto a chair and wanted to play in the splashing water.

Another surprise was a tiny water closet, a private little place. It was a crowded three by five feet, with an indoor toilet like those she had seen on the ship, but never in Maida. The copper-lined wooden water tank was high up, near the ceiling. A long chain hung down. "Go ahead," Michele told her. "Pull the chain."

She did, and with a roar that made her jump in alarm, fearing she had broken it, five gallons of water rushed through the pipe from tank to bowl, and in a violent little whirlpool disappeared down the pipes hidden beneath the floor.[3]

"And down the cellar," Michele explained, "is the furnace, *u fornace*. In the wintertime I load in the wood and start the fire, and the heat comes up, through the pipes, out these grates in the floor, see? That warms up the whole house."

Michele had arranged with the aging landlord, who lived on the first floor, that he would cut firewood, tend the furnace, shovel the snow, and in summer cut the grass and tend the garden, in return for reduced rent. The saved money would be banked toward the future purchase of their house.

"*Com' è meravigliosa* (How marvelous)!" Teresa said. "All these American inventions." Two thousand years earlier, her Roman ancestors enjoyed central heating, indoor plumbing, and faucets with hot and cold running water. But those amenities had long been denied to the common people of Italy, and seeing them for the first time, Teresa thought they were wonderfully new American inventions, *le cose americane.*

Michele guided Teresa through Nyack, walking along tree-shaded, paved streets to visit and to shop in stores. Maple trees were brilliant in their fall colors, delighting Teresa. "I never knew," she thought, enjoying autumn's paintings, "that America was a land of so many trees. How nice if we could send a few to shade Maida in the hot summer!"

She was overwhelmed by the abundance heaped on the long counters of the two five-and-dime stores on Main Street, in Signor Raso's grocery, in the Italian butcher shop on Franklin Street, and in Mr. Appelbaum's dry goods store. "What kind of name is that, Appella-bomba?" she wondered. The hubbub of Nyack was also astonishing compared with the pastoral quiet of Maida. Here were great, chugging locomotives rolling along steel tracks and noisy airplanes flying low overhead. Factory whistles hooted every noon and at three and five o'clock. The deep bellowing of the town fire alarm woke one up at night, followed by the wailing of the answering fire trucks. Everywhere was the crackling static of radios. Along every street moved honking automobiles, clomping horses, rattling wagons, and so many busy *americani*, jabbering away in their foreign tongue! Who could understand what they were saying? Teresa despaired that she would ever be able to.

Michele walked proudly with Teresa through Nyack's streets. Here he had found the beginnings of success and respect that had not been available to him in Italy. It had not been easy to come this far, and he knew that more struggles lay ahead. But Teresa's delight was his reward.

Teresa soon learned the street names and the routes to friends' and relatives' houses.[4] In time, more Italian families would settle in Nyack, on Mill

---

3. Modern "water-saver" toilets require only 1.5 to 2 gallons of water.
4. The families included Asaro, Barone, Biancini, Cervodoro, Conace, D'Auria, Dellolio, Delpizzo, Gallo, Fatale, Fiola, Lanzana, Maiorano, Paone, Pugliese, Renella, Serratore, Scheno, Sutera, and many others whom I did not know until years later.

and Prospect Streets, on Brookside, Cedarhill, Depue, Elysian, High, and Ross Avenues. Their homes were not crowded together, as in many ethnic enclaves, but separated, at some distance from each other. The Italian families had no telephones—indeed fewer than a third of all the homes in Nyack enjoyed that amenity—so communication was always in person. To do that, people walked several blocks and sometimes several miles from one home to another. Walking was a necessary part of each day, the kinetic energy weaving together that little Italian community that lay scattered among the streets of Nyack.

For Teresa, it was not the new things and people that were the most wonderful, but the familiar ones. Here was Michele's sister, Macrina, whom she had not seen in 17 years, and his young brother, Giuseppe, who had left Maida six years ago, and his new wife, Nunziatta, whom Teresa met for the first time. Teresa's father had come by train from Ocean City to welcome her, as did her sister Anna with her husband, Giuseppe, and their little Rosina. And here, walking into her new apartment with smiles, tears, and open arms, were her two oldest friends, Angelina Pillegi Conace and Caterina Cuci Serratore, playmates since babyhood in Maida. They cried with happiness after so many years of separation. New friendships, too, would soon develop, like those with the Asaros, Cervodoros, Fiolas, Schenos, and Lanzanas.

"Tonight," Teresa promised, "I will write to *mia madre* and tell her all about Nyack and the happy reunions." By nine o'clock, however, worn out with excitement, she fell asleep. The letter would wait another day.

My family was now in America—except for me, of course, since I would not be born until 1932, five years after Teresa and 'Nando arrived. The family settled in, establishing ties with relatives, friends, and neighbors, learning the ways of Nyack, starting their transformation into *americani*.

Within a few weeks, 'Nando's intensive American acculturation began in kindergarten in the Nyack Public School on Liberty Street. Teresa had wanted to enroll him in the Catholic school, but friends warned them about the priests, nuns, children, and parents. "*Tutti sono irlandesi* (they are all Irish)," they said, "and the Irish, they don' like Italians." Anyway, they cautioned, it would cost too much money.

In the 1920s, the public schools had a mission to transform immigrant children from what the Americans saw as ignorant, slovenly, immoral, and outlandish into well-behaved Americans. Whatever one may think of that mission, the public schools provided enormous benefits for immigrants. Most teachers were patient, supportive, and competent professionals who were committed to public education. The American public school system was a rich resource offered by this country to its immigrants.

'Nando quickly learned the new language and was soon telling his parents about Americans. He had become Teresa's personal six-year-old guide to America, an enthusiastic little filter through which American culture flowed into her home. He brought his crayon drawings and his first attempts at printing his name, which he informed his parents was no longer 'Nando, but Freddie. Teresa was annoyed at that, seeing a presumptuous intrusion, usurping the very name of her little boy. "Ferdinando is your name, and to me you are always *'Nando Bello*," she said, "and I don' care what the teachers say; we name you, not the teachers!" But Freddie insisted on his new American name, and even Teresa finally slipped into the habit of saying "Fred," which always came out as "Freh," although she frequently lapsed back to his real name, *'Nando Bello*.

Freddie brought home notes from teachers, but they were in English, and Teresa took them for translation to *Zia* Jennie Asaro, who was literate in both languages, and who became the secretary, interpreter, and go-between for the Italian community in Nyack. Freddie, she explained, had become a favorite of the teachers. An engaging, curly-haired little boy, bright and eager to learn, he progressed quickly, mastering the language, even surpassing many American-born children. Freddie had so much to learn in his new country that his academic growth was visible from one day to the next. He responded enthusiastically to his teachers and discovered new words, ideas, and skills as if he was in a store where wonderful new things were all free. The teachers, happy at the little boy's progress, attributed his rush of achievement to their efforts and felt personally rewarded for bringing it about.

Like Freddie in school, the Italian families in Nyack settled into their new lives, building their knowledge and skills, banking daily lessons in personal competence.

The Italian immigrants whom I knew in the 1930s were highly supportive of a good education for their children, even though they had received little or none in their own childhood. They realized that *l'uomo che sa leggere sta bene in america* (the literate man does well in America)!

Arriving in America, they found Italian newspapers, radio programs, even churches campaigning to educate the immigrants. The message "keep your children in school" was printed and broadcast. Italian-language newspapers posted registration deadlines and opening days, and explained how to fill out forms, the laws mandating school attendance, and the penalties when parents failed to heed them. Italian newspapers[5] publicized the academic achievement of Italian youngsters and praised the families when their children graduated. Education became a mark of success and *rispetto*, an important ladder toward better jobs and an ascent beyond the lowest levels of labor of their fathers. To become a telephone operator, railroad conductor, bank teller, insurance salesman, store clerk, or manager required an education—and the marvelous, free public schools of *la bell'America* provided it.

5. See Briggs (1978).

These immigrants were determined that their children would graduate high school, but formal education ended there. Thoughts of higher education brought awareness of other barriers, like money for tuition and other expenses. Nevertheless, the distance from my father's four years of formal schooling in Italy to the 13 full years offered to his sons was a magnificent opportunity, unheard of back in Maida. If our formal education ended after the 12th grade, it was still a marvelous achievement for anyone who had "come from the old country."

5. "Everybody Ought to Be Rich!"

Six years earlier, when Michele had returned to the United States, he had found a puzzling country, different from the one he had known before the war. By 1920, after the constraints of war had eased, the country seemed to have exploded into a million pieces. One piece was the apparent intent of young people to tear away the old generation's inhibitions. It was a revolution, a boiling mix of fast-breaking, explosive events. The country was thriving in a post-war economic boom. In 1920, women, after 75 years of campaigning, were allowed to vote for the first time with the ratification of the 19th Amendment to the Constitution. Warren G. Harding won the presidency in 1920, and his Republican friends promptly plundered the country by stealing its oil reserves. They were eventually exposed in the greatest scandal yet to hit the country—the Teapot Dome Scandal of 1921–1927.

Thieves were not limited to the Republican administration. Prohibition was in force.[6] Criminal mobs like Al Capone's Chicago syndicate grew into powerful crime organizations. Speakeasies, shadowy places selling illegal booze and playing the new jazz, proliferated, eagerly supported by the public and happily protected by the police. Largely thanks to the radio's rapid reporting, racketeers and gangsters became infamous public villains and exciting popular heroes. America of the 1920s was a coast-to-coast sky-high wild party, flowing with illegal booze and throbbing with sexuality, the black man's jazz, and prohibition's gangsters.

It was not all decadence, however. The 1920s also saw an explosion of global exploration and discovery, stunning inventions, record-breaking daredevil feats, vibrantly muscular capitalism, a torrent of shining consumer goods to make everybody happy, and an upward-zooming stock market that created overnight millionaires. The mood was an intense demand for excess in everything, seemingly fueled by youth's love of new fashions, by behavior designed to shock the elders, by the era's greed for money and, most characteristically, by the search for excitement. The young had determined

6. After a long campaign that stretched back to the early 19th century, beginning with prohibiting the sale of liquor to "Indians," prohibition became the 18th Amendment to the Constitution in 1919. It did not take long for the country to realize the social disorder and economic loss it created, and prohibition was repealed in 1930.

that the world had no limits, and the avaricious of all ages and social levels grabbed at opportunities to use any means to gain wealth and/or power. It was a 10-year feast of unrestrained optimism, self-indulgence, graft, greed, corruption, and gangsters, and not much sober thinking. It was an exciting time.

The 1920s were gloriously prosperous years for many. A postwar boom of industrial expansion and extraordinary profits nearly doubled worker productivity, and new consumer goods poured into the market. To keep the factories humming, people were encouraged to abandon traditional frugality and consume all they could. Sober workers who had long been prudent savers now became imprudent spenders. To lubricate unrestrained spending, credit, a mysterious resource traditionally reserved for the affluent, was extended to everyone. Now one could buy a marvelous new radio, toaster, automobile, or virtually anything, including houses and stocks, with only 10 to 20 percent of the price in hand. The rest was carried on credit. With only $100 one could own $1,000 of stock, and many became "rich" on paper. People were inflated with feelings of importance when they were treated with such respect and trust. It had become acceptable to owe money, and many did not realize that credit was a sanitized debt into which they were being lured. Being suspicious of the practice, Michele refused for a long time to buy anything on credit, although almost everyone was doing so. "If I don't have the dollar, then I wait until I do," he said. Benni Maiorano, an older man who had been in America for nearly 30 years, was another exception, and warned anyone who would listen: "When you buy on credit, you turn into a debtor; then if you lose your job, you turn into a beggar. And when you turn into a beggar, you turn into a nothing!" Although Signore Maiorano held fast to his beliefs, Michele eventually bought on credit, like everyone else. The consumer society flew high. Buying on credit and becoming a debtor was the new patriotic responsibility.

American exports were flowing, largely to South America in the absence of healthy industrial production by war-crippled Europe. Electricity was the new industrial power, and increasingly it was found in homes and small business.

Linking everyone was another new marvel, perhaps the single most important revolution of the age: the radio. Battery-powered or plugged into the expanding electric grid, or even a crystal set made at home, the radio turned Americans into devoted listeners, albeit to scratchy and often unintelligible sounds. By 1924, radios broadcast boxing matches, baseball and football games, political speeches, lectures with moral messages, debates on issues such as "how the new daylight saving time will destroy the country," live classical concerts, dance bands, operas, Broadway musicals, and church services. That year the whole country could hear Calvin Coolidge read his acceptance speech at the Republican National Convention, an amazing event for Americans, who could not quite believe that voices and music could fly hundreds of miles through the air and emerge from little boxes in their own homes. Americans were so taken with this new invention that they happily tuned in to anything that was broadcast, with little discernment. By 1927, there were more than 6 million radios in the United States and 30 million regular listeners. Radio brought entertainment and information, and the power to create a new unity, a modern togetherness of people all across the country sharing important events simultaneously.

Popular culture flourished through the radio, and into every home that owned a receiver came the static-tattooed jazz that had traveled from New Orleans to Chicago, thumbing its nose at social conventions, exciting the young and alarming the old. Carried into white society, the "black man's music," with its exciting rhythmic drive and powerful emotions, shocked the middle classes and appealed to the vibrant young. They appreciated its improvisation, its on-the-spot personal creativity, its joyous freedom from old restraints. In jazz there was no stuffy etiquette, no dusty scores that had to be performed as written by previous generations. This was new music by new composers and new performers, with new freedom from constraints. It was a brilliant model of the new identity of young Americans, and for a brief time it seemed that everything in the culture—from pop music to business to professional sports to gangsterism—was another form of exciting, hard-driving, creative improvisation.

Automobiles, introduced 30 years earlier, offered exciting new ways to break old limits. Only the wealthy had been able to afford autos at $5,000 each, but Henry Ford's assembly line turned out 15 million Model T Fords from 1908 to 1927, bringing the price down to $360 by the mid-1920s. A car was now within the reach of most working men. If one could not afford a new car, then buying a used car for $100—equivalent to six or seven weeks' work—was possible for men like Michele. With credit, a mere $10 or $20 could put one behind the wheel of a car. Automobile registration in the United States climbed from 8 million to 23 million, and the old horse barns behind houses became garages for family cars. Soon automobiles defined not only transportation, but also social status. America became infatuated with automobiles and was well on its way to outright addiction.

The most exciting of the postwar developments was the airplane. Only 20 years after Orville Wright hopped through the air for 12 seconds, airplanes were crossing the sky at more than 100 miles an hour. In 1919, the navy's NC-4 Curtis Flying Boat made the first transatlantic flight, followed in two weeks by Alcock and Brown's nonstop transatlantic flight. An English airship then made a transatlantic round trip. Eight years later, in 1927, Charles Lindbergh completed his solo nonstop transatlantic flight. A month after that, Hegenberger and Maitland flew across the Pacific, a much longer flight. In 1929, Lt. Apollo Soucek reached an altitude of 39,140 feet. "That's almost eight miles high!" an astounded public exclaimed. Barnstorming pilots, men and women, took off from cow pastures in surplus World War I biplanes, terrifying animals and thrilling the public. Continental airmail and cargo flights and shorter trips for passengers were started. Airplanes were used for dusting crops, fighting forest fires, and evacuating victims of natural disasters.

The military showed that wood-and-canvas biplanes could sink steel-armored battleships,[7] that airplanes could fly from ships, and that paratroopers—the first a unit of marines—could leap upon their enemies from the sky. Lt. A. J. Williams set a speed record of 266.59 miles per hour. Could anyone have imagined that humans would ever propel themselves at such incredible speed? Airplanes flew over the North Pole (1926) and South Pole (1929).

A new industry and an exciting, powerful symbol of America's future where even the sky was no limit had been created. If Americans once flew metaphorically on the wings of eagles, now they were flying higher, faster, and farther on the wings of airplanes—the new metaphor for progress.

However, the greatest optimism and excitement, and belief in an unlimited, grand, and prosperous future, was found in the extraordinary successes of stock market investors. It was a long-running bull market; stock prices continued climbing, as did the personal wealth of many investors. In 1929, John Raskob, the CEO of General Motors, said "everybody ought to be rich"[8] by investing only $15 a week in common stocks and managing it wisely. The core of his suggestion was truly innovative—a person need not have great wealth in order to earn a good income from investments. Of course $15 a week was all that the average worker earned. But no matter, it was the idea that was important, the possibility that with a little money one could become "rich." Most workers could not, but a minority of the population could. For the workers it was reassuring to know that they lived in a country where such success was possible, perhaps someday available to them. The eagerness to trade in the prosperous stock market showed the country's confidence and optimism for its great industrial machine.

Herbert Hoover had been Secretary of Commerce and, like Presidents Harding and Coolidge before him, was a Republican, committed to laissez faire economics. In his 1928 speech accepting his party's nomination, Hoover reminded people of the decade's successful capitalism that had brought prosperity to so many. He told the excited nation:

"We in America today are nearer to the final triumph over poverty than ever before in the history of any land. The poorhouse is vanishing from among us!"

---

7. In July and September 1921, U.S. Army officer "Billy" Mitchell, using Army MB-2 biplane bombers, demonstrated to a skeptical military the potential power of aircraft by bombing and sinking four surrendered World War I German battleships. "Impossible!" the rigid military men had said prior to the demonstrations. "Irrelevant!" they said afterward.

8. Raskob (1929). By "rich" Raskob did not mean excessively wealthy, but earning enough from investments to support a family "in a decent and comfortable manner."

The voters agreed, and he was elected to the presidency. On New Year's Day 1929, *The New York Times* editorialized about the "unprecedented advance" of the stock market and the ''wonderful prosperity" that would surely continue.

In 1929, with his family in their new apartment, Michele continued to work at The Mill. Like many workers, he had started in the "Glue Room," that boiling corner of industrial hell,[9] a steamy, malodorous concrete area where large vats of glue were mixed and cooked and where exploding bubbles sent hot, choking, and undoubtedly toxic fumes into the air and into the workers' lungs. But who knew about such things in those days before OSHA and the EPA?[10] However grueling the Glue Room may have been, it provided steady and welcome work that earned Michele a weekly pay envelope of just over $17, the heftiest he had ever received.

The wild world of flappers, jazz, millionaires, airplanes, and mobsters was exciting, but for Michele and his family and friends it was no more than an interesting background, far from their real world. They knew of that glamorous world from newspapers, radio, and discussions in their kitchens, but it had little to do with their lives. Everyone knew about "flappers"— "*i flopperi,*" *Comare* Cervodoro called them with a dismissive wave of her hand—but no one had seen any or behaved like them. Certainly there were no "*flopperi*" among the young ladies of the Italian immigrant social set in Nyack. Theirs was a world of work, family, and everyday concerns such as children's health and bills. They shared the sense of the country's well-being but had no part of the great excitement or the big money, like the stock market investors whom they heard about but did not comprehend.

In truth, their lives were better and more comfortable than before. They began to share an optimistic thought that this vibrant America of 1929 was becoming everything they had heard about back in Maida. It seemed that their long search for security, freedom, and personal respect was nearly over, that the war and the deadly poverty of Southern Italy were finally behind them.

6. 79 Elysian Avenue

Michele's adjustment to America had progressed in stages. His five years in America before the war (1909–1914) had made him familiar with the country and convinced him to make it his home. The six years following the war (1921–1927) helped him smooth out his adjustment, gain skills, save money, earn his citizenship, and finally settle his family here. By the

9. Many years later the author would experience the Glue Room during his first factory job.
10. OSHA (the Occupational Safety and Health Administration) and the EPA (Environmental Protection Agency) began operating in 1970. Both were generated in President Lyndon Johnson's (1963–1969) "Great Society" and were signed into law by President Richard Nixon (1969–1974).

summer of 1929, not two years since Teresa's arrival, Michele decided that conditions were right to buy a house, furniture, and perhaps even an automobile. It was a marvelous time, with a level of prosperity not possible in Maida. For Teresa, it seemed like one of the romantic stories she had enjoyed as a child.

Owning a home would elevate them to the status of solid American citizens, responsible property owners with a substantial stake in Nyack, finally equal to their American neighbors. A comfortable home for his family, the fine home he had so long ago promised Teresa, would enhance his growing *rispetto*.

"We need to buy a house," he told Teresa, "big enough to make two apartments, one for us, one to rent and help pay the mortgage." He walked through Nyack inspecting houses, rejecting several because of deficiencies in the houses themselves, or in the neighborhoods, or because they were too expensive. Early in 1930, Michele saw a house on Elysian Avenue, just two blocks from their apartment on Washington Avenue. It was a substantial house on a nice residential street lined with maple trees. The neighbors were first- and second-generation German, English, and Irish, in a mix of middle-class and working-class families. They included a retired engineer, the police chief, a railroad conductor, a chauffeur for one of Nyack's wealthiest families, a pharmacist, a local retail store owner, two schoolteachers, the county's district attorney, and a judge. It occurred to Michele that if he purchased the house they would be the first Italian family to live on that street, bringing Southern Italians, those whom Americans had already branded as undesirable, to this nice neighborhood of Real Americans.

"Elysian Avenue," he thought, looking up at the street sign on the corner. It was an unusual name, not like Maple, Elm, or Mill Street. He wondered what the name meant and asked a few neighbors, but no one knew. "Well now, hmm, I haven't given it much thought," Mr. McMahon, who lived next door, told him. Elysian Avenue, Michele would learn many years later, when his youngest son had gone off to college and read it in a book, probably derived from the Elysium Fields of Greek mythology, the final place of rest for the souls of heroes and the virtuous.

Michele took Teresa to inspect the house, although the decision to buy would be his. "It needs work," he told her. "The wiring, the old furnace and heating system, the plumbing, it all needs to be fixed or replaced. Downstairs needs a bathroom, another bedroom, maybe two. Upstairs needs a kitchen and a bathroom to make a nice apartment. The front steps are broken and gotta be rebuilt. Needs a new front entrance for the people upstairs. The roof needs some new slate. The kitchen needs a new window in the corner. Plaster gotta be fixed all over, and needs lotta painting. The cellar gotta be bigger, fixed up. Lotta work it needs, inside, outside."

Carpentry, masonry, plastering, and painting were skills that he knew well, and Michele was confident that he could transform the house into two apartments. His family would occupy the larger first-floor apartment, taking advantage of the basement and yard, and he would find tenants for the upper floor. Even the attic and cellar had possibilities for future renovation and expansion.

The house had been built years before, on a former apple orchard that had been cut into small lots to accommodate the growing town. There was room for a vegetable garden and grapevines, and for some expansion of the house. The garage, he saw, needed new doors. It was also too small for a modern automobile and would have to be lengthened. Michele planned to buy a car in another few years—he liked the stately Packards with their long hoods and pointed grilles.

Michele looked at the house and those around it. Then he walked the four-block street from Highway 9-W at the top of the hill to Franklin Street and the railroad tracks at the bottom. He liked the neighborhood and the appearance of the house, with its front porch that right-angled around two sides, its high, peaked roof, the decorative Victorian woodwork, and the small, colorful, tinted glass squares around the edges of the windows. What Michele saw was not a turn-of-the-century house standing before him, but the house it would someday become after his renovations, the house he had promised Teresa. Michele had no qualms about the enormous amount of work or his skills, even though he had no experience with plumbing or electrical work. "If I don't know how," he told himself, "I'll figure it out."

As for the expenses, Michele had calculated closely and explained to Teresa that his factory wages would not be enough for the mortgage and other bills. Creating an upstairs income-producing apartment would be necessary.

Teresa, still new to the country, was worried. With the few dollars that Michele earned each week, how could they buy a house? "How we gonna pay for it?" she asked

For years Michele had sought extra work in the afternoons and evenings, small jobs around town, cutting lawns and making minor repairs for a number of homeowners. He saved those earnings in his bank account for a down payment on a house.

"I can keep on makin' extra money cuttin' grass and doin' those jobs for the people I already know. One day a week, Sunday, I'll work on Macrina's farm; she always needs the help. In the winter the town hires part-timers to shovel snow and clear the storm drains, the fire plugs, the fire alarm boxes on the corners. With all that, I can pick up another 20 hours a week, easy. And that, with the money from The Mill, will make the difference."

He felt confident with his plans and was not deterred by a work week of 75 or 80 hours plus the time to walk to the various work sites. It was a less demanding week than the farm work back in Maida and paid a good deal more. As for the upkeep and renovations needed in the house, Michele would do the work himself—no need to hire electricians, carpenters, masons, painters, or plumbers. Teresa would run the home and care for the family. Her Italian peasant's skills for economizing would be worth many extra hours of paid employment.

With steady employment at The Mill and their own determination and continuing good health, Michele knew that, working together, he and Teresa would succeed.

"God willing," Teresa[11] said with a sigh, making the sign of the cross.

"The Mill willing," Michele corrected, but silently.

Michele and Teresa made their decision to buy a home in a time of secure employment and high optimism. As 1929 opened, President Hoover and his predecessor, Calvin Coolidge, industrial and financial leaders, and influential newspapers like *The New York Times* had spread their assurances of continued prosperity. On the surface all seemed well. In reality, the toughest of times were rapidly approaching. Soon the Italian parents, talking quietly at night, would wonder if their choice of America over Italy had been the right one.

The 1930s were to become dark years. The immigrant families would be severely stressed, but they shared two survival factors: their willing immersion in hard work—at home for the women and on the job for the men—and their devotion to their families. Wherever the work might be, they would find it; whatever demands might arise, they would meet them. Few obstacles could defeat these families—they were survivors.

The powerful Southern Italian work ethic Michele had learned as a youngster now came into play. He could depend on the strength of his body and his willingness to labor as hard as might be necessary to work his way out of any economic problems and take care of his family. Knowing that it was a gamble but also confident in his ability to meet any demands that might come along, Michele decided to purchase the house.

In those days, even in small towns like Nyack, banks were designed as financial palaces to impress the public with the institution's solidity. The floors were marble and fat, fluted pillars reached high to a lofty ceiling that glowed with domed skylights. Tellers stood behind barriers of brass bars, as if in cages. Loan officers sat at impressive desks separated from the public by a wide, low marble balustrade. Applicants were admitted to that sanctuary through a small swinging gate held open by an underling.

My father was carefully respectful of power and authority—but not with a hat-in-hand, downward-glancing, foot-shuffling attitude. Rather, he knew that he was the equal of anyone. He might not have had as much money, education, or social status as others, but there was a quality of dignity and

---

11. Settling into America, Teresa soon adopted the American spelling of her name, Theresa, which she used for the remainder of her life, and which we will use in the remainder of our story.

honor that superseded mere station in life, and good men, he believed, cultivated those qualities. In those situations, Michele dressed carefully—suit, necktie, breast-pocket handkerchief, and polished shoes. He held his head high and, with his trimmed hair, neat clothing, and slim, athletic build, presented himself in a stately manner that was just this side of haughtiness. Were he six feet tall, he would have been an imposing figure, turning heads as he strode by with such seeming assurance. Alas, he was only five feet six inches tall, and slim, about 140 pounds.

On October 6, 1930, Michele placed a down payment on the house at 79 Elysian Avenue. A 20-year mortgage of $5,500 was arranged. He agreed to pay at least $25 a month, nearly 40 percent of his factory wages. The papers were signed, the title cleared, and their new life as property owners in *la bell'America* began.

III

The Great Depression

Chapter 13

The Depression (1932)

1. The Machine

Michele and his brother, Giuseppe, continued working at The Mill through 1929, but a murmur of troubles leaked from behind the mask of good economic times. For 30 years the country had been sinking into a swamp of jingoism and a mistrust of foreigners. New laws fueled by distortions to Darwinian theory[1,2] forced an enormous decline in immigration from Southern and Eastern Europe.[3] "Dago," "Ginzo," "Guinea," and "Wop" rolled easily from American tongues in ordinary conversation, as did "Heinie," "Honkie," "Bohunk," "Polack," "Mockie," "Kike," "Jew Boy," "Nigger," "Coon," "Jigaboo," "Greaser," "Chink," and "Slant Eyes." Immigrant men at work and their sons in school endured daily insults. We fought our tormenters on playgrounds and in the streets, winning some battles but losing most, because the bullies lined up two or three to one. To adults, that was normal, just "what boys do." Americans, however, would not tolerate grown men fighting back.

Each day insults and rejection waited in the background. There was no escape, except when safely at home with family and friends. Michele, now 35 and responsible for a family, could no longer retaliate with fists as in his younger days. That had brought satisfaction, but also more trouble, like the 1913 late-night escape in his brother-in-law's horse-drawn wagon, just ahead of the police. Now he must swallow insults, pretend not to hear them, laugh with his tormenters, remain dignified, and keep to his task of supporting his family. He hoped the derisive background would someday fall silent.

In 1929, two enormous events occurred. The first, on October 29, hit an unprepared nation and affected everyone. The second occurred just two weeks later, tearing into our family with a terrible ferocity. They occurred in tandem, rapidly, like the stunning jabs of a heavyweight boxer.

1. One classic book on social Darwinism is by Hofstadter (1992).
2. Dore (1968).
3. The Johnson-Reed National Origins Act, 1924. Italian immigration into the United States decreased from 283,738 in 1914, the year before the war, to 3,845, the new quota in 1929, the year the act went into effect, a 98 percent decline. See Chapter Four.

On November 15, a machine at The Mill ripped off Uncle Joe's[4] left arm. "An accident," it was said, "somebody was in a hurry, just a little push; not on purpose, of course. No one meant any harm; just an accident, nobody's fault."

Uncle Joe, 26 years old, drowning in the pain and horror of having his arm wrenched from his shoulder, was a long time recovering from that powerful trauma. No one knew then about post-traumatic stress, but it was no less horrific for lack of a name. Like a shark in the water, that machine had taken his arm—not once, but repeatedly, in terrible dreams that would not leave him alone. Rehabilitation services were primitive; good prostheses and counseling were not available. He would have to adjust by himself to that empty sleeve. My father and Aunt Macrina helped their brother and his family through their long ordeal, and somehow, he survived.

New York State paid compensation, perhaps generous for that time— $23 a week from 1929 to 1935, a little more than five years, for a total of 6,250 dollars, the lifetime economic value of a young working man's left arm in those days. Those who ran The Mill did not abandon him but, with some sense of compassion and responsibility, reemployed him despite his severe handicap. Uncle Joe asked nothing of anyone and worked as hard and as well as any two-armed man. But what work could a man with one arm carry out? He could not lift and carry heavy boxes nor operate machines that required two constantly moving hands to manipulate levers and switches and keep them running without jamming.

It took him years to climb out of his despair and pain, to reassemble a normal life. He found his healing in work, in earning wages to support his family, carrying out those most important tasks required of a man. Searching for tasks that he could manage, Uncle Joe learned to operate a forklift truck, driving the powerful machine with his one arm through The Mill's crowded corridors. Years later, when I worked at The Mill, I would see Uncle Joe drive by, sitting high up at the controls, maneuvering heavy pallets from one department to another, from production floor to loading dock and back, with never an error. He worked at The Mill for 48 years, retiring in 1969 at the age of 66. Through it all, Uncle Joe took care of his family and remained the gentlest, sweetest, and most generous man I have ever known.

He confided to his brother that as terrible as it had been, his falling into that machine might have had an even more hideous ending. Like his brother, Uncle Joe was not a religious man; he never claimed divine protection, but knew that through a twist of chance he was still alive, and for that he was grateful. I think that knowing what he had been spared, instead of dwelling on what he had lost, helped him to heal and to maintain his integrity and wonderfully benign view of life.

---

4. Uncle Joe was Giuseppe Graziano, Michele's younger brother.

2. The Paper Mountain

Just three weeks before that terrible event, the other disaster had occurred, affecting the entire nation, although most people did not immediately realize its impact. On October 24, the stock market had its most volatile day in history. Just five days later, on "Black Tuesday," October 29, 1929, 16 million shares were traded at far below their value of just hours before and the stock market crashed. It was the first loud public warning of the coming Depression. Over a two-month period, $32 billion of America's wealth simply vanished. Many thought the stock market crash caused the Depression, but recession or depression had occurred in 1902, 1907, and 1910.[5] The 1930s depression had been under way, unrecognized, for years. The 1920s postwar excitement and prosperity had masked the economy's real weaknesses, but they were about to be revealed.

America, unlike Europe, had been spared war's devastation and returned quickly to a civilian economy. There were problems as communist, socialist, and fascist appeals caught the attention of many Americans. But the government was stable, and while Europe spiraled down into economic depression, political chaos, and Fascist dictatorships, the U.S. economy steamed along. Stock values soared, commerce bubbled, men worked and supported their families, and investors prospered. The 1920s seemed a decade with no limits.

Postwar factories hired workers to produce a rich flow of consumer goods. Credit became easily available. Business and industries expanded, relying on their marginal stock investments and low-interest borrowing. From 1921 through 1929, the stock market's value ballooned. America was riding high and happily on a towering surge of prosperity, but it was all built on a mountain of debt, and debts must eventually be paid.[6]

While the debt grew, other things were happening—or failing to happen—out of sight of most Americans. Most destructively, there was little sharing of the new wealth. Instead, in accord with the values of successive Republican administrations, a small portion of the population appropriated the lion's share of the new wealth. It went into huge salaries, bonuses, and expense accounts for executives, high dividends for stockholders, and tax relief for the rich, but it did not increase workers' wages. While factory workers' productivity increased more than 40 percent and corporate profits 65 percent, wages for workers increased less than 10 percent, and the average working family received only a petty share of the nation's prosperity. At the same time, industrial monopolies were growing, giving even greater power to fewer groups and further reducing the range of income distribution. For example, by 1930 three companies controlled half the country's electrical output.[7] Adding to the inequalities, the government enacted huge

5. Primack and Willis (1980).
6. Phillips (1969).
7. Ibid.

tax cuts for the wealthy. In 1926, taxes for those earning more than $1 million a year were cut by more than 65 percent. By 1929, the top 0.1 percent of U.S. families had as much income as the bottom 42 percent.

Heavy industry, no longer producing for war, slowed and began to lay off workers. Europe, war-devastated, could not buy American products or pay wartime reparations. World demand fell; factory, farm, and coal mine production slowed; railroad and ocean shipping decreased. World trade staggered, and more workers were laid off.

At first, only a few groups were affected—farmers, railroad workers, and coal miners. Farmers were particularly assaulted, but were not easily visible to an increasingly urbanized country. Banks repossessed farms, forcing those families to auction everything for pennies on the dollar. By 1920, a dozen years before most felt it, American farmers knew economic depression. Farmers accounted for nearly a quarter of the U.S. economy, and hurting farmers hurt everyone. In the 1930s, when the already beaten farmers were further attacked by drought and pushed deeper into poverty, America turned against them, refusing to help. They blamed farmers for their own misery, driving them from "decent" towns where good people wanted no "Okies," "Bums," or "Hobos." Desperation grew in rural and coal-mining areas, but this was of little concern to most Americans, who continued to buy on credit and believe in unending prosperity for all.

The great American economic engine was beginning to sputter.

With falling income, families could no longer buy the river of consumer goods that had been so optimistically produced. Retail sales and savings began to slip. American products piled up in warehouses. Americans began defaulting on their debts. Banks, heavily invested in mortgages and the stock market, began to fail. Between 1921 and 1933, nearly 16,000 banks failed—more than half the country's banks—further reducing the money supply and choking off factories, farms, stores, and households.

President Hoover, industrialists, and financiers told Americans those events were merely postwar economic adjustments that would be ironed out by the normal workings of the free-market economy. As long as business was protected and taxes on the wealthy kept low, they said, prosperity would "trickle down" to everyone. Most people went about their normal affairs, and investors reveled as their paper wealth continued to climb.

The market's prosperity was built on a paper mountain of debt—10 cents on the dollar—and the mountain sat on nothing more than investors' promises to pay. As the economy slowed to match the depressed pace of the rest of the world and the country's money supply decreased, investors could no longer pay their debts. In 1929, feeling the first stabs of panic, they began selling their stocks at whatever price was offered.

The mountain began to tremble.

Few people noticed those events in the 1920s. My parents and their friends felt little threat. They were not economists or financiers, and they knew nothing of margins, shares, and stock market investment. They could not be expected to see clearly what others, who should have seen, failed to notice. They sensed some unease, hearing about shaky things going on in the mysterious stock market, but after all, this was *la bell'America*, and the president himself had said there was no problem. Their jobs were safe at The Mill, which seemed not to have been hurt, not like heavy industries elsewhere. The Mill continued running, and men collected their wages.

Then The Mill stopped hiring new workers. Hourly wages stagnated, and in some departments hours were reduced, but no jobs were cut. Because prices were declining, such cuts were not quite as threatening as they might have been.

It was too bad, though, that *Zio* Serratore would lose his grocery store on Main Street, because he had generously trusted too many people with credit and now they had no money to pay him. And it was unfortunate that some houses in Nyack became empty, their owners unemployed and gone elsewhere. Even on Elysian Avenue a house stood vacant, its family and its life shaken out of it.

On "Black Tuesday," the paper mountain collapsed. Thirty-two billion dollars of the country's wealth vanished like *Nonno* Peppe's money orders up in smoke.

Our folks talked about the market's crash but were more puzzled than concerned. Some had heard that the economy was grinding down and they might soon be out of work. But the men's concern was blunted. The crash was a distant event, far away on New York City's Wall Street, with little impact on them. As long as The Mill kept running, they were secure.

It was nearly a year after the crash that Michele and Theresa bought the house at 79 Elysian Avenue, not understanding that the Great Depression had already set in. In early 1930, after he purchased the house, Michele still had no recognition that average people would be affected, even after the stock market crash of a few months earlier. In fact, he had heard that economic recovery had already begun. Newspapers carried President Hoover's continued faith in the "power of the free market" to correct any problems. Financiers spoke of regained confidence in the economy. The brief downturn was over, they said, and a depression would not occur.

In the final months of 1930, however, banking, manufacturing, farming, and retail crumbled. Bank failures averaged nearly 2,500 a year from 1930–1933. Within three years, a million farms were foreclosed and unemployment, which had lingered around 3 percent for nearly a decade, exceeded a quarter of the work force by 1933. A million farmers, 15 million workers, and their estimated 70 million dependents fell into poverty. Homeless, despondent men roamed the country, to be chased away by the police or by frightened citizens. More jobs disappeared from Nyack and more people became desperate. Two more houses were abandoned on Elysian Avenue.

3. Hoover's Disgrace

In 1932, Michele heard of food riots in Detroit and St. Louis, and of a shameful incident where President Hoover set the army against World War I veterans in Washington. There was talk of a "revolution" about to explode. What was happening to the country? It seemed to be tearing apart—on one side there was the euphoria of mindlessly happy pastimes like professional sports (*u pazzo americana*), Broadway shows, popular songs, new automobiles, flappers, speakeasies, gin, and jazz. On the other side, jobless men roamed the country in a grim army of despair.

"The economy is fundamentally sound!" President Hoover repeated. "The Depression is just a passing incident in our national life," he said. In 1932, the Chairman of the Board of U.S. Steel assured the country that American industry was already recovering, that the Depression would soon be over. The radio and newspapers urged people to banish their "doom and gloom." They told uplifting stories of Americans who battled the Depression by going to work, running their businesses, and refusing to give up. "Go out and buy! Be a patriot. Spend money and put America back to work!"

My father and his friends heard the messages. They looked at each other. "What do they say?" one asked.

"They say, 'Go spend your money. Buy, buy!' And that makes everything all right."

The men paused, puzzled. "*Ma, sono tutti pazzi, no?* (But they are all crazy, no?)"

"*Si, tutti sono pazzi.* (Yes, they are all crazy.)"

"And is it true? Food riots in *la bell'America*? Can that be?"

"*Si, è vero.* Just like we used to have years ago, in *Torino, Milano*, and *Napoli*."

"What's going on? They say Mussolini is putting Italy right again, fixin' the depression. But over here, we go in the other direction!"

Eight years earlier, in 1924, Congress had acknowledged World War I veterans' contribution to the country and awarded them U.S. bonds of up to $1,000, based upon their length of military service. The bonds were to mature in 20 years, 1945. However, by 1930 the Depression had set in. Millions were out of work and desperate. Many were veterans, and they asked that their bonds be redeemed now, when they needed the money. In 1931, a few congressmen agreed, but there was so much opposition by conservative Republicans that the measure failed. The next year, another attempt was made and a bill was scheduled for vote. To show support, veterans converged on Washington—at first a few, soon a torrent of 20,000 veterans, wives, and children.

They were a desperate lot—broken by the Depression, destitute, hungry, and with little hope. All had served their country and now asked their country to help them. With scavenged material from a nearby trash dump, they built a shantytown of cardboard and tarpaper near a row of condemned downtown buildings. "Tent City" and "Bonus City" it was called. For three months, the veterans, calling themselves the BEF (Bonus Expeditionary Force), walked peacefully in small groups, carrying American flags and asking their congressmen to support the "bonus legislation."

The bill passed in the House of Representatives but was overwhelmingly defeated by the more conservative Senate.

About half the veterans, defeated, left Washington. Others remained, hoping for another try. In July, a minor encounter escalated into tragedy when a policeman opened fire on the unarmed veterans, killing one. The veterans responded with stones, and the police appealed to the army to control what they said was a "riot," instigated by the marchers. A frightened President Hoover gave the order.

Army Chief of Staff General Douglas MacArthur and his aides, Majors Dwight D. Eisenhower and George S. Patton, commanded the troops. This was a "communist revolution," MacArthur said and, ignoring President Hoover's direct orders, armed his soldiers with fully loaded weapons. At 4:30 p.m. on July 28, 600 infantrymen with fixed bayonets, mounted cavalry with drawn sabers, six tanks, and a machine gun unit advanced in disciplined order against the veterans and their wives and children, who sat in their makeshift huts and tents. The soldiers lobbed tear gas grenades at the families, hit them with the flat sides of their sabers (cutting off the ear of one man), and, as it was described, "pig-stuck" and victoriously drove the veterans and their families up Pennsylvania Avenue and out of the city. Then they burned down whatever was left in the camp, destroying the families' few belongings.

The army was praised for its discipline that kept down the number of casualties and for not firing a single bullet. Two veterans and one baby had been killed, an 11-year-old boy was blinded, and several women suffered miscarriages. More than 1,000 people were severely sickened by the tear gas. All in all, it was quite a successful operation, and President Hoover later said, "Thank God there is a government in Washington that knows how to deal with a mob."[8] The veterans and their wives and children had been defeated. A few years later, in 1936, a more liberal Congress approved the veterans' bonus bill, overturning President Roosevelt's surprising veto and allowing the veterans to cash in their bonds.

4. The Mill

In 1932, as Hoover drove the veterans out of Washington, Mussolini was in the 10th year of his Fascist rule. Adolph Hitler, impressed by Mussolini, became Europe's next Fascist dictator, followed by Spain's Franco

8. Phillips, page 5.

and Portugal's Salazar.[9] Japan continued building its military and extending its empire. Nationalism, militarism, and industrialism flowed together, and World War II was but a half-dozen years away.

For Americans those were background events, mere whispers from beyond two oceans and not important in the face of more immediate catastrophes. By 1932, Americans knew they had fallen into the Great Depression, and all the president's men could not put the economy back together again. Nor could Hoover's optimistic reassurances and armed cavalry chase away the frightening realities confronting the American people. Outrageous things like Hoover's dreadful action against American veterans were happening in the country. Everyone was growing frightened, not only about the economy, but of the government and of President Hoover himself. The 1932 presidential election in November promised to be a referendum on whether the country would continue Hoover's conservative Republican policies or turn to something else.

In Nyack, local factories were cutting back, several stores on Main Street closed, and youngsters began dropping out of school, seeking work to help their families, usually without success. The Mill closed for several weeks. Some men were recalled later, for part-time work, but others were not, and their desperation grew.

My father and Uncle Joe were among the fortunate, and resumed working at The Mill after it reopened. Their lives seemed normal, but the background was ominous, like a swarm of angry bees, Michele thought, still far away, but growing closer, louder. Perhaps the swarm would never arrive, but if it did, what then?

It was 1:00 on a cold Monday afternoon in mid-January 1932, a few months before the Bonus Army's march on Washington. Michele had left for work as usual at 5:30 that morning. Fred, midway through the seventh grade, was in school. Theresa, having finished the laundry that now dried on wooden racks in the furnace-warmed cellar, added coals to the kitchen stove to heat the oven. She floured the breadboard, preparing to make dough. Theresa looked up when she heard the side door open, felt the brisk intrusion of winter air into her warm kitchen, and was surprised to see Michele home at that early hour. He stamped the snow from his shoes, removed his hat and gloves, hung his coat on its hook in the lower back hall, and slowly came up the three steps into the kitchen. He seemed distracted and, unlike his usual careful manner, carelessly dropped his metal lunchbox onto the wooden table. It slammed with the solid thud of fullness, not the hollow sound of emptiness that told of a good lunch enjoyed. He said nothing and stood with his back to Theresa, warming his cold hands over the stove.

9. After World War II, Spain and Portugal, under the dictatorships of Francisco Franco (1936–1975) and Antonio Salazar (1932–1970), remained Fascist states.

Theresa, puzzled, brushed a strand of hair from her forehead, leaving a streak of white flour. "Why are you home so early?" she asked. Michele was slow to answer, and she felt a warning wave of anxiety.

"Your lunch?" she asked, quickly looking away from him, distancing herself from the terrible idea that was forming in her mind. Theresa released the two metal snaps on the lunchbox, opened it, and saw that everything she had packed that morning was still there, undisturbed, neatly wrapped in waxed paper.

"Michele, you don' eat your lunch today?"

He pulled out a chair and sat down at the table, slumping with a weary resignation that she had never before seen in him.

"Michele, what's the matter? You don' eat your lunch, and you're home too early. What's happen'?" He started to say something, but no words came out. He looked at her with a sad, puzzled expression.

"Oh, my God, your job?" Theresa sat down, suddenly, as if her legs had folded under her. Her arm brushed a little white blizzard of flour from the breadboard, spilling it down over her ankles and shoes and onto the floor, but she did not notice.

"Michele, your job?"

Theresa was frightened and she could no longer keep the thought away by fumbling with the lunchbox. She looked at her husband and put her hands protectively over her rounded belly, just a month from the expected birth, leaving white, floured handprints.

Michele reached over and gently brushed at the flour. "Look at you," he said, quietly. "You look like your bread dough, all covered with flour." He smiled, urging along his little joke, but the smile kept flickering out.

Theresa would not be diverted. "Michele, tell me. The Mill. What? You lose your job?"

"No," he said, slowly shaking his head and holding her hand, wanting to reassure her. But, in truth, how much reassurance could he give her?

"I still have my job, some of it anyway. Don't worry. Everything will be OK."

But Theresa did worry. "Some? Some of it? What do you mean, some of it?"

"They cut our hours," Michele told her, still holding her hand. "And now we gonna be down to only three and a half days. Joe, too, his hours been cut. At least we have some work. We're lucky; some don't have any work. They don't know what they gonna do. My friend Tom, he rides with me on the bus; now he's gonna lose his house. The bank is takin' his house away. He just bought it three years ago. Tom, he been fixin' it up. Lotta work they put in that old house, Tom and his wife, lotta work. Now they gonna take it away from him. What's he gonna do now? What's gonna happen to his family?"

That night they sat at the kitchen table, their coffee growing cold, ignoring the *biscotti* Theresa had baked. Uncle Joe and Aunt Nancy were there, staring at the same reality—how were they to survive with their wages cut by 40 percent? Uncle Joe, a man with one arm, transformed two years before by a mindless machine that still whirred in The Mill, had even more to worry about, knowing that no other employer would hire him. What could they do but share their fears that what had happened to Tom and his family might now happen to them?

My brother, then 11 years old, listened, absorbing their worry, beginning to understand that they had been living just this side of poverty with only the men's jobs for protection. Now those jobs and the families' welfare were threatened by "the Depression." Fred had little understanding of what was happening, but he knew that life was going to be different. Were his friends Buster, Dessart, Joe, Jack, and Otto all going through the same thing with their families, sitting around their kitchen tables, feeling this fear and not knowing what to do about it? Yes, he would soon learn, they were.

Two years earlier, being in debt for a house had been an honorable condition, a sign of success, a patriotic action encouraged by the consumer society. For the immigrants, home ownership was a powerful symbol of their triumph. Their journey from *la terra di miseria* found its deepest meaning in their new status as free citizens in a free country, living in *homes of their own*. "*Finalmente, noi siamo arrivati* (Finally, we have arrived)!" they told themselves as they took possession of their new homes.

Now, Michele and Theresa faced losing their home; their success would be short lived. Less work at The Mill meant a lighter pay envelope, down to $11 a week. Mortgage payments would take $7, leaving but $4 a week for food, clothing, coal and firewood, taxes, doctors, medicine, and all else. This was not what *la bell'America* was supposed to be! Sitting at the kitchen table, calculating on bits of paper, comparing income and expenses, "so much a week for this, so much for that," Michele could not make the figures come out any better. He was not a big man, but he was lean, wiry, square-shouldered, and hard-muscled from years of physical labor. A family's strength, he knew, begins with the man. This was part of the ethic of *la famiglia*, that irreducible human group to which one paid allegiance above all else. Were he to put it into words, he might have said, simply, "That's just the way it is; it's for the man to be strong for his family." Nevertheless, one day Michele revealed to Uncle Joe, "You know why I keep my hair so short? So I can't get my fingers in and tear it out."[10]

As her fourth pregnancy neared its end early in 1932, Theresa's anxiety grew, and spiked in alarm when Michele told her of the work reduction. Between 1927 and 1930, a boy and a girl had been born but, as happened

---

10. Michele kept his hair neatly trimmed and short in a crew cut or flat-top.

frequently in those days, had died in infancy. Theresa was in good health during this pregnancy, but still grieved over her two lost babies and feared for this one. She promised herself that whatever God might bring about, she would have that operation and this would be her last pregnancy.

Michele, seeing her distress, tried to soothe her. "It will be all right," he said. "There's nothing to worry about." Even as he said it, he knew there was much to worry about. With the Depression deepening, his working hours and income cut, Michele feared that his first missed mortgage payment would be only a month or two away. How many missed payments would the bank tolerate before it took the house?

Theresa prayed each day, asking God to bless and protect her child soon to be born. God answered her prayers, and their son, to be named Anthony, was born in mid-February, and grew heartily. But for His own reasons, which Theresa never dared to question, God imposed a price—for this new life, He took two others from the family.

5. Francesca

We have an old photograph showing a smiling man in his 60s holding a tiny white bundle in the back yard of Michele and Theresa's house on Elysian Avenue. It was April 1932. The man was Michele Dattilo, Theresa's father, the family's patriarch, the migrant who had started the family's journeys to America in 1900. The bundle was Anthony, two months old, being held gently by his grandfather, who had traveled from Ocean City to meet his new grandson. The visit should have been a happy one.

The letter had arrived from Maida shortly before, and Michele Dattilo, a still-vibrant man of 64 years, not old even by the standards of 1930, was suddenly worn out, tired, dispirited.

"I'm going home," he told Theresa. "This time, to stay. I'm finished with America and will never come back. Why didn't I go back years ago, to be with my family? I had to stay here. Why? For money that we can't earn in Italy! Now I'm going home, but it's too late. How much time will I have with my daughter?"

"She's only 16, your little sister," he told Theresa. "*Tubercolosi, la malattia americana*, is taking her away, just like *il polmonite* took away *Zio* Giuseppe, Macrina's husband. It comes back to plague us again. But Francesca, she's only 16. Only 16."

He showed Theresa the letter from Maida, and she cried for herself, for her father, for her family, and for her little sister's final misery.

Before leaving for Italy, Michele Dattilo offered a generous price for the house in Maida owned by my father, who had bought it in 1921 for Theresa to live in while he worked in America. "I will need a house for me and Elisabetta," he said, "and you and Theresa can use the money for your house here."

The exchange was made. My grandparents now owned a house in Maidà, and Michele and Theresa had money for two more years of payments on their Nyack house. They were overwhelmed with gratitude for the older man's generosity, for they would gladly have given him the Maida house without payment. They would still have to struggle under the weight of the Depression, but the security of that financial cushion lifted much of the burden. The despairing mood Theresa had been developing retreated. She recognized her father's generosity, but also knew the hand of God had been extended in answer to her prayers. Michele, equally grateful, saw only the benign hands of his father-in-law. If the hand of God was there, it was not evident to my father.

In April 1932, my grandfather quit his job in Ocean City, gave away his few things, closed out his postal savings account, paid his bills, said goodbye to his brothers, and returned to Maida to be with his daughter. Within two months, Francesca died. Michele was despondent, convinced he had failed her by not being there to protect her. My grandfather never recovered from his grief and guilt and lived silently in his private misery for another three or four months. Then he too died. Michele Dattilo was 64, his daughter only 16. Both were too young for death in a family of long lives. She died of tuberculosis; he died, it was said, of a broken heart.

For my grandmother *Nonna* Elisabetta, 1932 was her *anno di miseria*, a year never to be forgotten or forgiven. Her husband, absent during much of nearly 30 years, had finally returned, but Death had taken him away. Always looking to take advantage when He could, the Dark Prankster also stole away her youngest child. Two other daughters, Anna and Theresa, lived in America with their husbands and children. *La famiglia* was being torn from her, some transported from *Italia* to America, others from life to death.

Michele Dattilo's generous payment for the Maida house (about $600) created a big margin of safety for the family. Their survival, however, would require at least $20 a week, or an additional $9 weekly. As people said, "*Non lavori assai, nessun dollaro hai, e non mangerai mai.*" It was as simple as that: without work there are no dollars, and without dollars there is nothing to eat. Michele began planning how to earn the dollars in those economically stagnated times.

In 1931, soon after buying the house and while still working full time, Michele started converting the second-floor bedrooms into an apartment. He found bargains in secondhand fixtures and worked late into each night. He also built a bedroom in the attic for Fred and a separate front entrance for the upstairs apartment. Then he was ready to install a tenant. The rent, $12 a month, would be a buffer against the Great Depression.

During the Depression, the tenants often came downstairs, hesitantly knocked on the door, and explained that they could not pay the month's rent. Michele allowed them to stay, and nearly all eventually paid their debts. I remember one couple, the Frederickses, older people who finally left, accepting the truth that they had no money and no prospects for earning any. Michele understood that theirs was a common plight and he supported them for several months, for which they were grateful. Out of work, their savings gone, too old to compete for jobs, they finally moved into their daughter's crowded apartment. For a while, Mrs.Fredericks would drop by to visit Mom, and soon, like everyone else from that era, she eventually passed out of my life.

To support his family, Michele needed more income. He developed a grueling schedule, working in The Mill three and a half days a week and then, during the late afternoons, evenings, and weekends, walking through town seeking extra jobs. He mowed lawns, cleaned yards, trimmed trees, chopped wood, shoveled snow, tended furnaces, and did carpentry and masonry repairs for people who were still fortunate enough to be able to hire others. When work was available, he signed on to village crews to clear ditches, patch roads, and, in the winter, shovel snow from the water hydrants and fire alarm boxes. On Sunday afternoons, he walked the several miles to Aunt Macrina's farm and helped tend the large garden that she shared with her two brothers. In the winter, he helped repair tools and machinery and prepare flower beds for the spring. In good weeks his extra labor earned the extra dollars the family needed to survive a few more days. Some weeks brought little or no extra work, and he returned home late at night, fatigued from walking, dispirited from failing. At those times, the world looked even more threatening, more out of his control.

6. The Larder

There was one area he could control—food for the family. Michele, like every Southern Italian immigrant with the space for it, created a garden in the back yard. The farmer of Southern Italy could not be suppressed, no matter how urbanized he might become. Cultivating one's own garden, however small, was an affirmation of identity, a grasp on one's family traditions. They would no more live without growing food in their own gardens than they would live in a house with no roof. The garden's produce was shared among the families, as was a friendly competition of growing the finest vegetables.

While our American neighbors maintained lawns, Michele worked a productive garden. Despite his extra jobs, he found the time and energy for his garden, and with skills learned as a child working on Italian farms he produced bountiful crops. From early summer into late fall he harvested peas, beans, lettuce, escarole, tomatoes, peppers, squash, pumpkins, carrots, scallions, onions, raspberries, grapes, currants, peaches, figs, herbs and spices, and more that I no longer remember. Fresh produce from Michele's garden and the farms of Uncle Joe and Aunt Macrina was shared, an abundance of food for the three families. He expanded his grape arbors, and within a few years was producing enough deep-purple concord grapes for Theresa to make jellies and jams for the whole year, and for Michele, of course, to make his wine.[11]

These Italian families were true to their peasant upbringing. Their gardens were small but abundant. Whomever we visited in the summertime, I always found a little forest of pole beans sprouting in the back yard, surrounded by a variety of other vegetables. Food production began with the sweet, fresh peas of early summer, but it was the months of September and October, *il raccolto* (harvest time), that saw sustained, high-energy activity. This was the celebratory reaping of good harvests, followed by the intensive labors of preserving food for the coming winter. Those few weeks of extraordinary activity, mostly by the women, seemed to a child with no responsibilities to be one long, happy celebration.

Those who owned automobiles drove others to local farms to pick bushels of fresh produce, adding to the harvest from their own gardens. For days, several families gathered in our large, cool cellar to boil jars; clean, peel, chop, and slice vegetables and fruit; fill sterilized jars and add spices and herbs; and seal the jars for winter's use.

It was a celebration, a sharing of abundance, gossip, and laughter, together banking security for the coming winter. Children dashed about the cellar, up the stairs and down, running outdoors, indoors, always noisy, engaged in their own important business, just this side of mischief. Our cellar shelves gradually filled with rows of vegetables and fruit in their sparkling jars. Their reds, whites, and greens, many dotted with black peppercorns and fat, white garlic, gleamed through the glass, colorful like Italian Christmas cookies. Jars of carrots, peaches, pears, and cherries added their splashes of orange, yellow, creamy white, and dark red. Oregano, parsley, sweet basil, mint, garlic, and hot red and green peppers hung from the ceiling, drying. On a wide, raised plank on the floor stood three thick earthenware crocks of pickled green tomatoes, peppers, and eggplant, all sliced, spiced, and salted, each crock weighted down with a heavy stone that added pressure and thus heat to fuel the chemistry of the pickling process.

In the fall, several families bought a butchered hog from a local farm. As I recall, families gathered at the home of *Zio* Antonio on Mill Street. Big pots of boiling water were set over a wood fire in the back yard; men with hatchets, saws, and long knives cut up the carcass. Chops, steaks, ribs, and loins appeared. With hand-turned meat grinders and wide copper funnels, long strings of sausages were made. Some of the meat was salted and smoked for long-term preserving; some was prepared for more immediate use. All was divided among the families.

11. Years later, when their economic condition had improved, Michele bought red and white California grapes for his wine making.

Wine making, another fall activity, was also a skill brought from Italy.
Like the grapes, it blossomed in *la bell'America*. This was a task exclusively
for the men, and each knew the skills well. Every year bottles were exchanged in friendly competition to see whose wine was best.

Michele climbed his ladder and picked the ripe purple grapes from his
overhead arbors, and then sorted, rinsed, crushed, and pressed them in a
hand-operated grinder and winepress. It was a long, loving labor that was
mysterious to me. My father tested and adjusted levels of acid, sugar, and
temperature, judged color, watched the fermentation. Nearly a year later,
he would siphon the wine into bottles, cork them, and store them slanted
downward on the dusty cellar racks for still another year. At dinnertime,
and when friends visited, bottles were uncorked and the wine begun two
years earlier was enjoyed.

Like his house, each bottle of wine was an important symbol for my
father. Bringing a bottle up from the cellar, wiping off the dust, holding it
to the sunlight and assessing its color, pulling the cork, pouring, swirling,
waiting a few moments, then sampling, composed as much of a ceremony
as the priests' reverent raising of the wine chalice during Sunday mass.
I think my father found more of God in his winemaking than in all the
church services that Mom made him attend.

Dinnertime required the family to gather at the end of each day in celebration of what we were privileged to enjoy—each other, and the food
and wine prepared and set before us by our parents. It was our daily celebration of *la famiglia*.

My father's dinnertime wine ceremony lasted only a moment, and I am
not certain that we recognized it as a ceremony.[12] It was a rich moment,
providing a soft transition from a day of work to our celebration of family.
The bottle of wine was a centerpiece of this ceremony. For all the men in
this small group of Italian immigrants, a glass of wine was much more than
a glass of wine.

There were no prayers at the table, no saying of grace at dinnertime,
even on holidays. Mom believed that God had helped bring our food and
comfort, but the rest of us knew it had been provided by our parents' labors. I recall asking my father why we never said grace, as did my American
friends. "Maybe," he said, "sometimes we give God too much credit for
the good things and not enough for the bad."

I have wondered if that was a point of friction between my parents.
If it had been left up to Mom, a prayer would have been recited before
each meal. My father was willing to accompany the family to church on
Sundays, stay awake during the sermon, and dutifully drop the family's

---

12. My attempts to continue this tradition have been largely unsuccessful. Our three children,
thoroughly socialized in American culture, find little meaning in it. Our son-in-law, Mark, and
daughter-in-law, Sabine, however, seem to understand, and I like to think that a bit of the tradition will survive through them.

envelope into the collection basket. That was fine for God's house. But I suspect he took being the master of his own table seriously, and would not tolerate any competition from outside or above.

As those weeks of *raccolto* ended and the cold weather settled in, our basement storage room and wine cellar filled with enough food and wine and, for me, home-brewed, sweet and bubbly root beer to keep the family going for a long time. In addition to the preserved food, Mom purchased basic items for her larder, like salt and sugar, coffee beans, flour, dried beans, imported olive oil, and heavily salted imported anchovies. The imported olive oil was expensive, but a necessity for Italian cooking. The imported anchovies, however, were a luxury.

My brother once told me that our cellar was like the hold of a big ship, its provisions standing ready for the hungry crew. His memory of crossing the ocean nearly 10 years earlier, in what must have seemed a giant ship, was blurring now. Perhaps seeing the cellar as a ship's hold served somehow as a needed reconstruction of his own passage to America, a review, to help him understand who and where he was.

As I think about it, I realize that the preparation of that extensive cellar larder was an expression of peasant independence and self-sufficiency. "*Tu lo devi fare. Solamente tu. Perché nessun altro lo farà per te.* (You have to do it. Only you. No one else will do it for you.)"

"Freh'," Mom asked, "you go down and bring up for me a jar of tomatoes?"

"Come on, Sailor," he would call to me, "we're going down into the hold."

"Aye, aye, Sir," I said, always ready to play the game. "But first turn on the lights. I don't want to go down there in the dark. It's too spooky!"

Going into the cellar, or the ship's hold as it became in our imaginations, brought us into a quiet and cool world where floating aromas greeted us, shifting as we moved from one room to the next. The wine room braced us with its intoxicating crushed grapes. In another room, the sharp, spiced acidic smells of green tomatoes pickling in their crocks mingled with the gentler aromas of hanging herbs and spices. It was a dazzling olfactory journey matched only by the tantalizing smells that greeted us in the Italian delicatessen on Franklin Street, and of course outdone by the fragrance of Mom's cooking in her warm kitchen.

I have asked how these uneducated and poor immigrants made it through the Depression in a new country with a strange language when so many others, with many more resources, knowledge, and experience in America, did not survive. I am convinced that, in those long Depression years, their traditional ties to the land gave these former peasants an important economic and psychological advantage over their non-Italian neighbors, who depended on food bought in stores. The preserved foods from our own gardens augmented our diets, significantly reducing what had to be purchased. In times without money, Mom could reach down into her cellar for flour, herbs and spices, home-canned tomatoes, fat green beans, sweet pears, peaches, and bottles of wine. From her own larder, Mom created hot bread and *pasta fresca*[13] and spicy tomato sauces, tasty dishes of green beans, olive oil, and onions, and, for dessert, home-baked fruit pies or cakes or her own preserved pears or peaches colorfully topped with a dab of homemade grape jam. Add, of course, a bottle of my father's wine. Depression or not, poor or not, hunger was never a problem, at least not that I, as a child, knew.[14]

The Great Depression defined reality and threatened survival. It created a situation over which most people had no control. For these families, however, the almost ritualistic preparation of extensive winter larders was one of their control strategies. The Depression, then, was not completely devastating; they could assert themselves and fight back against that giant enemy. When they asked, "Where is our next meal to come from?" these immigrant families knew that when all else failed, that next meal could come right from their own cellars. That sense of control over at least one aspect of the Depression created a stable mooring in their sea of desperation.

My father's task was to ensure that our home remained securely ours. Earning those extra few dollars a week to meet the mortgage payments became the focus of his personal economy. When the week was good, it produced those few dollars; when bad, it did not. Earning—or failing to earn –$7 dictated the anxiety level for each week. But if my parents knew constant weariness from their daily fight against the Great Depression, I knew little of it.

Oscar Wilde said, "There is only one class in the community that thinks more about money than the rich, and that is the poor. The poor can think of nothing else."[15] My father never thought of himself as "poor," and he would have been offended were anyone to suggest he was. To be among *i poveri*, to have crossed that line, was to have failed, to have negated the journey from *la terra di miseria* to *la bell'America*. Throughout the Depression, he was always aware of balancing on the edge of *la povertá*, trying to keep his family safely on the high side. Money for its own sake was never important, but concern for money as the means to maintain his family was a constantly intrusive companion. Had he known of Oscar Wilde, he would have agreed with him.

How different was this experience from that of the poor in Italy? In Maida, too, they had lived on the economic edge. But here, in *la bell'America*, one maintained his economic balance while living well—as long as one

13. *Pasta fresca* (fresh pasta) is a moist pasta made with flour and sometimes eggs. All the *pasta in casa* (homemade pasta) was this type. It is a very different eating experience from that with the semolina-based dried pasta bought in stores.
14. This, of course, is the view of a child. Reality may have seemed different to my parents.
15. Wilde (1891).

succeeded in staying on the right side of the line. Precarious economics was a constant reality in both countries, Michele knew, but here it was on a very different level. If you owned a home, almost every material aspect of life was better. One still struggled and worried, but here the resources and rewards were far greater. And my father relished the most important difference—America offered the children a future that was far better than that available in Maida. Was it worth leaving the struggles in Italy to join the struggles in America? "Yes," Michele concluded. "When you put everything on the scales—good, not so good, and bad—and you look at the balance, we see which side is better. Yes, it is worth it."

So, we did not think we were poor. However, at times my handed-down shoes were too large or too small, or the soles flapped for want of repair, and my clothes did not fit right or were a bit too worn and patched. The Italian children whom I knew were dressed pretty much the same as I, so there were no offensive comparisons made among us—those would come later when we entered school and began to meet children from other families. This was the accepted state of affairs, and no one was too concerned about it. It often happened that a running child tripped over a flapping sole that had folded under a foot and tipped him over. We laughed as he held up the offending foot, showing his toes wiggling through the broken sole. Jackets, hats, mittens, scarves, sweaters, trousers, shoes, boots, and every other frequently patched and repaired article of clothing was passed down through each family, from oldest to youngest, and then, with some wear left in them, to another family. "Hey, that's my old jacket you're wearin'!" a youngster might tell a child in another family. Such discoveries made one feel important, as if carrying out an adult responsibility, practicing their future roles as good providers.

One did not throw away used clothing. When the youngest in the chain of families had outgrown something, it was given to St.Ann's Church, for the poor. If it became too ragged to repair, pass down, or give to the church, it was carefully cut into rectangles and recycled as patches for other clothes, and eventually as cleaning rags. The rags then made their way through laundry cycles until only the trashcan was left for them. Torn mittens, scarves, and caps, knitted long ago by someone's mother, were washed, unraveled, salvaged, neatly tied together into long strands of wool, wound up into soft woolen balls, and recycled as new, if somewhat faded and not always color-matched, knitted mittens and scarves.

Recycling, although it was not called that in the 1930s, was an important part of our economy. Food left over one day was transformed into tasty new dishes the next, and home-baked bread, when stale, became spiced-up breadcrumbs for future use. Jars were used as glasses; metal food cans became containers for paintbrushes, nails, screws, and bolts. Large cans were cut open and carefully flattened, their edges laboriously bent over and hammered down to round off their sharpness, and then used in home repairs or fabricated into flour scoops, dust pans, radiator covers, and even toys. One toy that I remember my father making for me was a small locomotive. It was crafted from a cylindrical food can mounted on a rectangular scrap of wood and fitted with six black wheels that had been salvaged from broken toys. Any salvageable items, such as bottles and jars, broken tools, wooden handles, old brooms, lengths of string, even cardboard boxes, were saved and refurbished into useful things. My father had several carefully washed jars in his wine cellar that he used as clear glass beakers for testing the color and other attributes of the wine as it seasoned. Another half-dozen jars, matched for size and shape, were lined up on a shelf as wineglasses for his visitors, who congregated in the cellar to talk, escaping for a few moments from their women, who gossiped upstairs, drinking coffee in the kitchen. Included in that array was my own jar for root beer, so I too could stand and talk with the men.

I now think of those things as my parents' resourceful armament of self-sufficiency. If they could not have jobs that provided good wages, then they would either fall under the weight of Depression-era economics, as had so many others, or assert whatever independence and personal control was allowed by their circumstances, skills, and unflagging capacity for hard labor. If they chose the latter, then their peasants' code and skills came forward. These were drawn from their long experience as poor people who had learned well the skills of farming and stretching resources for maximum use. If they were fortunate enough to settle in an American community where those skills could be applied, they did well. Such, I believe, was the case for my parents and relatives, and their friends, who chose a small town surrounded by farms, which allowed them to develop some control over their lives and thus a degree of self-sufficiency. Those who settled in urban areas like New York City would not have so readily found opportunities for growing food or owning and renovating their own homes. In order to survive, they had to develop in other directions, and their peasants' skills would weaken from disuse.

An important urban route to survival was being involved with groups beyond the family and learning to magnify individual power through concerted action on shared needs—concepts that were not common in Italy. People created active organizations such as neighborhood and church societies, fraternal groups, craft and labor unions, political parties, and so on. It is no wonder that those second- and third-generation Italians who became important political figures did so from the power of their urban bases.

For those like my parents who settled in more rural areas, the more traditional peasant values and skills prevailed. They preserved their view of the primacy of family and home—developing a new-world version of traditional Italian *campanilismo*.

There was a willingness to labor long and hard; a shared sense of each couple's partnership and clearly defined parental roles; a diligence in maintaining homes and property; a skillful recycling of whatever could be recycled; a bountiful growing and preparing of food; and the creation of a substantial winter's larder. Were they to abstract and verbalize their set of fundamental beliefs, they might have voiced a credo like this:

"Love, protect, enjoy, and be loyal to your family above all, because nothing, not even God, is more valuable than your family.

"Work hard and succeed, because America, this great country, like no other in the world, will let you do that.

"Tend to your own business. Take care of your family and yourself, because no one else—no person, charity, union, church, government, politician, judge, pope, saint, or God—is going to do it for you. You and your family are on your own!"

Thus, we survived the Depression.

For the first few years after buying the house in 1930, Michele had little time to improve the family's apartment. He was too busy working at The Mill, creating the second-floor rental apartment, tending his garden, and scrabbling for work to earn those needed $7 each week. In addition to the economic issues, they had also to deal with illness. The high fevers and deep chills of malaria, Michele's invisible wound from the war, increased, each frequent attack leaving him weak and shaking for days. Every few weeks he suffered severe, debilitating attacks. The pain, chills, fever, and nausea often made him so doubled over that his boss sent him home from The Mill, accompanied by Uncle Joe. The two of them sat together on the Piermont-to-Nyack bus, Michele wretched in his illness and Uncle Joe wretched with worry, using the one arm The Mill had spared him to hold his brother and keep him from falling. One wonders what the other people on the bus thought of that repeated scene.

Of course, both men were docked for the hours of lost work, dropping them even more deeply into economic trouble and forcing them to work even harder at extra jobs in the following weeks.

Michele lost weight and grew weaker. His body seemed to shrink, but his furious schedule of work never slowed for very long. Theresa fretted over his health but could do little to help him. She took care of the house, saw that Michele and the two youngsters had good meals, remonstrated with him to slow down, and worried and prayed a good deal. Theresa's health began to fail too, adding more stress, and her mood swung toward emotional depression in the continuing battle with illness and economics.

In that accumulation of assaults over several years, the most dispiriting for the family was Death's attention. During the six years from 1926 to 1932, Death visited the family six times, carrying away Macrina's husband and Theresa's grandfather, her two infants, her father, and her 16-year-old sister, Francesca.

"I am here for my annual visit," Death seemed to whisper as he drifted through the family. Theresa was battered by the losses. It was Michele's strength and the loving support of their friends, those Italian families who rushed to the house, listening, crying, and praying with her, that bolstered her own resiliency and brought her through those trials.

Michele soon realized that their optimistic purchase of the house in 1930 had been superbly ill timed. The economy had changed with a suddenness that caught people unprepared. Michele, Theresa, and everyone they knew were now struggling for survival.

The year 1935 was the Depression's darkest, the depth of personal despair for millions of people. Nearly a quarter of the workforce remained unemployed. Homeless men, reduced to poverty and vagrancy, roamed the country. Bank failures and foreclosures of farms, homes, and businesses soared. Millions of people were uprooted, lost, and desperate. Michele and Theresa had so far managed to survive and keep their home, but the day-by-day effort eroded their energy and they wondered how long they could continue. Horrified at Uncle Joe's terrible injury, battered by so many deaths, weakened by Michele's worsening health, they were wearing down under the weight of the struggles to keep their home.

That's the year that opens my memories of the turquoise room described in the first chapter. If the anxiety and despair that filled the room came from Theresa, my mother, I now begin to understand why. Indeed, I am no longer certain if the furniture that was being moved was being brought in or taken out of the house.

Franklin Delano Roosevelt had become president in 1932 and was succeeding, through extraordinary social and economic reforms, to employ millions of people and recapture some optimism. He understood what the Republicans refused to see—that a greater sharing of the country's resources with the masses of working people was an essential move to combat the Depression and maintain a healthy nation. By 1936, the Depression was easing—17 percent of workers, instead of the previous 25 percent, were unemployed.[16] Life was still rough, but there were hints of hope.

In Europe, the power of dictators grew stronger. Mussolini created modern Fascism. By 1935, Mussolini's political philosophy and social organization had been selectively adopted by governments in Germany, Portugal, Spain, Austria, Hungary, Bulgaria, Romania, Greece, Poland, Japan, and Brazil, culminating in the coalition of the Axis Powers centered around Germany and Italy. Fascist political groups emerged in the United States, England, South America, and Eastern Europe (including, for example, Slovakia), and Hitler became the ultimate Fascist dictator. Mussolini invaded Africa to expand his empire, just as the French, English, Germans, and others had done. Modern Italian bombers and tanks savaged the mud-hut

16. Dunlop and Galenson (1978).

villages of Ethiopia, and by mid-1936, Mussolini claimed that he, too, was a colonial ruler. The expanding Japanese Empire had defeated China in the Sino-Japanese War of 1894, and 10 years later had defeated Russia. By 1937, Japan was a major military power that had invaded Manchuria, precipitated another war with China, distanced itself from the United States and other democracies, and signed an anticommunist pact with Germany and Italy, forming the Axis Powers of World War II.

Fascism, the intertwining of big business with a strong, militaristic, centralized government and fanatical, flag-waving patriotism, was on the march by 1936. The next World War was only two years away, but Americans were too busy struggling with their Great Depression to notice.

Chapter 14

The Lady from Rochester (1932–1936)

1. Mixing Cement

After purchasing their house in 1930, Michele and Theresa began their personal struggle with the Great Depression, and by 1936 had survived the worst of it. FDR, having defeated Hoover and his Republicans in 1932, was finishing his first term. My parents revered *u Presidente Rosabelta* for saving the country. They became loyal Democrats, and *Rosabelta's* party could always count on votes from our house. Michele remembered that November day when he proudly entered the booth and cast his vote for FDR.

Michele was excited, walking up Cedar Hill Avenue after work, because that evening he was going to vote for *u presidente*. Before dinner, he washed away the grime of The Mill and carefully shaved with a wicked-looking folding straight razor, the kind that men used at that time. He put on his new suit, made of a beautiful gray material with thin, light-blue stripes, well-shined shoes, a starched white shirt, and a necktie that puffed slightly above a discreet little stickpin, as was the fashion. A small handkerchief peeked out from his breast pocket. When he walked into that polling place he would make a statement, not only by casting a ballot, but by his very presence. "*Come ti vedonu, ti tratonu* (They treat you the way they see you)," a Calabrese adage, came floating back to him. Voting was a serious responsibility for a citizen of *l'America*, and it demanded that one present a suitable figure.

"Ahh!" Theresa exclaimed, clapping her hands when he walked into the kitchen. "*Michele mio, come sei bello* (My Michele, how handsome you are)!"

She brushed nonexistent lint from his shoulder and smoothed an invisible wrinkle from his lapel. "My handsome husband. If only they could see you now in Maida!" But Maida was no longer Michele's concern. Maida was the old life.

If purchased new, Michele's suit would have cost the impossible sum of $40 or more. The magic of *Zio* Antonio Asaro's skilled Italian tailoring made it affordable. He had measured Michele every which way and cut, sewed, and reformed a suit that had been sold by one of his customers. Sponged with cleaning fluids, aired, and carefully steam-pressed, it fit Michele like a fine custom-tailored Italian suit, which indeed it had become.

Zio Asaro charged $12 and allowed Michele to pay 50 cents a week. The poll watchers would never guess that he was but a mill worker, and that is exactly the way Michele wanted it.

"Wow! Hey, Pop! Zap! Flat-out! Where're you trottin' all snazzy?" Fred asked. At 12, he was enamored with the high school students' slang. "Jeepers, you look a zillion!"

Even Anthony, the baby, was impressed. The eight-month-old dropped the soggy *biscotto*[1] that he had been gumming and with a gleeful "Ya!" reached his moist and sticky little hands toward his father's handsome suit. Theresa rescued it just in time. The compliments made Michele feel a little embarrassed, but pleased. He was ready for *u Presidente Rosabelta.*

From 1930 through 1935, they were so busy working in order to buy groceries and pay the mortgage[2] that Michele had little time for the renovations he had planned. However, they repaired or replaced everything that was broken, cleaned everything that was soiled, and built or bought whatever else was needed. My father's large renovation projects that I remember did not begin until the late 1930s, after the Depression's economic strain had begun to ease. Into the 1950s, Michele seemed always to have a big project going.

I recall my farther working in the kitchen, repairing and painting the ceiling, walls, and woodwork and installing new linoleum. I knew the constancy of that work, the old stepladder that was part of the family, and the smell of fresh plaster and paint. I wanted to help, but Mom, fearing I would get hurt, sent me outside with Mary or Laura Serratore, or Mary Fiola, the *big girls* who sometimes came to watch me. But I kept returning to the kitchen and getting in the way, until Pop gave me a little pan of water and a wet cloth and set me to cleaning a spot on the wall. I lasted but a minute or two before going back outside, but I had made my important contribution. Pop smiled and said I had done a very good job.

One of the enduring images that I have of my father shows him balanced on the wobbly stepladder with his arms raised overhead, eyes squinting from the cascading white dust. He wears a light paint cap, the kind the store gave to its good customers. It has a small brim and a picture of a gigantic paint bucket upended over the earth, with paint oozing down the globe, flowing from the North Pole all the way past the equator. A message reads:

We Cover The World
Sherwin-Williams Paints

Pop replaced wooden lath, plastered and painted, repaired doors and window frames, installed electric wiring and light fixtures, and mended

1. *Biscotti* and *taralli* are hard Italian cookies, best when dunked in a cup of coffee.
2. The money from my grandfather's purchase of my parents' Maida house was a great help in meeting mortgage payments. See Chapter Twelve.

broken pipes. I remember the "water closet," a small windowless enclosure that held a tiny sink and a toilet, the kind with a tank high up the wall and a long pull chain to flush it. One day it was gone, replaced by a large new room with a new bathtub, toilet, and sink, and a window that let in air and sunlight. He added two new bedrooms and years later installed a new coal-fired central heating system, with cast-iron radiators throughout the house. I never wondered how he had acquired those skills; I simply accepted that all fathers did all those things for their own families. For the next 20 years, he maintained, improved, and expanded the old house, usually working alone.

In the summer of 1936, when I was four, Pop dug a large addition to the cellar with the help of his friends and my brother Fred, then 15. They used picks, shovels, wheelbarrows, and buckets on ropes to hoist out tons of soil and stones. When they were not working on their dig, I liked to climb down the ladder into the vast excavation to explore the new and strange world deep blow the surface. I discovered tiny waterfalls that dropped down the sides to make muddy little pools at the bottom. It was fun stamping in them. I found interesting stones, roots, worms, and hard-shelled bugs, and even some small bones. Mom would not let me bring the bones into the house, and she sprinkled holy water on my hands before she let me touch anything.

Horizontal layers of varying color and consistency were exposed where the men had cut through the soil. Carefully climbing down the ladder, I saw a dark, almost black top layer, from which the grass grew. A lighter brown layer followed, and then several that were dry and almost white in color, and one that seemed made of tiny pebbles. It was like climbing down the side of a giant's layer cake. Clinging to the ladder, I dug out some gray clay to play with, but it turned out to be dry and hard, not like the moist, pliable clay that Fred sometimes brought home from school. One day I tried to moisten my dry clay by putting a hard lump of it into a cup of Mom's olive oil and then rolling it out on the kitchen table, like bread dough. Given the mess of clay, oil, soil, pebbles, and insect particles, and the waste of expensive imported olive oil, Mom was not pleased.

Neither did she appreciate my solitary explorations of the big hole. Running out of the house and waving her arms in alarm, Mom ordered me to climb out. "*Affretti! Affretti! Fuori! Sei laggiù troppo vicin' u diavolu. Voi stringere la mano con il diavolu?* (Quickly! Quickly! Out! You are too close to the devil down there! Do you want to shake hands with the devil?)" Of course Mom was more concerned with possible cave-ins than with the devil, but by conjuring *u diavolu* she created a scary enough image to get me out of there. My father, properly chastised by Mom, would pull up the heavy ladder so I could not climb down again. What good was having a big, interesting hole in the ground if you were not allowed to play in it?

Along the four sides of this deep excavation, Pop built wooden forms into which he dropped large stones that had been hauled out. This was puzzling, and I asked my father why, after pulling out the rocks, was he throwing them back in?

"The rocks been in the ground a long time."

"How did the rocks get in the ground?" I asked.

"God put them there," Mom offered, God's works being her answer to most questions.

"Then why'd you take them out?" I asked my father.

"I need the hole to make the cellar. So I took out the dirt and rocks to make the hole."

"Then why did you put 'em back in?"

"Because to have a cellar, we need a hole, a floor, and walls. So, I put the rocks back in with the cement to make the walls and the floor strong. Now I have the hole for the cellar, the rocks are in the ground where they belong, and the cellar has the walls and the floor it needs to stand up. Everybody's happy. See?"

"But won't God be mad because you moved the rocks from where He put them?"

"No. The rocks are for us to use. I think God likes it when we build things."

I even helped with this manly work, throwing small stones down into the wooden forms. I watched as the men, using long-handled hoes and shovels, mixed sand, water, and Portland cement. They poured countless wheelbarrow-loads of cement into the forms to make the walls and floor of the new cellar.

The process of transforming the soft, gray powder into hard concrete fascinated me. Pop lifted a hundred-pound sack of Portland cement and dropped it into the large metal slant-sided mixing box that looked like one of Mom's cake pans, only much bigger. Then, with what seemed to be a good deal of satisfaction, he slashed the bag with a vicious stab of the shovel's blade, and the gray limestone powder flowed into the mixing box.

He shoveled in brown sand, mixed it together with the hoe, back and forth, light gray and dark brown swirling together and gradually transforming into a uniform dark gray. When he was satisfied with the color, he mounded the dry mixture into a crater, like a volcano, and filled it with water from the hose. Using the hoe, he folded the dry mix into the water, pulling it down, bit by bit, into the crater. This, I thought, was just what Mom did with her little white mountains of flour that she folded into the wet center of eggs, water, and milk to make pasta or bread. But out here, everything was bigger, heavier, noisier, more powerful—somehow more in keeping, I felt, with a man's world. The cement made loud squishing noises as the hoe pulled and pushed, scraping against the sides and bottom of the box, turning the dry mix and cold water into smooth, gray, wet cement.

Two wheelbarrows, parked like small trucks, waited to be filled. The wet, heavy cement was shoveled from the mixing box into the wheelbarrows. Here the men paused to pray, or so I thought. "Jesus Christ!" each would exclaim, grasping the handles, lifting the enormously heavy cement-filled barrow off its rear supports, and pushing with great effort to overcome its inertia and get it moving. This brief prayer, I imagined, was to ask God for help in lifting such a heavy weight. It was what strong men did—pray when extra strength was needed. The wheelbarrows were pushed along wooden planks, the ground being too wet and soft. On reaching the wooden forms in the excavation, the men tipped the wheelbarrows and the cement poured down. They added rocks and, using shovels and a long handle with a flat board fastened across its end, pushed and tamped the cement to make it flow evenly down into the form, to fill all the air spaces. Then they went back for more cement.

After the cement cured into concrete, my father built a wooden floor across the top. It was like a big stage, and I jumped around on it until he ruined it with two-by-four studs to frame the walls for the two bedrooms and a bathroom that emerged on this new floor, eight feet above his new cellar. Earlier, he had made the garage several feet longer to accommodate his first car, a boxy, black, 1929 Packard that he proudly drove and kept running for years.

In the kitchen, Pop tore out the old linoleum and battled the dark turquoise that I disliked so much, forcing it to retreat behind the advancing layers of glossy white paint. I was happy to see them go, the turquoise and the dark red stuff and black squares in the linoleum.[3] He covered the floor with shiny new yellow and white linoleum. Mom sewed white muslin curtains for the kitchen window and tied them back with a white ribbon. The clean window let in bright sunlight and became my little window in the corner, just for me, to watch the world outside.

The oppressive turquoise room was gone, replaced by a bright, warm kitchen that became the center of our lives. My impression is that the turquoise room was transformed overnight, but that cannot be; a long time must have been needed to complete so much work.

The kitchen was the core of our family life. Other rooms were appendages, for temporary use like sleeping. The "front room" was used on Sundays and for special visitors. The dining room held our holiday meals, warmed by cheerfully noisy people crowded around the big table.

One evening, Mom asked Fred to lift a heavy box from the kitchen floor. "Freh, *bello mio*," Mom asked, "you pick up that for me, please?"

"I will, I will!" I said, pushing in front of my big brother. A skinny little five-year-old, I strode to the box, my arms bowed out with my imaginary bulging muscles. I did succeed in moving one end. It was heavy and I staggered. I knew the appropriate thing to do at this point, having learned

3. As described in Chapter One.

it from the men who pushed those loads of cement. Straining to lift the weighty box, I shouted, "Ah! Jesus Christ! Jesus Christ!"

Fred began choking on the piece of bread he was eating. Pop raised his eyebrows and smiled his quiet little smile but said nothing. Mom was not pleased.

2. The Great Stove

A brick alcove, once a kitchen fireplace, held a black cast-iron stove with a large oven and a flat cooking surface big enough to hold six bubbling pots. Above the stove was a wide metal shelf on which food was kept warm and wet mittens dried. The oven door swung open sideways, not downward as in modern ovens. A narrow metal shelf to support hot pans taken from the oven extended under the door. The shelf was a decorative open grill of curling metal vines that sprouted leaves and flowers. With my finger I could trace the vines along their curves, into dead ends and out again, and along lengthy runs that gently curved like tiny railroad tracks. I pretended the metal flowers and leaves were the railroad stations for various towns. My finger became a little train that could run all the way from one end of that narrow little country to the other and back again, stopping at which-ever towns I wanted to visit. My railroad was mapped out: First there was Nyack, the biggest town in the world. Next, the train came to Maida, and in sequence, New York City, Calabria, Rome, Piermont, and Ocean City. My train connected all the places that I had heard of, my whole world, all in a line, in my little country. "*La Ferrovia Piccola* (The Little Railway)," Mom called it. Far out at the other end, at the very edge of the world, was Rochester.

Comare Bettina's cousin, The Lady from Rochester, swirled in annually, down from the far north, with a big voice that spoke always to the other side of the room. She had the most engaging smile I had ever seen. The Lady from Rochester did not merely enter our kitchen, she invaded it, took possession, and ruled over everyone. Her high, loud voice danced, sang, and laughed, and everyone felt good when she visited. She told us hilarious stories of the people in Rochester, convincing me that it must have been the most wonderful place in the world.[4]

We loved her visits. I liked to listen to her talk, because she had a funny accent, unlike that of any other person I knew. By the time each of her visits was over, I could imitate her quite well. Sitting at the kitchen table I became, for a few moments, The Lady from Rochester, making the adults laugh, but they cautioned me that it was not nice to make fun of people, especially people whom we love so much. And if we did engage in such guilty acts, it must always be with the understanding

---

4. In his wonderful account, Jerre Mangione (1942) describes his Sicilian immigrant family as they lived in Rochester at about that time. See also Mangione and Morreale (1992).

that poking fun at a cherished member of our little group did not diminish the person or the friendship.

So we had to reaffirm each time that we were not making fun of The Lady from Rochester, only of the way she talked. What I did not understand was why her funny accent appeared only when she spoke English. Her spoken Italian sounded pretty much like every one else's—louder, perhaps, but otherwise quite the same. Our relatives and Mom's friends convened in our kitchen to renew their acquaintance with The Lady from Rochester on her annual visits. The discussions were long, loud, and lively, and these spirited ladies vied with one another to out-talk, out-gesture, and out-laugh the others. Everybody seemed to speak at once. Their arms swept through the air with punctuating gestures, each with its own meaning. Their conversations were vocal and visual, with everyone listening to and watching what the others had to say. In what must have appeared to outsiders to be total confusion, they shared news and stories—usually scandalous—and some intense feelings, particularly hilarity or righteous judgments.

In the 1930s in faraway Rochester, several groups of Sicilian and mainland Southern Italian families were forming a number of communities that were far larger than our own in Nyack. Our visitor talked of those people from Sicily and their lives and adventures. I never fully appreciated all the details, but her reports must have been like the soap operas on the Italian radio station, WOV, and the ladies in our group were eager to know about this or that person and his or her family's problems. We never did visit Rochester. It was far away up north, and my parents were content just to listen to her entertaining reports.

It was mildly disappointing, though, when *Comare* Cervodoro, who could not understand English, was among the ladies who came to our house to visit with The Lady from Rochester. Then all the talk was in Italian for *Comare* Cervodoro's benefit, and the funny accent I liked so much was not heard. "Talk American!" I would plead silently, willing them to do so. I wondered where such a funny way of talking came from, and I asked Mom about it. As Mom explained it to me, "*Così parlano a Rochester* (That's the way they talk in Rochester)." Mom pronounced it "Roe-CHEST-dreh."

The lady's name was Mrs. Materazzo, "mattress" in Italian. I thought that was pretty funny, but given the way Mrs. Materazzo talked, it seemed right. In deference to this lively lady whom I liked so much, I put Roe-CHEST-dreh on my *Ferrovia Piccola*, so I could visit her whenever I liked.

On the stove's cooking surface were four round cast-iron lids. Each had a small square depression into which the tip of a curved handle was inserted to lift out the lid, revealing the firebox and heating chamber beneath. At the front of the stove was another door, like a tiny oven door, that also allowed access to the firebox. That door had a sliding grate to control the flow of air into the fire. A short spindle protruded under the firebox. When the ashes needed to be cleaned out, my father attached a metal handle to the spindle and gave it a few turns to rotate the grates in the firebox, sending the ashes down into a metal box. He pulled out the box and discarded the ashes.

Then into the firebox went paper, wood, and coal. On the floor was a box of kindling and a pail, which I would learn later from our neighbor Mrs. Kinsella was called a "coal scuttle," both of which Pop kept filled. The coal scuttle had a child-sized metal shovel that I liked to play with, scattering coal dust on the floor, much to Mom's distress. I noticed that the scuttle had almost the same shape as Mom's delicate little cream pitcher that she put on the table for special company, like The Lady from Rochester. Both containers had a handle on the back and a spout in front, for pouring out their contents. One day I put them side by side on the floor—the big, dirty coal scuttle and the small, delicate cream pitcher—to examine their similarities more closely. Mom rescued her cream pitcher before any damage was done.

The kitchen was the center of the house, and the black stove was the center of the kitchen. The stove was huge, heavy, an unremitting black. Silent and motionless though it was, it imposed itself upon the room. It was a dark, implacable creature, squatting there, taller than I and so wide that my outstretched arms could not reach from one side to the other. When I stood in front of it, the stove filled my entire field of vision. In order to see what was on top, I had to stand on a chair or back up all the way across the room. I was attracted to this great stove but also a little afraid of it. "Be careful, don't let the stove burn you!" Mom warned. Why would it burn me? I liked the stove. As long as I stayed at arm's length, how could it reach me? I soon learned not to touch the top of the stove—that's where all the pots bubbled and the cooking was done. When I was a few steps away from it, the stove was comfortably warm, but when I stepped closer, the stove responded by becoming very hot, like the warning growl of an old dog who doesn't want to be bothered. A good amount of respect developed in my mix of feelings about the great stove.

The stove was the most important thing in the kitchen: the emperor, the king, enthroned in his brick alcove. It was more than that; it watched over us and warmed us in cold weather. When I awakened in the morning and went into the kitchen its warmth caressed me; it dried leggings, coats, hats, scarves, and mittens that had been water-saturated from our playing in the snow. When we came in on a cold day in winter, we went directly to the stove to soothe our chilled bodies. On rainy Mondays, the wet laundry was draped around the stove on wooden drying racks and the kitchen became a maze, a warm labyrinth of washday tents.

In the fall, the stove boiled canning jars. In the winter, it set kettles steaming that humidified the room and cleared nasal passages, and all year its energy helped create the cornucopia of roasted, toasted, boiled, broiled, steamed, fried, and baked foods that Mom skillfully created and carried to our table. The great stove was a multitalented creature demanding only a little respect, some fuel, and a bit of cleaning. It was our kitchen's heart.

Six days a week, my father was up at five o'clock, getting ready to go to work. I tried to listen for him so I could get up, too. My bed was a folding canvas cot in the dining room, next to the kitchen doorway. If I was awake, I could hear when Pop was up and moving around. He drank black coffee that he made by tossing fresh-ground beans into a small pot of boiling water. Pop always ate two soft-boiled eggs and a piece of Mom's crusty bread. I sat with him at the table, drinking the milk he had warmed for me. Sometimes he stirred a few drops of his coffee and some sugar into my cup. In those quietly shared moments early in the morning, side by side, we men of the house drank our coffee together, protectively alert, while the rest of the family slept securely. On some mornings, however, Pop had already gone by the time I awoke, and that was always disappointing, as if my day was starting out wrong.

On cold mornings, Pop first attended to the needs of the stove. He shook down the cold ashes in the grate from the previous night's fire, added newspaper and thin pieces of kindling, and applied a match. In a few moments, with the fire well established, he added larger pieces of wood and a half-shovel of coal. Soon, the cooking surface was hot and the room was warming. Through the spaces in the small sliding grate in the front of the firebox, I could see the bright heart of fire glowing, ready to provide the warm comfort of the kitchen and the shifting aromas of baking and cooking that would soon arise.

3. The Secret Cave

Our kitchen largely defined my preschool world, and my space in it was the broad plane of the floor. Adults functioned at a level that was, literally, above my head. Perhaps because that was my play area, Mom kept the floor very clean, sweeping it several times a day. Each night the mop and pail were brought out, too. I never minded the broom, but Mom's washing the floor was an annoying inconvenience, because I had to leave the room and not return until it had dried. Of course the floor's drying time was short whenever the great stove pulsed with its heat.

My indoor toys consisted of anything unbreakable that I could pull out of the cabinets and drawers. Among my favorites were the pot lids and Mom's wooden clothespins. Each lid had a knob in its center. My brother, much older than I, showed me how to spin a lid and send it skittering and spinning like a top across the linoleum. Sometimes we dropped a small object, like a clothespin, onto the whirling lid and watched as it was grabbed, whirled around, and spat out at great velocity across the floor.

"That's force," Fred explained. "It's called centrifugal force. See, because of the spin, it pushes things away from the middle of the pot cover."

That was fine with me, as long as it was fun. One of our games was trying to see who could best predict where the clothespin would land after it had been grabbed and hurled by the lid. By dropping the clothespin at different points on the spinning lid, we tried to control the direction of the missile, but never did get too skillful at it.

We had spinning duels. One of us sent his lid spinning, and the other tried to hit it and knock it over with his own spinning lid. There were also contests to see who could make a pot lid spin for the longest time. Fred always won, until I complained that it was not fair and Mom intervened. Then I began winning those contests. That was fair.

The clothespins, wooden pegs about five inches long, were like little people, each with a vague head at the top, a rounded torso, and two legs that flared out slightly in a suggestion of feet. I could draw eyes and a mouth on each head, imagining the clothespins were soldiers, albeit with no arms. Mom had a cloth bag filled with clothespins—an endless supply— and I once determined to make whole armies of wooden soldiers and have them fight each other. However, after penciling in rudimentary features on one or two clothespins, I grew tired of the effort and my poor soldiers remained faceless, armless combatants.

Best of all, I could make things by hooking the legs of the clothespins together. I had seen pictures of airplanes with double and even triple wings, and was able to make credible suggestions of those aircraft by pushing clothespins together in various configurations. My double- and triple-wingers, I thought, were pretty impressive, and given the number of clothespins in the bag, I could make whole squadrons of aircraft. The ones that I liked best were those with pontoons, although I did not know they were called pontoons. They allowed the airplanes to land in water. Of course my wooden aircraft floated in water anyway. Mom never did appreciate finding her saturated clothespins floating in the kitchen sink or in muddy puddles in the back yard. Unfortunately, my clothespin airplanes tended to fall apart whenever I launched them across the room.

My carefully constructed squadrons sometimes littered the floor. They were short-lived, though, because of Mom's frequent floor washing. Also, every Monday, Mom had to negotiate with me to disassemble and give up my airplanes so she would have enough clothespins to hang the wash on the clothesline. That, too, I thought, was not fair. After all, what are clothespins for?

Opposite the stove on the other side of the room stood the kitchen table. It had a long, hinged leaf on each side. When the leaves were raised and secured with wooden dowels that slid out to support them, the table could accommodate 10 or so people. They were crowded, but that increased the intimacy and thus the warmth of any conversation.

The kitchen table was an important setting for afternoon socializing. Taking a break in their daily work, or just walking by on their way to or from shopping, four or five ladies would gather for half an hour or so. There were perhaps two dozen Italian immigrant families in our group, and the composition of these impromptu gatherings around our kitchen table changed each time. However, there was an effective continuity from one day's gathering to the next, and the news shared at one time made its way to all the ladies.

Southern Italians had traditionally ignored the government's rules and laws. Instead, they negotiated based on *la famiglia, campanilismo*, and *la relazione*. Most everything had to be discussed at length and survive complicated and lively negotiations. The kitchen was the arena for important negotiations. They were exuberant people, happiest, it seemed, while crowding around the kitchen table, everyone talking at once. Gestures were essential, expressing meaning and emotion, clarifying issues, emphasizing points. If one could not hear the words because of the vocal din, then one could understand just by watching the gestures.

Often one of my little American friends and I would play in the kitchen while the adults enjoyed their lively discussion. Surrounded by loud voices, arm-flailing, and occasional table thumping, my friends sometimes asked, a little concerned, "How come they're always fightin'?" My surprised explanation that they weren't fightin' but "jus' talkin'" never seemed to convince them. I wonder what those kids reported to their American parents about our family.

While the ladies sat around the kitchen table, talking, laughing, and rattling spoons in coffee cups, I appreciated the space that was created underneath. With a large tablecloth thrown over the table and hanging down at all four sides, the space below became my secret cave. So intent were the adults on their sharing of the latest gossip that they sometimes forgot about this small boy in his cave, listening.

I learned a great deal while I hid quietly in my secret cave. One of the most important facts I learned was that when a lady wanted a baby, she went to the hospital and bought one. "*Maria Caldone ha cattata u bambino nell'ospedale!*" *Zia* Angelina announced one afternoon, smugly triumphant in having shocked the other ladies into instant and intense interest. This was colloquial Southern Italian—it meant, literally, that Maria Caldone had purchased a baby boy at the hospital. The phrase, of course, was figurative. The ladies knew she had not truly purchased a baby, but I, knowing little of metaphors at the age of four, heard only the literal meaning.

I had several times asked my parents where I had come from, not understanding that they were embarrassed by the question. In the 1930s, sex, pregnancy, and childbirth were not subjects that parents discussed with their four-year-olds. Apparently, they much preferred to trust that I would eventually absorb the knowledge as part of the general information that was imparted to children without effort, or I would learn it in the streets from my older and wiser playmates. I suppose the expectation was that I, in turn, would educate the next generation of little street friends. They believed that in the normal course of life children would gain the truth and parents would no longer be held responsible for dealing with such sensitive issues. It was a stalling tactic, a bit of parental cowardice.

Pushed by my insistent questions, Mom told me several variations of "God sent you to us." My father, a quiet man of discretion, simply kept himself out of these discussions, sometimes glancing sideways at us as he read his newspaper, *Il Progresso Italo-Americano*.[5]

Mom explained that I had been sent down from heaven in a wicker basket, much like our creaky laundry basket. Sometimes she said the basket and I drifted on a cloud or came sliding down a rainbow. At other times she explained that I had floated down to the post office and Willy Cook, our mailman, had dutifully delivered me to the front door. Some versions even included a note from God that had our address—79 Elysian Avenue, Nyack, New York—written on it, presumably in heavenly script. Usually, that detail was omitted. In different versions, God left me on our front porch or back steps, next door at Mrs. Kinsella's house because no one was home at the time of delivery, or at the Nyack hospital, where my parents picked me up.

Being a mailed package from God seemed a good way to be launched in life and was a satisfactory explanation for me, because everyone knew that God did all sorts of things. But my mother's demeanor was not convincing and the explanations varied too much, so I became pretty skeptical. And anyway, there was one occasion when Mom was explaining about my being God's little gift to the family and my brother Fred—who at 16 knew everything—intervened. He stood right behind Mom, looking at me over her shoulder. Waving his arms and shaking his head from side to side, he silently mouthed, "No. No way!" Fred communicated pretty clearly that there was some big secret here and our parents were not about to tell me the truth. He, of course, knew the truth and was willing to tell me. All I had to do was ask him.

So, increasingly frustrated by Mom's inconsistent explanations, I turned to my big brother and demanded, "Freddie, you tell me. Where did I come from?"

Fred became very serious. He slowly rubbed his chin and wrinkled his forehead like a bearded old sage. "Well," he answered, with grave thoughtfulness and a manner that said I was about to be enlightened, "the truth is, we found you in an old shoebox right out at the curb down on Franklin Street. Me and Mom and Pop were walking home from Raso's grocery, and there you were."

While I tried to picture that, Fred added, for my further enlightenment, "It was Thursday."

---

5. *Il Progresso Italo-Americano* was the longest continuously published daily Italian-American newspaper in the country (1880–1989). With a daily circulation in the 1930s and 1940s of 90,000 to 100,000, it was the most influential of the ethnic newspapers.

I did not miss the significance of its having been Thursday, because Thursday was "junk day," and anything left out on the sidewalk was for the Junk Man to pick up and toss into his truck.

"And we almost left you there," Fred continued, "because we were already carrying bags of groceries. But after a while, we decided it was a pretty good shoebox, so we picked you up and brought you home.

"Of course," he added, "we had to leave a whole sack of perfectly good potatoes just so we would have room to carry you home."

Mom was horrified at this explanation, and while I tried to deal with the flood of new and troubling images that Fred had created, she hurried to assure me that he was only teasing—a fact that became clear from his averted gaze and innocent expression.

"No, no, Honey!" Mom said with great feeling, getting right to the core of what was most troubling in Fred's account. "Nobody t'row you out! Nobody!" Mom hugged me and reassured me that her "God's gift" version was the correct explanation and, that being settled, gently pushed me outside to play. By then I knew that neither one was telling the truth.

But now, hiding in my secret cave under the kitchen table, I had heard the truth from the very ladies who were so successful in having obtained their own babies. They, of all people, would know the truth!

"So that's where babies come from!" I realized with a bright, new clarity. "The lady goes to the hospital and buys one!" It seemed reasonable and even explained why the term *l'ospedale* (hospital) frequently accompanied references to new babies. I imagined several ladies in the lobby at Nyack Hospital on Midland Avenue, all dressed up with little hats and carrying their handbags, carefully looking through a display case, like in Mr. Raso's grocery store. They picked out the babies they liked, and probably even haggled over the prices. Maybe the babies were sold by the pound, weighed on a scale that hung on three chains from the ceiling. I supposed the chosen baby, boy or girl, would then be carefully wrapped up, bagged, and handed over the counter to the new mother, who would pay for her purchase and happily carry her bundle home. My knowledge of the world outside of our kitchen was certainly expanding.

I learned, too, that when a lady went to the hospital to make her purchase, she was supposed to take her husband with her—presumably, I thought, so he could have some say in which baby to choose from the display case. This, I gathered, was a hospital rule. But poor Maria Caldone, a young lady from Cedar Hill Avenue whom I knew only slightly, had apparently ignored the rule! She had sneaked off to a hospital in a distant place called Paramus, New Jersey, to buy a baby but had not taken her husband with her, and now she was really in trouble! I was a little confused, however, because as far as I knew, Maria Caldone did not even have a husband. So how could anyone be mad at her for not taking him with her to the hospital when he did not exist at all? It seemed so terribly unfair to poor Maria and her new baby. And anyway, if everybody was so mad at her, how come all these ladies sitting around outside my cave were snickering so much?

True, some of the knowledge gained in my secret cave was more distortion than enlightenment. Nevertheless, my cave was an important source of worldly information, and its secret nature made the knowledge even more valuable.

4. Gabriel's Birthday Present

I knew that other kids also liked to eavesdrop on adults' conversations. When we visited other Italian families, children sometimes hid behind furniture in order to listen to the adults. Actually, it was only the boys who did this. When girls wanted to hear what their parents were talking about, they went into the room, climbed onto their mothers' laps, and listened. When they heard what they wanted or grew bored with the conversation, they climbed down and returned to their more interesting little girls' pursuits.

But this was too direct for boys. We knew life was more complicated, mysterious, and filled with intrigue and that, unlike girls, we had to be willing to break the rules in order to learn The Truth. The adults, we thought, would be off guard, not knowing we were hiding within earshot. Thus whatever we might overhear was not meant for our ears, and therefore would be the Real Stuff.

In these Italian homes in the 1930s, children were part of the natural landscape, and parents would never banish them to other parts of the house in order to hide adult subjects from them. One of the unstated rules was that adults could speak freely of most adult things, even when children were in the room. Of course one did not use foul language when in mixed company, but any subject could be discussed. They liberally used metaphors that could sanitize any topic and obscure some of the more interesting things for little ears. A corollary rule was that the children were not to intrude into adult conversations, because such intrusion would shift the focus from the adults to the children, and that was not why the adults gathered together.

As long as the children did not intrude, they could remain within the orbit of adult conversation. We knew the unstated rules—everyone pretended that the children were not listening to the adults, or, if they were, probably did not understand everything. If some subjects were unsuitable for children, then the adults would hold abbreviated conversations using code words, euphemisms, and metaphors; if the children still understood, so be it, they had to learn sometime.

The natural state of things—played out repeatedly in these Italian families—was the multilevel social setting. Adults ranging into the 90s shared space with teenagers, children, and infants. In the Asaro family, for example, *Zia* Maria, who must have been the oldest person in the world, sat in the kitchen on a large, cushioned chair that had a high back and wide armrests, like a throne for a queen. She wore a long, black dress and a hand-crocheted white lace shawl. Her wooden cane rested against the chair. *Zia* Maria's family and visitors for the evening sat around the large kitchen table, talking and drinking coffee. The big stove in the corner, much like our own, kept the room warm on cold evening visits.

The men laced their coffee with *Zio* Antonio's *anisette*,[6] and occasionally one or two smokers would go out to the back porch to light up. Smoking in the house was not allowed by most of the women. Looking through the window, I could see the sudden red glow in the dark as cigarette tips blazed into momentary brilliance. A face floated there in the dark, briefly bathed in a scary red glow, so distorted by shadows that I could not identify to whom it belonged, a leering Red Devil in the shadows. Then the face would silently fade away into the night, returning to its underworld lair, still staring at me as it receded. Better for me to stay in the kitchen, I thought.

Several loud conversations would occur simultaneously. Laughter and surprise, delight or skepticism exploded here and there as some interesting bit of information was shared. While the adults talked, the children played among them. Here were different worlds coexisting, sliding by each other in the same frame of space and time. I was impressed that *Zia* Maria could so easily fall asleep in her big chair near the warm stove in the midst of the noise and bustle. Her family kept a respectful and careful watch over her, frequently talking with her, gently touching her shoulder, moving a bit of white hair that had fallen down across her eyes, rearranging her pillow, or bringing her a bit of the soft pastry that she liked. Looking up, *Zia* Maria would smile, nod, say something, and seem pleased to find she was still there with everyone, the respected *Nonna* and center of the family that she had created.

Young adolescents coalesced into little groups, the girls giggling and looking at movie magazines or gossiping about their friends, the boys bragging, punching each other's arms, showing off, and stealing glances at the girls. Younger children occupied the floor—rolling wheeled toys, playing with puzzles, turning the pages of comic books, and so on. Colorful books of paper dolls were popular. Each book included some famous person—here was Shirley Temple in her underwear—and subsequent pages would feature clothes and hats to be cut out and fastened to the paper dolls with little fold-over tabs.

There was usually at least one infant in arms, passed around the table for each lady to hold for a while. I do not remember much crying from those babies—they looked around, kicked, waved their chubby arms, smiled, laughed, and gurgled at whoever was fussing over them at the moment. The women and girls paid attention to them, but I did not think they were worth much fussing. They seemed dull, did not do much of anything, and at times smelled pretty bad. And anyway, they all looked pretty much the same to me.

---

6. *Anisette* is a colorless, sweet, anise-flavored Italian liquor, first developed as a substitute for absinthe. Anisette is about 25 percent alcohol, compared with 40 percent for most liquors.

This multilevel gathering was characteristic wherever these families came together—in homes for an evening, in the fire hall to celebrate weddings, even at wakes, which in those days were held at home where the deceased, quiet and waxy-looking, was on display for two or three days. Of course, if the occasion were a funeral, there would be no boisterous games or playing on the floor. Italian men were properly subdued; the women cried softly; the widow, *madre* or *Nonna*, wailed loudly, thumped her chest, and waved her arms about while well-meaning persons poked smelling salts under her nose, making matters worse. A proper Italian funeral was lachrymose, "*non come gli irlandesi* (not like the Irish)," who, as everyone knew, "sit around leaning on the coffin, drinking whiskey, telling jokes, and laughing!" But even at wakes, the occasion was shared by Italians of all ages.

These many-leveled interactions with a multitude of simultaneous themes were intensely social; the participants were focused on each other. There was none of the isolation that we now see in our age-segregated, Little League, television- and computer-dominated children's world.

These settings were reminiscent of Italian operas, probably the most complex form of theater. In a single operatic scene, there can be several levels of emotion, action, thoughts, story lines, and music, all in beautiful coexistence. Three or four characters might be singing at once. Two can be expressing their shared joy in their love for each other. A third might be crying over his or her black despair, while still another will express intense jealousy, even hatred, and sing of nefarious plans to teach everyone a terrible lesson. While all that is going on, the orchestra plays several themes, expressing all those conflicting emotions and warning the audience of the doom soon to come. Then the chorus sings to remind the audience of the young heroine's lost innocence. Meanwhile, in the background, the extras are going about their normal activities, acting out numerous sub-plots—shopping in the square, drinking in the tavern, flirting in doorways, laughing at some story, or running from the *carabinieri*. A group of children are on stage also, playing games, getting into mischief, marching, singing, and so on.

With all those complexities, the swirls and eddies of emotion, the thoughts, sights, sounds, melodies, rhythms, and action weaving and flowing onstage, one might expect complete chaos. But it all works together in beautiful harmony. So too did the multilevel social settings work for these immigrant families.

While everything else was going on, the boys and girls behaved pretty much according to expectations. The young boys, as all the adults knew, crawled behind the couch to listen to the parents' conversations. We believed that the adults could not possibly be aware of our presence as we clandestinely listened. In truth, they knew what we were doing and sometimes used the situation to deliver powerful messages to the snooping kids—powerful because, we believed, children were not supposed to overhear them.

While Italian families occasionally used a "smack on the behind" to discipline their children, their major controls were verbal, such as oblique threats that something quite nasty would happen if we did not shape up. Parents' teasing humor and children's skepticism were contained in such threats. Children understood that they and their parents were playing a game of sorts, and if it was negotiated skillfully, within the mutually understood rules, then the threatened events were unlikely to occur. But we also knew not to take too many chances, and we treated the threats as serious possibilities. It was a process of negotiation from which usually came satisfactory compromises.

One evening while visiting *Zia* Angelina's family, four of us, about five years old, having exhausted other forms of entertainment, crowded behind the living room couch to listen to the adults who sat talking in the adjacent dining room. Stifling our giggles and settling into the cramped space between the couch and the wall to overhear all sorts of good things, we noted a brief silence among the adults. Then Gabe's mother loudly announced to the other mothers, in a carefully enunciated, over-formal manner so we would be sure to understand, "In a few weeks is Gabriel's birthday. Six years, he gonna be."

"Bravo, bravo," answered Joey's mother. "And you gonna have a nice party for him? We gonna bring lots of presents?"

"*Ah, ma no. Io sono molto spiacente, ma no. Nessun di compleanno per Gabriel quest'anno. Niente.* (Ah, but no. I am very sorry, but no. No birthday presents for Gabriel this year. Nothing.)"

"*Oh, ragazzo sfortunato. Nessun regalo di compleanno? Nulla? Neanche un piccolo regalo? Eh, ma, perché.* (Oh. Poor little boy! No presents for his birthday? Nothing? Not even one little present? Eh, but why?)"

"*Perché. Vi dico perché.* (Why? I'll tell you why.) Because he's been so fresh lately that all he's gettin' for his birthday is two pieces of coal that he can put in the stove. Two pieces!"

"*Ah, Dio mio. Povero Gabriel! Neanche una piccola cosa?* (Oh, my God. Poor Gabriel. Not even one little thing?)"

"Eh, OK, then, maybe three pieces of coal.

"But maybe, just maybe, if he's really good the next few weeks? Then maybe we have a little party and we give him some nice presents. But if he keep bein' so fresh. . . ." Her clear, loud voice trailed off, but not until it had unerringly reached us in our hiding place behind the couch.

"*Ahh, si,*" answered Solly's mother, loudly. "*Saccio io.* I know! My Salvatore, too, he's been getting so fresh that I went and got this medicine from *Zia* Maria. She got it just last week, from Italy. They use it on the boys who don't be nice."

Then she leaned toward the other mothers and added, in a loud whisper that penetrated the very wall between us, "This medicine, it makes them behave!"

We became rigid behind the couch.

She continued, in a loud voice, "This medicine, it tastes so bad they don' even give it to the men in the army! Imagine? So bad it tastes! And you know *Compare* Ciccone's little dog, Cavallo? He took a sip by mistake and it was so bad, that poor little dog, he run away crying in the woods and don' even come home for two weeks! That's how bad!"

"Ahh," the other mothers said, smiling appreciatively at each other and nodding their heads in full approval. "It must be very good, that medicine. Anything that tastes that bad!"

We looked at each other and saw the fear on our faces. That poor little dog! Imagine what the medicine would do to us! They're not really gonna make us take it, are they?

Solly's mother answered our silent question. "So, I went and got this medicine in a Big Black Bottle from *Zia* Maria. I'll give alla' you some of it to take home so you can give it to Gabriel, and Anthony, and Joseph, when I give it to my Salvatore." She clearly emphasized our names.

"You give 'em three big tablespoons every morning and every night." She paused thoughtfully for a moment, and then added, "For a month!" She punctuated her prescription with three loud raps on the table, presumably one for each big tablespoon.

"Yes!" she added for emphasis, not wanting to end the moment too quickly, "*Ogni giorno, sei cucchiai molto grandi!* Every day, six great big tablespoons!"

The message had been delivered. Our very futures would be defined by a whole month of evil-tasting Black Bottle Medicine from Italy! Every day would be defiled not once, but twice, morning and night! Twice a day, three big tablespoons each time! We figured it out, counting on our fingers. That would be six big spoonfuls a day!

We knew that to avoid the dreaded medicine, we must reform, mend our ways, be good. But first we had to get out from behind the couch where Solly's mother, Black Bottle in hand, could easily trap us. Scrambling and pushing, we crawled out, banging loudly against the wall, almost knocking over the lamp and sending the standing ashtray rocking on its base.

"Oww! Get off! Get off! You got your foot on my finger!" Joey shouted.

"Be quiet!" demanded Solly. "We gotta be quiet or they'll hear us!"

We escaped from behind the couch and safely made it around the doorway into the hall without, we thought, being detected by the mothers. Composing ourselves, we plotted our strategies—how readily we could agree when so much was at stake! Settling into desperate expressions of innocence, we walked sedately in single file into the living room and sat quietly on the couch with our hands neatly folded. Our angelic reformations had already begun, and the mothers silently smiled and nodded at each other.

Chapter 15

The Sewing Machine (1936)

1. The Patio

One of my father's many projects was a shaded back yard patio under the cooling leaves of the grape arbor. I thought it was magnificent. The patio was small, perhaps 10 feet square, and was made of thick, smooth-surfaced slate flagstones that were too expensive for us to buy. They had been salvaged from sidewalk repairs on Ross Avenue, near our house. In the 1930s, Nyack's residential streets were lined with maple and elm trees. Their expanding roots had lifted the flagstones, causing them to break. New sidewalks were installed as part of a WPA program. The Works Progress Administration was one of the many programs, which also included Social Security, created by FDR in 1935 to combat the Depression. The idea was to invest federal dollars in employing people to carry out socially useful work.

The WPA employed nine million persons—laborers, artists, craftsmen, teachers, and others—from 1936 to 1943. Although many of their creations have since been destroyed, thousands remain, including murals, sculptures, bridges, parks, poetry, and plays. One example, a heroic mural of Hudson River colonial scenes painted in 1936 by artists Jacob Smith and Jacob Peltzman, still marches across the walls of the Nyack Post Office on Broadway. I saw the mural for the first time shortly after its completion, when I was four or five years old. Many times while my parents conducted their business at the barred windows, I walked around the edges of the big lobby, gazing up, following the picture story and trying to find where it started and ended. I saw forests, animals, the Hudson River, Indians with bows and arrows, sailing ships, soldiers with long rifles, settlers with plows, and log cabins. It was a compelling presentation, and I felt an appreciation that, at one time, all of it had existed right where I was standing.

The intent of the WPA was to pump federal money into the lower levels of the economy, to help working people directly to earn money and survive the Depression. This idea would never have occurred to the Republicans—Harding, Coolidge, and Hoover. They may not have caused the Depression, but they had certainly been guilty of ignoring and even increasing the people's suffering. The Republicans' business-first approach had been to pour federal money into the top of the economy, from which it would supposedly "trickle down" to everyone else. Of course, that did not happen. Our little group of working families recognized and appreciated FDR's attempts to help us, and for two generations remained loyal to the Democratic Party.

While walking home from work one day in 1937, my father saw the sidewalk repair crew. He stopped and asked the workers what they were going to do with the broken flagstones.

"Throw 'em inna dump," they said, "for landfill."

"Well, if you gonna just throw 'em away," my father asked, "OK if I take a few?"

The Irish boss was a big man with an impressive stomach and a red face. He looked a lot like the Red-and-Black Man of my imagination. Later we came to know this man and his family, who lived not too far from us. His name was Mike, just like my father's.

"Sure," Mike said, looking down at my father. "Whatever ye' take'll be less for us t' carry. And if ye' kin carry 'em, ye' kin have 'em."

The crew laughed at that, knowing that four men were needed to lift a thick slab and set it in place. Pop was small and slim, and was going to cart off a ton of stone by himself. Although he would take smaller, broken pieces, it would still be an impressive feat.

Pop walked home and pushed his wheelbarrow from the garage. The wheelbarrow, too, had been salvaged, thrown out by a man for whom my father worked on weekends, trimming and cleaning his yard. Pop had pushed it home—despite its nearly inoperative wheel, broken supports, and loose handles—10 blocks, across the railroad tracks and up Cedar Hill Avenue. He had repaired, cleaned, and painted it, gaining a heavy-duty, steel-box, oak-handled wheelbarrow.

When Pop returned with his wheelbarrow to the repair site, the crew had gone, leaving the broken slabs. They expected to find them still there the next morning when they returned to the job. But they did not know Pop.

Except for a short distance up Ross Avenue, the trip home was downhill—Maple Street to Elysian Avenue, around the corner, a few houses, and home. After many trips, pushing the heavy wheelbarrow while I ran ahead, Pop brought the pieces home and piled them in our back yard. In the evenings for the next few weeks, he labored on his patio. I can still hear the ringing of his mason's hammer and cold chisel as Pop carefully straightened the edges, breaking several slabs in the process. He set lines to define the edges, dug the patio bed, shoveled in cinders from the furnace and a layer of sand, and began fitting the pieces together. I watched as the patio took shape, piece by piece, a big, gray jigsaw puzzle. Finally, his back yard patio under the grape arbor was completed.

Pop built a wooden bench and painted it gray. Even the paint had been salvaged, from discarded material at The Mill, and for a while everything Pop painted was gray—wheelbarrow, bench, the patio furniture that he later made, and the front porch steps. Pop said I was to be the first to sit on the bench. I thought it was beautiful, and every day I played on my new patio. I knew, of course, that Pop had made it just for me. The hard, smooth surface was perfect for bouncing a ball and for some furious circular pedaling on my tricycle.

The patio added a little elegance to our home. We enjoyed summer nights sitting on the bench and the wooden patio chairs that Pop made. He never talked about the patio or his countless other projects, but I know that he enjoyed creating things for his family. Here was something that I did not yet understand, satisfaction in one's labor and manual skills, defining what it means to be a man.

Creating his patio was a little victory for my father against the endless depression. By 1932, 10 million savings accounts had disappeared and 25 percent of the labor pool was unemployed—12 million to 15 million people. Hundreds of thousands of families roamed the country, drifters searching for work. Public school youngsters and 80,000 college students[1] left school to work for pennies. Lacking funds, 20,000 rural schools closed, dumping children into the streets. A quarter-million teenagers joined the country's wanderers. Children became sick and starved. Many died, and mothers wept.

Prices dropped as consumer demand fell. In 1935, with $10 in his pocket, a man was "king for a day." He could buy new trousers, a shirt, a necktie, a sweater, shoes, socks, and a hat. Then he could relax in a barbershop for a haircut and a shave. Neatly dressed and barbered, he could buy and enjoy a dinner of pork chops or sirloin steak, with one vegetable, bread and butter, coffee, and pie, and still have half a dollar left for breakfast and lunch the next day.

With $10, Mom could buy a five-pound rib roast, two plump chickens, six pounds of lamb chops, six pounds of pork chops, five loaves of bread, two pounds of butter, and four quarts of milk. Pork chops cost 25 cents a pound; bread was a nickel a loaf; onions, potatoes, bananas, and rice were all under six cents a pound. Milk was 10 cents a quart, and eggs 29 cents a dozen.

Of course, 45 million people did not have even $10. The unemployed earned nothing, and the underemployed were hard-pressed to earn $10 working two or three weeks.

By 1936, wearied people knew the Depression was an economic monster with no visible end. Nyack had its share of desperate men seeking any work in return for a meal. They dropped from the freight trains at the station on Franklin Street and ran from the railroad guards. Hungry men stopped at houses like ours, properly at the back door, knocked gently, and asked if they might do some work—not for money, just for "a bite to eat, please." Their words were not always familiar to Mom. But their expressions, threadbare clothing, and dejected, hat-in-hand politeness of defeat

1. See Cohen (2002).

communicated perfectly. One did not need sophisticated language skills to understand despair.

Mom fed them. Whatever we had, we gave. Sometimes the meals were meager, as were ours. "*Dio mio. Perché? Poveri uomini, poveri uomini* (My God, why? Those poor men, those poor men)," she would say, holding her hands flat together as in prayer, thumb against thumb, fingers pressed to fingers, swiveling her hands up and down at the wrists, as if the movement would better catch God's eye.

Mom's romantic 19th-century view of the world was strained by this American Depression, and her question to God was as near as she ever came to religious doubt. Some people, in the face of misfortune, turn against God. For Mom, however, such things deepened her belief. In her own way, she faced her God and tried to bring His attention to the misfortunes that He seemed to be ignoring. Her distress was real, and even as a child of four, I understood that it had to do with those ragged men who came to our back door asking for food.

I remember one man who sat quietly on Pop's wooden bench. Mom was in the kitchen preparing a glass of milk for him and two sandwiches of *ricotta* and jelly on thick slices of fresh-baked bread. I had eaten the same lunch earlier, although barely a quarter of a sandwich had been enough for me.

"But Ma," I asked, "why don't you give him a sandwich of good stuff, like meat and stuff, like you do?" I had the uneasy feeling there was something vaguely wrong and embarrassing about such meager fare as jelly and *ricotta* sandwiches. What would the man think of us?

Mom shrugged her shoulders. "Here," she said quietly, in Italian, "take this out to that poor man and tell him I'm sorry, but this is all we have right now. I wish we had more to offer."

Mom opened the screen door for me, and I walked very carefully down the three concrete steps that Pop had built. I carried the glass of milk slowly, so as not to spill it. Then I went in and brought out the sandwiches. I often took food to men who waited on our patio, and I cannot recall many details about the others, but I will never forget this man.

He had taken off his hat and placed it on the bench. His hair was long, thick, and tangled, his skin wrinkled and tanned. The hat had a wide, circular brim with a curved piece cut out of it, as if someone had taken a bite from it. I wanted to ask him about that bite, how it got there, but then, caught up in my job of delivering the food, I never did ask. A stained handkerchief was tied around his neck. His hands were rough, grimy, and very large. He was a big man, and looked strong. He did not smell nice; he did not smile; he did not speak. His eyes narrowed. He watched me, a little four-year-old boy in short pants, walking so carefully so as not to spill and being very serious, because I had an adult's task to carry out.

I stopped in front of him and carefully set the plate down on the bench, next to the glass of milk. "Ma says she's real sorry, Mister," I told him in my best grown-up voice. "Ma says this is all we got right now. It's on'y jelly 'n stuff. I hope it's OK for you."

The big, tough man with the rough, strong hands stared at me and began to cry.

I was astonished and embarrassed. I had never seen men cry. Ladies cried; girls cried; little kids cried. I even cried. Well, maybe sometimes. I quickly retreated into the safe kitchen. When I tried to peek out at him around the curtain of my corner window, Mom made me stop. "No now, Honey," she said. "We don' look on him now. *Povero uomo.*" I could see tears in Mom's eyes, too. There was something here that Mom understood but I did not.

In a few minutes, the man knocked gently at the door, passed in the empty glass and plate, and quietly thanked Mom. I remember that he tipped his hat, the one with the bite out of it. Then, like all of the other drifters, he walked around the corner of the house and disappeared.

I did not ask then, but must wonder now, what is the nature of a ragged and hungry bum who cries softly at the sight of a child, who politely thanks you for your kindness, and tips his hat to a lady?

That night, when Mom was putting me to bed in my corner of the dining room, I asked, "Ma, why was that man crying?"

"Ah, *Tesoro mio*,[2] maybe he was thinking of another little boy he loves very much, and he was sad."

"But if he loves that little boy very much, why was he sad?"

"Because he miss him, and to make it worse, he was hungry."

"Well, why was he hungry?"

"Because he have no food."

"So why don't he go buy food in the store?"

"Ah, because he no have no money."

"Well why don't he have no money?"

"Because he no have no job."

"So why don't he have no job?"

"Only God knows, *Tesoro*, only God knows."

"Well then why don't God give him a job?"

"Ah, that I don' know. That, I just no understand. We can only pray for him."

And pray I did, being careful to move my lips the way I saw people in church praying. I prayed that God would give him a job, or maybe even a good sandwich. I prayed for the man that night, and the next, but I never was convinced that it did any good at all.

2. Mom's New Toy

"The Depression" was something I heard about frequently in my cave

2. A term of endearment; literally, "my treasure."

under the kitchen table. I pictured a big, dark, formless thing out there, like thick storm clouds rolling over us. Its men had no work, no money, no food. Its people wandered the country, searching because they had lost their homes. I did not understand that; homes were big, how could anyone lose their home? I knew exactly where mine was.

For me the Depression was a distant dark thing, a problem for other people. We never lost our home; it was still there, where it had always been. Food was plentiful, as far as I could tell. My plate was always filled and I was never hungry. Sometimes my parents just weren't hungry and they put their food on my plate and on Fred's. I had no complaints about that.

I understood that money was necessary to buy things, but there always seemed to be plenty of money around. Didn't I have my jar with pennies nearly covering the bottom? We always seemed to have more than enough money. When Mary or Laura Serratore came on Saturday to take me to the movies, Mom opened her pocketbook and took out a little purse. It was black and had two little silvery knobs on top that made a sharp click when it was snapped shut. Mom's purse always had money in it, pennies, nickels, and even some dimes. Mom reached in with two fingers and gave Mary a dime for her ticket, and sometimes a penny for candy. Mom's purse had a never-ending supply of money—what more could we need?

For the next two or three hours, my friend Nils Mathsen and I would remain under the watchful eye of Mary or Laura at the Saturday afternoon movies. We merged with the boisterous audience of not-quite-civilized youngsters while our caretaker sat between us, dividing her attention between the two of us and the great screen. In those days, children were admitted without charge. The dime was for Mary or Laura's ticket, and the occasional penny or two bought candy for all of us. Mom and Mrs. Mathsen shared the costs, each paying her dime or 11 cents on alternate Saturdays. Seventy years later, Mary and Laura reminded me of those Saturday afternoons. "In those days," they told me, "dimes were hard to come by."

I knew that Pop went to work every day and was paid money. I supposed it was the money that we used to buy food. But what else did we need money for? We already had a house and a yard; there was always plenty of coal in the coal bin. Mom was always sewing our clothes, even making some. I supposed that except for the pennies and dimes for our Saturday movies and the new steel-toed work shoes that Pop bought every two years, there were just not many things we needed to buy. That was a comforting thought.

At night, falling asleep on my cot in the dining room, I listened to my parents talking in the kitchen, often about "the payment." They seemed worried.

One day a stranger brought in a big sewing machine, several large bundles of cloth, and a box with spools of thread and metal parts. The machine was an impressive apparatus, with a thick wooden table standing on four hefty iron legs. Their decorative scrollwork looked like my metal railroad track on the stove's shelf. These two big black objects—the stove and the sewing machine—must be related, I thought. This machine, a smooth and shiny affair of rounded black metal, was bolted to the top of the thick table. I had never seen one before and wanted to try it out, to see how it worked. Mom said to be careful, because it could pinch me. So the stove could burn me and the sewing machine could pinch me. I guess they really were related.

One end of the machine held a smooth, shiny wheel—like a car's steering wheel, but smaller and silvery-looking. When Mom turned the wheel, a needle on the other end of the machine went up and down into a little metal slot, pulling thread along with it, unwinding from a spool on top. The thread stretched across the top, passed through two guide hooks, and went down to the needle and through a hole near the needle's point. As the wheel turned and the needle moved up and down, the thread was pulled and the spool spun around, unwinding. This was an amazing machine.

I knew that when Mom sewed, she used a needle and thread, and on one finger wore a shiny thimble that looked like a fancy little cup. I once insisted, against Mom's attempts to dissuade me, on drinking my milk from that little cup, but soon gave it up because it was taking too long and I was spilling too much. "See, *Tesoro*," Mom said, wiping up the spilled milk. "Non I tella you?"

It was fun to put the thimble on my finger and wander the house, tapping things with it, making sounds—musical tinkling and solid thuds. It was like a little piece of armor, like the old knights wore. When Mom wanted to sew something, we had to look for her thimble all over the house, because I never remembered where I had left it.

Under the machine's table, near the floor and connected to the legs, was a large pedal about a foot wide and two feet long. A brown leather belt looped from one end of that pedal up through a slot in the table and around the shaft that held the shiny wheel. When Mom pumped the foot pedal up and down, the belt moved, causing the shaft to spin, the wheel to turn, and the needle to run up and down in its slot, pulling the thread through the cloth. The shiny wheel hummed with smooth precision, and the whole apparatus worked quietly and rapidly—a precisely engineered, wonderful machine. It made small sounds. There was a steady, light, metallic whir as the needle stabbed up and down, its speed depending upon how rapidly Mom pumped the foot pedal. The spool or bobbin made little clicks as it spun around. These were soft noises, pleasant and reassuring, because as long as I could hear them, that meant Mom was there, in the room, near me. The only loud noise was the rhythmic clacking of the foot pedal as it swiveled up and down, banging against one of the metal legs on each upswing. Although loud, it had a predictable regularity, and it too signaled that all was well in the kitchen.

Fancy writing and leafy gold decorations ran along each side of the shiny black machine. My brother Fred, who knew everything, explained that they were letters—all but the flowery stuff—and that letters made words. If you knew your letters, he told me, you could actually read not only this word but all words. That, I thought, was impressive. On this machine, he explained, the word said "Singer." "See, the first letter is S." He put my finger on it and I traced the letter. I started at the top of the S and moved my finger down its curves, like riding down a slide at the park. I traced it again. "When you read it, it has the sound ess," Fred explained. I repeated "ess." It looked like a little snake—and even sounded like a snake is supposed to sound, "essss, essss."

This was impressive! I had learned a letter, and now I could read! S was a really neat letter, and I looked all over for more of them. On a shelf there was a round cardboard box that contained "esssalt." There were three "essteps" into the back yard. The kitchen had an "essstove" and an "esssink." In the drawer were "esspoons." Mom would "esssweep" the floor. At dinner we might have "essspaghetti" or "essscarole," and in the garden Pop had "essscallions." At night I could see "essstars," we washed our hands with "esssoap," and when it was dark, we all went to "essleep." All of this I eagerly explained to anyone who came to visit, walking them all around the house tracing S's in the air, announcing the names of objects and sounding like a little snake. Mom thought I was pretty clever and cute, and I kept it up until one day Fred looked at me and announced that the kitchen also contained a little "esss-Stupido." I hit him in the leg. What else do you do when you're insulted by your big brother?

Mom sat at the smooth sewing machine making it hum, sending the needle rapidly up and down. Her feet swiveled alternately on the foot pedal, right, left, right, left. She bent over the table, squinting to see better, feeding the cloth under the needle, turning it this way and that, and stopping now and then to break off the thread, sometimes leaning down to break it with her teeth, or to put on a new spool. Her hands flew rapidly around the machine, engaging and disengaging the needle, tightening or loosening the thread's tension, maneuvering the cloth under the needle, turning the wheel, stopping the wheel. All the while her feet pumped up and down, up and down, as if she were running, never stopping. The shiny wheel spun, the thread raced down, the bobbin clicked, and the needle blurred, stabbing through the cloth over and over. It was a fascinating machine.

It must have been fun to use, and it was not fair that I was not allowed to. Mom could use it any time she wanted, but I had to wait until no one was looking, and then I could give the shiny wheel a few rapid turns and watch the needle on the other end magically respond. One day when Mom was out of the room, I kept spinning the wheel as fast as I could, until it suddenly stopped and refused to move anymore. When Mom returned she found a large, tightly wound knot of black thread jammed under the needle. It took her a long time to clear the machine, all the while shaking her head at me.

When Mom finished clearing the machine, she gave me a hug. I guess that was the signal for me to feel OK about it. Even though all was forgiven, I was careful never to jam up the machine again.

I liked the machine. I liked its sounds and the smooth way it operated. It was Mom's toy and she sat at it sewing for hours every day, having a good deal of fun, I imagined. At times she stopped sewing long enough to prepare meals, clean the house, make the beds, attend to me, do the laundry, or go shopping for groceries.

After a time, however, I began to feel resentful of the machine and of all the time Mom played with it. It was in the kitchen, my kitchen, and the machine and its piles of material took up a good deal of my play space on the floor. Ever since the sewing machine had come into the house, Mom had less time for me and the ladies no longer came to drink coffee and gossip in the afternoons, so I had few occasions to spend time in my secret cave anymore. However, many nights as I lay in my cot in the dining room, I was comforted and soon lulled to sleep by the gentle whir of the machine as Mom pedaled and sewed long into the night.

Mom began soaking her hands in warm water, and her fingers had little cuts all over them from the thread. She pressed them together frequently and flexed her fingers, trying to ease the cramps, and winced when she did so. After sitting for long periods bent over the machine, she slowly pushed herself up from the chair and, with exaggerated stretching, tried to ease the tension in her back. I would imitate her, even the groans, always making her laugh and briefly relieving her fatigue.

Once a week the Sewing Machine Man arrived, bringing more piles of material and spools of thread. He looked through the things Mom had sewn and separated them into two piles. Sometimes Mom would protest mildly, asking if some piece shouldn't be in the other pile, but he would shake his head and say "Oh, no, Missus, it's not done right. It don't count!" He wrote some figures in his book, reached into his pocket, and handed Mom some money. Sometimes Mom would just look at the bit of money in her hand and sigh and shake her head. The Sewing Machine Man would say something like, "You did OK this week, Missus." Then, putting the book in his pocket, he would gather up the finished pieces and take them away in his car. I noticed that he even took the ones that "don't count."

I never quite understood what was going on, but began to sense Mom's fatigue. As a result, I did not like the Sewing Machine Man and grew to dislike the machine itself. Pop didn't like it either, and once I heard him say he was going to "throw the Goddamn thing out the window!" I wanted to see that, but he never did it.

The sewing machine was with us for a long time, but one day it was gone, and I never saw it or the Sewing Machine Man again. That was good, because now I had my floor back. Around that time, Mom began taking me with her to other people's houses, and my world expanded. There, she settled me with a few toys and told me to play quietly until she finished cleaning the house. Mom washed windows and floors, dusted, swept, vacuumed, did laundry, and made beds for those other people.

I did not like the vacuum cleaners. They were big, much taller and heavier than I. Each had a big black bag that could, I was sure, wrap me up and take me away. The machine stared at me, quietly docile, waiting, and then suddenly roared to life, the black bag ballooning to gigantic size, and I could feel its rushing air pulling at my feet, trying to pull me in. I was glad we did not have one in our house. Whenever Mom switched on the monster in someone else's house, it was my duty to jump up and down on the couch and kick my feet and protest loudly until Mom turned it off.

It was sometimes boring waiting for Mom to finish cleaning, and I would get restless and demanding, adding to Mom's burden. Most of the time, however, it was a pleasant change from my own house. It was fun to see the interiors of other people's houses and peek at the fine furniture in rooms I was not allowed to enter. The people either ignored me, and that was all right, or were kind. Sometimes a lady gave me a cookie or even a piece of sweet, icing-covered cake, but she always made me sit out on the back steps to eat it.

When Mom finished her work, we walked home, where she did more of the same chores.

I knew that women toiled in their homes, and sometimes outside too. But women's homemaking activities were simply not "work." Women took care of the home and raised the children, but they did not "work." Mom did the laundry, cooking, sewing, bed-making, shopping, and house cleaning, and generally functioned as the physical and emotional caretaker of the family. She could labor as hard as any man, over a day that often stretched more than 15 hours. But that was just what women did. It was impossible not to recognize how much Mom did at home—but it was not "work."

My father worked. He was a man who worked long, hard hours at The Mill, at home, and at his many extra weekend and evenings jobs. Everything he did was "work." His energy was prodigious. I recall warnings by relatives telling him to "slow down," "take it easy," "Michele, don' work so hard," "relax a little," "you gonna make yourself sick, you keep working like that!" But I do not recall anyone saying any of that to Mom.

Men competed in the labor market and earned money to support the family. If they failed, the family failed. Women controlled the home, using the money earned by the men to create the best possible quality of life for the family. If the women failed, the family suffered. This division of responsibility was clearly understood and maintained. My father never washed a dish, cooked a meal, did the laundry, made a bed, swept the floor, or darned a sock. My mother never raked a leaf, shoveled snow, cut the lawn, cleaned the furnace, dug the garden, fixed the roof, climbed a ladder, or painted a wall.

There were some exceptions to that division of responsibility. Aunt Nancy and Uncle Joe raised my cousin Fred on a small farm, and Aunt Nancy did much of what would ordinarily be considered "man's" work. Aunt Macrina was widowed, and to maintain her flower crops she dug the soil, moved rocks, and trundled wheelbarrows. For a number of years during the Depression, when families were economically teetering, Mom and most of the other women altered their traditional roles to work outside the home and earn extra money. This flexibility seemed always to involve women's assumptions of some male responsibilities, but I do not recall men assuming women's responsibilities to any great extent.

Mom's realm was our home and social life. She did all the housework, decided what food we consumed, when medical attention was needed, how to furnish and decorate, whom to visit, and how to clothe the family. She ran the home, making the family's daily decisions. No one argued or questioned them. Mom was in charge of those things.

Pop's realm included his jobs, the yard, the garden, and the cellar, and all repair and renovation of the house. I think he was happiest when he was down in his cellar, king of his subterranean domain, with his homemade winepress, barrels, and racks of bottles, his tools and workbench, and the huge coal furnace that he tended like some underworld god of fire. The dark cellar was big, and Pop had dug and constructed most of it, the original having been only a small furnace room. It was truly his subterranean kingdom, and he was responsible for keeping it functioning.

It became clear to me that the responsibility for what was considered to be real work, the work that the family depended on for its existence, rested fully on the men. Americans today can feel pride in their successes, in their ownership of homes and cars and bank accounts. This was true, too, for my father and the other Italian men in the 1930s, at least to the degree that they were acquiring a few of those things. But overriding that was pride in their labor, in their capacity for labor and the results of their labor. Indeed, physical work was so much a part of my father's life that the very definition of manhood seemed wrapped around two major ideas: work and responsibility for one's family. As a child I had little understanding of how hard both of my parents worked, or of how committed they were to the rightness of personal labor and the overriding importance of one's family. Indeed, the moral lives of men and women were largely defined by how well they could, through personal labor, wrest from the indifferent world a safe and happy home for their family.

3. The Clothesline

Monday was wash day on Elysian Avenue, and it had its own excitement for me. Mom and I began working early in the morning, after Pop had left for The Mill and Fred for school. I had not yet started school, so I stayed home, where my world was still well within Mom's sphere.

After breakfast, Mom cleaned up the kitchen while I played on the floor, and then we were ready for the laundry. The soiled clothes were gathered up, loaded into the big wicker basket, and carried down into the cellar, the wicker creaking with each step. It was a nice sound, that rhythmic creaking, reassuring, rather like the rocking chairs on the porch, and it made me feel good. I wanted to carry the basket, but Mom, puffing after the third trip, said it was too heavy for me. I insisted, and found that I could not reach all the way around to the two handles at the ends of the oval basket. As usual when in conflict, we negotiated and compromised. Mom and I each grasped one handle and carried the basket to the top of the stairs, where I relinquished my hold and Mom took it the rest of the way down.

Pop had installed a large double tub in the cellar. He had found it in a house that was being demolished and had been allowed to cart it home in his wheelbarrow, without having to pay anything for it. Mom had a wooden washboard with a corrugated metal scrubbing surface, a large wooden paddle, and a creaking, hand-operated wringer that was clamped to the side of the tub. Bleach, soap, water, and little cubes of "blueing" were swirled together in the tubs of hot water. A great deal of effort with the paddle set it all into circular motion. The clothes were separated—the whites here, the coloreds there, each pile in its place (the language of that separation, whites and coloreds, bore no irony at that time). The clothes were first soaked in hot soapy water and swirled with the paddle. Then, with sleeves rolled up, Mom plunged both arms in and rolled, squeezed, pushed, pulled, and prodded the clothes, also using the wooden paddle to stir them around in a circle, first in one direction and then the other. Her skin turned red. Each article was scrubbed with soap against the washboard, then washed again in the tub. After a while, at Mom's signal, I reached in and pulled the plug, and the gray water rushed down the drain, making a whirlpool that grew smaller and smaller, finally disappearing with drawn-out gurgling noises. Mom rinsed and refilled the tub, and washed the clothes again. Her sweat mingled with the wash water and her hair, pinned up when she had started, began to escape and to drop, wetly, down around her eyes. The cellar became hot and damp; the concrete floor was slippery with soapy water.

Rinsing in clean water was the next step, then draining and rinsing some more. I am not sure, but it might have been at this point that the blueing was added. This was a chalky blue substance that came in a little cube, or sometimes it was in a liquid or in crystalline form. Whatever the form, it was added to the water at some point because it supposedly made white clothes look whiter. My preferred brand was Bull Dog Blu. I insisted that Mom buy that particular brand because each package contained a little blue plastic bulldog. For a while I had quite a collection of tiny blue bulldogs, but eventually I lost them all.

Wet laundry, I discovered, was heavy, especially the sheets. They were big, and it was difficult to pull a soaked heavy sheet out of the tub. To reduce the weight and drying time, and to remove more of the soapy residue, each item was wrung out first by hand. It must be fun, I thought, for Mom to twist the clothes into the long oblong that was thick in the middle and tapered toward the ends, almost to points. You could follow the spiral of the twisted material around and around. They looked like the drill bits that Pop had in a box on his workbench or like giant De Nobili cigars, those smelly black twists of tobacco that some of the men smoked, but not in the house. Wringing out the wet clothes was two-fisted, strong-armed, grunting, hard labor. Mom usually gave me a sock to wring out, and I gauged my success by seeing how much water I could squeeze out as I wrenched, twisted, and grunted in complaint, imitating Mom, making her laugh.

The wringer was a large machine attached to the tub. It had three rubber rollers placed one above the other, a big metal crank with a wooden handle, and a lever that changed the tension between the rollers. Inserting one corner of a wet item between two rollers, Mom tightened the tension and turned the crank with both hands, making big circles with her arms. An intake of breath on the upswing, and a long exhalation on the down stroke, "Hnnn . . . ahhh! Hnnn . . . ahhh!" rhythmically paced Mom's labor. This was hard work; the big crank did not turn willingly. I watched as a towel, a shirt, or a huge bed sheet was fed into this machine. The wash went in one side, wet, soft, fat, and seemingly alive. What emerged from the other side was flat, stiff, squeezed-out, and dried, a dead suggestion of its former self, all haphazardly folded up and wrinkled, like a flat board. Some things came out looking like the flat slabs of *baccalà*, the dried and salted codfish that we bought at Christmas time. Those poor fish! At one time they had been fat and alive, too. I was always a little afraid of this machine, having seen what happened to the clothes that went through it. Whenever Mom used the wringer, I kept my distance and held my hands clasped tightly behind my back.

Wet laundry, even after it went through the wringer, was still heavy, and carrying several basket-loads up the concrete stairs to the back yard to hang on the clothesline was a considerable task. The clothesline was a marvelous piece of machinery, a top and bottom rope slung between two creaky pulleys. Pop had attached one pulley to the house, about seven feet off the ground. The other pulley was attached 20 feet high on a huge elm tree that grew at the far end of the yard. I wondered why Pop had put the pulley so high up on that tree, so far out of reach, and learned later that it had been placed high so the hanging wash would clear the pole beans that grew in Pop's garden.

Mom draped a sheet over the lower rope of the clothesline and secured it with clothespins. A few grinned at me with their little faces that I had penciled in.[3] With a few easy tugs on the line, Mom moved the sheet farther into the yard, making room for more laundry. The pulleys squealed and the clothes flapped with sharp snapping sounds, making me think of big flying birds. There was one bird, a beautiful blue and gray long-tailed bird, with an insistent, loud voice like he was imitating the squeaking pulleys. I called it The Clothesline Bird. My brother thought that was pretty funny and said it was a "blue jay."

"There are different kinds of birds," he said, "like jays, sparrows, ducks, and hawks."

"And chickens!" I said, catching the meaning of his impromptu lecture. "Like at Uncle Joe's farm."

"Right," he said. "They're in different families—like the jay family and the sparrow family. See those little brown ones over there? They belong to the English sparrow family. Then there is a song sparrow family and a chipping sparrow family. Your clothesline bird's in the blue jay family. There's a western jay family, but they don't live around here. Your bird is a blue jay."

I thought that was interesting, and it led to an activity that we continued for many years: identifying birds by sight and sound and checking my answers in Fred's bird books. I became pretty good at it. But my beautiful, noisy, blue and gray bird remained The Clothesline Bird.

The clothesline apparatus suggested some very interesting possibilities. Not so much at the house, but at the other end, at the tall elm tree where the clothes swung high, way up, where the birds lived! If sheets and pillowcases could be moved along that line to such great heights, why couldn't I? Imagine being transported all the way across the yard, higher and higher off the ground, like a bird! What would the world look like from up there? I told my best friend, Freddie, about this. Freddie Ogden lived next door. He was my first friend outside of the other Italian families, all of whom were more like cousins than friends. We would remain close until after high school graduation. There was a clothesline in Freddie's yard, too, but it did not have pulleys and could not be moved along, like mine.

Freddie liked my idea. "We'll take turns," we said, plotting enthusiastically. While one of us pulled the line, the other would hang on and be transported across the yard to soar high up into the sky, all the way up into the elm tree! We lugged the heavy old kitchen chair with the split seat outside and placed it under the clothesline's lowest point, where the pulley attached to the house. We climbed onto the chair and teetered there, rocking on its uneven legs. Freddie, being more than a year older and wiser—he was already in kindergarten—decided that he would be the "puller" and I would be the "flyer." That was fine with me; after all, it was my idea. I reached up, grabbed the clothesline, and stepped off the chair, fully expecting to find

3. As described in Chapter Thirteen.

myself dangling in the air. Instead, the clothesline stretched and sagged, and my feet were on the ground.

"You run," yelled Freddie, not deterred by seeing me firmly grounded instead of hanging in the air, "and I'll pull. And when your feet go off the ground, lift them up and I'll pull you all the way up the tree!"

I ran, holding on to the line. Freddie hauled, the pulleys squealed, the clothesline raced upward toward the elm tree, and the ground streaked by under me. I was fast approaching the hedge that ran across the yard and yelled to Freddie that he better get me into the air soon, or I would crash right into it! Mom heard the commotion, looked out the window, and saw the charging little two-legged airplane trying to fly. She dropped a dish on the floor and ran into the yard, desperately yelling at us to stop. Too late—I was airborne! I lifted my legs as high as I could, like a bird tucking up its feet for flight. Freddie pulled faster, the line stretched and snapped, and the clothesline and I collapsed to the ground while Freddie Ogden fell off the chair.

I never did clear the hedge, reach the tree, or look any birds in the eye. In fact, I had been airborne for only a fraction of a second before the line snapped, dropping me those few inches to the ground.

When he came home from work, Pop shook his head at his destroyed clothesline, explained how dangerous it might have been for me, and, gently shaking his finger, made me promise not to do that again. I realized that I had done something wrong, but I also saw Pop's little smile and the bemused shake of his head. Then he set up his tall ladder against the elm tree, climbed up, and repaired the clothesline. I watched him working up there, high up the tree where the birds perched, where I still wanted to go.

Pop climbed down, and while he was putting away his tools in the garage, I began scooting up the ladder, determined to reach the birds one way or another. Before I had managed two rungs, my big brother reached out a long arm, grabbed me by the collar, hauled me down, and advised me that I was already in enough trouble.

"Boy, are you lucky this isn't Monday!" my brother told me.

"Monday? Why Monday?" I wondered.

I do not know how many hours it took Mom to complete the laundry each week, but it seems to have been a good part of the day. I know that it took too long for me. I became bored and had to seek other activities while Mom finished. I don't suppose it took all day, however, because Mom still had all those other things to do—cook, clean, make beds, sew, attend to me, and go shopping for groceries. With all that stuff for Mom to do, it was a good thing, I decided, that women did not have to work.

Tuesday was ironing day on Elysian Avenue. Mom had three heavy irons of different sizes, each with its own decorative cast-iron trivet to be set on when not in use. Even my favorite, the small iron, the baby of the other two, was pretty heavy. Mom heated them on the stove, then glided the irons smoothly over each clean item that was stretched out over the long-legged, skinny ironing board. She sprinkled the clothes with water to dampen them and sometimes added dry cornstarch so the iron moved more smoothly. Periodically she would put one iron back on the stove to heat and pick up another.

In those preschool years, children spent their time primarily with their mothers. There were no day care or nursery schools for us. A few blocks away on Route 9-W was a big house with a large fenced yard where many children played, having been deposited there by well-dressed people who drove Buicks, Packards, Cadillacs, and La Salles. Mom and I walked by frequently when going to visit *Comare* Cervodoro or *Zia* Fiola on Brookside Avenue, and we could see the penned-in children watching us as I watched them. "Boy, what a big family," I thought.

Our mothers stayed home, and we children shared our first five years in close association with them. The families were not exactly the same, but I think that the second-generation children came away from their first five or six years with pretty much the same sense of values. We could not have verbalized them if asked, but they had been securely planted.

We learned a clear, uncluttered, deeply rooted idea of the primacy of family.[4] To the young child, family and home filled nearly all the world. In the slim margins that bordered the remainder were other neighborhoods and people, even God, but nothing as important as one's family.

This was a small-world view, suited to the needs of young children. But its narrow focus had serious limitations, which we later realized as we were assailed and altered by experiences in school and work. The world would grow larger for us; the family would recede in relative size and other values would crowd in. But even after the family had made room for other allegiances, it would remain our primary focus of life and responsibility. It was a powerful lesson, permanent, the basis on which we formed our later relationships.

What also came through in those early years was the ethic of work. It is interesting that these Italian Roman Catholics would have so powerfully espoused what is generally considered to be the Protestant work ethic. Everyone had to work, even if women's work was not labeled as such. Hard work over long hours was a fact of life. Men were largely defined by their work and by how responsibly they carried it out. Devotion to work was fully expected, even if you were ill. This dovetailed with the family ethic, because family survival depended upon the responsibility, skill, and success with which you carried out your work. Preteen boys were expected to mow neighbors' lawns, rake leaves and shovel snow from sidewalks, take out the trash and the furnace ashes for elderly neighbors, run errands, walk dogs,

---

4. A child's world today is far larger, due to the more than 10,000 hours each child spends watching television. One must wonder what this has done to the sense of family such as we experienced.

and so on, and add their earned nickels and dimes to the family finances. Young girls took care of neighbors' children and helped to clean houses, and their coins were added. Teenage boys found part-time jobs in local stores as early as possible, and brought home their earnings. It was an important mark of maturity when, at age 14, a boy finally received his "working papers."[5] All of us knew about working papers, despite the fact that as many jobs as we held, none of us had actually seen such papers. A boy's first steady job was a mark of passage, a family event to be recognized and praised. As girls matured, they assumed more of the homemaking responsibilities. Although they received no wages for their work, they were recognized as contributing to the family welfare. It was a mark of arrival, maturity, and pride when a teenage girl produced a meal for her family that rivaled what her mother might make. When those things happened, much was well with the world.

Devotion to work was not a grim or loveless duty. The point of work was to maintain the family, the family was the ultimate source of all meaning, pride, love, and satisfaction, and responsibility for work took on a positive character. *La famiglia* was to be enjoyed; it housed much to be proud of, to laugh about, to share, and to love. There was sadness too, disappointment, failure, hurt, and anger. All were part of life. One worked hard, knowing without question that work ultimately brought family health and joy. And that, after all, is what this very short life is all about.

This morality that rested on the twin foundations of work and family was a carryover of the rural Italian peasant view of life. For men and women, the important relationships, *le relazione*, were among the family. My cousins might disagree, but I believe that, given life's realities in those Depression years, one's relationship with God was of secondary importance. How much one person could succeed in his or her interactions with the world on behalf of his or her family depended not on God, but upon that person's capacity for labor. Success was limited to what he or she could reach, in a very physical sense. In modern America of the 1930s this meant that each man's success—and therefore the fate of his family—was limited by the reach of his own personal labor in an uncertain market.

That philosophy of personal strength and self-sufficiency also carried limitations, leaving each family susceptible to any conditions that affected the man's ability to work. For my father in the 1930s, two major threats constantly rumbled in the background, like live volcanoes ready to erupt. If he became ill and unable to work, our family would be in jeopardy within one week. The Great Depression was the second threat, and it generated constant anxiety in all the immigrants. It was always there, in the background. It would, it seemed, never let them go.

5. Federal and state laws defined permissible ages, wages, and conditions of employment for youth still in school. At age 14 we were supposed to obtain "Employment/Age Certification" (working papers), but nearly everyone ignored this.

Chapter 16

The Truss (1937)

1. The Smoky Room

The truss was a formidable object, introduced solemnly to me by Mom after a visit to Dr. Monteith's office when I was five years old. It was a smooth, nicely curved wooden affair, about an inch wide and half an inch thick, with soft white cloth padding on its inside surface. It was to be worn around my waist and carefully positioned so it would support a weak place on my abdomen, where my brother happily told me my guts were pressing from inside, trying to get out. If I wasn't careful, he said, they'd pop out all over the kitchen, like those of the poor chickens that Mom cleaned in the sink.

This was not happy news, and the first thing I did was throw the thing away, thereby in some perverse manner believing that I was protecting my innards from serious scattering around the kitchen. Somehow what Dr. Monteith had prescribed as a benevolent aid for my insides had taken on the character of a clinging fiend biting at my stomach.

Mom chased Fred out and assured me that she would allow no scattering of any parts of me anywhere in her kitchen. She said that I had to wear the truss until Dr. Monteith could get around to fixing up the hernia, for that is what the innocent-looking little bump was called. I made my peace with the truss. It was actually a rather nice-looking construction of smooth wood and contrasting white and brown surfaces, and nothing else in my life was quite like it. My initial embarrassment gave way to some sort of pride when I realized that neither of my closest friends, Freddy Ogden and Bobby Greggs, had a truss of his own. So I wore it dutifully most of the time, sometimes taking it off to play with when Mom was not looking. Whenever Fred caught me waving my truss in the air, playing, he made faces at me, wiggled his fingers, and made wet, slurping noises that were intended to suggest slippery intestines sliding around the kitchen floor. I could not even complain to Mom about him, because then she would know that I had taken it off. So I just hit him with it, happily discovering that its slight springiness added a nice sting if I got him just right.

One day Mom took me on a visit to an ailing elderly friend, and my shaky acceptance of the truss dissolved. The lady had been in her bedroom for a long time, helped by her daughter into bed at night and to a large chair during the day. The windows were tightly closed, and the shades were pulled down against *la mal aria* that always threatened from the night air. It was a hot, dark, stuffy room with unpleasant smells that I will forever associate with old age and infirmity.

A large crucifix hung on the wall at the head of the bed. Two strings of black rosary beads were draped over the bedposts, while another string was crawling its way among the lady's fingers.

The tortured little figure hanging on the crucifix was carved in white ivory. A brilliant red, bloody circle under the crown of thorns, the glistening crimson wounds in his hands and feet, and that terrible red slit in his side, oozing more blood, stood out against the stark white body.

On the wall opposite the bed hung a large picture of a handsome Jesus with beautifully barbered and combed shoulder-length chestnut-colored hair, lustrous beard, and moustache. He wore a pure white robe neatly tied with a golden cord and stood serenely with his arms out, palms up, and his blue eyes turned to heaven. Jesus apparently did not mind that his chest had been split open, revealing an over-large crimson heart that sprayed bright drops of red blood and golden rays of beatifying light. I had seen the image countless times in other homes, framed or on calendars, always conspicuously displayed. Tacked to the wall next to Jesus was a small dried palm leaf crucifix, such as we made on Palm Sunday.

On a bureau stood a familiar plaster statue of the Virgin Mary, painted in soft white and blue, Mary's lovely colors. A single fat candle in a red glass spluttered and smoked at her feet, the candlelight gently waving across her features. Another string of rosary beads circled the Virgin, as if constraining her, a holy chain keeping her from stepping away. In front of the statue was another plaster model, a realistic, full-sized human foot. It sat there upon its sole, pink and healthy, its toes pointing at the Virgin. Tied around the stub of the ankle were strings of colored yarn, each ending in a piece of paper on which Italian words had been penned, each carefully turned toward the Virgin, so she could read them. Unknown to me, it was a common practice of older Italians to place before the Virgin wax or plaster models of organs that were ailing, and beseech her intercession to make the organ healthy again. In Italy these were brought out on festival days, particularly those honoring the Virgin Mary. In this room, however, the foot seemed to be on more permanent display. I was intrigued by that foot, stared at it, and wondered if it might be a real one. I looked at the lady to see if it might be one of hers, but she had both. Anyway, it looked too smooth and shiny and, unlike most of the other figures in the room, had no blood coming from it.

The air of religious intensity and prayerful desperation was so thick in that hot, smoky, twilight room that upon entering Mom reflexively made the sign of the cross, just as she did at church.

The lady was thin, too thin, I thought, to be an Italian lady. Her white hair was sparse, wispy, like a translucent cloud floating around her head. She was propped up in a big chair; one foot was bandaged and resting on a stool. I could see a dark band on her shin, just above the bandage—black, purplish, striated with lighter streaks. At first I thought she was wearing a purple sock, but it was her skin. I shuddered.

Clearly, she was lonely and in pain, but when she saw us, she smiled and made her own sign of the cross, ending it with a light kiss to her fingertips. She held out her arms in welcome, speaking softly in Italian, and smiled at me.

"Come," Mom said, urging me gently. "Come give *Zia* a kiss."

Reluctantly I moved toward the lady. She gently touched my shoulders. Her hands were shaky, their weight as light as a cloud. *La Zia* gazed at me for moment, smiled softly, and slowly kissed me once on each cheek, gently tugging me toward her. I had expected the exuberant, loud, wet kisses of Italian ladies, but la *Zia's* kisses were dry and light, just feather touches, as if she were very tired.

Mom and *La Zia* talked and sighed quietly, and for a while held hands. They took up their rosary beads and prayed together softly, advancing the rosaries through their fingers from one bead to the next, progressing through the ritual.

While they prayed I stood, ignored, hands behind my back, looking around the room, feeling increasingly oppressed by the heat, the gloom, the smell of the smoking candle, and the sense of age and illness. It seemed that everywhere I looked, crimson flowed against white. This room, a despairing and dark monument to blood and suffering, was not a place I liked at all.

Then I saw it, leaning against the wall. It was the same construction as mine: smooth, curved, brown wood with white padding. *La Zia's* crutch. It was not the same as mine. It was a different shape and much bigger, but the crutch and my truss were clearly of the same family of things, related in their construction and materials. I immediately felt, in a rush of emotional understanding that needed no words, that these were alternate expressions of the same condition—human infirmity and desperation. My truss was a smaller statement of *La Zia's* crutch, and I had become, in an instant of recognition, a young version of this ailing lady. I had been joined with her in her misery, had entered, via ownership of my truss, into a companionship with her. We were together, sharing the class of objects that defined our sad linkage.

Is this where I was headed by virtue of my seemingly innocuous little truss? Was this room, or one like it, someday to be my room?

Of course I did not think this in so many words. Rather, I felt a rush of alarming emotions and images, and an irrational certainty that somewhere in God's plans there was a room like this for me. I could not have voiced or understood it, but neither could I dismiss the overwhelming feelings that now centered on that little wooden truss, that now hateful, frightening, ugly thing.

The dark room and crimson blood, the smoking candle, the oppressive warmth, the smells, the air of despair and finality pressed over me, and I wanted to run, but held still until they finished their prayers.

Mom must have realized my distress and was angry at herself for taking me into a setting that was much more disturbing than she had expected, so she did not delay our departure. They said goodbye; Mom, still vibrant, and *La Zia*, very tired, looked into each other's eyes, remembering the sweet years shared in their little town so far away in Italy. They quietly held each other's hands for what seemed a long time.

"*Grazie*, Theresa," she whispered. "Goodbye. Goodbye, Theresa. Goodbye."

La Zia's daughter quietly thanked Mom, gently patted my cheek, smiled sadly, and solemnly let us out, softly closing the door after us. Mom was crying.

The sudden fresh air felt wonderful, but the proximity of the oppressive room that we had just left and Mom's tears mixed everything up. I was not sure what to feel.

"Will we go see *La Zia* again?" I asked as we walked home. After a long silence, Mom said what I wanted to hear, but it did not feel very good.

"*No, Tesoro mio*," she said, sighing quietly, holding my hand more tightly. "*Mai più. Mai più.* (No, my treasure. Never again. Never again.)"

2. The Ward

Over the next week, Mom could not understand my adamant refusal to wear the truss, or why I would not even touch it or remain in the same room with it. I did not have the clarity to explain it to her. But Mom was not to be defeated. She tore a strip from an old sheet and tied it around my abdomen, providing at least some support. She lovingly tucked a small picture of the Virgin Mary into the bandage. In my mind, I was finished with the truss. This solution was far better, and knowing that little picture was there made me feel safe. Then Mom and Pop, with Fred as interpreter, consulted Dr. Monteith in his office.

"Well," he said, approving of Mom's makeshift truss, "keep this young fellow as quiet as you can. No jumping around for a few days." He smiled and looked at me over his glasses. "We'll get him in early Monday morning." As usual, he gently patted my head and gave me a red lollipop—the real reason I had agreed to go and see him. He said I was getting to be a "big, strong boy."

For the next few days, everyone was solicitous. Even Fred refrained from teasing me. Each day after coming home from school and on that weekend, Fred played quietly with me and generally helped to keep me as physically inactive as is possible for a five-year-old to be. He told stories, read from books, built a tent in the basement out of a clothesline and a blanket. In it we camped together on an African plain and found ourselves cowering in the middle of a great herd of wild animals that had suddenly appeared, galloping right through what had been the furnace room.

My memories of the hospital are incomplete, images running like bits of film snipped here and there from a large reel. What I remember best is not this hospital stay, but the time I had my tonsils out. I am in a bed at about the center of an enormously long room filled with kids in two rows of beds set perpendicular to two long walls. Nurses and an occasional doctor walk between the rows, checking on their little patients. The hospital bed is a marvelous contrivance that can be rolled around the floor and even cranked up and down by the nurses. By standing on my bed, I can see the kids at the far ends of the room. However, standing on your bed is forbidden, lest it lead to jumping contests that would inevitably pitch some kid head first onto the floor.

One boy down at the end always seemed to be causing some mischief. He would be discovered trying to crank his neighbor's bed up or down when the nurses were not looking, running around the ward or out into the hall and the main waiting room, and being chased back by the despairing staff.

All of us, boys and girls, had to wear gowns that came down to our knees and, with every little move, immodestly peeked open in the back.

"This is a dress!" complained the mischievous boy at the end of the row. "Boys don't wear dresses! I won't wear it!" he shouted, jumping up and down on the bed, his little gown popping open and closed with each jump. "I won't! I won't! And you can't make me!"

He did, though, just like the rest of us.

That ward became our world, and the nurses our caretakers. In their white dresses, white stockings, white shoes, and perky little white caps, they moved, smiling, around the ward to each child. Nurse Barbara, Nurse Jennie, and Nurse Margaret were our cheery providers of food, comfort, and even entertainment.

Then there was Meannurse—she had no other name. The bearer of the ping-pong paddle, the children's disciplinarian, Meannurse was a giant, scowling woman whose very entrance into the ward caused a marvelous quiet to descend on the children. She stalked the long aisle between the two rows of beds, slapping the paddle against her left hand, announcing that she would "tan every little backside I find out of bed!" Kids scurried right and left before her, always managing to leap back into bed just before she reached them. Occasionally, in the haste to find sanctuary, one would find oneself in some other kid's bed, and then had to face the terror of trying to explain to Meannurse how that could have happened. We all knew that when she paddled you, they had to send you right up to the operating room so the doctors could sew you up again. Every day we heard the slap,

slap of the paddle against her palm, but never saw her actually paddling a child. That was proof, we concluded, that Meannurse snuck in and did her serious paddling at night while we were asleep and defenseless.

A girl my age was in the bed next to me. She was at the end of the girls' section and I at the end of the boys'. Her name was Aggie, for Agnes. I called her "Eggy," because that's what I thought she told me. We talked a lot, laughed, shared coloring books and crayons. Our parents brought little gifts for both of us. Eggy and I became fast friends in those few days, and promised to visit and play at each other's homes after leaving the hospital.

One by one the children were taken out of the ward on a rolling cart, looking scared, surrounded by unfamiliar grown-ups dressed all in white. The rest of us would wave reassuringly from our beds and say things like, "Don't cry, Joey, it's OK" and "See you later!" and then watch them disappear. We became silent and serious each time. Then they were gone, around the corner, taken to the mysterious Operating Room. Wheeled back some time later, the children were groggy or asleep, soon waking up and crying, or complaining and calling for their moms, who could not be there until visiting hours at seven o'clock. Each of us knew our turn would soon come, but we never talked about it.

In the 1930s, every kid I knew had his or her tonsils sliced out. It was an accepted part of the culture of growing up, a rite of passage and so common as to be barely worth bragging about—like measles and chicken pox, which everyone had to catch sooner or later. Mumps were more serious and less common, and only the lucky few could brag about having mumps. If you still had your tonsils, you were obviously still just a little kid.

I had gone one better than most kids—I had tonsils, appendix, and hernia. Here was something to brag about. Later, when it was all over, I discovered an unanticipated bonus: an impressive crosshatched scar on my abdomen to show off to Bobby and Freddy.

Suddenly, it was my turn. The rolling cart with the tightly stretched white sheet had arrived for me. The white-clad giants had come to get me. I waived an uncertain goodbye to Eggy, promising again to visit her when this was all over. My filmstrip images show me lying on a narrow cart that was wheeled into a tiny room with a sliding door. Then the room hummed and began to slide upward—or down, I could not tell which—and the White Giants now had white masks hiding their faces, making their voices distorted and rumbling. That was more than enough for me, and I jumped off the cart to escape, catching the White Giants by surprise. They returned me to the cart, this time with two straps holding me down. Then a round black thing descended over my face, and I remember kicking one of the masked figures. There was a funny smell.

The time I had my tonsils taken out, I was told that after surgery, my throat would be sore and I would not be able to speak above a whisper. But, they said, the sore throat would soon disappear and my voice would return. And, they promised, every kid who had his tonsils out would get a big dish of wonderful ice cream when he woke up!

Ice cream was a major treat in those Depression years, something we might buy at a fancy soda fountain perhaps once a year, on some special day, sitting on dainty wire chairs around a tiny table and eating cool vanilla with fancy little round-bellied spoons. The promise of ice cream in the hospital—as much of any flavor I wanted—was an anticipation of pure delight.

Waking from the surgery, however, brought a series of disappointments. The one happy thing was that when I opened my eyes I saw Mom, Pop, Fred, Uncle Joe, Aunt Nancy, Aunt Macrina, and Cousin Mary, all standing around my bed to welcome me back. Apparently not even Meannurse had been able to stop Mom's determination to bring so large a crowd into the ward—and against all regulations, not even during proper visiting hours—just to be there when I woke up. Meannurse scolded and grumbled. Cousin Mary and Fred just rolled their eyes in embarrassment and distanced themselves from their parents while the adults shrugged at each other, pretending they could not understand a word of English.

Everyone had a big smile for me, except Mom, who was tense and worried-looking and clutched a damp handkerchief all wadded up in her hand. There were gentle hugs, all carefully mindful of my recent surgery, and soft kisses on my forehead from everyone, even Fred, who shut his eyes and said "Yuk!" as he kissed me. There was also a bag of *taralli* —hard homemade cookies—which Meannurse immediately took away, shaking her head and saying, "Tsk, tsk." Mom did not care about losing the *taralli*; she could make plenty more. Maybe, she thought, Meannurse would go somewhere to eat them and not bother us for a while.

I guess the crowd around me was just too rowdy for Meannurse, because she came over and yanked the curtain all the way around the bed, enclosing us and hiding my Italian relatives from the more sedate Real Americans who visited the other kids in the ward.

Coloring books, crayons, and two thick picture books of Tom Mix and his horse, Tony, were offerings in recognition of my brave journey through the Operating Room. Each page of the picture books had a large drawing, and in each upper corner another small drawing. When the pages were fanned rapidly from front to back, the small figures moved, just like in a movie, and Tom Mix leaped into action, riding, roping, and shooting his gun at bad guys. When you fanned them from back to front, the figures did everything backward! Bad guys, shot down just a moment ago, now jumped up; Tony ran backward, and the lasso lifted itself off the bad guys and snaked back into Tom's hands!

I was still too groggy and tired to appreciate all the gifts, but I clearly remember the books and one other gift. Fred reached into his pocket and pulled out a small jar. "Look," he said happily, holding it up and shaking it for us. "Dr. Monteith pickled your tonsils, and we can take them home to look at them!"

"Aiee, Freh! My God!" Mom said with disgust, and made him put it away. I don't know what Meannurse thought about that exchange coming from behind the curtain, but I think she had had enough of us by then and was not about to get involved.

I learned later they were not really my tonsils, just two bright-orange slices of carrot that Fred had whittled down and put into a jar of water colored with a little red Jell-O, suspended like red filaments of flesh. Not having my real tonsils to look at was the second disappointment, the first being Meannurse's removal of the cookies.

Meannurse redeemed herself, however, by bringing the ice cream that I had selected prior to surgery: one scoop of vanilla, my favorite, and one of peach, because I had never heard of peach ice cream and it sounded exotic. But the ice cream was the next disappointment. Whether because of medications or the condition of my throat, it tasted terrible. The whole point of going into the hospital—to get cool ice cream in exchange for infected tonsils—had been subverted.

Disappointments kept piling up. After my family had gone and the curtain had been pulled back so I could rejoin the ward, I saw that Eggy was gone, her bed empty, the white sheet stretched tightly, its edges tucked neatly under the mattress, waiting for the next child.

"Where's Eggy?" I asked Meannurse. She smiled at me, handed me a picture, and gently brushed my hair back from my forehead. "Agnes went home this morning. She's all better now. And she said to be sure to give you this picture that she drew for you."

The picture had a big yellow sun, little squiggles in the sky that were probably birds, and two kids playing in a meadow of green grass filled with dots of every imaginable bright color—flowers. By any measure it was the happiest picture I had ever seen. I was pleased with the picture, but even more surprised at this gentle side of Meannurse.

I thought of Eggy for some time after that, but never saw her again.

My final disappointment was that upon awakening, I had realized that, try as I might, I could not get my throat to hurt. In addition, when I first saw all the people around my bed, I had said, without sufficient thought, "Hello" and "Where's my ice cream?" in a perfectly normal voice. I had neither a sore throat nor a pitifully weak voice, as had been promised! I had been depending on the sore throat and whispery voice to coerce weeks of sympathy, attention, and indulgence from Mom. But what now? I would just have to fake it.

I quickly developed subtle facial expressions of pain and discomfort and just the right weak, wavering voice. They worked wonders on Mom. At times I had only to whimper and point vaguely, and Mom instantly leaped away to do whatever it was that she thought I wanted. After I returned from the hospital, my friends Bobby and Freddy came to visit. I whispered at them, barely audible, indicating unbearable pain that they would never understand. I communicated clearly that I was too sick even to think about anything other than lying in bed all day, listening to my favorite radio programs, playing with toys, and being the center of attention, getting whatever I wanted to eat and being waited on by Mom. They were very impressed.

My general malaise, apparent sore throat, and failure to marshal any more than a whispery voice continued long beyond Dr. Monteith's promised "few days." Mom became worried and distressed. After all, it had been her decision to follow Dr. Monteith's advice, and she had delivered me up to the hospital's operating room. Thus, she was responsible for my suffering. Mom's assumption of guilt pressed her to redouble her solicitousness and try harder to help me get better. She worried, and showered me with even more pampering and concern. I, of course, loved it all and had no idea that my fakery was causing such distress for Mom. But Fred knew it and tried to explain it to her. Mom could not accept the idea that her sincere mothering was turning me into a pretty smooth malingerer, a sick-role convert, a weak-voiced, limp-bodied whiner with wide, beseeching eyes and a woebegone expression that pleaded for comfort and deliverance from my ordeal. However, she was willing to try Fred's suggestions, "just for one day," she said.

That afternoon, Fred came to my bedroom corner of the dining room, where I sat on my folding cot, happily playing with toys and listening to one of my favorite radio adventures, "Jack Armstrong, the All-American Boy!"[1] brought to me by "Wheaties! The Breakfast of Champions!"

"You know," my brother said, with no introduction, "from now on if you want to eat, you gotta come to the table. No more maid service."

We looked at each other.

"And we're going to put the radio back in the kitchen, so Mom can listen to her programs. I think you've had it long enough."

"Oh, and another thing," Fred said. "If your regular voice isn't back by, say, after supper when 'The Lone Ranger' is on, Dr. Monteith says to wrap you up in a blanket and take you back to the operating room, and he'll go diggin' around inside your throat to see where your voice went. So if you know where your voice is, you better find it real soon."

By seven o'clock, I was whoopin' "Hi Ho Silver, awaaaay!" even more robustly than the Masked Man himself.

3. The Priest and the Doctor

My hospital and recovery experience mirrored the culture of illness and health that Italian families created as they adapted to their new country.

---

1. One of the most successful of all radio programs, this juvenile adventure series ran from 1931 to 1951.

My sick role performance was my version of what I had seen many times in ailing adults. Theirs was a powerful social construction that brought together the settings and roles of hospitals, sick rooms at home, doctor, patient, priest, and the power of fervent prayer. It grew in the new country, conceived from the values and beliefs of the old country.

Being ill was serious business, and one had to behave appropriately. The most powerful idea was that being ill brought one nearer to God. Thus, the proper role of the ailing person would include a respectful awareness of that nearness, a heightened level of religiosity, and a deeper appreciation that life was mysterious and fleeting. The sickrooms were quiet, darkened with drawn blinds. The patient was the center of concern; everyone else enacted complementary roles, respecting that mysterious aura of the patient's proximity to God, treading quietly, speaking softly, and giving the respect and indulgence owed to the afflicted person.

Everyone prayed with and for the person lying in bed, and since almost every ill person eventually recovered, praying obviously worked. Even the very old who left this world at the end of their illness had recovered in the most important sense—being transported into that sweet eternity with their God. The circle of prayers had worked for them, surrounding each *Zia* or *Zio* with love, gentle friendship, and respect in this, their final journey.

To be in the state of illness was to become a passive object of the will of God. The person had no part in becoming ill, no responsibility for it. Illness was an affliction sent by God, by fate, by unfortunate luck or other forces that we could never understand. It was mysterious. Praying to God and never knowing whether God would choose to intervene deepened the mystery. Illness was an issue between the person and God; whatever God and his angels, the devil and his demons determined to bring about fell upon the person. That reality was not necessarily the direct result of the power of either of the warring sides, but most often was a compromise in which one side or the other won a bigger share of the outcome.

In its ultimate expression, this view leads to a pervasive fatalism—the fate of the person is determined by outside forces. The person has little control over his or her own well-being. Bearing no responsibility for being ill or for getting better, the person sinks deeply into submission to the condition and dependence upon God to bring back a state of health and upon the family to nurture him or her while God exercises His will. Absolved of all responsibility, the ailing person could, for the duration of the illness, control any number of people into becoming bedside servants, while the aura of Godliness and benign virtue flow all around.

In 19th-century Italy, this construction was reinforced by visits by the priest and ladies with their rosary beads, and the undeniable fact that there really was not much that one could do in the face of severe illness except to pray. But in 20th-century America, that construction of religion and superstition, a bit of primitive medicine, and much love soon changed, and *il dottore americano* began to nudge aside *il prete*[2] in matters of illness and health. When the doctor made a house call—doctors did that in the 1930s—he was treated with great respect. I was allowed to greet the doctor at the front door and struggled to carry his heavy medical bag for him into the bedroom, where his patient, the family, and their circle of friends waited.

Il dottore americano was the bearer of science, medicine, knowledge, and objectivity. He played out his role as the kindly-but-stern, finger-shaking, no-nonsense man of authority whose sole function was to help God make one better again.

"It's good to pray," *il dottore* would tell us, "and hope that God will hear us."

His patients from Maida agreed, liking *il dottore's* sentiments.

"But," he added, "we have to give God a little help. Now, I want you up and out of this bed for two hours tomorrow, and each day you stay up a little longer. And take the medicine three times a day, like I told you. If your temperature goes up again, you call me right away."

The women, being more accepting of religion and mystery, tended to fall most readily into that near-fatalistic role. But the men, less religious, more cynical, more disposed to taking direct action in their own lives, responded differently. While they agreed that ultimately God or some other force greater than themselves might control their illness, they tended to stand up to it, fight it, refuse to be subdued by it. As ill as my father often became with attacks of malarial pain, chills, and fever, he refused to bend to it, until it overwhelmed him and his body would no longer function normally. Dreadfully sick, he went to work or performed hard jobs at home, such as the time he dug a large trench in the yard in order to free a clogged drain pipe, even though he was bent over with pain and misery. In a sense, this too was a fatalistic acceptance of events. It was, of course, a gross denial, a delusional attitude that maintained, despite countless prior experiences, that the problem did not exist, or it would "go away." It was an expression of the Southern Italian man's sense of responsibility—he must continue to work or his family would suffer. It was an expression *della virilità e della forza maschile* (manly virility and strength). And finally, it was an expression of independence—standing alone, against the world, with no help from any other agencies. Packed into the Southern Italian man's reaction to illness were all the prized male characteristics learned in that culture.

However, according to my mother and the other Italian women, it was none of that. Instead it was evidence that each man was *u testaduro* (thick-headed), as were all the Calabrese, but most decidedly the men.

In those migrant families, the doctor played a complicated role. He

2. The doctor replaced the priest.

knew that his medicines alone would be less effective than their careful blending with his patients' religion and family, and his treatment must include all of it. He was a man of wisdom and skill, a man to be respected. Like the priest, he became an intercessor between God and mankind, thus standing closer to God than did other humans. This, of course, conveyed to him a status considerably above anyone else. Unlike the priest, his role was not to help us along to that other plane, but to keep us in this one. *Il dottore* became part of that complex mix of mystery, religion, science, respect, and hope.

The doctor often addressed one of the adolescents in the family, to be sure his instructions were understood. In our family it was Fred, even though my father was capable of understanding instructions. If the doctor was the intercessor between God and man, then Fred assumed that role between *il dottore* and *la famiglia*. It was an important role. Not only did it place responsibility on Fred, but I think it turned his interests in the direction of science and medicine. He never talked about becoming a doctor, something that was not possible given our family's status and finances. But it was a factor that guided his choice of high school studies.

Visiting and comforting those who were ailing was a duty respected by everyone. In those days, patients were at home more than in the hospital, and bedside visitors were frequent, an ordinary part of normal life. When one person in the group became ill, everyone became involved. Illness, like death, was a mystery that must not be left to solitary endurance. It was a call for support, encouragement, loyalty, and love—as much a healing tonic as the best of *la medicina*. It was a home-centered event, a circle of concern and love, a gathering of the extended family, another iteration of *la forze della famiglia*.

Chapter 17

The Visitors (1937)

1. The Truck

The five years prior to 1937 were my childhood immersion in Italian life, our continuous celebration of family. The language, gestures, food, morality, music, humor, and love, even the arguments and Mom's radio soap operas—the very rhythms of life—were Italian in nature.

The years 1937 through 1939 were pivotal, a time of transition during which the whole world changed. For our parents, *la bell'Italia* ebbed while *la bell'America* flowed into our homes through a dozen daily channels. By then, immigrant families owned radios and read newspapers, deep channels for *le cose d'America*.

The second generation helped to usher *l'America* into their families, forcing changes by challenging their parents' behavior, clothing, food, and even religion. They brought their ease with English and their knowledge of the world gained in school. They introduced non-Italian friends to the family, and some even married persons who were neither Italian nor Catholic. The parents, fathers in particular, resisted some of the pressures, not to prevent *il diluvio americano* (the American deluge), but only to slow it down a bit, so they could catch a breath before moving on. Despite frustrations with their children, parents were genuinely proud of their youngsters and how well they were becoming *americani*. I think that all the intergenerational confrontations, no matter how intense and seemingly intractable, were eventually resolved through acceptance and compromise. *La forza della famiglia* was usually reaffirmed.

I recall the final years of the 1930s as those of The Visitors, who brought new images into my life. Mrs. Materazzo, The Lady from Rochester,[1] was an eagerly anticipated annual visitor, bringing tales of that distant northern city. A friend of my father, whom he had not seen since leaving Italy many years earlier, came all the way from a place called Camden, New Jersey, to spend a day recalling their youthful adventures. Another special visitor arrived from Maida and told a dramatic tale of the town's invasion by wolves, convincing me that Maida must have been the most exciting place in the

---

1. See Chapter Fourteen.

world. With each visitor, I ventured further from my familiar world, into new images of exciting places. Most visitors brought good news, but some was less pleasant.

Our honored guests sat in the kitchen, surrounded by our friends. During everyday visits, the women remained in the kitchen with their coffee and gossip. The men, tiring of their wives' topics, which of course dominated the discussions, drifted down into the cellar, where my father made wine and, for me, root beer. Although tempted to stay and listen to the women's lively discussions, I usually chose to follow the men downstairs, careful to stay close to them because, for a five-year-old, the cellar had a million dark and scary corners, and anything could be hiding in there.

In the cellar's slight gloom, the men talked quietly and sipped wine, using recycled jelly jars for glasses. On a shelf under a long line of windows Pop kept a dozen clean jars, each with its lid to keep out the dust. My jar was special, with a smiling Shirley Temple on it. Pop selected a bottle of wine from his shadowed shelves and, being careful not to shake it, held it up to a window, squinting in critical inspection. Satisfied, he gently wiped down the bottle, pulled the cork, poured wine for his friends and then root beer for me. Appreciatively, the men swirled the wine in their jars, helping it to "breathe," and peered at its color and clarity. "Good color," they would say, "nice and light," or, "good color, nice and dark," comparing it with their own wine. Carefully squinting, I too held my jar up to the light. My root beer always looked good to me. "Good color," I said, nodding with grave authority. It was dark brown, a little bubbly, with a floating fluff of light tan foam—nicely balanced shades of brown, as though an artist had arranged it just for me. I looked up at Pop with my silent "thanks," and he smiled at me.

We men stood in our circle. "Salute," we said, raising our jars to each other.

They talked about their jobs, gardens, and houses, and the Depression that was supposed to be over soon, but no one knew when. The men's discussions were not as lively as those of the women. They spoke softly, with no loud laughter, dramatic gestures, or snickering over some bit of gossip. They were not, I thought, having as much fun as the women. But of course, the topics men shared were more important, more serious issues. Men and women, I was learning, were different.

Zio Domenico usually stood with his left thumb casually hooked over the edge of his belt. None of the other men did that, so I thought it must be special. I had no belt, but could hook my thumb over the top of my short pants and walk casually around the house, looking pretty grown-up. But I soon discovered that it hampered my ability to play with toys, and I gave it up, except when standing in the cellar with the other men, holding my jelly jar of root beer.

One day, something unusual happened. Five men came to visit my father, and they sat in the kitchen. I was in my cave under the table, ringed by their heavy work shoes. Clearly, this visit was different—they were still in work clothes, right from The Mill. That was not done when visiting, because it would be disrespectful to the lady of the house—one must clean off the grime of work and dress up a bit before entering another's home. "Where are the ladies?" I wondered. These men sat in the kitchen instead of standing in the cellar, and drank coffee instead of wine. Their words crackled with sharp anger, like the whiff of ozone after a lightning strike. I heard no soft discussions of gardens and wine, not even the usual sighs over the continuing Depression. Angry phrases in mixed Calabrese and English swirled around the table, switching back and forth between languages like the flicking tail of an angry cat. Someone pounded on the table, making me look up to make sure the roof of my cave was not about to fall on top of me.

"They fired him! The bastards fired him. Without no notice, just fired him! *Figli di cane! Eh, perché? Non ha fatto niente, Marco, niente! Hanno fatto così a Marco, eh poi così faranno a tutti di noi.* They think we're just stupid Italians. Dumb immigrants. We don't know no better! That's why they do it to us. *Figli di puttane!*"[2]

"Fired?" I thought, sitting up, more attentively. "Somebody fired poor Marco? Fired, like in the stove? And they might do that to all the men, even to Pop?" The image of someone being "fired" in the stove frightened me. I knew the men were angry, but I did not understand that they were also terribly afraid. For working men with families in those Depression years, there were few things that could generate more desperate fear than the threat of losing their jobs. Slim pay envelopes were all that kept their families from hunger, homelessness, and bottomless poverty. These men were tough, strong, and proud, but they were vulnerable. No one had savings, because everything was spent living from one payday to the next. If the job was lost, everything was lost. The thought of their homes reclaimed by the bank, their families thrown into the streets, their furniture strewn on the sidewalks, with no aid from any quarter, was unbearable.

"We can't let the bastards do this to us. We gotta do something, now!"

Gianni (Johnny) Lucasso, the youngest man, was a hothead. "I'm tellin' you," he said, "the union. The union gotta do something! They gonna have a meetin' next week. We all gotta go, make demands, show 'em we got strength."

"You crazy! We mess with this, they do to us what they done to Marco."

"That's why they do whatever they want," Johnny shouted back. "Because we got no strength. We gotta demand, we gotta use our strength. That's what it's all about. You don' wanna do it? I will! I'm gonna show the sons a' bitches!"

2. "The sons of bitches! Why? Marco didn't do anything. They did it to Marco, and then they'll do the same thing to all of us! The sons of whores!"

"Johnny," said *Zio* Paolo in reasonable tones. "You young, you no got no wife and kids to worry about. We do. What we gonna do if we start makin' trouble and get fired? Look what happened at the Valley plant a couple years ago, when they tried to unionize, to that young Polack who was organizing. They busted his head! They damn near killed the poor guy, scrambled his brains, and he can't even talk right no more, and all he wanted was decent pay. Then they fire him, for Chrissake. First they break his head, then they fire him! What the hell's gonna happen now to his wife and kid?"

"Listen," added *Zio* Totó, his voice louder than usual, "when they throw him outta his job, there was 20 men waitin' in line to work for the company without no union. You think they worried about him? You think anybody gonna worry about us if we get fired? You think some union gonna do anything to help us after we get thrown out in the street? Don' mess with this. Don' mess with our jobs!"

"So what the hell you gonna do?" shouted Johnny. "Goddamned nothing? You gonna sit on your asses and think everything's fine, and let 'em screw you up the ass and run your life? You call me crazy, but you do that, you're the crazy ones!"

Uncle Joe's calm voice came in. "Johnny, I know we gotta ask the union what to do about this, but it don't help to go wild and stir everything up. That only gets their backs up. We gotta take our time, calm down, think about this, use our heads, figure out what happened here, why he got fired, who got him fired. Let's find out, think about it, and then figure out what to do."

"Shit on that Goddamn horse shit!" Johnny shouted, just as Mom stormed in, her face angry, her high heels clicking across the floor. Chagrined, the men looked at each other and quieted. She scolded them for "talking like that when the little boy is in the room! Come out from under there," she called to me. "Right now!"

How did Mom know I was in my secret cave? Actually, I was relieved. All that talk about breaking heads and men getting fired in the stove had me worried, and I needed some serious comforting. Without complaint, I crawled over the work shoes and out of my cave, and was swept up by Mom and carried from the kitchen. The men glanced at each other with guilty looks. But *Zio* Totó was not daunted.

"Teresina!" he shouted to Mom, who by then had taken me out to the front porch. "Leave the boy alone. He gotta know what goes on. He gotta grow up, no? Better he learn here than inna streets."

It was a presumptuous statement, a man telling a mother how to raise her child. Only *Zio* Totó could have carried it off, but even he would pay for it later, when *Zia* Angelina found out.

On the porch, Mom calmed herself and resumed her sewing. "Ma," I asked, after awhile, "why did they fire poor Marco in the stove? That's not nice!"

"No, Honey, no," Mom explained, setting down her sewing. "No in the stove. It means they chase him from his job, take away his job, so he no work there no more."

"No stove?" I asked.

"No, no stove, and no fire. Is just a word people use. Is just a way to talk."

I thought about that, relieved that no stove or fire was really involved. But "they"—whoever "they" were—took away his job, and that was not nice, either. Without understanding, I began to feel some of the men's anger. It stewed for a while, grew, and then burst out: "*Figli di putane!*" I muttered.

"*Oh, Dio mio!*" Mom said, looking up to heaven. Setting aside her sewing again, Mom turned to me and made me promise never again to say such "bad words."

Marco's problems had started two days earlier and had worsened since. He had been walking along Franklin Street near Mr. Streppone's store. Like many young men from small towns in Southern Italy not yet matured by family responsibilities, he held a shallow view of the good life of a bachelor, seeing himself in a handsome suit, a hat, and well-polished shoes. He and his friends would sit at a table in the *piazza*, drinking *espresso* in elegant little cups, perhaps with a drop or two of *strega* or *anisette* for flavor and to give it a little kick. They would talk leisurely about women. Ah! That would be a civilized life. Of course he had never lived like that in Maida, and in America they didn't even have *una piazza*!

La bell'America! he thought. Where are those gold-paved streets and *gli scudi* (dollars) raining from the skies? Look at old Franco, and the Rassos, and Mr. Streppone. They had opened stores and now had great wads of money. Everyone who lived in *l'America* in the 1920s, he had been told, owned a car and a house and had plenty to eat. The factories ran full time and jobs were easy to find. If you didn't like one job, you found another. It was a treasure house for the older men with families, and for the young men, he had heard, *l'America* was one long party! There was "prohibition," an American word that meant plenty to drink for everybody, a good time every weekend, and women with short dresses, sitting with their legs spread, looking for fun wherever you went.

Poor Marco. For most people, such high-living America had not been true in the 1920s, and by 1936, all pretense of it had disappeared. There were no gold streets or raining *scudi*, no long party. Jobs were scarce and insecure, and pay was low. Families were thrown into poverty; men left home to find work, children quit school to earn a few pennies, women despaired and spiraled down into bitter hopelessness, or worse. The government, Marco had heard, didn't even like Italians anymore, wouldn't even let them in now.

Marco was handsome but seemed unaware of it. He was pleasant, had an engaging smile, but was of light intellect, with little capacity for thoughtful reflection. Marco had a good-natured belief in God, because he had been taught to believe, but had no theology. He attended church on Sunday if other people did, and stayed home if others stayed home. Friends came to know him as an uncomplicated young man with a pure heart but an insubstantial mind. He was open, obliging, generous with what little he had. Marco was, at his very deepest, exactly what one saw on his surface. He was inoffensive, naïve, gentle, and gullible. The older men in our group recognized his limitations and protected him, like uncles. Thus my father and a few other men had to step forward, risking themselves, to rescue Marco from his crisis.

One could not say, as Marco walked along Franklin Street, that he was thoughtfully reflective about his own limited prospects or those of the country. But he felt some disquiet. His vision of good living, as simple as it was, was not to be had. He did not complain of the unfairness of fate. He did not understand or ask why things were as they were, but knew it would be nice if they were not. That was as profound a thought as Marco would ever have.

Thus, when he found the paper bag of money on the ground near Streppone's store, he did not question the circumstances or implications of finding treasure in this time of poverty. It was, in Marco's understanding, just an instance of good luck. Why should it not happen to him?

It was an ordinary brown paper bag, not large, with its top neatly folded down. The bag was several inches deep, but not heavy. He brought it to his ear and shook it, and nothing metallic rattled inside. Slowly he opened it and peered in, to find an astonishing number of dollar bills, neatly stacked in three bundles and bound with elastic bands. There were also some slips of paper with numbers written on them.[3] Marco was so excited at finding so much money that when he pulled out the bills, the slips of paper fell to the ground, unnoticed. He tried to count the bills, but in his excitement kept making mistakes and had to count all over again. "Sixty dollars. Maybe 70, maybe more!"

He ran into Streppone's, shouting and waving the money. "Look what I found—$60, $70, maybe $100!"

"What?" asked the old man. "That's a lot of money, Marco. Where you find all that?"

"Out there. Onna sidewalk. A hundred dollars, maybe! Let me have some cigarettes, Mr. Streppone. The fancy kind, not those over there." He laid a dollar bill on the counter.

"Marco," the old man started to say, "Marco, you gotta be careful. . . ."

"And a cuppa coffee," Marco interrupted. "No, not coffee, ice cream. Vanilla, inna dish! With one of those little spoons. Yeah, vanilla."

---

3. These were betting slips in an illegal lottery.

"Marco, . . ." Streppone began.

"Vanilla," Marco said again, liking the sound. "*Vaniglia*-vanilla. Vanilla-*vaniglia*," he sang, turning his hand over in the air, palm up, palm down, each time he switched between Italian and English. "There oughta be a song, you know? *Vaniiiglia*—Vaniiiilla," he sang happily in his excitement.

"Listen, Marco, listen to me," Mr. Streppone tried again, leaning across the marble counter. "Calm down and listen. Don't go wavin' that money around like that. And don't tell nobody you find it in a paper bag, you hear me? Marco, you know what that money is? Was there pieces of paper and numbers with it?"

But Marco was not listening. Without even scooping up the 70 cents change from his dollar bill for the cigarettes and ice cream, he danced from the store in his excitement.

"Marco!" called Streppone. "What about your ice cream? And here's your change. Marco!"

But Marco had gone, heading for Main Street and the clothing stores. Within a few hours, he had left $25 as down payment on a new $40 suit and shoes. Marco bought drinks for some strangers in the Nyack Tavern, and ice cream and candy for some kids. He spent $5 for a fancy hat. Walking along Main Street, Marco tipped his new hat to two nuns and handed them $10 for their church. Then Marco bought dinner for himself and four friends at the Main Street Diner. By the time he returned home, Marco had spent all but $14 and had been observed by countless people as he happily disbursed his new riches.

Late that night, two narrow-eyed, tight-lipped men visited Marco at his rooming house. "It's not right to keep something you find on the street that ain't yours," they told him quietly, lecturing him on the virtues of honesty. "You supposed to give it back to the owner. Ain't that right, Marco?" They took his remaining $14 and, because he had no more to give them, twisted his arms behind his back until his joints cracked, and so ferociously slammed their fists into his midsection that he threw up all night, retching blood and his fancy meal. For days he remained doubled over, barely able to move.

"We're real patient," they told him, slowly, so he would understand. "We're reasonable people, you know? We don't want no trouble. We gonna give you a whole week to come up with $200. For the money you shoulda gave back, with interest, for all the trouble you made for us. One week. We'll be back. You don't have the money, then we take a nice little ride in the country. You know? Eh? You understand?"

They patted his cheek, gently, like an uncle might. Then they smiled and left.

The next day, my father and his friends met at our house after work. Mom decided she had something else to do—shopping, a church service, or visiting. No matter how much I protested that I wanted to stay home and find out what was going on, she made me go with her. The next two days formed a crisis around Marco's dread of his visitors' return and his desperation over the impossible demand for $200. Not knowing what to do, he did nothing, and the hours marched on toward his "nice little ride in the country."

His friends explained the seriousness of taking that money and discarding the numbered slips. "Those people," they said, "are bad people. You don' want to mess with them." But poor Marco had already done so.

Marco's generous spending had been witnessed, that information had been passed on, and the night visitors had arrived. By early next morning, the leaders of Marco's labor union had been notified, and they passed a discreet word to The Mill's personnel manager. That afternoon, while Marco groaned in his room, a co-worker brought him the news of his dismissal.

"Marco, I'm sorry. The boss, he fire you when you don' show up today."

Marco, in a fog of pain and fear, only glimpsed his predicament. His friends, however, had a good idea of what was going on. The local numbers runners, the rightful owners of the money, had put Marco in a bind. They had made an impossible demand for a $200 payback in a week, knowing that he would never be able to do it. Then they had seen to it that he lost his job. Finally, they beat him, making it impossible for him to work and earn any money at all.

"They want something from him," my father said. "They know he can't pay, and it don't do them no good to hurt him anymore. They're making it so he gotta do something for them. But what?"

"We only got a few more days," another said. "Suppose they come back and hurt him? If we gonna help him, we gotta do it now."

They asked their union steward, who sent them to another man at The Mill, who put them in touch with someone else, who arranged a meeting with *Il Padrone*. In the early days of immigration, *i padroni*[4] had been important mediators, but were disappearing as immigrants learned to rely on each other. This padrone had been given the old title as a matter of respect and some sense of cultural continuity. Whatever the rumors may have been about his enterprises, he liked to present himself as a sympathetic businessman with many connections, willing to assist any worthy person, particularly Italians, whose problems could not be solved through the usual channels. He loaned money, settled disputes, brought unions and management together—or apart—as needed, provided services for business and governments, and seemed to have his hand in all local activities that involved large sums of money.

Il Padrone was a soft-spoken elderly man, like a gentle grandfather. My father and two friends, feeling anxious, were taken to him, but when they saw his grandfatherly demeanor much of their anxiety evaporated. They

4. See Chapter Seven.

were respectful, and he was gracious to them, inviting them to sit down, addressing each man by name.

"Your friend Marco," he said, "I understand he's in some trouble. I think some people, they got offended by what he did, and maybe they were too rough on him. They didn't have to do that, but what's done is done. They say he messed with their business. Now, I been told that your friend, he don't understand things too good, he really don't know what he was getting into. You know, he's lucky in a way that he don't understand, because those people, if they thought he really knew and was being a 'wiseguy' . . . ."

He let that dark idea hang for a moment, then continued. "So, maybe it's not his fault. Still, it's too bad he made all that trouble for so many people."

"Now, your friend Marco, no way he can get himself out of this trouble, so you come here to help him. That's good. Helping your friends, I like to see that. *Siamo paisani*, we have to stick together, no? So, what it looks like to me is if we can come to an agreement, you and me, then I can talk to those people, maybe straighten it out for Marco. Fix it all up. We can help each other and help your friend, too. Like they say, '*una mano lava l'altra* (one hand washes the other).' I have nothing to do with this business, but you asked for my help, and I'm happy to help. OK?"

He looked at them for a moment.

"*Allora, abbiamo un accordo, come gentiluomini?* (Well, then, do we have an agreement, like gentlemen?)"

The three friends had no idea what the "agreement" was, but were relieved to learn that *Il Padrone* was willing to straighten out Marco's problems. It was not until they were politely ushered out that they realized the interview had lasted barely five minutes and they had said virtually nothing, except to agree, "like gentlemen." However, they understood clearly that they were now committed to whatever indelible "agreement" *Il Padrone* had contrived. They had no more choices. If they failed to carry out their side of the agreement, then, like Marco, they would suffer.

One of *Il Padrone's* men gave them instructions. Early that Saturday morning, my father and two friends, Al and Vince,[5] drove 20 miles south on 9-W to Fort Lee, New Jersey. They parked at 6:00 a.m., as instructed, in a restaurant parking lot on the west side of the road. Within 15 minutes, a truck crossed the still-new George Washington Bridge[6] and pulled in next to them, followed by two men in a 1936 Buick sedan. The high-sided truck was covered with a tarpaulin that hid its cargo. On its side, a sign

5. I never learned who the other men were and have simply picked these two names, Alberto and Vincenzo (Al and Vince), from among those of my father's friends.
6. Groundbreaking for the George Washington Bridge connecting upper Manhattan with Fort Lee, New Jersey, occurred in October 1927. The bridge opened almost exactly four years later, in October 1931.

said, "New Jersey Farm Produce Cooperative." The driver climbed down and entered the sedan, which drove off, back over the bridge into New York City, leaving the truck with its motor running. Neither the truck driver nor the men in the Buick had said a word or acknowledged the three friends waiting there.

My father and Vince climbed into the truck and drove 85 miles north on 9-W, while Al followed in his car. The drive was long and tense on the narrow, twisting, dangerous two-lane road. Impatient drivers passed them on blind curves. My father gripped the big steering wheel; his face and hands were sweating, and he felt the start of a sharp, tension-induced pain in his left side. With anxiously discordant movements instead of his usual smoothness, he depressed the clutch and shifted gears, gritting his teeth as the transmission screamed in protest.

It was not the driving that made them sweat but the reason for the journey. As instructed, they made no attempt to identify their cargo—it was enough to suspect that whatever it was, they were not supposed to be hauling it. They worried that if they made even a minor traffic violation, they would be stopped and surely arrested for hijacking the truck and its cargo. The winding road cut through dozens of small towns. In each one, the men were sure, a police car was waiting for them. What could they do then, plead ignorance? Tell the judge, "We don't know anything, your honor, we're only drivers for *Il Padrone*"? Most distressing was the unstated question, "If we get caught, what will happen to our families?"

They, and not *Il Padrone* or his men, were taking the risks. Marco's mistake, their responsibility for helping him, and *Il Padrone* had made them the potential patsies, the fall guys, if it all went wrong.

When they reached their destination, an innocent-looking warehouse just outside a small mid-state town, they left the truck, dropped the keys through a slot in a locked box as instructed, and drove back to Nyack in Al's car. The all-day, anxiety-ridden trip had worn them out.

"That's finished!" they told each other, celebrating their relief after they had returned home. "Now we relax. Marco will be all right."

But it was not finished. Eight more times over the next year they received instructions—different routes, different pick-up and drop-off destinations, never knowing if this trip would bring their arrest or if it was the last to be demanded of them. Finally, it was over. No one told them; they simply received no more instructions.

To his credit, *Il Padrone* saw to it that Marco's debt was canceled. Marco was never bothered again, and his job was restored the day following the meeting at which the agreement had been made, "like gentlemen." Marco, still too sick to work, had to delay nearly two weeks before returning to The Mill.

The friends decided not to tell him about how he had been rescued.

At first, Marco was reluctant to talk about his ordeal, but in time, he began to feel safer and spoke more about it. With each telling, it seemed that Marco had defended himself ever more valiantly; in one version he described how he had so completely routed the five thugs—in the retelling, their number had grown—that they never came back.

2. Angelino Diavolino Returns

Another memorable visit was set in motion in the early summer of 1937. My father opened a letter at the dinner table and smiled. "It's Angelino," he announced. "Angelino Diavolino, my old friend from 30 years ago!"

He continued to smile, looking up at the ceiling, seeing in its white-painted plaster the scenes of his friend and their adventures so long ago in Italy.

"Angelino Diavolino? That's some name," Fred said. He looked inquiringly at Pop. "You sure that's his name? Sounds weird to me. Angel Devil? Boy, I don't know, Pop, I don't know. . . ."

I did not understand what they were talking about, or why Fred was so skeptical. In 1937, Fred was almost 17, and at five, I was convinced that he knew everything. So I was puzzled, because here was something that Fred admitted he did not know. "What?" I kept asking. "What? What?" To me, it was a perfectly fine-sounding Italian name, "Angelino Diavolino." It had a nice, rolling musicality. "Angelino Diavolino," I repeated to myself. Yes, I liked it.

"He was my friend," my father explained. "We worked on the farm when we were boys, and he was a couple years older than me. When I was 14, we quit the farm, and the two of us went away to Naples to make our fortunes. He was going to be a great actor. I just wanted to get away from Maida. I don't know why he thought Naples was the place for great actors. Pretty soon, we were back in Maida—no great actor, no fortunes. Another couple years, Angelino went to America and we lost touch. Then I came here too, and worked on Aunt Macrina's farm. Then the war came in 1914, and me and your Uncle Joe from Ocean City, we went back to Italy to join the army. Now, 25 years since I seen him, Angelino finds out I live in Nyack. He lives in Camden and wants to come visit. Isn't that something? After all these years."

This was the longest speech I had ever heard my father make. I was impressed; there must have been something very special about this Angelino Diavolino, this friend from the past with the musical name. I was intrigued.

Pop wrote back to Angelino, or rather, he asked Mom to write the letter, and arrangements were made for the visit to Nyack.

One evening, about two weeks before the visit, some of my parents' friends dropped in and were sitting around the kitchen table with coffee and *taralli*, those wonderfully hard, home-baked cookies that were perfect for dunking. *Zio* and *Zia* Conace, he with his booming voice and she with her marvelous laughter and sense of humor, were there. The Asaros and Barones were also visiting. I was in my cave under the table, listening. Pop told them about Angelino's coming visit and entertained them with tales of Angelino's exploits as a boy.

"This Angelino," I thought, "is really something." I could not wait to meet this boy who got himself in so much trouble all the time.

After a while, Pop and the other men went down to the cellar to check out his wine. The four women stayed in the kitchen rattling their cups, talking all at once and laughing, as usual. I crawled out of my cave and went down to join the men, and that's when I heard the unedited story from a man's appreciative view. Pop told about *La Bella Renella*, 10-year-old Angelino Diavolino, and the trick he'd played on a man named Tito many years ago when Pop was just a kid working on a farm.[7]

Now I was really intrigued. Any kid who would wear hay on his head and jump around in front of everybody without any clothes on just to play a trick on some guy must be crazy. I had never seen a crazy kid, and I was eager and a little afraid to meet this boy.

On the day of the visit, we waited, expecting Angelino and his wife to arrive shortly after noon, which they did. Their car, a beautiful, new, shiny blue Packard with a long, pointed hood and distinctive grille, pulled up to our house. I ran to our front door and saw a man and a woman step out, but I did not see Angelino. Thinking they might have left him in the car, I ran out the back door, around the house, and to the street where the car was parked. Stepping onto the running board, I peered through the open window. But there was no Angelino Diavolino. It was a disappointment. The car had brought only a lady and a tall gray-haired man who looked a lot like everyone else. *Il Signore* Angelo Perrino certainly did not look like someone who would dance naked with hay on his head.

They talked all day about Maida and what they had done as youngsters. Our friends came, and everyone talked together while I sat in my cave until Mom hauled me off to bed. That was all right, because lying in my cot in the dining room next to the open kitchen doorway, I could still listen to them.

Angelo had left Maida before World War I and had gone to America. Unlike many of the other young men, he had not responded to Italy's call for their return to fight in the war. Instead, he was among those immigrants who joined the American army, and he had seen battle in France. After the war, Angelo had returned to America, where he and many other foreign nationals who had served in the U.S. military were granted citizenship. He worked in the Italian theater in New York and eventually at the growing Italian radio station, WOV. At first a radio actor, he moved

---

7. See the account in Chapter Nine.

behind the scenes into programming. Although his voice was no longer heard on the air, he knew the stars of the popular Italian soap operas. That gave him great status among the ladies, most of whom listened to the daily stories and had their own favorite characters and actors. They asked, "Do you know so-and-so, the one on this or that program? What is she really like?" That Signore Perrino had come to our house to visit brought considerable status to our family, and Mom was smugly pleased for many weeks after the Perrinos had gone.

Some months later, we visited the Perrino family in Camden, where we were treated to the usual gregarious, ebullient, and crowded Italian hospitality. It was a wonderful day in a big city that was so far from but not so different from Nyack.

3. "*I Lupini* Are Coming!"

Contact with Italy was maintained by letters and through newly arrived immigrants. There were Italian communities in many New York cities, including Rochester, Syracuse, and New York City. Many communities were in New Jersey, and some were as far away as Ohio. Trips between those communities required time, but there was good train service and some long bus rides. Except for our relatives in Ocean City and Mrs. Materazzo, The Lady from Rochester, my parents had no direct ties with other communities. However, there was always someone in our group who knew someone in another community, who in turn knew someone, and so on.

By 1936, when I was four years old, immigration from Southern Italy had dropped to fewer than 3,000 people a year, from the peak of nearly 300,000 in the year just before the war. This was the result of restrictive legislation passed by Congress in 1924, aimed at keeping out Southern Europeans such as Italians and Greeks and encouraging the more desirable northerners. By 1939, with the advent of the Second World War, immigration stopped and the only new Italians coming into the country would be a handful of prisoners of war in the mid-1940s, who were held at Camp Shanks, a nearby military base. In the waning years of the 1930s there was still a trickle of Southern Italian immigrants. Our contact with new immigrants usually began with a letter from Italy to one of the families.

> May 15, 1937
> My Dear Niece,
>   Rico DeAngelo from Maida, who married your cousin Beatrice's sister-in-law, Marianna Paoli, from Bari, is sailing next week from Napoli to work in Cleveland with his uncle Gennario Cippone, who went there from Maida in 1923. Rico is going to send you a letter after he gets there. You remember Rico. He lived in town by *la Chiesa di Santa Maria*.

This news was quickly shared among the families, and everyone looked forward to Rico's letter. Months passed, and the letter arrived. Rico had enjoyed a good voyage and was safely in Cleveland, working at the factory with his *Zio* Gennario. Rico dutifully relayed greetings from persons in Maida and Bari to their relatives in Nyack. He said that when the plant closed for its annual retooling during the first week of August, he and *Zio* Gennario would board the train and visit Nyack and Montvale, New Jersey, where many former Maidese and Barese lived.

Such visits were memorable. Rico and his uncle were treated royally, and the contact family was responsible for hosting them. There was great excitement, for we were about to talk with a man who would bring firsthand news of home. In particular, the parents wanted to ask about the disturbing speculations of a war in Europe. On these occasions, elaborate meals of celebration would be prepared at the host's home, despite the constraints of the Depression. Those meals strained small budgets, so several families shared the expense and labor of preparation. The hosts' children would be crowded into one bed so the visitors could have their own room for sleeping. An evening celebration was held, attended by all the families, honoring the two guests.

The guests were obliged to visit each family—relatives, friends, former neighbors in Maida. The little troupe of Rico and his uncle, their host and hostess, and several children set out from the hosts' home and walked through Nyack, from one Italian home to the next. Other families joined them, and the troupe grew in size as the day progressed. Some of our American neighbors became slightly uneasy, having never before seen so many Italians at one time.

When Rico and his uncle visited us in 1937, I was five years old and still small enough to fit in my secret cave under the table. I scurried in there when I heard them at the door. Three loud raps on the wooden screen door. "*Teresina! O, Teresina! Siamo qui!* (Teresina! Oh, Teresina! We are here!)" When calling at a friend's home, no one waited for the owner to open the door. The practice was to announce oneself and walk in. Doors, in that time and place, were never locked. Our flimsy wooden screened doors were meant to keep out flies, not people. The group came into the kitchen and was greeted by Mom. Pop had gone down the cellar to draw a few bottles of wine for the table, from his best barrel. Later he would take the two guests down into the cellar, proudly show off his little winery, and urge a few bottles on them to take back to Cleveland.

Effusive greetings, hugs, handshakes, kisses, back slaps, spirited gesturing, and talking all at once greeted our guests in the kitchen. One would think they had not seen one another in years. In truth, for all but the guests of honor, it had been only days or hours since their last contact.

Some members of other families soon showed up, and the kitchen became crowded, the festivities spilling over into the adjacent hallway and dining room. Sitting in my cave, I soon realized that I had a problem. Three children my age had been brought along with their parents. I was expected to play with them. The three were bending over, peering at me under the table. We were eye to eye, just a foot or so apart. I wanted to stay in my cave, and there was no room for them in there with me, so I pretended not to see them. This was pretty difficult to manage, and became impossible after one of the kids tugged at her mother, pointed under the table at me, and asked loudly, "Ma. Why is he under the table?" Not for the last time, I wondered, "Why are girls like that?"

So, at Mom's insistence and to my great annoyance, I crawled out of my cave to sit on the floor and play with those nosy kids.

Our guest brought news of Maida, delivered letters written by relatives, and passed around snapshots. Someone had died; babies had been born; daughters had been married. Best of all for the people gathered in our kitchen were the personal messages from relatives. Mom was reassured by Rico's account of visiting her old home and spending an hour with my grandmother *Nonna* Elisabetta and Mom's brother and sisters, and finding them all in good health and fine spirits. Each time another friend entered the house and joined us at the table, Mom made him tell about her family all over again. Mom's younger brother, my uncle Joe, was trying to emigrate to America, but new restrictions made the wait very long. It would be almost 20 years before he was allowed in.

Not much happened in Maida, I thought. I was getting bored trying to follow the Italian conversations while also carrying out my duties as host to those three nosy kids. I was trying to show them how to make neat airplanes out of clothespins, but they just thought it was stupid. Suddenly a word leaped out from the adults' conversation—"*i lupi!*" I did not know what it meant, but the adults' reactions to the word were dramatic.

I knew that *lupini* were large beans that we enjoyed at holidays. Salted and served cold at the end of a big dinner, they accompanied fruit, nuts, wine, and conversation. I ate them one at a time, savoring the cool and salty taste, then reaching for the firm crunchiness and the delicate, nearly hidden flavor of each bean. I knew what *lupini* were, but our guest was telling us *that "i lupini"* were attacking the sheep!

"Beans attacking the sheep?" I thought. "How can that be?"

The sheep, he said, were going crazy, bleating and panicked and running all over. The shepherd, just a young boy, was scared to death. He came screaming into the town, and men grabbed their guns and raced up the hills to shoot *i lupi* and save the sheep. The whole town was in an uproar. Mothers ran around grabbing their children; gleeful boys ran from school ignoring *il professore*, who shook his fist, swished *il fischio*[8] menacingly through the air, and shouted at them to come back. Old Paiolo, the

8. "The whistler," as *il professore's* switch of correction was known. See Chapter Nine.

shoemaker, left his bench and tools right there on the street and hobbled home to get his gun, having forgotten that he had sold it years ago. The three old dogs that usually dozed in the sun jumped up and barked in wild excitement for a moment before going to sleep again, and the whole town was crazily energized.

"Will *i lupi* come into town?" the people asked, "and go after the children?"

"Wow!" I thought, with approval. "This is really exciting!"

"Beans?" I asked my brother. "They were scared of the beans?"

"*Lupi!*" Fred exclaimed. "Wolves! *Lupo* means wolf! Big, shaggy, wild wolves with yellow eyes and great sharp teeth, and they were really, really hungry!"

Fred narrowed his eyes and gnashed his teeth so convincingly at the little kids sitting on the floor that they all ran to their mothers. I tried to use the opportunity to sneak back into my cave, but could not get past the close-packed legs of the adults.

Now that, I thought, was exciting. Hungry wolves with big teeth, sheep going crazy, people running around screaming, dogs barking, boys escaping from school, the teacher hollering, and shouting men with guns racing up the mountains! Wow! Had I been there, I would have taken my gun and run up the mountain to hunt the *lupi*, too. I suddenly had a new respect for that place called Maida. Nothing like that ever happened in Nyack! Even those three nosy kids were impressed.

"*Non c'erano lupi da cinquanta anni, ma* . . .(There had been no wolves for 50 years, but. . . .)," Rico continued. "Gino, Germaio Busconi's youngest boy, he came running, yelling the wolves were eating his sheep up in the hills. This was just the day before I was going to Napoli, for the ship to come here!"

"We spent all morning in the hills, hunting the wolves," Rico continued, "but all we found was some footprints and a couple of chewed-up bones. We shot our guns to scare the wolves away and somebody shot a bird, maybe by accident. He brought it back for supper, but it was too skinny to be much good. And poor Gino, he was so scared he didn't want to go back to the flock. But his father made him go anyway."

People were surprised that any wolves were left in the area and were concerned that *i lupi* might return and ravage the town. It was, I guess, a reminder that the hills of Southern Italy were very different from the streets of Nyack, New York.

The next day, after effusive goodbyes, the two men left to visit Montvale. I wondered how they would carry all the bottles of wine they would collect by the time their visits were over. *Compare* Cervodoro, who owned his own business, took time from work and drove them the short distance to Montvale.

The adults now had plenty to talk about, and the story of the wolves had made it a memorable visit for me. Fred and I made a joke about the "wild *lupini*" laying waste to Maida. "The *lupini* are coming!" I shouted, galloping through the house. For the next few days, Mom had to explain it to puzzled visitors as I excitedly warned them of the impending threat. "*I lupini?*" they would ask. "*Ma, che cosa?* (The beans? But what is this all about?)"

Mom did not think it was funny. "Is easy to be brave here in Nyack," she said. "But you no laugh if *i lupi* come after you!"

I do not know if my parents maintained contact with Rico and *Zio* Gennario. For me, they were two more people who entered our lives briefly and then moved on.

Chapter 18

A Midsummer Knight's Dream (Nyack, 1938)

1. The Knight

Several dozen Italian immigrant families lived in Nyack in the 1930s, and about two dozen formed our closest group. The women, born around the turn of the century, were in their 30s, and their husbands, consistent with Italian custom, were some 10 years older. They had similar histories—poverty, child labor, little formal education, wartime experience, resentment and distrust of *u guverno ladro* (the thieving government), and emigration to *la bell'America*, where they found hope, work, and the Great Depression.

My father was one of the tens of thousands of veterans who had been driven out of Italy by Europe's postwar disorder. He had been in combat, but seldom spoke of it. The only evidence of his service was in a small box that I found in the attic: one brown photograph of a uniformed young man, a military citation naming *"Il Caporale Graziano Michele di Ferdinando,"*[1] corporal's stripes, and two medals. Impressed by the medals, as young boys will be, I carried the box carefully downstairs and, wide-eyed, asked him about it. "That," he said, "is what I earned in five years of war—two cloth stripes, two circles of tin hanging on some colored ribbon, and a piece of paper with my name on it."

The second generation, my generation, included some 60 children, infants to 25-year-olds. Our parents had kept close friendships for decades, but the age spread in my generation meant that the youngest in some families would never know the oldest in others. A gap had opened, loosening the old people's ties and creating my generation's more tenuous alignments. Our parents, seeing their customs eroding, knew they must bargain with *l'America*—what to give up, what to embrace, what to reject, how to become *un'americano* without losing one's heritage.

Most Italian immigrants settled into cities, forming distinct ethnic neighborhoods. Our group, however, had chosen a town small enough for close associations without the need to cluster in a single enclave, and no concentrated "Little Italy" grew in Nyack like the "colored section" down

---

1. Corporal Michele Graziano. The form *"di Ferdinando"* was a common identification, meaning "of Ferdinando Graziano," his father.

on Franklin Street. Italian families were distributed throughout the town, most within a few blocks of each other, a few several miles apart. This was a good arrangement, avoiding an Italian concentration that would have maximized our negative visibility. Each family settled into a neighborhood without tipping the ethnic balance and kept a low visibility of the Italian immigrant presence. Older German, English, and Irish homeowners who had preceded the Italians grumbled, but I was not aware of outright opposition to the sale or rental of homes to Italians.

The Italian homes in Nyack were oases in a desert, strategically placed as we walked through the neighborhoods. They were safe ports to warm us on a cold winter's walk from stores, to give us a cooling lemonade on a hot day, or to let us set down our bundles, rest, and talk a while.

With a few exceptions, like the homes of Mrs. Kinsella, Bobby Greggs, and Freddie Ogden, the houses between the Italians' homes were those of strangers. So little did those other houses matter to me as a preschooler that they may as well have been empty lots. Had I been able to draw a map of Nyack, it would have shown only a dozen streets, each with one or two Italian homes. Whoever resided between them was of little importance.

When I was four, Fred tried to teach me to play chess. My chess master's career, however, was summarily nipped by my immediate fascination with the knights, whose horses could make prodigious leaps over their enemies' heads and land precisely where they liked. My knights jumped all over the board, enthusiastically knocking over pawns, rooks, bishops, and even an occasional king or queen. Try as he might, Fred could not convince me to honor the rules about when, how, and where the knights were allowed to jump.

"Rules!" I complained to my brother. "No fair! My knight can jump anyplace he wants!" I gleefully dashed across the battlefield, knocking down the enemy's army with my knight, sometimes with both of my knights together.

"Hmm," Fred said as he put away the board and pieces. "Maybe we'll try again in a few years."

In my imagination, my knights, undeterred by rules of civilized warfare, broke from the constraints of the board. If I were a knight, I thought, I would leap over streets, buildings, and my neighbors, all the way to Mr. Streppone's store to buy ice cream.[2] Then I would leap up to Mill Street to show off my horse to Angie Conace and Divino Serratore. Another bound would take me to Brookside Avenue, and then to Cedar Hill, where Mary Fiola, Joey Sutera, and Joey Asaro would be so impressed that they would fall over. Such was my concept of Nyack—a few solid Italian homes with little of importance in between.

In the final years of the 1930s, those empty spaces in my Nyack map

2. For kids in our 1930s depression families, ice cream was the grandest and most rare of all treats.

began to fill in. Mom rushed about, trailing me in the air like a flapping banner gripped firmly in her hand, and I discovered the town's stores. Best, however, was walking with my father to the hardware stores and to the bank, which at first I thought was another church. There were several churches in Nyack, but we were allowed to enter only St. Ann's, because going into any other would be a pretty big sin. A park was near the river and a railroad station on Franklin Street. *Zio* Jimmie Fiola ran one of the powerful steam locomotives. When we visited *Zia* Fiola during the daytime, I was reminded, finger-to-lips, to be very quiet so as not to awaken him—he was the only man in the world who worked at night and slept all day.

Nyack had several schools—two public, one Catholic, a few other private schools—and a movie theater on Broadway, where Mary Fiola or Mary or Laura Serratore took me on countless Saturday afternoons.[3]

Frequent visiting was the families' recreation. That meant a good deal of walking, since few of the first generation owned automobiles. Walking a mile or two to visit friends posed no burden to people from Maida, who had walked five or six miles each day, down and up the mountain, to work the farms. Mom, who insisted on wearing high heels, walked everywhere. Until the late 1940s, walking was Nyack's rhythm. On most Sundays, for example, *Zio* Antonio Conace walked a circuit that included Mill Street, Elysian Avenue, Brookside, Maple, Cedar Hill, Depue, and Washington, stopping to visit each family for the personal renewals that he could not manage during the work week, helping to maintain the group's cohesion. I looked forward to the lively visits of this vibrant man, and our Sunday mornings would not have been complete without him. Families came together at different homes on different days. Italian families were often on the streets of Nyack, carrying covered dishes and bottles of wine, on their way to visit friends.

2. The Rich, The Poor, The Colored, and Us

By the time I began school in 1937, I had a hazy understanding that Nyack was organized in distinct economic levels identified by our neighbor Mrs. Kinsella as "The Rich," "The Poor," "The Colored," and "Us." There were Upper Nyack mansions on walled estates along the Hudson River, large homes scattered throughout the north end of town and on secluded properties on South Mountain, and some stately old homes on Broadway. The rest of the town—commercial, residential, middle and working class, poor, and "colored"—spread from the top of the hill at Highway 9-W down to the eastern docks of the Hudson River.

Nyack maintained a small, segregated colored section, bordered by Franklin Street, Main Street, railroad tracks, stores, and warehouses. Families lived above dark little stores in old, wooden, paint-flaking apartment

3. See Chapter Fifteen.

buildings that pushed right up to the sidewalks, with no softening lawns, flowers, or trees. That neighborhood included factories, some abandoned, decaying stables, and a live-poultry store that burned down, leaving a thick smell of charred feathers and flesh for weeks. For a brief time I had a little friend, Barbara, who lived above one of those stores on Franklin Street. After school we walked together, hand in hand, carefully crossing the streets and the railroad tracks to her home. Then, waving goodbye, I continued, alone, up the hill to my home. Barbara was assigned to Nyack's segregated classes,[4] and I soon lost track of her.

The town was crossed by avenues running east and west, and by nicely shaded north-south streets. The farther from the railroad tracks, stores, factories, and the colored section, the more substantial were the neighborhoods, with larger houses, newer cars, and smaller families.

While The Rich, The Poor, and The Colored were separated from the rest of us, middle-class and working-class white families lived on the same streets. Our four-block neighborhood included a judge, a district attorney, and a police chief, making us all feel pretty safe. We had two store owners, a school teacher, a boat builder, a secretary, a life insurance salesman, a railroad conductor, a chauffeur for a wealthy family, two plumbers, a postal worker, retired couples, and several blue-collar families like ours. Our block, with its two dozen houses, contained 18 youngsters—ranging from infants to older adolescents—and seven of them were my companions. Each block or two defined its own nation of children, aware of each other, occasionally mingling, sometimes competing but mostly keeping apart, each "nation" savoring its own self-defined superiority over the others.

Most of the families were second- or third-generation English, Irish, or German. We were the only Italian family on our block until nearly 1950.

In small-town style, there was a clear social hierarchy. To our higher-status neighbors such as the district attorney and his family, my parents were Mike and Theresa. My parents, however, addressed them as Mr. and Mrs. This irked my father. He used the polite form of greeting because it was proper when addressing people who were not personally close. What bothered him was the Americans' presumptive casualness in using his first name while accepting his polite use of their titles. He was the gentleman, he concluded, while they were ill-bred, ill-mannered, impolite, and disrespectful *Americani*.

Despite economic differences, everyday interactions were cordial. My parents, however, seldom entered the homes of higher status people. (Mom did, when she cleaned house for them.) Instead, they socialized with other blue-collar families, mostly with the Italians in town.

Neighborhood children ignored the social class strictures. My "second home," for example, was next door with Mrs. Kinsella, her brothers Tom

4. See also Chapter Nineteen.

and John McMahon, and her daughter Mae. I was allowed free entry without knocking, and enjoyed snacks, meals, even afternoon naps, and uncounted hours with my beautiful septuagenarian neighbors as they shared tales of Nyack's earlier years.[5] After I began school, Mrs. Kinsella was always the first to see my report card.

Invited by their playmates, children entered each other's homes, in a social mixing tolerated by the parents, breaking through social barriers within neighborhoods. However, neighborhoods of different social classes remained separate. Children from a working-class neighborhood were not allowed entry into upper-class homes in other neighborhoods, and upper-class parents would not have allowed their children to enter working-class homes anywhere.

A stranger could not have easily identified which homes in a neighborhood belonged to which people at different status levels because, with few exceptions, all were well-tended properties. Our street was a gentle hill four blocks long. The higher-status families tended to live at the top of the hill, the lowest-status at the bottom near the railroad tracks, and the rest of us in between. Two houses near the tracks were abandoned, victims of the Depression. Except for this gradation from the top of the hill to the bottom, the homes were not significantly different. In this respect, we enjoyed a democratizing leveling of comfort and life quality. For my parents, living as successful American homeowners was a validation of their choice of *la bell'America*. My father was proud of the house, our success, and our equality with our neighbors, even if he did address some with more politeness than they showed to him.

Ours was a safe neighborhood; doors were seldom locked and the few automobiles drove by slowly and carefully. Several times each week a farm wagon clattered down our street, pulled by a snorting horse tossing his head from side to side. The driver sat high on the swaying seat, powerful arms straining, reins clenched in big fists, controlling the huge animal. To me, the driver was heroic and strong.

A white and black milk wagon with a poor old horse that I thought always looked tired still delivered to a few homes. Horse-drawn wagons had not yet been displaced by motorized milk trucks, which were just beginning to appear.

The streets were not the exclusive territory of motor vehicles as they are today. Neighbors strolled, greeting others relaxing on porches or tending their small front lawns. On summer evenings, the mildly tranquilizing fragrance of Mr. Ogden's cigars or his honey-and-rum pipe tobacco drifted from his porch to ours. The street became a safe playground, and from the early darkness drifted the intense sounds of innocence that only children can produce in their dedication to the moment. Hide-and-seek,

---

5. See Chapters Twenty-Two and Twenty-Four for Mrs. Kinsella.

ring-o-leerio, kick-the-can, jump rope, Rover-come-over, hopscotch, dodge ball, and countless other games were played, repeat performances on our street's stage by small, age-ordered groups.

In the wintertime, Ross Avenue was closed to automobiles and became one of the town's designated slopes for children to race their sleds down the steep hill, into the big snow bank in Miss Storey's yard. Several "nations" of children from nearby neighborhoods converged on this slope. A snow-packed winter evening found dozens of unsupervised youngsters self-directing their own vigorous activities, with no coaches or hovering parents. Sometimes the children's exuberance brought on a collision of sleds, a snowball thrown too accurately, a brief argument over someone's failure to respect the rules about taking turns. Somehow, we survived.

Roving vendors brought merchandise and news of other neighborhoods. Housewives gathered around the trucks to bargain and gossip while their children sought mischief. Twice a week, Bill Pozefsky parked his Chevrolet truck in front of Mrs. Garrison's house and displayed the fruits and vegetables that he had arranged early that morning. He counted oranges, lemons, and ears of corn by the dozen and weighed bananas, apples, and cabbages in a round-faced scale that looked like a rattling old one-handed clock swinging on three chains. Potatoes, onions, and string beans were sold by the pound or the peck, measured in baskets of three sizes—one peck,[6] a half peck, and a quarter peck. Bill's twice-weekly visits over the years were equal parts socializing and retailing.

Mr. Sutera brought fish. Blowing into a little trumpet, he alerted the housewives that fresh fish had arrived. I always felt sorry for the glazed-eyed, open-mouthed fish lying on their beds of chopped ice.

For a while he had a competitor, a man who outdid Mr. Sutera's tin horn by singing heartily to entice the housewives:

"Halloww! Halloww! Halloww!" he always began his song, cupping his hands around his mouth for greater distance.

"We got fresh fish, nice an' co-ohld,
Fresher'n your hubby, so I been to-ohld.
Better buy one for him
'Fore he gets too o-ohld!
Halloww! Halloww! Halloww!"

The Ice Man parked his truck and looked for the big diamond-shaped cards hung in his customers' windows. Turned one way or another, they showed a number in the upper corner for the size of the block of ice that was required that day—10, 15, or 20 pounds. Six huge blocks of ice were covered with burlap in his pickup truck. The blocks, sliding around as he worked, made deep rumbling sounds. A leather holster hung on his belt, holding a long, wicked-looking ice pick for stabbing the big blocks, splitting

6. A peck is a now little-used dry measure, equivalent in volume to eight U.S. quarts or two gallons. A peck of potatoes, as measured by Bill, weighed out at 15 pounds.

them into smaller ones. Each stab sent zigzagging fingers crackling inside the block, streaking like lightning, creating frozen, internally etched works of art. The Ice Man never weighed his blocks, but knew just the right size for each weight. He clamped big pointed tongs into the desired block, hoisted the ice to his leather-draped shoulder, carried it into the kitchen, and slid it into the upper compartment of the wooden icebox.

While he was away from his truck, kids took small pieces of ice, diamonds splintered from the blocks, and ran off to enjoy their cooling magic. The Ice Man, with his holstered ice pick, pointed tongs, and muscles, and his envied job that kept him cool on the hottest days, was an impressive man. We all wanted to be the Ice Man when we grew up.

The vendors were appropriately named—the Cheese Man, the Mailman, the Rug Man, each attracting the ladies to check the merchandise and haggle over prices. Working people like everyone else, they paused to chat and accept a glass of cool lemonade on a hot day or hot coffee on a cold one. They lived in other neighborhoods but were part of ours, adding to the pulse of the rhythm of the street.

Wally the Bread Man drove a green 1932 Model A Ford panel truck with "Widman's Bakery" painted on its sides. I don't know how Wally made it through his route—he was always stopping to talk to customers, children, even to the neighborhood cats and dogs.

Willy Cook, the Mailman, was known for his sunny smile, despite his burden of a heavy leather mail pouch, shiny brown like the color of his skin on a hot day. Fifteen years later he would lose his oldest son in Korea and, it was said, his smile as well.

My cousin Joe, the Milkman, rattled bottles loudly in his metal carrier. He sometimes paused long enough to give kids a bottle of cool chocolate milk on a hot day.

Mr. Dropkin, the Newspaper Man, told funny stories when he came into the kitchen for his weekly payment. His brother and sister-in-law, Isador and Doris, were our upstairs tenants.

The Scissors Man, who sharpened blades and mended metal pots and tools, traveled like a comet, appearing only once a year. There was also a man with a little pony and a big box camera. A photograph of a child on the pony cost 25 cents. I was afraid of the pony, because he always looked at me sideways, clearly with malicious intent. Try as she might, Mom never did get a picture of me on that pony.

By the 1940s the Good Humor Man had begun his rounds. A string of bells jingled as he slowly drove along the street. Like that of the first robin of spring, his initial appearance each year in his white truck, white hat, white shirt, white trousers, white socks, and white shoes—all vanilla, we thought—was exciting, signaling the coming glories of summer. At the bells' first tinkling, children looked up, stopped their play, and streaked home. In each house, the intense scene was repeated: a desperate child pleading for a dime. "Before he goes away! Please, Ma, please, please! Pleee-us!" Usually, there were no dimes. But two or three youngsters dashed back to the Good Humor Man, waving their dimes and shouting, "Wait, wait!" Then the wonderful man opened the thick door that always made a loud click!—the door with the picture of a huge chocolate-covered ice cream bar with a bite out of one corner, revealing the luscious creamy inside. Just looking at that wonderful picture was a summertime delight— imagine having an ice cream that big!

Even those with no dime strained to glimpse the glistening arctic landscape inside the wondrous truck, its silent wisps of cold fog curling up among the jumbled treasures. There were mountains of ice cream cups in all flavors, forests of chocolate-covered bars on thin wooden sticks, and streams of high-priced sundaes with sweet toppings and chopped nuts that we never did get to taste. Glistening snow sprinkled the landscape of that enchanted world inside the truck. A dime bought a paper cup of smooth, sweet ice cream and a small, paper-wrapped wooden spoon. Vanilla was always my choice, defended spiritedly against the derision of my friends, who claimed the superiority of chocolate. Only girls chose strawberry, such being the etiquette of ice cream. The few lucky kids took their ice cream home to enjoy. The rest, disappointed, slowly walked away, hoping that next time we might be the kids with the dimes.

Other vendors conducted their business at kitchen tables over coffee and, like Bill Pozefsky, were welcomed visitors. The Insurance Man collected payments of 25 cents a week. Later, in the 1940s, when men and women were working steadily during the war and began to feel more prosperous, the Ring Man with his glorious jewelry display cases became a regular visitor. It was not expensive jewelry and was undoubtedly overpriced, but it was affordable because it required only a small weekly payment. I think that small touch of gold was important to my parents, a bit of luxury, a small ostentation suggesting success and the end of hard times.

By the close of the 1940s, the street vendors had nearly all disappeared. Some had put away their trucks and opened stores in town. Others just faded away. Bill Pozefsky was one of the last to go, and the Milkman and the Good Humor Man continued for quite a while. Soon, only the Mailman, a new one replacing Willy Cook, visited our neighborhood.

3. The Butcher Shop

Sunday's preparations in the late 1930s began with Saturday shopping. The small butcher shop held gleaming white cases displaying an assortment of meat, much of which I did not recognize. It had a unique atmosphere of spicy and pungent aromas. Three men in freshly stained white aprons moved behind the counters, pulling long, sharp knives out of slots in thick butcher's blocks and wielding them with alarming precision. Every now and then one honed his wicked-looking knife by running its blade back and forth against a tapered steel rod, holding his arms above his head like a sword fighter in the movies. The scraping of steel on steel made the back of my neck shiver. It was a flashy display, as much to entertain the customers as to sharpen the knives.

I did not like the viciously pointed ceiling hooks with their hanging carcasses that had ominous black stains running down their sides. I could identify only the poor chickens, looking so small and sad, hanging upside-down, their skinny little naked stubs of wings held out as if they were trying to fly away from their torment. They hung next to huge, vaguely animal-shaped white slabs. It would be a long time before I realized there was some affinity between those woeful carcasses in the butcher shop and the friendly, softly nuzzling little animals that I cradled, petted, and crooned to on Uncle Joe's farm. That realization created a sharp rebellion at home—a shocked, angry, and stubborn little kid refusing to eat any more "meat stuff." Mom, of course, had to deal with that.

The small butcher shop was crowded with women, mostly Italian, a few German and other Real Americans, all preparing for the Sunday meal. They greeted each other, gossiped, laughed, complained about the prices, and respected some silent code for taking turns at the counter.

Children held onto their mothers' skirts. At first reticent, we soon sought out each other while our mothers harangued the butchers. We liked to drag our shoes through the deep sawdust that was scattered on the floor, wending our way in and out among the preoccupied ladies. It was like plowing a field or making tiny roads that ran all over the floor and between the customers' feet. The ladies ignored us and inconsiderately kept obliterating our roads in the sawdust with their no-nonsense black shoes.

Sometimes, if he was not too busy, the butcher cut slices of bologna for us. This was a major treat for me, because Mom would have none of that in our house. "You don' know," she insisted, "what they put in the grinder to make those things." I think that Maxie, the youngest butcher, knew of Mom's displeasure, and he liked to sneak those bologna slices to me as another way of tweaking his customers.

Mom was fastidious about food. She wanted only fresh food that she had preserved or prepared herself or picked from her own garden, or that was clearly recognizable in its natural form. With few exceptions, any food from a can, the butcher's meat grinder, or a factory was barred from our house. Mom loved America, but some things about America were evil and revolting, like liverwurst, mustard, butter, mayonnaise, and condensed milk. Down the list, but still banned, was moist and mushy American white bread, the kind that you could take a whole slice, roll it into a small, dense ball of dough, and throw at your brother. I think the most horrendous meal imaginable for Mom, undoubtedly served by *i diavoli* to torment sinners in hell's deepest circles, would have been a sandwich of liverwurst and mustard on buttered, mushy white American bread, smeared with mayonnaise.

To signal that a treat was coming, Maxie made question marks with his eyebrows. I smiled eagerly and nodded yes, and the treat was handed over. One day when Maxie gave the sign, I shook my head to the bologna and pointed instead to a long grayish roll that I had seen many times but had never tasted. Italian ladies never bought any of this, but Mrs. Scherer, who lived across the street, did. Maxie's eyes rose in surprise, then darted over to look at Mom. She was busy talking with *Zia* Angelina and had not seen our exchange. Maxie cut a slice and handed it to me. I did not know it was called liverwurst, but it was delicious! Then I saw Mom's horrified expression when she realized what I was eating. She tried to cross the floor in time to save me, but there were too many ladies in the way, and I quickly gobbled the rest of my treat and licked my fingers. What could Mom do about it? Make a scene in public? No, she wouldn't do that. She clenched her teeth and shook her fist at Maxie. He just looked up at the ceiling, innocently. Mom wiped my hands and face with her handkerchief, none too gently. Later, as we marched home, Mom kept asking if I was sick to my stomach yet.

Mom's transformation on entering the butcher shop was a marvel to witness. My sweet and placid Mom instantly became a woman whose hardened expression warned, "Don' fool with me today!" When it was her turn to be waited on, Mom carefully chose the beef and pork she wanted. "No!" she demanded, pointing into the case. "Not that one. This one!" I could never see any difference, but apparently Mom did. With upraised fist and gritted teeth, Mom threatened the butcher with unnamed horrors if chop, steak, or chicken turned out to be less than pristinely fresh. "But, Signora," he would plead. "This is so fresh you gotta hold it down so it don' run away!"

There was nonstop banter between ladies and butchers, a lively, adversarial but friendly relationship, respecting a code that I never understood. The ladies' intent was to get the best cuts at the lowest price, and their standard tactics included complaints and outright threats. Older ladies had known the butchers' families for years. "Listen to me, Maximilliano," a tiny, blue-haired lady warned, leaning on her cane with one hand and shaking a small, thin fist at him. "That better be a good cut! Remember, I paddled your behind when you was a kid, en' I can do it again!"

Maxie, big enough to carry a quarter of a steer under one arm, smiled. "Si, Signora, I know. And why do you think I always stay on this side of the counter?"

In any store, shopping was interactive, and personal.

"Twenny-nine cents a yard," Mr. Shapiro said. "See, good strong material. And a nice pattern. Make a nice dress, Mrs."

"Twenny-nine cents? Is too much. Too much. Look, is only junk, this. You give me 10 yards for a dollar and a half."

"What? Fifteen cents a yard? That's half price! I go broke, I sell you this fine material for half price."

"That's all is worth. Is junk. See, junk!"

"Missus," Mr. Shapiro said, quietly, with a sly look, "so tell me, if it's so much junk, why you want it, eh?"

Slowed for moment, Mom had only a weak reply. "So, why? Hmm. Eh, mebbe sometimes you just need a little junk."

"No, no, missus. Nobody need junk. You don' want junk and I don' sell junk. Look, it's not junk. It's good, strong material." He grabbed it up in his two big fists and pulled with such might that I held my breath, waiting eagerly for it to tear in half, which would have been pretty funny. But it never did.

"See?" he said. "Strong! Good material."

"Hmph," Mom said, not impressed.

"You're a good customer," Mr. Shapiro said. "For you, I make a special price. Twenny-five cents a yard, if you buy 15 yards. That's three seventy-five. It's a bargain, missus. Where you gonna get a bargain like that?"

"And what I'm gonna do wi' fifateena yards?" Mom replied, shaking her hands at him in front of her face, fingertips together, in the gesture that said, "But what's the matter with you?"

"I don' need no fifateena yards," she went on. "Look, I give you twenny cents a yard, no more."

"But I don't make nothing on twenny cents a yard. Havaheart, missus! I got kids to feed, and my wife. . . ."

"Ah, ah, ah! No tella me that. Mrs. Shapiro, she look pretty healthy to me. And you kids, they already graduate, they out of the house, and you no gotta feed 'em no more. I give you twenny-one cents a yard and then I buy two yard of that ribbon over there, and two skeins of that blue wool for knitting."

"Ah, missus, missus. You're a tough lady. You gonna send me to the poorhouse!" he said, putting his hand on top of his head to continue his lament. "And they gonna lock the door an' never gonna let me out! But, OK, since you gonna buy the ribbon and the wool, and you're a good customer, I let it go for twenny-four cents a yard, just for you. And I'm losin' money on every yard."

"Twenny-two," said Mom, opening her pocketbook.

"OK, OK. You win," Mr. Shapiro conceded. "Twenny-two cents a yard. Then I'm gonna close up my store and go live in the street!"

"*Va bene*," Mom said, concluding the deal. "Twenny-two cents a yard. And I want fifateena yards instead a' 10."

"Oy!" said Mr. Shapiro. "Fifteen yards. Now I lose even more money!"

"And take 10 cents off the wool, too," Mom added.

"Five."

"Seven!"

"Oy!"

Mom had won. Mr. Shapiro had won. Both were satisfied, having played out their roles very well indeed.

4. Sunday

There was excitement on Sundays, because the weekday routine changed. Pop started each Sunday by cleaning the ashes from the stove and setting a new fire. Soon the kitchen was warm. In winter, Pop stoked the furnace, added coal, and built up the fire to heat the house. I waited for him, sitting on the floor in front of the heating vent in the kitchen wall, and soon felt the warm air rising from the revived fire. As we ate our breakfast, Mom began preparing dinner,[7] moving between table, icebox, sink, and stove. She set a big pot on the stove and added olive oil from the gallon can, one of the few canned foods she allowed in the house. A few crushed cloves of garlic went in. The kitchen began to fill with successive aromas that told me of each stage of the dinner preparation. The warming olive oil gave off its own light aroma. Peeling and slicing onions, Mom made me think she was crying. She was glad when that job was done, and the onions went into the pot with a prodigious sizzling. She stirred them with a long wooden spoon, and their aroma signaled the next stage of preparation. As the onions slowly turned translucent, I knelt on a chair at the table, ready to carry out my important job, turning the handle of the pepper grinder. Mom added salt and the fresh-ground black pepper to the cooked onions, stirred well, and then filled the pot with water. Immediately the sound of sizzling stopped, and the aroma of cooking onions faded. The pot became neutral, with nothing interesting emanating from it anymore. It had reached another stage in the preparation—boiling water. This was always disappointing, as if something had been lost, diluted by tasteless water. But I knew that more good stuff was coming. Mom stirred it, covered it, and let the water come to a boil.

While the water heated, Mom cut up more onion, and some celery and carrots, and chopped a cup of fresh parsley and sweet basil that Pop had just brought in from the garden. She covered them with waxed paper and set them aside, my signal to snitch a piece of celery or carrot. Later, when Fred came down from his room in the attic, he took some too. Mom anticipated our larceny and cut up more than she needed for the pot. Spreading a piece of waxed paper on the big wooden board that Pop had made, she cut up a fat chicken. This, Mom explained to me, was the kind of chicken we ate, not the kind that I hand fed and carried around on Uncle Joe's farm, cradling their surprisingly solid, warm little bodies, petting their impossibly soft, dark-red feathers, and answering their "crrrrk, crrrrk" as they talked to me.

When the water boiled, the chicken was added. Later, in went the vegetables, along with salt, pepper, and other spices, including bay leaves tied in a little sack like a homemade tea bag. Soon the pot was boiling again, and Mom moved it to the back of the stove to simmer for the rest of the morning.

---

7. Sunday dinner was always at about 1 p.m., soon after church.

The toughest job came next. Pop carried the meat grinder up from the basement and attached it to the wooden table. The top of the grinder looked like a bugle, and into it went cubes of pork and beef that Mom and I had bought at Maxie's butcher shop the day before. A crank and a wooden handle protruded from the back of the grinder and, when turned, set in motion a big spiral shaft that looked just like the drill bits that Pop had on his workbench, only bigger. The spiraling action pulled the meat down into the grinder, forcing it through holes in the front with loud, wet, squishing and crackling noises as the fibers were broken down.

Interchangeable flat metal disks attached to the grinder with a wing nut. The first disk had the largest holes, and the meat came out in large, tough bits. The disk was changed several times, each time progressing to smaller holes and finer meat. In the final pass, the finely ground beef and pork were thoroughly mixed together.

Mom was able to grind the finer stages, but starting the process with the large chunks of meat required more power than we mistakenly believed ladies were able to exert. This was a job for the men of the house. I always insisted on being the first man to try, but despite my mightiest effort, I could not budge the handle. Every Sunday I tried and failed, and the grinder became my Sunday adversary. Someday, I knew, I would defeat that dumb grinder and its stupid meat. Pop was usually working down in the cellar by then, so it fell to Fred to supply the power. Respecting the seriousness of the meat-grinding ceremony, Fred stepped up to the handle. He bowed to Mom, very formally, then to the machine, and winked at me. Anticipating his weekly performance, I began to giggle. Mom glanced up at the ceiling with her exaggerated look of annoyance. Fred carefully rolled up his sleeves and stretched both arms above his head several times, flexing his fingers, getting his muscles and mind ready. He flexed his right biceps, then his left, each time resting his forehead on the back of his hand, like Charles Atlas. My part of the ceremony was to applaud my big brother's performance and be consumed with laughter. Fred remained serious. Mom, with her eye on the clock, knew we had to get to 10 o'clock mass. She might have been amused, but what she really wanted was to be irritated.

"C'mona, c'mona!" Mom urged. "My God, Freh'! Alla time you gotta be so, so, mmmmm!"

I never knew what the "so" was. Apparently, neither did Mom, so she just said "mmmmm!"

Finally, Fred ground the beef and pork together. Mom could have had the butcher grind the meat, saving us all the work. But nothing that came out of someone else's grinder would ever be allowed to enter our house.

Mom crushed dried bread into crumbs, and in a big bowl mixed them with the ground meat and eggs. She added salt, the black pepper that I had ground, some finely chopped garlic, plenty of Pop's fresh parsley and sweet basil, a pinch of hot red pepper, and some imported pecorino Romano cheese that she had grated earlier. Nothing was measured with precision, just added according to her own measurement scheme—a dash, a bunch, a drop, a bit, a pinch, some, a little, a lot, or a sprinkle—and everything always came out balanced and tasty. Mom plunged both hands into the bowl and mixed thoroughly, making loud squishing noises, adding a dash of olive oil if it felt too dry.

Mom now had the basic ingredients for her *propetti* and *bracciole*.[8] The *propetti* (meatballs) were made in three forms by rolling a generous table-spoon of the mixture with the palms of the hands. Some of the mixture was rolled into the size and shape of golf balls. Another batch of much smaller spheres was rolled out. Finally, a batch was made in an elongated shape, fat in the middle and tapering to pointed ends, looking like those malodorous little black De Nobili cigars that some of the men smoked. The rolled *propetti* were placed on a large platter, covered with waxed pa-per, and left to "set" for awhile. The *bracciole* were more complicated, involving steak that had been thinned and tenderized by pounding with the flat side of the heavy cleaver, then brushed with olive oil, salt, and pep-per and cut into strips about six inches wide. Mom placed some of the beef, pork, and bread mixture on the flattened steak and rolled it up into a cylindrical shape about six inches long and two inches in diameter, then tied it up with string, tucking the loose flaps in at each end. Before rolling and tying, she pressed an egg, hard-boiled and shelled, down into the cen-ter of the mixture, its long axis parallel with that of the roll. "See," Mom explained. "We hide the egg, like this," and the egg was gone, swallowed up by the *bracciola*. After it was cooked in her savory red sauce and served, it was sliced in cross-section. This produced round disks, each with a rim of tender steak surrounding the spiced meat and bread filling, and in its center, a round slice of pure white hard-boiled egg with its own golden bull's eye. I thought it was magic when Mom cut into each *bracciola*, re-vealing those delicious, colorful circles of egg that had been hidden there. It was my favorite part of the meal. I always wanted the slice from the very center of the roll, because that was the largest, most dramatic, and best-tasting slice.

"Aha!" Fred would announce at dinner, squinting with great concentra-tion into his plate and pretending to measure his slice with a tiny pocket ruler he always carried. "The diameter of my *bracciola* is a millimeter and a half bigger than yours!"

"Is not!" I answered, waving him away with my fork, unimpressed by whatever a millimeter or a diameter might be.

"And not only that," Fred continued, "that means it tastes a millimeter and a half better than yours!"

That grabbed my attention.

8. I have spelled these as they were pronounced at home. Italian cookbooks spell *bracciola* as *bresaola*, and *propetti* is a Calabrian idiomatic form of *polpetta*, meaning "meatball."

"And furthermore," he finished, "it also means that my *bracciola* will last a millimeter and a half longer than yours!"

That accumulation of millimeters and halves was intolerable, and my loud complaint of yet another gross unfairness at the hands of my older brother was quickly corrected as Mom switched our pieces. Now, that was fair.

But before we could eat the meal, the preparations had to be completed.

The *propetti* and *bracciole* were browned in hot olive oil and garlic, carefully so as not to break them. The small *propetti,* to be added later to the soup, were browned only slightly, the larger ones more thoroughly. The *bracciola* was browned longest, probably because it was the thickest. They were removed from the pot and set aside.

The olive oil, garlic, and flavored meat juices were left in the pot, to which was added rich home-canned tomato paste. This was cooked for a few minutes, continually stirred so it wouldn't burn. Then Mom added her home-canned whole tomatoes with their spices of basil, parsley, garlic, salt, and pepper. Just enough water was put in, all was stirred together, and the pot was left on the hot stove to simmer slowly over the next several hours or so to be transformed into Mom's smooth red pasta sauce. The soup simmered in another pot, and the browned meat was left to keep warm. A large covered pot of lightly salted water was placed on the stove. While we were in church it would warm up, and by the time we returned it would be ready to be moved to the hottest part of the old stove and brought to a hard boil to cook the pasta. While we were gone, we knew, the old stove would take care of everything.

On our return from church, Mom went back into the kitchen, where she stirred her pots, clattering their lids, and added the browned meat to the pot of sauce to cook for another hour. She then made one or two vegetable dishes, put together the ingredients for a salad, made the dressing (olive oil, a few drops of Pop's red wine vinegar, a sprinkle of fresh oregano, shredded sweet basil, and a little salt), and set the table. About 20 minutes before calling us for dinner, around one o'clock, Mom put the pasta, usually ziti on Sundays and homemade *pasta fresca* on major holidays, into the boiling water. By then, the chicken soup was hot and ready to be served.

Sunday dinner always included soup, meat, pasta, two green vegetables, salad, home-baked bread, and, for my father, a glass or two of his red wine. I was allowed a little wine in my own glass so I could join in the toast, raise my glass, and say "*a salute!*" On weekdays, the menu was built around fresh greens, beans, chicken, some seafood, and a little beef or pork. The staples, always present no matter what the menu, were olive oil, greens, and home-baked bread. Desserts were rare, other than homemade *taralli* and Mom's home-canned pears or peaches topped with a little dollop of her sweet grape jam. As noted earlier, the Great Depression surrounded us, but as far I knew, it never showed itself at our dinner table.

5. The Funnies

After Sunday mass and dinner, I read the funny papers with Fred. My father briefly suspended his usual work around the house and sat with us in the living room, relaxing, if only for a bit, reading *Il Progresso*, the Italian-language newspaper.

The "funnies" were a part of Sunday. Immediately on returning from church I took up my post at the kitchen window, looking eagerly across to where Mr. McMahon, who liked to be called "Uncle Johnny," lived. He must have watched for signs that we had returned from church, because he soon came out onto his back porch with the Sunday funnies folded into a narrow rectangle. Uncle Johnny looked over at my window, waved the paper like a signal flag, and wedged it under his porch railing so the wind would not blow it away. I ran over to get the paper whatever the weather, shouted a loud "thanks!" to Uncle Johnny, ran back home, and demanded that Fred read the funnies to me.

I loved the funnies and followed the perfectly colored pictures that were like a very neat kid's coloring book, and the words as Fred read them aloud, slowly so I could follow. Each comic had a story that was told in just a few colorful boxes with a handful of words. Some of the comics were serials, like Prince Valiant. "No, not cereals like we eat," Fred explained. Those were not as interesting, because you had to wait a whole week to find out what happened next, so I ignored them. There was Lil' Abner and his Mammy, a tough little lady who smoked a corncob pipe. Gasoline Alley seemed dull. Joe Palooka, I think, was a boxer. Mutt and Jeff and Felix the Cat were pretty funny, and I felt an affinity with the Katzenjammer Kids, because they were always into mischief. Mandrake the Magician and the Phantom were a little scary, not funny. I skipped them. Smilin' Jack and Tailspin Tommy flew airplanes, which I liked, and poor old Mr. Casper Milquetoast never seemed to have anything turn out right. Alley Oop and Peter Piltdown did not look like people should look, and I never understood why. I never did like Little Orphan Annie with her vacant eyes. Her dog, Sandy, who always said "arf," was a lot more interesting than she was. Dick Tracy's nose was too sharp. He was always saying dumb things like "Ye Gods!" and Mrs. Ogden, Freddie's grandmother, yelled at us whenever we repeated swear words like that. Anyway, it seemed to me his whole comic strip was much too serious. One comic strip, whose name I do not recall, had a recurring character, a little man with a big beard. He wore a coat that was so long it came down over his shoes, which stuck out, pointing sideways in opposite directions. He was always hitchhiking and he seemed to say nothing but "*Nov schmoz ka pock*," or something on that order.

It was easy following Fred's narratives, and I began to identify letters and some words. I was only vaguely aware that I was learning how to read, Sunday by Sunday, with Fred and the funnies. Usually I enjoyed the comics from two newspapers, the *New York Daily Mirror*, which I thought had the superior funnies and was supplied by Uncle Johnny, and the *Daily News*, brought to me by Mr. Dropkin, our upstairs tenant. Later I discovered *The New York Times*, but it wasn't any good because it had no comics.

Pop sat in the living room, *Il Progresso Italo-Americano* on his lap, a little smile on his face, watching Fred and me sprawled on the floor with the funnies spread under our noses. When Fred finished reading to me, I "read" the funnies to my father. I was sure he wanted to hear them all over again. Remembering the sequence of actions and most of each brief story line, I pretended to read to him. Every now and then Pop would say, "My, my" or "You think so?" and he always told me how well I could "read."

Later, I walked down the street, two sets of funnies tucked under my arm, to Bobby Gregg's house. Older than I and already in school, my friend Bobby could not yet read either. So I "read" the funnies to him. Bobby liked the stories but always got mad when his mother said how nicely I could read, pointing with her nose at Bobby and adding ". . . and being a lot younger than you-know-who." Of course I could not read, and I knew it. I faked it, remembering the story lines and putting on a convincing show for Bobby's benefit. His mom saw through my act, but Bobby, who could not check my accuracy, never did catch on, and I was not about to tell him.

Sundays were holidays, weekly celebrations of family, throughout the 1930s. Church, visitors in the kitchen while Mom cooked, and the comics were all part of it, but the heart of our celebration was the family. In church we sat together as a family, and for Mom at least, that hour was a deep religious thankfulness for our family's health, happiness, and continuity.

My father dutifully took us to church every Sunday. But I cannot recall any suggestion of religious intensity such as Mom displayed, or as shown by some of the men in our group, like *Zio* Serratore. Pop did not go to confession on Saturday or line up for the communal host on Sunday. He belonged to no religious societies, as Mom did, and never entered church except on Sundays or Christmas, or for funerals or weddings.

I never saw him pray as many of our friends prayed. Nor did he ever say grace at a table, refer to religious teachings as moral guides, or utter phrases like "thank God," "God knows," or "God's will" that would suggest some acceptance of religion. If my father prayed at all, he did so privately, silently, never sharing his prayers with others. But I believe that he neither prayed nor believed in God, as Mom did. Young Michele's life from 1892 to 1927 had left him with a passionate commitment to *la famiglia* and a deeply held alliance with *l'America*, his chosen country, but had driven out any budding religious reverence. I think that attending Sunday mass was an important responsibility for him, not so much born of faith but as a contribution to the weekly celebration and reaffirmation of *la famiglia*. In that sense, then, one might say he was a sincerely religious man.

As for me, going to church was a family event. I neither understood nor particularly enjoyed the services, although the singing and organ music were nice, and I was always impressed that some older boys carried out important duties assisting the priests during mass. Sometimes I thought it was all pretty silly—as when the priests and altar boys marched solemnly down the center aisle wearing long, fancy dresses and swinging gold lanterns with smoke coming out that made the whole church smell funny.

However, I thought Saint Ann's Church was beautiful, with its lustrous wood and serenely hued, sun-glowed stained-glass windows and its aura of lovely peacefulness. Most beautiful, I thought, were the wondrously smooth, curved, glowing wooden posts and arches that rose up to the vaulted ceiling high above. I wondered if those burnished posts had grown that way, sprouting from the floor, as if God had lovingly smoothed and polished special tree trunks that branched out in such beautiful symmetry, reaching, perhaps, for heaven. There is no doubt that I felt awe, wonder, and mystery—which some might consider the stirrings of religiosity. I think those feelings came from my innocent recognition of the sheer beauty of St. Ann's church and the tranquility that it seemed to create in the gathered parishioners and in myself.

6. Fireflies and Mandolins

Another celebration of *la famiglia* was the back yard gatherings on summer evenings. Invitations were unnecessary; people just attended, somehow knowing that "this Saturday we go to *Zia* Jennie's" or *Zia* Angelina's or whoever was hosting. Families came, parents and children. My friends and I, all about five to 10 years old, were known collectively as *i giovani* (the youngsters) or, later in the evening, after we had unwound, as *i piccoli diavoli* (the little devils). We formed our own autonomous group, busy with our own involvement, operating for the most part in the social and physical spaces between the other groups. Those were the adolescents, whom we labeled "the big kids"; the "babies," children under five years, whom we did our best to ignore; and the "Old Folks," who headed families and were in charge, like my parents. The older the person, the greater the deference given, such as the honor always paid to *Zia* Maria.

When such a gathering was at our house, people carried our kitchen chairs out to the back yard lawn and to Pop's little patio under the grapevine. They laughed and joked. The men drank wine and beer. The women drank coffee, although a few savored a glass of cold beer. Everyone ate the homemade cookies brought by each family. The women shared details of their various ailments, told each other hilarious stories about anyone not present, and kept watch on their husbands and children. *I giovani*, mutually absorbed, unremittingly busy, and continually accelerating, wove in and out, propelled by our own aims and needs.

As the evening deepened, a mandolin emerged from its round-bottomed case, soon joined by a guitar, a clarinet, and, on rare occasions, *la tromba*, although the trumpet was always played very softly. Sometimes an accordion appeared and was soon squeezing out music more or less in concert with the other instruments. Later in the evening, spurred by the accumulation of wine, one or two unsteady men decided to entertain us with their off-key and, at some point in the evening, off-color singing. They embarrassed their wives but were applauded by everyone else, appreciated more for their good-natured willingness to play the clowns than for their music. The musicians always performed more quietly than raucously, out of deference to the neighbors.

The warm evening grew more softly around us and gently wore on. The friends grew closer in the shared family celebration.

Too soon, one of the old folks announced, "I think it's bedtime for *i piccoli diavoli.*" That was the signal for us to run in all directions, like bugs in a room when the light clicks on. Some of us ran behind the hedge, others into the house, a few into the garage. None ever hid in the cellar, because that was scary. Our general rule was, "Keep movin', then they can't catch you!"

We didn't know it, but the bedtime announcement was a control strategy, putting us on notice that we were approaching the threshold of adult tolerance. For probably the next 15 minutes, we were very quiet kids indeed, out of earshot, out of sight, restrained by crafty self-interest. After we were quiet for some time, the old folks seemed to forget about us. Soon we were cautiously emerging from our various hiding places, flowing together like raindrops on a windshield, pooling into an ever-growing and more formidable force, feeling our increasing power that would soon be unleashed on the old folks. We were snickering, exulting in our victory and already winding ourselves up for more atrocities. Ah, the evening was not just young, it was unending.

For seven- and eight-year-old boys in those days, the greatest value of girls was in their capacity to be victims. They squealed, screamed, and reacted wonderfully when we put worms in their hair. But in those who had grown up to become "big kids," a monstrous metamorphosis occurred: they not only looked different, they were different. No longer intimidated by our outrageous behavior, they made us their victims, for in their evolution from about 12 to 14, they had cast their lot with the old folks. They had turned into the old folks' lieutenants, and this gave them power. They had become Big Sisters!

There were at least three of them at any gathering. Three big sisters facing a dozen *giovani* meant that the kids didn't have a chance. The rules were stacked against us. A Big Sister was Mamma and Papa, and *Nonna* and *Nonno,* in one exuberant, authoritarian proxy, with the righteous certainty, physical enthusiasm, and stamina of a healthy adolescent. Invested with two generations of authority, she relished her role! With near apoplectic pleasure she pounced on us, curtailing our perfectly normal activities, like when we were pulling up *Compare* Barone's garden. She was making us calm down, for God's sake, and she wielded her new power with a terrible righteousness.

Like knights on Fred's chessboard, the big sisters could move at will in any direction; they could jump, pounce, and grab. The authority vested in them not only was unlimited and unilateral and allowed no appeal whatsoever, but was universal, extended to any kid—they didn't even have to be your own big sister. They were interchangeable. After collaring a sufficient number of kids, they would sort us all out, and we'd end up with our own genetically determined jailer. If you didn't have your own family big sister, as I did not, any one of them could rightfully take you into custody. Those were the rules.

Once, in affronted defiance when I was collared by one of the Big Sisters, I shouted at her, "You're a sadist!" I had heard the word somewhere and had some vague understanding of its meaning. I pronounced it "saddest," just as I had heard it. "You," I said, trying to hold my head high in dignity, but with great difficulty against the powerful restraint of her talons in my collar, "are a saddest!"

"No," said a subdued Joey, who had just been taken into custody by another Big Sister and was being marched off to his waiting mother. "They ain't sad. They're just plain mean!"

When they were turned loose on us, it was like the unleashing of guard dogs—the kind with big spikes on their collars. By the end of the evening, sheer fatigue had thrown us into a hyperactive peak of uncontrolled frenzy. As the old folks were rising from their chairs, the men taking that last drink of wine and packing up their mandolins, clarinets, and guitars, one of the old folks, always someone's mom, would give the signal to the Big Sisters. "*Trovateli!*" she would say imperiously, pointing her prodigious nose vaguely in our direction. "*I diavoli piccoli sono stanchi, e sono come animali!* (Find them! The little devils are tired, and they are like animals!)"

"*Trovateli*" loosed the Big Sisters on us. It made no difference how far or fast we ran. The rules were that we could run but had to stay within the boundaries of the property, and hiding at this point in the evening was strictly forbidden. So we all played out the rules for kids and Big Sisters, and after brief, frenzied chases, we were inevitably caught, sorted, and herded into the appropriate family groups.

Soon, all the kids were properly allocated, subdued, and grudgingly cooperative. Our drooping eyes revealed our sudden acceptance of the fact that we really were tired. The games were over. Obligatory animosities between kids and Big Sisters were put away. Hugs and kisses swirled all around, the girls behaving sedately while we boys wiped wet kisses off our faces, saying "Ugh!" and "Gaah!" and rolling our eyes.

At this time in the evening, some of the men walked funny and bumped into chairs and laughed at themselves and each other.

We understood what was going on. It was the wine; it had gone to their heads. But if it had gone to their heads, then why were their feet so tangled? Perhaps the wine flowed down to the feet before turning and making the journey up to make the head dizzy? It was another minor mystery understood by the old folks. We learned that drinking a little wine was OK, as long as everyone had a good time and there were people around who were not dizzy to take care of you.

Grinning at each other over the heads of their wives, the men raised their hands, holding imaginary glasses, giving each other one last "*salute.*"

"Again, you drink too much wine," a *comare* would scold her husband. In a pleasantly mellow state by then, he would reply, "*Ah, bella moglia mia, se vuoi stare giovane, anni e bicchiari e' vinu no si cuntanu mai* (Ah, my beautiful wife, if you want to stay young, never count the years or the glasses of wine)."

Zio Gino burned his fingers with his cigarette again, so that he jumped around, shaking his hand in the air and saying things like, "*maledetto!*" and putting his fingers in his mouth, making us all laugh. Every party, it seemed, ended with *Zio* Gino's *canzone e ballo* (song and dance).

Like the kids, the men, too, now were submissive, willing to recognize the authority of their women to take over and direct their walk home. They looked at each other, silently communicating satisfaction with their lot in life. "This is as it should be," they seemed to say to each other.

Family groups made their way home, each in a different direction, some walking six or seven blocks through the warm, dark night of the small town, the men chuckling, sometimes softly singing or trying to throw an arm amorously around a protesting wife. The kids stumbled in their fatigue and whined in minor complaint. The mom, always fearful of embarrassment in public, kept them all in order. With a pull on an arm or a whispered correction, she glanced around, concerned that neighbors, rocking in the darkness of their porches, catching a cool breeze, might see and hear them. The men, realizing they were now in public, walked carefully, straight-legged, leaning back slightly to aid their balance, with precision and dignity, and passed through the gauntlet of our Real American neighbors.

Later, supposedly asleep, I am quietly kneeling at the little window in the corner of the kitchen with my chin on my arms and my arms on the sill, looking out at the moonlit yard. It is quiet, now that everyone has gone home and my family is all in bed. Even the echoes of the music have faded away. Empty chairs are scattered in the shadows, waiting for Pop's cleanup in the morning. A paper napkin, like a little white ghost, waves in the slight breeze. The night is soft, like dark velvet. Fireflies—"lightnin' bugs" we called them—dance silently in the air, making little trails of light, signaling each other.

"That's how they say goodnight," Mom had once told me.

"What a neat way to talk," I think, watching those tiny creatures blinking their little messages. "Maybe if I blink my eyes at them, the lightnin' bugs'll answer me."

I blink, and blink, and am soon asleep.

Chapter 19

The Stranger on Sidney's Porch (1939)

1. Miss McElroy

My grammar school was an 86-year-old[1] two-story yellow brick building on Liberty Street in Nyack. It stood in the middle of two playgrounds, one with swings and climbing bars for the younger children and the other with a baseball diamond for the older ones. Each playground was surfaced with concrete and black asphalt and surrounded by a chain-link fence. The school was near the post office, across the street from the Nyack Journal News building, and a block from the library on Broadway. Each day, hundreds of youngsters converged on the school. They ranged from kindergartners through sixth graders, boys and girls, immigrants and Real Americans, blacks, whites, Protestants, Jews, and Christians, rich and poor, entering together through two doors on the north and two on the south side of the building.

For all of the diversity that poured in, this was no egalitarian melting pot of American social equality. As early as kindergarten, I began to see a social order that became more evident to me with each grade promotion. By second grade I felt annoyance and, soon, anger—not because I thought it was unfair to minorities, like the black kids who were segregated, but because I thought it was unfair to me. A sense of something being wrong and blatantly unfair began to grow.

Those of us in the "A" sections seldom saw the "B" kids. We did not interact in classrooms, on the playground, or even during school assemblies. We knew that a "B" section existed, invisible, hidden across the hall and lost in a different schedule, with teachers we never knew. This was a grammar school cleaved in half, segregated, the "As" kept apart from the "Bs." I was always assigned to the "A" section—something, I suppose, to be thankful for.

The "A" and "B" sections were further divided. Our second grade, for example, consisted of 2 A-1, 2 A-2, 2 B-1, and 2 B-2. The system was applied for kindergarten (K A-1 through K B-2) through sixth grade (6 A-1

---

1. Built in 1851, the school was 86 years old when I entered kindergarten in 1938. It continued in operation another 30 years, until 1968.

through 6 B-2), and was carried into middle school. No invidious comparisons were admitted, no social segregation acknowledged, but the divisions were undeniable, a clear-cut social ordering.

Each morning about half the children[2] disappeared into the "B" section, and about half of those children were further dropped down into the B-2 quadrant. No one ever said that at each grade level A-1 was the best, the preferred and highest status, and B-2 was the lowest and least desirable. In my mental map of this organization, A-1 was located "up there" and B-2 "down there." The A-1 students, I thought, were the elite, the same youngsters kept together throughout their years in school and kept remote from the rest of us. My own A-2 assignment throughout grammar school was near, but never at, the top. No one had to tell us who counted in that school; the message was in the very existence of that ordering of sections.

Perhaps I was mistaken, but by third grade I had developed my own understanding of that organization: the grade divisions in school reflected the class distinctions of Nyack society. As I saw it, the children of middle- and upper-class white families—the children of politicians, doctors, old-line county families with venerable surnames, and important professional and business people—were assigned to the A-1 sections. They remained in A-1 through grammar school, seldom mixing with us in A-2, and never with those down in the Bs. They were the elite. We all knew that.

Working-class white children such as myself, from reasonably clean families of acceptable repute, were assigned to the A-2 sections. We were a pretty good lot of youngsters, despite a few cutups, such as myself.

The lowest-status white kids, the poorest, those from socially marginal families, or those who were not academically "strong," were generally assigned to the B-1 sections. We understood, correctly or not, but with unspoken clarity, that they were not only the poorer but also the "slower" white kids in school. Finally, it seemed to me, the B-2 sections were reserved mainly for the black kids.

Once made, these assignments remained throughout one's grammar school career. There were a few exceptions. I recall two or three black kids in my nine years of A-2 sections, and I think there might have been one or two in the A-1 section. Other than those few, there was a clear separation of the children, who were categorized primarily by social class and skin color and only secondarily by perceived academic ability.

My resentment of this social organization increased as I moved through the grades. I was convinced that I was just as smart as the brightest of the A-1 kids but, because of my family's low social status, I would never be admitted into their elite level.[3] This, I thought, was an egregious unfairness, an affront to me and to all Italian families. Perhaps something of

---

2. My sense at the time that half of the children were placed in the B section might not be accurate. It is more likely that the A section was larger than the B section.
3. This might not have been true, but I was convinced that it was.

the immigrant's search for *rispetto*, so important in their motivation to leave Italy and to succeed in America, had been communicated to me early on, probably by my father. My resentment grew, and centered on perceptions of unfairness and the school's disrespect for my ethnicity. Perhaps this helps to explain my repeated acts of rebellion against classroom and school rules, so that despairing teachers kept sending me to the principal's office for discipline.

Miss McElroy's first floor office was in the northeast corner, at the bottom of the stairs. Her secretary, a quietly smiling lady, occupied a little anteroom and looked at me with kindly eyes and silent compassion each time I showed up.

"I'm s'posed to see Miss McElroy," I told her, subdued. "Again."

In my child's eyes, Miss McElroy was impossibly old and superlatively mean. Those of us who were the favored recipients of her discipline thought of her as being "older'n sin and meaner'n a snake." I cannot recall a single thing she ever said to me, but through my many visits over the seven years in her school, I came to know her office well. A sharp image, still with me, shows the lower right-hand drawer of her wooden desk, always slightly open. In its darkness lay the wide, brown leather strap, coiled, waiting like a viper in its nest. She beckoned to me, silently, with a cold smile, to come around her desk, closer to her, closer to that dark drawer.

I enjoyed a fantasy that one day when she reached in for the strap it would bite her. It never did.

I think this principal's one-dimensional understanding of her role was embedded in that stinging ribbon of leather. Half a dozen lashes of the strap across the backs of bare legs, sometimes across the buttocks when she forced you over her lap, was her solution to youthful insubordination. I was sure that this treatment was only for children who were made vulnerable by their placement in the lower social categories. Occasionally as I returned to my classroom, rubbing my stinging rear or legs, I passed the next worried little kid slowly coming down the stairs, heading for his own "private lesson," as we called those sessions.

"Did you cry?" he would ask, whispering.

"No way!" I'd say, a little too loudly, lifting my chin. I would not cry, and neither would he. It was our solemn agreement. Of course I told him in grossly exaggerated detail how particularly sharp, mean, and forceful the stinging strap had been that day, and that he was "really in for it." With certainty we agreed that "Ol' McElroy would never dare do that to an A-1 kid!"

In spite of "Ol' McElroy," school was a good experience. The teachers were competent professionals who worked hard to guide their pupils. Learning went beyond academics, and we gained knowledge about a wider world that was populated by people of different types. Miss McElroy, for example, represented to me a menacing, purely American type, the antithesis of all the values of *la famiglia* taught to me at home. There was no one in all the Italian families I knew who was remotely like Miss McElroy. I suppose that was one of the good lessons for me at the Nyack Grammar School—my experience with Ol' McElroy reinforced my certainty that, compared with Americans, Italians were a good deal more civilized.

2. Sidney's Wonderful Steps

Sidney and I, classmates in Miss White's 2 A-2, walked home after school on a still-warm October afternoon in 1939. Having exploded through the doors to the freedom of Liberty Street, we pumped our legs homeward. "Liberty" had real meaning at three o'clock, when kids flew away from school in all directions, like little honed arrows shot from bows.

We had decided to play at Sidney's because his house, perched high above the sidewalk on Cedar Hill Avenue, had wondrously steep and endless wooden steps—hundreds of them, it seemed. The steps invited seven-year-old boys to propel small toy cars across the porch so the cars would shoot into the air over the top step and bounce down, hopefully to the bottom. We had endless contests. The car that made it to the bottom won. The one that made it closest to the bottom without falling off the last step won. The car that hit the most steps won; the one that hit the fewest steps won; the one that made the most noise won; the least noise, the most damage, the least damage; the fastest, the slowest, and so on. We played these mindless games in sequence, invoking one set of rules for winning and then another. Sometimes, in our eagerness to hurl the cars down the stairs, we failed to specify the rules. Then, of course, we would each loudly invoke whatever rule was most advantageous.

"I won! My car went all the way down and yours didn't!"

"No! I won. Mine stopped on the last step and yours fell on the sidewalk!"

Resolving such disputes required a kind of formula that we had worked out over many afternoons, consisting of a lot of shouting, demands to "prove it!" challenging shouts of "Oh yeah?" and the inevitable bargaining that would leave both of us satisfied. "OK, we'll call it a tie." It would have been a disappointing afternoon had there not been at least one good dispute.

We had our little cars in our pockets, our own favorites, our champions. Mine was a sadly battered 1934 Ford Roadster that was missing its left rear wheel. Sidney had a yellow Auburn convertible, the one with the neat boat-shaped tail.

3. The Telephone

Sidney's wonderful steps would wait, but first we had to go to my house to tell Mom where I would be that afternoon. I would not think of using a telephone to call her. In 1939, fewer than half of the homes in town had telephones. Our first telephone, with the number 1993-J, made us proud members of a multiple-party line. The J distinguished us from the other party line subscribers. My father, suspecting another snub against Italians, wondered why we could not have been A or even B. "At least B is close to the top. But J? J," he said, "is the bottom of the list!"

Had we really been insulted, I wondered. But a glance at Pop's fleeting little smile revealed his joke. "Boy," I said, agreeing, "that phone company!" But J we remained.

After the telephone had been installed, Pop said each of us could make one call, to see how it worked. I remember the operator's voice: "What number, plee-uz?" I wasn't ready for that voice. I had never before heard a voice so cultured, so refined, so enviably Real American, and so completely attentive to me, as if I were as important as any adult. I was startled. I clutched the phone to my head until my ear turned red, and was immediately convinced that I was in love with this wonderful lady. Maybe she was next door, a neighbor? An image appeared in my mind. She must be a member of an exclusive sisterhood of refined, beautiful ladies with upswept, neatly arranged hair, all wearing elegant, long white dresses and bright little smiles, and maybe white gloves. The ladies would be sedately answering telephones all day, sitting somewhere in a carpeted parlor with subdued table lamps that had strings of beaded frills on their domed shades. I resolved to find out where this elegant lady was and someday knock on her door and say hello to her in person, and tell her that I was 1993-J, and maybe she would smile right at me.

"Number please," she asked again as I gripped the handset. She was so very patient. I was a little nervous this first time and had to repeat the number so she could understand it. "One four seven oh," I said very carefully. "Thank you!" she said, and my heart fluttered.

There was no J on the end of that number, because it was not a party line. That was my friend Bobby's number, and he did not have to share it with anyone. Bobby's family, unlike my own, had always had a telephone, as Bobby frequently reminded me. So Bobby was the first person I called, thereby removing forever at least this one small insult. Of course he pointed out that his phone "don't need no J."

Our new telephone was in the front hall, on a little wooden table that my father had made for it. Mom had taken up her crochet hook in anticipation, and had created a beautiful little doily. With ceremonious flair, Pop brought up the table from his workbench in the cellar, positioned it just right in the front hall, and stepped back. It was shiny, dark-stained wood and still had that nice smell of new shellac. Then Mom came forward with the doily held out in both hands, palms upward. She carefully placed it on the table, smoothed it, and stepped back. Then I came forward with the telephone. It was surprisingly large and heavy, a shiny black two-piece instrument tethered by a thick brown cloth-covered cord that disappeared into the baseboard. Carefully I set it down precisely in the center of the little table, feeling proud to have been given such an important part in this little ceremony, and feeling vaguely like an altar boy at Sunday mass. Then Mom said, quietly, "*Preghiamo Dio.* We pray to God that this little machine brings us always only happy news." For a moment I did feel like an altar boy, a scary position of responsibility that I never did attain.

My brother happened to come in just then. At 18 and about to become a high school graduate and a working man, Fred was already a hardheaded realist with no patience for such sentimentality directed at a telephone. He went out on the porch, mildly disgusted with all of us. But I noticed later that he used the phone more than the rest of us.

My parents and I formed a circle around the telephone, a little awed. I was still thinking about the telephone operator somewhere at the other end of that machine. Maybe if I followed the brown cord I could find her? And Pop was thinking that back in Italy, in their hometown of Maida, only one or two families, the very richest, would have telephones. But in *la bell'America,* we owned our own, right here in the front hall, on a little white hand-crocheted doily, on a homemade table, just like the millionaires had theirs.

Pop said that this telephone was an important piece of equipment and was to be used only for serious things. Calling Mom to tell her we were going to play cars on Sidney's steps did not, in my understanding, qualify as a "serious thing." So I did not telephone Mom. Instead, we ran past Sidney's house to mine, four blocks up the hill.

When we banged through the back door, Mom was already preparing supper. We heard sizzling and bubbling and pot lids bouncing on puffs of steam. Mom's kitchen was warm and comforting; the windows were steamed up, and we floated on the aromas of the magical transformation of raw things into savory dishes that Mom would soon place lovingly on the table for her family.

Mom's cooking was one of the reasons why Sidney and all the other kids liked to come to my house. Mom fed them all with a missionary's zeal, knowing absolutely that American mothers did not know how to cook or how to feed their families, and their children were all too skinny. Mom would pinch a kid's upper arm. "*Ah, Dio mio!*" she would say, her eyes heavenward. "Here, (Bobby or Freddy), sit, *mangia!* Eat, eat!"

But Sidney was properly filled out and obviously well cared for. Her discerning eye saw a good mom in Sidney's life—an exception to her view of American mothers. She felt an affinity with Sidney's Real American mom, although they had never met, and she clearly approved of this unknown woman. She fed Sidney anyway, because he loved the food, and Mom rejoiced in the sight of any kid so happily consuming the treats she put before him. It might be bits of freshly made *propetti* or *bracciole*, or a tasty *frittata*, or fresh, home-baked bread topped with bubbling tomato sauce that seeped into warm little valleys, making tiny pools of sublime taste in each slice.

As we finally left to go to Sidney's steps, Mom reminded me to be home by five, no later. "*Diritto a' cinque, eh! Senti?* Fi' o'cluck! You hear?"

Sidney did not understand many of Mom's words, and one day he confided, "You know, your mom's really nice, but sometimes she talks funny."

And so she did. I was often embarrassed and pretended not to be with her, if we were in a store and some Real American mother with her Real American kid stopped to say hello and chatted with easy confidence. Tommy, Freddie, Bobby, and Buckles all had Real American parents who did not talk funny. They knew how to talk American, and they did so with such elegant and enviable self-assurance that I was embarrassed in those public encounters.

On Sidney's porch we had completed several races and our argument for the day and had eaten freshly baked cake his mom brought out for us. It was sweet, sticky, and delicious. I was sorry when I licked the last of it from my fingers.

Sidney's mom talked funny, too. Not like my mom or all the *comare* drinking coffee at our kitchen table, and not at all like Mrs. Kinsella, our neighbor, who we said was "Irish, but really nice anyway." Everything Sidney's mom said sounded like a question. Her sentences all seemed to inflect at the end. And she used a lot of V's, as in, "Ven ve go?" Like me, Sidney was sensitive about this, and he wouldn't discuss it. I wondered if he, too, pretended not to be with his mother when they met people in the store. But Sidney's mom had a nice smile and cooked wonderful food that was different from my mom's, and when she tousled my hair it was like my mom doing it. So they both talked funny, each in her own way. Maybe that was the nature of moms, but maybe only some moms.

4. The Stranger

A man walked up the street. I paid no attention to him until he came up Sidney's sidewalk. We had to stop our car races while he climbed the high stairs. I had never seen him before, so therefore he was a stranger, and he just walked right onto Sidney's porch!

Now I began to pay serious attention to him. The stranger was dressed in black—black shoes, black trousers, long black coat, and even a very hairy black beard. A bunch of strings hung down from his belt, under his coat. To top it off, he wore a black hat. It was a puzzling hat, something like a cowboy hat, with a wide brim. Like a citified cowboy hat.

Now here was a puzzle, and I struggled to understand who or what this man was. I reasoned that if this stranger's hat was really some type of cowboy hat, then he was not only a stranger in town, but a Bad Guy! Otherwise, why would he wear a black hat? All the Bad Guys in the cowboy movies wore black cowboy hats. The Good Guys wore white cowboy hats. This whole thing was getting to be a little scary.

Pretending to move my car around in little circles, I kept my head down and strained my eyes up and to the left as far they would go, and with eyeball-wrenching effort, I secretly watched this stranger. Then, without even knocking, he opened the door and walked right into Sidney's house!

I looked at Sidney. He was completely unconcerned about what had just happened and was revving up his car, ready for the next race.

"Hey," he said. "You gonna race, or what? Waddya, dreamin'? You just been sittin' there! And anyway, why are your eyes like that? You look goofy!"

"But Sidney," I said, trying to uncross my eyes, "that man, he just walked right in your own house! And din't even knock!"

"So?" said Sidney. "He don't gotta knock. He's my fodder!"

Sidney's father! So one mystery was solved; the Stranger–Bad Guy had been transformed into Sidney's Father–Good Guy, and now all was right and safe again on Sidney's porch. I was relieved. But life is never simple. New puzzles keep jumping out at you, as I was about to learn.

After several minutes and some satisfying car crashes, Sidney's father came onto the porch, smiled at us, and asked if we had a good day in school. Sidney and I looked at each other, knowing that if one had to be in school, then it could not possibly have been a "good day." But we answered politely and, satisfied, he sat down, unfolded a newspaper, and began to read.

He had taken off his hat and coat, and was wearing a long-sleeved white shirt, buttoned all the way up to the collar, except it did not have a collar. That was strange; in my world men came home from work wearing blue shirts, with blue collars. And they were never buttoned all the way up. But Sidney's father and my father apparently agreed on one thing—no necktie.

Most intriguing, however, was the newspaper. It was the size and shape of a regular newspaper, and had white pages and black printing. I was a second grader and knew how to read. In fact, I could read some big words. But as I looked up at this newspaper I realized that not one word or letter—if those marks were letters—could I read. But Sidney's father was content and seemed quite able to read whatever was on the pages of that very strange newspaper.

In my house, the newspaper proclaimed across the top of the front page, "*Il Progresso Italo-Americano*." Its horizontal lines arranged in narrow columns and separated by photographs looked just like those of any Real American newspaper, like the one Mr. Ogden read on his front porch after supper. It was only when one looked closely at *Il Progresso* that one realized the familiar letters were formed into unfamiliar words, Italian instead of English. However, *Il Progresso* clearly belonged in the same family of newspapers as the Real American newspapers that I had seen.

But the newspaper Sidney's father read defied comprehension. This man presented more questions just by being there, on the porch, than even Miss White did when she was interrogating our class! Here was another puzzle, and I had to solve it. What kind of strange newspaper was this, and what kind of man was able to read it?

I plumbed my second grader's store of knowledge about newspapers and languages. This paper was neither American nor Italian, so it must have been something else. But what else was there? What language had funny marks that Americans and Italians could not read? I pondered, lost all contact with car crashes, and then, with sudden knowledge, jumped from the floor. An image had appeared in my mind—a small and mysterious store on Broadway that Mom and I often walked by after shopping but never dared to enter, Mom grabbing my hand in a grip like a plumber's wrench until we had safely passed by. The door was painted glossy red. Inside it was all murky, and there were big gold dragons motionless on the walls, ready to go slithering all over. People sat at little tables eating funny food—with sticks! But my focus in this memory was on a sign in the window—it had strange black marks that to me looked pretty much like those in the puzzling newspaper. Aha! The answer was revealed to me, explaining everything about Sidney's father—the beard, the clothes, the newspaper! The strings! I was elated. The problem was solved!

"Hey, Sidney," I said, with the light of reason and logic illuminating my sudden understanding and my insightful solution of the puzzle. "Hey, Sidney. I din't know your fodder was Chinese!"

Sidney looked at me for a moment and sighed quietly as if he had known this would come up eventually. Then, with a quiet patience, he explained, "My fodder ain't Chinese. He's a tailor."

So I learned something new about my expanding world: Tailors wore all black, had big beards, shirts without collars, cowboy hats, and strings hanging at their waists, and they read Chinese newspapers. I was learning that the world contained all kinds of people, like Ol' McElroy and tailors, not just Italians and Real Americans.

Some days later, Bobby and I were walking home. Bobby was older and wiser than I and knew many things, because his family was Real American. As we walked past Mr. Smith's ice cream store, on the corner of Main Street and Midland Avenue, a page from a wind-blown newspaper scurried across the sidewalk and wrapped itself around my leg.

"Hey, Bobby," I said, shaking my foot, trying to dislodge the persistent newspaper. "Look, it's a Chinese newspaper with all the funny Chinese writin', see? It's like the one Sidney's fodder was reading. When I thought he was Chinese."

"You dope!" Bobby said. "That ain't Chinese. It's Jewish. It's Jewish writin'. Sidney's father is Jewish."

"No he's not!" I said, standing tall, looking up into Bobby's eyes, certain that, for once, I knew something that Bobby, despite his advanced age and Real American family, did not know. "He ain't Jewish," I said authoritatively. "He's a tailor! Sidney even tol' me himself!"

Chapter 20

An Angel Passes By (1939)

1. The Lady in the Box

By the time I started school in 1938, my world had grown larger, more complicated. At first I could arrange the world along my Little Railway[1] on the stove—from Nyack through Maida, and to faraway Rochester. As I experienced more of Nyack and heard more about Italy, the two became defined and separated. Nyack grew larger, and Italy, even as it gained in definition, diminished in importance and appeal.

I had little interest in my parents' origins and seldom asked about their childhoods in Italy. Parents just were; I did not question their origins. I had a child's certainty of the never-ending presence of parents long before the lesson taught to me by Sister Rosaria in our third-grade religion class. "But," I asked the holy lady, "If everything comes from God, then where did God come from?"

Sister Rosaria's eyes pinned me to my chair. She held me there for a long time, and the class was quiet. Then, with the precision of absolute certainty, she informed me: "God always has been and God always will be! Forever and forever!"

That was a definitive, no-nonsense, eye-opening, dispute-ending declaration. It left no room for doubt. The clarity, certainty, and power of the concept were thunderous and wiped away any uncertainties that this nine-year-old may have had—at least for the moment. A few years earlier, I must have felt some anticipation of that sentiment as it applied to my parents—Mom and Pop always have been and always will be, forever and forever. Given that implicit faith in my parents' eternal presence, there was no need to question their origins.

The adults seldom talked about their lives in Italy, although they discussed the plight of their families there. It was as though our parents had invested their energy in this new country, focusing on the here and now, in this house on this street, at this time. They were from Italy but were now of America.

Letters from Italy were shared—who married whom, what new babies were born, who was ill, who died, who left for America, who had returned,

1. See Chapter Fourteen.

defeated, who had been called to the military or killed in war. Weather, crops, employment, and economic conditions were all discussed. If a new priest arrived in Maida, or a shop changed hands, someone in our Nyack group learned about it and shared the news.

Some letters included monochrome photographs of elderly ladies in long, dark dresses, their hair severely pulled back, making their heads look abnormally small and round. I could see their houses, each with its single open doorway, a dark rectangle in a white wall, an opening so shadowed that it seemed impenetrable, discouraging any thoughts of entry. I saw the pebbled and dusty streets, the antiquated clothing, and the people, whose faces seemed old, and none seemed happy.

I remember pictures of a lady in a box—funeral processions and close-ups of a very old person lying in a plain coffin with hands crossed over rosary beads and crucifix. The face, wreathed in a lacy white shawl made lovingly by her saddened relatives, was sharp and angular, not looking at all soft and "*in pace*," as everyone said.

Relatives stood around the box, staring sorrowfully at us through the camera. One rested her hands on the woman in the box, as though, I feared, they had to hold her down. I was always a little afraid of those pictures of gaunt people in boxes. Tears were shared when these photographs were passed around, but so too was a sense of celebration, because while mourning a death, they also praised a long and pious life and a successful passage to a better world. "Better? I don't know," I thought. Being held down in a box did not look "better" to me. I preferred to be here in my kitchen, in my house, on my street.

I sensed that the box could not hold her spirit, which had drifted away to join all the others that coexisted invisibly with the people of Maida. Were those spirits roving the hills, maybe with the wolves? Perhaps they stayed inside the small, dark houses. Maybe that's why every photograph showed people outside, in front of their houses, even the pictures of the woman in the box. Death, it was explained to me, was the final step in this life, not to be feared, but welcomed at the right time. I would need some convincing about that. I clung to Mom as those gray pictures were passed around.

Other pictures of Italy were happier. Mom described scenes painted in the warm sun of *il mezzogiorno*, with white clouds carefully placed as if for pleasing contrast to the blue sky. Rolling mountains were softly covered with living green and decorated with flowering fruit trees. Figs, grapes, and oranges were fat, sweet, and juicy, and the olives were green jewels filled with golden oil. Even *i limone* were beautiful and tasty in their sour way. In Teresa's world, little girls laughed and played in the sun all day long.

In contrast, the photographs that tumbled out of those letters revealed a more somber place. I saw a land, miles and years distant from us—a land of the past, before there was color, perhaps, when people were subdued. It did not seem a happy place; my picture of Southern Italy always remained tinged by those gray-toned scenes, and I developed no desire to go there.

Thus, while the adults avoided talking about Italy's past, they communicated to me that their country was set in a static and somber monochromatic past. For me, Italy existed in a time before, a time that was gone.

Italy was not our country. We lived here now, in America, a country modern and alive. Without realizing it, our parents showed us such vivid contrasts with America that they hastened my generation's American acculturation and growing distance from their Italy.

In return, the children's unenthusiastic reactions to the descriptions of Italy reflected to the parents a different picture from the one they remembered. The children became teachers to the parents, providing information and guidance. Adults had to craft new identities not only in their interaction with the American society, but also with their children and other immigrants. We had become "Italian-Americans" and we hated that label. Later generations would be "American."

Children were funnels, open to the culture, bringing *l'America* into our homes. Adults without children could more readily keep American culture away from their center. They were disadvantaged with no children to interpret America, to share their growing sophistication gained from school and from their American friends. Immigrants' children were socializing agents, educating their parents. Childless couples missed that education and seemed to hang on to their original Italian culture, and had difficulty learning English and the ways of America.

Children were surrounded by talk of relatives in Italy, and we absorbed it. It was incidental learning, a soaking up of information in a passive way while we were intent on other things. Gradually, a picture of Italy was transmitted to us, and we began to see the place from which our parents had come, without asking about it or receiving formal instruction. None of the parents spent time reading to their children, reading not being a skill of people with little or no formal education. Had they done so, we would have learned more about Italy and probably would have formed more positive ideas and images.

This transmission of culture was limited in its historical scope. As children, we did not know that the modern, independent, united Kingdom of Italy[2] was 100 years younger than the United States. Nor did we know much about the Italian Peninsula's 2,000 years of civilization, or of Italy's creation of the Renaissance and thus of much of Western civilization. We never heard of the Italian heroes who fought for independence and national unification. We had no historical framework for appreciating the country of our parents. Our view of Italy was, on balance, mildly negative, one of a depressed, sad, gray country with only a few flashes of color, humor, and excitement, which were, after all, not sufficient to have held our parents to their homeland.

2. Not many years later, in 1946, Italy would become a democratic republic.

A delight of my childhood in the 1930s was hearing Mom's stories about Maida. In 1901, the year of Mom's birth, Maida had a population of about 3,500. Except for Sicily, Calabria is the southernmost of Italy's 20 *regioni* (regions), and it stretches from the Adriatic to the Tyrrhenian and south to the Mediterranean, once known as the Roman Sea, linking Europe, the Middle East, and North Africa. Calabria includes the narrowest part of Italy, and today one can drive coast to coast in two hours.

2. The Owl

Southern Italy was called *mezzogiorno*, or noontime, because it was sunny and hot, as if it were always midday. It also harbored *mal aria*, the mysterious "bad air" that lifted silently out of the swamps and spread up the hills. If caught by those vapors, one was left sick, shivering with chills, fever, pain, tremors, and even convulsions and death.[3] One could curse *la mal aria*, but that did little good; one could take *medicine* from *il dottore*, but that was useless. One could only stay indoors, away from the night air, light holy candles, and pray.

Nighttime posed dreadful threats and required special alertness. Old ladies prayed at night that their families would survive to praise the next day's sunlight, and to prevent frightful visitations and *la mal aria*. Prayers were murmured and rosary beads clicked well into the night in any home where *una Nonna* lived. Moths were among the nighttime visitations. Moths, it was said, were the souls of the dead, of those consigned to *purgatorio*. They were frightened, lost souls, innocents in an evil world, fluttering weakly through the darkness, seeking the light, drawn to the flame of the candle, where their sins would be purged by the fire. One must never kill a moth, that tiny and vulnerable vessel of some poor soul.

The owl also called at night. Sent by the devil or God, no one knew which, the owl flew on silent wings out of the darkness and came to announce an imminent death. The owl was patient, watching with luminous eyes, waiting to fly with the departing soul of the dying *cristiano*, even of those who did not know their time was up. When the call of the owl made its way through the shadows, everyone felt the dread, knowing that a life would end that night. "*Il gufo siede sulla porta* (The owl sits over the door)." When *Zia* Romina died, an owl had perched there all night, and people were afraid to enter or leave the house. The family said that at the moment *la Zia* died, *il gufo* flew off. Most distressing was when an owl visited the home of a sick child. Then the terrible anguish gripped the family through the long, dark hours, as they waited for the departure of the owl with the tiny soul. Sunny Italy was not always so sunny.

---

3. In many regions of the world, malaria remains a major scourge, with 300 million new cases—mostly the poor, children, and pregnant women—and one million deaths each year. With global warming, the mosquito carrying the disease organism will spread to parts of the world formerly too cool for its survival.

It is also earthquake country. People feared that one day the earth would shake and split and throw the houses down the mountain. Even more frightening, some warned that when the earth splits, *i diavoli* rise out to snatch unwary children. When Teresa asked her father about *i diavoli,* he assured her in his gentle voice, "*No, bella figlia, non è vero. Quelle sono solamente superstizioni. Solamente le storie delle nonne; storie delle vecchiaia. Le nonne credono in molte cose che noi sappiamo non essere vere. Ma loro sono cresciute molti anni fa, quando i cristiani credevano in quelle cose sciocche. Dio non ha creato il mondo per spaventare le piccole ragazze. No. I diavoli non escono dalla terra.* (No, my pretty daughter, that's not true. Those are only superstitions; only grandmothers' stories, stories of old age. The grandmothers believe all sorts of things that we know are not true. But they grew up many years ago, when people believed such silly things. God has not created the world in order to frighten little girls. No. Devils do not come up from the ground.)"

Teresa nestled in his strong arms, reassured that no demons could get her as long as her father was there. The superstitious ramblings of old ladies would not frighten her. But still, a moth at the candle flame made her feel sad for the poor creature, and her spine still quivered at the call of an owl. And while boys examined every crack in the ground and challenged every large hole, Teresa avoided those passages to the demonic world, even though she most certainly did not believe such silly tales.

3. Nina's Story

The region is mountainous, bordering the sea with steep cliffs falling to rocky shores and sandy beaches. Some cliffs are so high that one can look down and see the gracefully soaring seagulls from above. Mom's town, Maida, was inland, and only twice did her family make the journey to the seashore. Those were memorable trips to hear the rolling waves and feel the warm softness of the sand. It was beautiful but threatening, because the tireless ocean was deep and the tides were powerful.

The beach, the sea, and the grand horizon, as in a beautiful painting, showed a world unlike the hills of her home. Many in Maida would never see it. Some, the more affluent landowners, took their families to the seashore each year, a mark of status.

However, despite their limited contact with the sea, the Maidese shared an ocean-based heritage and, in one way or another, the sea called to them. The ocean was not a barrier to the rest of the world, but a connecting route. I sometimes think that part of going to America was the sailor's lure of crossing the ocean, and that if the Atlantic had not been there, the journey would have been less appealing. It is no accident that *Cristoforo Colombo,* however historical revisionists might try to reinvent him, is one of the heroes for Southern Italians. I remember once asking my Uncle Joe why he had not been seasick when he came across the ocean in that ship that he said had "tossed all the way, like a leaf in the brook." With a shrug, he answered simply, "*Ah, in cuore siamo tutti marinai* (Ah, we are all sailors at heart)."

In spite of the threats of *mal aria*, earthquakes, and demons, Mom recalled her little town in idyllic terms. At first I was puzzled, but then I found it amusing to hear my parents' conflicting descriptions of their town. They agreed on the quality of *la famiglia*, and that losing those relationships was their greatest sorrow upon leaving Maida. Beyond that, they seemed not to be describing the same place. Mom's Italy was a place of softness, beauty, love, happiness, nourishment, romance, and song, the secure envelopment of *la famiglia*, the comforting blanket of religion, the rich harvests, blue skies, and happy festivals and celebrations. Mom was a romantic and she loved music—operas by Puccini,[4] of course. In her idealized version, Maida was brightly beautiful, uncomplicated, and filled with love.

My father was a realist. His world was one of child labor, poverty, a personal world war, and in America the sharp stings of prejudice and recurrent, debilitating illness. With his cynical realism, Pop recalled homes— huts, actually—that were small, dark, dirty, and crowded, smelling of the chickens, goat, and cow that lived on the ground floor. He recalled working—when work was available—from the age of five, just as other boys had done. He remembered unremitting work for men that brought few rewards and the feeling of entrapment in an economically depressed region that was best when it was left behind. My father's Italy was a place of hard labor, unending poverty, deadly drought, and oppressive heat. He recalled superstition and ignorance, children forced to work in the fields instead of attending school, and feudal oppression by the rich and the Church. He knew firsthand the lack of opportunities for a poor person, the mindless and vicious militarism that killed young soldiers and drained the country, and the lack of respect for any man or woman who was not of the upper classes. Certainly he liked much about Maida, but there the life that a man could make for his family was meager and brittle, not up to the promises in the accounts of those who had returned from America.

What was I to do with such contrasting realities? My solution was to accept both, for I could not believe that either of my parents could have been so thoroughly wrong in their recollections. Italy, I concluded, must have been everything they described: beautiful, loving, hard, and ugly.

Years later, I understood that their views depended on how much one was shielded from or exposed to one side or the other. If placed in circumstances of a relatively comfortable family, sheltered from the hardness that my father recalled, then one could paint life in positive hues. But if placed in a family exposed to the harshness of poverty, then my father's hard worldview would prevail.

---

4. Many Italians maintained that Verdi, not Puccini, was the greatest composer.

Mom's favorite story of Maida was about a young lady named Giovannina who had been born nearly 100 years before Mom. It was not my favorite story. I preferred the story about the wolves; that was an exciting story.[5] But Giovannina's story was all about a girl and love. It would be many years before I began to hear and appreciate the mystery and romanticism that appealed to Mom. "Is that story really true?" I asked. Mom answered: "*Se non è vero, è buona trovata*," which means, in essence, "If it isn't true, it is well-invented."

When Mom was six years old, in 1907, *La Nonna Giovannina* was perhaps 97. Mom often saw her sitting quietly in the sunny doorway of her house up on the hill. *Nonna Giovannina* had been born around 1810 and lived to 1907, her life spanning nearly the entire 19th century! That part of the story did impress me—my mom actually knew a lady who had been born well over 100 years ago. I was not sure how long 100 years was, but 100 of anything seemed to me a vast amount, almost too much to imagine, like $100. Who could ever, in this world, have a hundred dollars? Giovannina's story fueled Mom's romanticism, although nearly a century separated their youthful years. The 97-year-old and the six-year-old had reached across time, and delicately touched.

Giovannina, called Nina, was a pretty child. She did all that young girls were supposed to do—played with dolls, and learned to sew and knit and how to behave and speak nicely, as a young lady should. But Nina was different. Like Mom, she was a romantic, and that's understandable, because in those days Romanticism was still alive in Europe. In her imagination, she heard the music of the sea and dreamed of distant places and wonderful ships that traveled to all ports. Nina seemed always to be listening, trying to hear something that no one else heard. She loved hearing her mother and sisters singing at home, and the musicians performing in the *piazza*. When birds sang, Nina listened with eyes closed and a little smile on her lips. But those were sounds that everyone could hear. Most attractive to Nina was the music others could not hear, the music for which she searched. At the end of each day, Nina walked up the highest hill. With her face raised to the wind and her eyes closed, she listened for the music.

On Nina's seventh birthday, her father made a little wooden sailboat for her.

"What kind of a present is that, for a little girl?" asked her mother. "*Perché non hai fatto una bambola? Per un ragazzo una nave è buono. Ma, per una ragazza piccola* (Why didn't you make a doll? For a boy, a boat is good. But for a little girl?)"

"*Ha molte bambole, Nina*," her father replied. "*Io ho già fatto molte bambole. In ogni modo, so che le piacerà questa piccola barca.* (Nina has plenty of dolls. I already made lots of dolls for Nina. Anyway, I know she will like this little boat.)"

5. See Chapter Seventeen, "The Visitors."

Nina did like it. It had a nicely curved hull, three sticks for masts, and six white sails made from scraps of cloth. With strings, the sails could be pulled up and down, and when they were unfurled the white sails made Nina's own elegant little sailing ship complete. Indeed, it was the only one she had ever seen, because even though Calabria was nearly surrounded by ocean shoreline, she had never traveled from Maida to the edges of the world, to see the ocean and watch the ships. But she knew about ships, and how their sails, blossoming with air, pulled the boats over the oceans like great birds soaring over the water, propelled by the same winds that carried music to her across the hills.

Listening for something silent gave her an air of detachment. Her raised chin and gaze seemed always to point to the horizon, creating an aristocratic bearing in the little girl, but there was nothing snobbish about Nina. She was sweet and sociable; she talked, laughed, played, and worked like any little girl, but she moved with a graceful demeanor, like a little princess.

When she was 15 or 16, around 1825, Nina seemed in all manner and appearance a princess. Young men began to loiter around her house, to call and to sit with her, under her mother's alert supervision, and to watch as Nina, her mother, sisters, and aunts walked to church. But, so the legend goes, she would have none of the young men. The son of the shoemaker, or the mason, or even the rich tailor, was a fine catch for any young lady, but not for Nina. She heard the music; she had her dreams, she was a romantic, and she was waiting.

"*Bella Nina mia*," her exasperated mother implored, her hands together as if in prayer, swiveling up and down at the wrists, her eyes turned to heaven. "*Tutti sono buoni giovani* (They are all fine young men). The tailor's boy will soon own his father's shop and will be a rich young man! *Mi senti? Ricco!* (Do you hear me? Rich!) Why do you send them all away?"

But Nina only smiled.

"Ah, Nina, Nina, your nose is in the air! Come down to earth, stop dreaming all the time!" Thus her mother frequently reminded Nina that reality, not fantasy, was the rightful domain of life. "Sometimes we all have to dream," she said, "but you have to keep your feet on the ground."

Shaking her finger, she warned her daughter, "*Naso all' aria, i piedi non trovare!*" meaning, "If you keep your nose in the air, you cannot find your way in life!" But Nina listened for her music, and not to her mother.

And then one day, the music was real. He was new in the village, a young musician who had given up his life as a sailor. He played the guitar and sang about the sea and love, and once he saw Nina, he sang all his songs for her.

It's an old story. Of course they were married and, as Mom told it, had many fine children and enjoyed long and satisfying lives. He lived to be 75, and Nina lived some 20 years more. In her widowhood, Nina was not unhappy, because she continued to enjoy each new generation of her family.

As she grew older, *La Nonna Giovannina* began to listen, again, just as she had so many years before. While still able, she slowly climbed the high hill, helped by her grandchildren, and listened to the breeze. When no longer able to walk those steep slopes, she sat in the sunshine and listened for the music that someday would come for her.

And what is the legend? The legend is that when *Nonna Giovannina* died at age 97, three generations gathered sorrowfully at her bedside. They had heard the owl that evening and rushed to her house to pray and to say their goodbyes. In her final moments, *La Nonna Giovannina* opened her eyes, smiled at everyone, and said just one word, "*Senti!* (Listen!)" And everyone heard Nina's music. It rose and glowed, and flowed over them, and slowly faded away across the hills on the little breeze.

Mom said that the wind had embraced Nina's music and never let it go. Each day in its unending journey, circling the sea and across the mountains, the gentle wind brings Nina's music back to life for just a few moments.

"Ever since then in Maida," Mom concluded, "when you feel sad, when your spirits need lifting, you can climb any high hill. And at the top, if you catch the breeze and you hold your breath and are very quiet and listen carefully at just the right time of day, you can hear the sweet songs to Nina from long ago. And if, perchance, you cannot hear them, you can lift your voice and sing your own sweet song, and when you are finished, you will feel so much better."

My mother, the romantic, would smile and sigh. "*Allora, come è bella, quella storia* (Now, isn't that a beautiful story)?"

"Huh!" my father, the cynical realist, would answer. "If you ask me, it's all a lot of baloney."

4. My Father's Social Science

My father did not tell many stories of Italy. One that he did tell, about a lazy farmer, is more of a parable, and may have been less about Italy and more about my father's view of America and his personal beliefs that drove him to work so hard.

Maida, my father said, had been so poor for so many generations that every man despaired of being able to maintain his family. Despair and passivity had become men's common conditions, so that even when things were promising some could not see beyond their habitual pessimism, and thus missed the few opportunities that did come along. Not so in America, he said, where there were endless opportunities and a culture that pushed men to reach for them. The parable was a straightforward contrast between what he saw as the vigorously optimistic ways of America and the passively pessimistic ways that Italy had fallen into through generations of oppression.

America, unlike Italy, offered rewards and the resources to obtain them, and every person was free to work for them. Perhaps this sounds trite to our more cynical ears today, but for those Italians, it was a powerful message: "America is the place of opportunity." With all its problems, unfairness, prejudice, violence, corruption, and greed, "only in America is there such opportunity for people like us; only here in America. *Solamente qui, in America.*"

If one did not take advantage of the opportunities and climb out of poverty, then, except in an overwhelming catastrophe like war, death, injury, or illness, any failure to overcome poverty was a personal failure, a father's inexcusable moral failure that brought loss of respect for the family. It was a hard, demanding, unforgiving wisdom.

The parable tells of a poor farmer who was blessed with wonderful fig and nut trees, but his family lived in poverty and had little to eat. The fruit was there, he had only to harvest it, but he had been immobilized by generations of pessimism. A friend just returned from America told him:

"Pick your figs, Girardo, and pick the chestnuts. Then sell them in the market or trade them, and your family will have food."

"I can't pick them; they are too high up the tree."

"Use your ladder."

"I don't have a ladder."

"Buy a ladder."

"I have no money for a ladder."

"Build one."

"I don't have the wood."

"Buy the wood."

"I have no money to buy the wood."

"Go work in the fields, earn the money."

"There are no jobs in the fields anymore."

"Then, from that scrap wood, make a ladder."

"I don't have tools to make a ladder."

"Here, I loan you my tools."

"I don't know how to build a ladder."

"Then use my ladder."

"But I don't have a pail."

"I'll give you a pail."

"Thank you, but now it is too late. All the fruit and nuts have fallen to the ground and the pigs have eaten them."

The parable voiced my father's uncomplicated view of a dynamic American society and its contrast with an Italy that was depressed economically and psychologically. In America, he believed, resources were all around. If you aimed for something, you had to work for it. If you did not achieve it, work harder and try again. If you did not succeed, then, barring debilitating illness, the failure was due to your own laziness or incompetence. He was suspicious of people who remained in poverty, disdainful of those who, like the lazy farmer, made excuses or complained about how ill-used they were. He rejected those who expected charities or governments to do it for them.

According to my father, any people still in poverty after a generation in America had only themselves to blame.

My father had little understanding of the complexities of American society, and no patience for failure. This seems a hard position, but it was not born from a soft life with no hardship. He had known years of poverty and struggle. Illness, too, was no stranger: malaria made him repeatedly ill during most of his years in America; he was often bedridden with pain, chills, and fever. Although he had experienced a good deal of anti-Italian prejudice, he could not understand that such events could control one's life. He recognized that such things—poverty, illness, prejudice—are hateful realities and sharp-edged obstacles, but if they dominate your life, it is only because you allow them to do so.

"We are the boss of our own lives. Succeed or fail, find happiness or not, we do it ourselves. Nobody does it for you." That, right or wrong, was his simple social philosophy.

"That's why we came to America," he told me. "Here, there is much fruit to pick. And the more we harvest, the more the tree makes. But if you don't harvest it, plenty of others will."

As I moved through high school, Pop and I often discussed Nyack's people and society, particularly those minorities who were still struggling and, as he saw it, still complaining. I was learning about social science and explained to him how some people, because of social factors that were as powerful as debilitating illnesses, were locked into whole generations of poverty.

Pop was tolerant of my social science and admired how many other things I was learning. But drawing from his own experience, he politely maintained that social science and I were wrong. His message remained constant.

"But, Pop," I would try to explain. "For some people it's not possible. The barriers are too great. They just can't get out from under them. They have no chance!"

Pop's arguments were straightforward and did not have the formality of education, but he held his views with quiet conviction.

"Everybody gets a chance," he said. "Everybody. But not everybody takes it."

I never did convince him.

5. *Zio* Antonio and *Zia* Rose's Grocery Store

At the end of the 1930s, our family—my parents, Aunt Macrina, and Uncle Joe and Aunt Nancy in Nyack, and Uncle Joe, Aunt Annie, and the Dattilos in Ocean City—were doing well, considering the ravages of the Depression. In Ocean City, my great uncles and aunts, Antonio and Rosa and Giuseppe and Bettina Dattilo, raised their families. By then, we were 15 cousins in the United States. Others would be born in Italy, but I would not know them until the 1950s.

Zio Antonio and *Zia* Rosa established the first Italian-owned grocery store in Ocean City. I recall wooden steps leading up to a green-painted screen door that opened into the dark, cool store on West Avenue. At the back of the store, to the right and three steps up, was the door to the apartment where my great aunt and uncle lived.[6] I felt privileged, very adult, being allowed to go behind the counter. I was introduced to a new treat of sparkling sweetness in a cool, green, long-necked glass bottle that was just the right size for me and bore the name 7UP. I never had to pay for it, a truly magnificent bonus, I thought.

The counter ran along the back of the store, so high that I could not see over the top. When I stepped into that privileged space, before me was a long, dark tunnel flanked on one side by the high counter and on the other by shelves. I marched down the tunnel to the refrigerator door under the counter at the far end. It had a big, shiny silver handle that you pulled to the side, and the thick door swung open to reveal cool, upright bottles of cola, ginger ale, orange crush, chocolate milk, and, of course, my 7-Up. The door was thick, a shiny black metal outside and a gleaming white inside. It opened and closed with a loud click! That unmistakable sound and thickness must have been, I thought, a shared characteristic of very special doors, all of which, when opened, revealed some sweet delight. How did I know this? Because the only other door in the world that was as thick and that gave off the same definitive noise upon closing was on the Good Humor Man's ice cream truck! Clearly there was order in the world.

My uncle took items off the shelves as requested by the customer and set them down on the counter. When the customer had finished, my uncle pulled out a brown paper bag, carefully smoothed it, and, using a stubby pencil, wrote down the prices and added them up.

I stood near the counter and watched the numbers flowing from the tip of his pencil to their final summation. I watched particularly for the number seven to appear—my favorite number, because he always wrote it with a short horizontal line through the middle of its single, curved leg. There was only one other place where such decorated sevens appeared: in the letters that came to us from Maida. Those sevens always had the little horizontal line, making them look rather like backward F's, and that letter, in its forward form, was the first letter in my brother Fred's name. In a moment of great insight, I realized there must be some deep connection: the crossed seven, my brother's initial, and, of course, the label on the beauti-

6. As noted by my cousin Joseph Dattilo, this was actually a comfortable "back room," a living-and-dining area where our aunt and uncle relaxed and took their meals when the store was not busy. Their living quarters were in a huge house on their substantial property—they had to be large to accommodate their big family.

ful green 7UP bottle must all share some momentous meaning. Why not? To a youngster, all things are possible.

6. *"Pass u Angelu!"*

While in the early grades of grammar school, some of us came to picture Italy as an old-fashioned place of poverty and superstition. I began to suspect that even Mom's happy recollections were fantasies and the gray pictures revealed Italy's reality.

At the same time, we saw America as modern, rich, colorful, and rational. Those were the contrasting images before us—one was old and depressingly negative and the other was modern and boundlessly optimistic. Faced with the clear superiority of America, we began to feel ashamed of our parents' homeland, manners, and speech, and we turned more sharply away from Italy and toward our allegiance to the United States. This process was encouraged and rewarded by the general air of intolerance and specific instances of anti-Italian prejudice, by the repeated lessons taught in school about the superiority of the United States over all other countries.

One of the ways that youngsters showed their rejection of *le cose Italiano* was by ridiculing their parents' superstitions. This was America; we did not believe old folks' superstitious nonsense. For example, boys often pretended many of the most tragic things in their play. We shot each other, and when we were the bad guys, we groaned loudly, dramatically clutching our chests, falling to the ground and writhing in agony until we died. Freddy Ogden always did the best spastic death scenes. Of course, if we were the good guys, then we remained stoically unconcerned about multiple bullet holes through our arms or chests—"just flesh wounds," we said—and continued shooting, riding, fighting as if they were mere mosquito bites.

At other times we screwed up our faces into wonderful agony, hung out our tongues, drooled, and made loud choking sounds. We twisted our limbs into grotesque positions and stumbled around with rigid, uncooperative legs. We stammered, stuttered, and growled, and generally practiced precisely those grotesque positions, behaviors, and afflictions that our parents knew too well were very real in some children but, "thank God," they said, had not befallen their own. Such theater, of course, was saved until we were in full view of our mothers.

"That's no' funny!" a mother would shout, angry and alarmed for our safety. "God spared you such things!" she would say, vigorously shaking a fist at us. "Don' make fun on those *poveri sfortunate* (poor unfortunates)! You are making fun of God, too!"

In our mothers' view, we were mocking God, contemptuously jeopardizing our good fortune, tempting fate, inviting disaster, coming dangerously close to asking for some terrible retribution. It was, the mothers knew, critically important to get this across to these ignorant and disobedient little savages before their disrespect of God and nature brought ruin down upon their lives.

A Depression-era song repeated the refrain, "Hallelujah, I'm a bum." I do not recall anything else about that song, but that phrase stuck with me, and I roamed the house singing it, enjoying Mom's irritation because she believed that if an angel happened to pass by, such utterances truly invited disaster. This was one of the superstitious beliefs that we took great joy in debunking—the passing angel. This was apparently a chance event, since angels did not pass by all the time. We reasoned that, even if the silly story had some truth, there was a pretty good chance we could get away with it without an angel passing by right at that moment and seeing us. But if, while we were behaving in such depraved manner, an angel came by and caught us mocking God and unfortunate people, then, according to our mothers, the angel might point to us and in an instant freeze us forever into that grotesquely distorted position. "*Pass u' angelu* (an angel will pass by)!" the mothers warned, vigorously shaking a fist. "*Si. Pass u' angelu!*" And then, presumably, we would be forever afflicted, forever sorry, never released from the wretchedness that we had brought upon ourselves.

As soon as we succeeded in forcing from the mother that phrase "*pass u' angelu!*" we offending boys began pointing and shouting in mock fear, "Look, look, there. Right behind you. *U' angelu! U' angelu!* Aghhh!"

If we were in a particularly disrespectful mood and sufficiently out of the mother's reach, one began hopping around, flapping his arms like wings and shouting "I'm *u' angelu*! I'm *u' angelu*! Bam! You're dead!" or "Ka-pow, you're a gimp!" sending the rest of us disrespectful little devils into great doubled-over fits of laughter.

And then, one day the angel did pass by, and it was suddenly no longer fun to mock anyone. From that day on, the two of us who witnessed the event no longer joined in with other boys to shout degrading things like, "Hey, Peewee Head! Ha! Ha! Peewee Head" or "Looka the midget! Hey, midget, when ya gonna grow up?" and otherwise torment poor kids with disabilities, of whom there were so many in town. I don't suppose we believed it was really an angel, but then why take any more chances?

Solly was the one who was punished by the passing angel. A low wall, about two feet high, held back the tiny raised lawn that lay between Solly's house and the sidewalk. Whenever we walked by, of course, we had to teeter along the top of the narrow wall rather than on the secure sidewalk. Solly's mother was sitting on the porch, happy with life, shelling peas, enjoying the sunshine, watching her son and his friends playing.

The opportunity could not be passed up, Solly realized. In one performance he could bait his mother, bravely tempt fate, and entertain his friends. Why were these mothers so easily baited? Why did they not simply ignore the boys' foolishness? It was their responsibility to react, because in their world, angels really did fly around and dispense retribution. For mothers, the situation was a truly dangerous one, and they had to protect their children. So they reacted, each time.

Solly began his act. He twisted himself into a most wonderfully grotesque, hump-backed, claw-fingered, stiff-legged, tongue-lolling, slackjawed, brutish posture and began painfully crawling his way across the wall, dragging a useless left leg behind and croaking, "Arrgh! Arrgh!"

"Sol-lee!" his mother shouted, as predicted, shaking her fist at him. "Stop that right now! *Pass u' angelu!*"

There! She said it. "*Pass u' angelu.*" There it was, our cue to become hilarious fools, which we did, gleefully. But suddenly, as if propelled by some unseen force, Solly flew off the wall and fell with a heavy thud onto the cement sidewalk. It was only a short drop, the kind we had all experienced many times with no harm done. But I guess this time it was not the distance of the drop, but the way he landed—or, we wondered later, the way he had been shoved by an unseen, otherworldly hand?

Solly screamed and tried to hold his left leg. It looked funny, the way it was twisted under him. Of course we thought it was still part of his clowning around and we laughed even more. But his mother, hearing something else in his screams, knew it was for real, and soon we, too, began to have our doubts and feel a few fingers of fear.

With amazing speed for such a big woman, Solly's mom ran off the porch, screaming, her arms held out in front of her. Peas—some shelled and some not—flew through the air; the metal pot clanged onto the floor, bounced down the steps, and wobbled noisily onto the sidewalk. In her concern and agitation, the first thing she did when she reached poor Solly, who was screaming even more loudly now, was to shout at him, "Non I tella you? Non I tella you?" which added to his already sharp misery. Then, crooning to comfort her son, she picked him up and ran into the house, kissing his face the whole time. A moment later, the door banged open, slamming hard against the wall, and his big brother, Jimmie, ran out, leaped down the four steps in a single impressive jump, and ran to a neighbor's house on Midland Avenue, where we learned later he used their telephone to call his father.

It seemed only moments later when Solly's father came racing up Cedar Hill Avenue in his truck, with his paint cans, ladders, and tools rattling and clanging in the back, and bounced to a stop at his house, with one front tire up on the curb. Still clutching Solly, who was now moaning and wrapped in a blanket, his mom exploded out of the house and ran down the porch steps so fast that we thought surely she, too, was about to fall and break her leg.

His father leaped from the truck and took his son gently in his arms, holding him while Solly's mom climbed onto the seat. He handed Solly in to her, closed the door, ran around the front of the truck to the driver's side, jumped in, and without even closing his door went roaring away to the hospital. An empty paint can fell from the back of the truck and wobbled across the street, making hollow, circular sounds.

We were stunned. We had never before seen so much unexpected action and heard so much noise and yelling in so short a time, and we were truly scared and worried about Solly. Exhaust smoke, kicked-up road dust and pebbles, and the fading echoes of the brief but wild commotion settled down over us in the suddenly quiet street.

We looked at each other, serious, not yet certain if we should be frightened, but we were not laughing anymore.

"An angel? You think?"

We looked around, warily.

"Nah. He just tripped . . . didn't he?"

Chapter 21
'Nando's Wonderful Shoes (1939–1940)

1. The Hot Dog

As a child I had little interest in my brother's life in Italy. I never asked him if he remembered Maida before coming to America in 1927, at the age of six. When I had the opportunity to ask, I was not interested; now that I am interested, I no longer have the opportunity. Mom said that Fred was the most beautiful, perfect, brightest child in the whole province, and she was the envy of all the mothers in Maida. Who am I to doubt Mom's unbiased assessment? At the age of five I knew, with the unquestioning certainty of solid hero worship, that my big brother, like my father, knew and could do everything. In addition, they were the two strongest and bravest men in the world.

I recognized Fred's vast superiority over me and attributed it to his advanced age and experience; after all, when I was five, Fred was 17. It seemed a proper arrangement in life that older brothers knew more than younger kids. I was confident that, on reaching Fred's age and experience, I would match him in all things. Therefore, I insisted to everyone that I harbored no envy of my big brother. I had no resentment, I told them, of the privileges that were attendant upon his maturity. In particular, I said, I did not resent that Fred had his own room in the attic, while I had to sleep on a folding cot in the dining room. Nor did I resent that he stayed up late whenever he pleased while I had to go to bed, or that he took girls for rides in Pop's car but refused to take me with them.

Aunt Annie, however, who lived in Ocean City, often pointed out that my eyebrows came together over the bridge of my nose, indicating great jealousy of my brother. "Yes," she said, with absolute certainty, "you jealous on you brother." This so infuriated me—because I knew it was blatantly untrue—that I punched Fred in the leg. He thought it was funny. He laughed and playfully held me at bay with his long arms while I flailed in the air, which of course made me even angrier, causing me to punch the air with even greater vigor. That, I knew, would show Aunt Annie that I harbored no jealousy—not a single drop! She, however, pursing lips that had a little smile flitting behind them that I did not recognize, repeated with solemn certainty, "See? Non I tella you? You jealous on you brother!"

There was one area, however, in which I admit to feeling resentment. It always began with an ominous statement that told me some invidious comparison was about to be made—"When your brother was your age"— usually accompanied by a finger shaken at me. I seldom heard this from my parents, but did hear it from my teachers and neighbors, and even the priests at Saint Ann's Church. Fred had preceded me through school, and at each new grade when the teacher saw my name on the roster, they were reminded of my brother. Nyack was a small and stable town, and the teachers welcomed younger siblings of their former students, thereby getting to know the nature of many families. My teachers remembered Fred and had a good impression of our family. The teachers, athletic coaches, principals, and even the school nurse, Ms. Riley, had good memories of Fred. Many had been impressed by the six-year-old who had come to America without knowing its language or customs, had entered school with enthusiasm and good humor, and had quickly outpaced most of his American-born classmates. He was an honor student and a member of several academic clubs and varsity teams. He left two of his paintings in the school building. One, of dinosaurs, became a permanent mural. The other, showing two pheasants, was displayed for years in the art room, and finally made its way to our house, where my father proudly featured it in our living room.[1]

I went to a football game once just to see Fred play, but I could not tell which of those identical uniforms clothed my brother. My interest in the game was soon replaced by my fascination with the hot dog that I had earned by promising an older kid I would take his place in the sweep-up crew after the game. Mom never allowed things of such suspicious composition as hot dogs to enter our house, so this was a superb treat. With my eyes closed and the warm aroma of hot dog, mustard, relish, and mounds of sauerkraut rising into my nostrils, I was about to take my first-ever bite of the forbidden treat when my private little world of bliss was invaded.

"Tony! Stop! You can't eat that!" Tessie Conace shouted. "Today's Friday! It's a sin. You can't eat meat on Friday! You better throw that away!"

I suppose that Tessie was trying to save my soul, but it was not gratitude that I felt. Had I eaten the hot dog in ignorance, having forgotten that it was Friday, I think that God would have overlooked it. But now, consuming the hot dog and, worse, enjoying it with full awareness of committing a sin, was a direct affront to God's Friday rules. I would have to enter the confessional booth on Saturday and tell Father Farrelly about the hot dog and all the other nasty things I had done all week, and he would make me say a bunch of Hail Marys and Our Fathers. I knew that once it was on your soul, a mark like that could never be erased. Even with confession and kneeling at the altar rail, fervently reciting numerous Acts of Contrition,

---

1. Fred's painting of pheasants has long since disappeared, but it can be glimpsed in the background of a black-and-white photograph of my family in our living room. See photo number 6-5 in the Photo Album section of this book.

and maybe even lighting a candle (which cost a dime), there would always remain a little smudge, like a faint stain of spiritual mustard, on the slightly tarnished breast of one's soul.

Tessie stood there, arms crossed, tapping her foot and watching me. I looked at her, and then at the aromatic, tantalizing hot dog, only inches away.

"Well?" said Tessie, drumming her fingers on her crossed arms, her forehead furrowed with accusation.

The moment of decision had arrived. The hot dog was here now, but confession was not until tomorrow, and God was far away, busy somewhere up in heaven. I looked at Tessie; I looked at the hot dog.

It was delicious. Never since, although I still search for it, have I encountered a hot dog to rival the splendor of that Friday's sin. As I licked the final drips of mustard and grease from my fingers, Tessie could say only, "Ooooh. You're gonna get it!" and ran off with her friends.

Although she might have thought it, Tessie did not remind me that I was going to go to hell. Had she said so, I suspect that I might have had at least a momentarily defiant thought that it would be worth it, just to have tasted that hot dog. To her credit, Tessie never told Mom about my Friday hot dog. She might have been a vigilant Catholic girl, concerned for my soul, but she was no snitch. I guess she recognized that my indiscretion was an issue between God and me, and it was out of her hands.

If I was going to have a hero, my brother Fred was the likely one. It is not that he was such a good boy—after all, he and Otto Gottesman did set fire to our garage once while messing around with the great jars of chemicals that they had acquired and kept on a high shelf, supposedly out of my reach. As long as he was so much older, I could accept his superior knowledge and skills, and could even believe that someday I would be his equal. The big age difference meant that we were not serious rivals. The problem was that teachers and others made a point of presenting to me his exemplary behavior when he had been my age! Clearly, I suffered by comparison. I gladly accepted him as my 17- or 18-year-old hero, but these people were telling me he had been a five-, six-, and seven-year-old hero, too! How can one compete with that?

At some point, I must have decided that I would keep the 18-year-old Fred as my hero, model, and mentor, and someday I would be as much like him as possible. In the meantime, I would be as much unlike the seven-year-old Fred as I could. My teachers often wondered how Fred and I could have come from the same family.

2. 'Nando, il Calzolaio

I liked Mom's often-told story of 'Nando's wonderful shoes, but always felt uncomfortable with it. In 1925, Fred and Mom lived in Maida while my father worked in America, trying to get them on the immigration list.

One day Mom told her mother, *Nonna* Elisabetta, "'Nando needs new shoes, but I can't afford them."

"Go talk to *il calzolaio*, (the shoemaker)," *Nonna* Elisabetta advised. "He'll let you pay him little by little. Pay him something first, so he can buy the leather for the shoes."

Mom hesitated. "No," she said. "I don't like to do that. Suppose he makes the shoes and I can't pay him? Then what's the poor man to do? He has to feed his family, too. No, I don't have the money now."

The four-year-old 'Nando began watching *il calzolaio and* asking questions whenever he passed by with his mother. "Let me try?" 'Nando asked one day. The shoemaker gave him some thin leather pieces and tools, showed him how to use them safely, and told him to be careful not to hurt himself. Over the next week, sitting on the floor of the shoemaker's shop and using tools that were big in his small hands, 'Nando crafted a pair of shoes that were just his size. The shoemaker was astounded at this precocity, and displayed the shoes for weeks, telling everyone about this amazing event. People agreed that this little boy had a fine future. He could apprentice to *il calzolaio*, they said, and someday might even own the shop. Mothers with daughters as young as two and three began musing of a future wedding with prosperous 'Nando, *il Calzolaio*. Old ladies crossed themselves and thought of the young Jesus lecturing to the philosophers, although the priest, perhaps catching a little whiff of blasphemy, insisted that while it was certainly a wonderful achievement, it was not really the same thing. 'Nando's shoes were briefly famous in the little town.

"Is that really true?" I asked Mom.

"Of course it's true," she replied. "I was there. I know."

Even Pop, who never strayed far from the truth, corroborated most of the story. When he returned from America, he said, the famous shoes were still in the house.

Mom added, turning to my father, "Those shoes, they were perfect, the most beautiful little shoes that you ever saw! Weren't they, Michele?"

"Hmm ...," was all he answered, recalling that however "perfect" the shoes may have seemed to Mom, 'Nando had never actually succeeded in wearing them. I guess Pop knew better than to dampen Mom's ebullient memory of the perfection of 'Nando's wonderful shoes.

"Well," I thought, "I can make shoes, too!" But by that time, I had already decided that I was not going to be the young Fred, and therefore I definitely was not going to make shoes, although, obviously, I could were I interested in doing so. And that would show everybody!

3. Carter's Blue Ink Bottle

It was exciting to receive letters from Italy with their spidery writing. Our relatives lived in Maida, *Provincia di Catanzaro, Regione di Calabria, Italia!* Now *that* was an address!

I think that Mom felt sad each time she wrote to her family, even when writing of happy things. Mom found quiet times to pen letters to her mother. Sometimes, on waking from a nap, the first thing I heard was the soft scratching of Mom's pen. The kitchen table, the roof of my cave, was Mom's desk. She dipped her pen into a bottle of Carter's Blue Ink, and as she moved her hand across the paper, words flowed out from the metal nib, communicating with family across the ocean. In that bottle of ink, I thought, was stored all the words to tell of our family. The pen seemed to guide Mom's hand and to pour out the words in a continuous chronicle.

Sometimes Mom gave me a pencil and let me scrawl some Xs at the end of the letter and print my name. "Antonio," Mom insisted, although I knew that was not really my name. My printing took up a large space and was undoubtedly illegible.

Over the years, Mom wrote about our lives in *la bell'America*; about our friends, the Great Depression, the house, the fears that we would not meet the mortgage payment this month and the relief when we did. She described our 1929 Packard and Pop's pride in owning it. The relatives were told, too, about all of Pop's projects. "Michele built a new cellar. Then he made two more rooms upstairs, and now we have seven rooms! Can you imagine? . . . And now Michele put in a new bathroom for us, and it has a wonderful long bathtub, and you can stretch out in it. . . ."

"He made the garage longer for the car . . . the garden this year was very good, so many beans and tomatoes for canning. He's so proud, this year for the first time, the two fig trees have fruit! . . . Michele is painting the house. You can't imagine how high it is, up to the roof, 40, 50 feet high! I worry about him, up there on the ladder, on top of the roof. But he won't listen to me. 'Terese,' he says, 'you want to paint the house?' So, what can I do? . . . Michele put in another grape arbor. We'll have lots of jelly next year, and wine. . . . He put in new heating pipes and radiators all over the house, and a new furnace for coal instead of wood. . . . Antonio had to go to the hospital for his tonsils. He's all better now. . . . He's growing so fast. . . . I still have my stomach problems but, pray to God, it won't get worse. Even so, I feel good, and we are happy. . . . I miss all of you. . . . My poor Michele had more attacks. Now they are coming sometimes every week. The doctors give him medicine but don't know what to do. They say maybe it is from bad air—*u mal aria*. They say there is a lot of *mal aria* in *Italia* and that's where he got sick. Or maybe when he was in the army. Sometimes he's so sick, but he goes to work anyway. More and more his brother Giuseppe brings him home on the bus, too sick to stay in The Mill. I beg him to stay home, but no. I pray for him to get better, but he is so sick sometimes and I don't know what to do for him. . . . *Zia* Paolina has been called to God, 92 she was. Amelia, *Compare* Gerace's daughter, she had a baby girl. . . . Michele bought a washing machine for me. No more washing clothes by hand. I wish I could send a machine to you.

"Ferdinando was first in his class again. They gave him another certificate. His report card says he is one of the best students. He will go far, his teachers say. Soon he will graduate. He wants to go to the university in New York City. Columbia. The best university. We are so proud. But how? Columbia is only for rich people. Maybe someday he can go. But first, after he graduates, he will work in the coat factory down by the river and bring home some money, a big help. . . . Ferdinando graduated high school, *con honore*, we are so proud. Now he works every day in the factory. He watches the newspaper for a better job."

Letter by letter, week by week, year by year, from 1927 right into 1997, the year she died, Mom recorded our family's living history on thin sheets of paper and sent them across the ocean to Italy, where in time they were all lost.

I wanted to dip the pen in the ink and write letters, too. What I found was that the bottle of Carter's Blue Ink, so remarkably stable when Mom used it, became a round-bottomed little devil in my five-year-old hands.[2] The resulting large blue stain remained in the wooden tabletop until Pop, with my help, used sandpaper to remove most of it. Sandpaper, I found out, was interesting material. It could make wooden things smooth. After working on the stain with only partial success, Pop gave me a piece of wood and showed me how to use the sandpaper. I also learned, on my own, that you do not want to rub it on your skin.

I was not finished with the ink, and returned to it later, when Mom was busy elsewhere in the house. This time I was careful with the Carter's Blue Ink bottle. Something remembered? Made up? Whatever the origins of the idea, I was clear on what I wanted to do. The pen, I found, with its metal nib, was too hard, too pointed, and did not work well on my writing surface. I found that by chewing the end of a wooden matchstick, I could make a small although inefficient brush that I dipped into the Carter's Blue Ink and set to work. When I finished, I carefully screwed the cover back onto the bottle, put everything neatly away, and admired my creations. They were beautiful, even with the splotches where my impromptu brush had spewed forth too much ink. It was taking a long time to dry because it was thick in those places, and I was becoming impatient. My lips and chin were a deep blue from keeping my brush smoothed out, but because I had not looked in the mirror, I did not know it. Eventually my beautiful work dried.

I squared my shoulders, clenched my fists, and bunched my powerful muscles, ready for action. I swaggered and stomped through the house, peering around doors, looking for Mom, pretending that I wore big, tough, black work shoes that made a lot of noise.

"*O, Dio mio! Honey, bello mio. No! Che hai fatto? Guardi questo! O, Dio*

---

2. This was six or seven months before I started kindergarten in 1937.

mio! Perché? Non devi scrivere così sulle bracci! L'inchiostro ti fa male! È veleno. Veleno, mi senti? Veleno! Non fare più cosi, bello mio! Per piaccere, ti prego, No, no!"

Mom's admonishments were not as bad as they perhaps should have been, because some of her reaction was amusement. The rest was made of equal portions of annoyance, concern for my health, and tolerance of my explorations. What she had said was, "Oh my God! Honey, my handsome boy. No! What have you done? Look at this! Oh my God. Why? You should not write like that on your arms! The ink will make you sick. It is poison. Poison, you hear me? Poison! Don't do this anymore. Please. I beg you. No, no!"

Mom saw blue lips and dirty arms covered with shaky lines and thick blobs of ink, and, I am sure, the threat of some terrible systemic poisoning of her youngest son. But what I had drawn on my arms were the serpents, eagles, and flags that were dredged up from someplace in my memory,[3] and I was determined to keep them. We were headed for conflict. Pulling me to the sink, Mom began to wash off my artistry. Pulling away, I was determined to save my creations. As usual, we negotiated and eventually agreed. Mom would wash off only the top layer of ink so it would not be so thick and I would not be so poisoned. There would be plenty left, she said, that had already soaked into my skin, so I could show my friend Bobby, and Fred and Pop that night. Then, after I had enjoyed my tattoos all day and showed them to everyone, Pop would help me wash them all off before bedtime.

That night, I tensed my arms to make the biggest muscles that I could, and strutted up to Pop to show him my tattoos. Pop's reaction when he saw what I had done to my arms was his characteristic little smile. After carefully admiring my work, he led me into the cellar to the big sink where he washed up after working in the garden. With a big bar of hard, brown Octagon soap, we washed my arms. I was not happy about this, but I had agreed.

To my pleasant surprise, even the powerful Octagon could not remove all the ink, and there remained enough of my blue creations for me to continue to strut around and show them off. My friend Bobby was so impressed that he went home and did his own arms, only he got "walloped," as he called it, by his mother. My wondrous pictures remained on my arms for several more days, and then, like so many good things, they faded away.

4. Freddie, Where Did I Come From?

Years earlier I had asked my brother, "Freddie, you tell me. Where did I come from?"[4] I was asking for a biological explanation and sensed embarrassment in discussing that information. There is another meaning of the

---

3. See the Red-and-Black Man described in Chapter One.
4. See Chapter Fourteen.

question, one of cultural heritage, asking, "Where did we, as a people, come from?" I do not recall asking that. A child's world is the family, in the present, and the past was not an issue for me.

Our parents were proud of being Italian, but seldom talked about it. In my secret cave under the kitchen table or standing with the men in my father's wine cellar, I never heard discussions of Italian history or heritage. They talked of current things close to home: relatives, neighbors, jobs, prices, gardens, illness, deaths, children, politics, and the year's wine.

That is not surprising. They were not educated, literate people and they had little personal experience with an Italian nation. When my father first came to America, the Kingdom of Italy was not even 40 years old. The peninsula had a long, rich history, but that was not shared by everyone. *Campanilismo*, not nationalism, defined the southerners' heritage. *La famiglia* was the central circle, the town was next, and the region, Calabria, formed the outer circle.

For some 50 generations, Southern Italians had conducted their lives through complex social relationships without the aid of centralized government,[5] and allegiance to a nation or a central government held little meaning. These people came to America not as Italian nationals, but as *Calabresi, Sicilani, Napolitani,* and so on. Americans, not knowing those regional distinctions, saw only "Italians." As the newcomers accommodated to the new country, they came together in common need across regional distinctions, as they had never done before. They accepted the label "Italian," and they diminished, but never eliminated, regional identities. In essence, they came to America, where they found their identity as Italians.

By accepting that label, they moved into closer agreement with their American hosts and accelerated their transition to being "American." The adults whom I knew in the 1930s were in that process. My father, for example, had accepted the label by the time of his U.S. citizenship in 1926, and since then thought of himself as "American." Mom took longer, maintaining her Italian identity for many years, but she eventually completed that cultural transition.[6]

Countless times I raised my glass of milk or my diluted wine in a toast at the crowded dining room table, or tilted my root beer to men in the wine cellar. "*Salute!*" we said. "To your health," and held our glasses or jelly jars high and gently clinked them together. The salutations were to those who were present, and not to people outside our circle. Never did we raise our glasses to da Vinci, Columbus, or Garibaldi. On several occasions, however, we did raise our glasses to *u presidente Rosabelta*, who had

5. See, for example, Dore (1968), pages 95–122.
6. As noted in Chapter One, in 1996, her 95th year, Mom would explain to her grandchildren, "Italia is beautiful. I was born there and I grow up there. With my family. But Italy is no my country no more. Now, this is my country, the United States. America. I love this country. I love this country."

already made well-appreciated progress combating the Great Depression. We enjoyed gatherings at our overflowing table, but had no special holidays to celebrate Italian national history, no carefully preserved ceremonies designed to teach children about a common Italian heritage.

What took me years to realize was that our heritage was the context itself, the family. To be Italian was to be a member of a family and of our small group. Our culture was being created by the Italian families day by day in the 1930s.[7] Our second generation would stand in two worlds—Italian and American—and live in the present without an appreciation for the roots of either world. As young adults, we would have little knowledge of Italian history and cultural traditions other than our family experiences.

As we gained experience outside of our families, Italian influences became secondary to American culture, as they should in a host country. For my generation, being Italian was an earlier condition from which we had journeyed and to which we no longer aspired. We had been Italian as young children, but we were becoming Americans as we matured, paralleling the experience of our parents. We did not think of it in these terms, but it seems as though we children, like our parents, were also immigrants, leaving our old culture and entering a new one.

Our parents had chosen the United States and were now in transition between two cultures. They needed to learn the ways and language of America but, unlike their children, would never become fluently American. Being mature adults and bearing full responsibility for their families, they found themselves in a strange position for mature adults—developmentally suspended, still learning, still struggling, and trying to sort it all out. However sophisticated or mature they might become, their broken English would remain a clear sign of their difference from everyone else. They made errors, sometimes humorous, often costly. They failed or succeeded at this or that, felt frustration at times and elation at others. Men and women who were mature and competent were often patronized and treated with condescension by Real Americans. They endured the subtle slights and blatant insults. They struggled to define themselves, to maintain dignity in this new world—*la bell'America*—but often failed, and they did not understand many of the issues facing them. It was as if these mature adults were struggling through an imposed and demeaning cross-cultural second adolescence.

We children—the second generation—did not understand or appreciate our parents' cultural balancing act. We quickly learned the new language and American ways and outdistanced our still-struggling parents. As we gained fluency in English, we gladly gave up fluency in Italian. In some

7. The Asaros, Barones, Bianchinis, Cervadoros, Cianciminos, Cicalonis, Cilibertos, Conaces, Cosentinos, D'Aurias, Dellolios, DelPizzos, Farsettas, Fatales, Fasanos, Fiolas, Giacobes, Grazianos, Lafascianos, Lanzanas, Maioranos, Paones, Pettinatos, Puglieses, Renellas, Schenos, Serratores, Suteras, and others whom I, as a child, had not yet met.

perverted way we embraced the idea that our growing distance from the Italian language and culture was a clear measure of success. Simply put, we had to "get over" being Italians.

As the years progressed, we grew less interested and less fluent in spoken or written Italian, and retained only a weakened ability to understand colloquial *Calabrese*. We were, in effect, willingly moving over to the other side. We did not understand that, by actively aiding the erosion of the language skills we had acquired as young children, we were throwing away important ties with our parents' heritage. We were effectively removed to only secondary contact with Italian culture, to secondary experiences through English language commentary about Italy. We had removed ourselves from inside to outside the circle of the tolling bells—*campanilismo* was fading from us.

Our second generation acculturated quickly, moving to adulthood and surpassing our parents, who were still caught in their difficult cultural adolescence. Children, even those in grammar school, were called upon to interpret the culture for their parents. They translated letters and documents, explained to their parents about appointments, and helped in discussions and negotiations with landlords, clerks, doctors, and bankers. In some ways, these young Italian-Americans were maturing faster and becoming more knowledgeable and sophisticated than their youthful American friends, who knew little of such adult activities.

Too often, children became impatient and patronizing toward their parents, an insufferable reversal of roles and status. American parents are often patronized by their teenagers and feel puzzled, amused, and sometimes angered by their children's supercilious "know-it-all" attitude. But there is a significant difference: the American teenager is a "work in progress," still immature, still learning, and without his or her parents' experience and skills. Therefore the slings, slights, and insults launched by today's teenagers toward their parents can be attributed to the adolescents' immaturity rather than to the parents' lack of sophistication. But this face-saving interpretation was not available to the Italian immigrant parents in the 1930s, because in many ways the roles had been reversed. The parents were, in fact, those with less skill and knowledge; the adolescents were more sophisticated in many things that were important for the family. The parent had to seek the child's help and advice. It was often the child who advised the parent to be cautious and thoughtful before taking action, to carefully think through business propositions or purchase agreements before signing a contract. For those people who valued their independence and their responsible caring for their families, this role reversal must have been a difficult, rankling, and poorly understood trial of life in *la bell'America*. How must those parents have felt?

Their survival task was to fit their identities into an American culture that was not completely welcoming. They traveled the route from being

Calabresi to becoming Americans. In the process they created their Nyack culture of close friendships among families, a carryover of the relationships they had enjoyed in Maida.

Here, then, was the culture they passed on to us—not a nationalistic, flag-waving allegiance to a nation, but their own Italian-American culture that they created, day by day, with *la famiglia* as its core. As children, we were protected by the family; as adults, we became its protectors. In either event, *la famiglia* was the center of life.[8]

Any interference with the family disrupted the functioning of the world. Divorce was unacceptable; a mother who did not take good care of her children, a father who neglected his family, or a man who abused his wife were disruptive and debased. Young people who showed disrespect for their parents, who fought with them and abandoned their homes, were in violation of precious values. Parents who beat their children proclaimed their own disgrace. If one was arrested, or cheated a friend, he brought dishonor on the family. The most reviled person of all, however, was the man who beat his wife; he was the most despicable of men, for he violated *la madre*, the very core of *la famiglia*, undermining the entire family.

This is not to suggest that those Italian families were models of perfection. They had their problems and family conflicts. We knew that some of the parents hit their children, and that husbands and wives, pressed by economic problems, argued hotly.

But hitting children was rare, a quick swat across the behind before the child managed to elude the parent. None of the Italian parents assumed the task of physical discipline with the righteous certainty that spanking or whipping was a parental duty, such as espoused by some millions of American Protestants[9] and practiced by our grammar school principal, "Ol' McElroy."[10]

To be disgraced by behavior such as wife-beating was to suffer social rejection and permanent loss of honor among friends and relatives. Americans, not Italians, were wife-beaters. These Italians appreciated that *la bell'America* offered employment and opportunities, but who could respect a people who harbored wife-beaters?

5. Where Have All the Redwings Gone?

Success was judged not only by external criteria—wealth, status, prestige—but also in terms of its effects on the family. If the pursuit of success interfered seriously with the family, then success was not worth pursuing. "*Che*

---

8. This theme is common in Italian children's stories, such as Carlo Collodi's classic Pinocchio.

9. See, for example, Samuel Butler's novel *The Way of All Flesh* (1884) and Philip Greven's historical study, *The Protestant Temperament* (1980).

10. See Chapter Nineteen for a description of Miss McElroy.

vale la ricchezzia *senza famiglia* (What good are riches without a family)?" Even children's small victories could bring a measure of honor to the family, as did my redwings in 1940, when I was eight years old.

Fred found the contest in the *Nyack Journal News*. The prize for the first correct answer was a ticket to the Saturday afternoon movies, and the winner's name would be featured in the newspaper the following week.

"Look at this," Fred said, handing me Cousin Emma's page for youngsters.

I saw a black and white picture of a bird and a description: "This fellow has black feathers all over, and a bright red patch on his shoulder. What is his name?" I knew immediately that "this fellow" was a redwing blackbird.

Many times Fred and I, quietly concealed at the old Ice Pond framed by Route 59 and Highland Avenue, had watched the redwings swaying on the brown cattails that grew around the shoreline. Those beautiful birds were "Admirals of the Pond," I thought, with their bright shoulder patches and loud warnings to interlopers. The most dramatic actor of the pond, however, was the belted kingfisher, a funny-looking blue and white bird whose head and beak seemed too big for his body. Perched on a high limb, he suddenly dropped straight down into the water and, with hardly a splash, disappeared.

"The poor bird!" I said, alarmed. "He's gonna get drownded. He fell right in. Help him, Freddie! Go help him!"

"Just watch," Fred said, laughing. "Right over there." He pointed.

The water erupted. The kingfisher broke through the surface and flew back to the tree branch, a small fish wriggling in his beak.

"The poor fish!" I said. "He's gonna get ate! Go help him, Freddie!"

"Hmm," Fred said. "It must be Friday."

"No it isn't!" I told him, not understanding his joke. "It's Saturday, that's why you're not in school."

During our outings at the Ice Pond, we observed and discussed what different animals ate for dinner, how they made their nests, hunted, raised their families, and generally conducted their lives in and around that busy pond. The nature lesson continued over several years, as Fred led me hiking into the woods of South Mountain or to the Ice Pond or the West Nyack swamps. We even went to the cemetery on Highland Avenue to spot birds. I wasn't too sure that I liked that.

The best time for our hikes was early in the morning, starting at five o'clock. On those quiet Saturday mornings, Fred and I seemed the only inhabitants of a still-sleeping world. We were stopped once by a policeman, who asked what an adolescent and a little kid were doing up so early, wandering along Highland Avenue. In time, the policemen all recognized us, and waved as they drove by in Nyack's green-and-white patrol car.

In the 19th century, the pond had been a true ice pond, shimmering in the winter with shouting men and snorting horses, ice sleds, ropes, and long ice saws. After the commercial ice plant was built at the railroad tracks near Clinton Avenue in South Nyack, the ice pond was no longer needed. Cattails advanced into the water, nearly hiding the pond from Route 59. It became a jungle pool, a rich place for exploration, a treasure of life and learning. Birds, fish, mammals, and all kinds of slithery things abounded. Who knew what lion or rhinoceros might come charging out from that tall grass over there? In the wintertime the hard-frozen ice was a slick stage. The scenes and sounds of a generation of ice-skating youngsters and the warming campfires on shore rivaled any Currier and Ives image.

In the 1950s, the Ice Pond was defeated by the wisdom of commerce. "Nothing but a useless swamp," they said, and our old ice pond was filled in, paved over, and turned into a gasoline station, tavern, and access ramps for an overhead highway. I sometimes wonder, paraphrasing the song, "Where have all the redwings gone?"

But back to my contest. I filled in the row of boxes under the picture— just the right number to print "Redwing Blackbird," and carefully added my name and address. Advised by Fred that I could deliver it more quickly than the U.S. mail, I took it that afternoon to the *Journal News* office. A lady stood behind a counter that was so high I stood at the low swinging gate for her to see me. She smiled and accepted my entry.

I won the contest, saw my name and picture in the newspaper, and, with pride, claimed my movie ticket. I won the next contest, and the next, each time eagerly reading the description, leafing through Fred's bird books until I found the right one, and personally delivering my entry.

Each win, each ticket in its little white envelope, each posting of my name right there in the newspaper, was a measure of family honor. Each time I showed my father my name in the newspaper and Cousin Emma's congratulations for a well-done job, he smiled and told me how proud he was.

"This is easy," I thought. "Free movie tickets for the rest of my life!" It never occurred to me that it might not be fair to kids who had no access to Fred's bird books.

My winning streak ended. The next time I delivered my entry, the lady behind the counter opened the gate, invited me into a big room with desks and busy people, and led me to an office, where I met Cousin Emma herself. She smiled, shook my hand, and congratulated me on winning so many contests. Then she explained how unfair it was to other kids if I kept on winning. "We know you can win them all," she said. "That will be our secret." Handing me a little envelope with two or three more tickets to seal the bargain, she told me that I could still identify the birds but would not be awarded any more prizes. Her message was disappointing. Silently, I thought, "Sure, it's unfair. Unfair to me!" But being in a real newspaper office, talking with the actual and unexpectedly pretty Cousin Emma, was heady and a bit intimidating. So I said "OK," and the agreement was sealed.

Cousin Emma[11] gave me the tickets and a wonderful smile, then took me to each desk in the big room and introduced me to the reporters, secretaries, and editors. "This is the young man who is winning all my contests," she told them, her hand resting on my shoulder. They smiled, shook my hand, and congratulated me, and I began to feel pretty important. This might have been even better than winning more contests.

I was conducted through the newspaper building and was fascinated by a ticker-tape machine punching out messages under a glass dome like an upside-down fishbowl. Downstairs, I met the pressman himself. There in his noisy domain, I saw a gigantic roll of white paper unwinding, racing through the roaring press in a complicated sequence of twists and turns, and, in a lightening-fast transformation, becoming the finished pages of the *Nyack Journal News*.

My parents and Fred were pleased that I had been treated with such respect. As they saw it, our whole family had been respected. I had brought *l'onore alla famiglia*.

6. A Fact of Life in Nyack

My parents appreciated two streams of Italian culture beyond *la famiglia* and passed them on to me. For Mom, they were her religion and Italian opera. For my father, it was mainly Italian opera. Except for those two cultural areas, they knew little of Italian history, art, or literature. Their knowledge was not sophisticated, but consisted of faith and emotion for Mom and a genuine love of the opera for both.

Perhaps I am unfair, but as best as I can recall, it seemed as if no national past existed for that first generation or, if it did, they had set it aside, separated it from the practical realities of life. Perhaps this was a necessary dissociation from the disappointing country they had left, a strategy to aid their efforts in becoming American. Perhaps it reflected their lack of education.

Italian youngsters were being pushed by our culture, at school in particular, to become American. I entered school in 1937 and began learning to appreciate what it meant to be American. We were taught that it meant living in a country of orderly laws rather than individuals like kings and dictators; freedom and opportunities for personal and family achievement; a heritage of great men like Washington and Lincoln. It meant, also, pride in knowing that we had fought and won a revolutionary war against a despotic king, a civil war to free the slaves, and World War I to save the world. To be an American was to be part of the greatest nation that ever existed. America, we were taught, was bravery and honesty and goodness—the Pledge of Allegiance to the flag, "The Star-Spangled Banner," and the Boy

---

11. Some time later, Cousin Emma became my real cousin by marrying Joe Conace, my first cousin. Joe's parents were my Aunt Macrina and Uncle Giuseppe Conace, whom we discussed in Chapters Eleven and Twelve.

Scout's Oath. All of this was repeatedly presented to us and seemed to have been particularly aimed at the children of immigrants, perhaps as part of the great public school attempt to assimilate these little foreigners quickly and completely.

Beyond the recitation of idealized history, we were also guided to develop a personal relationship with American historical figures. Through repetition in little storybooks with those clear-edged illustrations and our classroom celebrations of patriotic days, we learned that even as a child George Washington never told a lie. Abraham Lincoln walked miles through the snow to school and, after chopping a ton of firewood every day, studied long into the night bythe dim and smoky candlelight. Betsy Ross created our beautiful flag, sewing it with her own hands. Benjamin Franklin was a brilliant scientist, philosopher, and statesman who flew kites, just like we did, on windy days. I wondered if his kites, like ours, became tangled in the telephone wires. The Wright brothers, we learned, through sheer "Yankee ingenuity,"[12] tinkered in their bicycle shop and invented the airplane all by themselves. Those were real people; they had been children, like us; they had played games, grown up, had families, worked with their hands, and overcome obstacles, as we had. Our teachers had done an excellent job of creating our affection for those people. We learned our lessons well. Americans shared a great past, enjoyed the finest present, and anticipated a future with no limits. We were proud to be Americans.

My neighborhood friends were secure in being American, but children in Italian immigrant families had to deal with the question of what it meant to be Italian. We had no school to teach us of Italian history and heroes. We read no stories of young Mazzini or Garibaldi, no idealized Italian mythology like that for George Washington or the Wright brothers. Once a year, we were reminded of *Cristoforo Colombo*, but most of what we learned about Italian culture was incidental, and during the war in the 1940s was severely distorted by wartime propaganda. But even before the war, my Italian past was already dimming, and was suffering in comparison with the expanding heroic picture of Americans and the United States. In many ways, we were being pushed not only to become Americans, but also to deny our Italian past.

One dimension of that pressure toward denial was the anti-Italian prejudice readily expressed by many Nyack residents in the 1930s and 1940s. In grammar school, I found that casual ethnic prejudice was so pervasive that at times the only escape was to defuse it by joining the tormenters in demeaning my own Italian heritage.

12. This is one of the persistent myths of America. The Wrights' research was based on others' research over hundreds of years. The Wrights maintained they were not "tinkerers" and "mechanics," but scientists who researched, experimented, and understood the physical and mathematical principles of flight that had been developed by many before them (See Oppel, 1987, page 18).

That, however, caused guilt and self-criticism for cravenly abandoning my heritage, and that, in turn, caused a rebound, a reassertion of my Italian background and a truculent defense, fighting with the bullies, real or imagined, even seeking them out. This aggression caused more problems for me, because the bullies were older and bigger, and outnumbered me. It also caused the labels "troublemaker" and "discipline problem" to be applied to me in school.

To me it was complicated and fatiguing, turning first one way and then another, trying different strategies. I sometimes wondered if my father and brother were subjected to similar insults and shared my feelings and problems. However, ashamed of how I was treated, of how many fights I lost, and of my inability to stay out of trouble in school, I never wanted to tell them about my demeaning experiences or ask them about theirs. This part of our lives was something we never discussed—it became an unacknowledged secret, shared but never aired.

Italians were succeeding economically in the 1930s, despite the Depression, but were still regarded by some as interlopers, inferior people who should remain in their place as unskilled laborers. When they did succeed, such as in business, they were often denigrated for being too assertive, reaching beyond their "proper station."

My world was expanding beyond the safety of my home, and I was meeting youngsters from families with other ethnic backgrounds. Those youngsters were like funnels—what their parents poured into the wide end came out from the children in narrow, toxic concentration, and I heard what their parents were teaching them.

It was the derision and rejection, the insults that smoldered in the face of Italians' obvious success that was so dispiriting. It was not just denial of respect, but the repeated active assertion of disrespect that was so bad.

Many factors contributed to the anti-Italian attacks that I experienced. First, there was the ordinary human "cussedness" of targeting victims on any convenient basis—ethnicity, religion, skin color, physical or mental disabilities, economics, and so on. Two ideas were specific to the anti-Italian sentiments. The most pervasive throughout my experiences in the 1930s was our very presence in the United States. It made some sense, I suppose, and was expressed as variations of the challenge, "If Italy is so good, why did you come here?" Within this lay the usually unspoken demand to "go back where you came from!" To many Americans, Italian immigration was an admission that Italy was a failure. There was no getting around this assumption. For me the message narrowed down to this: my parents were here because they had been failures in their own country! They expected the United States to make up for Italy's deficiencies. They could not "cut it" in their own country. Our presence in the United States was proof of Americans' superiority over Italians. How could one argue against such solid reasoning and certainty?

The second factor bore down on us a few years later, concentrated from about 1942 to 1945, when Italy and the United States were enemies in the Second World War. I was nine years old when that war began for the United States. Our two nations' antagonism would complicate the already difficult position of every Italian-born person in the United States.

For children, the preeminent dimension was America's rampant propaganda. Quite correctly, American propaganda was a wartime stream of criticism and ridicule aimed at Tojo, Hitler, and Mussolini.[13] It surfaced in newspapers, magazines, and comic books, on the radio, and, with the most impact, on the Saturday afternoon Movietone News. Tojo, "the Jap," was a sneaking, sinister, sibilantly hissing, back-stabbing, bush-whacking, slant-eyed little snake. Hitler, "the Kraut," was a screaming, goose-stepping, obviously insane, vicious little dwarf with hair combed down over one eye and half a black comb glued under his nose. Mussolini, "the Wop," was a fat, pompous, strutting buffoon with a bulbous chin and a wonderfully comical name. They were shown standing on balconies spewing spit and gibberish down on cheering mobs of hysterical people, who were so stupid that they believed every lie their leaders told them. Each of the three men represented his own country, and certainly every single countryman was just as ridiculous as the leaders.

Children, with little skill for rational skepticism, were openly receptive, vulnerable to the propaganda, believing it as truth, or at least as great fun. Caught up in the excitement of the war, they took it as their patriotic duty to spread those caricatures, like the duty of collecting aluminum pots, old tires, and scrap paper for the war effort.

Somehow, the patriotic zeal became entwined with racism. In our neighborhood and school, there were no "Japs" conveniently at hand to ridicule. "Krauts" did not really exist, because kids of German descent were from families that had been here so long they became Real Americans, and they blended in. In any event they were not about to ridicule themselves. But there were plenty of "Wops" around, and Mussolini was too tempting a comical caricature to ignore. It was the Italian kids living in predominantly Irish, English, and German neighborhoods who became the convenient targets.

The bullies, and there were many, were armed with those two certainties: Italians were in all ways inferior to Americans, and Italians were the comic enemies of America. The Mussolini caricature—the fat, silly, strutting buffoon—begged for derision. A bully needed only to puff out his chest, strut like a rooster, and hurl insults in a loud, burlesque Italian accent: "Hey, Guinea, Guinea, Mussolini!" "Hey, Pastafazoo, wacha do?" and "You eata da' spaget' today, eh?" were shouted for the amusement and approval of friends, and brought up bitter shame and anger in the victim.

What was hard to take were the daily assertions of Italians' inferiority,

---

13. The leaders of Japan, Germany, and Italy.

the ridicule, the Dago jokes, the name-calling, the demeaning parodies of Italian speech, and the refusal by some middle-class adults to have anything to do with Italians.

This was particularly true of one Irish family in my neighborhood. One tormenter, Tommy, was the major bully, always backed up by his younger brother Francis, both enjoying their loud derision and name-calling. In my anger and desperation, I fought with him, trying to punish him, but he was older and bigger than I, and always had his brother with him. I always lost those fights.

The anti-Italian prejudice of the 20s, 30s, and 40s was a pervasive fact of life outside of *la famiglia*. For a boy growing up in Nyack there were far too many incidents to recount, several each week, often daily face-offs, and not only with youngsters. The following incidents might convey a bit of the experience.

The first incident that I recall, although I did not understand it then, occurred in 1937. Fred was 16 and I was five. We had walked up the hill to spot birds and explore the woods across 9-W just west of Elysian Avenue. I was a little worried about getting lost in the woods, having heard what happened to those two kids, Hansel and Gretel. As we began to walk down the hill, heading home, a man came out of his house at the top of the hill. I remember that he slammed his wooden screen door and wore a long-sleeved striped shirt with no collar and what looked like garters around his arms. He wore suspenders, and no belt.

"Where do you two belong?" he asked.

"We're just walking home," Fred replied, responding to something going on that I did not understand. Fred took my hand and edged us away from the man.

"You from that Eye-tal-yin bunch down the hill?"

I looked up at Fred, puzzled because he did not answer the man. Instead, he gripped my hand more tightly and walked faster, making me run alongside.

"You better remember where you belong!" the man shouted after us, pointing either at us or down the hill—I was not sure which.

"Why are we going so fast?" I asked Fred. "That man was worried that maybe we're lost and wanted to help us find our way home."

"Yeah," Fred said. "Sure. Come on, Mom's got supper for us."

A few years later, in third grade, I had just made a new friend, Jimmie, who lived about six blocks away. As we rode our bikes in front of his house on Prospect Street, his father came home from work. He stopped and looked at me.

"What's your name?" he asked.

"Tony," I said.

"Tony what?"

"Tony Graziano."

"Oh Christ!" he answered, looking up at the sky. "Not another Wop!" He stormed into his house, slamming the door.

Jimmie was not sure of what had just happened, but I had long ago become aware of ethnic insults and had already experienced too many to count. I ended our new friendship on the spot, permanently, and poor Jimmie, puzzled, kept asking me for the next few days in school why I was "mad" at him. I could not get back at his father, so I guess I took it out on Jimmie. Both of us were hurt.

Another incident shows a subtler context for the pervasive anti-Italian prejudice than the coarse views of Jimmie's father. Mr. Bergman, a widower, long retired, lived quietly across the street in his well-kept house. He bought a new Buick every few years and was visited by old friends. He was a responsible homeowner, a quiet neighbor, and a good citizen. Although we lived across the street, we had no contact with him.

One afternoon in 1942, when I was 10 years old, my father was trimming the backyard hedges and I was raking up the cuttings. He was proud of our yard and kept it neatly groomed, rivaling any of the neighbors' gardens. We did not talk much as we worked, but I think he enjoyed our quiet companionship. I know that I did.

Into our back yard walked Mr. Bergman. Pop and I were surprised by the unexpected visit of our neighbor, whom we knew only by sight and name. I must have stared at him, seeing him up close for the first time.

"Hello, Mr. Bergman," my father said politely, in welcome to our home as one neighbor to another.

"Mike," he answered with a meager nod and the use of my father's first name, underscoring their status difference. "My cesspool needs cleaning. How about comin' over tomorrow and cleanin' it out?"

My father's lips turned white. I saw his hands tighten around the hard oak handles of the long, sharp hedge shears. His arms, muscled from years of physical work, bulged.

In front of his young son, my father had been tagged a "cesspool cleaner." It was honest work, a job that needed to be done, and he certainly could use the money, but in this context it was an insult. What must have been going through my father's mind? He was a successful homeowner, proud of having achieved equality with our American neighbors despite the damnable Depression, and yet he, of all the men on Elysian Avenue, had been singled out to clean Mr. Bergman's cesspool. Would Mr. Bergman have asked our mutual neighbor, the county district attorney, to come over and clean out his cesspool? My father's dignity and his cherished equality with our neighbors had been trashed.

As young as I was, I knew that something significant for my father was being played out right in front of me. He had been insulted, and I felt it too, but without full understanding. I looked at my father, wondering what he would do. I had no idea how I would handle the situation. I felt embarrassed for him, because he had been demeaned, and I was disappointed in him too, because I feared that, facing this Real American from across the street, my poor father just did not know what to do. I waited, looking at both men, unaware that my body had tensed and I was holding my breath.

Slowly, my father set his shears down on the bench. His arms relaxed. Politely, he answered, "No, Mr. Bergman, I don't do that kind of work. You should call a septic tank company, they can come and pump it out for you."

Mr. Bergman seemed truly surprised and, for a moment, confused. He glanced around our yard, at its neatly trimmed hedges, lawn, and garden, the carefully swept little patio and slate walk, as if this was not what he had expected to find.

"Oh. Well, then," he said. "Er, yes, that's what I'll do. Yes."

My father remained silent.

"Yes," Mr. Bergman repeated, beginning to recognize, but not understand, the tension he had caused. "That's just what I'll do. Yes. Well, then. Ah, yes, um, all right."

He left, still looking puzzled. My father stood there, watching, as our neighbor retreated. Then he picked up his shears and resumed trimming the hedge.

My sudden exhalation told me how tense I had been during the brief, quietly played out confrontation. My feelings of relief were then swallowed up by an enormous pride that I felt at that moment for my father, and a surge of guilt for having doubted that he could handle the situation. He had known what to do, how to handle Mr. Bergman's insult, and how to do so with dignity. I wanted to jump up and down and shout, "Hooray, Pop!" and I wanted to rush over and hug my father. But that would not have been in keeping with the dignified tone of his response to Mr. Bergman. So, after a moment, I merely said, "I guess he just don't know us, huh?"

"Hmm, I guess not," my father said. He turned, looked at me, and smiled. We understood each other; we both knew what had just happened. That's when I threw down my rake, ran across the yard, and hugged him.

Chapter 22
The Depression Eases (1940)

1. FDR and Better Years

The hard decade of the 1930s was ending. The Depression slowly eased for most of the country's 132 million people, but it continued to plague several million still unemployed. Most people were lifting from the Depression, trying out a new, if mixed, outlook for the new decade.

The last half of the 1930s brought a slow economic recovery and uplifted hopes, since FDR had put through one daring reform after another. The Democratic president created new and robust policies that radically changed the country, permanently in many respects. He was faced with a great deal of opposition. The United States of the 1930s played out in microcosm the liberal versus conservative conflicts of Europe in the 19th century—liberal pressures to share resources and power and to extend democratic participation versus conservative pressures to keep resources, power, and participation within an elite class. This was evident in FDR's support of labor unions, such as his National Labor Relations Act (1935), which gave labor unions the right of collective bargaining and extended to millions of working people, for the first time, direct participation in the country's industry and commerce. FDR's liberal social and economic agenda included creation of the Works Progress Administration (WPA), which helped millions of families and created an artistic legacy. The Social Securities Act (1935) continues, nearly 75 years later, to keep millions of retirees above poverty.[1] He also inaugurated reforms of public utilities, the Federal Reserve, and the tax code. Roosevelt's liberalism was a continuation of the Progressive era of the late 1800s[2] and the policies of his mentor and rival, Al Smith, New York's former governor, who had lost the 1928 election to the Republican Herbert Hoover. For working families like ours, FDR was a hero; to bankers, the wealthy, Republicans, and conservatives in general, he was an outrage.

For his enemies, FDR's outrageousness was made even worse when he

---

1. In 2009, political conservatives are still trying to dismantle this most successful of all liberal social programs.
2. Levine and Levine (1970).

defied the term-limit tradition created by George Washington and sought a third and fourth presidential term. He won by big margins, further enraging the conservatives. FDR became the conservatives' iconic Hated Liberal. My father and other working families enthusiastically voted for FDR in 1932, 1936, 1940, and 1944.

"Why not?" my father said. "When you have a good man, keep him!"

Beyond politics, many popular events also lifted the nation's pulse. Admiral Byrd returned in triumph from two years' exploration of the Antarctic. The magnificent new luxury liner *Normandie* made its maiden voyage across the Atlantic. Detroit's glittering auto shows urged Americans to buy new Chevrolets, Fords, and Plymouths for $465, and top-of-the-line Cadillacs for $3,500. In a 1938 rematch, Joe Louis defeated the German heavyweight Max Schmeling with a first-round knockout, attracting the world's attention and boosting America's honor. Babe Ruth, Lou Gehrig, Joe DiMaggio, Ted Williams, and Bob Feller electrified baseball fans. Airplanes and streamlined luxury trains crossed the continent, setting speed records and new levels of comfort. Movies, plays, and musicals thrived. Everything seemed to proclaim the country's exciting awakening from the Great Depression.

Business, the stock market, jobs, and wages were slowly improving. Labor unions, with the help of FDR's Democrats, were becoming a significant economic force, and working men began to feel a new confidence and hope.[3] The Mill was back to full-time production. My father and Uncle Joe were now earning 67 cents an hour, bringing home a pay envelope of nearly $27 a week. Now, with more than $100 a month coming in, plus the $5 to $10 weekly from his extra work around town, my father increased his monthly mortgage payments, sometimes to $55. He soon made his final payment, and 79 Elysian Avenue belonged to Michele and Theresa. In terms of their goals and hopes at their wedding in Maida in 1919, they had finally arrived.

Mid-1940 brought another important family event: Fred graduated from high school. My parents were proud, and their appreciation of *la bell'America* grew. Here, a lad from Maida could complete 12 years of formal education—an impossible accomplishment had they remained in Maida. What helped to make this so wonderful and exciting for them was that here, in America, it was an ordinary event—every young cousin, nephew, and niece, every son and daughter of our friends, would do the same. This was *la bell'America*.

2. Does Helen Hayes Make Sausages?

In June 1940, when Fred graduated from high school, I was eight years old and had just completed Miss White's second grade. I was no longer

---

3. The average annual wage for a working man in 1940 was $1,500. Members of Congress gave themselves a salary of $10,000.

a small child, not yet a teenager, still pretty naive, but learning. Fred was learning, too. In September he watched his schoolmates go off to college, but his closest friends were in the same situation—bright, capable, and industrious enough, but with no money for college.

Fred had talked about Columbia College, but after seeing the tuition figures he threw out the college catalogue and stopped talking about it. Our parents encouraged him, said they would help, saving a little from Pop's wages. Mom would work at the pocketbook factory while Fred earned money for college. It would take a few years, they said, and Fred would just be a bit older than most beginning college students.

I would have been resentful in his place, seeing less studious classmates going to college just because their parents had money. But Fred never talked about it, at least not to his eight-year-old brother.

Fred's friend Otto Gottesman hoped to become a chemist or an engineer. In their shared enthusiasm for chemistry, Otto and Fred had almost burned down Pop's garage two years earlier, while trying to make something spectacular with their big jars of chemicals. Otto lived with his parents above their small upholstery shop on Broadway. It would take a lot of Mr. Gottesman's sewing and tacking to save enough money to send Otto to college.

Buster Ogden lived next door and was Fred's best friend. His young brother, Freddie, was my best friend, a convenient arrangement. Their father, Amos, had an enviable job as chauffeur to some of Nyack's most distinguished citizens, the Blauvelts and Judge Patterson of the Supreme Court, who was known to me only as "the Judge." I knew they were rich, because they owned magnificent automobiles, driven by Mr. Ogden. What made the judge even more important in our view was that he apparently lived near Nyack's most distinguished citizen, Miss Helen Hayes, the famous actress. I was not quite sure why the job of actress was so well regarded by everyone. After all, anybody could act—I knew my friends and I did every day in one way or another, and our performances were often convincing enough to get us whatever it was that our act had aimed for. Helen Hayes lived in Upper Nyack, in a grand mansion on a brick-walled estate on the banks of the Hudson. It was far from our house, and Pop had once driven us there to see the impressive brick wall that hid everything else from our view.

Mr. Ogden had told us that rich people owned their own motorboats, with boat garages built right in the river that had floors of water, so at night the boats could be driven inside! I wanted to know if Freddie's father also drove the Judge's boats, speeding up and down the river and making great white waves, but Freddie did not think so, because you had to be a boat captain to do that.

Most impressive were the two large automobiles that Mr. Ogden drove. Mrs. Patterson owned a stately LaSalle, with a window separating the chauffeur from the passengers. We knew that Miss Hayes, too, must have had great cars and a chauffeur just like Mr. Ogden. After all, she lived on a great estate, and great estates always had great cars. The fact that we often saw Mr. Ogden driving one of the Judge's cars but never saw Miss Hayes or her chauffeured car made her all the more mysterious. Her cars must have been truly magnificent if no one ever saw them.

Mr. Ogden drove slowly through Nyack in one of the softly purring autos, sometimes stopping at his house for lunch. The automobile we liked best, a Packard Landau owned by the Judge, we named "the Double Car." It had beautifully curved front fenders that flared out from its long, pointed hood, a running board on each side, and big white-walled tires that Mr. Ogden scrubbed clean no matter what the weather might be. Sitting high in the driver's seat, Mr. Ogden wore a peaked black cap. He looked bigger there, more important than when he was just Freddie's father sitting on his porch, his shirtsleeves rolled up, reading the *Nyack Journal News*. The car was a magic machine that transformed Freddie's father into the great captain of that grand vehicle.

Those cars allowed a glimpse into a world that, despite the hesitantly growing optimism of 1940, was impossibly out of our reach.

While Mr. Ogden occupied the open section of the automobile, his passengers rode comfortably inside. In his private compartment, the Judge had his own windshield, separate doors, and even window shades to pull down for privacy. The big seat looked soft and plush, much nicer than the couch in our living room. There was even a table and a shiny footrest that folded out, and two extra little seats that folded away when not needed. Freddie told me it had two cigar lighters that pulled out from the armrests. The Judge had only to touch the glowing tip to his cigar and, like magic, he was soon puffing fragrant white smoke. Most intriguing were two metal funnels, one in the back compartment and one in Mr. Ogden's section. They looked like the fat funnels that Mom used to stuff sausage casings with the mixture of meat and spices she had so laboriously ground up. "If Helen Hayes has a car like this one, then, does she make sausages?"

"I dunno," Freddie Ogden said. "Maybe."

"I guess only when she's not bein' a actress," I suggested.

"Yeah," Freddie said. "Prob'ly."

The funnels, however, were not stuck into sausage casing but into a fabric-wrapped hose. It was, Mr. Ogden explained, a speaking tube, through which the Judge in the back seat could talk to Mr. Ogden in the front and give him instructions about where to drive. What a marvelous invention, I thought—an improvement over telephones, with which, in order to speak to anyone, you first had to catch the attention of the telephone operator, that mysterious, invisible lady.

We sometimes caught a glimpse of someone in the back seat as Mr. Ogden drove by, but we were never sure about that. There was one thing, however, that we knew with certainty: there could have been only one other car like it in the whole world, and it must have been owned by Miss Helen Hayes.

One day as Freddie and I walked home from school, his father stopped and invited us to ride in the grand car with him. There was no one in the private compartment, and Freddie wanted to sit in the back and give his father orders through the speaking tube. But Mr. Ogden said no. Only the Judge could invite people into the back compartment.

So Freddie and I sat up as tall as we could in the open front, pretending that our hair was flying in the wind like in the magazine advertisements showing sporty red roadsters racing through the countryside, carrying handsome men and pretty ladies. Their hair was streaming in the wind, but here there was no wind because Mr. Ogden always drove so sedately. We rode up Cedar Hill Avenue, turning our heads in excitement, eagerly looking for our friends so we could ignore them and pretend that we did not see them at all. But we saw none of our friends and had to be satisfied with waving imperiously at a little kid who was sitting on a tricycle in front of his house. He stared at us, obviously impressed, and we were certain he would later tell his mom about the really rich kids in the big car that he had just seen. Later, when Freddie and I told our friends about our magnificent ride, they did not believe us.

Unfortunately, even with his association with Nyack's wealthy, Mr. Ogden still could not afford to send Buster to college.

3. The Pocketbook Factory

After graduation, Fred began working full time at the coat factory down by the river, just below Main Street and Broadway. He had a small blue book with numbers written in it. Once a week, Fred carried that little book and some of the money he had earned to the bank, where a lady behind some bars—when I had first seen her I thought she was in jail—took the money, wrote some numbers in the book, and smiled at us. Pop decided that I, too, ought to have a bank book. When I walked to the bank with Pop, I handed up my blue book and the quarter he had given to me. The smiling lady wrote it all down. After a couple of years, my balance had grown to well over $6, and that, I thought, ought to buy a good portion of Columbia College for Fred.

In 1938, Mom began working at Mr. Katz's pocketbook factory, where ladies sat at long rows of electric sewing machines making pocketbooks and gloves. It was a big, hot, noisy, dusty place, with heavy sewing machines bolted to thick wooden tables. Men hurried in and out, bringing stacks of flat leather and taking away armfuls of completed pocketbooks.

Sometimes Mom brought home leather scraps that were fun to play with. I tried to make things with them like holsters for my cap pistols, but somehow my sewing never held together for very long. Mom used the scraps to repair the elbows in the sleeves of our coats.

Occasionally one or two of the sewing machine ladies came home with Mom for lunch, our house being only a short walk from the factory. The ladies lived too far away to walk home for lunch and were happy to come to our house and briefly escape the dust and din of the factory. They opened their brown-paper bags and smoothed the waxed paper on the table, like crinkly place mats. The ladies ate their sandwiches, gossiped, laughed, and drank coffee that Mom made. Mrs. Bremmer, a soft-spoken Real American lady, was particularly nice. She had a pretty smile and always shared with me a generous piece of her sandwich of bologna, mustard, and wonderfully soft white bread. Why couldn't Mom cook like that?

After lunch, they walked back to the factory and I returned to school, usually walking with Bobby Greggs or Freddie Ogden. Sometimes Mom returned to the factory with her friends; on other days she stayed home. During those years, 1937–1941, I was in school, releasing Mom so she could go to work. At lunchtime, I too returned home, looking forward to the occasional visit of the sewing machine ladies and Mrs. Bremmer's wonderful sandwiches.

I suspect that Mr. Katz, who owned the factory, might have been the same man who used to bring sewing for Mom to do at home, but I am not sure of that. If so, I suppose that Mr. Katz was moving up in the world, owning his own factory and all.

4. Fred's Bookshelf

Fred went to work early in the morning and returned late in the afternoon. I never knew what work he did at the coat factory, but I began to notice that Fred was different, having changed from my big brother in high school to a working man of the world. He no longer played with me or took me on bird hikes. He had become quiet and private, and spent a lot of time away from home in the evenings, with his friends, I guess. Because I was in school by then, I was finding my own new friends and interests. But I began to miss him and to resent that coat factory, which was taking so much of his time away from me.

Early one evening, Fred was nicely dressed up and went out, driving away in Pop's car and not even inviting me for a ride. In a short while he returned home to get his wallet, which he had forgotten. There was a girl in the car, someone I had never seen before, and she was sitting right there, in my car! I did not like that at all. Fred was my brother, not hers. It was my car, not hers! This girl had long blonde hair, and, to make it worse, she began combing it as if she thought the car belonged to her! I wanted to tell her to get out of my car, but all I did was hide behind a porch post and watch her and become more annoyed.

When Fred came out on the porch, I glared at him but said nothing. His eyebrows went up, silently asking, "What?" I just pouted.

"Well, OK, then." He smiled. "See you later." He walked down the steps and drove off with that girl, who was still sitting in my car.

Fred's bank account did not grow very much, and remained too small for any reasonable assault on Columbia's tuition. Fred must have realized that Columbia College was not to be in his future, and I think he decided he would have to educate himself. From yard sales, used-book stores, and discards from the local libraries, he brought home many books. They bore titles like *Trigonometry*, *Practical Mathematics*, *The Calculus*, *Plane and Solid Geometry*, *The History of the World*, *Basics of Photography*, *Modern Physics*, *Chemistry in Your Life*, and *How to Paint in Oils*. He carted in an old set of encyclopedias that had two volumes missing. Years later, when I started to use them myself, I could never find any information on "Wagner," "Walrus," or "Waterloo, the Battle of." He also acquired several wooden slide rules and even tried to teach me how to use them, with little success.

He accumulated more books than the old house had ever seen, and Pop built a long shelf on the wall in the narrow back hall behind the kitchen. It became known as Fred's bookshelf. Pop attached a swinging reading lamp to the wall and painted the old wooden kitchen chair that had been in the house my entire life. It barely fit at the end of the narrow hall, but it provided a private, quiet, snug place to sit and read. Pop never quite succeeded in making the legs of the old chair level, so you could even rock a little as you read.

I investigated every book that Fred added to his shelf. He gave me permission to browse freely, as long as I treated the books respectfully and returned them to their proper places. Two sets on mathematics, however, were disappointing. Each set had six volumes, their imitation-leather covers embossed in red and gold letters that you could actually feel by moving your fingers across them. The 12 volumes were identical in appearance, making a neat and impressive mathematics section on the shelf, but their contents made little sense to me. Fred and Otto, however, studied those books for hours, working their slide rules and comparing results. They might even have worked through all the volumes.

Of all the books, four were my favorites, and I went through them countless times over several years. *Microbe Hunters* by Paul de Kruif, a 1932 edition that had been written or edited for young readers, had short chapters about famous scientists. At first, Fred read these to me, and later I read them to myself. Those scientists had discovered important things, but they were real people, like me, and I came to believe that Leeuwenhoek, Pasteur, Koch, Spallanzani, Reed, and all the others could easily have been my neighbors and friends. The man who invented the microscope, for example, Mr. Leeuwenhoek,[4] was really a janitor, just like Mr. Walmsley at school. Paul de Kruif introduced me to some important and compelling

4. Antony van Leeuwenhoek (1632–1723) lived in Delft, Holland, had no advanced education, and, as I learned later, did not invent the microscope. However, he made some of the most important early scientific discoveries in biology, using the single-lens microscopes that he constructed.

ideas about the world outside of Nyack, a world of science that no one else seemed to know about but Fred, Dr. de Kruif, Otto Gottesman, and me.

Birds of America was filled with beautiful full-color paintings that held my attention for hours. *How to Draw* by Arthur Zaidenberg was a large book with instructions on drawing animals and human figures. I actually learned something about drawing and began to make credible sketches of all sorts of things, such as Aunt Annie's collection of cute ceramic figures. The human figures in the book were drawn without clothes. When I showed the book to my friend Bobby, who was older than I, he became very interested in the drawings of naked ladies. Every once in a while Bobby would ask if we might look at Fred's drawing book again.

My favorite book was a slim volume about our solar system.[5] Each glossy page was in brilliant colors, like vivid paintings of the sun's blazing surface with orange and yellow flames curling far out into black space. Turning those pages, I could see what Mercury, Venus, Saturn, Mars, and Jupiter looked like up close. There, too, was our green and blue Earth, floating, as it must appear from space, and a series showing the phases of our moon. On a double page was our solar system, with its planets swinging around the brilliant yellow sun at its center. Paintings that needed no written text showed me how eclipses occurred and explained why the moon seemed to grow and shrink as each month progressed due to the changing angles of illumination. I learned some new words, like "umbra" and "penumbra," meaning shadows such as those cast by planets or moons, and I told my friends, most authoritatively, "It's bad luck to step on your own penumbra!" But they were not much impressed.

Fred went through the book with me, page by page, reading aloud and explaining those marvelous pictures. Later I sat with my father, showing him the pictures and explaining what was going on far out in space, in our solar system. These were lessons, however distorted my presentations may have been, that Pop had never learned in his three years of school in Maida at the end of the 19th century. Pop listened to me with his quiet little smile, and every now and then said, "My, my." He was pleased and proud that I could explain so much to him. Neither of us understood the significance of this role reversal for Italian immigrant families—the child teaching the father—or that it would continue to grow.

Sharing what I was learning from Fred's books was fun, but not always successful. I tried to explain to Mrs. Kinsella, my favorite neighbor, who lived next door, that the "new moon" each month was not new at all, but was actually the same old moon with just a part of it that we could see. She was not convinced, I think, by such nonsense.

But then, Mrs. Kinsella taught me some of the things she had known in her long life. For example, she told me that when she was my age, real

5. Wagner (1936).

Indians had sometimes come into town, at the corner of Franklin and Main streets. The "brave" was always wrapped in a colorful blanket, she said, and had a feather or two in his hair. He rode on his horse, followed by his squaw, who walked and carried bundles. They were trailed by a bunch of little kids. I was interested but disappointed, because when I asked her, she said, "No, they did not go whooping about, shooting people with bows and arrows." For some time, when Mom and I walked downtown to the stores in Nyack, I looked around for those Indians, but I never saw any. "Well," Mrs. Kinsella explained, "after all, that was a long time ago, in the 1860s, when I was a little girl."

"Is it really true?" I asked. "There were really real Indians right here in Nyack?"

"Of course it's true," she answered with a little smile. "I ought to know. I was there."

Her most impressive story was about seeing President Lincoln. Mrs. Kinsella was not sure if she remembered seeing him or if she was recalling her father's repeated story. They were in a big field, she said, filled with people. She was a tiny girl, and her father swung her up on his shoulders and pointed to some men standing on a high, flag-draped platform. "Look, Sarah," he said. "That's President Lincoln!"

Years later, long after Mrs. Kinsella died, I began to appreciate that I had known someone who had seen Abraham Lincoln! A vague idea of historical continuity was tantalizing me, just outside of my reach. In some way, through my wonderful neighbor, I was linked with history and could reach all the way back 100 years to the time of Lincoln and the Civil War!

Two of the pictures in the astronomy book were particularly impressive. One showed a spectacular array of northern lights, shimmering and slanting down through the night sky like rippled ribbons of crunchy sugar candy. These, Fred read to me from the book, were the aurora borealis—I pronounced it "roraballis"—"the shimmering, spectral lights that soften the polar darkness."[6] That sounded nice when Fred read it aloud, like poetry. How was I to know that in only a couple of years, on a warm summer night in my back yard, I would see the beauty of the real thing? The *Nyack Journal News* would explain that it had been a rare display of the northern lights and had never before occurred over Nyack. In great excitement, I watched the magnificent nighttime display of flashing lights while Mom, Mrs. Kinsella, and Freddie Ogden's grandmother clutched their rosary beads and wailed into the night sky as the end of the world descended upon us.

The other picture showed a man in old-fashioned clothing, in a dark, shuttered, high-ceilinged room. Through a small hole drilled through a shutter, a narrow shaft of sunlight slanted through the room and struck

6. Ibid., page 135

a glass object on a table. It was a "prism," Fred explained. That slim ray of white light stabbed into the prism and burst from the other side, split into a wide rainbow of brilliant colors. "White light isn't white," Fred said. "Things aren't always what they might seem."

Fred's bookshelf grew, and Pop added another. I think this narrow back hall was Fred's college, in place of what had become impossible for him. My favorites were the books with pictures, but there were others that I ignored and did not get to know until years later. Fred read them, and when I finally did, they helped to explain something about Fred's growing seriousness and his self-education. Books like Upton Sinclair's *The Jungle*, Steinbeck's *The Grapes of Wrath*, Veblen's *Theory of the Leisure Class*, and some pamphlets on Marx's *Das Kapital* opened up worlds far different from my sheltered life on Elysian Avenue.

The year moved toward its close. Mom, Pop, and Fred were all factory workers now, and I was halfway through the third grade. The mortgage on our house was paid off that year, and Pop cut back his extra work around town. He urged Mom to quit her job at the pocketbook factory now that the mortgage was paid and Fred had decided to forgo college.

"We'll see," she said. "One more year, that's all. Then I stop."

Now Pop could focus his energy on enlarging and improving the house for his family's comfort, and he did so with an unrelenting energy that drove everyone who knew him into a state of instant fatigue. Our lives settled into regular rhythms.

On Tuesday, November 5, 1940, my father donned his fine gray suit, the one tailored eight years earlier by *Zio* Antonio Asaro. A good-quality new suit in 1940 cost two weeks' wages from The Mill. It was better, Pop thought, to keep the old one for a while longer. That evening, he walked to the South Nyack fire station and voted for the third time for FDR whose liberalism, as my father saw it, had defeated the Republicans' Great Depression, rescued working families, and opened up better possibilities for our future. Interestingly, Wendell Wilkie, the Republican opponent, had campaigned vigorously that FDR had failed to end the Depression. Mr. Wilkie had not convinced my father or 27 million other voters.

5. Echoes

By the summer of 1941, I was nine years old and Fred had been a workingman for a year. He was busy evenings and weekends, away from home. Something called "the union" was becoming important to Fred, and I heard talk of organizing and meetings. When he left for those meetings, he seemed to march away with some powerful determination that I did not understand. Mom was worried and told him, "Be careful what you do!" and Pop, in his quiet way, cautioned him about "things" that could "happen." Mrs. Kinsella, who was then in her 80s, one day pointed at Fred and told him that if he wasn't careful, "they gonna put you in a corner and fire you!" I had heard the phrase "getting fired" before. The image of Fred being "cornered" and "fired" was upsetting, but then I recalled earlier discussions and was reassured that it was only a way of speaking, that no real fire was involved. Nevertheless, something was going on. The people in my world were becoming tense and preoccupied, and I could feel their tension, even though I did not understand what was happening.

Then, without warning, Mom was injured at work. While she was sewing leather at the factory, the thick needle pierced her left thumb, driving down through the nail and into the bone, embedding a knotted mass of black thread. Mom was rushed to the hospital, where the needle and knotted thread were removed, and she returned home in throbbing pain that lasted for weeks.

Pop was furious about the "Goddamned factory." I had never seen him so angry. His quiet smile was gone; my patient and soft-voiced father was briefly transformed. But there was little he could do, except try to help Mom through the pain of healing.

Fred, too, was angry, even though Mom's injury at the pocketbook factory seemed to have had nothing to do with his job at the coat factory. Fred said it was no accident under those conditions, and he became even more deeply involved in whatever was going on at his factory.

Small things are sometimes echoes of larger events, light shadows of things past, reminders, ripples in time started long ago and now reaching us, more faintly but enough so we won't forget. Mom's agony was such, or so it seemed to my father when they brought her home from the hospital. He had been there in 1929 when they took Uncle Joe from The Mill, and he was the one who told Aunt Nancy what had happened, and her screams still echoed inside him. "An accident," they had told her. "A machine. Nobody's fault. Accidents happen." A whole young man had gone to work on the morning of another ordinary day. An accident, the men told her, but they kept their heads down when they said it. Nobody meant any harm, a little touch, maybe a small push, just kidding around; who knew? An iron and steel machine that roared with whirling shafts, toothed spinning wheels, and wide, thick, loudly slapping leather drive belts that became invisible blurs when running at full speed. How long did it take to clean the remains of his arm from the innards of that machine?

Mom's ordeal was an analogue in miniature of what had happened to Uncle Joe 11 years before. The elements were the same—powerful machines running at top speed, a factory intent on high production, inadequate or nonexistent safety measures. Workers were cogs in the machine, flesh and blood components. The scenario of agony was repeated across the country and the years. Each family in our group had its own version of the story. They told of an uncle crippled when run over on a poorly managed construction site. Another was severely burned by a broken electrical cable. A young cousin had his legs broken by a collapsed ladder. A son fell

20 feet from a power pole when a defective harness gave way. A father's back was broken when a scaffold collapsed. They were real people, relatives and friends; they had all experienced it, knew what it was like. They came to console and help Mom and to cook for our family, and they brought their love and support as well. They knew about pain, and they shared a collective anger and sadness that such was the nature of their work world here in *la bell'America*. They also knew there was little one could do about it.

Uncle Joe survived, that sweet man, gentle as a spring rain. He lived out his long life as a one-armed man and never complained. Mom also survived, and returned to work at the factory. For most of us, the incident receded into the background, but Fred seemed the most affected, the angriest. His meetings with workers from the coat factory became more intense; something was about to happen. It was as if we were all waiting for a storm. But that storm in Nyack never came, because another, much greater storm rolling across Europe and the Pacific was about to break over us and reduce all other problems to mere inconvenience.

IV

War

Chapter 23
The Map (1940–1941)

1. *Compare* Domenico Cervodoro

It looked rather like a picture of a high-heeled boot tacked to the wall.

"See, see here?" *Compare* Cervodoro urged, pointing to the big map, his enthusiasm spilling out. "This is Italy. This is where we come from. Here. . . ." He tapped his hand against the map and looked at me to make sure I was paying attention. "Here, in the Mediterranean, between Europe and Africa, here is *Italia*, the center of the world. This, right here, is *la bell'Italia*!"

It was 1939. I was seven years old, in second grade, and interested in playing outdoors with my friends. I had to admit, however, that visits to *Compare* Cervodoro's small apartment on Brookside Avenue held their own adventures, very different from the daily Americanizing process that swept over our second generation. In school we conversed, read, and wrote in English and played American games. We listened to American radio programs, watched American movies on Saturday afternoons, and idolized great American heroes like George Washington and the "Long" Ranger, as I called him. We were becoming Americanized, moving away from the Italian center of our families, leaving our parents behind. However, my gruff-voiced *compare*, with his insistent gestures and passion, directed me to his great map of Italy, pulling me back.

I was not very interested in lectures about Italy, but could never dodge *Compare* Cervodoro's enthusiasm. The huge map, beautifully multicolored, was so tall that I had to angle my head upward to see northern Italy. There were cities, mountains, green hills, white surf, and beaches. I saw railroads and trucks, and great ships steaming to and from the coasts. Sleek airplanes and squadrons of ominous tri-motored bombers flew across the map. At the top, factories poured smoke, fields were neatly combed by tractors, dams generated electricity, and power lines webbed the country, and all was framed by blue water and white-frosted Alps.

A box in the margin showed grapes, olives, barrels of wine and olive oil, fish, variously shaped pastas, cured meats, and thick wheels of cheese. Another box pictured statues, paintings, orchestras, and magnificent buildings. The largest box showed columns of marching Roman soldiers—powerful, thick-armed men with plumed helmets, leather breastplates, shields, swords, and lances. Moving down this picture, the soldiers became a modern army in khaki uniforms, with tanks, cannons, great battleships, and warplanes all around. I noticed that the powerful soldiers of the Roman legions and those of the modern army looked like the same men.

Prominently pictured at each compass point was a bundle of sticks tied together with the blade of an axe protruding. I did not know what it was, but it looked important.[1]

The glorious map presented Italy as a grand country that surely must have dominated the world. I tried to tell my friends about Italy's grandeur as revealed by *Compare* Cervodoro's map, but they had never heard of Italy doing anything great, like America did every day. Few of them even knew where Italy or Europe was. Miss Storey, my third grade teacher, helped me locate Italy on the globe in the library. There it was, the high-heeled boot. On the globe, it was not the world-dominating country suggested by *Compare* Cervodoro's map, but was a skinny appendage that stuck down from the underbelly of Europe. I was not going to push that imagery any further.

Which picture was true, my *compare*'s great map or the tiny peninsula on the globe? I think it was about then that I began to feel embarrassed by my association with all things Italian. The pressures toward Americanization had started several years earlier. As I began playing with neighborhood children, entering their homes, meeting their families—*Real American* families—I began to realize that we were different from everyone else. We talked differently, ate different foods, listened to different music, had different pictures on our walls. Real Americans were uniformly competent in the ways of America. They knew their way around and conversed without funny pronunciations. Nothing was more embarrassing than being in a store with Mom and meeting another Italian lady. They stood, speaking Italian, while my friends' Real American mothers walked by and looked at us. "Talk American!" I pleaded with Mom. Had she not held my hand so tightly, I would have slunk away to hide.

School taught us that all things American were superior. American history, government, wars, industry, cars, food, sports, and all else were the best. We had beaten the English in the Revolutionary War, the Indians in the Wild West, the Mexicans in Texas, the Spanish in the Caribbean, and the Germans in the Great War, and had even invented the airplane. Our daily lessons moved us, step by step, to accept the superiority of all things American, and what was "correct" became entwined with what was "American." Correct behavior, speech, manners, and thoughts were, by definition, American. All else, by implication, was incorrect.

1. The *fasces*—the ancient Roman symbol of the power of Roman magistrates, the axe representing their power over life and death. The symbol was adopted by Mussolini's *fascisti*. This map, I learned later, was intended to glorify Mussolini's Fascist dictatorship.

That meant that whatever our parents did, said, or believed that was more Italian than American was wrong. Each day in Italian families, children came home from grammar school and edited their parents' language, values, knowledge, and behavior. It was an impatient bigotry of youth, a thoughtless assumption that our folks, with their broken English, were not as refined, capable, or proper as Real Americans. We developed an intolerance of our parents, and that grew into embarrassment, and that led to rejection of much of their identity. Why couldn't they just be more American?

I never considered how my growing impatience with my parents' limitations might have affected them. They tolerated their children's criticisms but must have been distressed as we showed a disrespect that would not have been allowed in Italy. And yet, caught between cultures, they had to admit that the youngsters were often right. It must have been difficult for them. We loved and respected our parents, but the negative feelings grew and would soon be fueled by world events that would brand Italy as our enemy.[2]

While my second generation was struggling with our identity, *Compare* Cervodoro had no doubts. For him, the magnificent map was reality: Italians were the world's most civilized, cultured, artistic, creative, and intelligent people. He was not modest in those opinions, nor did he hide his contempt for those who denigrated Italians, now that we were, temporarily, at a low point in history.

Compare Cervodoro was not a blood relative, but because of close friendship and valued personal qualities, our families had been, in a sense, merged. *Compare* and *Comare* are terms that respect an honorary family connection. *Signore* and *Signora* also imply respect, but are less personal. Children always used the respectful terms when addressing adults.

When I was nine, in 1941, I asked Domenico Cervodoro to be my *padrino* (godfather) for my confirmation ceremony, thus joining our families and becoming my *compare*. "*Comparello* (Little *Compare*)," he thenceforth called me.

Although not tall, he was a compelling man. He was thick-chested, heavy-armed, with a deeply tanned, weathered face and the roughened hands of a lifetime of outdoor work. His shoulder muscles were heavy, giving him a slightly hunchbacked appearance. My *compare*'s voice was loud, gruff, matching his one or two years of school. But to the astonishment of people who met him for the first time, this rough-cut laborer had wide interests and self-taught knowledge.

He read Italian poetry, novels, and history, and political tracts in Italian and English. He studied the Renaissance and loved good music, especially Italian operas. He was proud of his phonograph records, thick, heavy,

2. See Gallo (1974) and Crispino (1980*)*.

single-sided 78-rpm discs that were a foot in diameter and played for three or four minutes. An operatic album held half a dozen discs in heavy paper sleeves between thick cardboard covers. Each six-disk album, 15 inches long, 13 inches wide, two or three inches thick, and so heavy that I could safely carry no more than one at a time, gave us 15 to 20 minutes of music, interrupted about every few minutes as we changed the record.

With no record player of his own, *Compare* Cervodoro brought his albums to our house to play on our Victor Talking Machine. Pop had bought it in 1939 at an estate sale at one of the mansions on Broadway. It was a beautifully crafted, polished wooden cabinet, five feet tall, three feet wide, two feet deep, and so heavy that Pop, Fred, and *Compare* Joe Lanzana strained to bring it into the house. When raised, its heavy lid revealed the gilded RCA Victor trademark, "Nipper," the little dog, sitting with ears cocked, attentive to "His Master's Voice." It had been Victor's top-of-the-line home entertainment center and the cutting edge in acoustical technology.

This marvelous machine was electrically powered and did not need to be wound up manually, like the older one owned by Mrs. Kinsella. A single record was placed on the felt-covered metal turntable, and a heavy tone arm holding a shiny steel needle was carefully lowered onto it. The music flowed through the arm and into a wooden horn built into the cabinet below. The volume control was no-nonsense technology: we simply opened or closed two little doors in front of the horn. After spinning for a few minutes at 78 rpm, the machine wondrously shut itself off.

It was in mint condition, but there were no buyers for the outmoded machine until my father offered a few dollars in the final hour of the sale. "Sold!" they said happily, and added four large boxes of records—operas, symphonies, Broadway shows, and popular songs. My father and *Compare* Joe set it in our living room, where it became the grandest piece of furniture we owned. Pop had bought it on impulse as a surprise gift for me. For years I explored the music in those records, playing them repeatedly, undoubtedly ruining them with my careless handling, and I became the acknowledged *capo* of the machine.[3]

The Cervodoros and my parents relaxed in our tiny living room, facing the Victrola. I put my *compare*'s records on the turntable, changing them every few minutes and adjusting the doors for the best sound. Out from that great cabinet came Caruso, Galli-Curci, Alma Gluck, Correlli, and John McCormack, who was an Irishman but, according to my *compare*, had a beautiful tenor voice. We were enveloped by the magnificent music that poured out from underneath the crackling and hissing of those old recordings.

Compare Cervodoro's favorite composers were Giuseppe Verdi, of

---

3. The records were from the 1920s and early 1930s, with a few World War I recordings. Most have been lost over the years. About three dozen remain in my collection.

course, and Beethoven. Years later, he would purchase an oil portrait of Beethoven and display the composer's heroically glowering face on his dining room wall.[4]

Once a year, Mom, Pop, Fred, the Cervodoros, and I walked down to the Franklin Street railroad station and climbed aboard a train to New York City. The conductor always set a little stool on the platform so the ladies could more easily step onto the train. As telephone poles whipped by, we shared the brown-bag lunch that Mom had prepared, including my favorite, hard-boiled eggs with lots of salt. The conductor, Mr. Hartwick, a neighbor who lived three houses down the street but had little to do with our family, was a tall, sharp-faced, imperious man. Standing there in his pressed black uniform with the shiny buttons and flat-topped cap, he checked our tickets and punched little cloverleaf holes in them so we could not use them again. Mr. Hartwick always frowned when he heard us unfolding our lunch bags and cracking eggshells in his train. I began to think that maybe we were doing something wrong, but he never said anything about it.

A stop-and-go bus ride through crowded New York City streets followed. Then we were seated at the rear of the balcony among an enthusiastic matinee audience, waiting for Aida, Musetta, Butterfly, Lucia, or some other Italian heroine. The best, I thought, was when real horses and camels pranced onto the stage in a glorious parade of victorious returning warriors who carried real swords and shields. The soaring music made me want to pump my feet in martial rhythm, swing my arms, and march down the steep aisle to join the parade. The next day, my friends, accustomed to Nyack's wavering high school band and our tiny grammar school stage, refused to believe me when I told them about the great pageantry that had poured across that vast operatic stage.

Compare Cervodoro drove a gargantuan squared-off 1932 Pierce Arrow that could have doubled as a bulldozer. He gripped the big wooden steering wheel, glowered unwaveringly straight ahead, stomped on the accelerator, and rocketed down the middle of the road with the same vigor he applied to everything in life. He could be seen rushing about town in his unique car. Not everyone moved quickly enough out of his path, but none of his automotive mishaps were very serious. Typically, after banging into another car, he sued the offending driver and usually won. He often complained, "*Gli americani,* they don't know how to drive!" He seemed perpetually in litigation about one thing or another, but never against Italians.

One of his passionate beliefs was that the world had always recognized

---

4. The oil portrait was painted by Signor Tomasso Gallo, an artist just emigrated from Italy. He sold several of his paintings with the help of *Compare* Cervodoro and my brother Fred, but it was not enough. After a few disappointing years, he returned to Italy in about 1965. I have two of his paintings but the others, including Beethoven's portrait, have long since disappeared.

the superiority of Italians by plundering everything that Italians had creat-ed. "Why do you think everybody wanted to own Italy, to steal everything Italian? Because they don't have anything like it in their own countries! We created Europe's culture—art, philosophy, government, science, the whole Renaissance, all created by Italians!" Being seven years old at that time, I had no idea what "the Renaissance" was, but it sounded impor-tant.

He was proud, he said, that Italians had given the world "every cultured and civilized idea that we have today." It was intolerable to him that the world now refused to give Italians proper credit. "They insult us and steal anything of ours they want." It was, he complained, "outright thievery by the ignorant barbarians!"

"And the French," he added, "they looted Rome, stole our art. Took it away to the Louvre, that thieves' nest!" He had been fortunate enough to visit that gallery when he was much younger. "It was truly magnificent," he admitted, but still "a thieves' nest."

He did not simply complain, but with his high-energy certainty, he waged campaigns to right the wrongs. My *compare* was a crusader, raising local consciousness about Italians' cultural contributions, to the annoy-ance of his fellow Rotarians, whom he harangued at monthly luncheon meetings. Books, pamphlets, correspondence, and notes about this or that Italian who had been egregiously wronged were strewn across his dining room table, to the annoyance of *Comare* Cervodoro.

"*Comparello*," he would ask, digging through the pile on his table, his hand burrowing paper tunnels like a determined little mole, "do you know who really invented the telephone?"

He sometimes aimed his Pierce Arrow down 9-W to New York City, to meet with a group of Italians demanding that the Hudson River be re-named to honor its true discoverer, Giovanni da Verrazano, who had sailed into the river 80 years before Henry Hudson. "The Dutchman, he even used Verrazano's charts!" *Compare* Cervodoro complained, waving this or that magazine article at me as proof.[5] He did not succeed in that project, but was overjoyed at the outcome of another of his campaigns, which he shared with *Zio* Antonio Serratore. Together at their kitchen tables, they wrote countless letters. *Zio* Serratore "shoulda been a lawyer," people said. His beautifully flowing penmanship and mastery of English compellingly laid out their case. In 1964, the world's longest suspension bridge was completed, connecting Brooklyn and Staten Island, a major link in Robert Moses' parkway system. John La Corte[6] led that campaign, persisting for years against powerful opposition, including a drive to name

5. Hudson was actually English, but many of his crew were Dutch, and he often sailed for Dutch companies.
6. Professor John La Corte, founder of the Italian Historical Society in 1949, long campaigned for public recognition of the many Italians who had made significant world contributions.

it after President John F. Kennedy. La Corte and his many supporters, including *Compare* Cervodoro and *Zio* Serratore, succeeded, and the bridge was named the Verrazano-Narrows Bridge.[7]

"*Comparello*, tell me, who invented airplanes?" he asked me on another occasion. "And submarines?"

"I know all about airplanes," I answered. "The Wright brothers, in their bicycle shop."

"No," he corrected, his voice a bit sad, disappointed at my ignorance. "Leonardo da Vinci. Hundreds of years ago. And submarines, too."

Another time he asked, "*Comparello*, who started the work on the American Constitution and Bill of Rights, and who wrote the words in the Declaration of Independence, 'that all men are created equal,' eh? Who do you think?"

"Umm, well, George Washington?" I guessed, fully expecting that my answer would be wrong.

"No," he said, reaching for a book under the scattered papers. "It was Filippo Mazzei. An Italian immigrant. He's the one who taught his friend Thomas Jefferson all about democracy."

While embroiled in another of his campaigns, he asked, "*Comparello*, who invented the telephone?"

"Alexander Graham Bell," I answered, this time with certainty. "Everybody knows that."

"No," he said, shaking his head. "It was Antonio Meucci, another Italian immigrant and a friend of Garibaldi. Meucci, he had the telephone patent years before Bell. They stole it from him, and he died a poor man, a sad man. Here, you should read this."

Although his assertion about Leonardo was somewhat stretched, his claims about Mazzei and Meucci were correct.

My *compare*, Domenico Cervodoro, shared with me his great map and his passion for Italian culture. With no children, he gave to me all his stored-up paternal affection and concern as my *padrino* and *compare*. I was the only son he would ever have. But with the callowness of the young, I failed to recognize, appreciate, or acknowledge that. I realize now that my *compare*'s insistent enthusiasm had a braking effect on my continued distancing from our Italian background, and I owe to him an important measure of my "rehabilitation" that was to come later.

2. *I Fascisti*

Compare Cervodoro's great map remained on his dining room wall until 1942, when he tore it down in disgust. I never saw it after that. His initial

---

7. Upon its completion in 1964, this was the world's longest suspension bridge. Since then, six other, longer, bridges have been built. It remains the longest suspension bridge in the United States.

pride in what the map represented and his later rejection of it paralleled the career of Italy's final dictator, Benito Mussolini.

In 1919, Italy was deep in crisis. The Allies' shabby postwar treatment of Italy, the incompetence of the king and parliament, government corruption, privileged treatment for the rich, and poverty and unemployment for everyone else had churned up a continuing turmoil. Banks failed and labor strikes, food riots, and political uprisings exploded. Right and left radical groups, as well as those at the center, demanded different solutions to the country's problems and fought against the constitutional government and one another. Socialists, Bolsheviks, laborers, and the unemployed, desperate for jobs, had taken over many northern and central towns. Businessmen, landowners, monarchists, churchmen, professionals, and the rich in general were alarmed by the growing power and demands of labor and were ready to support any effective anti-left movement. By 1922, Italy's increasing bloody civil strife had brought it near collapse. It was a perfection of chaos, just right for the appearance of a charismatic savior.

For years Mussolini, a journalist, had been a Marxist and a socialist leader. By 1919, however, seeing that power lay on the political right, he had become a right-wing nationalist, intensely opposed to communist and socialist organizations and labor unions, his rivals for power. Packaging his new stance in militaristic nationalism, he attracted the bourgeoisie, the rich landowners and industrialists, all of whom feared liberalism, labor, and left-wing politics. In 1919, enamored of the glories of imperial Rome, he formed his private army of Black Shirts and the Fascist Party, which he named *i fasci di combattimento* (the Fraternities of Combat). Although a virulent opponent of left-wing political groups, he maintained socialists' prolabor demands: universal suffrage, an eight-hour workday, a national minimum wage, a progressive tax on capital, and confiscation of 85 percent of war profiteering.[8] Four million jobless workers and desperate war veterans who had returned home to unemployment and poverty joined the party, willing to wear the Black Shirt and march for the Fascists' program. It is a measure of Mussolini's demagogic genius that he gained the support of the right by attacking labor, communism, and socialism while maintaining the enthusiastic following of millions of workers. Fascism, as it ultimately developed, was an unwieldy amalgam born of far left, far right, and centrist ideas.

In 1921 Mussolini and a few other Fascists were elected to parliament. With that foothold, Mussolini was ready to take over the government.

By the fall of 1922, Italy was near civil war. Socialists had gained significant election victories; the king and the right wing feared disaster. Seeing his opportunity, Mussolini accelerated his attacks on the left, thus increas-

8. Kirkpatrick (1964).

ing support from the right while at the same time courting the socialists on the left. He used both groups to his advantage. Then he threatened the constitutional government with a revolution.

The king had the constitutional power to stop Mussolini by establishing martial law and ordering the army to restore order. However, while this crisis boiled, the king stayed away from Rome, visiting a neighboring country and relaxing at one of his many vacation homes.[9] When he returned to Rome, the situation had worsened, but there was still time for him to act.

Fascists had taken over the town councils of Ferrara, Cremona, Parma, Ravenna, Bologna, and Leghorn, and by September controlled most of the north and much of central Italy. In October, Prime Minister Facta resigned, his government collapsed, and Mussolini made his move, his famous "march on Rome."[10] Threatening to send 20,000 armed Black Shirts to the capital, he demanded that the king appoint him prime minister or his troops would take the government by force. Mussolini, the people heard, was marching his army to Rome for a violent coup. In fact, the marchers were a much smaller, mostly unarmed group, and Mussolini's own "march" was a comfortable overnight ride on a sleeper train from Milan to Rome.[11] However, Mussolini had made his point, and awaited the king's answer.

October 1922 was a decisive time. Parliament and the military high command, alarmed by the Fascists, supported the monarchy.[12] Mussolini knew that the army was stronger than his marchers and would crush them on the king's order of martial law. He had to avoid a battle. But he thought the monarch might be too frightened or befuddled to give the order, and a bluff might work. Thus, Mussolini announced—safely distanced at the Swiss border and ready to flee north if necessary—that his troops were ready to "march on Rome."

The Fascists moved toward Rome. The generals and the army were ready to meet them. The people expected a violent confrontation and a sure defeat of Mussolini. The king agreed to declare martial law. Parliament drafted the order, and at 9 a.m. delivered it to the king for his signature.

9. During Mussolini's career, the king had several opportunities to stop him, but failed to act. Only at the very end, when the Fascists had been roundly defeated by the partisans and the Allies and Mussolini was a broken and powerless man in hiding, did the monarch take a stand. See Smith (1997) for detailed discussions.

10. This famous "March on Rome," apparently the creation of one of Mussolini's lieutenants, Gabriele D'Annunzio, was a magnificent and effective bluff, more theatrical choreography than military force. The similarity of Mussolini's rhetoric and tactics to those of Garibaldi's private army of *camicie rosse* (Red Shirts) and their famous march on Rome in 1860 cannot be ignored.

11. Smith (1997).

12. Apparently some high-level military officers as well as some influential people in the king's court and family privately favored Mussolini, largely because of his strong antisocialist actions. The Queen Mother, it was said, was an enthusiastic supporter of Fascism.

Now, Mussolini could be stopped. But to everyone's astonishment, the king refused to sign the order. Mussolini had bluffed, the king blinked, the army was blocked, and the Fascists won.[13]

The king feared a Fascist revolution and, even more, the toppling of his monarchy. Pushed by members of his family and by business interests, who favored the Fascists, he gave in and appointed Mussolini to the position of prime minister. In accord with the constitution, Mussolini formed a new government. The monarchy, having become the Fascists' co-conspirator, survived.

With the king's complicity, the Fascist revolution had succeeded. Mussolini had expected more of a fight, knowing he would have lost had the army faced his troops, and was surprised at the easy capitulation. Later, he expressed his contempt for the king's weakness.

Mussolini was a complete pragmatist, a superb opportunist, using and discarding any opposing camp or position, depending on which would give him the advantage. He accurately read the moods of the people, the weakness of his rivals, and the opportune moments for action. With convincing showmanship, he told the people what they wanted to hear—that Italy's chaos could be ended, life could be improved, the nation's weakness overcome, and respect restored. All will be achieved, he declared, through strength, discipline, and devotion to the state.

With apparently no limit to his energy, Mussolini traveled Italy spreading his vision. He understood the value of public performance and was good at it. He posed in military uniform, in diplomatic attire, as a farmer plowing a field or a laborer swinging a sledgehammer alongside sweating workers. He sat grandly astride his white stallion, Atlantico, played his violin for the photographers, posed at the controls of a new bomber, drove armored tanks, and piloted airplanes. The people heard of his skill as a violinist and his legendary abilities at fencing, horsemanship, skiing, and swimming.[14] He loved to address huge crowds, from whom, he said, he gathered his power. Mussolini's public appearances were staged theatricals, vulgar and common according to some critics, but the people cheered. He connected well with the masses, gaining supporters wherever he went, convincing many that he was a strong and unstoppable leader, the only one who could save Italy and build a powerful modern nation. The time was right for Mussolini. With the country in chaos, Italians were willing to give him a chance, to see if this supposed "strong man," as their legitimate prime minister, could help them out of their turmoil.

In 1933, the world was still deep in economic depression. In Nyack, my father and everyone we knew was struggling, and many had been defeated. Millions of Americans could not feed their families. Industry and

13. For an excellent discussion of this repeated failure of the king, see Smith (1997), chapter 14.
14. Smith (1997), page 344.

commerce were stagnating, not yet recovered from the war. Europe was in chaos, from which emerged one great leader, Benito Mussolini, who was showing the world how to solve its problems. In only a few years, his "modern Fascism" achieved economic miracles of recovery. *Fascismo*, he claimed, was the "new capitalism," the future for all governments, an assertive, powerful, no-nonsense, reality-based approach to governing.

Most appealing to the Western nations was Fascism's powerful opposition to the Bolshevism that was growing in Russia. Mussolini was the new champion of the right, defending Europe against Marxism.

Mussolini reduced the violence in Italy's cities, energized industry and agriculture, and built hydroelectric plants, highways, railroads, and airports. He modernized cities, ports, and the postal system, created a modern air force, and strengthened the army and the navy. Determined to end Italy's plague of malaria, he drained the Pontine Marshes near Rome and on the reclaimed land created five agricultural towns and 3,000 new farms. For the first time, funding for education flowed to the south and compulsory education was enforced, with the aim of lifting the south to the level of the rest of the country.[15]

The most popular of Mussolini's many triumphs was the 1929 Lateran Accords, his masterful healing of the 70-year-old Vatican-government schism. Mussolini recognized the Vatican as a sovereign state, paid reparations for confiscated Vatican property, declared Roman Catholicism to be Italy's state religion, and adopted the church's marriage rules as national law. In praise of Mussolini, Pope Pius XI said, "He has given God back to Italy, and Italy back to God!" It was an astute and timely political move that brought Mussolini, who was privately an atheist, adulation at home and the admiration of the world's Catholics for his inspired statesmanship.

Far ahead of other leaders, Mussolini recognized the potential of air power, and in the 1930s built Italy's *Regia Aeronautica* into Europe's most advanced air force. Italian pilots and aircraft were setting new speed and distance records and winning the world's coveted air trophies. Italian aeronautical engineers designed highly advanced aircraft, and Italian pilots were among the world's most skillful.[16]

In 1933, Mussolini sent 24 sleek, twin-hulled Savoia-Marchetti S-55-X seaplanes across the Atlantic to represent Italy at the Chicago World's Fair. At that time, flying even one airplane across the Atlantic was a great achievement, but bringing an entire squadron with 96 crewmen was a momentous triumph of technology and courage. The astounded and delighted world ap-

15. As of 2007 Italy has an adult literacy rate of 98.4 percent, somewhat higher than that of the United States.
16. Early in World War II, Italian pilots, flying 1930s Fiat CR.42 Falcon biplanes, were able to outmaneuver Britain's advanced Spitfires and Hurricanes. However, the Falcons' limited numbers, speed, firepower, and spare parts, and lack of protective armor, radios, and radar, soon grounded those old fighters.

plauded the Italians' tour de force. Wherever the squadron stopped—Orbetello, Amsterdam, Reykjavik, Montreal, Chicago, and New York City—it was cheered by thousands and given enormous coverage by the excited press.

The aviators were feted in rallies and parades. In Chicago, a monument was dedicated to them and a street was named for their leader, Italo Balbo. President and Mrs. Roosevelt hosted them at the White House. Madison Square Garden roared with cheering Americans. Unlike my father and other poor immigrants of a few years before, these triumphant Italian aviators presented a very different image to America.

The flight was an international sensation, glorifying Fascist Italy. Mussolini was viewed as Europe's greatest leader and statesman. His "new Fascism" became the model for several European regimes[17] and stimulated new political parties in the United States, Great Britain, Europe, and South America. Millions of Italian migrants around the world were enthralled by this powerful leader who was bringing honor to Italy. "Now," *Compare* Cervodoro said, "we hold our heads high!"

In the 1920s, the American journalist Lincoln Steffens lauded Mussolini. Nicholas Murray Butler, president of Columbia University and a Nobel Peace Prize recipient, found Fascism "a form of government of the very first order of excellence." Otto H. Kahn, a leading American financier, said, "Not only his own country, but the world at large owes a debt of gratitude [to Mussolini]." Winston Churchill, following a meeting with Mussolini in 1927, declared, "Anyone could see he thought of nothing but the lasting good of the Italian people." On a later occasion, Churchill told Mussolini, "If I were Italian, I am sure that I would have been with you from beginning to end in your victorious struggle." Churchill praised Mussolini as the world's "greatest living legislator." In 1929, United States Congressman Milford Howard wrote, "I want to go on record for . . . avowing my faith in Benito Mussolini, Italy's great premier, and fascism . . . as the highest expression of a pragmatic philosophy of government."[18] Sigmund Freud, on the request of a client, sent Mussolini an inscribed copy of one of his books.[19] The Manchester *Guardian* declared in 1939 that Mussolini was "the greatest statesman of our time." The Archbishop of Canterbury said that Mussolini was "the only gigantic figure in Europe." In a 1940 radio address to the Italian people, Churchill, by then at war with Italy, told the Italians that Mussolini was "a great man."[20] Sir Anthony Eden later wrote that Mussolini was "a man whose personality would be felt in any company."[21]

If those worldly people were so impressed, then we can see how Italian-Americans, ready to welcome any *honore* for their former country, would

17. Austria, Germany, Portugal, Romania, Spain.
18. Quoted by Diggins (1966).
19. See the account of the inscription in Jones (1953). It is not clear if Freud was praising or cautioning Mussolini.
20. For the quotations, see Adams (1982), page 27.
21. Kirkpatrick (1964), page 190.

look favorably on Mussolini. Most people did not understand what Fascism was, but it was working, and Benito Mussolini was the man of the decade. By 1935, Italian-Americans were proudly in support of Mussolini and saw Fascism as Italy's creative solution to modern problems. *Compare* Cervodoro tacked his great map to the wall, and his Italian pride soared.

In 1935 Mussolini was at the peak of his acclaim, but by the next year that would change. Another picture, hidden or ignored for over a decade, of a man willing to use any means to gain power—including murder—had started to circulate through Italy.

Mussolini understood that to maintain power he had to control public discourse. He did so by developing a Propaganda Ministry, complete with a Hollywood-modeled *Cinecittá* (Cinema City) dedicated to "spreading the spirit and civilization of Fascism."[22] The Ministry produced radio broadcasts, posters, books, newspaper articles, lectures, and propaganda films. Added to the indoctrination of schoolchildren, mail censorship, and total control over schools, newspapers, and radio broadcasting, the Ministry kept the public focused where Mussolini wanted.

The Propaganda Ministry created the twin myths of Italy's military strength and Mussolini's physical, intellectual, and political prowess. "*Il Duce* can read and write a dozen languages, you know," people told each other. "He stays up all night reading great literature and writing books," they repeated. "He is a master violinist, a great horseman, an unbeatable swordsman, and he's as strong as three men!"

Millions of people slid into the growing cult of personality, cheering the myth of the man without rational understanding of the nature of his government. The letter M became a symbol of patriotism, perhaps a greater one even than the national flag. It was carved in stone, painted 20 feet tall on walls, emblazoned in huge archways in glowing lights, and worn on the skinny chests of proud little five-year-olds in their new Fascist uniforms. As had happened with other successful demagogues, the intense adulation of the person blinded the people to the truths of his regime. Later, from reports leaked to the foreign press and from their own soldiers returned from other countries, Italians would learn more of the realities.

Once in office, Mussolini solidified his power through violence, demagoguery, and the complicity of the befuddled king. In 1922, Fascist Black Shirts led by Italo Balbo[23] invaded northern cities, attacking socialists and labor groups and killing hundreds, and making bonfires of their literature and their meeting halls, which of course endeared the Fascists to the right wing. Armed Fascist thugs roamed parliament, waving pistols and beating up opponents. There was evidence, too, that Mussolini had ordered the beating and murder of Giacomo Matteotti in 1924, and of Giovanni

22. Adams (1982), page 12.
23. Italo Balbo was a charismatic Fascist leader, considered to be Mussolini's heir and possibly his rival.

Amendola a year later. Both were members of parliament and critics of Fascism. Although he knew of Mussolini's involvement in those murders, the pusillanimous king did nothing. Indeed, starting in 1923, he issued a series of decrees that gave Mussolini total dictatorial power. Under growing criticism, Mussolini, in a January 1925 address to the nation, admitted his "full responsibility" for Matteotti's murder. It had been "necessary," he explained. "Italy wants peace and quiet and to get on with its work. I shall give it all of these, if possible in love, but if necessary by force."[24] The speech was meant for all who might have considered opposing Mussolini, and parliament became his tamed accomplice.

After 1925, there remained no pretense of working in concert with parliament and the king. Mussolini abolished free elections, outlawed all political parties but his *fascisti*, had his opponents beaten by thugs, and threatened to kill any minister who criticized Fascism. As his regime unfolded, he abolished all individual liberties—the right to vote, freedom of speech and assembly, equality before the law, and freedom of the press. His government censored mail and his police officials began to call in citizens and warn them that their loyalty seemed less than desired and, if not corrected, would gain more serious official attention. Such was the case for Signora Farina, who balked at buying a military uniform for her eight-year-old son until her interview at the Provincial Police Headquarters convinced her to be "more cooperative."[25]

With the king's support, Mussolini closed parliament and restructured the government. He created the "corporative state," a system of "corporations" to control all industry and labor and indeed all aspects of Italians' lives. He took control of every agency, including the media and education, and even demanded loyalty oaths from all teachers. Children from age four were pressed into his Fascist Youth Brigade for political indoctrination, "to develop ... an aptitude for combat and for sacrifice."[26] Youngsters, pledging their loyalty to Mussolini, marched in military uniforms that their poor families were forced to buy from the government.[27] Boys began at age six practicing with scaled-down Model 91 infantry rifles,[28] and later advanced to machine guns.

Mussolini had contempt for the masses, disdain for liberalism, and a fear of democracy. To him, democracy and republicanism were absurdities at best, and he was determined to destroy them. "The masses," he said, "are

24. Smith (1997), page 332.
25. Farina (1999).
26. Adams (1982), page 17.
27. See the remarkable description by Guido Farina (1999), who lived through this period.
28. Military and political indoctrination through the Fascist Youth Brigade began at age four for the sons of party members. Preschool boys, the "Wolf Cubs," wore uniforms and were taught to march and sing patriotic songs. By six, they became the "*Ballila*" and began training with scaled-down rifles. At 14, they continued training in the "Advanced Guards," and they received full-sized rifles at 18. At 21, they were admitted into Fascist party membership and they "pledged their lives to the Duce." Adams (1982), page 17.

nothing but a herd of sheep. ... I deny that they are capable of ruling themselves,"[29] and, "The individual only exists in so far as he is a member of the
state and is subordinated to the interests of the state."[30] In 1926, celebrating
his "march on Rome," he cheered the Italian people, whom, he declared,
"thirsted to obey, thirsted for discipline ... wanted to be governed."[31]

He became a master crowd pleaser. "Everything," Mussolini said, "turns
upon one's ability to control the masses, like an artist. The crowd is like a
woman. The crowd loves strong men."[32] The Propaganda Ministry fabricated information, distorted and suppressed facts, and fed its products to
the people like fodder to so many bleating sheep. As for free elections, he
reportedly said that half a million rifles outweighed five million votes.[33]

Mussolini's disdain for the people continued the traditional arrogance
of Italy's Royal House of Savoy, with the concept that only the elite can
rule; that the people "want" to be ruled and their only responsibility is
to obey their rulers. That was a powerful belief, shared by all Italian sov-
ereigns from the King of Sardinia in 1859 through the three[34] monarchs
who reigned into the 1940s, and it was central in Mussolini's beliefs. That
concept was both the backbone and the corruptive weakness of Italy's autocratic governments. It was the core of what Mazzini had fought against,
the price the country paid for having turned its back on Mazzini and republicanism. It was the path the Italians chose through their revolution,
rejecting Mazzini and supporting the monarchy, and bringing the nation
to the quintessential autocratic rule of Mussolini, *il Dittatore*.

Being a literate man of some skill, Mussolini harbored intellectual pre-
tensions of authoring a new political philosophy that would be studied by
scholars and would replace democracy, capitalism, and communism. What
developed, however, was not a rational philosophy but a repressive regime
of state control, militarism, and colonial adventure. It was pursuit of power
above all, and its operating mode was expediency rather than constancy of
principle.

Mussolini's Fascism was a centralized, authoritarian regime, and Mussolini made himself the final authority on everything. From village mayors
to the parliament, elected officials were replaced by Mussolini's appoin-
tees. All business, industry, agriculture, labor, trades, professions, and arts
were assigned to "corporations" under the absolute control of the central
government. Individuals had no rights. The king, allowed by Mussolini to
keep his crown, slid from the status of a Fascist collaborator to that of a
Fascist puppet.

29. Kirkpatrick (1964), page 158.
30. Ibid., page 178.
31. Adams (1982), page 26.
32. Kirkpatrick (1964), pages 158–159.
33. Ibid.
34. The fourth, Umberto II, had a more egalitarian view, but was monarch for only a few
months in 1946.

The extraordinary attempts to organize and control everything created a tangle of bureaucracy too cumbersome to be effective and so convoluted as to provide hidden nooks and crannies for corruption, incompetence, and minor acts of rebellion. In time, the people learned that the Fascist bureaucracy invited extraordinary levels of thievery and bumbling, making it the most corrupt in Italian history. Dennis Mack Smith, a historian of Italy, noted that many Fascists believed in their mission to improve Italy, but "most of their leaders were adventurers of the worst sort, either ignorant bullies or mercenaries in search of booty."[35]

Mussolini became more militaristic, shouting his crowd-pleasing, flag-waving patriotism. In 1923, he boasted that in another decade his military would number five million men and his air force would "darken the skies."[36] He spoke of creating a "New Italian Empire" in Africa, the Balkans, and the Middle East. He talked of "owning" the Adriatic and dominating the Mediterranean, which he called "*mare nostri* (our sea)." In moments of unchecked grandiosity, he even spoke of defeating England. Strangely, England welcomed Italy as a rising military factor, a useful balancing of European power and defense against Russia's Marxist expansionism.

In the 1920s and 1930s, Mussolini had a powerful influence on Germany, Portugal, and Spain. Hitler sought the Italian dictator's leadership and used Mussolini's Fascism as the model for Nazism. Hitler's German variant included the nationalization of industry, a major propaganda machine, a youth brigade to indoctrinate the young, suppression of all individual rights, militant nationalism and expansionist plans, and even the stiff-armed, Fascist salute. In 1948 Churchill would write, "As Fascism sprang from Communism, so Nazism developed from Fascism."[37]

Portugal, after nearly 100 years of antimonarchy revolution and counterrevolution, had become a constitutional republic in 1910. Antonio Salazar became prime minister in 1932; he, like Hitler, admired Mussolini and modeled much of his own repressive police state after the Fascists. Salazar, however, was loyal to the Church and the upper classes, to the detriment of the workers, the poor, and general education. He turned Portugal into a corporative state, but insisted its foundation was Roman Catholic philosophy rather than Mussolini's Fascism. Salazar maintained his dictatorship until 1968.

The antifascist Italian underground had begun almost simultaneously with Mussolini's rise, as his opponents were forced to operate clandestinely. Underground newspapers circulated, including *Non Mollare,* founded in 1925 by Gaetano Salvemini and the brothers Nello and Carlo Roselli. Another was Leone Ginzburg's *L'Italia Libera. Il Partito d'Azione* and other organizations became active underground resistance movements, and in the 1940s as many as 200,000 Italian partisans fought against the

35. Smith (1997), page 315.
36. Ibid.
37. Churchill (1948), page 15.

Fascists and Nazis in World War II.[38] In the 1920s, underground leaders were captured and imprisoned, as was former prime minister Francesco Nitti. Others were murdered, including the Roselli brothers, Leone Ginzburg, and Antonio Gramsci. Some antifascist writers, such as Carlo Levi and Gaetano Salvemini, survived in exile and continued to fight Fascism.[39] Although underground antifascist activity continued, after 1925 it had no effective power against the Fascists' tightening control. It was not until World War II that the underground antifascists had grown strong enough to have any significant effect.

Throughout Mussolini's rise, many Italians were dismayed at his growing authoritarianism, and in the end would claim they never did support him. However, as has been pointed out,[40] the dictator could hardly have gained so much power without the active and tacit support of the Italian people. The Church, too, was an ardent supporter of Fascism. Pius XI and Pius XII both praised Mussolini and Fascism, and thousands of sermons were preached from Catholic pulpits urging the people to respect and obey the Fascist regime. Supporting Mussolini's authoritarianism, Pius XI proclaimed in 1931, "We cannot allow freedom of discussion, for that might imperil the faith of less enlightened hearers and damage the established religion."[41]

By 1935, however, Italians were losing their zeal for Mussolini, resenting the control he pressed down upon them and beginning to fear his propensity for war. They began to wonder if their earlier willingness to support him had been an error.

While doubts were growing within Italy, Mussolini's international prestige was shattered by his 1935 invasion of Abyssinia (Ethiopia). He believed that France approved of his invasion plans and England had no objections. The Church voiced no opposition to the prospect of spreading Roman Catholicism to East Africa.

With the active support of the king, Mussolini invaded that peaceful country to expand his empire, just as the French, English, Germans, and Portuguese had pursued their colonialism. Italy needed room to expand, he said, especially since the United States' 1929 restriction on Italian immigration. Mussolini claimed that the occupation would also correct the Allies' egregious treatment of Italy after the war. Finally, and here was the crowd-pleaser, it would avenge Italy's humiliating defeat by the Ethiopians at Adowa 40 years earlier.

In the summer of 1935, Mussolini sent warplanes, tanks, trucks, guns, and troops across the Mediterranean and through the British-owned Suez Canal to Italian-controlled Eritrea and Somaliland in East Africa. The British

38. Smith (1997), page 421.
39. See the Reference List for Levi (1982) and Salvemini (1942).
40. Smith (1997), page 380.
41. Ibid.

knew what was being shipped through their canal; they protested mildly but did nothing. Perhaps they were distracted by Hitler's unexpected announcement that, despite the Treaty of Versailles, he was rebuilding the German army and adding 36 divisions.

With no opposition, Mussolini continued his military deployment, assuring the Abyssinians that he had no intention of invading their country. When he was ready, he did invade, using a trumped-up "act of aggression" as an excuse. In September his bombers, tanks, cannons, flame-throwers, and poisoned gas—which had been outlawed by the Geneva Convention—destroyed Ethiopian villages. The defenders, with no modern military and no help from the world, were overwhelmed. In only six months, it was over. Ethiopia's monarch, Haile Selassie, fled to England, an exiled victim of 19th-century-style colonial aggression.

Mussolini's four colonies in Africa (Libya, Eritrea, Abyssinia, and Italian Somaliland),[42] a land area five times the size of the Italian Peninsula, provided a staging ground from which to threaten future expansion into Egypt, Algeria, the Sudan, Greece, the Balkans, and the Middle East. To cheering crowds, he claimed the Abyssinian victory as the rebirth of the Roman Empire after 15 centuries. A pleased Victor Emanuele III accepted Haile Selassie's crown, awarded Mussolini the nation's highest decoration, the Grand Cross of the Military Order of Savoy, and added Abyssinia to the Italian Empire.[43] Vittorio Emanuele could now claim he was King of Italy and Emperor of Abyssinia.

The world, having done nothing to help the Abyssinians, condemned the invasion as colonial aggression. The League of Nations voted mild economic sanctions against Italy. The world's mood was not sweetened when Mussolini's son Vittorio published his account of how much he enjoyed bombing tribesmen who were fleeing on horseback and watching gleefully as each exploded "like a budding rose."[44]

While most of the world criticized Mussolini, Hitler praised him and treated him to magnificent rallies that fueled Mussolini's expanding delusions of military power. The world's condemnation pushed Mussolini closer to Hitler's beckoning welcome and broke his precarious ties with England and France. By that time, Mussolini, Europe's preeminent military dictator, had cast his lot with Hitler.

Japan, also a growing military dictatorship seeking empire, had already formed a pact with Germany. By edging closer to Germany, Mussolini tacitly joined with Japan, and defined the Axis powers of the coming World War II.

To most of the world of 1936, the Abyssinian venture unmasked Mus-

42. The modern Italian Empire was created over many years: Italian Somaliland, 1889; Eritrea, 1889; Libya, 1912; Rhodes and other Greek Isles, 1923; Albania, 1920 and 1939; most of Somalia, 1934; Abyssinia (Ethiopia), 1936; Montenegro, 1941.
43. Kirkpatrick (1964), page 331.
44. Smith (1997).

solini as the brutal colonial oppressor of a free, peaceful, and defenseless people. He dismissed the world's criticisms while his Propaganda Ministry praised the troops, twisted the facts, and barraged the nation with distorted accounts of noble military triumphs.

At first, Italians enthusiastically supported the war, proclaiming their patriotism, savoring the Fascist propaganda that told of victory over unprovoked African aggression. Soon, however, they learned of the world's contempt that had destroyed Italy's good image and turned so many against Mussolini and Fascism. Smith described the Abyssinian venture as one controlled by a few men who honestly believed in their mission, but also by many who were corrupt opportunists.[45] The adventure was a mix of propaganda, personal aggrandizement, and profit for the cynically opportunistic. There was enormous corruption, many no-bid contracts, and no government oversight. It was an unchecked free-for-all for greedy Fascists and businessmen, who gleefully siphoned all the money they could from the national treasury.

Originally supportive, Italians and Catholics in the United States, with the advantage of America's uncensored news and reports from those who had escaped, were horrified at the brutality, inhumanity, and slaughter. In Italy, returned soldiers told distressing accounts of thousands of captive Abyssinians massacred on Mussolini's orders to kill prisoners and gas whole villages, because by defying his invasion of their country, they were "rebels."

For many Italians, the great victory soon crumbled to a sorry adventure, and their regard for Mussolini decayed. The Fascist police state was by then so powerful that citizens dared not criticize openly, but beneath the surface, disillusion and dissatisfaction percolated. Thirty thousand Ethiopians had been killed in the brief war, and "genocide" was whispered.

Mussolini, elated at the victory, complained that only 1,500 Italian soldiers had died. Not enough young Italian blood had been spilled, he said, for a truly noble victory. One must wonder what Italian mothers would have felt had they known that their leader wished more of their sons had died.

Mussolini had defied England, France, and the League of Nations and shown that Europe was powerless against his military aggression. His invasion helped to destroy the League of Nations and tear the fragile peace in Europe, and to speed Hitler's own schedule of conquest. The Abyssinian invasion was the opening salvo of World War II.

By then, Mussolini was blinded by delusion, like the kings of the House of Savoy, believing that he commanded a formidable military power. His military, particularly the *Reggio Aeronautica* and the navy, were among the most advanced in Europe, but only for the moment. In truth, Italy did not have the natural resources or industrial capacity to sustain that level of

45. Smith (1997), page 387.

military strength. It had neither coal to fuel industries nor oil to power war machines. Also, the Fascist government was so corrupt that it could not focus on the nation's needs, as is required for an operation as complex as a general war.

Military expenses had depleted the treasury. Supply problems, especially of fuel and spare parts, had been known to the military in Abyssinia, but Mussolini would not listen to his generals. As vehicles were stilled and airplanes grounded for lack of fuel and repair, Mussolini saw expanding glory. He was bankrupting the nation, but his war machine was already running down.

For a decade, Mussolini had supported Fascist movements in Europe while denying any intention of "exporting" Italian Fascism. In 1937, ignoring the economic drain of the Abyssinian war, he sent 60,000 troops, 700 aircraft, and 750 tanks to aid Franco's Fascist revolution against the Republic of Spain, further impoverishing the Italian treasury. The already stressed people suffered more taxes *"per le guerre di Mussolini* (for Mussolini's wars)."

In 1931, the Spanish people had voted for a democratic republic to displace the Habsburg king, Alphonso III. The new constitution created universal suffrage, an elected representative government, and secularization of all schools (formerly church dominated). The Church was stripped of political power and much of its land was seized for distribution to the people. In 1934 and 1936, the republic was reaffirmed by free elections.

To Mussolini, this was an outrageous assertion of liberty, a rejection of his declaration that Fascism, not democracy, was the world's future. In Spain, the Fascists, monarchists, and church leaders, and the political right in general, began undermining the new republic. When Franco launched his Fascist revolution in 1936, Mussolini helped him destroy the young republic and its seditious ideas about democracy, freedom, and liberty.

Mussolini's interference in Spain angered France, England, and some in the United States, nearly breaking their already strained relations with Italy. Hitler, seeing an opportunity to pull Italy closer to his side, supported Mussolini's intervention and also sent military aid to Franco. Germany and Italy thus became aligned, and, in 1936, stated clearly to the world that they intended to wage war in order to destroy democracy and foster Fascism in other countries.

The Spanish Civil War, one of the most important events of the 20th century, was a three-year (1936–1939) bloody struggle of Fascism against a democratic republic. Mussolini, Hitler, the Vatican, the Spanish Catholic Church, Catholics around the world, Italians and Germans in the United States, and conservatives in general supported Franco. Liberals, socialists, and communists aided the republic, and hundreds of Americans volunteered to fight against Franco's Fascists.

The final battle occurred in 1939 at Barcelona, where Italian troops and

German tanks and warplanes defeated the republican remnants. Franco then executed or imprisoned thousands of opponents and established his *Falangista Española* (Spanish Fascists). Franco rescinded the republican constitution and abolished political opposition, trade unions, the right to vote, and workers' right to strike. He restored the Church, the aristocracy, and landowners to their previous advantages and withdrew Spain from the League of Nations, and would later affirm his support of the German-Italian-Japanese pact of 1940. Like Hitler, Franco based his rule on Mussolini's model.

By 1937, Hitler was the dominant Fascist leader. Early in 1938, after a triumphant visit to Germany, Mussolini adopted the Nazi's goose-stepping march and directed the Italian Ministry of Culture to decree that there was a "pure Italian race" that was closely related to the "Aryan race," and that Jews were not included. He imitated German racial policies, albeit in significantly watered-down form. Jews were removed from all literary, artistic, scientific, and professional societies, and from civil and military posts. Jews were not permitted to teach in or attend Italian schools and universities, to serve as notaries, to own more than 123 acres of land, or to employ more than 100 workers. Jews of foreign origins could not marry Italians and had to leave Italy within six months. Jewish refugees had always been welcomed by Italians, but now, desperately fleeing German persecution, they would be turned away by *i fascisti*.

The racial manifesto and anti-Semitic laws shocked the Italian public. Pope Pius XI, despite his earlier support for Fascism, condemned the laws and denounced radical nationalism, saying that German racism was not in accord with Italian nature, and chided Mussolini for imitating Hitler's racist ideas. Apparently, with this exception, there was little concern among the church hierarchy over anti-Semitism and no support for a strong stand against it. [46]

The concept of a "pure Italian race" was an absurdity to many Italians, who saw the idea as another indication of the depths of delusion into which Mussolini had sunk. For 3,000 years, Italians had been a variegated blend of humanity—hostile invaders, peaceful immigrants, and visitors, light and dark-skinned—from all over the world. It was a denial of all reason to believe that there could now be a "pure Italian race." What was Mussolini thinking, many wondered, to proclaim such nonsense?

Unlike Germans, most Italians would not accept Nazi anti-Semitism. Mussolini's imitation of Hitler further eroded the people's regard for him and strengthened their opposition to Germany and to his tightening ties to Hitler. The Fascists, however, were in control and carried out the policies, although never reaching the Germans' levels of inhumanity.

By 1938 Hitler had made his first moves, surprising everyone, including

46. Ibid, Smith (1997)

Mussolini, and was intent on a general war. Mussolini knew that Italy, having consumed so many resources in Abyssinia and Spain, could not sustain a larger war. However, in light of Hitler's successes, he needed another military victory. He eyed Albania, just across the Adriatic Sea. Albania, long under Italy's military and economic influence, was a good target for an affordable, limited war. A successful invasion would keep Mussolini somewhat on pace with Hitler, and would provide a secure base in the Balkans, control of the Adriatic, and some time to prepare for a future general war.

Italy invaded Albania in April 1939. Success came quickly, because King Zog had no defenses. However, Italy's depleted military, lack of basic resources, and demoralized troops caused immense problems with deployment, equipment breakdowns, supply shortages, and unnecessary casualties. The army's already low morale was further eroded. When a leader already viewed with less than complete confidence sends his troops into unwanted wars and fails to provide ammunition, fuel, spare parts, and supplies—even food and boots—then troop morale erodes. Soldiers returning from Abyssinia, Spain, and Albania, and later from Greece, North Africa, the Adriatic and Mediterranean Seas, and France, told the people at home of their predicament—ordered to fight but not given the means to do so. They privately voiced their increasing opposition to "*la guerra di Mussolini*," now beginning to be called "Hitler's war," and "*la guerra tedesca* (the German war)." Neither the troops nor the people supported Hitler's war. A low buzz of rebellion began among the troops and the people at home.

By 1940, Hitler's armies had slashed through Czechoslovakia, Poland, Denmark, Norway, and France. England's cities were bombed unmercifully, and the Germans would soon invade Russia. Mussolini became a secondary associate, more observer than participant, a follower of Hitler.

Midway through 1941, after years of managing a doubtful neutrality, playing off advantages with Germany on one side and France and England on the other, and making a pretense of being the peace-keeper of Europe, Mussolini announced his formal decision to join with Hitler.[47] His military and policy advisors pointed out to him that Italy had few tanks, armored cars, and warplanes, and an industrial capacity too limited to provide for war. Military supplies had been drastically reduced in the Abyssinian, Albanian, and Spanish wars, and no steps had been taken for civilian protection, such as the building of air-raid shelters. Troop morale, they said, was too low to be dependable, and the civilians did not want war.[48] Going to war, they cautioned, would be national suicide.

By then, however, Mussolini's delusions were overpowering—he believed his own propaganda, the lies about Italy's military strength. He

47. Actually, Mussolini's actions since 1936 were clearly on Hitler's side.
48. In the run-up to World War II, Mussolini had consumed industrial and military resources in Spain, Africa, and the Baltic. Italian industrialists had profited by producing war equipment and selling it to other countries, all of which depleted Italy's military strength.

seemed to believe that he was history's instrument to recreate the Roman Empire, to carry on the noble military tradition of the Royal House of Savoy and complete *il risorgimento* as promised in the 19th century. As Smith suggested, Mussolini fell into the trap of believing his own lies, the "inevitable result" of totalitarianism.[49] His delusions were his realities and his downfall. He was convinced by the Nazis' successes that it would be a short, manageable war. Dismissing all contrary advice, saying the war would be won in a few months and Italy would gain great profit from victory, he made an unbelievably bad decision to join Hitler and declare war on England, France, and Russia and their allies.[50]

Hearing that war declaration, *Compare* Cervodoro finally lost his respect for Mussolini. In his ignorance of the facts, my *compare* had admired the man, but now he ripped his great map from the wall. I was not there when he tore it down, but later, noticing its absence, I asked him where it was. He looked at me for a long time, the only time I had seen him with nothing to say. Finally, he shook his head no but said yes in a slow, dispirited voice. I was confused at his double message of "no" and "yes" and I think now that he was admitting his own confusion over how the world had turned.

Compare Cervodoro would later say that a crazed man and his thieving associates had taken "our beautiful country" to its ruin. The "Fascist crooks," he said, were plundering everything in sight before the people of Italy finally woke up and destroyed them. He said they were "even worse than the French!" and he hoped the Italian people would rise up in a new *rivoluzione* and destroy Mussolini and his Fascist government.

Mussolini took his unprepared and unwilling country into World War II. It was economically and physically impossible for Italy to sustain military operations at that level. But Mussolini went ahead, led by his delusions, spurred by Hitler, blind to the people's lack of support for war, deaf to the growing undertone of resentment and rebellion. Questions were raised quietly about Mussolini's health, his deteriorating judgment, and his deepening delusions. The antifascist underground grew stronger.

In the Pacific, the Japanese had waged their own empire-expanding war, defeating China in the Sino-Japanese War of 1894, and 10 years later defeated Russia. By 1938, Japan was the major power in the Pacific. It had invaded Manchuria, precipitated another war with China, and distanced itself from the United States and other democracies. In 1940, Japan formally declared unity with Germany and Italy, forming the Axis powers of World War II. The Japanese were moving rapidly toward a government in-

49. Smith (1997).
50. The Tripartite Axis powers were Germany, Japan, and Italy, joined later by Romania, Bulgaria, Slovakia, Hungary, Yugoslavia, Croatia, and Finland. Numerous cobelligerent states, puppet states, and collaborator states were also involved. See Weinberg (2005) and Dear and Foot (1995).

distinguishable from the autocratic dictatorships growing in Europe. The next world war was but a year away. Some would say that the First World War had never ended, but had smoldered, unacknowledged, until it burst out once again. In 1941, General Hideki Tojo, in a takeover of the government by the military faction, became Japan's prime minister. Although not a Fascist in name, Tojo was an autocratic dictator who, like Hitler and Mussolini, fused autocracy, patriotism, militarism, and industrialism in his regime. Tojo pressed for war against England and the United States and was the force behind the 1941 Japanese attack on Pearl Harbor. The 20th century's Fascist revolution, the intertwining of political conservatism and big business with powerful, militaristic, centralized governments and fanatical, flag-waving patriotism, was overrunning Europe and the Pacific with aims to destroy and supplant democracy.

Many of those who recognized the spread of autocracy and militarism applauded, admiring military strength and seeing the dictators as powerful barriers to bolshevism, and viewing their regimes as the flowering of big business and conservative values. Throughout the 1930s, Fascism appealed to many Americans, Englishmen, and Europeans. In 1940, a year after France, Britain, Australia, Canada, and New Zealand had entered the war against Germany, the United States still asserted its neutrality. In 1941, most Americans held to the belief that it was not their war and the US should stay out of it. Americans were too busy struggling with their Great Depression to notice.

3. The Abandoned Cave

Many of the Italian immigrants in Nyack had left Italy in the decade following World War I, when the country was in political turmoil and the Fascist revolution was under way. Between 1920, when my father came to America to stay, and the final months of 1927, when he succeeded in bringing in Mom and Fred, Mussolini and the Fascists had taken over the country. In 1929, about a year after Mom's arrival, the new American law severely restricted Italian immigration, and my father knew how fortunate he had been in bringing his family out of Italy in time to avoid the new regulations.

Years later, in a rare disclosure about his war experiences, he told me he had had enough of war. He saw militarism growing in Italy in the 1920s and 1930s and wanted none of it for his family. Like most, he did not know what Fascism was, but admitted being impressed by its successes and feeling proud of Mussolini's accomplishments. He was no more prescient than anyone else in seeing its viciousness, the loss of freedom, or the disastrous war that was soon to explode. But in the 1920s, as he watched from across the ocean and saw a mixed picture of Mussolini's accomplishments and growing militarism, he began to fear for his old country. Escaping Fascism had not been among his original reasons to emigrate, since modern Fascism had not yet taken control. His escape had been fortuitous rather than planned.

In the 1920s and 1930s, Italians in America watched Mussolini's career grow and Italy rise to a European power. At first they were cautious, but by 1933, as America's Depression deepened, they began to admire Italy's economic progress—Mussolini was succeeding where America was failing! Their tentative support blossomed into an enthusiastic embrace of Mussolini as Italy's savior and Europe's hero. *Compare* Cervodoro pinned his great map to the wall and savored what was, surely, Italy's rebirth.

After 1936, their pride turned to disappointment, rejection, and shame. They recognized Italy's industrial weakness and saw Mussolini for what he was, a deluded *braggadocio* who was now making Italy look bad in the eyes of the world. It was hard, however, to abandon their recent hopes, and they were left with a jumbled ambivalence toward Mussolini, and an ebbing desire that perhaps he would still make it come out well.

In 1940 I was eight years old. I had completed nearly three years of school, and was feeling pretty grown up. I had long ago abandoned my secret cave under the table, and now sat with the adults in the kitchen or stood with the men in the cellar and heard their talk of families, The Mill, a now-tarnished Mussolini, and a threatened Italy.

I recall one discussion in the kitchen. Mom was especially upset, for she understood everything in personal terms—her family, herself, her world, and her God. She spoke of "Mr. Appella-bomba," one of her bargaining adversaries for so many years. Doris and Isidor Dropkin were our upstairs tenants and friends, and Mr. Levine and Mr. Brown were the retailers from whom we had bought all our furniture over the years. The Gottesmans were hardworking people whose son, Fred's friend Otto, was *un buon ragazzo* (a good boy) who was often at our house. Bill Pozefsky came by twice each week selling fruit and vegetables and sat in our kitchen with a cup of coffee. Mrs. Giessmann was one of the hardworking ladies at the pocketbook factory who came home with Mom at lunchtime.[51] All spoke in their own funny ways and struggled alike to raise families in our adopted country. Together we helped make the America that the immigrants, whatever their origins, had sought.

"They work hard," Mom said. "Like us, they have families. Now Mussolini wants to chase them out of Italy. Why? What did they do to him?" These were things Mom could not understand. "Only God knows," she concluded. "Only God knows."[52]

The rumored plight of Jews in Italy was distressing, and so were our

---

51. See Chapter Twenty-Two. I recall that Mrs. Giessmann never ate lunch with the other ladies. She clearly enjoyed being with them and joined in their lively conversations, but she never ate lunch and I never knew why.
52. The true horrors of the Holocaust were not revealed until the war's end. See Piper (1994) and Polaikov (1956).

fears for the safety of our relatives in Italy. People could not even turn around, we heard, without policemen or government officials watching them, warning them, telling them what to do and what not to do. They were now being taxed on everything, and each year it became more difficult to make a living. "*Sulle spalle, u guverno* (the government sits on our shoulders)," the people said.

Most distressing were Mussolini's forays into war, taking young men from their families and throwing them into East Africa, Spain, the Balkans, and Egypt, and later Greece, France, and the North African desert. Mom's brother, Giuseppe, had been sent to Africa to help colonize and tame the natives, and the family had not heard from him in a long time. Even the children wear uniforms now, they said, and they practice with real guns. Even the children!

That year, 1940, my father paid off the mortgage. He and Mom must have felt proud and relieved at having weathered the Depression and kept their home. That must have been an important event, but I do not recall any particular celebration. That year, too, Fred graduated from high school, gave up on college, and began his career as a working man at the coat factory down by the river. The great jars of chemicals remained on the garage shelves, luring me into some dangerous eperimenting when no one was watching and probably leaking hazards into the neighborhood. The books on science and mathematics remained on Fred's bookshelf in the back hall. He and Otto no longer tackled mathematical problems in their six-volume set, and Fred's slide rules became my wooden playthings.

The final years of the 1930s prodded my parents in contradictory directions. The Depression seemed lighter and the future looked better, but war had become real for Europe and might soon swallow up America, too. The news from Italy was alarming. In the contradictory pull toward elation and despair, people continued to work, to live. Four topics—the Depression, imminent world war, Mussolini's probable destruction of Italy, and the fate of relatives and friends—consumed the adults gathered around our kitchen table.

For my parents, 1940 was a year that capped a decade of accomplishments and some disappointments, but mostly it was a year of apprehension. People knew that world-altering events were emerging, but they did not know which direction would prevail. For me, 1940 was another ordinary year. It snowed in January, school dragged on to its blessed end in June, family dinners were as good as ever, Uncle Johnnie waved the comics at me every Sunday morning,[53] and Freddie Ogden and Bobby Greggs were still my best friends.

---

53. See Chapter Eighteen.

Chapter 24

"Time goes slow when you don't do nothin'!"
(Nyack, 1941–1945)

1. Summer, 1941

While his more affluent high school classmates completed their first year of college, Fred left the coat factory to work at Lederle Laboratories in Nanuet, where he met a young lady, Marie Palazzollo. We were delighted with her beauty and vibrancy. Mom happily welcomed Marie and was already counting the chubby grandchildren who would be scampering around her kitchen.

By 1941, the Democrats had overcome much of the Republicans' Great Depression, and FDR had won a third term. The Mill had been running steadily for a year. My father and Uncle Joe were working regularly and felt a lifting of the Depression's weight.

My father's health continued to decline. Controlled most of the time, the malaria erupted periodically into pain, chills, and fever that kept him curled up in bed for days, assailed also by mind-numbing pain medication. Dr. Relland finally sent him to specialists in New York City. They did no better controlling the malaria, but discovered other problems that complicated his condition. In the weeks between those terrible episodes, he threw himself into his work, as if trying to outrun an adversary. Pop enlarged the cellar, built more bedrooms, added bathrooms, dug his garden, replaced the heating system, rewired the house, patched, painted, and repaired, and kept his home in a constant state of improvement.

The war in Europe was in its third year, and we feared that America would soon be entangled. Hitler's armies had overrun Western Europe, pushed into Russia, defeated France, and driven the English into the sea at Dunkirk. Goering's bombers were pounding British cities into rubble. Mussolini, neutral until 1940, rejected the repeated invitations to join England and France and sided with Hitler. His troops moved into Greece, British Somaliland, and Egypt.

The Italian navy, much smaller than the English navy, caused them significant losses in the Mediterranean, and tied up much of the English navy for three years. In the first year of war, the Italian 10th Light Flotilla destroyed 30 British ships including two battleships.[1] Recognizing the threat

---

1. England's losses included the battleships H.M.S. *Queen Elizabeth* and H.M.S. *Valiant*. By the end of the war the Italian air force had destroyed 72 additional Allied warships and damaged 500 others. Bradagin (1957).

of the Italian navy, the English decided to strike quickly to weaken it. In November 1940, the British launched a surprise attack on the Italian fleet anchored in the harbor at Taranto. It was a carefully planned raid using new tactics combining aircraft and ships. Twenty Swordfish Torpedo Bombers, 1930s biplanes, were launched from the carrier H.M.S. *Illustrious*. Attacking at night in two waves, they destroyed nearly half of Italy's navy, including three major battleships. With limited industrial resources, Italy could not easily replace the ships. The Italian navy never fully recovered, but continued to be an effective force against the English in the Mediterranean.[2]

That fall I entered Miss Copper's fourth grade and resumed my private lessons with Ol' McElroy, although not as often as in the previous year. I cannot say that I missed our more frequent private times with the coiled leather strap behind her closed door. We had developed a certain pathological rapport, Ol' McElroy and I. While the sessions did not improve my behavior, they made me a more resistive kid, and that, I thought, was valuable. Our confrontations were driven by Ol' McElroy's determination to make me cry, opposed by my even stronger determination never to do so, no matter how resolutely she wielded the strap. Wearing her out became my grammar school career goal; my obstinacy would triumph over Ol' McElroy's malevolence! One thing was certain: school would never be the same if Ol' McElroy ever retired.

Concerns about the war in Europe occupied my parents, but I was caught up in more important issues, like my father's decision that I should no longer sleep on a folding cot in the dining room. "You're growing up," he said. "Nine years old. I'm gonna build a room for you."

Space was limited. Pop's additions over the years had stretched the limits of Nyack's zoning regulations. I eagerly monitored progress as he added my new room to one of the remaining unoccupied corners of the house, just off the back steps to the kitchen. With Fred's occasional help, Pop dug the cellar, built the forms, and mixed and poured cement. He attached the base plate and framed in the studs and joists. He added flooring, walls, and a ceiling, and installed a window, a ceiling light, and a flat corrugated metal roof. Upon that roof, I discovered, raindrops tapped out marches and lullabies. So pacifying was the patter of rain on the metal roof that I was disappointed whenever evening approached with a cloudless sky.

At the end of August, with the last nail pounded, the last bead of joint compound smoothed down, and the final stroke of Pop's paintbrush, my wonderful bedroom, four feet wide by eight feet long—a closet, really—was finished, and I claimed it as my own. With my cot unfolded, there was not much space for anything but myself, my treasures in a flat cardboard box under the cot, and a small stool to reach the narrow shelves that Pop

2. Caravaggio (2006).

had built into one wall. Mom made a curtain for the doorway, and I could pull it closed to create a cozy privacy. My window looked out at our patio under the grapevines. My new room was an intimate and safe place of my own. Even Fred was impressed.

To keep me safe while I slept, Mom blessed my new room with a prayer to my namesake, St. Anthony, and a liberal sprinkling of holy water purloined from the font at St. Ann's Church. Pop, as usual, stayed quietly in the background, gently tolerant of Mom's mysticism, and just smiled at me, pleased because I was pleased.

Except for my new room, the summer of 1941 was like other summers, not particularly notable and too quickly ended. My new bedroom was the high point; the lowest was our summer vacation's final week. As the last days approached, my friends and I sought desperately for ways to delay our return to school. "There gotta be a way!" we told each other. Tommy, the oldest, had heard that "time goes fast when you're busy." "So," he reasoned, with the deductive logic of his Catholic school education, "time goes slow when you don't do nothin'." Convinced by such clarity, we decided that "nothin'" was exactly what we would do the next day, the final day of summer vacation.

That morning, five friends, third and fourth graders, gathered in Bobby Greggs's back yard and climbed onto the slanted, tar-paper roof of his mother's chicken coop. We stretched out on our backs, soaked up the warm sun, and blinked into the blue sky. In the dry soil below, a dozen glossy Rhode Island Reds clucked and scratched, penned in just as we would soon be in school. "Don't even move," we cautioned each other, lest we use up too many moments of our last day of freedom. "If we hold our breaths and close our eyes," Freddie Ogden suggested, "that'll really slow everything down."

Unknowingly, we were echoing Paolo's lament half a century earlier. "*Polli sfortunati* (unfortunate chickens)," he had called himself and his friends, an appropriate label for us.

Our inactivity lasted only a few minutes before we jumped from the roof and dashed off to more typical high-velocity consumption of our final hours. In abandoning the rooftop, we may have glimpsed a metaphorical lesson that, on a grander scale, was about to be thrust on the nation— seeking freedom through inactivity is not a good idea.

Freedom is the most valuable of human conditions. It is sought by revolutionaries and immigrants, and by schoolchildren in the final week of summer. The summer of 1941 was our pivotal time—just a few months later, every part of every life would be different: more somber, fretful, fearsome. Every day of normal life would become but a footnote to the overriding issues of another world war. The demands made on youngsters to master the challenges of normal childhood would be overshadowed by war, and children would be robbed of the normal pleasures of their own developmental dilemmas. Whatever we faced at home was not as important as the issues facing the young men who would soon fight in a horrific war that was to kill more than 60 million people.

We knew none of that when school began in September, but our parents had long feared it. With mixed reluctance, eagerness, and innocence, we returned to school, to our new teachers and old friends. We settled into familiar routines, starting with the adventures of our morning walk down the hill to school to face whatever would be offered up that day, including Ol' McElroy. The best thing about school was our explosive three o'clock release and the enthusiastic running and jumping among the dangerous, sharp rubble of the collapsed factory building across the street. We dashed through the cavernous Nyack Coal and Lumber Company and ran past the Singer Sewing Machine factory, where Wally Fredericks waved at us from his second-floor window. We ran across the railroad tracks, often between the slowly moving trains, and past the Cedar Hill Tavern that was always dark inside, like a cave.

On the way, we paused at Franklin Street to pound on the big metal sign swinging at the corner gas station, making it boom like a Chinese gong, just like in the movies. That made the owner come running out of his little house, blowing smoke from his cigar like an angry steam engine, yelling and shaking his fist at us as we ran away up the steep hill to the safety of home. I thought he was rather like the cuckoo clock in Mrs. Kinsella's kitchen—whenever she moved the big hand to the number 12, a little bird would pop out and make funny noises.

On Washington Street, we loitered at Fritz's house to pat his head and talk to him, a huge gentle German shepherd. On some days we ran an extra block to Maple Street in order to dash past Mr. De Revere's house and make as much noise as possible, because he hated kids. On trash collection days our journey took longer, as we explored our neighbors' more interesting castoffs, searching for treasures that we happily carted home and our parents later threw out in our own trash. Our summer was over; autumn had begun and there was nothing we could do about it. September rolled on into December.

2. The Radio

Mom's radio, a 1930s Philco, sat high on a kitchen shelf near the back door and brought to us, mainly from WOV, the Italian station, Italian soap operas for Mom, and excerpts from real operas. It brought the news for my father and, for me, Mel Allen's spirited play-by-play call of Yankees games.[3] Its wooden cabinet was rounded on top, like a Roman arch, and nicely balanced by a small arched dial in front, with two control knobs. Some years later, I would save up money I earned after school working at cousin Joe Conace's grocery store and buy Mom a shiny white plastic AM/FM radio

---

3. For Yankees fans, Mel Allen (Melvin Allen Israel) was as much part of the team as any player. Allen broadcast Yankee games and countless other events from 1939 to 1964.

that I placed on top of the refrigerator. I appropriated the old Philco and painted it red, that being the only paint I could find in the garage. Carefully writing "Lorraine" across the front in honor of my 1948 girlfriend, I placed it on the wooden stool in my crowded little bedroom.

Our kitchen was the family's center, where loud voices swirled with laughter, news, gossip, and strong opinions. Hands swept through the air, speaking their own language, while spoons clattered in coffee cups and coffee cups clinked against saucers. Friends and even some strangers came into our kitchen, always a place of robust sharing.

One day I walked into the kitchen and found a somber, silent, and gray-faced trio. My father was standing; Mom and Aunt Macrina were seated. Mom was twisting a handkerchief in her hands, always a sign of distress. They stared at the old radio, high on its shelf like a prophet on the mountain delivering an apocalyptic message to his people below:

"Yesterday, December 7th, a day which will live in infamy, the United States of America was suddenly and deliberately attacked by naval and air forces of the Empire of Japan."

There was more in the brief address, and President Roosevelt finished with:

"I ask that the Congress declare that since the unprovoked and dastardly attack by Japan on Sunday, December 7th, a state of war has existed between the United States and the Japanese Empire."[4]

"War," my father said, quietly. In the stillness of our kitchen it sounded like thunder.

The Japanese attack on Pearl Harbor was patterned after the British raid on the Italian fleet at Taranto a year earlier, which the Japanese had carefully studied. In a two-hour raid, Commander Isoroku Yamamoto's fleet of 30 warships launched 400 carrier-based airplanes that bombed, torpedoed, and strafed the 94 American ships trapped in Pearl Harbor, killing or injuring more than 3,000 Americans. Seven of America's eight battleships were sunk or damaged. Three cruisers, three destroyers, 200 warplanes, and the naval base were destroyed. Our navy was crippled. Our war had begun.

With Pearl Harbor, the reputation of the Japanese was instantly sealed— it was a "coward's sneak attack," a "bushwhacking," a "vicious stab in the back," an attack on a country that did not even know it was at war. Most deplorable was the Japanese duplicity. As Yamamoto surreptitiously moved his fleet into attack position, Japan's ambassadors were holding peace talks in Washington to keep the Americans unaware of the impending attack.[5]

Throughout the war, the drumbeat of our propaganda would portray Tojo, Hirohito[6] and all Japanese as cowardly, devious, and uncivilized. On

4. Address to Congress by President Franklin Delano Roosevelt, December 8, 1941.
5. See Prange (1988).
6. Hirohito was the Japanese hereditary emperor, and Tojo was the prime minister and virtual dictator of Japan.

the home front, we were told to view this war not as "Freedom versus Fascism," like our fight against Germany and Italy, but as a death struggle of civilized humanity against Oriental savages. Such deep loathing for the Japanese was created that Americans felt little sympathy when, starting in 1942, 120,000 Japanese-Americans—all loyal American citizens—were rounded up and locked into concentration camps. Four years later, in 1945, two nuclear bombs destroyed Hiroshima and Nagasaki, ending the war in two moments of horror, flattening cities, melting buildings, burning up more than 100,000 men, women, and children, and horribly sickening tens of thousands more who died slowly of radiation sickness. Americans showed little concern for "the Japs," who "deserved whatever they got."

"War," my father had said. I had some idea what it meant—we were going to fight a war, and that would be exciting, but I had no real understanding. The adults knew, and silently faced their fears—Aunt Macrina's sons, Fred, Joe, and Frank, would be taken away to war. My brother would go, as would my cousins Fred Graziano and Joe Dattilo. Our family's friends Frank Fiola and Joe and Greg Conace would go (their younger brothers, Dominick and Frank, would go later, to other wars). The Asaro, Ciancimino, Colarito, Maiorano, Raso, Renella, Serratore, Scheno, and Sutera families, who had sat at our kitchen table, were all targets for war. More than 100 young Italian-American men from our small town were taken away to war. Fred's friend Otto Gottesman and Bobby Greggs's older brother Glen; our neighbors Brad Hartwick, Bernie Garrison, and Bobby Hilton—all would be called, as would many others whom I did not know. All over the country, people listened to our president, knowing that many young men would go but not knowing how many would return.

3. War

There were no ceremonies to mark the day Fred left for the army, except that my father delayed leaving for work that morning in order to see him safely on his way. My brother walked up Elysian Avenue to Maple Street, where he met two friends walking in the same direction, casually, as if heading to another day at work. Mom, Pop, and I stood huddled together on the porch, Mom twisting her handkerchief. Mrs. Kinsella and Uncle Johnnie came out onto their porch and she called out, "God bless you, Freddie. God bless you."

At the corner, Fred turned and waved at us, then walked on, beyond Mr. De Revere's house and out of sight. Others must have joined Fred and his friends, forming a small parade to Main Street, where a military bus waited to take them away. I wondered what those young men talked about as they walked together, away from Nyack, toward the war.

After a while, my father picked up his lunch box that Mom had packed, tucked it under his arm like a football as he always did, and walked down the street to the bus stop. He was late for work at The Mill, but on that day the boss would understand.

About a week later, Mom unpacked a cardboard box addressed to us in Fred's handwriting. Mom's eyes were red as she lifted out Fred's civilian clothes that he had worn the day he left and shipped from whatever boot camp the army had taken him to. He would not need them for a while. I carried the shoes to Fred's room in the attic and put them away. I took his clothes down to the laundry and stored the empty box in the garage with a vague idea that it was special and should be preserved. Then I took a long walk in the shadowed woods up on South Mountain, where Fred and I had hiked so often, now feeling afraid for my brother.

Our lives were taken over by the war. Each day brought reminders of Fred. We knew where he was while he was posted in the United States. Soon his letters bore the return address "ETO," for European Theater of Operation, but we never knew exactly where. Fred wrote V-Mails (Victory Mails), one-page letters with words blacked out before the pages were microfilmed for compactness. Under those precise black rectangles were hidden things we were not allowed to know. I tried, with no success, to see what was hidden, but the censors had been clever. My cousin Joe Conace, home on leave from the navy, told me that because Fred was only an enlisted man, he had to give his letters to his commanding officer to be censored, but the officers were allowed to censor their own. That, I thought, was not fair.

Newspapers and radio broadcasts kept the war in public view. Popular music, songs of bravery, faith, patriotism, and the patience of young ladies waiting at home took on jazzy martial rhythms or measured sentimental romanticism. For me, the two most evocative and memorable of all the songs of the war were "We'll Meet Again," recorded in 1942 by Vera Lynn, and "When the Lights Go on Again," recorded by Vaughn Monroe in 1943.[7]

Schoolchildren bought war stamps and pasted them into booklets to reach $18.75, the cost of the least expensive war bond. Classrooms competed for stamp sales, and their weekly totals were displayed in the corridor near Ol' McElroy's office. The week's winner pinned a paper cutout of a Japanese Zero on the board.

Government posters told us "Loose Lips Sink Ships," "Let's Hit the Bull's Eye—Buy U.S. War Bonds," and "A Half-Filled Stamp Album Is Like a Half-Equipped Soldier!" A message our family readily understood was "Use It Up, Wear It Out, Make It Do!" The poster that I liked best, because of our scout troop's scrap drives, shouted, "Salvage Scrap to Blast the Jap!"

---

7. "When the Lights Go on Again" was composed by William Benjamin, Sol Marcus, and Eddie Seiler and recorded in 1943 by Vaughn Monroe. "We'll Meet Again" was recorded by Vera Lynn in 1942, and was written by Ross Parker and Hughie Charles. Both compositions have become classics of wartime popular songs.

One that I did not like at all was displayed in the post office. It was menacing, and it pointed right at my family. I hated that poster and tried to warn my parents about it, but they only shrugged their shoulders. The poster featured caricatures of Hitler, Tojo, and Mussolini. "Don't Speak the Enemies' Language!" it commanded. "Speak American!" My parents' language and, by implication, my parents, were "the Enemy." I have sometimes wondered if that poster influenced my growing resistance to speaking Italian.

We conserved and recycled everything we could for the war effort. When paper became scarce, one of our teachers, Miss McKenzie, searched her closets at home and brought in dozens of white paper plates. Happy with this novelty, we pounded them flat on our desks, making more noise than was necessary, and for several weeks wrote our assignments on those wonderfully unconventional round pages. Mr. Rittershausen, the high school principal and Troop 6 scoutmaster, supervised our collection of newspapers, aluminum pots, lead pipes, foil wrappers, metal food cans, copper wire, and rubber tires. Pulling a large, two-wheeled covered wagon that some unknown craftsman had built for us, we journeyed through Nyack collecting newspapers for the war effort, bundling and storing them in Mr. Burnweit's Pontiac agency on Main Street.

Small flags appeared in windows. A blue star in a red-bordered white rectangle showed that this home had sent a young man to war. Our own short block on Elysian Avenue displayed five flags. One day I noticed that a flag on Midland Avenue had been taken down and replaced by a gold star. Others began appearing around town. "They must be special," I thought. "Maybe we can get one for our window." I did not know yet what sadness surrounded those gold stars.[8]

The war seemed endless, and following its progress became a major daily activity. *Compare* Cervodoro no longer had his map on the wall, but *Zio* Jimmie Fiola, one of the 400,000 Italian immigrants who had served in the American military in World War I,[9] had his maps—two centerfold newspaper war-zone maps of Europe and the Pacific. Throughout the war, until his son came home, *Zio* Jimmie marked the European map wherever he thought Frank might be fighting. "It makes Frankie safe," he said, "to know where he is," but I was not sure if he really believed that. While *Zio* Jimmie marked his map on the wall and thought of his son, *Zia* Vittoria prayed for Frank in front of her candles.

Like other youngsters, I was caught up in the fear and frenzy of war. We absorbed information from our "Weekly Readers," the Saturday afternoon movie newsreels, our parents' discussions, and the trading cards that came in bubble gum packets. Each card had a color drawing of a battle, weapon, or person, and on the reverse side a brief description. We collected and

8. The blue star indicated that a person in that home was serving in the military. The gold star meant that he or she had been killed.
9. Belmonte (2001).

traded those cards, studied the pictures, and learned about the war. For example, an American pilot had dropped a single bomb right down the funnel of a Japanese cruiser and destroyed the whole ship. "So," I thought, "that's all we have to do to beat the Japs—just aim for the funnel!" It seemed easy enough.[10]

Everyone was exhorted to work for the war effort. My friends and I decided that our contribution would be to collect scrap with the Boy Scouts, watch for suspicious enemy aliens in Nyack, and become airplane spotters. Our official lookout post was the slanted roof of Mrs. Greggs's chicken coop, from which we could spot any Italian, Jap, or Nazi airplane that threatened Nyack. I studied the silhouettes, insignia, and performance facts of military aircraft of all countries, memorizing such information as armament, payload, crew requirements, maximum speed, range, and altitude. I could recite more facts about warplanes of the world than about the Yankees' batting and pitching records.

Balsa wood had "gone to war," and our model airplane kits were made of paper. We folded, rolled, cut, pasted, and produced striking paper models. Two dozen, prefinished in their authentic colors and insignia, flew tethered to my ceiling by black thread from Mom's sewing basket. Among my favorites were the Curtis P-40 with the white sharks' teeth, the gull-winged Corsair F4U, the twin-tailed P-38 Lightning, and England's DH 98 Mosquito bomber, which amazingly was constructed of plywood. When the Republic P-47 Thunderbolt was introduced, a fighter-bomber that was bigger, heavier, and faster than any built before, I excitedly told my friends about its heavy armament and unbelievable speed of 470 miles an hour![11] With that airplane we would surely win the war. My favorite, however, was the outmoded and slow (250 mph) Douglas Dauntless SBD, the dive bomber that would win the Battle of Midway in 1942, turning the war with our victory over the Japanese.

Mrs. Greggs's chicken coop began to groan under our boisterous weight, threatening the hapless chickens below, but no malevolent silhouettes appeared over Nyack. Nevertheless, we knew that ours was an important job.

In our youthful understanding of the proper order of things, wars were fought by men. We were shocked to learn that in 1942, an army unit was formed for women![12] For the first time in the United States, not counting

10. As I recall, the card identified a U.S. Navy pilot as having dropped that bomb on a Japanese ship, but I have been unable to verify this in military records. The only reference I have found is to R.A.F. Flying Officer Kenneth Richards, who destroyed a 3,000-ton German ship by dropping a bomb into its funnel. Richards received the Distinguished Flying Cross for this and other actions.
11. This was the top speed of a later version, the P-47M. The XP-47J, an experimental version that never went into production, exceeded 500 miles per hour.
12. The Women's Army Auxiliary Corps (WAACS) was formed in 1942 against great opposition. As in the rest of the military, the women were racially segregated—the few black women allowed were restricted to their own units. Other branches formed women's units, and by war's end more than 350,000 women had served. See Gruhzit-Hoyt (1995) and Merryman (1998).

the nurses' corps, women were joining the military—and causing consternation. Around kitchen tables, in churches, in Congress, and over the airways, the decadent morals of those loose women who joined the army were discussed with much sputtering, clucking, and head shaking. However, even that became an accepted normalcy of war. By 1945, 350,000 women were in U.S. military auxiliary groups.

If we were shocked by the intrusion of women into a man's war, we were incredulous on seeing a young black man walking along Main Street dressed like a soldier. "Do they really let the colored in the army?" we asked. "The colored," we learned, were indeed allowed in the army and navy, but not in the marines or the Coast Guard. Some were even given guns and sent overseas to fight. Most were assigned to kitchens, laundries, mess hall cleanup, and to be officers' personal servants. "Of course," we were told, they had to stay in their own units and "never mix with the white boys."

How had we youngsters acquired the astonishing idea that "the colored" were not allowed in the army? Largely by omission, by what we had not been told. Every patriotic poster in town, every picture in the newspaper, and, most powerfully, every Saturday matinee film with our great American military heroes, like John Wayne, showed only white men marching off to save our country. African Americans were simply not part of the universe of heroes and soldiers. This was in accord with the reality of racial segregation in the military and of the social system that we knew in 1930s and 1940s Nyack. Our amazement at seeing a black soldier was a testament to Nyack's 19th-century socialization of children in the mid-20th century. I cannot recall a single adult in Nyack criticizing or questioning military segregation practices. Even the new women's auxiliaries were segregated by color! By the social standards of Nyack, the official policy of the military, the president, the Congress, and the entire country, racial segregation in the military was, simply, "right."

We knew little about the feeble demands for integration in the military in the 1940s, and the changes that grew under the liberal influence of Eleanor Roosevelt and Harry Truman. Those World War II issues helped build the civil rights movements of the 1960s and 1970s.

But the discovery that "coloreds" were placed in segregated military units did bring back my rankling displeasure of my school's social organization.[13] Here was the A-1, B-2 social grid all over again. I had long been aware and resentful of that, not because I had empathy for the kids who were kept down in the B-2 sections, but because of its blatant unfairness to me. I would never be allowed A-1 status. Now, however, I saw that the A-1, B-2 mentality was not limited to Ol' McElroy's Liberty Street Grammar School, but pervaded the whole country. It was not about unfairness to me, an Italian kid. It was much greater, and I began to glimpse some of

13. See Chapter Nineteen.

what black kids in school, their families in those dim buildings on Franklin Street, and the segregated black soldiers must have been feeling—pretty much the same resentment that I felt, but much more so.

We remained focused on news of the fighting, on Fred's safety, and on all the men we knew who had gone to war. The country's leaders were caught up in logistics and tactics and the primary aim of destroying the enemy. For civilians, there were rationing, scrap drives, war bonds, rallies, and parades. Youngsters, all safely distanced from the battlefields and ignorant of reality, enjoyed the perverse excitement and exultation of war. Our growling imitations of tanks and airplanes, whistling bombs, exploding shells, and speeding bullets were immensely satisfying. The Saturday afternoon newsreels of enemy planes making corkscrew trails of black smoke and crashing in blinding flames made us cheer happily and caused not a single moment of thought for the men being roasted inside.

Malevolent brutality is the overriding dimension of war. That was not recognized by youngsters, or by some adults. Such is the power of rationalizing that war's inherent barbarities can be viewed through the lens of patriotism and appear noble. We knew with certainty that we, the Allies, conducted a moral and noble war. We knew, also, that the Japanese committed barbaric atrocities against civilians and soldiers. We knew little about German atrocities, and surmised that the Germans were like us, more civilized than the Japanese. There were rumors that the Germans were deporting a few people, including some Jews, to special places, but that seemed benign in comparison with the Japanese atrocities. It would not be until near the war's end and the opening of the gates at Bergen-Belsen, Buchenwald, Auschwitz-Birkenau, Dachau, and the other concentration and extermination camps that the horrors were revealed.[14] We were then filled with disbelief, revulsion, and new hatred of the Germans who had done such things.[15]

4. Hopeful Signs

After crippling the American fleet at Pearl Harbor in 1941, the Japanese continued to destroy American and British ships in the Pacific.[16] They invaded Malaya, Hong Kong, Guam, the Philippines, and Midway, and in 1942, landed on U.S. territory (the Aleutian Islands). U.S. troops surrendered unconditionally to the Japanese in the Philippines; British forces

14. The Germans had detention camps, work camps, and extermination camps throughout Europe, in which millions of people were murdered, many with cyanide gas, and cremated or bulldozed into mass graves. Gutman (1990) and Bauer (1982).

15. It was the British in the second Boer War (1899–1902) who originated the practice of incarcerating civilians into concentration camps. An estimated 220,000 civilians were imprisoned, blacks and whites in separate camps. Because of the horrendous conditions, 46,000 people died. Eighty percent of the deaths, 39,000, were children. Packenham (1979), Smith (1996).

16. From December 1941 to October 1945, the U.S. lost more than 700 vessels, including 300 major ships, in all war fronts.

surrendered in Singapore and Burma; and our Dutch allies surrendered in Java. In April, the Japanese forced 76,000 Allied prisoners on the Bataan Death March, 60 miles in blistering heat without food or water, causing 5,000 American prisoners to die along the way. In an August naval battle north of Guadalcanal, Japanese warships sank an American destroyer and four heavy cruisers. Three other Allied ships were damaged and more than 1,200 Allied crewmembers were killed in the one-hour nighttime battle—a major defeat for the Allies. Tojo was rapidly spreading his empire around the Pacific, steaming closer to our West Coast.

Across the Atlantic, the Axis armies advanced in Europe and Africa. By the time Japan attacked Pearl Harbor, the Germans had taken Austria, Czechoslovakia, Poland, Finland, Denmark, Norway, Belgium, France, Luxembourg, the Netherlands, Romania, Yugoslavia, and Greece. They were moving rapidly across Russia toward Moscow and continuing their merciless bombing of England's cities. German submarines were sinking the British navy and merchant fleet and began attacking American ships along our Atlantic Coast. The news for us was grim.

By mid-1942, however, there were hopeful signs. The Germans had gotten bogged down in the Russian snows and were retreating from Moscow—a replay of Napoleon's retreat in 1812 and that of the Germans in 1917. In 1943, the German and Italian armies surrendered in North Africa and the Allies began their assault on Sicily. The Germans retreated across the Straits of Messina, and the battle for the Italian Peninsula began.[17]

In 1942, Jimmie Doolittle led carrier-based Mitchell B-25 bombers in the first air raid on Japan. Of little strategic value, the raid was a morale booster for the Allies and a morale breaker for the Japanese. Then, in the naval and air battles of the Coral Sea and Midway, so many Japanese warplanes and ships were destroyed that Japan's planned invasion of Australia was averted, and the war in the Pacific began to turn in our favor.

It was not over, however. There remained bloody island-hopping battles for Guadalcanal, Tarawa, Kwajalein, Saipan, Guam, Leyte, Okinawa, Bataan, and Iwo Jima, bringing the Allies within a few hundred miles of Japan.

In July 1943, news of the Allies' victories in Sicily brought hope to my parents that the war might soon be over. It also caused concern, because the fighting was a short distance across the strait from Calabria, and it would not be long before the war moved into their town of Maida. We wondered if Fred would be there, in the invasion of the mainland.

In that month Mussolini's 21-year Fascist dictatorship was overthrown. The Italians had finally moved against him as *Compare* Cervodoro had hoped they would. However, this was neither a general revolution nor

17. The campaign in Sicily was a victory for the Allies. There were criticisms, however, because the Germans had been allowed to escape to the mainland instead of being forced to surrender on Sicily, thus prolonging the war.

an anti-Fascist movement. It was carried out by the Fascists themselves, who recognized that Mussolini's increasingly irrational and incompetent behavior threatened their comfortable and lucrative government positions. Mussolini had made one disastrous decision after another, and now seemed completely deluded about the war. He was increasingly superstitious, expressing fear of the "evil eye" and consulting astrologers.[18] He refused to accept the facts of Italy's lack of war resources and stubbornly rejected all advice that contradicted his delusions. In 1941, for example, believing that the war would be over in a few months, he demobilized 200,000 men while sending others into new battlefronts. In a completely irrational move, Mussolini sent his only motorized division to fight the French in the Alps, where those mobile units could not even maneuver properly. Over his generals' objections, he sent troops into France without adequate equipment and supplies. Smith notes the infamous "cardboard boots" fiasco.[19] His navy had excellent ships and crews but little fuel or ammunition, and he still expected them to defeat the powerful English navy. He ignored the fact that at the start of the war his air force had fewer than 900 operational warplanes, many of which were 1930s biplanes. (In comparison, the U.S. alone deployed 160,000 modern warplanes from 1942[20] through 1945.)[21]

Mussolini seemed unable to understand that this world war was not another small colonial venture, like the wars in Abyssinia and Albania; it required resources he did not have and demanded careful planning that he did not even recognize. When his troops ran out of ammunition, equipment, spare parts, supplies, food, and clothing and could no longer fight, he called them weaklings and cowards and blamed them and their officers for the defeats.

For 20 years, the Fascist Council (*Gran Consiglio*) had been a powerless formality. Now, seeing the growing wartime disasters and threats to its own well-being, it knew that something must be done—at least the military ought to have an opportunity to make military decisions. It voted some limits on the dictator. The military leaders, too, with their traditional allegiance to the monarchy, saw that Mussolini was a danger to them, and they too wanted to stop him.

As for the king, *la Casa Savoia* (the House of Savoy) had survived nearly 1,000 years as a ruling dynasty. For the last 83 years, it had been Italy's ruling monarchy. Its most recent kings, Umberto I and Vittorio Emanuele III, little more than figureheads, knew that their primary responsibility was to maintain the privileged status of *la Casa Savoia*, whatever else might happen to the country. In 1943, the king agreed with the council and the

18. Smith (1997), page 411. Many years later our own President Ronald Reagan, through Mrs. Reagan, reportedly also consulted an astrologer!
19. Smith (1997).
20. The FIAT CR.42 Falcon biplane was the best biplane fighter of the 1930s, but could not compete with modern 1940s warplanes.
21. Bierman and Smith (2002).

military that Mussolini must be curbed. Fearing that Mussolini's continued ineptitude not only would lose the war but, worse, might bring down his monarchy, the king appointed Marshal Pietro Badoglio, a longtime Fascist official, as the new prime minister and ordered Mussolini's arrest. The military, always loyal to the monarchy, obeyed.

This was not an anti-Fascist revolution or the creation of an enlightened democratic government. It was the king's attempt to save his Royal House of Savoy. For 20 years the king had been Mussolini's willing collaborator, granting him ever-increasing power, helping to create the Fascist dictatorship. In return, Mussolini left the monarchy alone, thus maintaining the fiction that a constitutional government with king and parliament still existed. This new, 1943 government was an association of the monarchy, military officers, rich landowners, industrialists, and virtually the entire Fascist bureaucracy. Censorship and control continued, and except for Mussolini and a few others, the same Fascist officials remained in control.

Prime Minister Badoglio declared martial law, outlawed the Fascist party while keeping former Fascists in their government posts, negotiated peace with the Allies, and declared war on Germany. By September 1943, Italy had cut ties with Germany, and what little was left of her military fought against the Germans. Italians were jubilant over Mussolini's arrest and the end of Italy's alliance with Germany.

Two months after his arrest, Mussolini was dramatically rescued by German paratroopers and installed as the head of a new Fascist regime. From 1943 into 1945, Mussolini maintained his delusions with his irrelevant Nazi puppet government in Northern Italy—*La Repubblica Sociale Italiana*—hiding from the Italian partisans and Allies. Now in command only of his puppet regime, he ordered five colleagues, including his son-in-law, Count Galeazzo Ciano, shot in the back for their insufficient support the previous year.[22]

Guido Farina, a youngster in the 1940s, described life in Southern Italy. The people were bitter over Mussolini's war and his restrictions of their lives. They resented military training for their four-year-olds and mandatory expensive uniforms to burden already poor parents. They were helpless as officials poked into their private lives and the police detained and threatened them. They hated the Fascists for telling them not only what to do and what not do, but also what to think and what not to think. Mussolini continued killing their young men and raising taxes to pay for it. Poverty was worse than ever.

People were told by soldiers on leave and men returned from Germany, where Mussolini had sent them as conscripted laborers for the Nazis, that the Germans were hateful, inhumane, and dangerous people who viewed Italians as inferior beings.

---

22. Smith (1997), page 430.

"Those are the people that Mussolini has thrown in with?" Guido's neighbors asked each other. "Is that the path we are to follow? We are Italians, not Germans!"

After the 1943 overthrow of Mussolini and the armistice with the Allies, Southern Italy became a chaotic jungle. The poor struggled to live, and thousands of soldiers sorted themselves into predators and prey. As they retreated northward, the Germans committed a mix of barbarities, seeking revenge on the Italians who had turned out Mussolini. They searched for Jews, Italian soldiers, partisans, escaped prisoners, anyone with sympathies for the Allies, and destroyed whatever they could. Italian soldiers, leaderless, wandered the south, trying to return home and avoid capture by the Germans. American and British soldiers, former prisoners in Sicily who had escaped during the Germans' retreat across the straits, tried to find their way back to their units.[23] Italian, American, and British soldiers found themselves allied, fugitives wandering together, aided by the people, eluding capture by their common enemy, the Germans.

The Germans shelled the countryside against the advancing Allies, and the Allies shelled the countryside against the retreating Germans. German airplanes bombed the countryside, American airplanes bombed the Germans, and the civilians were caught between. "The Americans came to liberate us," Guido's parents said, hiding from bombs. "Now they come to kill us."[24]

The war raged northward up the Italian Peninsula, westward from Russia, eastward across the English Channel and France, all aimed at Germany. As 1945 opened, the retreating Germans still occupied Central and Northern Italy, treating their former allies as defeated enemies.

5. Prisoners in Our Kitchen

After Italy's 1943 realignment with the Allies, a curious thing happened that briefly touched our families in Nyack—prisoners visited our kitchens. They were detainees at nearby Camp Shanks, young men from Italy who wore U.S. Army fatigues and "POW" stenciled on their jackets. Of the 425,000 prisoners of war held in the United States, 51,000 were Italian, and most of the remaining were German.[25] I do not know how many were at Camp Shanks.

After 1943, Italy was no longer our enemy and Italian prisoners were no longer held as enemy combatants. They could not be returned to the wartime chaos of Italy, so they became detainees in the U.S., but with considerable freedom. Most volunteered for work details in the camps, and some even held jobs on local farms, where they found warm acceptance by Americans.

23. Farina (1999).
24. Ibid.
25. See U.S. National Archives WWII POW Records.

They had been in war, seen and done things that I could hardly imagine, and were happy to be safely out of it and in the United States. I was 12 years old at the time, and those young men, barely beyond high school, seemed just like my brother and cousins. Some were strikingly good-looking and the young ladies in our group were pretty excited.

Two or three visited each time, unguarded and on their honor to return to camp by 5 or 6 p.m. I do not recall their names or who arranged the visits. I knew that *Compare* Cervodoro brought them from Camp Shanks to Nyack in his Pierce Arrow and made sure they returned on time. They sat in our kitchen surrounded by our family and friends, spoke in our familiar Southern Italian accents and gestures, and fit easily into our families, like visitors from another city.

Mom prepared Calabrian meals, and the young men consumed them with such pleasure and praise that we smiled and felt good just watching them enjoy a meal from home. At first, Mom was "Signora," but she soon became "Mamma" to these soldiers, most barely older than teenagers. As each *piatto* was set out, a young man would jump from his seat and give Mom another Italian hug. Pop brought his wine from the cellar, and the visitors stood appreciatively and raised their glasses to him. "*Salute!*" they said. I raised my glass of wine, being allowed to have a little, but to be honest, I preferred Pop's sweet root beer.

Our kitchen filled with friends eager to meet the young men and talk about Italy and the war. The soldiers hoped to return to America someday, to live here just like us. Mussolini, they said, had long ago become Italy's hated man. Hitler was more a demon than human, and the Fascists were greedy and repressive. The Germans, they said, were not civilized, and their soldiers were "like machines, without souls, never thinking, never feeling, only obeying. We are Italians," they said, "not Germans. The German way is not our way," they repeated. It was "Hitler's war. Mussolini's war. Those madmen pushed us all in it. It was our mistake to join Hitler."

I do not recall who asked the question that every adult had thought about for so long: "But if you know that Mussolini was so bad, then how did you let him take over the country, tie everybody up like that? Lead you by the nose? How?"

The question brought silence around the table. "I don't know," the young men finally answered. Then, defensively, they tried to explain. "We were not even born yet when Mussolini started. We were maybe four, five years old when he was already dictator! What could we do? It was already too late."

They spoke with sadness and shame about the greed of the men of their own government and the shameful weakness of the king, their parents, and the whole country, for having let themselves fall to this terrible level. Italians, they said, had only themselves to blame. They hoped that their country had learned a lesson.

"To tell the truth," they confessed, "we had no more heart to fight for Mussolini." They spoke of the demoralized troops forced to fight without weapons or supplies and then blamed for failure. "In North Africa we been fighting long enough. We could not wait for the Americans to get close enough so we could surrender to them. That was where we would find honor in this war, by telling Mussolini to go to hell, not by starving in the desert to die for him."

"What about the Germans?" someone asked. "They didn't surrender."

"The Germans. They always said they were strong, they would never surrender, they would fight to the last man. But when the time came in the Sahara Desert and the Germans, too, had no more water and felt the dry rasp of thirst they, too, surrendered by the tens of thousands, right along with us."[26]

"And," one young man added, "I think maybe the German soldiers knew by then Hitler was crazy, too, another madman like Mussolini."

Despite such depressing talk, their visits were celebrations, harmonious reconnections among people who had for too long been at odds. I recall only two visits, although there may have been more. By war's end in 1945, the young men would be returned to Italy and, like all the other strangers who had visited our kitchen, disappeared from our lives.

6. The Anti-Fascist Revolution

The Allies liberated the south. The Germans retreated and occupied Central and Northern Italy. For two years, Allied troops and 200,000 Italian partisans fought the Germans.[27] Following Mussolini's removal in 1943, the German occupation forces retaliated against their former allies, executing partisans and searching for escaped Italian soldiers.

Until late 1943, Jewish refugees from German-occupied areas had been relatively safe in Italy and Italian territories. Italians had refused to join the Germans' genocide and had not allowed the deportations of Jews.[28] However, in 1943, the Germans, now the occupiers of Italy, asserted their racial policies of arresting and deporting Jews from Italy.

During the German occupation, an estimated 10,000 Italian Jews were rounded up in Italy and sent to concentration camps, where nearly all were murdered. From 1943 to June 1944, some 1,800 Roman Jews were murdered in extermination camps. It was a brutal occupation and genocide. However, thousands of Jewish Italians, particularly those who were citizens of Rome, were protected and hidden by Italian partisans and families, and survived the occupation. In all, with the help of partisans, citizens, and

26. In May 1943, the combined German and Italian armies surrendered in North Africa.
27. It is estimated that by late 1945 as many as 200,000 Italian partisans fought against the Germans in Central and Northern Italy, attacking and pinning down German divisions as the Allies fought northward. See Smith (1997), page 421, and Wilhelm (1988).
28. Holocaust Encyclopedia (2007).

government officials, more than 40,000 Jewish Italian citizens and refugees survived the holocaust in Italy.[29]

Questions remain about the complicity of Italians in the Germans' slaughter of Jews and others, and of the role of the Church, particularly of Pius XII, the pope throughout the war and beyond (1939–1958). Many claim that, in order to protect itself, the Church actively helped the Germans or did little to protect the victims.[30] However, partisans and Italian families did much, at high personal risk, to protect and save tens of thousands of targeted Italian Jews.[31]

Several points[32] seem clear: 1. From the start of the Holocaust in the 1930s, Pius XI, Pius XII, and other Church officials knew of the Germans' atrocities; 2. numerous official in-person appeals were made to the pope by the world's religious and government officials, asking for a public denunciation of the atrocities; 3. the pope repeatedly refused, asserting the Church's official position of "neutrality" on the issue of Jewish persecution; 4. at no time did the pope or the Church take a clear, moral public stand to denounce the atrocities and demand their end; 5. many Church officials, priests, and nuns, as well as private citizens, worked clandestinely to protect potential victims by hiding them in monasteries and other cloisters, helping them change identities and helping many to escape to safer places; and 6. Pope Pius XII quietly ordered some of those actions. Many were successful, thus suggesting that he could have done even more, had he chosen.

In defense of the popes, it is claimed that a public denunciation of the atrocities would have triggered terrible reprisals, causing even more death and destruction, and that the popes acted behind the scenes and saved many thousands from deportation and death. Perhaps they did, but might not a more vigorous, courageous public stand and assertion of their avowed humanitarian and Christian values have saved more people, perhaps changed history? We must wonder what might have happened had Pius XII instructed his 400 million Catholics around the world to oppose the brutal slaughter. What might have been the impact had the pope been courageous enough to offer himself to the Germans, saying, "Stop the slaughter or do to me what you have done to my fellow human beings!" It is a naive idea, I suppose, a pope offering himself to martyrdom, but might it have changed the course of events?

By April 1945, Allied victory in Europe was near. By war's end, tens of millions of people had been killed. In that month, however, the deaths of just three persons demanded the world's attention. On April 12, 1945, so

29. Farina (1999).
30. For example, Cornwell (1999) and Zimmerman (2005).
31. For example, Gallo (2006), Dalin (2005), and Smith (1997).
32. For example, Bauer (1982), Cornwell (1999), Dalin (2005), Gallo (2006), Gutman (1990), Holocaust Encyclopedia (2007), and Zimmerman (2005).

near to victory, President Roosevelt died of a cerebral hemorrhage. Just weeks earlier he had returned, fatigued and ill, from a summit conference at Yalta. FDR, Churchill, and Stalin had met to discuss the war's end and postwar issues of territories, reparations, and the development of a United Nations organization.

On April 26, 1945, two weeks after Roosevelt's death, Mussolini was captured by Italian partisans near Lake Como as he and his mistress, Clara Petacci, tried to escape across the border. The anti-Fascist revolution had reached its peak in the partisans' hatred of Mussolini. This time, the rebellion against Mussolini was a true revolution of the people, not a contrived tactic by the Fascists, the king, and the military to save their own skins. On April 28, the partisans executed Mussolini, Petacci, and a dozen other Fascist leaders. The bodies of the dictator and Petacci were hung upside down in Milan's Piazza Loreto, a brutal statement of the people's loathing for Mussolini and his *fascisti*.

Two days later, on April 30, as Russian troops neared, Hitler murdered Eva Braun, his long-time mistress and wife of just a few days. He killed her with poison, and shot himself in the head. Earlier he had poisoned his little dog, Biondi, presumably to test the substance that he was planning for himself and Braun. Eight days later, on May 7, 1945, Germany surrendered.[33]

Millions of Americans mourned for Roosevelt, their revered president who had brought working people through the Depression and led the country to victory in the war. Newspapers and newsreels were filled with images of weeping Americans standing along the railroad tracks from Warm Springs, Georgia, where he died, to Hyde Park, New York, as the funeral train slowly steamed northward for FDR's burial.

In contrast, Italians celebrated Mussolini's death, cheered his executioners, and praised their God for the dictator's removal from their lives. There was little mourning for the man they had come to despise.

The war with Japan continued another three months. On August 6, by order of President Harry Truman, the first atomic bomb was dropped on Hiroshima, and three days later the second was dropped on Nagasaki. Japan surrendered on August 14, 1945. World War II was over. More than 62 million people had been killed.

7. The Ice Man's Customers Melt Away

The horrors of German concentration camps continued unfolding. In our family, however, safely distant from those terrible events, 1945 to 1950 were five good years. Most of Nyack's young men had come home. Fred had returned safely and married Marie. I was 13 in 1945 and had been working for more than a year with Bill Pozefsky, riding high on the curved

---

33. A classic book, highly recommended, is Shirer (1962).

front fender of the old Chevy or standing on the running board as we circulated through Nyack, selling fruits and vegetables. My job was to help load and unload the truck, carry purchases into kitchens, keep Bill company as we drove from one street or town to the next, and watch that mischievous kids did not steal our apples. In the summertime, we loaded the truck at 6 a.m. and began our rounds. During the school year, I traveled with Bill on Saturdays, met his truck after school, and helped him complete his route and unload at night, getting home after dark.

It was a heady experience, a nomadic freedom of movement through town, the independent feeling of being a real working man. When I returned home at night, I was not a 13-year-old tired out from playing, but a wage-earning young man helping to support my family. For my labors Bill paid me $6 to $12 each week, depending on my hours. I dutifully—and proudly—handed my wages to Mom, who accepted my contribution to the family's well-being. It was our weekly ceremony in recognition of my growing maturity and responsibility for adult things.

Produce was always left over after we unloaded the truck on Saturday night. Bill's family used some of it, and Bill gave me an overflowing bushel basket, a cornucopia of fresh food to take home. It was an enormously satisfying experience to return home on Saturday night with my dollars in my pocket and that bushel basket on my shoulder, filled with fresh peas, beans, lettuce, peaches, peppers, and tomatoes. It was particularly satisfying when I walked into our kitchen and found not only my parents, but friends or relatives. When I set the overflowing bushel on the floor, everyone saw with approval that I was now a family provider, a good son shouldering family responsibilities, *un uomo, veramente* (truly a man)!—the highest praise a boy could then receive in those Italian families. Mom shared the abundance, and I remember how much *Comare* Bettina Lanzana particularly liked the crisp, fresh peas.

I worked regularly with Bill for just over three years, and then one weekend, as he relaxed at home, my employer and friend died. I had not even known he was ill. It was a crushing, sad time.

One reward of working with Bill was being part of the colorful cadre of Nyack's mobile vendors, briefly sharing in that vibrant culture that had helped drive Nyack's life for half a century. By the 1950s, however, it was over. People had become more affluent, sophisticated, and mobile in the postwar boom. New cars were on the roads, and people no longer needed the roving merchants. Refrigerators replaced iceboxes, and the Ice Man's customers melted away. Wally the Bread Man and his green Model A stopped at our street for the last time. All the itinerant vendors and their wares disappeared as if they had marched off in silent procession, led perhaps by the plodding old milk-wagon horse that had always looked so tired.

V

Promises Kept

Chapter 25

Good Years (Nyack, 1945–1950)

1. Liberal Legislation at Its Best

The war was over. America grieved for the 407,000 men and women who would never return. Our weariness of war merged into a greater excitement for peace, and the armistice presented a new beginning. Veterans returned, thousands through Camp Shanks, their jumping-off point to war just a few years earlier. They were heroes to us, unassuming, saying little about their war experiences and nothing about their heroism. Consider Joe Conace, best man at my brother's wedding. Joe's father, *Zio* Antonio, an immigrant, had served with the U.S. Army in World War I. Joe's parents were among my family's closest friends and shared hours socializing in our kitchen. Wounded in France, Joe was awarded many military honors including the Purple Heart, the Conspicuous Service Medal, the Bronze Star for "heroic achievement in combat," and, years later, the French *Legion d'honneur*, given at that time to only 16 veterans of the war. None of us knew that until 62 years later. Joe was 84 in 2007, when a newspaper reporter discovered the story of our local hero.[1] In 1946, when Joe and his brother Gregory returned from the war, Joe had just wanted to get on with his life with his bride, Vickie.[2]

Families were reunited, empty spaces filled. We were energized by images of a brilliant future. Each day, it seemed, a young veteran launched a new business—my cousin Joe's grocery store in Central Nyack, the Pugliese brothers' plumbing company, Jerry D'Auria's tobacco shop, a radio repair shop, a new pharmacy, a new restaurant, young Dr. Ingrassia's new practice. Veterans rattled by in prewar cars, horns blowing, white streamers flowing, tin cans bouncing, and "Just Married" painted all over. Even strangers waved, sharing the happiness. Young men reclaimed old jobs, began new jobs, entered school and training programs. New houses sprouted all over the county and suburbs expanded, eating up the old farms, and there was work for everyone. The mills were running; people filled the stores, buying

1. Padnani (2007).
2. Belmonte (2001) has estimated that in World War I, 300,000 to 400,000 Italian-Americans, most of them immigrants, served in the American military, and between 500,000 and 1,500,000 served in World War II.

everything in sight. The radical, low-slung 1947 Studebakers and Kaisers appeared, and a high-spirited little renaissance blossomed in Nyack.

In 1945, Fred came home from the war, married Marie, and lived with us at 79 Elysian Avenue before moving to a fifth-floor walk-up in New York City's Lower East Side. Pop happily took up his tools and added a new bedroom and bathroom for them, swallowing Fred's bookshelf and shrinking our back yard that much more. Pop also built a larger bedroom for me just off the front hall and turned my old, tiny room into the family's bathroom.

Fred's bookshelf had served well as his de facto university since 1939. Now, he would attend a real university thanks to the G.I. Bill, the Servicemen's Readjustment Act of 1944.[3] In 1943, FDR's National Resources Planning Board predicted unemployment at war's end for 15 million returning veterans. FDR feared a repeat of the errors following the First World War—the desperation of unemployed veterans, Hoover's shameful 1932 act of sending tanks and machine guns against American veterans and their families, and, of course, the Great Depression.

Determined to avoid those Republican postwar catastrophes, Roosevelt outlined new legislation. The American Legion, by no means a liberal group, took up FDR's ideas. Working with the Democrats, they drafted a bill to fund veterans' education and training; home, farm, and business purchases; and health and unemployment insurance, and guided it through Congress. It was an extraordinary and brilliant social contribution, liberal legislation at its best. Unfortunately, it was the last of Roosevelt's New Deal. In concept, it was like the WPA that had helped millions survive the Depression.[4] While conservative politicians still clung to the "trickle-down" approach of first aiding the wealthy, FDR's liberals and the American Legion understood the value of putting federal money into the hands of ordinary people.

The proposed legislation was criticized as ushering in socialism. Handouts, they said, would only "encourage sloth," "create a welfare state," and "keep men from seeking jobs." The universities, they warned, would be swamped.[5] The president of an Ivy League university argued that it would allow the "most unqualified people of this generation" to go to college.[6] Those "unqualified people" were, of course, the veterans who had just saved him and his family from Fascism! I don't suppose one should expect gratitude from everyone. Nor do I expect to find many more blatantly

---

3. For discussions of this legislation and its impact on the United States, see Bennett (1996), Greenberg (1997), Keane (2001), Mettler (2005), Olson (1974), Roach (1997), and Ross (1969).
4. See discussion of the WPA in Chapter Fifteen.
5. Conservatives were opposed to this legislation; their criticisms have been discussed by Bennett (1966), Goodwin (2000), Greenberg (1997), Mettler (2005), and others.
6. Recalled by historian Doris Kearns Goodwin in a televised discussion on *The News Hour* with Jim Lehrer, "Remembering the G.I. Bill," July 4, 2000.

undemocratic and ungrateful statements than that one.

The bill easily passed in the House and the Senate, but nearly died in conference committee, surviving by a single, tie-breaking vote. FDR signed it into law on June 22, 1944. It would not have succeeded without the American Legion's extraordinary efforts.[7]

Some historians consider the G.I. Bill "the best piece of legislation ever passed by the U.S. Congress."[8] A generation of young men and women from blue-collar families, with little hope of higher education—like my brother—could now afford college and enter the professions. In 10 years, eight million veterans received education and/or job training benefits. University enrollment doubled; the housing industry, business, professions, and the entire American middle class were expanded and reshaped. The G.I. Bill had an enormous impact, bringing more people into the middle class than has any other congressional action. One of our greatest liberal, democratizing policies, it transformed the country and powered the American postwar renaissance.

The system had weaknesses, not in concept, but in its uneven application. All veterans were included, but decisions about who would receive funds were made locally—with prejudice and favoritism often mixed in. Many black veterans found themselves facing bankers who refused to give them loans and universities that refused to admit them. Local customs of discrimination distorted the intent of the legislation, and although some African American veterans and their families did benefit,[9] thousands were barred from this historically unparalleled democratizing process.

We knew nothing of the system's bigotry, recognizing only its advantages. My father, with his three years of school a half-century earlier, and Mom, with her self-taught literacy, saw Fred's high school diploma and enrollment in Columbia University as a marvelous accomplishment that was unimaginable in their former world. "Only in America, *la bell'America*," they said, can such splendid things occur for so many ordinary people.

2. Bobby and the Baby Brownie

In the 1930s, college was unlikely for youngsters like my brother and me. Sons of Italian immigrants were guided into a man's world of work, taught to earn money to help the family. As a youngster, I earned nickels and dimes from neighbors—shoveling ashes from furnaces, rolling trash barrels to the curb, clearing snow, mowing lawns, working magazine and newspaper routes, and even taking Patrick Henry Hartwick—our neighbor's frisky little brown dog—for walks around the block.

---

7. Fifteen years later, Republican president Dwight D. Eisenhower, the same man who fought the veterans in 1932, opposed extending the G.I. Bill to the peacetime military.
8. Historian Steven Ambrose, in a televised discussion on *The News Hour* with Jim Lehrer, "Remembering the G.I. Bill," July 4, 2000.
9. Roach (1997).

We also thought up money-making schemes. Most fizzled out, but one was a great success. Around my 10th birthday, I answered an advertisement in a comic book for selling chances on punch cards. The prize was a new camera for the winner and another as the seller's commission. My sales packet arrived—two punch cards, instructions, a page for record keeping, and an envelope to mail in the names, addresses, and money. Each card held a hundred small, perforated circles, 200 in all. It cost 25 cents—a lot of money, I thought—to punch out a circle and reveal the number beneath. With both cards sold, I would have $50 to mail to the company, which would determine the winner and ship the prizes. I did not even know 200 people, so I invited my older and wiser friend Bobby Greggs to join me. Together, we would surely find enough willing chance takers.

Door-to-door selling was tough going, but we made progress. One afternoon, as we walked past the pharmacy on Main Street, Bobby stopped and stared into the window. I saw a crafty look gathering on his face. It usually meant trouble.

"What?" I asked.

"Look," he said, pointing to a black plastic Kodak Baby Brownie camera on sale for $5, complete with a roll of film.

"So?" I asked.

"So, this," Bobby said, poking his palm for emphasis. "We sell all the chances and get $50 right?"

"Um, OK."

"Then, we buy that camera for $5, and give it to the winner."

"Ahh," I said, looking at him with admiration, seeing where he was going with that idea.

Bobby continued, "We're doin' all the work, right?"

"Right!"

"So, we really don't hafta give the money to the company, right? And we get to keep"—he counted on his fingers—"$45! That's, um. . . ."—he went back to his fingers—"20, 21, no, 22 ... $22 and . . . um . . . um . . . 50 cents: $22.50 each!"

"Wow!" I said, sold on Bobby's scheme, trying to picture $22.50 in my pocket.

Wasting no time, we put down a dollar on the camera and asked George, the pharmacist, to set it aside for us. George refused to buy a chance, saying it would not be right if he won. Energized, we sold all the chances, happily counted the $50, and ran into our first problem.

"How do we know who's supposed to win?" I asked. Even Bobby was stumped, so we took our problem to Bobby's brother, Glenn, who was home on leave from the army. "Write the numbers on pieces of paper," Glenn said. "Put 'em in a hat, close your eyes, and pick one out, and there's your winner."

"I got a hat!" Bobby said, running into his house and emerging a few moments later with a baseball cap, two pencils, and a box of his mother's very expensive embossed stationery, which we tore up into small pieces. We carefully copied the numbers from the punch cards onto those 200 bits of fine stationery, tossed them into Bobby's hat, and stirred them up with a little stick. To be absolutely fair, we asked Glenn to close his eyes and select the winning number, which turned out to belong to my cousin Mary, who lived on the corner of Elysian Avenue and Maple Street.

Mary was pleased to have won, but suspicious, because the little camera that we gave her did not look like the impressive one pictured on the punch card. Bobby and I divided the remaining money, $22.50 each, and strutted around like big business tycoons. We even pretended to smoke fat cigars, which were really brown cattails that grew in the old ice pond. We had several hanging on the cellar door, drying. Our sales enterprise was so successful that we planned to send for more punch cards and rake in even more money. "Man, oh man!" we told each other. "We'll be rich!"

"You know," Glenn said, overhearing our plans to become millionaires. "What you did is illegal, and if they catch you, they'll probably throw you in jail for the rest of your lives."

That was a sobering thought. Each of us had suspected perhaps a bit of shadiness in our scheme but hadn't wanted to raise the issue. Now, with our new honesty, we decided to forgo the punch-card scheme and seek our fortunes in other ways. But that's another story.

Another problem arose. Having equated illegality and sinfulness, I confessed our enterprise to Father Farrelly. He told me to repent, say 10 Hail Marys, and consider giving the tainted money to some good charity. Bobby thought that was pretty funny, because he had no such problem; he was a Protestant.

As we grew older, we progressed to more formalized work. For example, local farmers hired youngsters to pick crops. We gathered early in the mornings at the corner of Main Street and Midland Avenue, waiting for the farmer's truck with its open back and wooden-stake sides. We climbed up and, standing as we rode, were transported to the farmland to spend the day picking peas, beans, peppers, or tomatoes, depending on the season. I recall that a bushel of string beans, for which we had to work a rather long time, brought 20 or 30 cents. There was always a brief debate when we presented each filled basket to the overseers. They shook our bushels vigorously, until the beans settled down below the rim, then sent us back among the rows to pick more and top off the basket with a generous mound of additional string beans.

"But that's more than a bushel!" we complained.

"That's the way it is," they said, recording the transactions in their little books.

It was not onerous work. The farmers treated us well, and except for standing up in the open truck as it drove along the highway, we faced no dangers. It seemed a rather nice country outing, and we created as much fun for ourselves as we could. We noted that some of the older adolescents sneaked off, two-by-two, and we could hear them giggling. The youngsters among us had only an incomplete notion of what was going on between the bean rows. I am not sure that our employment was even legal, but it was a fact of growing up in working-class Nyack. I had no idea that I was experiencing a pale echo of my father's 19th-century world of child labor—from which he had escaped by coming to *la bell'America*.

My next step in training for a life of work was taken in 1943 when, at age 12, I began working with Bill Pozefsky on his rounds through town selling fruits and vegetables.[10] By 1945, Fred was home from the war, married, and enrolled in Columbia—an impossibility turned reality. I too had an academic transition, from grammar school to middle school, a new building and new principal. I had moved on, and had survived Ol' McElroy's grammar school cauldron—she and her coiled strap were out of my life.

The A-1, B-2 social class divisions remained through middle school, and the same kids were assigned to the same high and low status groups. In my freshman year, however, classes became more democratic, and I finally met my A-1 schoolmates on academically, but not socially, level ground.

For my parents, our completing high school was an imperative. The immigrants' discovery long ago that *l'uomo che sa leggere sta bene in America*[11] was taken seriously. When they found a full 12 years of free education offered to everyone, they gratefully accepted it as another wonderful resource provided by this country. By coming to America, they had discarded their old restrictions and had stepped up to a higher standard for their children.

Prior to the G.I. Bill, the career path for most Italian boys was to complete high school and "find a good job" in a local mill. That was true for me, step by step, starting with jobs at home, informal work for neighbors, hiring out as a field hand, caddying for golfers at the Rockland Country Club, running a newspaper route, delivering the then-popular weekly magazine the *Saturday Evening Post*, and clearing snow from the town's fire hydrants. Regular part-time work began with Bill, followed by after-school and Saturday hours in Cousin Joe's grocery store, working the concession stand at nighttime minor league baseball games, and washing dishes and bussing tables at the Rockland Country Club, to name some of the jobs. With some of my more affluent classmates, I attended dances at the country club. They danced; I cleared tables and washed dishes.

As a senior in high school, I moved up to working with a contractor, razing old buildings. I discovered that demolishing old structures, wielding crowbars, and swinging sledgehammers without the demands of turning out finely crafted work appealed to my adolescent vigor and my idea of what real men did.

10. See Chapter Twenty-Four for a description of this job.
11. Meaning "the literate man does well in America." See Chapter Eight.

My parents were clear on the relative importance of work and school, both being necessary preparation for a successful adult life in *la bell'America*. When conflicts occurred, such as during examination periods, school took precedence. They had little realistic expectation of affording college for their sons, but demanded that we finish high school, thus moving from the level of *bracciante, giornalieri,* and *contadini* to a level approaching *il gentiluomo.*

Lest I create the impression that life was all study and after-school jobs, let me say that it was not. With the enviable energy of youth, my friends and I participated in all the adolescent rites—clubs, dating, socializing, varsity athletics, keeping old Fords, Chevys, and Plymouths running, unveiling the mysteries of sex, and getting into various kinds of trouble. The latter was carefully kept from my parents, just as I had never told them about Ol' McElroy in grammar school. Bobby Greggs, Freddie Ogden, Eddie Verville, and I frequently conspired, in various combinations at different times, to skip school and sneak off to do more interesting things.[12] Later, as older adolescents, we veered toward some stupidly dangerous activities on our days of truancy, usually involving cars, but that's another story.

The days stolen with Bobby were often instructive. (It was Bobby who had thought up our punch-card get-rich scheme.) One of our repeated adventures was to cross the Hudson River on the Nyack-to-Tarrytown ferry, a small motor launch that carried about a dozen passengers. The captain of the ferry was a circumspect man who accepted our 25-cent fare and never questioned why we were on his boat and not in school. Our school day was then devoted to exploring the Hudson's eastern bank, up and down the hills of Tarrytown, safely distanced from our principal, Mr. Rittershausen. We were careful to return to Nyack's shores by three o'clock to join our homeward-bound schoolmates, in innocence, as if we had been with them all day.

On our most memorable crossing of the river, Bobby and I determined to find the gravesite of Washington Irving, whose stories about Rip Van Winkle and the Headless Horseman we had read in school. After asking directions and searching through Tarrytown, we climbed to the top of a hill and stared in disbelief at an unkempt family gravesite and a thin, slanted old stone so weathered that its carving was hard to read.

"Look!" we said, our indignation swelling. "It's full of weeds, and the tombstone's falling down, and the railing is all rusty and busted. Somebody better fix the place up!"

"That's no way to treat a famous writer!" Bobby complained to a friendly counterman when we stopped that afternoon for a five-cent soda before rushing to meet the ferry.

---

12. These often-in-trouble kids nevertheless completed high school. Bobby eventually retired from a long U.S. Air Force career, Freddie became a college director of academic computing, Eddie became a physician, and Anthony became a university professor.

"You're right," he answered, slapping his palm on the counter. "And I'm gonna do something about it! And you know," he added, leaning close and whispering so no one else could hear, although no one else was there, "down the street"—he pointed—"on the next corner is the very spot where the horrible ghostly horseman threw his head at poor, terrified Ichabod Crane!"

Energized by that information, we finished our sodas, dashed down the street and, standing on the corner, dared the "horrible ghostly horseman" to "just try" and scare us. Of course we knew it was only fiction, but it was great fun.

We never returned to find out if that man really did fix up the monument. Moreover, when we touched Nyack's shore, we realized that we could not boast to our teachers or anyone else about our discovery of Tarrytown's shabby treatment of Washington Irving, because that would reveal our truancy! So with great discipline, we reined in our excitement and kept our discovery secret, until now revealed only to that anonymous counterman and the ferry-boat captain.

Fifty-five years later, in 1997, North Tarrytown was designated as Sleepy Hollow. This historically interesting place was refurbished and Washington Irving rediscovered. I like to believe that so many years earlier Bobby and I, and our friend the counterman, had influenced that revival.

3. The College Alternative

By 1945, five years before I graduated from high school, while I was working with Bill Pozefsky and occasionally crossing the river with Bobby, Fred's enrollment in Columbia had raised our expectations of higher education to a new level. Fred's new status brought an enormous measure of *rispetto* to our family. It generated pride in my parents, marked a significant success for them, and helped to define who we were in America. Their pride in Fred's acceptance by Columbia may be difficult to understand today, when college attendance is so commonplace and many youngsters assume, without much hard thought or, too often, effort, that they will attend college. In 1940, that was not the case—only the privileged attended university. Fred's acceptance to college was an immense achievement for Michele and Theresa, magnified by their certainty that Columbia was not "just another college," but the world's preeminent university. That their son had been accepted was a family honor, and it helped to ease much of the disdain that they, as immigrants, had borne for so many years. The scales were shifting, finally. Our family's *onore* was one of the many unpredicted bonuses of the marvelous G.I. Bill that my parents credited to their revered *Presidente Rosabelta*.

When Fred started at Columbia, I was entering the eighth grade and was well into my workingman's career path, in my third year of working with Bill Pozefsky after school. Fred's admission was an overwhelming and happy event, so much affecting our family's view of itself that college as a possibility for me was becoming less remote. The workingman image, however, was still paramount.

By my senior year, the college alternative began to rival my march toward The Mill. Fred had graduated from Columbia and was studying medicine at New York University, still on the G.I. Bill. "You know," he advised me, "you should apply. Columbia needs another Graziano." I took the requisite standardized tests, filled out the application, and, to the astonishment of the guidance counselor (who had recommended that I might try a local junior college) and all but two of my teachers, Columbia admitted me.[13]

By then, however, I was well along the route to work and was looking forward to independence and a steady paycheck. The college option was but an alternative to my main direction.

4. Dancing with Florence

After high school graduation, I was ready for my first full-time adult job, which I started at The Mill. Like most new hires, I began, as my father had in 1922, in that malodorously toxic and hot introduction to factory life, the Glue Room.[14] After a month, I was moved to another department, one of the noisier places in The Mill. I was taught to fan flat boxes into the feeder of a long machine that roared with blurring speed, spitting still-flattened boxes—now complete with scored lines, cut-outs, and glued-in cellophane windows—into the hands of a co-worker at the other end. As the feeder, I was the responsible operator of the machine, aware that a careless, slightly askew insertion of cardboard would impact the bowels deep in the machine, destroying many boxes in the split second before I slammed my palm onto the red panic button to cut the power.

While the machine was shut down, cleared, and reset, production time would be lost. But even worse was the sledgehammer abuse that pounded down upon one's head, hurled by Florence, the floor boss.[15] "Dancing with Florence" we called it. Her job was to keep the machines running, and woe to any man who interfered. Florence was the toughest lady I had ever met, tougher even than Ol' McElroy, because Florence's job was to abuse grown men, not little boys. I wondered sometimes what it would be like to put Florence and Ol' McElroy in a roped ring and let them go at each other. I liked thinking that Ol' McElroy, even wielding her coiled leather strap, would have been humiliated, decimated, flattened, scored, punched out, and stripped, just like one of The Mill's cardboard boxes. Go, Florence!

---

13. Vivian Krum, chairperson of the school's biology department, and Robert Schilds, teacher of history and social studies, had always been particularly encouraging of my academic work. It was Miss Krum who interceded on my behalf following our most flagrant truancy escapade, bringing the punishment down to sub-draconian levels.
14. The Glue Room is described in Chapter Twelve.
15. Florence was the only woman in that department, and one of the few in the entire mill.

I proudly joined the union, paid my dues, ran my machine, and, like everyone else in the hot Stamping Room, oozed gallons of sweat. Blue-and-white dispensers encouraged us to swallow large salt tablets with plenty of water from the cooler. My first day at the machine seemed interminable, and the next morning I awoke with throbbing wrists and hands stiffened into the splayed up-and-down positions needed to fan thick cardboard into the feeder eight hours a day. My hands adapted to the machine's demands, and soon I was dancing with Florence no more frequently than any other machine operator. At noon I ate the lunch Mom had packed, played nickel poker with my co-workers, smoked unfiltered Camel cigarettes, and exchanged lies about weekend sexual triumphs. Every two weeks, we lined up at the pay window.

My father worked in another part of the factory, but once or twice each day he walked through my area, just to make contact with me. I was too busy tending my machine to stop and talk, but I was happy to know he was there. One morning I was enormously embarrassed when Pop walked through just as I had jammed my machine and was in the middle of a dance with Florence. When Florence saw my father, she stopped her tirade and helped me clear and reset the machine. I think she did that out of respect for Pop. He and Uncle Joe were older workers, men still at The Mill after nearly 30 years. I do not know what my co-workers thought of Florence's special treatment of me, but I felt protected by my father's presence.

For years Pop had been a stripper at The Mill, a job title that I thought was pretty funny. It was a tough job, however, standing over a dense pile of flat boxes that were tightly strapped together, using a heavy pneumatic drill to pound down through the pile and strip out each of the scored areas that needed to be removed. A slight misalignment of the heavy, rapidly firing drill, and 50 boxes could be ruined. About two years before I began working at The Mill, Pop's age—nearly 60—and declining health had prompted his supervisor to assign him to less strenuous work, in the Maintenance Department. At that time the union was strong, The Mill's management was responsive, and the workers were treated well.

Uncle Joe sometimes drove to work, coming by at 6 a.m. in his 1940 brown Chevrolet. Pop and I climbed in with two other workers, and we rode the few miles to The Mill. I marveled at Uncle Joe's deft, one-armed maneuvering of the car. At The Mill, I saw him throughout each day, sitting high up in his massive yellow forklift, the one-armed master of that powerful machine. Expertly guiding its huge prongs into the slots of the laden pallets, he lifted them, backing and turning the big truck with precision, and safely carrying the load, threading his way through long aisles of busy men, roaring machines, and stacked pallets. The three of us, I thought, were Graziano family representatives, a mini-union of our own. It was satisfying, being included, and I gradually settled into the life of a working man.

As weeks became months and the paychecks continued, my college option seemed to fade. It was my parents who kept reminding me, saying I had better decide soon; Columbia was not going to wait forever for my answer. "But Columbia's real expensive," I said. "I'll work for a year, save money, then maybe I'll go to college."

"Here," Mom said. Pop smiled. Mom handed me a slim little book, with my name handwritten on the cover. "We alla' time know you was go to college," she said.

"Nyack Savings and Loan Association, Certificate No. 6081" was typed across the top. It was a savings account with enough money for tuition and fees for my first two semesters at Columbia, that very expensive rich man's Ivy League college. Here were the nickels, dimes, quarters, and dollar bills that I had earned and turned over to Mom for so many years, my manly contributions to the family, of which I had been so proud. While I believed that I had been helping to pay the family's bills, my parents had been quietly depositing the money for me, for college.

Mom read my mixed feelings of surprise and pleasure, and my disappointment at learning that I had not been so important a family provider after all. As usual, she smoothed it out for me. "Sometimes," Mom said, "we hafta use some of you money to pay the bills. Is good thing you give to us, no? But mostly, is all here."

5. Good Years, Michele's Promises Kept

The six years of 1945 through 1950 were good years for Michele and Theresa. The war was over, Fred was safely home and married, and our family was together again. We merged with Marie's family—sister, parents, uncles, aunts, and grandparents. Family gatherings became even more warmly crowded around the dinner tables. Marie's grandparents, now in their 80s, had immigrated in the 1920s from Eastern Europe, and they were the oldest of our family. A dozen or more persons, stretched across four generations, sat at our dinner tables. With my complicity, my friends Bobby and Freddie often wormed their way to our crowded table, sharing a single chair to fit in. Good friends, like the Conaces, Fiolas, Cervodoros, Serratores, and Lanzanas, dropped by in the afternoon, increasing the crowding and the conversation.

Mom prepared her Sunday family feast. People arrived around noon and antipasti were set out. As was the custom, the women helped set the table and serve food while the men sat around, sipped wine, and discussed politics. The next day, while the men were back at work, the women had their afternoon coffee. The many course dinner began about 1:00 and continued through dessert, coffee, cheese, fruit, nuts, and liquors until around 5:00. Soon after, Mom would ask, only partly in jest, "Who's ready for supper?

Conversation around the table never lagged. When one person slowed, three others picked it up. Everyone had strong opinions on everything.

Despite the hard work, Mom was pleased to create the meals she set on the table. "*Mangia, mangia*," she urged, although we needed no urging. Pop was *il capo di tavola*, pleased with knowing that in America he had become, in fact, *u padronu*, beaming proudly in his quiet way over everyone's pleasure at the welcoming table.

It had been a long, half-century journey from poverty in Maida, and these recent few years in Nyack were a time to reflect, relax, and enjoy. They had traveled the ocean, survived the long economic depression, and, sadly, known grief when death came to loved ones, some much too young. Life in Calabria had been intensely social, filled with daily reassertions of warm ties. What, after all, was the purpose of life? They had feared it would be lost in America, but it had not been. The little Southern Italian community they created in Nyack enveloped them in friendship and affection, an echo of Maida, like a big, extended family.

They were proud of their successes—citizenship in 1927 for Pop and in 1943 for Mom, and home-ownership. Michele had delivered on his promise to Theresa of so many years ago: "I promise you a big, beautiful house in America, with many rooms, like none in Maida! ... You will have *una cucina grande* to cook in like you never seen, with a big stove like you can't imagine, and no more cooking outside over a handful of charcoal."

Michele had also realized a promise to himself: not to remain *uno bracciante impoverito*, laboring in poverty for *u padronu*. As an American homeowner and landlord, he had, indeed, become *u padronu*. Those thoughts must have warmed my father immensely as he sat at the head of his rich table, welcoming his family and guests.

As if it was a sweet topping for all their efforts, they especially prized the educational distance that Fred and I had traveled. This might not have been so remarkable to their American neighbors, nor did it seem so to me, but given my parents' worlds, it was the attainment of a virtual impossibility. All had been made possible by the nature of their adopted country, the resources provided by America. Their appreciation was boundless. "*Solamente qui, in America* (Only here, in America)," they said, over and over, were such marvelous things possible. They were good years.

By the start of 1951, however, the good years shared by Michele and Theresa would be coming to an end. My father's health continued to deteriorate, and that year cancer was detected. His work at The Mill was interrupted over the next four years by many surgeries. No previous hurdles had stopped or slowed him, but he had never before faced anything like this.

6. Traveling 9-W

Once I decided to leave The Mill and start at Columbia, I drew down my bank account, turning it over to the university. How quickly the balance tumbled to zero! Living at home relieved me of hefty dormitory bills. However, it meant a 20-mile daily commute along 9-W from Nyack to

Fort Lee, then a bus across the George Washington Bridge into the city, and a crowded subway ride down to 116th Street. Late each afternoon, I reversed the journey. For the first few months, I rode the Rockland Coaches' red and tan commuter bus to and from the bridge, sitting up front, talking with Harry, one of the drivers, about his favorite subject, the New York Yankees. But bus tickets eroded my tuition money, so I resorted to hitchhiking—40 miles each day—thus shifting some of my financial burden onto the public's shoulders. "Why not?" I rationalized. "Businessmen do it all the time."

Several times at night, as I hitched back to Nyack along a dark 9-W, Harry saw me with my thumb raised in the classic hitchhiker pose and stopped his bus as if for an ordinary paying passenger. When the door hissed open, I protested that I had no money for a ticket. Exasperated, Harry jerked his head back and rolled his eyes at me, silently mouthing, "Shut up and get in," without letting the paying customers know that he was giving me a free ride. "Boy," he whispered as I climbed the steps, "for somebody supposed to be so smart, you sure are dumb!"

Hitchhiking for four years was an educational experience. I once calculated, apparently having nothing better to do at that moment, that I had hitched 32,000 free miles. I guess I owe a lot of thanks to a lot of people.

Among my benefactors of the road were an elderly lady who must have been almost 40 and several young men, all of whom propositioned me. Once, a seriously inebriated man who was trying to get to Nyack lurched his fancy new 1952 Kaiser Manhattan to a crooked stop and handed me his keys. "Drive any place you want, ol' buddy, ol' buddy," he said, then crawled into the back seat and went to sleep. When we reached Nyack, I pulled off the road into a safe place and woke him up to return his keys and tell him where he was. Barely opening his eyes, he said it was the best driving he had ever done, and went back to sleep. I left him happily snoring.

My most anxiety provoking ride was when I saw, after getting into a car, that a dog as big as a sea lion occupied the rear seat. For 20 miles, my heart accelerated each time the great beast pushed its nose against the back of my neck and made loud snuffling noises. "This is it," I thought. "Any second, he's going to bite my head off." When we safely reached Nyack and I opened the door to get out, the monster wagged his tail and tried to lick my face. As the man drove off, I could see the dog peering through the side window, looking at me. His tail, ears, and eyes drooped, and he had a sad expression, as if he had just lost a friend.

The most disturbing ride was in November 1951, when a middle-aged man stopped his pickup truck. He lived in Nyack, not far from me, but we did not know each other. His son, about my age, had just shipped out to fight in Korea. "You think it's fair," he challenged me, "that you college students stay in school, and my boy goes to war?" At that time, the country was caught up in the Korean War and in hotly emotional arguments about the morality and wisdom of that undeclared "police action."[16] That spring, President Truman had sacked General MacArthur from the post of Allied Commander of the United Nations Forces in the Far East for insubordination, for usurping civilian control of the military. Half the country was on the general's side, the other half on Truman's. A sharply divisive issue was represented by the questions "Who stays? Who fights?" A political cartoon pictured two young men: a college student, loaded with books, with the caption "Too smart to fight?" and a soldier, loaded with armaments, with the caption "Too dumb not to fight?" It was that suggestion of a vicious elitism and unfairness that was plaguing that poor father, frightened for his boy. He was angry, afraid, and accusatory, but also apologetic, because he knew the war was not my doing. His son and I had both registered for military service and been declared "1-A," but the draft had spared me and scooped up his boy. It was a tense, 20-mile nighttime ride along 9-W. By the time we reached Nyack, I was feeling anxious and guilty, and was glad to climb out of his truck.

"Look," he said, as I opened the door and stepped out. "I'm sorry. I didn't mean to dump on you. I wish you success in school. Really. It's just that ... I mean ..." He shrugged and looked off vaguely into the darkness. We let it go at that. I am not sure why, but I closed the door as gently as I could.

In 1945, at the end of World War II, people hoped that all wars were over and the world had finally become a better place. But only a few years later, the Korean War (1950–1953) began, slaughtering 2.5 million Koreans, mostly civilians, and injuring millions more. There were 55,000 U.S. military deaths, plus 103,000 wounded and 8,000 missing in action. It was a terrible war, a stalemate that gained nothing for anyone. Our divided country wanted to push that war out of its memory, and disgracefully we have allowed Korea to become "the Forgotten War."

I learned later that the man's son had survived Korea and safely returned home.[17]

Freshman year ended, my bank account was emptied, and I would need to earn money that summer for next year's tuition. The few dollars I had been earning all year on Saturdays at Cousin Joe Conace's grocery store and at the Rockland Country Club's dishwashing sink in the evenings had been good for pocket money, but now a serious paycheck would be needed.

7. Ablondi's Bar and Restaurant

Across from the railroad tracks and the loading dock of the main post office in Pearl River, New York, stood Ablondi's Bar and Restaurant, owned

16. Anderson (2004) and Stueck (1995).
17. Just four years after the end of the Korean War, the country entered the Vietnam War (1957–1975) in which another 58,000 U.S. troops would die and 153,000 would be wounded.

by septuagenarian Alfredo Ablondi and his son, Mario. Mr. Ablondi was a short, pleasantly rounded man with a kindly face and wispy white hair. A quiet man, he carried a gentle smile. I still picture him coming through the swinging door from the kitchen, wrapped in his white chef's apron, carrying a home-cooked dinner to an old customer. His smile promised, "This, you gonna like."

An Italian immigrant in the 1920s, he had done well in *la bell'America*, operating his genial tavern for 20 years. "Blondie's" was a welcoming oasis, a refreshing stopover after work before one faced the domestic demands of home. He served many brands of beer and ale in bottles and cans, but a pull on the tap brought forth Rheingold beer exclusively. In big aluminum kegs in the cellar, the beer was kept at the right temperature and checked frequently each day. Fifteen cents bought a 12-ounce glass. A shot of rye, straight or mixed, was 25 cents. According to the house rules, after a patron had purchased three drinks, the bartender put up the fourth "on the house." Tavern etiquette obliged the patron to buy more drinks. After that the free drinks were presented less frequently. One night, I explained to Mr. Ablondi that, shrewdly, he had his customers on what psychologists call "an operant 1:3 fixed-ratio partial reinforcement schedule fading to variable intervals." He looked at me, his impish smile growing, and he said, in his soft Italian accent, "I knew that."

Fancy mixed drinks were seldom requested, Ablondi's being a neighborhood workingman's shot-and-a-beer or highball kind of place. Occasionally a stranger would wander in and call for something exotic, like a Tom Collins or an old fashioned, causing the bartender to surreptitious flip through the Mixologist's Handbook. The back bar was stocked with bourbons, scotches, and ryes; the bar whiskeys were to the left of the cash register, the better brands on the right. The glass-fronted display cabinets below held brandies and liqueurs that, for lack of demand, were seldom poured.

A swinging door opened to the kitchen, where sandwiches were made to order at any time. Sardines with spicy mustard, thick slices of onion, and a couple of pickled hot *pepperoncini* on a crusty, seeded roll was a favorite. Six days a week, Mr. Ablondi—"Pop" to his good customers—prepared a dozen servings of a substantial midday dinner for his regular customers of many years, most on their lunch breaks. The menu changed daily, but seldom varied weekly. On Monday we had pot roast; Tuesday, pork chops, mashed potatoes, and gravy. On subsequent days he served up spaghetti and meatballs, corned beef and cabbage, beef stew, and, on Friday, broiled or fried fish, or meatloaf with potatoes and gravy.

A big Zenith black-and-white television beamed down across the bar and the customers bathed in the flickering shadows of Milton Berle, Sid Caesar, Jack Benny,[18] wrestling, baseball, boxing, and hard, sinewy ladies

18. Other early 50s variety shows were those of Abbott and Costello, Eddie Cantor, Bob Hope, Fred Allen, Jimmy Durante, Red Skelton, and Dean Martin and Jerry Lewis.

knocking each other about in the roller derby. The bar opened at 8 a.m., after Axel O'Sean had swept and scrubbed the floor and washed the tables, bar, and booths. Axel was a crusty, wiry, long-retired merchant mariner with a Norwegian accent and a signature mustache that twitched from side to side under his nose whenever he became annoyed or excited. After finishing his work, Axel relaxed, always at the end of the bar that was farthest from the big window near the street. I asked him once why he sat there all the time. "Safety," he whispered mysteriously, and twitched his mustache. Axel smoked a cigarette and downed a few shots of blackberry brandy from his special bottle, which was kept under the bar for him. He was usually the day's first customer.

Business was slow most mornings except Saturday, picked up between 11 and 2, dwindled through the afternoon, and grew steadily from 5:00 to its 9-to-11 p.m. peak. The last customers said goodnight by about 1 a.m.; a few occasionally lasted to the 3 a.m. limit mandated by New York State.

Ablondi's was one of my most fortunate discoveries. Frank Ablondi was a fellow medical student with my brother at NYU. When Frank heard that I needed a job, he spoke to his uncle, who owned the restaurant and needed a bartender. I was introduced to Alfredo and Mario, was hired, and worked as nighttime and weekend bartender for the next four years, through college and into my first year of graduate school.

My schedule began at 6:30 a.m., when I walked up to 9-W lugging an old leather briefcase given to me by my Cousin Mary, to begin hitchhiking the 20 miles to the George Washington Bridge. Morning and afternoon classes followed, and daily practice for the wrestling team. Then came the return thumbing by about 5 p.m. After a quick supper that Mom always had ready for me, I borrowed Pop's Studebaker and drove the eight or nine miles to Ablondi's for my shift, 7 p.m. to closing. Every night brought its own adventures, but that's another story. After closing the door on the final customer, I locked the night's receipts in the safe and perishables in the refrigerator. Then, after checking the lavatories for anyone who might have fallen asleep in there, I drove home, usually around 2 a.m., to sleep and be ready to raise my thumb on 9-W by 6:30. Now, just thinking about that schedule makes me tired, but when one is 20 everything is possible. At that age, youth, strength, and endurance are forever.

Although the schedule was demanding and each shift behind the bar must have pumped several packs of secondhand cigarette smoke into my lungs, the work was pleasant. Over the years, a neighborhood tavern achieves a selective process of identifying compatible regular patrons, insuring that everyone is acquainted and everyone is tolerant of everyone else's peculiarities. Thus the mood at Ablondi's varied from soft tranquility to high-spirited good humor. Only once in four years did I need to break up a gathering fight. Two old friends had climbed off their barstools and were about to pound each other over some slur against Bobby Thompson, the hero of the October 3, 1951, final playoff game between the Giants and the Dodgers. The three-game series was tied, one game each, and the Dodgers were ahead, two to one, in this pennant-deciding game. The Giants were at bat in the bottom of the ninth, with one out and two men on. The Dodgers were just two outs from the championship when Thomson stepped up and hit his famous pennant-winning three-run homer down the left-field line, off Dodgers pitcher Ralph Branca. Sixty years later, Dodgers fans still say, "We was robbed!" The Giants, they accuse, had stolen Brooklyn's secret catcher's signs, and thus knew what pitch was coming at Thomson.

I was often reminded that working behind the bar was a good deal more educational than going to college. "You'll learn more right here than in all them books you read!" the patrons said. The acknowledged wisest man at the bar was Andy, the Philosopher. "Listen to Andy," I was told. "Throw away them books. Listen to the Philosopher; he'll teach you real-life philosophy!"

Andy was a skilled, highly paid tool and die maker, a man of objective measurement and mathematical precision. He was a soft-spoken, middle-aged widower, respected by all. It was Andy to whom the patrons turned to settle arguments about one thing or another. During the mellowing process of metabolizing nine or 10 beers through an evening, Andy would present his wisdom metaphorically, like the oracles of old. It was up to his listeners to translate and understand them. Late one night, he peered at me over the rim of his Rheingold with one eye closed against the smoke curling up from his cigarette. Andy pointed at me, preparing me for enlightenment. Silence crept along the bar; glasses stopped in midair; everyone focused on the Philosopher. Finally, when all was quiet, Andy looked around, pointed his finger, and announced, "You can paint oil over latex, but you can't paint latex over oil!"

"Oh, man. Ain't that the truth!" someone down the bar said, impressed once again by Andy's metaphorical eloquence. Then, looking at me, he added, "You better listen to Andy. You won't get *that* from no books!" Approving nods and words of agreement with the Philosopher flowed along the bar, followed by calls for more beer.

I knew that Andy was a working man's philosopher, and he was not really talking about oil and latex paint. His statement was an observation about man's eternal struggle in this mortal life. The best that I could make out of it was that some things in life are just not meant to be, they are impossible, and to aspire to them is foolish. Lewis Carroll may have had the Red Queen proudly believe the impossible—"Why sometimes I've believed in as many as six impossible things before breakfast," she told Alice[19]—but such was not for Andy. He was a realist. Some things simply cannot be.

Fifty-eight years later, I still don't know what Andy was talking about, but it sounded impressive at the time.

19. Carroll (1865).

Mr. Ablondi was a generous and tolerant man, allowing me to take off one or two weeks whenever I needed to study for midterm and final exams.[20] When Columbia reminded me that my scheduled $800 tuition payment was due, or there was a big bill at the bookstore, he advanced whatever money I needed. "Take your time," he said. "Don' worry about it. By the end of the year, we be all straighten' up." As I said, Ablondi's was one of my most fortunate discoveries.

On June 8, 1954, I graduated from Columbia College. That morning I drove Mom, *Comare* Bettina Lanzana, *Zia* Macrina, and a young lady, Florence Walmsley, in our old Studebaker into Manhattan, to Columbia's graduation ceremonies. My father by then was severely ill, fatigued and disheartened by repeated surgeries. As much as he had wanted to, he was not able to go with us. Pop had attended Fred's college and medical school graduations, and was sad at not being there for me. He was proud, however, that both of his sons were Columbia graduates.

Sixteen days later, on Thursday, June 24, I finished an 8–4 shift at Ablondi's and walked out, waving at the guys at the bar. They lifted their glasses in response. "Think great thoughts there, young man," Paul Ferguson called out. That was Paul's parting comment ever since I had become a Columbia graduate.

"See you guys tomorrow," I said, and drove home. When I reached our house, the front door flew open. *Comare* Bettina Lanzana, her face streaked and stricken, threw her arms around me and said, over and over, "Oh, oh, oh, oh." Her face felt hot, her tears washed over me. I could hear crying in the living room. Mom was sobbing and twisting her handkerchief, and although surrounded by her sweet friends, she seemed so alone. I hugged her. Mom held on and we cried together.

I knew what had happened. No one had to tell me. "Come," *Comare* Bettina said, softly. "Your father's in here." And she gently tugged me into the bedroom that Pop had so happily built 10 years before for Fred and Marie. Dr. Relland was slowly closing his medical bag. Like Mom's friends, he had come immediately. I knelt at the bedside, took my father's still-warm, work-roughened hand, and stayed there a while, just the two of us, silently saying goodbye.

20. Like so many other parents saddened by such blasphemies, Mr. Ablondi knew the grief of losing a son in the Korean War—his youngest son, Bruno, had been killed.

Chapter 26

At the Top of the Hill (Nyack, 2009)

1. The Family's "Second Wave"

We grieved for Pop. I still picture him, the proud *padrone, il capo di tavola,* uncorking his bottle of wine for the table, happily embracing his family and guests. I see him perpetually fixing things, building another room, standing on his ladder, climbing high on the roof, enlarging the basement, digging his garden, making his wine. I see him early in the morning stoking the kitchen stove, sharing his breakfast with me while the rest of the family safely sleeps, going off to work with his black lunch box tucked under his arm. Mostly I see him quietly smiling, pleased with all of our little successes. He is always there, always solid, steady and loving.

Grief never ends; it fades to a soft ache. For Mom, the past is alive; Michele died, but he would never be gone. Mom mourned, and when she returned to her living family and friends, Michele was there with her.

La famiglia and *amicizie*—family and friendships—formed the center of Michele and Theresa's world. Mom was the caretaker of all personal relationships, while Pop took care of all things financial and material. She loved being with people; he loved his tools and his building projects that made his family comfortable. They were happiest when doing, each in his or her own way, what nourished *la famiglia.*

My father's death in 1954 marked the end of the "first wave" of our family's migration. It had started in 1900 with my grandfather Michele Dattilo, continued with my grand uncles and aunts, and was followed in 1909 with my father and his sister and brother, and in 1927 with Mom and Fred. By 1946, my father had succeeded in gaining everything he had set out to find in *la bell'America,* all those impossible things that he had promised his young bride so long ago. We regret that he did not live longer to enjoy that success. That first wave of immigration—of Dattilos, Conaces, and Grazianos, the "old folks" who immigrated in the 1920s or before—was completed. "*La storia e finita!*" they might have said. But it was not finished; the "second wave" was about to begin.

Following the war's end in 1945, we shipped packages to relatives in Italy. The bundles were large, soft, rounded like great pumpkins, wrapped in white cloth, securely sewn together and tied with cord. They bore clothing, a few American dollars, and a note of love and hope. Some coffee was tucked in, a luxury for *Nonna* Elisabetta, who savored her daily *tazza di caffè*. My job was to print the address carefully on the cloth, using indelible ink. We carried the bundles to the post office, where Mom paid the postage and I visited the great mural on the wall.

In 1932, Theresa's brother, Giuseppe, had wanted to follow his sisters to America with his new bride, Maria Vittoria Tedesco, but U.S. immigration policy, Mussolini's dictatorship, World War II, and five years as a prisoner of war of the British in Africa and India intervened. In 1946, he returned to Italy's postwar poverty even more determined to take his family to America. Every day they talked of plans to emigrate, but America's restrictions and the hopeless number of visa applicants continued to frustrate them. For nearly 10 years, *Zio* Giuseppe in Italy and Theresa in America worked to clear the legal and bureaucratic barriers. Uncle Joe considered going to Argentina and Venezuela, and in 1954 almost led his family to Canada.

In 1951 and 1953, Southern Italy was struck by *u diluvio*—hurricanes, flooding, and volcanic eruptions. To provide relief, the American and Italian governments relaxed their restrictions; the family was rescued by waves of catastrophe. Leaving the family farm that had long sustained them, they traveled by train to Naples and sailed on the *Cristoforo Colombo*, the Italian Line's new flagship launched two years before.

Their voyage to America in 1955 was much improved over those of their forebears half a century earlier. Gone was the crowded steerage, the stacks of wooden-slatted bunks and the thin, crispy straw mattresses with creatures crawling inside. There were no food buckets, tin cups, and plates; no cold-water wash-up barrels; no lining up to select *u capo di rancio*, and no cross-legged sitting on the crowded deck for meals. No 7 p.m. curfew separated men from women. The family enjoyed the ship's luxuries along with 451 first- and cabin-class passengers and 604 in tourist class. They slept in clean four-bunk cabins, sat at tables in dining rooms, and were offered motion pictures, music, games, dancing, and other entertainment. Unfortunately, *u mal di mare* stalked even the modern ships, and many unhappy passengers remained in their cabins.

Uncle Joe, Aunt Vittoria, and the children—Elisabetta, age 20, Michael, 14, and seven-year-old twins Anna and Theresa—arrived at New York City's 48th Street pier on Good Friday, April 8, 1955. Mom, Fred, and Uncle Joe Graziano welcomed them at the dock and transported them to Nyack in two automobiles. After 28 years of separation, brother and sister were reunited, and the children had a happy first meeting with their *Zia* Teresina.

Michael, never before far from home, was entranced by his first sight of the city that floated toward them. There seemed more impossibly tall buildings here than trees in Italy! At dusk, the city began to glow; a million lights climbed and sparkled into the sky and spread along the streets, and there before him was a beautiful city of fantasy. He saw a man whose skin was black. "Look," Michael said. "That man, he must have just come up from the coal mines to be all black like that!"

Theresa welcomed, fed, and housed the family. Within three days, Uncle Joe began working at The Mill. In two and a half years he purchased a fine Victorian house on a large corner lot just two blocks away, formerly owned by Mom's friend Mrs. Cranston.

Uncle Joe Dattilo, a skilled Southern Italian farmer, cultivated his garden of vegetables, fig trees, peach trees, flowers of all kinds, and a large lawn bordered by a neatly trimmed hedge. What would an Italian garden be without a fig tree? My father's trees, carefully nurtured for so long, had been untended since his death. Uncle Joe revived them, took cuttings, and raised his own trees—a farmer's version of another Italian generation in America.

As Theresa had done 30 years before, Aunt Vittoria learned to manage what at first seemed an impossibly large house. Michael and the twins began school immediately, and the family thrived in Nyack's Italian community. The children grew, married, and established their own homes. Uncle Joe continued working at The Mill, retiring in 1973 at age 65, enormously pleased to be able to relax a bit and enjoy with Aunt Vittoria what had so long eluded them. For almost 30 years the house sheltered the family, until it was bought by Anna, who had married Vincenzo Ottaiano, and the cycle continued. Vincenzo and Anna's children grew, married, and brought their children to enliven the family. Truly, old houses, like people in a new country, can be made alive again. Were Mrs. Cranston and my father still there, she would have beamed in pleasure and he would have said, "Only in America, *la bell'America!*"

In 1956, one year after Uncle Joe arrived with his family, Theresa visited Italy for the first time since emigrating 30 years earlier. She visited her mother, *Nonna* Elisabetta, and her sisters, Caterina and Angela, who was by then *Suor* Eugenia. Caterina had married Giuseppe Bartolotti, who had helped Theresa learn to read many years earlier. Two of their four children, Francesca, 24, and Michael, 22, had decided to go to America, planning to travel that summer on the *Andrea Doria*, the Italian Line's magnificent new luxury liner, sister ship to the *Cristoforo Colombo*.

"Wait a few weeks," Theresa suggested, "and go back with me in October. We can all sail together, like a nice vacation."

My cousins delayed their departure and arranged to travel later with their *Zia* Teresina. Were *Nonno* Peppe still alive, he would have seen the hand of *San Francesco*, because on July 25, 1956, the *Andrea Doria* was sunk in a collision with the SS *Stockholm* off the coast of Nantucket. A superb rescue operation saved 1,660 passengers and crew, but 46 people were lost.[1]

---

1. For accounts of this rescue see Goldstein (2001), Hoffer (1979), Moscow (1988), and Simpson (2006).

In October, Theresa and Francesca and Michael Bartolotti boarded the *Cristoforo Colombo.* It was the season of storms. The sea was violent, the winds strong, and the passengers were ordered to wear life vests—not a reassuring order. *U mal di mare* was an insistent presence on the ship, striding the decks and slipping into every cabin. Theresa and Francesca clung to their rosary beads and refused to leave their bunks. They finally arrived safely in New York, but Theresa resolved never again to board any boat, no matter how large or magnificent it might be.

Michael and Francesca joined Uncle Joe's family in Theresa's house. Theresa sponsored a dozen relatives and the children of friends, sent money for tickets, helped them clear the U.S. bureaucratic hurdles, met them at the docks, transported them to Elysian Avenue, and housed and fed them until they established their own homes. Hesitant to leave her family in 1927, Theresa had become the central dynamo helping the rest of her family join her in *l'America.*

The old house was alive again. Theresa was pleased to be in the center of it all, like *la padrona superiore,* the cultural interpreter, protector, teacher, and guide surrounded by grateful family and friends. Theresa felt rejuvenated, given another opportunity to help her family and to guide young people. This must have been, she thought, the way her grandfather *Nonno* Peppe had felt when he became so important in the lives of the children. The fathers had left for America, and in his later years *Nonno* Peppe's paternal role had been resurrected. "Is this a small piece of heaven?" he had asked *San Francesco.* "Made again young in spirit, to help care for these children? Thank you, my Good Saint. Thank you." Now Theresa, the maternal elder of the family in Nyack, had taken on the central role in their new American lives. She too had been made young again, and in return, the family gave Theresa their love and *rispetto.* "What more could I possibly want in my old age?" Theresa asked herself. One might think that she would have been deeply sad that Michele could not be there to share in those final marvelous years, but in Theresa's world, Michele was there, right by her side at every moment.

Theresa had reason to be pleased and proud—her nieces Rose, Frances, Betty, Anna, and Theresa, all new to America, married hard-working, responsible men who knew well the traditions of caring for families.[2] Her two nephews soon showed what they could do. Michael Bartolotti had arrived on that stormy voyage with Theresa and Francesca with $11 in his pocket. Like Uncle Joe, he began work at The Mill immediately. He worked several years in that toxically malodorous Glue Room of my experience six years earlier.[3] Michael moved to a better job in another factory. In his off hours he began a three-year program of study in radiologic technology, supporting his studies by laboring nights and weekends washing dishes in restaurants and doing

2. Nicholas Pessolano, Vincenzo Colistra, Gino Delfino, Vincenzo Ottaiano, Frank Fiola.
3. See Chapter Eight.

other part-time jobs. The Italian immigrants' powerful ethic, "work hard and succeed; no one else will do it for you," was again in force. Michael's professional career spanned 40 years in hospitals, emergency rooms, and private practices before he retired in 2002.

For Michael, coming to *la bell'America* had been a good move. Here he found the opportunity to work, study, develop a profession, make wise financial investments, and purchase a beautiful home for his family. He also met and married Carol Blaikie, a nurse at the hospital. They raised a beautiful family and are now enjoying life with their grandchildren. The new generation has continued the successes set in motion in 1900 by our grandfather Michele Dattilo.

As with too many families, however, a wrenching tragedy left Carol, Michael, and our entire family with a deep and permanent sadness: an automobile crash in 1996 took the life of their beautiful young daughter, Michelle. Some pain never ends.

Theresa's youngest nephew, Michael Dattilo, had arrived in America in 1955 with his parents and sisters. Michael started school immediately but, without the language or socializing experiences of his peers, was puzzled by the maze of American adolescent society and high school culture. His sisters, Anna and Theresa, also began school without delay. They, being younger, did not yet need to face adolescent demands in the uniquely American world between childhood and adulthood, nor did they have the option of withdrawing from school.

His father, perhaps sensing Michael's discomfort, insisted in the old Southern Italian tradition that Michael had already achieved more than enough education and should now earn a living. Other family members urged Michael to remain in school, and Mr. Cook, a sympathetic teacher, was always available for him to talk with. However, Michael made his own decision and left school.

He worked on a local farm, picking beans and tomatoes—still close to the Southern Italian farmers' tradition. At the end of that season, Michael began working in a supermarket, advancing from stock boy to running the produce department. Still a youngster, he was soon functioning as assistant manager and was considered for training to assist in operating a new branch. Michael, however, already had bigger plans.

In a series of astute transactions, Michael built a large, complex, and highly successful business enterprise. For all his success, Michael now speaks modestly about his achievements. "If I had anything," my cousin told me recently, "it was persistence." Indeed, it was a good deal more than that. Intelligence, alertness, talent, and, as I have noted many times, the Italian immigrants' propensity for sustained hard work all entered the personal mix from which Michael crafted his successes.

I think that Uncle Joe did not realize the extent of his son's success. Nearly 50 when he immigrated, he understood the world largely in terms of his farming community in Italy. A story is told of his visit to one of Michael's enterprises, a spacious and elegant seaside property of beautiful new condominiums, a hotel, and a magnificent restaurant. Michael took his father on a tour of the lush lawns dipping to the sandy beach, the meticulous landscaping, tennis courts, flower gardens, even strolling guests. My uncle marveled at the scale and beauty of his son's resort. The parking lots were full; the carhops, bellhops, waiters, and waitresses bustled about. The spacious, multilevel seaside restaurant was filled with diners enjoying the feast set out for them on Michael's sumptuous grand buffet that drew people from many states.

My uncle walked through, not quite knowing how to respond to the respectful deference paid to him, the father of the owner. He saw everything and nodded in silent approval. But the old farmer saw possibilities missed by his son. After touring the restaurant and the kitchen—a cauldron of intense activity ruled by a lordly chef—he quietly took his son aside and gave him some business advice.

"*Figlio,*" he said, "you see all this food that comes back from the buffet that people don't eat? It's all thrown away, wasted."

His peasant life, early poverty, the threats and deprivations of war, and five hard years as a P.O.W. had taught him that nothing must be wasted. Those experiences had helped make him too cynical to be religious, but he knew that if a sin existed at all, wasting food would be it.

"You just throwin' it all away," he repeated.

"And look over there." He pointed out the banks of windows to the lush lawns and gardens. "See, you have all that empty land, and it don't produce anything. Now, I tell you what you do. You buy some pigs. You put 'em in a pen out there where you have all that land. Then feed 'em all this food you been throwin' away. That way, you don't waste the food, the pigs grow nice and big, and it don't cost you anything to raise 'em! See? And each pig, in the market, you could make some good money."

Michael's sister Theresa married Frank Fiola, a skilled tailor. Their family and business grew, and over the years they invested successfully in real estate. In the 1980s, having had enough of northern winters, Frank and Theresa moved their family to Florida.

Before leaving, Frank sold his tailoring business to our cousin Benedetta Bartolotti, who had immigrated not long before. Benedetta has continued to be a successful independent businesswoman sharing a comfortable suburban home with her sister, Elisabetta, who immigrated in 1987. Elisabetta's family includes three children and four grandchildren. Her husband, Domenico Martucci, died in Italy a few years later. During those years Betty, Michael's oldest sister, married Gino Delfino, who became an independent contractor. They raised their family in a beautiful new home, and soon enjoyed watching their grandchildren grow.

As graduate students in 1958, Sheila Ginsberg and I were married in a ceremony and reception that consumed all of our combined savings—$32. Our merging of Italian and Jewish cultures caused a brief stir of alarm in our families. "How can this marriage possibly last?" they worried.[4] "Those kids are starting out with a big problem, a mixed marriage, conflicting religions, alien cultures! Can't they see the troubles they'll have?"

However, acceptance and love prevailed, and the people of the "alien cultures" proved to be lovingly supportive. In the 1960s our children, Amy, Lisa, and Michael, were born, and the grandparents became happily immersed in their roles of teaching us how to care properly for little babies.[5]

Our children celebrated the traditions, love, crowded tables, and marvelous feasts of both cultures. The foods, prepared lovingly in each setting, were wonderfully complementary in their differences. Amid the welcomed variations in recipes and the refreshingly different accents heard around the tables, the "alien cultures" of Italians and Jews—*la famiglia* in one and *mishpocheh* in the other—proved to be wondrously compatible and equally rich in everything that mattered. Whatever was different just made life all the more interesting.

In the late 1950s and early 1960s Theresa helped to bring our young cousins, four-year-old Anne Marie Ceneviva and two-year-old Anthony (later named Jeffrey), from Maida to America. Fred and Marie adopted the children, and an overjoyed Theresa became *la nonna*.

Fred's medical practice was growing. He designed a large professional building that housed several medical and dental practices, a pharmacy, and a laboratory. For the next 40 years, Fred conducted his practice out of his building. Always interested in architecture, he also designed a house for his in-laws and another for his own family. It was a low-silhouette, Prairie style, modern brick ranch of earthen hues that fit beautifully into its sloped terrain, complementing the plateau-topped hill. It had been inspired by Fred's fascination with Frank Lloyd Wright's merging of buildings with their surrounding landscape, and it was like no other house in the area.

By the early 1960s, Theresa's family of newly arrived immigrants were in their own homes and 79 Elysian Avenue was quiet once again. Francesca (Frances), who had shared that violent voyage with her Aunt Theresa in 1956, had married Vincent Colistra. They purchased the house previously owned by our neighbor Mr. Hartwick, the elegant railroad conductor who used to admit us onto his coach on our annual trips to the opera in New York City and who rolled his eyes when we cracked open our hard-boiled eggs. Frances and Vincent raised their children, Anthony and Maria. Soon, grandchildren ran through those rooms, too.

Theresa moved to the small upstairs apartment and rented out the

4. At this writing, Sheila and Anthony are but a few weeks from their 50th wedding anniversary.
5. Theresa Graziano, Matilda Weisblatt, and Leon Ginsberg.

ground floor of 79 Elysian Avenue, taking over Pop's role of landlord. She collected rent, paid the bills, hired repairmen, and insisted on living independently, "in my own house," turning down all offers to move in with either of her two sons.

In the 1960s, Mom again visited Maida. Her first voyage, in 1956, had been by ship. "*No aeroplano!*" she had said. "I don' know how they stay up there!" However, that wild voyage on the *Cristoforo Colombo* with Frances and Michael was so violent that Theresa became more frightened of ships than of airplanes. Her subsequent trips were by air. They were, she said, *u circolo,* a line bending around and finding its own beginning. She was thinking of *u professore, u maestro di scuola* in turn-of-the-century Maida, who had predicted transatlantic flights.[6] While others scoffed, Theresa had listened. Sixty years later, she sat in one of the great machines, speeding across the ocean at 500 miles an hour and seven miles high. Theresa was much relieved, however, when the professor's *aeroplano* touched down safely in New York.

Theresa wanted to contribute something to her old town. She decided to purchase *una campana* for one of Maida's churches, to replace the bell that had cracked after years of tolling. There is no mystery as to why Theresa chose a church bell as her gift—the symbolic importance of *la campana* in defining the small towns of Southern Italy cannot be overstated. The town honored Theresa for her generosity, and she traveled to Maida for the ceremony.

Theresa journeyed several times to Maida, visiting with her mother, Elisabetta, who had entered her ninth decade. It was late in 1969 that I received the letter from Maida saying that *Nonna* Elisabetta had died at the age of 94. "Please," the letter said, "break the sad news to *Zia* Teresina." Mom never visited Italy after that.

In 1954, when my father died, Mom had no way of knowing she would live another 43 years. Around her revolved everyone she loved, all who mattered in the world, and she was tireless in keeping those relationships nourished. We joked—marveled, actually—that Mom was the "family encyclopedia," keeping in her memory the family stories and facts, and birthdays and anniversaries of every cousin, niece, nephew, grandniece, grandnephew, and friend—and she never failed to send each a card with a little gift folded inside. Each baby born into the family received a beautifully knitted set: a hat, a sweater, a pair of booties, unmistakably made by Theresa. Her telephone seemed always busy, keeping up with her web of *relazione.*

Friends and relatives visited Theresa in her little apartment, and in the summer, on the cool front porch, they relaxed in the wicker rocking chairs that I had played in as a child. Never having learned to drive an automo-

---

6. See Chapter Eight.

bile, although she often threatened to do so, Theresa continued walking through Nyack. When she was in her 70s, her nieces and friends came by to drive her to church, to stores, for lunch or dinner with their families.[7] She frequently visited her brother, my Uncle Joe, making up for their nearly 30 years of separation. Three or four times each year, Mom visited her sister Anna, my Uncle Joe Graziano, and my granduncles Antonio and Giuseppe Dattilo and their families in Ocean City. Several times a week, my other Uncle Joe dropped in, usually with some fresh produce from his farm in Central Nyack.

Theresa had many friends among her Nyack neighbors and Saint Ann's Church societies, including two very special nuns. One of Fred's high school friends from the 1930s, Jack Geist, had become a virtual family member. For Jack, Theresa was "Mamma." He continued visiting throughout the rest of her life, cheering Theresa with his wonderful humor and little presents of his fanciful artistic creations. "My number three son!" Mom beamed, giving Jack a big, maternal, Italian hug.

Theresa's old friends were aging. Some had died. Those remaining still enjoyed coffee in her kitchen, but not so often or with such spirited conversation as before.

So complete were Theresa's relationships with so many people, and so impressive was her undiminished ability to keep track of every person, date, and family event, that my cousin Michael Dattilo once proclaimed, "Aunt Theresa is the mayor of Nyack!"

In 1982, Theresa's sister, Caterina, widowed the previous year from Giuseppe Bartolotti, joined her children, Frances, Michael, and Benedetta, in America. Now, with grandchildren nearby, her sister newly arrived, and her close proximity to Fred and Marie, who took very good care of her, Theresa's world grew even richer. In her 80s, Theresa reached another important level in life. Kelly, Christopher, and Cameron were born to her granddaughter Anne Marie and Chris Keane. Theresa had become a great grandmother, elevated from *la nonna* to *la bisnonna*. In her world, Theresa had reached the highest status of motherhood.

In October 1991, the family celebrated Theresa's 90th birthday. She had many reasons for saying, "I been blessed in my life," attributing her happiness to a benevolent God, never voicing what Michele might have thought about such attributions. "Sometimes," my father had once told me, "we give God too much credit for the good things and not enough for the bad." But these were Theresa's years, and she could understand her world in any way she wished.

Theresa was the last survivor of a trio of ladies whose deep friendship spanned 103 years, 1894 to 1997, from Caterina Cocce Serratore's hun-

---

7. For example, Mary and Laura Serratore, Rose Maiorano, Theresa Serratore, Theresa Conace, my cousins Anna Ottaiano and Frances Colistra, and so many others.

dred years (1894–1994) through Angelina Pileggi Conace's long life of 93 years (1899–1992) to Theresa's 96th year. At the start of the 20th century, three little girls played together in Maida; at the dawn of the 21st century, three great grandmothers in Nyack continued sharing their lives. What a marvelous tenure—friends for 100 years! The magical "*cent'anni!*" bound together three people who shared so much life. *La relazione* is not a power to be trifled with.

I once asked my Ocean City Uncle Joe, "How come so many people in Maida live so long?"

"Because," he said, "we were poor."

That puzzled me. "Being poor makes you live long?"

"Ah," he said with a smile. "All we could afford to eat was beans, greens, olive oil, homemade pasta, with a little glass of wine, and fruits and nuts off the trees. And now and then, a poor chicken who didn't run fast enough. We didn't even know in those days we had the best food of all!"

Theresa's enthusiasm for *la famiglia* never lagged, and she was excitedly happy whenever her children, grandchildren, and great grandchildren visited. One weekend in 1994, in her 93rd year, Theresa awakened early, dusted, vacuumed, straightened her apartment, shopped, and created one of her magnificent home-cooked meals for her family's visit. That evening after dinner, as we cleared the table and washed the dishes, 93-year-old "Nanny" confided to her granddaughters Amy and Lisa, "I don' know why I gotta be so tire' out nowaday, when all I do is jus' clean my house and cook a little bit."

The families of my nearest relatives, the Bartolottis, Conaces, Dattilos, and Grazianos, and all those close friends with whom we became virtual family, the Cervodoros, Fiolas, Lanzanas, Serratores, and others—those turn-of-the-century *paesani* from Maida—had been transferred to Nyack and Ocean City. The post–World War II immigrants, too, had become Americans. They, the second wave, continued the patterns of hard work and success set by the family's 1920s immigrants. The older generation—my parents, aunts, and uncles and their friends—remained laborers all their lives, proud of their immense propensity for physical work. They had survived the economic battering of the Great Depression and become substantial homeowners, independent and responsible Americans.

In the family we now have homemakers, schoolteachers and university professors, Ph.D.s and M.D.s, artists, businessmen and businesswomen, engineers, lawyers, medical technicians, military officers, musicians, nurses, physicians, policemen, psychologists, scientists, and writers. All are self-sufficient and rich by Maida's standards. Many are rich even by America's standards. All are successful by any standards. The immigrants' message, "Only you are responsible for your own life; no one else will do it for you," has been carried through; the pattern continues. Each young family is indebted to those immigrants; each owns a share in what those journeys of the "old folks" have led to. Each family has its new stories, and I hope that someday some of the youngsters will pick up the threads of the narrative and bring us up to date into this 21st century.

2. The End of the Story

Mom died in 1997, her 96th year, and my story of Michele, Theresa, and Ferdinando is nearly finished. Were they here to look back at the miles and years they had journeyed since the turn of the 20th century, they would be pleased. They carried some dark burdens, the deaths of infants and a young sister. But as they would probably say, "*Cosi è la vita* (That's life)." They had heard the voices say, "*Oltremare!*" and had taken the path like millions of other immigrants to *la bell'America!* It may now seem naïve, but the praise "*solamente in America, la bell'America*" was heard often in my family, expressed with sincerity and always with appreciation and respect for this country.

My grandfather Michele Dattilo and my granduncles Antonio and Giuseppe Dattilo comprised our family's first generation in America. We are now in our fifth. This includes our grandchildren. Tegenya, our little princess, continues our family tradition of immigration. She was four months old in 2005 when Sheila and I and our daughter Lisa traveled to Ethiopia to bring her home. Benjamin was born in 2006 to Sabine Kastner and our son, Michael. Aaron Lucas joined us that same year, born to our daughter Amy and Mark Ring. Jeffrey Graziano, our nephew, and his wife, Donna, brought Ariel into our family. Were Theresa still alive, she would have loved these four additional great grandchildren.

The family grows; the next generation moves on. I like to think of those new arrivals as immigrants, too, and I hope that when they read this book in a few years, they will consider that the highest of compliments.

I have not said a great deal about my relatives who came here from Italy in the 1950s, or the children and grandchildren, including my own, who were born since then. My focus has been on the "old folks," the 1920s and Depression-era immigrants, those vibrant people to whom I was introduced more than 75 years ago. This final chapter is my farewell to them.

My brother, Fred, died in 2002 at 81 years of age, and was soon followed by Marie in 2005, in her 82nd year. My parents, aunts, and uncles, many of my cousins, and my best friends Freddie Ogden and Bobby Greggs are gone too. So are our old neighbors, Mrs. Kinsella and Uncle Johnnie, Isador and Doris Dropkin, the Ogdens, the Garrisons, the Greggs, my employers Bill Pozefsky, Joe Conace, and Alfredo and Mario Ablondi, and nearly all the young men who marched off to World War II. My *compare*, Domenico Cervodoro, with his intense Italian pride, is gone, as are all the "old folks," that first generation of Italian voyagers and homesteaders who had so vibrantly filled our kitchen. They have all flickered out, each in turn, like candle flames in a gentle wind.

3. At the Top of the Hill, 2009

I am standing at the top of the hill, looking down Elysian Avenue toward number 79, our home of so long ago. Surprisingly, the house looks much the same as it must have appeared 77 years ago when I was born, but the street has changed. A young brother and sister, Frank and Lisa, grandchildren of my parents' close friends Joseph and Elisabetta Lanzana, purchased our house. Theresa and Michele would be happy with that.

The top of the street that I once knew so well was sliced off in the 1960s, and it is not much of a hill anymore. Several of the houses are gone, removed to make way for the multilane highway that cuts across our old path up to the South Mountain woods that we had so often explored. Our tumbling little brook is gone, all the trees have been cut down, the tangled habitats of those busy little birds that used to live there have been cleared away, and the flowered meadow with our old baseball field has been paved over. Only cars and trucks now run across what once was the top of the hill.

I remember that sunny afternoon in the spring of 1937 walking down the hill, my brother and I, a lanky 16-year-old and a small five-year-old, on our way home after a hike in the woods. I can still hear the challenge of that man who came out of his house,[8] slamming his wooden screen door.[9] I can feel Fred's pace quicken and his hand tighten on mine, causing me to puzzle why. In a harsh voice, the man told us where we belonged—not up here, he said, not near his house, but down there, he said, pointing, "with that Eye-tal-yin bunch down the hill!" That's where we belonged, and that's where we should stay, he reminded us.

Now, after these many years, I think that in some ways he just might have been right.

---

8. His was one of the houses "sliced off" in the 1960s highway construction.
9. See Chapter Twenty-One.

Photo Album

1-1   [1890] *Una piazza* in Maida
1-2   [1900] Ice delivery wagon (Nyack Library Local History Collection)
1-3   [1900] Nyack, North Broadway (Nyack Library Local History Collection)
1-4   [1900] Michele Dattilo (1868–1932) leaving for America
1-5   [1909] Michele Graziano (1892–1954), age 17, leaving for his first voyage to America
1-6   [1910] Antonio Dattilo (photo courtesy Nicholas Regine)

2-1   [ca. 1916] Theresa Dattilo and Michele Graziano at their engagement
2-2   [1917] Antonio Conace and James Fiola in the U.S. Army, with Anthony Asaro and Jimmie Fiola
2-3   [1919] Michele Graziano, age 27, in World War I
2-4   [1927] Giuseppe Dattilo (*Nonno* Peppe, Theresa's grandfather) (1830–1927) and grandson Joseph Dattilo (Theresa's cousin)
2-5   [1925] Cousins Rosina and Ferdinando Graziano, Joseph Dattilo (center)
2-6   [ca. 1925] Giuseppe Dattilo (1908–1994), Theresa's brother, first enlistment

3-1   [1932] Francesca Dattilo (1916–1932), Theresa's youngest sister; died of "*tubercolosi, la malattie americano*"
3-2   [1932] Just prior to his final return to Italy, Michele Dattilo, Theresa's father, meets his new grandson (Anthony)
3-3   [1934] The Backyard Band at 79 Elysian Avenue
3-4   [1935] Michele and Theresa Graziano at Elisabeth and Joseph Lanzana's wedding
3-5   [1937] In the days of little angels. Theresa Graziano with Theresa Conace, Anthony Graziano, Mary Fiola, Mary Serratore
3-6   [1937] Some of The Coffee Ladies and Anthony. Front: Caterina Serratore, Angelina Conace, and Theresa Graziano. Back: Vittoria Fiola and Jennie Asaro. The lives of the three friends in front spanned the years 1893 to 1997.

4-1 [1938] Fred and Anthony in the backyard, 79 Elysian Avenue

4-2 [1939] Anthony and Frankie Lanzana inspect Michele's 1929 Packard

4-3 [1940] *Zio* Antonio Serratore entertaining his guests

4-4 [ca. 1940] Great Aunt Rose Dattilo, owner of first Italian grocery store in Ocean City

4-5 [1942] Pop's 1936 Packard. Joseph Lanzana, Theresa Graziano in background

4-6 [1943] Anthony with *Compare* Domenico Cervodoro (1884–1965), Confirmation Day

5-1 [ca. 1930] A construction crew in Ocean City. Third from right, Giuseppe Graziano, Theresa's brother-in-law (photo courtesy Nicholas Regine)

5-2 The Conace brothers: Joseph and Gregory (WWII, 1940s), Dominick and Frank (Korean War, 1950s)

5-3 [1942] Robert Lynch, Mary Serratore, and Robert Serratore

5-4 [1942] Cousin Fred, with parents Joseph and Nancy Graziano

5-5 [1943] Fred Graziano with his father, Michele

5-6 [1946] Michele builds another room at 79 Elysian Avenue

6-1 [1947] Main Street, postwar Nyack (Nyack Library Local History Collection)

6-2 [1948] A sunny day in the good years. Theresa and Michele at Aunt Macrina's farm

6-3 [1948] Anthony at work in Cousin Joe Conace's grocery store

6-4 [1950] Fred and proud parents, graduation day at Columbia University

6-5 [1952] The family at home. Fred's lost painting hangs behind them

6-6 [1954] Aunt Macrina and Anthony, another graduation day at Columbia

7-1 [1954] Anna and Theresa Dattilo with their aunt (Theresa's sister), *Suora* Eugenia, in Maida

7-2 [1954] Caterina (Theresa's sister) and Giuseppe Bartolotti with Frances, Theresa, Elisabetta, Benedetta, and Michael, in Maida

7-3 [1956] Frances and Michael Bartolotti with *Nonna* Elisabetta

7-4 [1956] Theresa and Elizabeth Lanzana visit *Nonna* Elisabetta in Maida

7-5 [1965] *La nuova campana,* Theresa's gift to Maida

7-6 [1965] Maida celebrates Theresa's gift

La bell'America

3-1

3-2

3-3

3-6

3-4

3-5

4-1

4-2

4-6

4-3

4-5

4-4

6-1

6-2

6-6

6-3

6-4

6-5

7-1

7-2

7-6

7-3

7-5

7-4

References and Index

References

Acton, H. M. (1961). *The Last Bourbons of Naples.* London: Methuen.

Adams, H. (1982). *Italy at War.* Alexandria, Virginia: Time-Life Books.

Ambrose, S. (2002). "Revisiting the G.I. Bill." *The News Hour.* PBS, July 4, 2000.

Anderson, D. (2004). *The Columbia Guide to the Vietnam War.* New York: Columbia University Press.

Anderson, F. (2000). *Crucible of War: The Seven Years' War and the Fate of Empire in British North America, 1754-1766.* New York: Knopf.

Bauer, Y. (1982). *A History of the Holocaust.* New York: Franklin Watts.

Belmonte, P. L. (2001). *Italian Americans in World War Two.* Chicago: Arcadia Publishing.

Bennett, M. (1996). *When Dreams Come True: The G.I. Bill and the Making of Modern America.* New York: Brassey's.

Bierman, J. and Smith, C. (2002). *The Battle of Alamein: Turning Point, World War II.* New York: Viking Press.

Bowen, R. (1948). "The French Revolution," in *Chapters in Western Civilization*, volume 1, pages 388–437. New York: Columbia University Press.

Bradagin, M. A. (1957). *The Italian Navy in World War II.* Translated by Gale Hoffman. United States Naval Institute.

Briggs, J. W. (1978). *An Italian Passage: Immigrants to Three American Cities, 1890-1930.* New Haven: Yale University Press.

Butler, S. (1903). *The Way of All Flesh.* Republished in 1998, New York: Random House, The Modern Library Edition.

Caravaggio, A. N. (2006). "The attack at Taranto." Naval War College Review, volume 59, number 3.

Carroll, L. (1865). *Alice's Adventures in Wonderland.* London: MacMillan.

Churchill, W. S. (1948). *The Second World War: The Gathering Storm.* Boston: Houghton Mifflin.

Cohen, R. (2002). *Dear Mrs. Roosevelt: Letters from Children of the Great Depression.* Chapel Hill, North Carolina: University of North Carolina Press.

Collodi, C. (1880). *Le Avventure di Pinocchio.* Published in weekly installments in *Il Giornale dei Bambini,* the first Italian newspaper for children. Republished in 1996, Florence: Edizioni Polistampa Firenze.

Columbia Electronic Encyclopedia (2007). New York: Columbia University Press.

Columbia Encyclopedia (2004). "Ferdinand II: King of the two Sicilies." *The Columbia Encyclopedia, Sixth Edition.* New York: Columbia University Press.

Cordasco, F. and Bucchioni, E. (Eds.) (1974). *The Italians: Social Backgrounds of an American Group.* Clifton, New Jersey: Augustus M. Kelley.

Cornwell, J. (1999). *Hitler's Pope: The Secret History of Pius XII.* New York: Viking Press.

Crispino, J. A. (1980). *The Assimilation of Ethnic Groups: The Italian Case.* Staten Island, New York: Center for Migration Studies.

D'Amico, J. (2005). *The Family/La Famiglia.* Buffalo, New York: Digita Batesjackson.

Dalin, D. G. (2005). *The Myth of Hitler's Pope: How Pope Pius XII Rescued Jews from the Nazis.* Washington, D.C.: Regnery Publishers.

Davenport, W. E. (1904). "The exodus of a Latin people." *Charities,* volume 12, pages 463–467. Reprinted in Cordasco and Bucchioni (1974).

De Kruif, P. (1926). *Microbe Hunters.* New York: Harcourt, Brace.

Dear, I. C. B. and Foot, M. R. D. (Eds.) (1995). *The Oxford Companion to the Second World War.* London: Oxford University Press

Di Franco, P. (1988). *The Italian-American Experience.* New York: Tom Doherty Associates.

Diggins, J. P. (1966). "Flirtation with fascism: American pragmatic liberals and Mussolini's Italy." *The American Historical Review,* volume 71, number 2, pages 487–506.

Dore, G. (1968). "Some social and historical aspects of Italian emigration to America." *Journal of Social History,* volume 2, pages 95–122.

Dunlop, J. T. and Galenson, W. (Eds.) (1978). *Labor in the Twentieth Century.* New York: Academic Press.

Farina, G. (1999). *Montecassino: The People's Real Battle.* Boston: Popular Technology.

Flores, G. (2007). "What killed Napoleon?" *Natural History,* April, 2007.

Foerster, R. F. (1919). "Coming of the Italians," *The Italian Emigration of our Time.* Cambridge, Massachusetts: Harvard University Press. (Reprinted in 1968, New York: Russell and Russell.)

Gallo, P. (1974). *Ethnic Alienation: The Italian-Americans.* Rutherford, New Jersey: Farleigh Dickinson University Press.

Gallo, P. (1981). *Old Bread, New Wine.* Chicago: Nelson-Hall.

Gallo, P. (Ed.) (2006). *Pope Pius XII, The Holocaust and the Revisionists.* Jefferson, North Carolina: McFarland.

Giordano, J. (Ed.) (1986). *The Italian-American Catalog.* Garden City, New York: Doubleday.

Goldman, E. (1952). *Rendezvous With Destiny: A History of Modern American Reform.* New York: Knopf.

Goldman, M. (1952). *City on the Lake: The Challenge of Change in Buffalo, New York.* Buffalo, New York: Prometheus Books.

Goldstein, R. (2001). *Desperate Hours: The Epic Rescue of the Andrea Doria.* New York: Wiley.

Goodwin, D. K. (2000). "Revisiting the G.I. Bill." *The News Hour.* PBS, July 4, 2000.

Graziano, A. M. and Raulin, M. L. (2010). *Research Methods: A Process of Inquiry,* Seventh Edition. Boston: Allyn and Bacon.

Greenberg, M. (1997). *The G.I. Bill: The Law that Changed America.* New York: Lickle Publishing.

Greven, P. (1980). *The Protestant Temperament: Patterns of Child Rearing, Religious Experience, and the Self in Early America.* New York: Alfred A. Knopf.

Gruhzit-Hoyt, O. (1995). *They Also Served: American Women in World War II.* Secaucus, New Jersey: Carol Publishing Group.

Gutman, I. (Ed.) (1990). *Encyclopedia of the Holocaust.* New York: Macmillan.

Hart, P. and Steel, N. (2002). *Defeat at Gallipoli.* New York: Macmillan.

Haythornthwaite, P. J. (2004). *Gallipoli, 1915: Frontal Assault on Turkey.* Westport, Connecticut: Praeger.

Hibbert, C. (1985). *Rome: The Biography of a City.* New York: W. W. Norton.

Hoffer, W. (1979). *Saved! The Story of the Andrea Doria, the Greatest Sea Rescue in History.* New York: Summit Books.

Hofstadter, R. (1992). *Social Darwinism in American Thought.* Boston: Beacon Press.

Holocaust Encyclopedia (2007). "Italy." United States Holocaust Memorial Museum, Washington, D.C. Accessed March 9, 2007, at www.ushmm.org.

James, R. R. (1999). *Gallipoli.* New York: Pimlico.

Jones, E. (1953). *The Life and Works of Sigmund Freud.* New York: Basic Books.

Keane, J. (2001). *Doughboys, the Great War and the Remaking of America.* Baltimore: Johns Hopkins University Press.

Kennedy, D. (1966). "Can we still afford to be a nation of immigrants?" *The Atlantic Monthly,* November 1996, pages 52–68.

Kirkpatrick, I. (1964). *Mussolini: A Study in Power.* New York: Hawthorne Books.

Krase, J. and DeSena, J. N. (Eds.) (1994). "Italian-Americans in a multicultural society," in Proceedings of the Symposium of the American Italian Historical Society, November 1993, State University of New York at Stony Brook. *Forum Italicum,* supplement number 7.

Lever, E. (2000). *Marie Antoinette: The Last Queen of France.* New York: St. Martin's Griffin.

Levi, C. (1945). *Cristo si e fermerto a Eboli.* Translated from Italian into English and republished in 1947 as *Christ stopped at Eboli.* New York: Farrar, Straus, and Giroux.

Levine, M. and Levine, A. (1992). *Helping Children: A Social History.* New York: Oxford University Press.

Lovett, C. (1982). *The Democratic Movement in Italy, 1830-1876.* Boston: Harvard University Press.

Mangione, J. (1942). *Mount Allegro: A Memoir of Italian-American Life.* Syracuse, New York: Syracuse University Press.

Mangione, J. and Morreale, B. (1992). *La Storia: Five Centuries of the Italian American Experience.* New York: Harper Perennial.

Margariti, A. (1980). *America! America!* Salerno, Italy: Galzerano.

Mazzini, G. (1831). "General Instructions for the Members of Young Italy," in N. Gangulee (Ed.) (1945), *Selected Writings,* pages 129–131. London: Lindsay Drummond.

Mazzini, G. (1844). "An Essay on the Duties of Man: Addressed to Workingmen." The Hanover Historical Texts Project (luttmer@hanover.edu).as

Meade, E. F. (1905). "Italian immigrants into the south." *South Atlantic Quarterly,* July 1905.

Mettler, S. (2005). *Soldiers to Citizens: The G.I. Bill and the Making of the Greatest Generation.* New York: Oxford University Press.

Mondello, S. (1980). *The Italian Immigrant in Urban America, 1880-1920, As Reported in the Contemporary Periodical Press.* New York: Arno Press.

Morgan, A. (1890). "What shall we do with the 'Dago'"? *Popular Science Monthly,* December, 1890, p. 172-179.

Moscow, A. (1988). *Collision Course: The Andrea Doria and the Stockholm.* Norwalk, Connecticut: Easton Press.

Nelli, H. S. (1983). *From Immigrants to Ethnics: The Italian Americans.* New York: Oxford University Press

Nicolson, H. (1967). *The Congress of Vienna: A Study in Allied Unity, 1812-1819.* New York: Viking Press.

Olson, K. W. (1974). *The G.I. Bill, The Veterans, and The Colleges.* Lexington, Kentucky: University Press of Kentucky.

Oppel, F. (Ed.) (1987). *Early Flight: From Balloons to Biplanes.* Secaucus, New Jersey: Castle Publishing.

Orsi, R. A. (2002). *The Madonna of 115th Street: Faith and Community in Italian Harlem, 1880-1950.* New Haven: Yale University Press.

Packenham, T. (1979). *The Boer War.* New York: Random House.

Padnani, A. (2007). "West Nyack resident honored by France." *The Rockland Journal News,* May 27, 2007.

Page, T. N. (1920). *Italy and the World War.* New York: Charles Scribner's Sons.

Peck, G. (2000). *Reinventing Free Labor: Padrones and Immigrant Workers in the North American West, 1880-1930.* New York: Cambridge University Press.

Phillips, C. (1969). *From the Crash to the Blitz: The New York Times' Chronicle of American Life.* New York: The New York Times Company.

Piper, F. (1994). "The number of victims," in *Anatomy of the Auschwitz Death Camps.* Bloomington, Indiana: Indiana University Press.

Polaikov, L. (1956). *Harvest of Hate.* Syracuse, New York: Syracuse University Press.

Prange, G. W. (1988). *December 7, 1941: The Day Japan Attacked Pearl Harbor.* New York: McGraw-Hill.

Price, W. (1917). "What I learned by traveling from Naples to N.Y. in the steerage." *World Outlook,* October 1917, volume 3, pages 3–5.

Primack, M. L. and Willis, J. F. (1980). *An Economic History of the United States.* Menlo Park, California: Benjamin Cummings.

Raskob, J. J. (1929). "Everybody ought to be rich." *Ladies Home Journal,* August 1929, volume 46.

Regine, N. C. (1999). *A View from Macaroni Street.* Absecon, New Jersey: MagicImage.

Richards, D. A. J. (1999). *Italian American. The Racializing of an Ethnic Identity.* New York: New York University Press.

Roach, R. (1997). "From Combat to Campus: G.I. Bill Gave a Generation of African Americans an Opportunity to Pursue the American Dream." *Black Issues in Higher Education,* August 21, 1997, pages 26–29.

Ross, D. B. (1969). *Preparing for Ulysses: Politics and Veterans During World War II.* New York: Columbia University Press.

Salvemini, G. (1942). *Italian Fascist Activities in the United States.* New York: Center for Migration Studies.

Schama, S. (1989). *Citizens: A Chronicle of the French Revolution.* New York: Alfred A. Knopf.

Sartorio, E. C. (1918). *Social and Religious Life of Italians in America.* Boston: Christopher Publishing House. Reprinted in 1974, Clifton, New Jersey: Augustus M. Kelley.

Schiavo, G. E. (1958). *Antonio Meucci, Inventor of the Telephone.* New York: Vigo Press.

Shirer, W. L. (1962). *The Rise and Fall of the Third Reich.* New York: Crest Books.

Simpson, P. D. (2006). *Alive on the Andrea Doria: The Greatest Sea Rescue in History*. Fleischmanns, New York: Purple Mountain Press.

Sinclair, U. (1906). *The Jungle*. New York: Doubleday and Page.

Smith, D. M. (1989). *Italy and its Monarchy*. New Haven: Yale University Press.

Smith, D. M. (1971). *Victor Emanuel, Cavour, and the Risorgimento*. London: Oxford University Press.

Smith, D. M. (1997). *Modern Italy: A Political History*. Ann Arbor, Michigan: Michigan University Press.

Smith, D. M. (1994). *Mazzini*. New Haven: Yale University Press.

Smith, I. R. (1996). *The Origin of the South African War, 1899-1902*. New York: Longman.

Smith, T. (2007). *The Crescent City Lynchings: The murder of Chief Hennessy, The New Orleans "Maffia" Trials, and the Parish Prison Mob*. Guilford, Connecticut: Lyons Press.

Steinbeck, J. (1939). *The Grapes of Wrath*. New York: Viking Press.

"Steerage" (1911). Italian emigrants en route: A proposed steerage reform. *Review of Reviews*, volume 44, pages 348–350. Reprinted in F. Cordasco and E. Bucchioni (Eds.) (1974).

Stueck, W. (1995). *The Korean War: An International History*. Princeton, New Jersey: Princeton University Press.

Talese, G. (1992). *Unto the Sons*. New York: Knopf.

Taubenberger, J. K., Reid, A. H., and Fanning, T. G. (2005). "Capturing a killer flu virus." *Scientific American,* volume 292, number 1, pages 62–71.

Travers, T. (2001). *Gallipoli 1915*. Stroud, England: Tempus Publishing.

Treadwell, M. E. (1954). *The Women's Army Corps*. Washington, D.C., Office of the Chief of Military History, Department of the Army.

U.S. National Archives: World War II POW records. See: www.gentracer. com/nara.html.

Veblen, T. (1927). *The Theory of the Leisure Class: An Economic Study of Institutions*. New York: Vanguard Press.

Von Borosini, V. (1912). "Home-going Italians." *Survey,* September 1912, volume 28, pages 791–793.

Wagner, N. (1936). *Unveiling the Universe: Where We Are and What We Are As Told by the Telescope and Spectroscope*. Scranton, Pennsylvania: The Research Publishers.

Weinberg, G. L. (2005). *A World at Arms: A Global History of World War II*, Second Edition. New York: Cambridge University Press.

Wilde, O. (1891). "The soul of man under socialism." *Fortnightly Review*, February 1891.

Wilhelm, M. B. (1988). *The Other Italy: Italian Resistance in World War II*. New York: W. W. Norton.

Williams, P. H. (1938). *South Italian Folkways in Europe and America*.

New York: Russell and Russell. (Reissued 1969.)

Wright, O. and Wright, W. (1908). "The Wright Brothers' Aëroplane." *The Century Magazine,* September 1908.

Zaidenberg, A. (1939). *Anyone Can Draw!* New York: Illustrated Editions Company.

Zimmerman, J. D. (Ed.) (2005). *The Jews of Italy Under Fascist and Nazi Rule, 1922-1945.* New York: Yeshiva University Press.

Index

The Author

Anthony Michael Graziano, professor emeritus at the State University of New York, Buffalo, is the author of 15 books and 50 articles on research methodology, childhood disorders, parent training, and many related topics. He is also known as an exceptional Italian chef. His brother, parents, and extended family emigrated from Italy. He says, "This is a book in celebration of immigrants. It speaks to us because we are all immigrants."

ABOUT THE TYPE

This book was set in ITC Galliard, a typeface based on the type of Robert Granjon (ca. 1513-1590), England. The ITC Galliard font is a work of Matthew Carter and a contemporary adaptation of Robert Granjon's 16th century design. The ITC Galliard font captures the vitality of Granjon's work in a graceful, modern typeface.

Composed at JTC Imagineering, Santa Maria, CA
Designed by John Taylor-Convery